Corporate Social Responsibility

Modern business is obliged to meet increasingly demanding ethical, environmental, legal, commercial and public standards as defined by wider society. Corporate social responsibility (CSR) has therefore become an important consideration for managers at all levels, as well as one of the most vibrant areas of study and research in the field of business and management. This important new book provides a comprehensive and student-centred introduction to the key themes and issues currently being addressed in CSR around the world.

The book brings together material by the most influential teachers and scholars working in CSR today, as well as many of the most cited and important articles, and is clearly structured in three parts:

- Understanding CSR
- Applying CSR
- Managing CSR

Each section includes an extensive and accessible editorial commentary that introduces the key debates and themes contained in the articles, as well as clearly defined learning objectives to guide the reader, and challenging and thought-provoking study questions to consolidate learning. The book also includes three major case studies to enable the reader to relate theory to the real world, focusing on Nike in Asia, Vodafone in South Africa and ABN AMRO in Brazil. Drawing on examples and issues from across the globe, this book is essential reading for all students and managers with an interest in corporate governance and business ethics.

Andrew Crane is the George R. Gardiner Professor of Business Ethics at the Schulich School of Business at York University in Canada.

Dirk Matten holds the Hewlett-Packard Chair in Corporate Social Responsibility at the Schulich School of Business at York University in Canada.

Laura J. Spence is a Reader in Business Ethics at Brunel University, UK. She is Deputy Director of BRESE (Brunel Research in Enterprise, Innovation, Sustainability and Ethics).

Corporate Social Responsibility

Readings and cases in a global context

Edited by

Andrew Crane, Dirk Matten and Laura J. Spence

Routledge
Taylor & Francis Group

LONDON AND NEW YORK

First published 2008 by Routledge
2 Park Square, Milton Park, Abingdon, Oxon, OX14 4RN

Simultaneously published in the USA and Canada
by Routledge
270 Madison Avenue, New York, NY 10016

Routledge is an imprint of the Taylor & Francis Group, an informa business

© 2008 Andrew Crane, Dirk Matten and Laura J. Spence for selection and editorial matter:
the contributors and publishers for individual chapters

Typeset in Bell Gothic by Keystroke, 28 High Street, Tettenhall, Wolverhampton
Printed and bound in Great Britain by TJ International Ltd, Padstow, Cornwall

British Library Cataloguing in Publication Data
A catalogue record for this book is available from the British Library

Library of Congress Cataloging in Publication Data
A catalog record for this book has been requested.

ISBN10: 0–415–42428–3 (hbk)
ISBN10: 0–415–42429–1 (pbk)
ISBN10: 0–203–08952–9 (ebk)

ISBN13: 978–0–415–42428–8 (hbk)
ISBN13: 978–0–415–42429–5 (pbk)
ISBN13: 978–0–203–08952–1 (ebk)

Contents

Acknowledgements

Writing and researching in the field of CSR inevitably brings one into contact with a lot of intelligent and creative people who inspire one to develop one's ideas in interesting and unexpected ways (one also gets to meet a good few weirdos and idiots, but that's another story). We have been extremely lucky to have worked with and learnt from some of the best CSR thinkers around, and so would like to take this opportunity to thank all the faculty, students and practitioners who have contributed to our understanding of this fascinating and sometimes exasperating subject. This applies in particular to everyone at the International Centre for Corporate Social Responsibility at the University of Nottingham, and also to our colleagues and students at Brunel University and Royal Holloway, University of London.

The genesis of this book can be traced to a cocktail bar in Honolulu, where our initial editor Jacqueline Curthoys encouraged us, during the course of a few Mai Tais, of the urgent need for a CSR textbook that didn't treat its readers as if they were stupid, but also didn't try to confuse them with too many long words. The course of the book was subsequently a little bumpy, seeing the production team get through three editors, two babies, one career change and two transatlantic relocations. Sometimes, things just don't go the way you plan, so it is with great pleasure that the final product now hits the shelves. In helping us get there, we would particularly like to offer our thanks to Pauline Seston at Brunel, Gemma Baker at Nottingham, Navneet Singh Chatwal and Michael Windle at York for their careful and detailed attention to various administrative matters, and of course to the team at Routledge for their editorial and production work.

The editors and publishers wish to thank and acknowledge the following authors, journals and publishers that have assisted us in allowing materials to be cited and shared in the readings:

1   Reprinted from *The New York Times Magazine* 13 September 1970, 'The social responsibility of business is to increase its profits' by M. Friedman, 13, 32–33, 122–126, ©1970, with permission from The New York Times News Services Division.

2   Reprinted from *Journal of Business Strategy* 4(2), 'The case for corporate social responsibility' by H. Mintzberg, pp. 3–15, ©1983, with permission from Emerald.

3   Reprinted from *Business Horizons* 34, 'The pyramid of corporate social responsibility – toward the moral management of organizational stakeholders' by A. Carroll, pp. 39–48, ©1991, with permission from Elsevier.

4   Reprinted from *Journal of Business Ethics* 53(1–2), 'Corporate social responsibility theories: mapping the territory' by E. Garriga and D. Melé, pp. 51–71, ©2004, with permission from Springer Science and Business Media.

5   Reprinted from *Stakeholder management: framework and philosophy* by R. Freeman, 'Strategic management: a stakeholder approach', Chapter 3, ©1984, with permission from the author.

6   Reprinted from *Academy of Management Review* 20(1), 'The stakeholder theory of the corporation: concepts, evidence, and implications' by T. Donaldson and L. Preston, pp. 65–91, ©1995 with permission from the Academy of Management.

7   Adapted from *The Market for Virtue: The Potential and Limits of Corporate Social Responsibility* by David Vogel, 'Is there a market for virtue? The business case for corporate social responsibility', Chapter 2, pp.16–45, ©2005, with permission from Brookings Institution Press.

8   Reprinted by permission of Sage Publications Ltd from R. Harrison, T. Newholm and D. Shaw (eds) *The ethical consumer*, ©2005, 'Meeting the ethical gaze: issues and challenges in orientating towards the ethical market' by A. Crane, Chapter 14, pp. 219–252.

9   Reproduced from *Business and human rights: dilemmas and solutions* by R. Sullivan, 'The development of human rights responsibilities for multinational enterprises' by P. Muchlinski, Chapter 3, pp. 33–51, ©2004, with permission from Greenleaf Publishing.

10 Reprinted from *Business Ethics: A European Review* 8(1), 'Corporate social responsibility as a participative process' by P. Maclagan, pp.43–49, ©1999, with permission from Blackwell Publishing.

11 Reprinted from *California Management Review* 44(2). 'The Next Wave of Corporate Community Involvement' by D. Hess, N. Rogovsky and T. Dunfee, pp. 10–125, ©2002, by the Regents of the University of California. By permission of The Regents

12 Reprinted from *Harvard Business Review* 80(12) 'The competitive advantage of corporate philanthropy' by M. Porter and M. Kramer, pp. 56–69, ©2002, with permission from Harvard Business School Publishing.

13 Reprinted from *Harvard Business Review*, 75(1) 'Beyond greening: strategies for a sustainable world' by S. Hart, pp. 67–76, ©1997, with permission from Harvard Business School Publishing.

14 Reprinted from *Non-state actors and authority in the global system* by R. Higgott, G. Underhill and A. Bieler (eds), 'Corporate politics and climate change' by D. Levy, and D. Egan, pp. 138–153, ©2000, Routledge. Reproduced by permission of Taylor & Francis Books UK.

15 Reprinted from *Accounting, Auditing and Accountability Journal* 10(3) 'Struggling with the praxis of social accounting: stakeholders, accountability, audits and procedures' by R. Gray, C. Dey, D. Owen, R. Evans and S. Zadek, pp. 325–364, ©1997, with permission from Emerald.

16 Reprinted from *Building corporate accountability: emerging practices in social and ethical accounting, auditing and reporting* by S. Zadek, R. Evans and P. Pruzan (eds), 'How to do it' by S. Zadek, P. Pruznan and R. Evans, Chapter 3, ©2003, with permission from Earthscan.

17 Reprinted from *Long Range Planning* 29(4) 'How corporate social responsibility pays off' by L. Burke, and J. Logsdon, pp. 495–502, ©1996, with permission from Elsevier.

18 Reprinted from *Corporate governance and sustainability – Challenges for theory and practice* by S. Benn and D. Dunphy (eds), 'Codes of conduct as a tool for sustainable governance in MNCs' by K. Bondy, D. Matten and J. Moon, Chapter 8, ©2006, Routledge. Reproduced by permission of Taylor & Francis Books UK.

19 Reprinted from *Harvard Business Review* 80(9) 'Serving the world's poor, profitably' by C.K. Prahalad and A. Hammond, pp.48–57, ©2002, with permission from Harvard Business School Publishing.

20 Reprinted from *Management International Review* 40(4) 'The downward spiral and the U.S. model business principles: why MNEs should take responsibility for improvement of world-wide social and environmental conditions' by A Scherer and M. Smid, pp. 351–371, ©2000, with permission from the publishers.

21 Adapted from *Harvard Business Review* 82(12) 'The path to corporate responsibility at Nike' by S. Zadek, pp. 125–132, ©2004, with permission from Harvard Business School Publishing.

The publishers have made every effort to contact authors/copyright holders of works reprinted in *Corporate Social Responsibility: Readings and cases in a global context*. This has not been possible in every case, however, and we would welcome correspondence from those individuals/companies whom we have been unable to trace.

SECTION A

Understanding corporate social responsibility

Corporate social responsibility (CSR) is a much discussed and debated subject in contemporary business. It is also frequently found in the discourse of governments, public sector organizations, non-government organizations (NGOs), and even intergovernmental organizations such as the United Nations, the World Bank or the International Labour Organization. CSR, it seems, is almost everywhere.

This means that, apart from anything else, there is much to gain from an academic study of CSR. After all, the different people and organizations that deploy the language or tools of CSR may well want, or even mean, different things when they get involved with CSR. For some, it represents a misguided attempt to divert money that should rightly go to shareholders; for others, it is little more than a smokescreen behind which large multinationals can maintain a discredited, unsustainable business model while appearing to be responsible to the outside world; for still others, it represents a genuine opportunity to help leverage millions out of poverty in the world's poorest countries. Ultimately, corporations may do good, or harm, or perhaps even very little, when they practise CSR.

The academic study of CSR therefore seeks to get behind the spin and explore some of these different perspectives with real substance. In this first section of the book, we will start this process by developing a robust understanding of CSR – i.e. what it means, what it looks like in different national and organizational contexts, what some of its basic underlying principles are, what kinds of ways we can theorize about it, and so on. We will also begin to explore some of the very different opinions on CSR that people have and, perhaps more importantly, what lies behind these different perspectives. To integrate and apply some of this knowledge, we provide an in-depth case study on Vodafone, the mobile telecommunications company, and its experiences in Africa.

In this section, then, we will develop an understanding of CSR in five main stages:

1   Introducing CSR
2   The case for and against CSR
3   CSR concepts and theories
4   Responsibilities to stakeholders
5   Vodafone Africa case study

It is important to recognize that, in building an understanding of CSR, our aim is not to convince anyone that CSR is necessarily right or wrong, or even that some approaches to CSR are better than others. Our aim is to explore different facets of the subject, and different perspectives, in an objective way that enables anyone interested in CSR to get a clearer picture of the area and make their own mind up as to what is good or bad about a particular approach. CSR is a complex and ultimately *contested* concept that is hard to pin down – but, at the same time, one that rewards greater investigation. Therefore, once we have built this foundation of understanding of CSR in Section A, we will turn in Section B to how CSR is applied in different arenas of the business – the workplace, the marketplace, the community, and the ecological environment – before exploring CSR management in Section C. This first section is crucial though: without an adequate understanding of CSR and its many guises, it is very difficult to evaluate specific responsibilities or management practices.

Chapter 1

Corporate social responsibility: in a global context

I N THIS CHAPTER WE WILL:

- Examine the recent rise to prominence of corporate social responsibility.
- Analyse different definitions of corporate social responsibility.
- Outline six core characteristics of corporate social responsibility.
- Explore corporate social responsibility in different organizational contexts.
- Explore corporate social responsibility in different national contexts.
- Explain the approach to corporate social responsibility adopted in the rest of the book.

Introduction: The Recent Rise of CSR

The role of corporations in society is clearly on the agenda. Hardly a day goes by without media reports on corporate misbehaviour and scandals or, more positively, on contributions from business to wider society. A quick stroll to the local cinema and films such as *Blood Diamond*, *The Constant Gardener* or *Supersize Me* reflect a growing interest among the public in the impact of corporations on contemporary life.

Corporations have clearly started to take up this challenge. This began with 'the usual suspects' such as companies in the oil, chemical and tobacco industries. As a result of media pressure, major disasters, and sometimes governmental regulation, these companies realized that propping up oppressive regimes, being implicated in human rights violations, polluting the environment, or misinforming and deliberately harming their customers, just to give a few examples, were practices that had to be reconsidered if they wanted to survive in society at the end of the twentieth century.

Today, however, there is virtually no industry, market or business type that has not experienced growing demands to legitimate its practices to society at large. For instance, banking, retailing, tourism, food and beverages, entertainment, and health-care industries – for long considered to be fairly 'clean' and uncontroversial – now all face increasing expectations that they institute more responsible practices.

Companies have responded to this agenda by advocating what is now a common term in business: corporate social responsibility. More often known simply as 'CSR', the concept of corporate social responsibility is a management idea that has risen to unprecedented popularity throughout the global business community during the past decade. Most large companies, and even some smaller ones, now feature CSR reports, managers, departments or at least CSR projects, and the subject is being promoted more and more as a core area of management, next to marketing, accounting or finance.

If we take a closer look at the recent rise of CSR, some might well argue that this 'new' management idea is little more that a recycled fashion or, as the old saying goes, 'old wine in new bottles'. And, in fact, one could certainly suggest that some of the practices that fall under the label of CSR have indeed been relevant business issues at least since the industrial revolution. Ensuring humane working conditions, providing decent housing or healthcare, and donating to charity are activities which many of the early industrialists in Europe and the US were involved in – without necessarily shout-ing out about them in annual reports, let alone calling them CSR. Even in a country like India, companies such as Tata can pride themselves on more than a hundred years of responsible business practices, including far-reaching philanthropic activities and community involvement (Elankumaran, Seal and Hashmi, 2005). What we discover, then, in the area of CSR is that, while many of the individual policies, practices and programmes are not new as such, corporations today are addressing their role in society far more coherently, comprehensively and professionally – an approach that is contemporarily summarized by CSR.

As well as the rise to prominence of CSR in particular companies, we can also observe the emergence of something like a CSR 'movement'. There is a mushrooming of dedicated CSR consultancies, all of which see a business opportunity in the growing popularity of the concept. At the same time, we are witnessing a burgeoning number of CSR standards, watchdogs, auditors and certifiers aiming at institutionalizing and harmonizing CSR practices globally. More and more industry associations and interest groups have been set up in order to coordinate and create synergies among individual business approaches to CSR. Meanwhile, a growing number of dedicated magazines, newsletters, email lists and websites not only contribute to providing an identity to CSR as a management concept, but also help to build a worldwide network of CSR practitioners, academics and activists.

Defining CSR: Navigating Through the Jungle of Definitions

In the context of such an inexorable rise to prominence of CSR, the literature on the subject, both academic and practitioner, is understandably large and expanding. There are now thousands of articles and reports on CSR from academics, corporations, consultancies, the media, NGOs and government departments; there are numerous conferences, books, journals and magazines on the subject; and, last but not least, there are literally millions of webpages dealing with the topic from every conceivable interest group with a stake in the debate.

How, then, best to make sense of this vast literature so as to construct a coherent account of what CSR actually is? After all, few subjects in management arouse as much controversy and contestation as CSR. For this reason, definitions of CSR abound, and there are as many definitions of CSR as there are disagreements over the appropriate role of the corporation in society. As McWilliams, Siegel and Wright (2006) recently declared: 'there is no strong consensus on a definition for CSR'. In February 2007, this lack of consensus blew up into something of a storm on the Wikipedia online encyclopaedia when the phrase 'corporate social responsibility' was nominated to be 'checked for its neutrality' following a series of disagreements about its meaning from supporters and critics (Ethical Performance, 2007).

Table 1 gives just some examples of the different ways in which CSR is described and defined by different organizations across the globe. As this clearly shows, there are some similarities in the way different actors understand CSR, as well as considerable differences. Moreover, although we often look to academic research to provide clarity among so much ambiguity, this diversity is also reflected in scholarly definitions of CSR. For example, one early writer on CSR, Keith Davis, described CSR as 'the firm's consideration of, and response to, issues beyond the narrow economic, technical, and legal requirements of the firm' (Davis, 1973, cited in Carroll, 1999), while a few years later Archie Carroll (1979) defined it much more broadly to include exactly those elements that Davis excluded: 'the social responsibility of business encompasses the economic, legal, ethical, and discretionary expectations that society has of organizations at a given point in time'.

This heterogeneity in CSR definitions has continued unabated. While the Carroll definition given above is arguably the most commonly cited, it remains contested, as we will see in Chapter 3. Therefore, others have taken a different route and, rather than specify particular responsibilities, have offered more general definitions which seek to include the different opinions on CSR that are evident across the literature. For instance, Brown and Dacin (1997) define CSR as a company's 'status and activities with respect to its perceived societal or, at least, stakeholder obligations', while Matten and Moon (2004a) offer the following: 'CSR is a cluster concept which overlaps with such concepts as business ethics, corporate philanthropy, corporate citizenship, sustainability, and environmental responsibility. It is a dynamic and contestable concept that is embedded in each social, political, economic and institutional context.'

In this book, we will not seek simply to follow one of these definitions, nor will we provide a new, improved one that will simply add to the complex jungle of CSR definitions. In the contested world of CSR, it is virtually impossible to provide a definitive answer to the question of what CSR 'really' is. Therefore, our intention is to identify some core characteristics of the CSR concept, which we hope will help to delineate its essential qualities, and provide a focus for the definitional debates that continue to surround the subject.

Table 1 Organizational definitions of CSR

Organization	Type of organization	Definition of CSR	Source
UK government	Governmental organization	'The voluntary actions that business can take, over and above compliance with minimum legal requirements, to address both its own competitive interests and the interests of wider society'	www.csr.gov.uk
European Commission	Governmental organization	'A concept whereby companies integrate social and environmental concerns in their business operations and in their interaction with their stakeholders on a voluntary basis'	EC Green Paper, 2001, *Promoting a European Framework for Corporate Social Responsibility*
Chinese Ministry of Commerce	Governmental organization	'A concrete action taken by Chinese companies to implement the political aspiration of the new Communist Party collective leadership – putting people first to create a harmonious society'	Ethical Corporation, 2005, 'Politics: A Chinese Definition of CSR', 15 September 2005: www.ethicalcorp.com
Confederation of British Industry	Business association	'The acknowledgement by companies that they should be accountable not only for their financial performance, but for the impact of their activities on society and/or the environment'	www.cbi.org.uk/
World Business Council for Sustainable Development	Business association	'The continuing commitment by business to behave ethically and contribute to economic development while improving the quality of life of the workforce and their families as well as of the local community and society at large'	WBCSD, 1999, 'CSR: Meeting Changing Expectations'
Gap Inc.	Corporation	'Being socially responsible means striving to incorporate our values and ethics into everything we do – from how we run our business, to how we treat our employees, to how we impact upon the communities where we live and work'	www.gapinc.com
HSBC	Corporation	'Means managing our business responsibly and sensitively for long-term success. Our goal is not, and never has been, profit at any cost because we know that tomorrow's success depends on the trust we build today'	www.hsbc.com

Organization	Type of organization	Definition of CSR	Source
Christian Aid	Non-government organization	'An entirely voluntary, corporate-led initiative to promote self-regulation as a substitute for regulation at either national or international level'	'Behind the Mask: The Real Face of Corporate Social Responsibility', 2004
CSR Asia	Social enterprise	'A company's commitment to operating in an economically, socially and environmentally sustainable manner while balancing the interests of diverse stakeholders'	www.csr-asia.com

Core Characteristics of CSR

The core characteristics of CSR are the essential features of the concept that tend to be reproduced in some way in academic or practitioner definitions of CSR. Few, if any, existing definitions will include all of them, but these are the main aspects around which the definitional debates tend to centre. Six core characteristics are evident:

● *Voluntary.* Many definitions of CSR will typically see it as being about voluntary activities that go beyond those prescribed by the law. The views of the UK government and the EC as shown in Table 1 certainly emphasize this characteristic. Many companies are by now well used to considering responsibilities beyond the legal minimum, and in fact the development of self-regulatory CSR initiatives from industry is often seen as a way of forestalling additional regulation through compliance with societal moral norms. The case of UK soft drinks companies introducing a code of responsible practice in 2006 (see Ethical Performance, 2006) is a good example of such a CSR initiative that has arguably been introduced to head off potential regulatory action. Critics of CSR, therefore, tend to see the element of voluntarism as CSR's major flaw, arguing that legally mandated accountability is where attention should really be focused, as the Christian Aid definition demonstrates.[1]

● *Internalizing or managing externalities.* Externalities are the positive and negative side effects of economic behaviour that are borne by others, but are not taken into account in a firm's decision-making process, and are not included in the market price for goods and services. Pollution is typically regarded as a classic example of an externality since local communities bear the costs of manufacturers' actions. Regulation can force firms to internalize the cost of the externalities, such as pollution fines, but CSR would represent a more voluntary approach to managing externalities, for example, by a firm investing in clean technologies that prevent pollution in the first place. Much CSR activity deals with such externalities (Husted and Allen, 2006), including the management of human rights violations in the workforce, calculating the social and economic impacts of relocation or downsizing, or reducing the health impacts of 'toxic' or otherwise dangerous products, and so on. For instance, a recent example of CSR in Asia was Unilever's collaboration with Oxfam to assess the positive and negative impacts of its business on the lives of poor people in Indonesia – this, in effect, was an attempt to account for one of the firm's main externalities in the region (see Clay, 2005).

- *Multiple stakeholder orientation.* CSR involves considering a range of interests and impacts among a variety of different stakeholders other than just shareholders. The assumption that firms have responsibilities to shareholders is usually not contested; but the point is that, because corporations rely on various other constituencies such as consumers, employers, suppliers and local communities in order to survive and prosper, they do not *only* have responsibilities to shareholders. While many disagree on how much emphasis should be given to shareholders in the CSR debate, and on the extent to which other stakeholders should be taken into account, it is the expanding of corporate responsibility to these other groups which characterizes much of the essential character of CSR, as illustrated by the CSR Asia definition in Table 1.

- *Alignment of social and economic responsibilities.* This balancing of different stakeholder interests leads to a fourth facet. While CSR may be about going beyond a narrow focus on shareholders and profitability, many also believe that it should not, however, *conflict* with profitability. Although this is much debated, many definitions of CSR from business and government stress that it is about enlightened self-interest where social and economic responsibilities are aligned (see, for example, the definitions of the CBI, the UK government and HSBC in Table 1). This feature has prompted much attention to the 'business case for CSR' – namely how firms can benefit economically from being socially responsible.

- *Practices and values.* CSR is clearly about a particular set of business practices and strategies that deal with social issues, but for many people it is also about something more than that – namely a philosophy or set of values that underpins these practices. This perspective is evident in both the Gap and the Chinese government definitions of CSR given in Table 1. The values dimension of CSR is part of the reason why the subject raises so much disagreement – if it were just about what companies *did* in the social arena, it would not cause so much controversy as the debate about *why* they do it.

- *Beyond philanthropy.* In some regions of the world, CSR is mainly about philanthropy – i.e. corporate largesse towards the less fortunate. But the current debate on CSR has tended to claim emphatically that 'real' CSR is about more than just philanthropy and community projects, but about how the entire operations of the firm – i.e. its core business functions – impact upon society. Core business functions include production, marketing, procurement, human resource management, logistics, finance, and so on. This debate rests on the assumption that CSR needs to be mainstreamed into normal business practice rather than being left simply to discretionary activity. The attempt to consider how CSR might be 'built in' to the core business of firms as opposed to 'bolted on' as an extra has become a major theme in the CSR practitioner world (Grayson and

Hodges, 2004). Even the then UK Minister for Corporate Social Responsibility, Nigel Griffiths MP, noted in 2004 that 'corporate responsibility must be ingrained into the ethos of every business, built in, not bolted on'.

These six core characteristics, we would suggest, capture the main thrust of CSR. However, as we will now discuss, the meaning and relevance of CSR will vary according to organizational and national context.

CSR in Different Organizational Contexts

The variety of definitions and perspectives on CSR discussed in the previous section is partly credited to the fact that CSR is practised in a broad range of different organizational contexts. In the following we will explore these contexts by analysing the role and relevance of CSR in all three main sectors of modern economies, i.e. the private sector, the public sector and the civil society sector (non-governmental organizations, or NGOs).

CSR and the private sector

The main arena of CSR, as indicated by the 'corporate' in CSR, is the business world. Within that arena, however, we have a plethora of different types, industries and organizational forms. In the following, we will look at one of the main distinctions, namely between large corporations and small and medium-sized enterprises (SMEs).

Arguably, the language of *corporate* social responsibility indicates that CSR is predominantly a concept that applies to large corporations, typically owned by shareholders and run by employed managers. Certainly the seminal contributions on CSR, as discussed in Chapters 2 and 3 of this book, conceive CSR against the backdrop of these large corporations. Therefore, as entities in which ownership and control are separated (Berle and Means, 1932), one of the prominent issues for thinking about CSR in the context of large corporations is the question of in whose interest the company should be run on by managers: just the interests of the owners or also the interests of society at large, represented by different groups such as customers, employees or local communities?

One could also argue that large corporations are far more visible and thus far more vulnerable to criticism from the public than smaller firms. A large company that wants to behave socially responsibly therefore may well have formal policies on its responsibilities, and how these are managed. On the whole, then, CSR in large corporations typically results in a fairly structured and formalized approach. CSR policies will be translated into codes of conduct for employees or suppliers; there will normally be committees and managers responsible for CSR; and many large companies involved in CSR will document their engagement in a dedicated annual report. In such a report, the corporation discharges accountability for how exactly it has dealt with different interests and expectations of society.

If we turn to SMEs, however, we will find a rather different picture. In a recent study in the Netherlands, only 20 per cent of SMEs reported on their CSR as opposed to 62 per cent of large businesses, and similar differences were found with regard to the implementation of codes of conduct or CSR committees (Graafland, Van de Ven and Stoffele, 2003). There are a number of reasons that account for these differences (see Spence, 1999). First, SMEs are normally managed by their owner(s), who delegate decisions on CSR to a small number of people or often to just one person. This will make the approach to CSR rather informal and ad hoc as opposed to the structured approach of large corporations.

Second, unlike large corporations – which due to size and branding are often quite visible and vulnerable to criticism – SMEs are generally rather small and go under the radar of wider society. Their key relationships with society are the personal relations developed between the owner/manager and, for instance, his or her employees, suppliers, customers or neighbours. These personal relations, however, are of crucial importance to the SME, and therefore much of what we could identify as CSR in this context is targeted at building good personal relations, networks and trust (Spence and Schmidpeter, 2002).

Overall, it is probably fair to say that given the importance of SMEs, which in much of the world account for the majority of private sector employment and Gross Domestic Product (GDP) in their respective countries, the CSR literature has so far paid disproportionate attention to larger organizations (Spence and Rutherfoord, 2003).

CSR and the public sector

At first sight, one would not necessarily expect CSR to be an issue for public sector organizations, such as government ministries, agencies or local administrative bodies. After all, it is 'corporate' social responsibility. However, in most industrialized countries, governments still supply a large amount of all goods and services – somewhere between 40 and 50 per cent of the GDP in many countries. Consequently, the same claims laid upon corporations to conduct their operations in a socially responsible fashion are increasingly laid on public sector organizations as well. For example, public sector organizations face similar environmental demands, similar claims for equal opportunities for employees and similar expectations for responsible sourcing as do private companies. Consequently, we increasingly find public sector organizations adopting CSR policies, practices and tools very similar to those of the private sector.

In some ways, these demands for CSR in the public sector could even be considered as more pronounced (Seitanidi, 2004). Public organizations, such as schools, hospitals or universities, by definition have social aims and are mostly run on a not-for-profit basis. This establishes the social dimension of their responsibility at the core of their operations. Furthermore, given the size of many public bodies and agencies, as well as their quasi-monopolistic position in many areas of services, they are likely to have an impact on society which is often far beyond the impact of a single large corporation. Consequently, the claim for responsible behaviour on the part of public bodies has grown, as has the demand for greater accountability to society in the public sector.

Just as private sector companies are exhorted to become more accountable in their reporting and communication to the public, so we now witness a steady rise in the use of typical CSR instruments, such as social auditing and reporting, by public bodies (Ball, 2004). For example, the publicly funded UK media organization, the BBC, now publishes an annual CSR report.

Apart from incorporating CSR into their own operations, many government organizations also take an active role in promoting CSR within their sphere of influence. While CSR as such is a voluntary business activity, governments have nevertheless tried to create incentives for and to facilitate the voluntary adoption of socially responsible policies by the private sector (Crane and Matten, 2007: 488–499). Thus, for instance, the US government, in issuing the US Apparel Industry Code of Conduct,[2] provided a regulatory basis for CSR by US companies in their overseas supply chains. Often, governments are also part of multipartite initiatives to further CSR, such as the UN Global Compact,[3] which is a set of principles issued by the United Nations for voluntary adoption by corporations globally. In particular the UK government, since the 1980s, has made considerable efforts to encourage CSR in British companies through a number of initiatives (Moon, 2004b), including the Ethical Trade Initiative (promoting fair trade practices) or the CSR Academy (educating business people about CSR).

A similarly pronounced role in promoting CSR has been adopted by the European Union. In a part of the world where CSR is still largely considered to be a novel and Anglo-Saxon idea, the European Commission has invested considerable effort in defining and promoting CSR in Europe, convening a multi-stakeholder dialogue which resulted in a widely discussed White Paper in 2002 (Commission of the European Communities, 2002). More recently, these efforts have continued in the establishment of the 'European Alliance on CSR', which, though facilitated by the European Commission, represents a significant step towards business taking charge of CSR in a more autonomous fashion (Gardner, 2006).

CSR and civil-society organizations

Intractably linked to the rise of CSR is the role of civil society organizations (CSOs) or non-governmental organizations (NGOs).[4] Many of the initial demands for more responsible business behaviour – such as the protection of the environment, improvements in working conditions in sweatshops in the developing world, or prevention of human rights violations in countries with oppressive regimes – have been brought to the attention of the wider public by NGOs such as Greenpeace, Save the Children, or Amnesty International. Traditionally, then, the role of NGOs in the CSR arena has been more that of a police officer or watchdog, a constant critic exposing corporate misbehaviour and mobilizing pressure against allegedly irresponsible practices. This role continues to be an important function of those CSOs whose skills in raising awareness and publicly exposing corporations can be such a major reputational risk for 'responsible' companies.

Increasingly, though, companies have responded to these challenges and have tried to take on board the criticisms of CSOs. In a considerable number of cases this has resulted in a changing relationship between business and CSOs: rather than just being critic and opponent, CSOs have also built up partnerships with business in order to contribute to more socially responsible behaviour on the part of corporations (Warner and Sullivan, 2004). Within these partnerships, corporations can bring their considerable financial resources to the table while CSOs can offer their expertise and public legitimacy, among other things (Elkington and Fennell, 2000). Moreover, a number of broader industry- or country-wide standards for responsible corporate behaviour have emerged from business–CSO partnerships. A prominent example here is the Marine Stewardship Council,[5] a set of rules and practices for sustainable use of fisheries, which was initially set up by the NGO Worldwide Fund for Nature (WWF) and the company Unilever. Indeed, many of the voluntary approaches to self-regulation seen today come into existence with some degree of NGO involvement (Doh and Teegen, 2003).

With the continued growth of NGOs such as Greenpeace, Friends of the Earth, or Amnesty International, many of which are global organizations with multi-million-pound budgets and thousands of members and employees, CSR has also become a topic for these organizations to think about for themselves. Since they claim to campaign 'in the public interest', there is a growing demand to improve their public accountability (Unerman and O'Dwyer, 2006). CSOs as well as corporations need to be transparent about their causes, their funding and their tactics, and to provide their supporters and the general public with some degree of say in how they represent these causes. This becomes more pronounced as business itself has moved increasingly towards setting up CSOs which represent specific business interests, such as the World Business Council for Sustainable Development (WBCSD), the Global Business Coalition on HIV/AIDS (GBC) or the Global Climate Coalition (GCC). While on the outside these organizations often resemble CSOs, they are in fact very different from normal grass-root CSOs, and have therefore been dubbed by some as 'astroturf NGOs' (Gray, Bebbington and Collinson, 2006). Arguably, the challenge of putting policies and practices in place for enhanced public accountability and transparency – in other words, implementing CSR – is one of the key future tests for CSOs.

CSR in Different Regions of the Globe

The meaning of CSR not only differs from sector to sector (as we have discussed in the previous section); it also differs quite substantially from country to country. To put CSR 'in a global context' (as our subtitle suggests) it is essential to understand the specific regional and national situations in which companies practise CSR. In the following, we will therefore discuss some basic characteristics of CSR in different regions of the globe.

CSR in developed countries

In its most well-known guise, CSR is essentially a US idea. It was in the US where the language and practice of CSR first emerged. In addition, most of the academic literature on the topic, and most of the key ideas discussed in the first section of this book, originate there. The main reason for this lies in the specific characteristics of the US business system (Matten and Moon, 2004b). As such, American society is characterized by fairly unregulated markets for labour and capital, low levels of welfare state provision, and a high appreciation of individual freedom and responsibility. Consequently, many social issues, such as education, healthcare or community investment have traditionally been at the core of CSR. Philanthropy is high on the agenda with, for instance, corporate community contributions by US companies being about ten times higher than those of their British counterparts (Brammer and Pavelin, 2005). In other parts of the world, most notably Europe, the Far East and Australasia, however, there has always been a stronger tendency to address social issues through governmental policies and collective action. Many issues that US companies would typically boast about as CSR on their websites, such as the provision of healthcare or fighting climate change, have not appeared on the screens of continental European companies until recently. The reason for this is that these issues have traditionally been considered a task for governments; or, in other words, the corporate responsibility for social issues has been the object of codified and mandatory regulation. CSR for European companies, therefore, has predominantly come on to the agenda through their overseas operations (where regulatory frameworks are different from those in Europe); and it is fair to say that, even up until the present day, multinational corporations (MNCs) rather than domestic companies can be considered to be the leading actors in European CSR. The US–Europe differences in CSR are likely to persist, and the manner in which corporations address CSR issues, such as global warming, the provision of affordable medicine to the developing world, or the use of genetically modified organisms in food production, remains markedly different on both sides of the Atlantic (Doh and Guay, 2006).

Countries such as Japan, and to a lesser degree South Korea and Taiwan, are considered fairly similar to continental Europe in terms of the institutional context for CSR. They are characterized by high bank and public ownership, patriarchal and long-term employment, and coordination and control systems based on long-term relations and partnerships rather than on markets. The Japanese 'Keiretsu', the Korean 'Chaebol' or the (mostly state-owned) Taiwanese conglomerates have a legacy of CSR similar to those of European companies – including lifelong employment, benefits, social services and healthcare – not so much as a result of voluntary corporate policies, but more as a response to the regulatory and institutional environment of business.

The reasons for the rise of CSR in Europe and in these developed economies in the Far East in recent years are several. To begin with, MNCs with their home base in such countries are challenged to implement more CSR in their operations located in countries with poor governance and low levels of state provision of public services, human rights protection or environmental protection. Furthermore, some of these developed economies have undergone substantial overhauls of their welfare systems and regulatory frameworks, resulting in lesser degrees of state attention to social issues and more discretion for private actors. The United Kingdom is probably the best example here, where radical reforms that liberalized labour and capital markets, together with the privatization of public services and publicly owned companies, contributed to a significant surge in CSR (Moon, 2004a). Increasingly, corporations in the UK have assumed responsibility for regenerating local communities, addressing unemployment, sponsoring schools and education, as well as improving public transparency and accountability.

In addition to these domestic political changes, globalization also represents a powerful booster of CSR – as we will discuss in more detail in Chapter 11. The rise of global investors linking their investment decisions to 'socially responsible investment' criteria, the growth in global NGO activism scrutinizing corporate behaviour, and intensified exposure of business by the media have all boosted growing attention to CSR in Europe and elsewhere (Matten and Moon, 2004b). It will also be observed that in most developed countries we have specific domestic CSR issues that shape the debate in the respective context. For instance, many European countries see CSR specifically with regard to the protection of the natural environment, while the CSR debate in the Far East prominently features issues of corporate governance and transparency in large conglomerates (Webb, 2006). Often the CSR debate in a country reflects long-standing and ongoing deliberations in society at large: for instance, in Australia and South Africa, considerable expectations have been directed towards companies to address and uphold rights of aboriginal and black people respectively, or to contribute to their economic empowerment more generally.

CSR in developing countries

The activities of Western MNCs in developing countries have also been a major driver behind the recent surge in CSR over the past two decades. Many companies use developing countries as a source of cheap raw materials and, in particular, cheap labour. Against this backdrop, it was, for instance, campaigns against Shell's role in Nigeria and Nike's labour practices in its Asian supply chains that triggered significant changes towards more responsible practices in many MNCs (see case study 3, pp. 492–3, for more on the Nike story).

Developing countries may at times be characterized by various features that can offer considerable scope for the exercise of CSR. These include low standards for working conditions and environmental protection, high corruption, oppressive regimes with low regard for human rights, poor provision of healthcare and education, as well as low levels of per capita income and foreign direct investment. Although this is not a fair representation of all developing country contexts at all times, the main challenge for MNCs from the developed world when they are faced with such circumstances lies in conducting their business in a way that would be considered socially responsible in their respective home countries. Reading 20 by Scherer and Smid in Chapter 11 (pp. 470–91) describes some of the approaches companies have applied to tackling such challenges.

It is important to recognize, though, that a growing number of *domestic* companies in developing countries have also developed an interest in CSR. The main CSR issues with which these companies are concerned include contributions to enhance the infrastructure of health, education and transport, and to serve as examples of good governance. Similarly, as the example of the Grameen Bank,[6] founded by Nobel Peace Prize-winner Muhammad Yunus, shows, a key topic on the CSR agenda is the encouragement of small scale entrepreneurship through micro-credit, and the economic empowerment of women and other marginalized minorities.

As the last example shows, the debate in the global South has begun to shift from understanding CSR as aid towards thinking of responsible behaviour more in terms of development. Arguably, one of the main reasons why these countries are poor is the absence of economic activity and growth – and it is here that one of the main responsibilities of business can be seen. Implementing CSR in this sense would therefore require MNCs to conduct business and bring FDI to developing countries in the first place, and then ensure that the wealth created is locked into development. Thus, for instance, the World Business Council for Sustainable Development recently issued an in-depth report on how business supports the implementation of the UN's Millennium Development Goals[7] (WBCSD, 2005). Many of the points raised in the report refer not to business 'sharing' its wealth with these countries but to business being present in these countries in the first place. Reading 19 by Prahalad and Hammond in Chapter 11 (452–91) develops one particular approach to poverty alleviation in developing countries that indicates a major potential role for business in development.

This role of MNCs, however, is not uncontested. Many critics argue that profit-maximizing corporations have only very limited interest in these more political goals, and that evidence of MNCs contributing positively in the developing world is at best sketchy (Frynas, 2005). Ultimately, according to the sceptics, responsible corporate behaviour in the developing world is an issue that cannot be left to the voluntary discretion of businesspeople but needs to be addressed by more stringent regulation in their home countries in the global North (Aaronson, 2005).

CSR in emerging/transitional economies

Between those two major categories of developed and developing countries there is a third category that deserves attention from a CSR perspective. Most countries of the former communist bloc have changed from a planned and government-run economy to a capitalist market system. While the social responsibility of state-operated business in the former model was far-reaching, including broad provision of education, healthcare, housing and a plethora of other services, the transition to a market economy has seen many of these former conglomerates dismantled and transformed into shareholder-owned companies. While there is a plethora of different approaches to CSR in these countries, one might argue that in some respects Russia and China represent the more extreme cases. Russia, on the one hand, has seen privatization and the turn to capitalism accompanied by rather weak and corrupt governmental institutions resulting in what some would refer to as a 'cowboy economy'. It is therefore little wonder that CSR is still a largely unknown concept in Russia (Grafski and Moon, 2004) and, for many Russian businesspeople, one which bears strong resemblances to communist times. China, on the other hand, has maintained a strong capacity for the state in controlling and regulating the economy and, while the role and responsibilities of business in society might not always be referred to in terms of the Western language of CSR, we still see considerable involvement of companies in the area. Many commentators expect that China, with growing economic development, will see a rise in CSR-oriented regulation over the next few years (Miller, 2005).

Conclusion

In this chapter we have discussed the development of CSR and its recent rise to prominence. We have also examined the maze of definitions that have been used to delineate CSR in order to develop some core characteristics of the concept. Finally, we have explored the meaning and relevance of CSR in different national and organizational contexts. What should certainly be clear by now is that the term 'corporate social responsibility' is very difficult to pin down precisely – it can have many meanings, applications and implications, and these are rarely agreed upon by those who take an interest in the debate. This may not make our lives any easier when studying CSR, but it certainly makes it more interesting!

In this book, we have adopted a deliberately broad perspective on CSR in order to provide a well-rounded introduction to the subject. Included in the following chapters are those that espouse a view of CSR as thoroughly embedded in a pro-corporate 'business case for CSR' as well as those that argue for a more political view of CSR that attends to the need to make corporations more accountable to the societies in which they operate. The point of this text is not so much to suggest that any of these perspectives is necessarily 'better' or more 'correct' than another, but more to provide an insight into the richness and diversity of the CSR literature. Editing a collection of readings on CSR allows us to present some of this heterogeneity while simultaneously providing some guidance as to how to 'read' some of the different contributions. After all, it is clear that many of the authors writing about CSR in this book are engaging in a discussion about CSR for different ends, and bring with them very different assumptions about the nature and purpose of the corporation. The introductions to the readings will offer some useful insight on these purposes and assumptions, at least as far as we see them.

The book is organized into three sections, dealing with respectively:

- Understanding CSR
- Applying CSR
- Managing CSR

In designing this structure, it is evident that our main focus is around the actual performance of CSR by organizations, although the book also offers considerable theoretical insight on CSR by bringing out key conceptual issues as they pertain to particular CSR practices and principles. The applied approach that we take is also demonstrated by the integrative case studies that appear at the end of each of the three sections. These are intended to bring together some of the main issues that arise in the different chapters in each section, and offer some fascinating insights into the challenges of CSR in a global context.

Ultimately, the theory and practice of CSR as presented in this book represents a work in progress. The subject has risen to prominence only relatively recently, and has been disseminated across the globe with remarkable speed. The way in which CSR is understood, practised and institutionalized in the global context is ever-changing and open to substantially different interpretations. This book offers a multi-faceted and relatively comprehensive account of CSR as it stands today, but this account is by no means the only or the final one.

Study Questions

1   What is CSR and why has it risen to prominence over the past decade?
2   What are the six main characteristics of CSR? To what extent do these characteristics delineate CSR from other concepts such as business ethics and corporate citizenship?
3   Select four corporations and four NGOs and research their perspectives on CSR on the web. To what extent is there overlap and divergence in their view of CSR? What can account for these similarities or differences?
4   'CSR is only relevant for private sector companies.' Critically discuss, providing examples from the public and civil sectors.
5   Can or should CSR be transferred to developing and emerging economies? What are the benefits and drawbacks of this for the countries concerned?

Notes

1   See e.g. the Corporate Responsibility (CORE) Coalition, a collection of UK NGOs including WWF (UK), Amnesty International, Action Aid and Friends of the Earth, that 'work to make changes in UK company law to minimize companies' negative impacts on people and the environment and to maximize companies' contribution to sustainable societies' (www.corporate-responsibility.org).
2   http://www.dol.gov/ilab/media/reports/iclp/apparel/main.htm (accessed February 2007).
3   http://www.unglobalcompact.org/ (accessed February 2007).
4   We use the terms CSO and NGO interchangeably in this volume.
5   http://www.msc.org/.
6   http://www.grameen-info.org/.
7   http://www.un.org/millenniumgoals/.

References

Aaronson, S. (2005) '"Minding Our Business": What the United States Government Has Done and Can Do to Ensure that U.S. Multinationals Act Responsibly in Foreign Markets', *Journal of Business Ethics* 59: 175–198.

Ball, A. (2004) 'A Sustainability Accounting Project for the UK Local Government Sector? Testing the Social Theory Mapping Process and Locating a Frame of Reference', *Critical Perspectives on Accounting* 15(8): 1009–1035.

Berle, A. and Means, G. (1932) *The Modern Corporation and Private Property*, New York: Transaction.

Brammer, S. and Pavelin, S. (2005) 'Corporate Community Contributions in the United Kingdom and the United States', *Journal of Business Ethics* 56: 15–26.

Brown, T. and Dacin, P. (1997) 'The Company and the Product: Corporate Associations and Consumer Product Responses', *Journal of Marketing* 61(1): 68–84.

Carroll, A. (1979) 'A Three Dimensional Model of Corporate Social Performance', *Academy of Management Review* 4: 497–505.

Carroll, A. (1999) 'Corporate Social Responsibility – Evolution of a Definitional Construct', *Business and Society* 38(3): 268–295.

Clay, J. (2005) *Exploring the Links between International Business and Poverty Reduction: A Case Study of Unilever in Indonesia*, Oxford: Oxfam GB, Novib Oxfam Netherlands, and Unilever.

Commission of the European Communities (2002) *Communication from the Commission Concerning Corporate Social Responsibility: A Business Contribution to Sustainable Development*, Brussels: EU Commission.

Crane, A. and Matten, D. (2007) *Business Ethics: Managing Corporate Citizenship and Sustainability in the Age of Globalization* (2nd edn), Oxford: Oxford University Press.

Doh, J. and Guay, T. (2006) 'Corporate Social Responsibility, Public Policy, and NGO Activism in Europe and the United States: An Institutional-stakeholder Perspective', *Journal of Management Studies* 43(1): 47–73.

Doh, J. and Teegen, H. (eds) (2003) *Globalization and NGOs: Transforming Business, Government, and Society*, Westport, CT: Praeger Publishers.

Elankumaran, S., Seal, R. and Hashmi, A. (2005) 'Transcending Transformation: Enlightening Endeavours at Tata Steel', *Journal of Business Ethics* 59(1): 109–119.

Elkington, J. and Fennell, S. (2000) 'Partners for Sustainability'. In J. Bendell (ed.) *Terms for Endearment: Business, NGOs and Sustainable Development*, pp. 150–162, Sheffield: Greenleaf.

Ethical Performance (2006) 'Soft Drinks Firms Sign Code Aimed at Fighting Obesity', *Ethical Performance* 7(10). Downloaded from http://www.ethicalperformance. com/europeamericas/articleView.php?articleID=3809 as at 3823/3808/3806.

Ethical Performance (2007) 'CSR Combatants Dig in for the Battle of Wikipedia', *Ethical Performance* 8 (9). Downloaded from http://www.ethicalperformance. com/europeamericas/articleView.php?articleID=4328 on 4315/4322/4307.

Frynas, J. (2005) 'The False Developmental Promise of Corporate Social Responsibility: Evidence from Multinational Oil Companies', *International Affairs* 81(3): 581–598.

Gardner, S. (2006) 'Pushing Business-driven Corporate Citizenship', *Ethical Corporation* April: 8–9.

Graafland, J., Van de Ven, B. and Stoffele, N. (2003) 'Strategies and Instruments for Organising CSR by Small and Large Businesses in the Netherlands', *Journal of Business Ethics* 47: 45–60.

Grafski, S. and Moon, J. (2004) 'Comparative Overview of Western and Russian CSR Models'. In S. Litovchenko (ed.) *Report on Social Investments in Russia*, pp. 13–22, Moscow: The Russian Managers Association and UNDP.

Gray, R., Bebbington, J. and Collinson, D. (2006) 'NGOs, Civil Society and Accountability: Making the People Accountable to Capital', *Accounting, Auditing and Accountability Journal* 19(3): 319–348.

Grayson, D. and Hodges, A. (2004) *Corporate Social Opportunity: Seven Steps to Make Corporate Social Responsibility Work for Your Business*, Sheffield: Greenleaf.

Husted, B. and Allen, D. (2006) 'Corporate Social Responsibility in the Multinational Enterprise: Strategic and Institutional Approaches', *Journal of International Business Studies* 37(6): 838–849.

McWilliams, A., Siegel, D. and Wright, P. (2006) 'Corporate Social Responsibility: Strategic Implications', *Journal of Management Studies* 43(1): 1–18.

Matten, D. and Moon, J. (2004a) '"Implicit" and "Explicit" CSR: A Conceptual Framework for Understanding CSR in Europe', *ICCSR Research Paper Series* (29–2004), University of Nottingham.

Matten, D. and Moon, J. (2004b) 'A Conceptual Framework for Understanding CSR in Europe'. In A. Habisch, J. Jonker, M. Wegner and R. Schmidpeter (eds) *CSR across Europe*, pp. 339–360, Berlin: Springer.

Miller, T. (2005) 'A Chinese Definition of CSR', *Ethical Corporation* November: 34–35.

Moon, J. (2004a) 'CSR in the UK: An Explicit Model of Business–Society Relations'. In A. Habisch, J. Jonker, M. Wegner and R. Schmidpeter (eds) *CSR across Europe*, pp. 51–65, Berlin: Springer.

Moon, J. (2004b) *Government as a Driver of CSR*, Nottingham: ICCSR Working Papers No. 20.

Seitanidi, M. (2004) 'Corporate Social Responsibility and the Non-commercial Sector', *New Academy Review* 3(4): 60–72.

Spence, L. (1999) 'Does Size Matter? The State of the Art in Small Business Ethics', *Business Ethics: A European Review* 8(3): 163–174.

Spence, L. and Rutherfoord, R. (2003) 'Small Business and Empirical Perspectives in Business Ethics', *Journal of Business Ethics* 47: 1–5.

Spence, L. and Schmidpeter, R. (2002) 'SMEs, Social Capital and the Common Good', *Journal of Business Ethics* 45: 93–108.

Unerman, J. and O'Dwyer, B. (2006) 'On James Bond and the Importance of NGO Accountability', *Accounting, Auditing and Accountability Journal* 19(3): 305–318.

Warner, M. and Sullivan, R. (eds) (2004) *Putting Partnerships to Work: Strategic Alliances for Development between Government, the Private Sector and Civil Society*, Sheffield: Greenleaf.

WBCSD (2005) *Business for Development: Business Solutions in Support of the Millennium Development Goals*, Geneva: World Business Council for Sustainable Development.

Webb, T. (2006) 'Is Asian Corporate Governance Improving?', *Ethical Corporation* May: 25–26.

Zadek, S. (2004) 'The Path to Corporate Responsibility', *Harvard Business Review* 82 (December): 125–132.

Chapter 2

The case for and against CSR

IN THIS CHAPTER WE WILL:

- Map out the long-standing debate in favour and critical of CSR.
- Highlight the nature of the modern corporation and its impact on CSR.
- Evaluate the role of governments with regard to the socially responsible behaviour of corporations.
- Understand and evaluate the key arguments against CSR.
- Examine the main points brought forward to counter the critics and understand the key arguments in favour of CSR.

Introduction

'CSR has won the battle of ideas.' This was the opening line of a special section on CSR in the business magazine *The Economist* in early 2005 (Crook, 2005). In many companies CSR is now a very visible element of management practice. This fact, however, does not necessarily imply that everybody agrees with this new corporate activity. A few lines later, in the same article, Clive Crook adds, regarding the surge of CSR, that its success in the battle of ideas 'is a pity'! When studying specific areas of business, such as marketing, finance or accounting, most experts would readily agree that these topics are a core part of what a professional executive should know. CSR as a special area of business studies, however, is somewhat different. After all, there are still many academics, managers and politicians who would argue vehemently that CSR should not be part of the curriculum for business students; nor should it be considered a legitimate activity of private companies. The debate about the legitimacy of CSR, then, is as old as the topic itself and it is vital to understand this contested nature of CSR.

We have already mentioned briefly that many activities labelled CSR today are by no means new (Cannon, 1994). When companies such as Cadburys in England or Krupp in Germany provided housing, healthcare or education for their workers and their families, or when industrialists such as Carnegie or Duke in the USA funded universities in the nineteenth century, they were doing similar things to what Vodafone or Nike (see Case studies 1 and 3 in this volume) currently feature as part of their CSR policies.[1] There are, however, two main differences which provide the basis for most of these heated debates about CSR. First, the nature of the corporation has changed significantly over the past two centuries: while most of these early activities were paternalistic in nature and chiefly initiated by the owners of those companies, today's CSR is carried out by huge corporations that are owned by hundreds and thousands of largely anonymous shareholders. Second, many of the early CSR activities by wealthy industrialists ultimately provided a standard for governments to issue legislation which made the provision of decent working conditions, fair wages and access to education a mandatory right for their citizens. These tendencies resulted in extensive welfare state provision in most industrialized countries, and as a result corporations had to comply with a whole plethora of mandatory expectations from society which led them to behave more responsibly – albeit not on a voluntary basis. The main points of contention, then, between advocates and adversaries of CSR focus on (1) the nature of the modern corporation, and (2) the adequate role of the state. We will have a look at both issues in turn.

Understanding the Nature of the Modern Corporation

As we discussed already in Chapter 1, the first major wave of debate on CSR started in the USA in the 1950s. By this time, most big corporations were no longer owned by individual businesspeople or their families but by shareholders with shares being traded on the stock market. The key debate in this context is in whose interest the company should be managed: should a corporation pursue just the interests of its owners (i.e. shareholders) or the interests of wider society as well? It is worth noting, then, that the terminology of *corporate* social responsibility reflects this focus on big businesses and, while many of the issues discussed in CSR also apply to smaller businesses, the key trigger of the debate was the rise of the modern corporation which became manifest following the Second World War in the US and beyond in most industrialized countries.

Much of the literature on CSR, in particular as discussed in Chapters 3 and 4 in this book, may be seen as making the case for the legitimacy of the interests of societal groups beyond (but including) shareholders. The reading by Henry Mintzberg in this chapter provides a powerful overview of this side of the controversy. On the other hand, there has always been the argument that a company should just do what its owners want it to do – and, as their chief interest is to maximize the value of the shares and/or the amount of their dividend, the economic goals of a business should be paramount.

The reading by Milton Friedman may be considered to be the most prominent voice on this side of the argument.

Interestingly, the more recent resurgence in the debate on CSR at the beginning of this century was triggered mostly by corporate *ir*responsibility towards shareholders in the context of corporate scandals in the USA (e.g. Enron, WorldCom) and Europe (e.g. Parmalat, Ahold). While the debate in essence did not surface fundamentally new arguments, it provided some more contextualization of the issues in the twenty-first-century business environment. In particular the compatibility of capitalism with wider societal interests (Child, 2002; Handy, 2002) and the need for change in business research and education (Gioia, 2002; Goshal, 2005) were centre stage of the debate. While these scandals have given considerable mileage to CSR in business practice, many critics eloquently reiterated the necessity of business to focus on its core economic functions of producing goods and services while maximizing the returns for their primary legitimate interest groups, namely shareholders (Henderson, 2001; Sternberg, 2000).

The Adequate Role of Government

In the above-mentioned article in *The Economist*, CSR critic Clive Crook quite eloquently rehearses another key argument of sceptics which is closely intertwined with the previous point (Crook, 2005: 18):

> The proper guardians of the public interest are governments, which are accountable to all citizens. It is the job of elected politicians to set goals for regulators, to deal with externalities, to mediate among different interests, to attend to the demands of social justice, to provide the public goods . . . and to organise resources accordingly.

The central point in this part of the controversy is that the chief arbiter of the wider welfare of society is the (democratic) government of a country. The decision on which social causes should be met, what labour standards are considered adequate, or what education should look like – to name some examples – is ultimately the domain of government. Private actors, most notably corporations, simply do not have the mandate to decide on these issues; rather it should be society as a whole through its democratically elected representatives. In essence, then, these critics argue that, if there is a problem in society which managers could potentially address through 'CSR', it should not be at the discretion of individual managers, dedicating their shareholders' money to these causes; rather it should be an issue taken up by regulators resulting in changes in the legal framework of the corporation – if that is what society as a whole wants.

This argument is quite powerful. However, it overlooks one of the key reasons which have put CSR on the agenda over the past two decades. As we will discuss in more detail in Chapter 11, globalization and other socio-political factors have fundamentally changed the way in which societies are governed. Many governments are now reluctant to impose extra regulation on business for fear of losing employment and tax income, since companies find it easier to relocate to more 'business-friendly' countries than to comply with unfavourable conditions. Furthermore, businesses in developing countries often face governments that are either undemocratic or are otherwise unwilling or unable to implement existing regulation to look after the public interest. It is no surprise that many companies – as the case studies in this volume illustrate – take up CSR because of their global operations in contexts of poor or non-existing societal governance on the part of politicians.

Introducing the Readings

The two readings[2] that follow offer a good introduction to both sides of the argument on CSR. As we have discussed above, the two key contested areas have remained much the same over the years and the two papers were accordingly written by very distinguished academics more than twenty years ago. In their own way, they represent simple but quite comprehensive overviews of the respective sides of the debate, and the arguments put forward still resonate strongly today in the contemporary debate on CSR.

The business of business is business

Nobel Prize Laureate Milton Friedman's article 'The social responsibility of business is to increase its profits' is one of the classics in CSR. Originally published by the esteemed economist for a non-expert audience in the *New York Times Magazine*, the article is written in very clear and simple language and sets out the key arguments of the CSR critics. In detailing the dominance of shareholder interests the article makes several important points about the nature of the modern corporation as a legal construct. To begin with, the corporation, in the same way as a building or any other construct of human activity, is unable to assume moral responsibility. This is only possible for human beings, Friedman argues, and thus only the human beings who set up and work in the corporation are morally culpable. Second, if the owners want to dedicate their money or their employees' time to social causes (as might be the case for the owner-managed small business) – fine: they are free to do what they want with their property. The employed managers, however, do not have a right to spend shareholders' money on what they, the managers, think should be the responsibility of the company. Friedman also quite powerfully argues that ultimately CSR is undemocratic: rather than letting society decide on what the public interest should be, managers who practise CSR assume a role for which they are neither trained nor can legitimately fulfil. The reading is particularly interesting as it is also a primer on Friedman's ideas on the economic organization of societies which so powerfully shaped economics and politics in the last two decades of the twentieth century.

The case for corporate social responsibility

Henry Mintzberg, the management guru from McGill University in Montreal, looks at the other side of the dispute in his article. Starting with an assessment of the debate and in particular with the critics of CSR, this reading provides some powerful arguments against Friedman's position on CSR. Mintzberg's defence incorporates both perspectives discussed above. Reflecting on the nature of the modern corporation, he argues that corporations are not only economic actors acting in the interest of their 'owners' but inevitably are also political or social actors as their economic decisions impact upon wider circles in society. As a powerful example he cites Dow Chemical's decision to sell Napalm to the US Army, later used in Vietnam. As an organizational scholar he also lines up convincing arguments against Friedman's claim of corporations being moral-free zones. With regard to the second aspect, the role of governments, Mintzberg highlights the limits of the legal framework to successfully enforce ethically and socially responsible organizational behaviour.

Study Questions

1   What are the key arguments for and against CSR? Answer the question by using Mintzberg's paper to address the arguments brought forward by Friedman against CSR.
2   Both Friedman and Mintzberg have different assumptions about:

  ● The nature of the modern corporation;
  ● The role and capacity of governments.

  Describe and discuss both aspects in the respective readings. Which approach do you think is most realistic for business in the twenty-first century?
3   Is there a difference between the social responsibility of a small family business and a large stock market-traded public corporation?
4   The UK government has for some time actively promoted CSR (e.g. through a government minister for CSR and other developments). In similar vein, the EU Commission has supported CSR in various initiatives over the past decade, for example, with the European Alliance for CSR. Think about reasons why governments could be interested in encouraging CSR. Do you see any problems with such an approach?
5   The debate for and against CSR as discussed in this chapter is based on papers written prior to the collapse of the communist bloc and its economic system, as well as before the rise of globalization. Suggest new arguments – on both sides of the debate – resulting from more recent changes in the global political economy of the past two decades.

Notes

1   All references to corporations reflect on their CSR-related reports and publications available from their websites as of December 2006.
2   The gendered language of some of the earlier readings is unfortunate and not an approach we advocate.

References

Cannon, T. (1994) *Corporate Responsibility*, London: Pearson.

Child, J. (2002) 'The International Crisis of Confidence in Corporations', *Academy of Management Executive* 16(3): 145–149.

Crook, C. (2005) 'The Good Company', *The Economist*, 374 (22 January 2005): 20pp.

Gioia, D. (2002) 'Business Education's Role in the Crisis of Confidence in Corporations', *Academy of Management Executive* 16(3): 142–144.

Goshal, S. (2005) 'Bad Management Theories Are Destroying Good Management Practices', *Academy of Management Learning and Education* 4(1): 75–91.

Handy, C. (2002) 'What's a Business For?', *Harvard Business Review* 80(12): 49–56.

Henderson, D. (2001) *Misguided Virtue: False Notions of Corporate Social Responsibility*, London: Institute of Economic Affairs.

Sternberg, E. (2000) *Just Business: Business Ethics in Action* (2nd edn), Oxford; New York: Oxford University Press.

A FRIEDMAN DOCTRINE –
THE SOCIAL RESPONSIBILITY OF BUSINESS
IS TO INCREASE ITS PROFITS

Milton Friedman

When I hear businessmen speak eloquently about the "social responsibilities of business in a free-enterprise system," I am reminded of the wonderful line about the Frenchman who discovered at the age of 70 that he had been speaking prose all his life. The businessmen believe that they are defending free enterprise when they declaim that business is not concerned "merely" with profit but also with promoting desirable "social" ends; that business has a "social conscience" and takes seriously its responsibilities for providing employment, eliminating discrimination, avoiding pollution and whatever else may be the catchwords of the contemporary crop of reformers. In fact they are – or would be if they or anyone else took them seriously – preaching pure and unadulterated socialism. Businessmen who talk this way are unwitting puppets of the intellectual forces that have been undermining the basis of a free society these past decades.

The discussions of the "social responsibilities of business" are notable for their analytical looseness and lack of rigor. What does it mean to say that "business" has responsibilities? Only people can have responsibilities. A corporation is an artificial person and in this sense may have artificial responsibilities, but "business" as a whole cannot be said to have responsibilities, even in this vague sense. The first step toward clarity in examining the doctrine of the social responsibility of business is to ask precisely what it implies for whom.

Presumably, the individuals who are to be responsible are businessmen, which means individual proprietors or corporate executives. Most of the discussion of social responsibility is directed at corporations, so in what follows I shall mostly neglect the individual proprietor and speak of corporate executives.

In a free-enterprise, private-property system, a corporate executive is an employee of the owners of the business. He has direct responsibility to his employers. That responsibility is to conduct the business in accordance with their desires, which generally will be to make as much money as possible while conforming to the basic rules of the society, both those embodied in law and those embodied in ethical custom. Of course, in some cases his employers may have a different objective. A group of persons might establish a corporation for an eleemosynary purpose – for example, a hospital or a school. The manager of such a corporation will not have money profit as his objectives but the rendering of certain services.

In either case, the key point is that, in his capacity as a corporate executive, the manager is the agent of the individuals who own the corporation or establish the eleemosynary institution, and his primary responsibility is to them.

Needless to say, this does not mean that it is easy to judge how well he is performing his task. But at least the criterion of performance is straightforward, and the persons among whom a voluntary contractual arrangement exists are clearly defined.

Of course, the corporate executive is also a person in his own right. As a person, he may have responsibilities that he recognizes or assumes voluntarily – to his family, his conscience, his feelings of charity, his church, his clubs, his city, his country. He may feel impelled by these responsibilities to devote part of his income to causes he regards as worthy, to refuse to work for particular corporations, even to leave his job, for example, to join the armed forces. If we wish, we may refer to some of these responsibilities as "social responsibilities." But in these respects he is acting as a principal, not an agent; he is spending his own money or time or energy, not the money of his employers or the time or energy he has contracted to devote to their purposes. If these are "social responsibilities," they are the social responsibilities of individuals, not of business.

What does it mean to say that the corporate executive has a "social responsibility" in his capacity as businessman? If this statement is not pure rhetoric, it must mean that he is to act in some way that is not in the interest of his employers. For example, that he is to refrain from increasing the price of the product in order to contribute to the social objective of preventing inflation, even though a price increase would be in the best interests of the corporation. Or that he is to make expenditures on reducing pollution beyond the amount that is in the best interests of the corporation or that is required by law in order to contribute to the social objective of improving the environment. Or that, at the expense of corporate profits, he is to hire "hard-core" unemployed instead of better-qualified available workmen to contribute to the social objective of reducing poverty.

In each of these cases, the corporate executive would be spending someone else's money for a general social interest. Insofar as his actions in accord with his "social responsibility" reduce returns to stockholders, he is spending their money. Insofar as his actions raise the price to customers, he is spending the customers' money. Insofar as his actions lower the wages of some employees, he is spending their money.

The stockholders or the customers or the employees could separately spend their own money on the particular action if they wished to do so. The executive is exercising a distinct "social responsibility," rather than serving as an agent of the stockholders or the customers or the employees, only if he spends the money in a different way than they would have spent it.

But if he does this, he is in effect imposing taxes, on the one hand, and deciding how the tax proceeds shall be spent, on the other.

This process raises political questions on two levels: principle and consequences. On the level of political principle, the imposition of taxes and the expenditure of tax proceeds are governmental functions. We have established elaborate constitutional, parliamentary and judicial provisions to control these functions, to assure that taxes are imposed so far as possible in accordance with the preferences and desires of the public – after all. "taxation without representation" was one of the battle cries of the American Revolution. We have a system of checks and balances to separate the legislative function of imposing taxes and enacting expenditures from the executive function of collecting taxes and administering expenditure programs and from the judicial function of mediating disputes and interpreting the law.

Here the businessman – self-selected or appointed directly or indirectly by stockholders – is to be simultaneously legislator, executive and jurist. He is to decide whom to tax by how much and for what purpose, and he is to spend the proceeds – all this guided only by general exhortations from on high to restrain inflation, improve the environment, fight poverty and so on and on.

The whole justification for permitting the corporate executive to be selected by the stockholders is that the executive is an agent serving the interests of his principal. This justification disappears when the corporate executive imposes taxes and spends the proceeds for "social" purposes. He becomes in effect a public employee, a civil servant, even though he remains in name an employee of a private enterprise. On grounds of political principle, it is intolerable that such civil servants – insofar as their actions in the name of social responsibility are real and not just window-dressing – should be selected as they are now. If they are to be civil servants, then they must be selected through a political process. If they are to impose taxes and make expenditures to foster "social" objectives, then political machinery must be set up to guide the assessment of taxes and to determine through a political process the objectives to be served.

This is the basic reason why the doctrine of "social responsibility" involves the acceptance of the socialist view that political mechanisms, not market mechanisms, are the appropriate way to determine the allocation of scarce resources to alternative uses.

On the grounds of consequences, can the corporate executive in fact discharge his alleged "social responsibilities"? On the one hand, suppose he could get away with spending the stockholders' or customers' or employees' money. How is he to know how to spend it? He is told that he must contribute to fighting inflation. How is he to know what action of his will contribute to that end? He is presumably an expert in running his company – in producing a product or selling it or financing it. But nothing about his selection makes him an expert on inflation. Will his holding down the price of his product reduce inflationary pressure? Or, by leaving more spending power in the hands of his customers, simply divert it elsewhere? Or, by forcing him to produce less because of the lower price, will it simply contribute to shortages? Even if he could answer these questions, how much cost is he justified in imposing on his stockholders, customers and employees for this social purpose? What is his appropriate share and what is the appropriate share of others?

And, whether he wants to or not, can he get away with spending his stockholders', customers', or employees' money? Will not the stockholders fire him? (Either the present ones or those who take over when his actions in the name of social responsibility have reduced the corporation's profits and the price of his stock.) His customers and his employees can desert him for other producers and employers less scrupulous in exercising their social responsibilities.

This facet of "social responsibility" doctrine is brought into sharp relief when the doctrine is used to justify wage restraint by trade unions. The conflict of interest is naked and clear when union officials are asked to subordinate the interest of their members to some more general social purpose. If the union officials try to enforce wage restraint, the consequence is likely to be wildcat strikes, rank-and-file revolts and the emergence of strong competitors for their jobs. We thus have the ironic phenomenon that union leaders – at least in the U.S. – have objected to Government interference with the market far more consistently and courageously than have business leaders.

The difficulty of exercising "social responsibility" illustrates, of course, the great virtue of private competitive enterprise – it forces people to be responsible for their own actions and makes it difficult for them to "exploit" other people for either selfish or unselfish purposes. They can do good – but only at their own expense.

Many a reader who has followed the argument this far may be tempted to remonstrate that it is all well and good to speak of government's having the responsibility to impose taxes and determine expenditures for such "social" purposes as controlling pollution or training the hard-core unemployed but that the problems are too urgent to wait on the slow course of political processes, that the exercise of social responsibility by businessmen is a quicker and surer way to solve pressing current problems.

Aside from the question of fact – I share Adam Smith's skepticism about the benefits that can be expected from "those who affected to trade for the public good" – this argument must be rejected on grounds of principle. What it amounts to is an assertion that those who favour the taxes and expenditures in question have failed to persuade a majority of their fellow citizens to be of like mind and that they are seeking to attain by undemocratic procedures what they cannot attain by democratic procedures. In a free society, it is hard for "good" people to do "good," but there is a small price to pay for making it hard for "evil" people to do "evil," especially since one man's good is another man's evil.

I have, for simplicity, concentrated on the special case of the corporate executive, except only for the brief digression on trade unions. But precisely the same argument applies to the newer phenomenon of calling upon stockholders to require corporations to exercise social responsibility. In most of these cases, what is in effect involved is some stockholders trying to get other stockholders (or customers or employees) to contribute against their will to "social" causes favored by the activists. Insofar as they succeed, they are again imposing taxes and spending the proceeds.

The situation of the individual proprietor is somewhat different. If he acts to reduce the returns of his enterprise in order to exercise his "social responsibility," he is spending his own money, not someone else's. If he wishes to spend his money on such purposes, then that is his right, and I cannot see that there is any objection to his doing so. In the process, he, too, may impose costs on employees and customers. However, because he is far less likely than a large corporation or union to have monopolistic power, any such side effects will tend to be minor.

Of course, in practice the doctrine of social responsibility is frequently a cloak for actions that are justified on other grounds rather than a reason for those actions.

To illustrate, it may well be in the long-run interest of a corporation that is a major employer in a small community to devote resources to providing amenities to that community or to improving its government. That may make it easier to attract desirable employees, it may reduce the wage bill or lessen losses from pilferage and sabotage or have other worthwhile effects. Or it may be that, given the laws about the deductibility of corporate charitable contributions, the stockholders can contribute more to charities they favor by having the corporation make the gift than by doing it themselves, since they can in that way contribute an amount that would otherwise have been paid as corporate taxes.

In each of these – and in many similar – cases, there is a strong temptation to rationalize these actions as an exercise of "social responsibility." In the present climate of opinion, with its widespread aversion to "capitalism," "profits," the "soulless corporation" and so on, this is one way for a corporation to generate goodwill as a by-product of expenditures that are entirely justified in its own self-interest.

It would be inconsistent of me to call on corporate executives to refrain from this hypocritical window-dressing because it harms the foundations of a free society. That would be to call on them to exercise a "social responsibility"! If our institutions, and the attitudes of the public make it in their self-interest to cloak their actions in this way, I cannot summon much indignation to denounce them. At the same time, I can express admiration for those individual proprietors or owners of closely held corporations or stockholders of more broadly held corporations who disdain such tactics as approaching fraud.

Whether blameworthy or not, the use of the cloak of social responsibility, and the nonsense spoken in its name by influential and prestigious businessmen, does clearly harm the foundations of a free society. I have been impressed time and again by the schizophrenic character of many businessmen. They are capable of being extremely far-sighted and clear-headed in matters that are internal to their businesses. They are incredibly short-sighted and muddle-headed in matters that are outside their businesses but affect the possible survival of business in general. This short-sightedness is strikingly exemplified in the calls from many businessmen for wage and price guidelines or controls or incomes policies. There is nothing that could do more in a brief period to destroy a market system and replace it by a centrally controlled system than effective governmental control of prices and wages.

The short-sightedness is also exemplified in speeches by businessmen on social responsibility. This may gain them kudos in the short run. But it helps to strengthen the already prevalent view that the pursuit of profits is wicked and immoral and must be curbed and controlled by external forces. Once this view is adopted, the external forces that curb the market will not be the social consciences, however highly developed, of the pontificating executives; it will be the iron fist of Government bureaucrats. Here, as with price and wage controls, businessmen seem to me to reveal a suicidal impulse.

The political principle that underlies the market mechanism is unanimity. In an ideal free market resting on private property, no individual can coerce any other, all cooperation is voluntary, all parties to such cooperation benefit or they need not participate. There are no "social" values, no "social" responsibilities in any sense other than the shared values and responsibilities of individuals. Society is a collection of individuals and of the various groups they voluntarily form.

The political principle that underlies the political mechanism is conformity. The individual must serve a more general social interest – whether that be determined by a church or a dictator or a majority. The individual may have a vote and a say in what is to be done, but if he is overruled, he must conform. It is appropriate for some to require others to contribute to a general social purpose whether they wish to or not.

Unfortunately, unanimity is not always feasible. There are some respects in which conformity appears unavoidable, so I do not see how one can avoid the use of the political mechanism altogether.

But the doctrine of "social responsibility" taken seriously would extend the scope of the political mechanism to every human activity. It does not differ in philosophy from the most explicitly collectivist doctrine. It differs only by professing to believe that collectivist ends can be attained without collectivist means. That is why, in my book "Capitalism and Freedom," I have called it a "fundamentally subversive doctrine" in a free society, and have said that in such a society, "there is one and only one social responsibility of business – to use its resources and engage in activities designed to increase its profits so long as it stays within the rules of the game, which is to say, engages in open and free competition without deception or fraud."

THE CASE FOR CORPORATE
SOCIAL RESPONSIBILITY

Henry Mintzberg

The concept of social responsibility – once known as "noblesse oblige" (literally nobility obliges) – has experienced a vigorous resurgence since the 1950s. As Elbing (1970:79) notes, citing references in each case, the concept has been discussed academically by professors, pragmatically by businessmen, politically by public representatives; it has been approached philosophically, biologically, psychologically, sociologically, economically, even aesthetically.

The cynic attributes this resurgence to what he sees as the illegitimate power base of the large, widely held corporation: Social responsibility is a smokescreen to divert attention from the disappearance of direct shareholder control (and some forms of market control as well). The "professional" manager – the individual who moved into that power vacuum left by the departing shareholders – sees social responsibility as a form of natural enlightenment, a reflection of the coming of age of the corporation, if you like. These two positions are, in fact, far less divergent than they seem: each tilts its own way based on similar premises. As Drucker puts the latter case, "to have a society of organizations with autonomous managements [later 'self-governing' institutions], each a decision-maker in its own sphere, requires that managers, while private, also know themselves to be public" (1973: 810–811). Milton Friedman begins with a similar premise – that social responsibility reflects a shifting of power into the hands of people less subject to traditional forms of control – but concludes, as a result, that it is a "fundamentally subversive doctrine" (1970:126).

Thus sits social responsibility, in the center, attacked from the left and from the right and supported by those who have the most to gain from the status quo of corporate power. Can social responsibility work? Does it work? Should it work? This article summarizes some of the overwhelming evidence that it can't, doesn't, and shouldn't, and then concludes that it must.

Forms of Social Responsibility

In its purest form, social responsibility is supported for its own sake because that is the noble way for corporations to behave. This leads to a posture Sethi (1975) has called "social responsiveness" – anticipating and preventing social problems as opposed to keeping up with them (his use of the term "social responsibility"), or doing the bare minimum ("social obligation"). Carried to its logical extreme – what Drucker has called "unlimited social responsibility" (1973:349) – social responsiveness postulates that "only business can do it"; in the words of George Cabot Lodge, "Business, it is said, is engaged in a war with the evils of our time, a war it must win" (1961:185).

Enlightened Self-Interest

Less pure are the postures that reflect self-interest of one sort or another that social responsibility pays. These are sometimes referred to as "enlightened self-interest," although, as we shall see, some are less enlightened than others. One broad argument postulates that the business community as a whole will benefit from socially responsible behavior. For example, "crime will decrease with the consequence that less money will be spent to protect property, and less taxes will have to be paid to support police forces. The arguments can be extended in all directions showing that a better society produces a better environment for business" (Davis, 1973:313). Others make the same case for the individual behaviors of individual firms. "Treat your employees well, get them involved, and you will make more money," we were told by a generation of industrial psychologists in the 1960s (e.g., Likert, 1961). Subsequent evidence (e.g., Fiedler, 1966:7) silenced these particular voices, but others appeared in their place about a host of other behaviors.

Sound Investment Theory

The argument that social responsibility is a sound investment has been developed most fully and literally by Edward Bowman of MIT. In a paper entitled "Corporate Social Responsibility and the Investor" (1973), he proposes the hypothesis that through the effect of a "neo-invisible hand," the market price of a company's stock is affected by its social behavior. He attacks two "myths" in his paper that "corporate social responsibility is dependent on either the noblesse oblige of the manager or the laws of the government," and that "corporate social responsibility is in fundamental conflict with investor interests" (1973:42). Sometimes a company must pay directly for behavior perceived as irresponsible; Bowman cites the case of the Dutch firm struck by unions all over Europe because of the disruptive local effects of shutting down one plant.

But Bowman's broader argument is that the stock market responds to the social behavior of the corporation, in terms of the market price of its stock, which affects its cost of capital and its earnings. To support this case, Bowman argues that many institutional investors view firms that are not socially responsible as riskier investments; also that churches, universities, and the like, as well as the "clean" mutual funds, by paying attention to corporate social behavior, influence the market for a corporation's stock. Furthermore, to the extent that investment portfolios are diversified, actions by individual corporations, which benefit the corporate sector as a whole – for example, by improving the environment – also benefit the individual investor (an argument Bowman draws from Wallich and McGowan, 1970).

The enlightened self-interest argument is certainly not new; its orientation has simply changed. In an earlier era, the point was religious and personal: "Be good or you will go to hell" – literally! Responsible behavior paid off, if not in this life, at least in the next. Today the case is made in economic terms (during this life), although it remains fundamentally the same. The gates of the treasury in this world, if not those of the heavens in the next, will open to those who are socially responsible. What has remained the same is the premise that one behaves responsibly not because of ethics – because that is the "proper" way to behave – but because it is to one's advantage to do so.

Avoiding Interference

A final argument from the perspective of self-interest is not economic but political, and it emerges as less "enlightened" than the others. We can call it the "them" argument. "If we're not good, they will move in" – Ralph Nader, the government, whoever. The problem with this perspective is that it tends to encourage rhetoric, not action. Typical of it is the report of the fifty-fourth meeting of the American Assembly (1978), a gathering of an impressive group of friends of the large corporation. Introducing the "them" argument – "if private initiatives fail, the issues of corporate governance are important enough that government will have to address them" (1978:5) – the report in a series of recommendations comes down solidly and repeatedly for social responsibility in general, the status quo in particular. For example, "employees should be regarded as a crucial part of the constituency of the corporation" but their "interests will be better served by various means, such as collective bargaining, direct communications, and participative management approaches rather than by direct employee representation on boards of directors" (1978:6).

To conclude, it should be noted that many of the self-interest arguments, by trying to make a case for social responsibility, in fact make a stronger one for other controls on the corporation – pressure campaigns from special interest groups, perhaps regulations from government. For Bowman, or those worried about "them," responsibility is a sound investment because pressure groups make it so. Only in its purest form – as an ethical position – can corporate social responsibility stand by itself.

Attacks on Social Responsibility

Social responsibility, as noted, has been subjected to attacks from the left as well as from the right (sometimes on the same grounds, as we shall see). Some of these attacks are based on the corporation's unwillingness to act responsibly; others on its inability to do so; still others on the lack of justification for it so doing. Let us look at some of these in turn.

Rhetoric, not action

The most elementary attack comes from those who simply do not trust the corporation. They view all of the talk of social responsibility as a giant public relations campaign. The head can pronounce; the hands do not necessarily respond. Thus, Cheit refers to the "Gospel of Social Responsibility," "designed to justify the power of managers over an ownerless system": "[M]anagers must *say* that they are responsible, because they are *not*" (1964:165, 172). And Chamberlain writes, "The most common corporate response to criticism of a deficient sense of social responsibility has been an augmented program of public relations" (1973:9).

Lack of personal capabilities

Another, more far-reaching attack is that by the very nature of their training and experience, businessmen are ill-equipped to deal with social issues. Theodore Levitt argues, for example, that the typical senior executive of the large corporation is there because he is an expert on his own business, not on social issues. By having had to devote so much time to learning his business, "he has automatically insulated himself from the world around him" (1968:85), denying himself the knowledge and skills needed to deal with social issues. Others make a related case by claiming that the orientation of business organizations toward efficiency and control renders their leaders inept at handling complex social problems, which require flexibility and political finesse. Harrington writes, for example, that "what cities need are 'uneconomic' allocations of resources. . . . Businessmen, even at their most idealistic, are not prepared to act in a systematically unbusinesslike way" (quoted in Ackerman, 1973:414).

Corporation's structure precludes social responsibility

Perhaps the most devastating of all, the third attack claims that social responsibility is not possible in the large corporation, given the nature of its environment, structure, and control systems. Appropriate or not, social responsibility, it is claimed, simply cannot and does not work. Proponents of social responsibility are dismissed as naïve: Corporations, by the nature of their activities, create social problems. How can they solve them?

> If we all understood the basic ground rules of private enterprise a little better, we would realize that the large corporation is not a rain god, and that no amount of prayer or incantation will unleash its power. The spectacle of otherwise sophisticated people going on bended knee to companies and pleading with them to have the kind of conscience and moral sensibilities only rarely found in individuals is nothing less than laughable (Henderson, 1968:8).

Others claim that socially responsible behavior is precluded in the economic system we have. Tumin (1964), for example, bases his argument on "the principle of least morality," that competition or greed causes some participants to depart from the rules (and the rules of social responsibility, as noted, are vague and not officially enforced in any event), forcing others to follow suit. Business, as a result, "tends to bring out, standardize, and reward the most unsocialized impulses of man" (Tumin, 1964:130). There is a good deal of evidence to back up the cynicism of these commentators, as we shall see. But before we turn to it, let us consider a final and more far-reaching attack on social responsibility.

No right to pursue social goals

The fourth attack is that the corporation has no right to pursue social goals. Here the left and right join forces to attack the center. Their argument is a simple and appealing one: Corporation managers lack broad public legitimacy: at best they are appointed by private shareholders; more likely they are self-selected. Therefore, they have no right to pursue broad social goals, to impose their interpretation of the public good on society. "Who authorized them to do that?" asks Braybrooke (1967:224). Public functions should not be exercised by private businessmen. They should be left to elected representatives.

Some critics ask what values will be embedded in the "socially responsible" choices of businessmen. How much of business ideology – bigger is better, competition is good, material wealth leads to a better society, etc. – will come along with these choices? Others ask to what extent business can be allowed, or expected, to dominate society. In a paper entitled "The Dangers of Social Responsibility," Levitt comments that "its guilt-driven urge" has caused the modern corporation to reshape "not simply the economic but also the institutional, social, cultural, and political topography of society" (1958:44). He sees the continuation of this trend as posing a serious threat to democracy: "business statesmanship may create the corporate equivalent of the unitary state" (1958:44). And then there is the argument that the function of business is economic, not social. Social responsibility (at least in its pure form) means giving away the shareholders' money: It weakens the firm's competitive position, and it dilutes the efforts of its managers, who are supposed to focus on economic productivity (Davis, 1973). The best known voice here is that of Milton Friedman:

> What does it mean to say that the corporate executive has a "social responsibility" in his capacity as businessman? If this statement is not pure rhetoric, it must mean that he is to act in some way that is not in the interest of his employers. For example . . . that he is to make expenditures on reducing pollution beyond the amount that is in the best interests of the corporation or that is required by law in order to contribute to the social objective of improving the environment. . . . Insofar as his actions in accord with his "social responsibility" reduce returns to stockholders, he is spending their money. Insofar as his actions raise the price to customers, he is spending the customer's money. Insofar as his actions lower the wages of some employees, he is spending their money (Friedman, 1970:33).

To Friedman: "[T]here is one and only one social responsibility of business – to use its resources and engage in activities designed to increase its profits so long as it stays within the rules of the game, which is to say, engages in open and free competition without deception or fraud" (1970:126; see also 1962).

Finally, the most pragmatic critics ask: How are businessmen to determine what is socially responsible? To whom are they responsible: the whole of society? the customers? the industry? the employees? the managers' families? the corporation itself? What happens when responsibility to one means irresponsibility to another? Should profit be given up to help needy customers? How much profit? Is lobbying for a stronger merchant marine – so that it will be available in the event of war – a socially responsible activity on the part of a shipping company? Is resisting government intervention responsible? Clearly, social responsibility involves a host of complex and contradictory needs in a perpetual state of flux. A common result is that sometimes the most well-meaning corporation is attacked for what it truly believed was responsible behavior while the most blatantly selfish act of another corporation, justified in the lofty terms of social responsibility, hardly gets noticed.

Thus, we have the arguments against social responsibility. Businessmen cannot be trusted; they are ill-equipped to deal with social issues; their corporations are not structured to do so; and they have no business even trying to do so. Let them stick to their own business, which is business itself.

The arguments are clear; what about some evidence?

The Evidence on Social Responsibility

Let us begin with some evidence from surveys, and then move toward studies of actual corporate behavior.

Surveys of corporate social responsibility

To test his contention that it pays to be good, Bowman teamed up with Haire (1975, 1976), using an interesting research methodology. They performed a line-by-line content analysis of the 1973 annual reports of eighty-two food processing companies in order to ascertain the percentage of total prose devoted to issues of corporate social responsibility. This figure was then used as a surrogate for actual company concern and activity, which they related to company performance.[1] Bowman and Haire found that those firms with some social responsibility prose performed significantly better than those with none (14.7 percent return on equity vs. 10.2 percent over the preceding five years, a difference significant at the 2 percent level).

But a breakdown of the data provides a more interesting result. As can be seen in Exhibit 1, firms that never mentioned social responsibility exhibited the weakest performance, the two groups closest to them (with 0.1 percent to 8 percent of the prose of the annual report) performed best, while those with the most prose (more than 16 percent of that in the annual reports) exhibited performance only slightly better than the first group (12.3 percent return on equity vs. 10.2 percent, compared with 17.1 percent for the second group). In other words, the relationship between the two factors had an inverse U-shape. Note that fifty-one of the eighty-two firms surveyed – almost two thirds – fell into the first category, with no prose at all.[2]

Bowman and Haire conclude with support for Bowman's original contention, qualifying it with the point that the stock market is willing to reward socially responsible behavior only to a point. It pays to be good, but not too good. Another conclusion seems perhaps more warranted, however: Don't

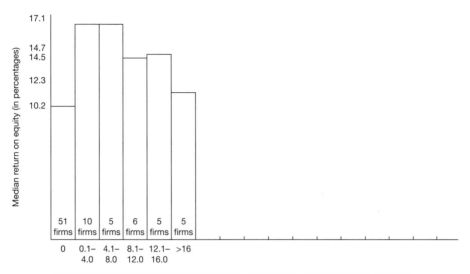

Percentage of prose on corporate social responsibility in the annual reports of 82 food processing companies

Based on figures from the study by Bowman and Haire, 1975.

Exhibit 1 Prose and profits

stand out from the crowd, do no more than is expected. In Bowman and Haire's own terms, "the mean really is golden" (1975:57). Note that the most profitable firms not only were not the most responsible (by their measure), but were not even in the middle. They were closest to the least responsible (again by their measure – the ones with no prose). And this latter group – the vast majority of firms surveyed – still managed a respectable 10.2 percent return on equity. Shall we accept Bowman and Haire's own measure and conclude that most firms do not care at all about social responsibility yet still remain viable?[3]

But taking these authors' central conclusion that the mean is golden, the question becomes: How good is the mean? Surveys of the general population, and especially of corporate managers themselves, give us some idea, and it is not very encouraging. For example, only 15 percent of those polled in a 1977 survey of the general population agreed that "business tries to strike a fair balance between profits and interests of the public" (in 1968, 70 percent agreed; in 1973, 34 percent). Asked to choose between social responsibility and regulation, the public came down strongly for the latter (Westlin, 1979:14, 16). In another general poll carried out in 1976, the "honesty and ethical standards" of business executives were rated "very high" by 3 percent of the respondents, "high" by 17 percent, "average" by 58 percent, "low" by 16 percent, and "very low" by 4 percent (2 percent had no opinion) (Gallup, 1978:838).

Of greater interest, however, are the results of polls of businessmen themselves. In the Gallup poll cited above, the "professional and business" respondents rated their own behavior hardly better than did the public at large: 2 percent, 22 percent, 55 percent, 14 percent, 8 percent, and 1 percent, respectively [23:840]. Other surveys of employees on the social responsibility of their own corporations, however, have been far more discouraging.

Brenner and Molander (1977) compared their survey of *Harvard Business Review* readers with a survey carried out fifteen years earlier and concluded: "Respondents are somewhat more cynical about the ethical conduct of their peers than they were [in their previous survey]" (1977:59). (And they hardly lacked cynicism to begin with, despite the finding that "[m]ost respondents . . . have embraced [social responsibility] as a legitimate and achievable goal for business," (ibid.) Close to half the respondents agreed with the statement that "the American business executive tends not to apply the great ethical laws immediately to work. He is preoccupied chiefly with gain" (ibid.:62). On a question of change in ethical standard over time, 32 percent felt that the standards of 1976 were lower than those of 1951 (and 12 percent felt considerably lower), while 27 percent felt they were higher (and 5 percent felt considerably so; 41 percent felt they were about the same). And only 5 percent listed social responsibility as a factor "influencing ethical standards," whereas 31 percent and 20 percent listed two sets of factors related to pressure campaigns by outside groups, and 10 percent listed government regulation.

On some specific questions, 89 percent of the respondents felt it "acceptable" to pad an expense account by about $1,500 a year if the superior knew about it and said nothing; 55 percent would do nothing in the case of a shady deal between a pilots' association and an insurance company whose board they have just joined (as an inside director; as an outside director, 36 percent would do nothing); and 58 percent would pay a "consulting fee" to a foreign minister to gain a lucrative contract (although a full 91 percent believe the average executive would pay, a reflection of the "real magnitude of [the] cynicism," (1977:65). Of the respondents, 43 percent attributed unethical practices to competition, and, more importantly as we shall see, 50 percent to superiors, who "often do not want to know how results are obtained, so long as one achieves the desired outcome" (ibid.:62). Brenner and Molander believe that two factors most likely explain these results: "ethical standards have declined from what they were or situations that once caused ethical discomfort have become accepted practice" (ibid.:59).

Other studies support these results, especially the ones pertaining to subordinate managers. Collins and Ganotis (1974) stress as one of the most significant findings in their survey of attitudes of managers toward social responsibility, "a sense of futility concerning the ability of lower- and middle-level managers to affect corporate social policy and a perhaps related attitude that social goals can best be achieved by individuals working outside their companies. These attitudes were particularly strong among lower-level managers" (1974:306).[4] Another survey, of managers within Pitney-Bowes, "a leader in [the] campaign for business ethics . . . reported that they do feel pressure to compromise personal ethics to achieve corporate goals"; similar results were obtained in Uniroyal (Madden, 1977:66). Even *Business Week* has concluded that "such pressures apparently exist widely in the business world" (quoted in ibid.). Finally, of the business managers surveyed by J.S. Bowman (1976), 64 percent agreed with the statement, "Private managers feel under pressure to compromise personal standards to achieve organizational goals," that belief being "particularly prevalent in middle and lower management levels" (1976:50). And 78 percent agreed with the statement: "I can conceive of a situation where you have good ethics running from top to bottom, but because of pressures from the top to achieve results, persons down the line compromise their beliefs" (Bowman, 1976:51).[5] One respondent wrote: "It is not people per se, but rather the structure of large organisations and the ruthless competition in them that develop unethical conduct" (ibid.).

The problem of structure

Let us take this comment as our point of departure. There can be little doubt that competition from within or without influences the corporation's ability to respond to social needs. (It also provides an excuse not to respond, but that is another matter.) This is the point of Tumin's "principle of least morality." But the results above may be better explained by problems inherent in the actual design of the large corporation. The corporation may be "'trapped' in the business system that it has helped to create" (Chamberlain, 1973:4).

In an important paper, Daniel Bell (1971) describes modern industrial society as "a product of two 'new men,' the engineer and the economist, and of the concept which unites them – the concept of efficiency" (1971:9). This concept gave rise to "a distinct mode of life," which Bell calls the "economizing mode" – "the science of the best allocation of scarce resources among competing ends" (ibid.:10). Economizing means "maximization," "optimization," "least cost." Underlying this was a concept of rationality, specifically "a rationality of *means*, a way of best satisfying a given end." The ends "were seen as multiple or varied, to be freely chosen by the members of society." But "the ends that 'became' given all involved the rising material output of goods. And other, traditional modes of life (the existence of artisan skills and crafts, the family hearth as a site for work) were sacrificed to the new system for the attainment of these economic ends" (ibid.:10). The new rationality and new goals needed "to be institutionalized in some renewable form of organization. That institution was the corporation" (ibid.:11).

The corporation, in other words, emerged as the rational tool to pursue economic goals. And the key to the functioning of that tool was its structure – specifically what we have elsewhere called machine bureaucracy (Mintzberg, 1979). The economic goals plugged in at the top filtered down through a rationally designed hierarchy of ends and means, to emerge at the bottom in a form that allowed workers to carry out highly formalized tasks designed according to the precepts of division of labor. These workers were impelled to put aside their personal goals and to do as they were told in return for remuneration. To ensure that they did, the whole system was overlaid with a hierarchy of authority supported by an extensive network of formal controls. And to keep this whole system on its economic track, society created its own controls – a price system, competition, and a stock market that measured results and watched the corporation's well-known bottom line.

Now, what happens when the concept of social responsibility is introduced into all this? The evidence from the surveys cited above suggests an answer: not much. The system is too tight.

In principle, social goals, instead of economic ones, can be plugged in at the top. Or else they can sneak in lower down, as employees ignore the demands of the hierarchy and instead do what they believe is right. But a number of factors work against such goals. External competition and the pressures to demonstrate economically effective performance are two obvious ones. Internal competition is another. According to Maccoby (1976), the pressure to get to the top of the hierarchy favors the "gamesmen" of the corporation, people to whom winning is all important. In Madden's summary (1977), the work of these gamesmen "does little to satisfy or even stimulate what Maccoby calls the 'qualities of the heart': loyalty, a sense of humor, friendliness, compassion. . . . Perhaps the key aspect of Maccoby's study is to note the decline since 1950 of an ideological or ethical basis for actions among the generation of executives born in the 1930s . . . Winning . . . turns out to be . . . 'the only thing'" (Madden, 1977:68). And winning is measured in numbers that favor the economic goals over the social ones. To quote Bell, the system "measures only economic goals"; the social goals such as "clean air, beautiful scenery, pure water, sunshine, to say nothing of the imponderables such as ease of meeting friends, satisfaction in work, etc. . . . in our present accounting schemes, priced at zero . . . add nothing to the economist's measure of wealth. Nor, when they disappear, do they show up as subtractions from wealth" (1971:14).[6]

Now what happens to the managers lower down, intent on performing in a socially responsible manner, when the numbers plugged in at the top of the system are economic? In fact, what happens from the top when the senior managers themselves try to plug in social goals alongside the economic ones?

Evidence from research on corporate behavior

In an important book entitled *The Social Challenge to Business*, Robert Ackerman (1975) addressed these particular questions. Ackerman looked at the effects on social responsibility of the divisionalized form – that structure used overwhelmingly by the United States' largest corporations (Rumelt, 1974; Wrigley, 1970). He studied two firms in depth, interviewing managers and specialists at different levels, analyzing documents, and investigating the functioning of their structures.

Ackerman begins with the premise that although some "rascals inhabit the executive suite," most business leaders "would like to avoid doing what they believe to be irresponsible" (1975:4). He then puts the rhetoric of social responsibility aside and concerns himself with behavior.

In the divisionalized form, the divisions are fully responsible for operating their individual businesses, while the headquarters controls them through systems that measure financial performance, thereby relieving itself "of the need to sift through and comprehend operating data from diverse businesses" (Ackerman, 1975:49). The division managers are, therefore, assessed in terms of the bottom line; specifically they "are encouraged to pay close attention to the near-term profitability of their units" (ibid.:50). What happens then when a new social issue comes along? Ackerman finds that it poses three major dilemmas for the corporation:

- Social demands subvert corporate-division relationships;
- Financial control systems are ineffective in explaining and evaluating social responsiveness; and
- The process for evaluating and rewarding managers is not designed to recognize performance in areas of social concern (ibid.:52).

A new social issue – say, concern about bias in hiring minorities – encourages headquarters management to intervene in the decisions of the divisions for two reasons. First, even local issues can have company-wide implications (as, for example, when the company's name is identified with a charge of racial discrimination). And second, in a hierarchical organisation it is the chief executive who is ultimately held responsible for its actions. But intervention violates the principle of divisional autonomy. And so the headquarters manager falls on the horns of a dilemma. If he hesitates, "it is probable that social responsiveness will lag." The division managers have already made commitments to their short-term financial targets. But if he acts, he will upset the system: "He may diminish the extent to which he can hold the divisions accountable for achieving agreed-upon financial results" (Ackerman, 1975:54). In effect, the neat separation of powers designed for economic performance impedes social responsiveness.

Of course, if the costs and benefits of the social issue could be measured, the well-meaning executive at headquarters would simply plug them into the control system. Unfortunately, however, although some of the costs can be measured, typically few of the benefits can. Citing the examples of "reducing noxious emissions into the atmosphere below the levels required by current law," Ackerman concludes that "from the accountant's point of view [the benefits, such as a rosier public image or pride among the managers], have the unfortunate characteristics of being largely intangible, unassignable to the costs of the organisational units creating them and occurring over an indeterminable future time period" (1975: 55–56).

Thus, even the chief executive at headquarters who wishes to incorporate social goals into his control system cannot easily do so. He may sing the praises of social responsibility, but his subordinates march to the tune of economic performance. Ackerman touches the heart of his argument with the following comment: "[T]he financial reporting system may actually inhibit social responsiveness. By focusing on economic performance . . . such a system directs energy and resources to achieving results measured in financial terms. It is the only game in town, so to speak, at least the only one with an official scorecard" (Ackerman, 1975:56).

To the extent that there is discretion in the system, of course, the division manager may still be able to consider social issues voluntarily. But when the screws of the financial reporting system are forever being tightened – as they are, increasingly, in the contemporary versions of these control systems – most of that discretion can disappear. Joe Bower, a colleague of Ackerman when he was at Harvard Business School, cites a well-known case of this:

> The corporate management of [General Electric before 1961] required its executives to sign the so-called directive 20.5 which explicitly forbade price fixing or any other violation of the antitrust laws. But a very severely managed system of reward and punishment that demanded yearly improvements in earnings, return, and market share, applied indiscriminately to all divisions, yielded a situation which was – at the very least – conducive to collusion in the oligopolistic and mature equipment markets (Bower, 1970:193).

Bower's conclusion seems to make the point of this whole argument precisely:

> In short, the same forces in a diversified firm that tend to strip away economic fat and social tradition from the management of the enterprise tend also to strip away noneconomic aspects of all issues facing division managements, even those that are not remotely economic in character. The result is that while the planning process of the diversified firm may be highly efficient, there may be a tendency for them to be socially irresponsible (Bower, 1970:193).

What of the ability of the manager lower down not even to act responsibly, but merely to avoid acting irresponsibly? Here too the evidence is discouraging, as we saw in the polls cited earlier. This issue was, in fact, investigated directly by James Waters (1978). Curious about how such things as General Electric's directive 20.5 could go unheeded, Waters studied testimony of various U.S. congressional investigating committees into corporate wrongdoing and interviewed some of the managers involved. He developed his conclusions in terms of seven "organisational blocks" – "aspects of organisations that may get in the way of the natural tendency of people to react against illegal and unethical practices" (ibid.:5). These blocks include:

- Strong role models, involving the socialisation of new employees into existing unethical practices and their identification with those responsible for them;
- Strict lines of command that discourage questioning such practices;
- Task group cohesiveness;
- Ambiguity about priorities, such as the "Catch 20.5" phenomenon that pitted vague social guidelines against specific financial targets;
- Separation of decisions, forcing employees to work in terms of given strategies and in contexts where unethical practices are the norm;
- Division of work, so that employees do not know about unethical practices, ignore them if they do, or are bypassed if they try to resist them; and
- The tendency for firms to avoid investigating their own wrongdoing for fear of public exposure.

This evidence suggests that the problems of social responsibility are inherent in the very conception of the large corporation and in the design of the structure and control systems it uses. Machine bureaucracy and especially the divisionalized form, by their very natures, seem to encourage people to behave in at best socially unresponsive, at worst socially irresponsible, ways. Were social irresponsibility restricted to the fly-by-night operator, it would be highly contained in today's economy. The problem is that it is not: specifically, unethical acts continue to be pinned on the largest and most prestigious of corporations, in the recent past on General Motors, General Electric, Ford, Gulf, Lockheed, ITT, and many others. A recent article in *Fortune* magazine concluded: "[A] surprising number of large firms have been involved in blatant illegalities" (Ross, 1980:57). Of 1,043 major corporations studied, 117 had been involved in one or more "serious crimes" within the United States during the 1970s – antitrust violations, kickbacks, bribing or illegal rebates, illegal political contributions, fraud, or tax evasion. One recent chairman of the Securities and Exchange Commission wrote: "There has been bribery, influence-peddling, and corruption on a scale I had never dreamed existed." And his words are echoed by another in reference to charges of illegal practices against nine large corporations: "Always there was direct involvement and participation by senior management officials" (quoted in Walton, 1977:3). And the president of Cummings Engine received a standing ovation when he told a group of top executives that "we are 'losing our freedoms' not because of the appetite of some monster government, but because we [businessmen] 'have abused our freedoms when we had them'" (ibid.). According to the evidence from the surveys, the problem seems to be getting worse, perhaps in good part because the divisionalized form of structure is becoming more pervasive and its control systems tighter.

But the root of the problem may go deeper than structure, at least if the conclusions of Singer and Wooton are any indication. They analysed Albert Speer's "administrative genius" as Minister of Armaments and War in Germany's Third Reich. Speer's organization was not a traditional bureaucracy, but an "adaptive, problem-solving temporary organization" that used a "matrix system with project management" and relied on "industrial self-responsibility" and "collegial decisionmaking" (Singer and Wooton, 1976:82–84), all characteristics of what we have elsewhere described under the label "adhocracy" (Mintzberg, 1979). Yet all of this – "advanced, participative, and 'humanistic'" – was used "to promote the goals of one of the most inhumane societies in the history of mankind" (ibid.:80). The implication is that the root of the problem may lie beyond structure, in the very concept of management itself: "It is not that managers are authoritarian themselves; rather . . . it may be that the process of management is authoritarian" (ibid.:100).

The "professional" manager is a "hired gun," so to speak, concerned with means not ends. But that very distinction may prove to be the problem, depersonalising relationships and breeding socially irresponsible behavior. Speer said: "The people [who suffered] became abstractions to me, not human beings" (Mintzberg, 1979:82). The "professional" manager can become encapsulated, insulated from the consequences of his actions; like Speer, he can come to see challenges "as tasks to be performed, as functions to be organized . . . as power to be exercised" (ibid.), a description reminiscent of Maccoby's gamesmen (who, by his description, are found in adhocracies). Singer and Wooton's message is that "many managers today are so caught up in the procedural demands of their work that they easily lose sight of the important end results of their activities" (Singer and Wooton, 1976:98–99).

All in all, the evidence on social responsibility is hardly encouraging. But before we spill away the bath-water, let us take a final look for the baby.

The Indispensability of Corporate Social Responsibility

The baby is indeed there (or at least we had better create one and put it there), for two fundamental reasons. First, the strategic decisions of large organizations inevitably involve social as well as economic consequences, inextricably intertwined (e.g., Mintzberg *et. al.*, 1976; Pfiffner, 1960). That is what renders the arguments of Friedman, and his echoes from the left, so utterly false. The neat distinction between private economic goals and public social goals – the one to be pursued by businessmen, the other by elected leaders – which sounds so good in theory, simply does not hold up in reality. Every time a large corporation makes an important decision – to introduce a new product line, to locate a plant, to close down a division – it generates all kinds of social consequences. Size alone makes economic decisions social. When a plant employing thousands of workers is opened or closed, the impact on a community and on many lives is direct and consequential. As a result, the corporation gets caught in its own web of power. It cannot claim neutrality. Consider the experience of Dow Chemical with the sales of napalm during the Vietnam War. The transaction was economic, but so too was it social. To refuse to sell napalm would have been a political statement, but so too was the decision to sell it (Chamberlain, 1973:189–192). In other words, there is no such thing as a purely economic strategic decision in big business. Every one is also social (or, if you prefer, political). Only a conceptual ostrich, with his head deeply buried in economic theory, could possibly use the distinction between economic and social goals to dismiss social responsibility.[7]

Business cannot solve society's ills

This is not to suggest that we must embrace social responsibility as the solution to our problems. It is nonsense to believe that business can solve the ills of society. It is also risky to allow business to use its resources without restraint in the social sphere, whether that be to support political candidates or to dictate implicitly how nonprofit institutions spend their money.[8] And social responsibility can never be relied upon alone. As we saw earlier, a good deal of what passes for social responsibility would disappear without other, countervailing forces on the corporation – pressure campaigns by activists, regulations by the government, and so on. Much so-called enlightened self-interest would become far less enlightened if the likes of Ralph Nader did not lurk outside the gates of every large corporation.

But given the immense power of large corporations – power not only to influence social issues in profound ways but also to circumvent government regulations and resist social pressures – the more ethical forms of social responsibility become imperative, at least if we are to have a humane society.

Where social responsibility can work

When business is involved in an issue to begin with and possesses some knowledge, social responsibility, alongside the other means to influence corporate behavior, has an important place: where government regulations are necessary but cannot work (e.g., where business creates externalities that cannot be measured and attributed to it); where regulation could work if only business could cooperate to help enact sensible legislation; where existing legislation needs compliance with its spirit as well as its letter;

where the corporation can fool its customers or suppliers or the government through its superior knowledge; where employees need the freedom to blow the whistle on unethical superiors or colleagues for the sake of the common good; wherever a choice must be made (e.g., in the selection of products and services) that can tilt the efforts of the corporation toward what is useful to society instead of what is useless or destructive. These are the places where society has a right to expect responsible behavior from its corporations. "[S]ocial responsibility is not telling society what is good for society but responding to what society tells the firm the society wants and expects from it" (Walters, 1977:44).

But can the businessman be socially responsible in these areas? All the evidence notwithstanding, the answer is that of course he can. Our second point is that there is always some "zone of discretion" in strategic decision-making. Ackerman, who uses the term, notes that managers have latitude as to "how soon and in what way to respond" to social issues (1975:33). That discretion can be used to subvert social needs, to ignore them in favor of economic ones, or to consider them alongside the economic ones. Contemporary control systems may reduce this zone, but they can never quite eliminate it. As the saying goes: where there's a will, there's a way. That is presumably what prompted 77 percent of Bremner and Molander's respondents to reject the statement that "every business is in effect 'trapped' in the business system it helped to create, and can do remarkably little about the social problems of our time" (1977:68).

There is little doubt that social responsibility in large corporations could be a great deal better. But it could also be an awful lot worse. We have no idea of the depths to which we can drop (although Singer and Wooton's description of Speer's "administrative genius" provides some indication). It is our ethics that keep us from falling any lower. Without them – without the pure form of corporate social responsibility, even such as it is – we would be in serious trouble. Those ethics need not define only a base level of social responsibility; they can also bring us up from where we are. In Waters's words, we must "tap into the tremendous reservoir of energy that exists among employees" in organisations, "unblock [their] natural ethical instincts" (1978:13). These can counter the forces pulling us down. Faced with a choice on Wednesday at 3:45 P.M. to decide how high to build that smokestack, what can counter the pressure of the financial controls is the manager's nagging sense of social responsibility, that there can be more important things in life than growth and profit.

The limits of legalistic approaches

To dismiss social responsibility is to allow corporate behavior to drop to the lowest common denominator, propped up only by external controls, by regulations, pressures, and the like. It is to give credence to the voices of gloom, such as Tumin. Instead, we would do better to listen to the words of Solzhenitsyn:

> I have spent all my life under a communist regime and I will tell you that a society without any objective legal scale is a terrible one indeed. But a society with no other scale but the legal one is not quite worthy of man either. A society which is based on the letter of the law and never reaches any higher is taking very scarce advantage of the high level of human possibilities. The letter of the law is too cold and formal to have a beneficial influence on society. Whenever the tissue of life is woven of legalistic relations, there is an atmosphere of moral mediocrity, paralysing man's noblest impulses (1978:81).

We shall certainly not be able to eliminate the regulation of business (current fashion notwithstanding). But legalistic approaches only set crude and minimum standards of behavior, ones easily circumvented by the unscrupulous. This applies equally to legalistic approaches within the corporation – General Electric's directive 20.5 being a good example. Bureaucratic procedures remind one of the Latin American countries that have passed laws to insist that previous laws be respected. As Waters notes, "A mechanistic approach – such as having everybody sign a standard affidavit like GE's '20.5' – can impersonalize and desensitize the issue"; "increasing the clarity of the control procedures may enable the bad guys to navigate their way around the system more easily" (1978:12–13). Socially responsible behavior will infuse the organisation not through procedures but through attitudes, not via directives but via examples, not because of "them" but because of "us." The question is one of simple, old-fashioned ethics.

And if the divisionalized form of structure proves to be too great an impediment to such behavior – as the evidence suggests – then our choice is clear: live with a low standard of corporate social responsibility or get rid of this form of structure. Bower has noted that "the best records in the race relations area are those of single-product companies whose strong top managements are deeply involved in the business" (1970:193). And Keim (1978) has found that small firms seem to be considerably more philanthropic than large ones, because for them, in his opinion, the sound investment argument really works: their commitment to specific, identifiable communities not only forces them to be more responsive but also offers them greater direct rewards from the localized benefits. (For example, "A contribution to the local hospital improves medical service for the firm's employees"; moreover, better health care facilities may make it "easier to attract new employees to the community and to retain existing workers" (Keim, 1978: 37–38). The point is that commitment – simple involvement on a *personal* basis – would seem to be at the root of true social responsibility. And the opportunities for this in the giant organization would seem to be increasingly limited. The more important social responsibility becomes to a society of free individuals – and in our opinion, such a society will not survive without it – the more that society will have to question the bureaucratisation, the diversification, and growth for its own sake of its organisations, public and nonprofit as well as private.[9]

Reversing long-term trends

There is a need to reverse the long-term trend toward impersonalism and utilitarianism in our organisations – toward squeezing out ideals, beliefs, feelings, ethics, and a sense of mission and purpose. Solzhenitsyn (1978) has experienced the natural finale to that trend. But the West is surely headed in the same direction, no matter that many of its bureaucracies are private. Social responsibility – that most naïve of concepts – represents our best hope, perhaps our only real hope, for arresting and reversing that trend. Without responsibility and ethical people in important places, the society we know and wish to improve will never survive.

Notes

1   The researchers were quick to address the obvious suggestion that arises, "that talk is cheap" [8:50]. They took a list of fourteen companies that had been identified by the editor of *Business & Society* "as being outstandingly responsible firms," and matched each with another firm in the industry, randomly selected, of approximately the same size. A content analysis of the annual reports of the twenty-eight firms found the percentage of prose content on corporate social responsibility to average 4.8 percent for the "premier" firms, 1.7 percent for the "neutral" ones, a difference that was statistically significant at the 2 percent level. The authors also present data comparing the mention of international activity with Standard and Poor's rating of actual international activity, by which they substantiate the use of the prose of the annual report as "a reasonable surrogate for real activity" (Bowman and Haire, 1976:15)

2   Other studies support this conclusion. Bowman and Haire (1975) refer to a study of companies ranked on an index of pollution control, in which their own breakdown of the results produced the same asymmetrical inverted U-shaped curve. Dent (1959) also found a similar relationship between the propensity of managers to express public service as a goal and the performance of their firms in terms of rate of growth. This relationship could also explain the combined findings of a study by Alexander and Buckholz (1978) together with two others that they cite.

3   This leaves aside the nagging problem of causation. While it seems reasonable to conclude that it costs to be too good, should we also accept that it costs to be bad? It is equally possible that poor economic performers cannot afford social responsibility, at least in the short run. Indeed, might poor performers not tend to act irresponsibly in order to try to catch up? Were these suspicions true, the corporation could interpret the Bowman and Haire findings in the exact opposite way they intended: It does not pay to be too good, and if one is weak, it may even pay to be bad. Obviously their data say nothing about irresponsible behavior, but the absence of prose in the annual report could just as well mean irresponsible behavior as minimally acceptable behavior. (See Bowman [1973] for a discussion of possible forms of causation in this relationship.)

4   More discouraging perhaps, they also found that the young managers experienced the lowest sense of personal responsibility for social problems and the weakest perception of the need for the corporation to involve itself in such problems.

5   Corresponding responses for public sector managers were similar but slightly lower.

6   For an elaboration of the argument that an emphasis on efficiency favors economic goals over social ones, see Mintzberg, "A Note on That Dirty Word 'Efficiency,'" *Interfaces*, Oct. 1982, pp. 101–105, or "Efficiency as a Systems Goal," in Mintzberg (1983: Ch. 16).

7   This is our main criticism of the Friedman doctrine. Others – the fallacies of (potential) shareholder control, of free markets, and of enterprise as private – can be found in Mintzberg (1983: Ch. 33).

8   Sethi falls into the contradiction of listing, among other forms of social responsiveness, taking "definite stands on issues of public concern" and avoiding "meddling in politics" (1975:63). He appears to be saying that managers should only meddle in the good issues, as if everyone knows what these are. Our position is that on behalf of their corporation, managers should involve themselves in no issues outside its own sphere of operations (and only carefully in the ones inside of it, so as not to abuse their power).

9   In this regard, it is of interest to consider how social responsibility has been studied in firms of different size. While the studies of the big firms found that the "responsible" ones used more prose in their annual reports, impressed the editor of a national magazine, replied appropriately in a questionnaire, or created yet another slot in the bureaucracy – this one programmed to make everyone else responsible – the one study we have of small firms found that they actually put more cash on the table. We are back to the point about the institution of more bureaucratic procedures to deal with the problems created by bureaucratic procedures, except that here it is the researchers who get caught up in the system, by using what are essentially bureaucratic research methodologies – that is, standardized, impersonal ones. How to measure the true social responsibility of a Beatrice Foods, with its 400 some-odd divisions? How to decide whether or not the hundreds of thousands of General Motors employees act responsibly? And if the researcher cannot even measure real social responsibility in the large firm, then how are its top managers to ensure it, let alone to think about it?

References

Ackerman, R. (1973) 'Public Responsibility and the Businessman: A Review of the Literature', in B. Taylor and K. Macmillan, *Top Management*, New York: Longman.

Ackerman, R. (1975) *The Social Challenge to Business*, Cambridge, Mass.: Harvard University Press.

Alexander, G. and Buckholz, R. (1978) 'Corporate Social Responsibility and Stock Market Performance', *Academy of Management Journal*, pp. 479–486.

American Assembly (1978) *Corporate Governance in America*, Fifty-fourth meeting.

Bell, D. (1971) 'The Corporation and Society in the 1970s', *The Public Interest*, pp. 5–32.

Bower, J. (1970) 'Planning Within the Firm', *The American Economic Review: Papers and Proceedings of the 82nd Annual Meeting*, May, pp. 136–194.

Bowman, E. (1973) 'Corporate Social Responsibility and the Investor', *Journal of Contemporary Business*, Winter, pp. 21–43.

Bowman, E. and Haire, M. (1975) 'A Strategic Posture Toward Corporate Social Responsibility', *California Management Review*, Winter, pp. 49–58.

Bowman, E. and Haire, M. (1976) 'Social Impact Disclosure and Corporate Annual Reports', *Accounting, Organizations and Society*, pp. 11–21.

Bowman, J. (1976) 'Managerial Ethics in Business and Government', *Business Horizons*, October, pp. 48–54.

Braybrooke, D. (1967) 'Skepticism of Wants, and Certain Subversive Effects of Corporations on American Values', in S. Hood (ed.) *Human Values and Economic Policy*, New York: New York University Press.

Brenner, S. and Molander, E. (1977) 'Is the Ethics of Business Changing', *Harvard Business Review*, January/February, pp. 57–71.

Chamberlain, N. (1973) *The Limits of Corporate Responsibility*, New York: Basic Books.

Cheit, E. (1964) 'The New Place of Business: Why Managers Cultivate Social Responsibility', in E. Cheit (ed.), *The Business Establishment*, New York: Wiley.

Collins, J. and Ganotis, C. (1974) 'Managerial Attitudes Toward Corporate Social Responsibility', in S. Sethi (ed.) *The Unstable Ground: Corporate Social Policy in a Dynamic Society*, Los Angeles: Melville.

Davis, K. (1973) 'The Case For and Against Business Assumption of Social Responsibilities', *Academy of Management Journal*, pp. 312–322.

Dent, J. (1959) 'Organizational Correlates of the Goals of Business Managements', *Personnel Psychology*, pp. 365–393.

Drucker, P. (1973) *Management: Tasks, Responsibilities, Practices*, New York: Harper & Row.

Elbing, A. (1970) 'The Value Issue of Business: The Responsibility of the Businessman', *Academy of Management Journal*, pp. 79–89.

Fiedler, F (1966) 'The Contingency Model: A Theory of Leadership Effectiveness', in H. Proshansky and B. Seidenberg (eds) *Basic Studies in Social Psychology*, New York: Holt, Rinehart & Winston.

Friedman, M. (1962) *Capitalism and Freedom*, Chicago, Ill.: University of Chicago Press.

Friedman, M. (1970) 'A Friedman Doctrine: The Social Responsibility of Business Is to Increase Its Profits', *The New York Times Magazine*, September 13, pp. 32, 33, 122, 124, 126.

Gallup, G. (1978) *The Gallup Poll: Public Opinion, 1972–1977*, American Institute of Public Opinion.

Henderson, H. (1968) 'Should Business Tackle Society's Problems?' *Harvard Business Review*, July–August, pp. 77–85.

Keim, G. (1978) 'Corporate Social Responsibility: An Assessment of the Enlightened Self-Interest Model', *Academy of Management Review*, pp. 32–39.

Levitt, T. (1958) 'The Dangers of Social Responsibility', *Harvard Business Review*, September–October, pp. 41–50.

Levitt, T. (1968) 'Why Business Always Loses', *Harvard Business Review*, March–April, pp. 81–89.

Likert, R. (1961) *New Patterns of Management*, New York: McGraw-Hill.

Lodge, G. (1972) 'The Utility of Ideology for Environmental Analysis', in R. Vancil (ed.) *Formal Planning Systems*, Conference for Planning Executives, Harvard Business School.

Maccoby, M. (1976) *The Gamesman*, New York: Simon & Schuster.

Madden, C. (1977) 'Forces Which Influence Ethical Behavior', in C. Walton (ed.) *The Ethics of Corporate Conduct*, Englewood Cliffs, N.J.: Prentice-Hall, pp. 31–78.

Mintzberg, H. (1979) *The Structuring of Organizations: A Synthesis of the Research*, Englewood Cliffs, N.J.: Prentice-Hall.

Mintzberg, H. (1983) *Power in and Around Organizations*, Englewood Cliffs, N.J.: Prentice-Hall.

Mintzberg, H., Raisinghani, D., and Théoret, A. (1976) 'The Structure of "Unstructured" Decision Processes', *Administrative Science Quarterly*, pp. 246–275.

Pfiffner, J. (1960) 'Administrative Rationality', *Public Administrative Review*, pp. 125–132.

Ross, I. (1980) 'How Lawless Are the Big Companies?', *Fortune*, December 1, pp. 56–64.

Rumelt, R. (1974) *Strategy, Structure, and Economic Performance*, Division of Research, Graduate School of Business Administration, Harvard University.

Sethi, S. (1975) 'Dimensions of Corporate Social Performance: An Analytical Framework', *California Management Review*, Spring, pp. 58–64.

Singer, E. and Wooton, L. (1976) 'The Triumph and Failure of Albert Speer's Administrative Genius: Implications for Current Management Theory and Practice', *Journal of Applied Behavioral Science*, pp. 79–103.

Solzhenitsyn, A. (1978) 'Why the West Has Succumbed to Cowardice', *The Montreal Star: News and Reviews*, June 10, p. B1.

Tumin, M. (1964) 'Business as a Social System', *Behavioral Science*, pp. 120–130.

Wallich, H., and McGowan, J. (1970) 'Stockholder Interest and the Corporation's Role in Social Policy', in *A New Rationale for Corporate Social Policy*, Committee for Economic Development, pp. 39–59.

Walters, K. (1977) 'Corporate Social Responsibility and Political Ideology', *California Management Review*, Spring, pp. 40–51.

Walton, C. (ed.) (1977) *The Ethics of Corporate Conduct*, Englewood Cliffs, N.J.: Prentice-Hall.

Waters, J. (1978) 'Catch 20.5: Corporate Morality as an Organizational Phenomenon', *Organizational Dynamics*, Spring, pp. 3–19.

Westlin, A. (1979) 'Good Marks But Some Areas of Doubt', *Business Week*, May 14, pp. 14, 16.

Wrigley, L. (1970) *Diversification and Divisional Autonomy* (DBA thesis) Graduate School of Business Administration, Harvard University.

Chapter 3

What is CSR? Concepts and theories

$\mathbf{I}$N THIS CHAPTER WE WILL:

- Establish some basic understanding of the notion of CSR.
- Examine the colourful language existing in the area of CSR.
- Understand the background and rationale behind different ways of talking about CSR.
- Discuss the core definition of CSR and its implication for various stakeholders.
- Explore the variety of theoretical avenues and the diversity of theoretical concepts in CSR.

Introduction

A few years ago *The Financial Times* reported on a survey among professors of the 28 top business schools in the USA about what they thought were the ten most important management books (Kellaway, 2001). It turned out that none of the respondents named a book which was published after 1973 – raising some suspicions about whether all those new management 'ideas', 'theories' or 'concepts' published within the past three decades were in fact nothing more than buzz-words or recycled versions of extant knowledge in the field.

Such a survey can make us somewhat sceptical about an area of business studies such as CSR, which has seen quite a prolific generation of new terms, concepts, theories or ideas over the past fifty or so years. While some firms extol their CSR programmes, others talk of being good corporate citizens (Matten, Crane and Chapple, 2003). Similarly, while some academics regard CSR as an important area of academic inquiry, others regard it as an unnecessary term that adds little to our understanding of the corporation (Van Oosterhout and Heugens, 2007). Perhaps most confusingly, different firms, writers and other experts seem to regard CSR as completely different things: some see it as corporate community initiatives; others view it as a moral obligation to multiple stakeholders; some think of it as a form of economic development; some consider it to be a way for companies to counter criticism of their activities while carrying on largely as usual; while for others it represents a repressive Western ideology that is used to protect business in the global North. The list could go on. There are almost as many different views on CSR as there are discussions about it.

This plethora of terms and meanings represents something of a problem for us in trying to understand what CSR 'really' is. There are, however, a couple of reasons which explain and justify this variety of language and concepts in the area of CSR. First, CSR is a relatively young field of practice, and academic research has only really taken off since the 1950s (Carroll, 1999). Consequently, there is still a lot of debate, new thinking and innovation in the field, which in turn demands some more experimental use of terms, concepts and ideas.

Second, CSR is a topic that has been very strongly driven by practitioners in business whose preoccupation is of course more about pragmatic use of language than the search for unambiguous, academically rigorous definitions and theoretical concepts. Even today one could argue that the generally rather conservative environment of business schools has been reluctant to embrace issues of social responsibility (Matten and Moon, 2004). Most notably, it was only really the business scandals in the USA and Europe at the beginning of this century that sparked greater attention from mainstream thinkers in business schools towards the issue (Ghoshal, 2005), and arguably many of the leading research centres and academic units dedicated to CSR in business schools are today still a result of funding and initiatives from businesspeople or corporations.

Third, corporate *social* responsibility is an idea that needs contextualizing in the relevant social context – the culture, country, region or society where the corporation is deemed to have responsibilities (Aguilera *et al.*, 2007). Since these contexts differ, especially in a global context, so do the perspectives and meanings applied to the underlying idea of CSR across the globe.

In the following we will highlight some of the most popular concepts that have dominated the debate in CSR over the past decades.

Corporate Social Responsibility

Corporate social responsibility may be considered as the most long-standing concept in the area and has been used by business and academia for more than fifty years (Carroll, 1999). Reading 3 by Archie Carroll in this chapter (pp. 60–76) probably provides the most widely accepted understanding of the concept. As such, the idea is a fundamentally American one and reflects strongly the Anglo-American business context. Interestingly, many companies – most notably outside the US, such as Bertelsmann, Nokia, GlaxoSmithKline or Siemens – have adopted this language;

however, they often omit the 'social' and just speak about 'corporate responsibility'. This shift in language is partly due to the intention to include a broader set of responsibilities into the concept, such as to the environment, which in part is reflected in the academic literature on the topic as well (e.g. Cannon, 1994; Tully, 2005). Furthermore, it hints at the fact that CSR needs to be located in a specific context; and in many such contexts, for instance, in Eastern Europe, the attribute 'social' still evokes reminiscences of the term 'socialism' – something businesses try emphatically to avoid. Similar trends towards 'regional CSR jargon' are visible in the growing literature on CSR in Africa (Visser, 2005), Asia (Birch and Moon, 2004) and Latin America (Haslam, 2004; de Oliveira and Vargas, 2006).

Business Ethics

In particular, within academic research and teaching the term 'business ethics' has often been used as an umbrella term to discuss CSR (Carroll, 1999: 291). Historically, in most universities, CSR issues were taught by a professor of business ethics or in a business ethics course, and in many business schools this is still the case today. Therefore, many issues in the relationship between business and society have been studied initially from an ethical perspective, and some of the leading academic voices in CSR today have a background in philosophy. Business ethics may be defined as 'the study of business situations, activities and decisions where issues of right and wrong are addressed' (Crane and Matten, 2007: 5) – and as such is concerned mainly with the rights and wrongs, or the morality, of different business practices. While this clearly forms part of the CSR agenda, there is also a whole set of CSR questions concerned more with how to manage, measure and implement CSR. Similarly, with the recent growth in areas of CSR we arguably see a bifurcation of the traditional business ethics field: while traditional business ethicists look at specific dilemmas and decisions of an ethical nature, such as payment of bribes, discrimination or ethical marketing, CSR is oriented towards the wider role of the corporation in the global economy.

Sustainability

The concept of sustainability or sustainable development is another bracket under which CSR is discussed in business, politics and academia. Originating from forestry and environmental management, sustainability in a business context aims at mapping out how an organization can successfully survive without compromising the ecological, social and economic survival of its current and future environment (for details, see Reading 4 by Garriga and Melé, pp. 76–107). Again, the language and concept of sustainability reflects the influence of different regional contexts on the understanding of CSR. In particular, in Europe, corporations had been forced to think about their impact on and responsibility to wider society in the context of the rise of the green movement during the 1970s and 1980s. Consequently, many corporations became involved in CSR through ecological issues, and still today many companies such as BMW, Danone, Daimler-Chrysler or Shell talk about their CSR in terms of sustainability. This concern with sustainability is also reflected on the political level: for instance, the seminal paper on CSR by the EU Commission (2002) equates CSR with sustainable development and has been influential in shaping the more recent interest in CSR in Europe quite significantly.

Corporate Citizenship

As Van Luijk (2001) has pointed out, the language of 'responsibility' or even 'ethics' has not always appealed to business since it might be seen as entailing a somewhat reproachful connotation. Conspicuously, then, since the early 1990s, we can observe a significant turn in language in CSR towards the terminology of corporate citizenship. In particular, companies which faced considerable public criticism and attacks in the past, such as Coca-Cola, Microsoft or ExxonMobil, have adopted this terminology, evoking a notion of corporations as a good neighbour, shoulder-to-shoulder with other fellow citizens, filling their rightful place in society. While this new terminology was primarily business driven, and represents not much more than a relabelling of CSR (Matten and Crane, 2005), the ongoing academic debate on corporate citizenship has focused on highlighting the political nature of CSR. For instance, many CSR activities of companies today, such as the global fight against HIV/AIDS, or responsible forms of advertising, are carried out in close cooperation with political actors, such as government departments, non-government organizations, and so on. This reveals the changing nature of the role of business in society towards some degree of participation in political governance (Cashore, 2002; Moon, Crane and Matten, 2005). The debate about the political nature of CSR is still relatively young but represents one of the currently most dynamic discussions in the CSR literature (Scherer and Palazzo, 2007).

Introducing the Readings

Both readings in this chapter represent seminal contributions in the CSR area, providing an in-depth explication of perhaps the most popular CSR concept in the extant literature as well as one of the most comprehensive overviews and analyses of the current academic debate on CSR.

The pyramid of CSR

Archie Carroll's reading provides us with a thorough introduction to the 'pyramid of CSR' – often considered to be one of the most long-standing and widely cited definitions of CSR. The model is convincing because of its comprehensiveness and plausibility. It starts with the economic responsibility of the firm to produce goods and services in a profitable manner. This 'foundation upon which all others rest' is pretty uncontroversial and fairly uncontested even by the harshest CSR critics. The next level of legal responsibilities also reflects this pragmatic approach – to abide by the law is a fairly uncontroversial business responsibility by any standards. The next two levels, the ethical and philanthropic responsibilities, go beyond these and represent the core of voluntary activities of corporations to live up to societal expectations. In the final part Carroll applies these different levels of responsibility and by way of examples spells out what these could mean with regard to different stakeholder groups of the firm. The model described by Carroll is therefore broad, but simple. Perhaps most significantly, it provides a way of reconciling some of the different perspectives on CSR, such as those discussed in the previous chapter – for Carroll, social responsibility does not mean forgetting about economic responsibilities in order to do good, but is about acting responsibly within a context of basic legal and economic obligations. This is not to say that the model is without its critics – for example, several authors have suggested that the model is less suitable for national contexts outside the USA (e.g. Maignan, 2001; Visser, 2005).

The theoretical debates in CSR

Elisabet Garriga and Domènec Melé succeed in their rather ambitious attempt to map out the different theories used in CSR. Their analysis is a brilliant overview of, foremost, the academic debate on CSR. While in the introduction to this chapter we have mapped out the core concepts of CSR predominantly used in business, this reading provides the various facets of the debate in academic research, regardless of its impact and clout in the real world. It also helps in understanding why CSR is often referred to as an 'interdisciplinary' topic: the array of theories used include business studies, economics, sociology, politics, law and philosophy. This is an indispensable read for any student of CSR, not least because it also provides references to most of the key contributions to the CSR literature over the past fifty-odd years.

Study Questions

1   What are the main labels used to refer to CSR? From the perspective of the geographic region in which you live, what would you consider to be the most useful one?

2   What are the core elements of CSR in Carroll's definition? Set out examples of companies that have upheld these specific levels of responsibility as well as companies that have violated them.

3   To what extent do you consider the plethora of terms and concepts in the CSR area to be a strength or a weakness for practitioners and researchers of CSR?

4   CSR originates from the USA and has only relatively recently entered the debate in other regions of the world. One of the largest European business newspapers has commented: '*The import of the concept of "Corporate Social Responsibility"*

should be "returned to sender" as quickly as possible, because it just describes a matter of course and things we knew all along' (*Frankfurter Allgemeine Zeitung*, 25 November 2006: 13). Discuss.

5 Think of Carroll's pyramid from the perspective of a small business. Would you suggest a similar hierarchy of responsibilities? Similarly, which theories of CSR as mapped out by Garriga and Melé would be most useful in a small business context?

References

Aguilera , R., Rupp, D., Williams, C. and Ganapathi, J. 2007. Putting the S back in Corporate Social Responsibility: a multi-level theory of social change in organizations. *Academy of Management Review*, 32(3): forthcoming.

Birch, D. and Moon, J. 2004. Corporate social responsibility in Asia. *Journal of Corporate Citizenship*, 13 (Special Issue): 18–149.

Cannon, T. 1994. *Corporate responsibility*. London: Pearson.

Carroll, A. 1999. Corporate social responsibility – evolution of a definitional construct. *Business and Society*, 38(3): 268–295.

Cashore, B. 2002. Legitimacy and the privatization of environmental governance: how non-state market-driven (NSMD) governance systems gain rule-making authority. *Governance*, 15(4): 503–529.

Commission of the European Communities. 2002. *Communication from the Commission concerning corporate social responsibility: A business contribution to sustainable development*. Brussels: EU Commission.

Crane, A. and Matten, D. 2007. *Business ethics: Managing corporate citizenship and sustainability in the age of globalization* (2nd edn). Oxford: Oxford University Press.

Ghoshal, S. 2005. Bad management theories are destroying good management practices. *Academy of Management Learning and Education*, 4(1): 75–91.

Haslam, P. 2004. *The Corporate Social Responsibility System in Latin America and the Caribbean*. Ottawa: Policy Paper FPP-4-01 of the Canadian Foundation for the Americas, www.focal.ca.

Kellaway, L. 2001. The oldies are the best. *The Financial Times*, 26 November 2001: 13.

Maignan, I. 2001. Consumers' perceptions of corporate social responsibilities: a cross-cultural comparison. *Journal of Business Ethics*, 30(1/1): 57–72.

Matten, D. and Crane, A. 2005. Corporate citizenship – toward an extended theoretical conceptualisation. *Academy of Management Review*, 30(1): 166–179.

Matten, D. and Moon, J. 2004. Corporate Social Responsibility education in Europe. *Journal of Business Ethics*, 54(4): 323–337.

Matten, D., Crane, A., and Chapple, W. 2003. Behind the mask: revealing the true face of corporate citizenship. *Journal of Business Ethics*, 44(1/2): 109–120.

Moon, J., Crane, A., and Matten, D. 2005. Can corporations be citizens? Corporate citizenship as a metaphor for business participation in society. *Business Ethics Quarterly*, 15(3): 427–451.

Puppim de Oliveira, J. and Vargas, G. 2006. Corporate citizenship in Latin America: new challenges for business. *Journal of Corporate Citizenship*, 21 (Special Issue).

Scherer, A. and Palazzo, G. 2007. Toward a political conception of corporate responsibility – business and society seen from a Habermasian perspective. *Academy of Management Review*, 32: forthcoming.

Tully, S. 2005. *International documents on corporate responsibility*. Cheltenham, UK, and Northampton, MA: Edward Elgar.

Van Luijk, H. 2001. Business ethics in Europe: a tale of two efforts. In R. Frederick (ed.), *A companion to business ethics*: 643–658. Cambridge, MA, and Oxford: Blackwell.

Van Oosterhout, J. and Heugens, P. 2007. Much ado about nothing: a conceptual critique of CSR. In A. Crane, D. Matten, A. McWilliams, J. Moon, and D. Siegel (eds), *The Oxford Handbook of Corporate Social Responsibility*. Oxford: Oxford University Press.

Visser, W. 2005. Revisiting Carroll's CSR pyramid: an African perspective. In E. Pedersen and M. Huniche (eds), *Corporate citizenship in a development perspective*: 29–56. Copenhagen: Copenhagen Business School Press.

THE PYRAMID OF CORPORATE SOCIAL RESPONSIBILITY: TOWARD THE MORAL MANAGEMENT OF ORGANIZATIONAL STAKEHOLDERS

Archie Carroll

For the better part of 30 years now, corporate executives have struggled with the issue of the firm's responsibility to its society. Early on it was argued by some that the corporation's sole responsibility was to provide a maximum financial return to shareholders. It became quickly apparent to everyone, however, that this pursuit of financial gain had to take place within the laws of the land. Though social activist groups and others throughout the 1960s advocated a broader notion of corporate responsibility, it was not until the significant social legislation of the early 1970s that this message became indelibly clear as a result of the creation of the Environmental Protection Agency (EPA), the Equal Employment Opportunity Commission (EEOC), the Occupational Safety and Health Administration (OSHA), and the Consumer Product Safety Commission (CPSC).

These new governmental bodies established that national public policy now officially recognized the environment, employees, and consumers to be significant and legitimate stakeholders of business. From that time on, corporate executives have had to wrestle with how they balance their commitments to the corporation's owners with their obligations to an ever-broadening group of stakeholders who claim both legal and ethical rights.

This article will explore the nature of corporate social responsibility (CSR) with an eye toward understanding its component parts. The intention will be to characterize the firm's CSR in ways that might be useful to executives who wish to reconcile their obligations to their shareholders with those to other competing groups claiming legitimacy. This discussion will be framed by a pyramid of corporate social responsibility. Next, we plan to relate this concept to the idea of stakeholders. Finally, our goal will be to isolate the ethical or moral component of CSR and relate it to perspectives that reflect three major ethical approaches to management – immoral, amoral, and moral. The principal goal in this final section will be to flesh out what it means to manage stakeholders in an ethical or moral fashion.

Evolution of Corporate Social Responsibility

What does it mean for a corporation to be socially responsible? Academics and practitioners have been striving to establish an agreed-upon definition of this concept for 30 years. In 1960, Keith Davis suggested that social responsibility refers to businesses' "decisions and actions taken for reasons at least partially beyond the firm's direct economic or technical interest." At about the same time, Eells and Walton (1961) argued that CSR refers to the "problems that arise when corporate enterprise casts its shadow on the social scene, and the ethical principles that ought to govern the relationship between the corporation and society."

In 1971 the Committee for Economic Development used a "three concentric circles" approach to depicting CSR. The inner circle included basic economic functions – growth, products, jobs. The intermediate circle suggested that the economic functions must be exercised with a sensitive awareness of changing social values and priorities. The outer circle outlined newly emerging and still amorphous responsibilities that business should assume to become more actively involved in improving the social environment.

The attention was shifted from social responsibility to social responsiveness by several other writers. Their basic argument was that the emphasis on responsibility focused exclusively on the notion of business obligation and motivation and that action or performance were being overlooked. The social responsiveness movement, therefore, emphasized corporate action, pro-action, and implementation of a social role. This was indeed a necessary reorientation.

The question still remained, however, of reconciling the firm's economic orientation with its social orientation. A step in this direction was taken when a comprehensive definition of CSR was set forth. In this view, a four-part conceptualization of CSR included the idea that the corporation has not only economic and legal obligations, but ethical and discretionary (philanthropic) responsibilities as well (Carroll 1979). The point here was that CSR, to be accepted as legitimate, had to address the entire spectrum of obligations business has to society, including the most fundamental – economic. It is upon this four-part perspective that our pyramid is based.

In recent years, the term corporate social performance (CSP) has emerged as an inclusive and global concept to embrace corporate social responsibility, responsiveness, and the entire spectrum of socially beneficial activities of businesses. The focus on social performance emphasizes the concern for corporate action and accomplishment in the social sphere. With a perspective it is clear that firms must formulate and implement social goals and programs as well as integrate ethical sensitivity into all decision making, policies, and actions. With a results focus, CSP suggests an all-encompassing orientation towards normal criteria by which we assess business performance to include quantity, quality, effectiveness, and efficiency. While we recognize the vitality of the performance concept, we have chosen to adhere to the CSR terminology for our present discussion. With just a slight change of focus, however, we could easily be discussing a CSP rather than a CSR pyramid. In any event, our long-term concern is what managers do with these ideas in terms of implementation.

The Pyramid of Corporate Social Responsibility

For CSR to be accepted by a conscientious business person, it should be framed in such a way that the entire range of business responsibilities are embraced. It is suggested here that four kinds of social responsibilities contribute total CSR: economic, legal, ethical, and philanthropic. Furthermore, these four categories or components of CSR might be depicted as a pyramid. To be sure, all these kinds of responsibilities have always existed to some extent, but it has only been in recent years that ethical and philanthropic functions have taken a significant place. Each of these four categories deserves closer consideration.

Economic responsibilities

Historically, business organizations were created as economic entities designed to provide goods and services to societal members. The profit motive was established as the primary incentive for entrepreneurship. Before it was anything else, the business organization was the basic economic unit in our society. As such, its principal role was to produce goods and services that consumers needed and wanted and to make an acceptable profit in the process. At some point the idea of the profit motive got transformed into a notion of maximum profits, and this has been an enduring value ever

Economic Components (Responsibilities)	Legal Components (Responsibilities)
1. It is important to perform in a manner consistent with maximizing earnings per share	1. It is important to perform in a manner consistent with expectations of government and law.
2. It is important to be committed to being as profitable as possible.	2. It is important to comply with various federal, state, and local regulations.
3. It is important to maintain a strong competitive position	3. It is important to be a law-abiding corporate citizen.
4. It is important to maintain a high level of operating efficiency	4. It is important that a successful firm be defined as one that fulfills its legal obligations.
5. It is important that a successful firm be defined as one that is consistently profitable.	5. It is important to provide goods and services that at least meet minimal legal requirements.

Figure 1 Economic and legal components of corporate social responsibility

since. All other business responsibilities are predicated upon the economic responsibility of the firm, because without it the others become moot considerations. Figure 1 summarizes some important statements characterizing economic responsibilities. Legal responsibilities are also depicted in Figure 1, and we will consider them next.

Legal responsibilities

Society has not only sanctioned business to operate according to the profit motive; at the same time business is expected to comply with the laws and regulations promulgated by federal, state, and local governments as the ground rules under which business must operate. As a partial fulfilment of the "social contract" between business and society, firms are expected to pursue their economic missions within the framework of the law. Legal responsibilities reflect a view of "codified ethics" in the sense that they embody basic notions of fair operations as established by our lawmakers. They are depicted as the next layer on the pyramid to portray their historical development, but they are appropriately seen as coexisting with economic responsibilities as fundamental precepts of the free enterprise system.

Ethical responsibilities

Although economic and legal responsibilities embody ethical norms about fairness and justice, ethical responsibilities embrace those activities and practices that are expected or prohibited by societal members even though they are not codified into law. Ethical responsibilities embody those standards, norms, or expectations that reflect a concern for what consumers, employees, shareholders, and the community regard as fair, just, or in keeping with the respect or protection of stakeholders' moral rights.

In one sense, changing ethics or values precede the establishment of law because they become the driving force behind the very creation of laws or regulations. For example, the environmental, civil rights, and consumer movements reflected basic alterations in societal values and thus may be seen as ethical bellwethers foreshadowing and resulting in the later legislation. In another sense, ethical responsibilities may be seen as embracing newly emerging values and norms society expects business to meet, even though such values and norms may reflect a higher standard of performance than that currently required by law. Ethical responsibilities in this sense are often ill-defined or continually under public debate as to their legitimacy, and thus are frequently difficult for business to deal with.

Superimposed on these ethical expectations emanating from societal groups are the implied levels of ethical performance suggested by a consideration of the great ethical principles of moral philosophy. This would include such principles as justice, rights, and utilitarianism.

The business ethics movement of the past decade has firmly established an ethical responsibility as a legitimate CSR component. Though it is depicted as the next layer of the CSR pyramid, it must be constantly recognized that it is in dynamic interplay with the legal responsibility category. That is, it is constantly pushing the legal responsibility category to broaden or expand while at the same time placing ever higher expectations on businesspersons to operate at levels above that required by law. Figure 2 depicts statements that help characterize ethical responsibilities. The figure also summarizes philanthropic responsibilities, discussed next.

Philanthropic responsibilities

Philanthropy encompasses those corporate actions that are in response to society's expectation that businesses be good corporate citizens. This includes actively engaging in acts or programs to promote human welfare or goodwill. Examples of philanthropy include business contributions of financial resources or executive time, such as contributions to the arts, education, or the community. A loaned-executive program that provides leadership for a community's United Way campaign is one illustration of philanthropy.

Ethical Components (Responsibilities)	Philanthropic Components (Responsibilities)
1. It is important to perform in a manner consistent with expectations of societal mores and ethical norms.	1. It is important to perform in a manner consistent with the philanthropic and charitable expectations of society.
2. It is important to recognize and respect new or evolving ethical/moral norms adopted by society.	2. It is important to assist the fine and performing arts.
3. It is important to prevent ethical norms from being compromised in order to achieve corporate goals.	3. It is important that managers and employees participate in voluntary and charitable activities within their local communities.
4. It is important that good corporate citizenship be defined as doing what is expected morally or ethically.	4. It is important to provide assistance to private and public educational institutions.
5. It is important to recognize that corporate integrity and ethical behavior go beyond mere compliance with laws and regulations.	5. It is important to assist voluntarily those projects that enhance a community's "quality of life."

Figure 2 Ethical and philanthropic components of corporate social responsibility

The distinguishing feature between philanthropic and ethical responsibilities is that the former are not expected in an ethical or moral sense. Communities desire firms to contribute their money, facilities, and employee time to humanitarian programs or purposes, but they do not regard the firms as unethical if they do not provide the desired level. Therefore, philanthropy is more discretionary or voluntary on the part of businesses even though there is always the societal expectation that businesses provide it.

One notable reason for making the distinction between philanthropic and ethical responsibilities is that some firms feel they are being socially responsible if they are just good citizens in the community. This distinction brings home the vital point that CSR includes philanthropic contributions but is not limited to them. In fact, it would be argued here that philanthropy is highly desired and prized but actually less important than the other three categories of social responsibility. In a sense, philanthropy is icing on the cake – or on the pyramid, using our metaphor.

The pyramid of corporate social responsibility is depicted in Figure 3. It portrays the four components of CSR, beginning with the basic building block notion that economic performance undergirds all else. At the same time, business is expected to obey the law because the law is society's codification of acceptable and unacceptable behaviour. Next is business's responsibility to be ethical. At its most fundamental level, this is the obligation to do what is right, just, and fair, and to avoid or minimize harm to stakeholders

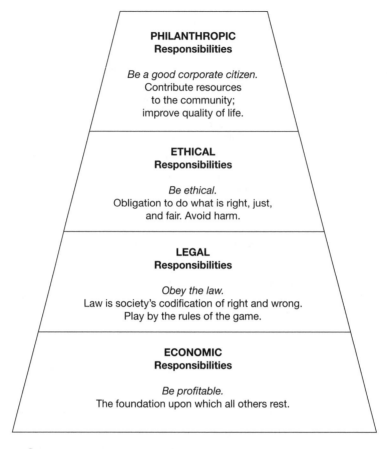

Figure 3 The pyramid of corporate social responsibility

(employees, consumers, the environment, and others). Finally, business is expected to be a good corporate citizen. This is captured in the philanthropic responsibility, wherein business is expected to contribute financial and human resources to the community and to improve the quality of life.

No metaphor is perfect, and the CSR pyramid is no exception. It is intended to portray that the total CSR of business comprises distinct components that, taken together, constitute the whole. Though the components have been treated as separate concepts for discussion purposes, they are not mutually exclusive and are not intended to juxtapose a firm's economic responsibilities with its other responsibilities. At the same time, a consideration of the separate components helps the manager see that the different types of obligations are in a constant but dynamic tension with one another. The most critical tensions, of course, would be between economic and legal, economic and ethical, and economic and philanthropic. The traditionalist might see this as a conflict between a firm's "concern for profits" versus its "concern for society," but it is suggested here that this is an oversimplification. A CSR or stakeholder perspective would recognize these tensions as organizational realities, but focus on the total pyramid as a unified whole and how the firm might engage in decisions, actions, and programs that simultaneously fulfil all its component parts.

In summary, the total corporate social responsibility of business entails the simultaneous fulfilment of the firm's economic, legal, ethical, and philanthropic responsibilities. Stated in more pragmatic and managerial terms, the CSR firm should strive to make a profit, obey the law, be ethical, and be a good corporate citizen.

Upon first glance, this array of responsibilities may seem broad. They seem to be in striking contrast to the classical economic argument that management has one responsibility: to maximize the profits of its owners or shareholders. Economist Milton Friedman, the most outspoken proponent of this view, has argued that social matters are not the concern of business people and that these problems should be resolved by the unfettered workings of the free market system. Friedman's argument loses some of its punch, however, when you consider his assertion in its totality. Friedman posited that management is "to make as much money as possible while conforming to the basic rules of society, both those embodied in the law and those embodied in ethical custom" (Friedman 1970). Most people focus on the first part of Friedman's quote but not the second part. It seems clear from this statement that profits, conformity to the law, and ethical custom embrace three components of the CSR pyramid – economic, legal and ethical. That only leaves the philanthropic component for Friedman to reject. Although it may be appropriate for an economist to take this view, one would not encounter many business executives today who exclude philanthropic programs from their firms' range of activities. It seems the role of corporate citizenship is one that business has no significant problem embracing. Undoubtedly this perspective is rationalized under the rubric of enlightened self interest.

We next propose a conceptual framework to assist the manager in integrating the four CSR components with organizational stakeholders.

CSR and Organizational Stakeholders

There is a natural fit between the idea of corporate social responsibility and an organization's stakeholders. The word "social" in CSR has always been vague and lacking in specific direction as to whom the corporation is responsible. The concept of stakeholder personalizes social or societal responsibilities by delineating the specific groups or persons business should consider in its CSR orientation. Thus, the stakeholder nomenclature puts "names and faces" on the societal members who are most urgent to business, and to whom it must be responsive.

By now most executives understand that the term "stakeholder" constitutes a play on the word stockholder and is intended to more appropriately describe those groups or persons who have a stake, a claim, or an interest in the operations and decisions of the firm. Sometimes the stake might represent a legal claim, such as that which might be held by an owner, an employee, or a customer who has an explicit or implicit contract. Other times it might be represented by a moral claim, such as when these groups assert a right to be treated fairly or with due process, or to have their opinions taken into consideration in an important business decision.

Management's challenge is to decide which stakeholders merit and receive consideration in the decision-making process. In any given instance, there may be numerous stakeholder groups (shareholders, consumers, employees, suppliers, community, social activist groups) clamoring for management's attention. How do managers sort out the urgency or importance of the various stakeholder claims? Two vital criteria include the stakeholders' legitimacy and their power. From a CSR perspective their legitimacy may be most important. From a management efficiency perspective, their power might be of central influence. Legitimacy refers to the extent to which a group has a justifiable right to be making its claim. For example, a group of 300 employees about to be laid off by a plant-closing decision has a more legitimate claim on management's attention than the local chamber of commerce, which is worried about losing the firm as one of its dues-paying members. The stakeholder's power is another factor. Here we may witness significant differences. Thousands of small, individual investors, for example, wield very little power unless they can find a way to get organized. By contrast, institutional investors and large mutual fund groups have significant power over management because of the sheer magnitude of their investments and the fact that they are organized.

With these perspectives in mind, let us think of stakeholder management as a process by which managers reconcile their own objectives with the claims and expectations being made on them by various stakeholder groups. The challenge of stakeholder management is to ensure that the firm's primary stakeholders achieve their objectives while other stakeholders are also satisfied. Even though this "win–win" outcome is not always possible, it does represent a legitimate and desirable goal for management to pursue to protect its long-term interests.

The important functions of stakeholder management are to describe, understand, analyze, and finally, manage. Thus, five major questions might be posed to capture the essential ingredients we need for stakeholder management:

1. Who are our stakeholders?
2. What are their stakes?
3. What opportunities and challenges are presented by our stakeholders?
4. What corporate social responsibilities (economic, legal, ethical, and philanthropic) do we have to our stakeholders?
5. What strategies, actions, or decisions should we take to best deal with these responsibilities?

Whereas much could be discussed about each of these questions, let us direct our attention here to question four – what kinds of social responsibilities do we have to our stakeholders? Our objective here is to present a conceptual approach for examining these issues. This conceptual approach or framework is presented as the stakeholder/responsibility matrix in Figure 4.

This matrix is intended to be used as an analytical tool or template to organize a manager's thoughts and ideas about what the firm ought to be doing in an economic, legal, ethical, and philanthropic sense with respect to its identified stakeholder groups. By carefully and deliberately moving through the various cells of the matrix, the manager may develop a significant descriptive and analytical data base that can then be used for purposes of stakeholder management. The information resulting from this stakeholder/responsibility analysis should be useful when developing priorities and making both long-term and short-term decisions involving multiple stakeholders' interests.

To be sure, thinking in stakeholder responsibility terms increases the complexity of decision making and may be extremely time consuming and taxing, especially at first. Despite its complexity, however, this approach is one methodology management can use to integrate values – what it stands for – with the traditional economic mission of the organization. In the final analysis, such an integration could be of significant usefulness to management. This is because the stakeholder/responsibility perspective is most consistent with the pluralistic environment faced by business today. As such,

| Stakeholders | Types of CSR | | | |
	Economic	Legal	Ethical	Philanthropic
Owners				
Customers				
Employees				
Community				
Competitors				
Suppliers				
Social Activist Groups				
Public at Large				
Others				

Figure 4 Stakeholder/responsibility matrix

it provides the opportunity for an in-depth corporate appraisal of financial as well as social and economic concerns. Thus, the stakeholder/responsibility perspective would be an invaluable foundation for responding to the fifth stakeholder management question about strategies, actions, or decisions that should be pursued to effectively respond to the environment business faces.

Moral Management and Stakeholders

At this juncture we would like to expound upon the link between the firm's ethical responsibilities or perspectives and its major stakeholder groups. Here we are isolating the ethical component of our CSR pyramid and discussing it more thoroughly in the context of stakeholders. One way to do this would be to use major ethical principles such as those of justice, rights, and utilitarianism to identify and describe our ethical responsibilities. We will take another alternative, however, and discuss stakeholders within the context of three major ethical approaches – immoral management, amoral management, and moral management. These three ethical approaches were defined and discussed in an earlier *Business Horizons* article (Carroll 1987). We will briefly describe and review these three ethical types and then suggest how they might be oriented toward the major stakeholder groups. Our goal is to profile the likely orientation of the three ethical types with our special emphasis upon moral management, our preferred ethical approach.

Three moral types

If we accept that the terms ethics and morality are essentially synonymous in the organizational context, we may speak of immoral, amoral, and moral management as descriptive categories of three different kinds of managers. Immoral management is characterized by those managers whose decisions, actions, and behavior suggest an active opposition to what is deemed right or ethical. Decisions by immoral managers are discordant with accepted ethical principles and, indeed, imply an active negation of what is moral. These managers care only about their or their organization's profitability and success. They see legal standards as barriers or impediments management must overcome to accomplish what it wants. Their strategy is to exploit opportunities for personal or corporate gain.

An example might be helpful. Many observers would argue that Charles Keating could be described as an immoral manager. According to the federal government, Keating recklessly and fraudulently ran California's Lincoln Savings into the ground, reaping $34 million for himself and his family. A major accounting firm said about Keating: "Seldom in our experience as accountants have we experienced a more egregious example of the misapplication of generally accepted accounting principles" ("Good Timing, Charlie" 1989).

The second major type of management ethics is amoral management. Amoral managers are neither immoral nor moral but are not sensitive to the fact that their everyday business decisions may have deleterious effects on others. These managers lack ethical perception or awareness. That is, they go through their organizational lives not thinking that their actions have an ethical dimension. Or they may just be careless or inattentive to the implications of their actions on stakeholders. These managers may be well intentioned, but do not see that their business decisions and actions may be hurting those with whom they transact business or interact. Typically their orientation is towards the letter of the law as their ethical guide. We have been describing a sub-category of amorality known as unintentional amoral managers. There is also another group we may call intentional amoral managers. These managers simply think that ethical considerations are for our private lives, not for business. They believe that business activity resides outside the sphere to which moral judgments apply. Though most amoral managers today are unintentional, there may still exist a few who just do not see a role for ethics in business.

Examples of unintentional amorality abound. When police departments stipulated that applicants must be 5'10" and weigh 180 pounds to qualify for positions, they just did not think about the adverse impact their policy would have on women and some ethnic groups who, on average, do not attain that height and weight. The liquor, beer, and cigarette industries provide other examples. They did not anticipate that their products would create serious moral issues: alcoholism, drunk driving deaths, lung cancer, deteriorating health, and offensive secondary smoke. Finally, when McDonald's initially decided to use polystyrene containers for food packaging it just did not adequately consider the environmental impact that would be caused. McDonald's surely does not intentionally create a solid waste disposal problem, but one major consequence of its business is just that. Fortunately, the company has responded to complaints by replacing the polystyrene packaging with paper products.

Moral management is our third ethical approach, one that should provide a striking contrast. In moral management, ethical norms that adhere to a high standard of right behavior are employed. Moral managers not only conform to accepted and high levels of professional conduct, they also commonly exemplify leadership on ethical issues. Moral managers want to be profitable, but only within the confines of sound legal and ethical precepts, such as fairness, justice, and due process. Under this approach, the orientation is toward both the letter and the spirit of the law. Law is seen as minimal ethical behavior and the preference and goal is to operate well above what the law mandates. Moral managers seek out and use sound ethical principles such as justice, rights, utilitarianism, and the Golden Rule to guide their decisions. When ethical dilemmas arise, moral managers assume a leadership position for their companies and industries.

There are numerous examples of moral management. When IBM took the lead and developed its Open Door policy to provide a mechanism through which employees might pursue their due process rights, this could be considered moral management. Similarly, when IBM initiated its Four Principles of Privacy to protect privacy rights of employees, this was moral management. When McCullough Corporation withdrew from the Chain Saw Manufacturers Association because the association fought mandatory safety standards for the industry, this was moral management. McCullough knew its product was potentially dangerous and had used chain brakes on its own saws for years, even though it was not required by law to do so. Another example of moral management was when Maguire Thomas Partners, a Los Angeles commercial developer, helped solve urban problems by saving and refurbishing historic sites, putting up structures that matched old ones, limiting building heights to less than the law allowed, and using only two-thirds of the allowable building density so that open spaces could be provided.

Orientation towards stakeholders

Now that we have a basic understanding of the three ethical types or approaches, we will propose profiles of what the likely stakeholder orientation might be toward the major stakeholder groups using each of the three ethical approaches. Our goal is to accentuate the moral management approach by contrasting it with the other two types.

Basically, there are five major stakeholder groups that are recognized as priorities by most firms, across industry lines and in spite of size or location: owners (shareholders), employees, customers, local communities, and the society-at-large. Although the general ethical obligation to each of these groups is essentially identical (protect their rights, treat them with respect and fairness), specific behaviors and orientations arise because of the differing nature of the groups. In an attempt to flesh out the character and salient features of the three ethical types and their stakeholder orientations, Figures 5 and 6 summarize the orientations these three types might assume with respect to four of the major stakeholder groups. Because of space constraints and the general nature of the society-at-large category, it has been omitted.

By carefully considering the described stakeholder orientations under each of the three ethical types, a richer appreciation of the moral management approach should be possible. Our goal here is to gain a fuller understanding of what it means to engage in moral management and what this implies for interacting with stakeholders. To be sure, there are other stakeholder groups to which moral management should be directed, but again, space precludes their discussion here. This might include thinking of managers and non-managers as distinct categories of employees and would also embrace such groups as suppliers, competitors, special interest groups, government, and the media.

Type of Management	Orientation Toward Owner/Shareholder Stakeholders
Immoral Management	Shareholders are minimally treated and given short shrift. Focus is on maximizing positions of executive groups – maximizing executive compensation, perks, benefits. Golden parachutes are more important than returns to shareholders. Managers maximize their positions without shareholders being made aware. Concealment from shareholders is the operating procedure. Self-interest of management group is the order of the day.
Amoral Management	No special thought is given to shareholders; they are there and must be minimally accommodated. Profit focus of the business is their reward. No thought is given to ethical consequences of decisions for any stakeholder group, including owners. Communication is limited to that required by law.
Moral Management	Shareholders' interest (short- and long-term) is a central factor. The best way to be ethical to shareholders is to treat all stakeholder claimants in a fair and ethical manner. To protect shareholders, an ethics committee of the board is created. Code of ethics is established, promulgated and made a living document to protect shareholders' and others' interests.
Type of Management	Orientation Toward Employee Stakeholders
Immoral Management	Employees are viewed as factors of production to be used, exploited, manipulated for gain of individual manager or company. No concern is shown for employees' needs/rights/expectations. Short-term focus. Coercive, controlling, alienating.
Amoral Management	Employees are treated as law requires. Attempts to motivate focus on increasing productivity rather than satisfying employees' growing maturity needs. Employees still seen as factors of production but remunerative approach used. Organization sees self-interest in treating employees with minimal respect. Organization structure, pay incentives, rewards all geared toward short- and medium-term productivity.
Moral Management	Employees are a human resource that must be treated with dignity and respect. Goal is to use a leadership style such as consultative/participative that will result in mutual confidence and trust. Commitment is a recurring theme. Employees' rights to due process, privacy, freedom of speech, and safety are maximally considered in all decisions. Management seeks out fair dealings with employees.

Figure 5 Three moral types and orientation toward stakeholder groups: owners and employees

Type of Management	Orientation Toward Customer Stakeholders
Immoral Management	Customers are viewed as opportunities to be exploited for personal or organizational gain. Ethical standards in dealings do not prevail; indeed, an active intent to cheat, deceive, and/or mislead is present. In all marketing decisions – advertising, pricing, packaging, distribution – customer is taken advantage of to the fullest extent.
Amoral Management	Management does not think through the ethical consequences of its decisions and actions. It simply makes decisions with profitability within the letter of the law as a guide. Management is not focused on what is fair from perspective of customer. Focus is on management's rights. No consideration is given to ethical implications of interactions with customers.
Moral Management	Customer is viewed as equal partner in transaction. Customer brings needs/expectations to the exchange transaction and is treated fairly. Managerial focus is on giving customer fair value, full information, fair guarantee, and satisfaction. Consumer rights are liberally interpreted and honored.
Type of Management	Orientation Toward Local Community Stakeholders
Immoral Management	Exploits community to fullest extent; pollutes the environment. Plant or business closings take fullest advantage of community. Actively disregards community needs. Takes fullest advantage of community resources without giving anything in return. Violates zoning and other ordinances whenever it can for its own advantage.
Amoral Management	Does not take community or its resources into account in management decision making. Community factors are assumed to be irrelevant to business decisions. Community, like employees, is a factor of production. Legal considerations are followed, but nothing more. Deals minimally with community, its people, community activity, local government.
Moral Management	Sees vital community as a goal to be actively pursued. Seeks to be a leading citizen and to motivate others to do likewise. Gets actively involved and helps institutions that need help – schools, recreational groups, philanthropic groups. Leadership position in environment, education, culture/arts, volunteerism, and general community affairs. Firm engages in strategic philanthropy. Management sees community goals and company goals as mutually interdependent.

Figure 6 Three moral types and orientation toward stakeholder groups: customers and local community

Though the concept of corporate social responsibility may from time to time be supplanted by various other focuses such as social responsiveness, social performance, public policy, ethics, or stakeholder management, an underlying challenge for all is to define the kinds of responsibilities management and businesses have to the constituency groups with which they transact and interact most frequently. The pyramid of corporate social responsibility gives us a framework for understanding the evolving nature of the firm's economic, legal, ethical, and philanthropic performance. The implementation of these responsibilities may vary depending upon the firm's size, management's philosophy, corporate strategy, industry characteristics, the state of the economy, and other such mitigating conditions, but the four component parts provide management with a skeletal outline of the nature and kinds of their CSR. In frank, action-oriented terms, business is called upon to: be profitable, obey the law, be ethical, and be a good corporate citizen.

The stakeholder management perspective provides not only a language and way to personalize relationships with names and faces, but also some useful conceptual and analytical concepts for diagnosing, analyzing, and prioritizing an organization's relationships and strategies. Effective organizations will progress beyond stakeholder identification and question what opportunities and threats are posed by stakeholders; what economic, legal, ethical, and philanthropic responsibilities they have; and what strategies, actions or decisions should be pursued to most effectively address these responsibilities. The stakeholder/responsibility matrix provides a template management might use to organize its analysis and decision making.

Throughout the article we have been building toward the notion of an improved ethical organizational climate as manifested by moral management. Moral management was defined and described through a contrast with immoral and amoral management. Because the business landscape is replete with immoral and amoral managers, moral managers may sometimes be hard to find. Regardless, their characteristics have been identified and, most important, their perspective or orientation towards the major stakeholder groups has been profiled. These stakeholder orientation profiles give managers a conceptual but practical touchstone for sorting out the different categories or types of ethical (or not-so-ethical) behavior that may be found in business and other organizations.

It has often been said that leadership by example is the most effective way to improve business ethics. If that is true, moral management provides a model leadership perspective or orientation that managers may wish to emulate. One great fear is that managers may think they are providing ethical leadership just by rejecting immoral management. However, amoral management, particularly the unintentional variety, may unconsciously prevail if managers are not aware of what it is and of its dangers. At best, amorality represents ethical neutrality, and this notion is not tenable in the society of the 1990s. The standard must be set high, and moral management provides the best exemplar of what that lofty standard might embrace. Further, moral management, to be fully appreciated, needs to be seen within the context of organization–stakeholder relationships. It is toward this singular goal that our entire discussion has focused. If the "good society" is to become a realization, such a high expectation only naturally becomes the aspiration and preoccupation of the management.

References

Ackerman, R. and Bauer, R. (1976), *Corporate Social Responsiveness*, Reston, Va.: Reston Publishing Co.

Carroll, A. (1979), 'A Three-Dimensional Conceptual Model of Corporate Social Performance', *Academy of Management Review* 4(4): 497–505.

Carroll, A. (1987), 'In Search of the Moral Manager', *Business Horizons*, March–April, pp. 7–15.

Committee for Economic Development (1971), *Social Responsibilities of Business Corporations*, New York: CED.

Davis, K. (1960), 'Can Business Afford to Ignore its Social Responsibilities?', *California Management Review*, 2(3): 70–76.

Eells, R., and Walton, C. (1961), *Conceptual Foundations of Business*, Homewood, Ill.: Richard D. Irwin.

'Good Timing, Charlie' (1989), *Forbes*, November 27, pp.140–144.

Frederick, W. (1978), 'From CSR$_1$, to CSR$_2$: The Maturing of Business and Society Thought', *University of Pittsburgh Working Paper* No. 279.

Sethi, S. (1975), 'Dimensions of Corporate Social Responsibility', *California Management Review*, 17(3): 58–64.

CORPORATE SOCIAL RESPONSIBILITY THEORIES: MAPPING THE TERRITORY

Elisabet Garriga and Domènec Melé

Introduction

Since the second half of the 20th century a long debate on corporate social responsibility (CSR) has been taking place. In 1953, Bowen (1953) wrote the seminal book *Social Responsibilities of the Businessman*. Since then there has been a shift in terminology from the social responsibility of business to CSR. Additionally, this field has grown significantly and today contains a great proliferation of theories, approaches and terminologies. Society and business, social issues management, public policy and business, stakeholder management, corporate accountability are just some of the terms used to describe the phenomena related to corporate responsibility in society. Recently, renewed interest for corporate social responsibilities and new alternative concepts have been proposed, including corporate citizenship and corporate sustainability. Some scholars have compared these new concepts with the classic notion of CSR (see van Marrewijk, 2003 for corporate sustainability; and Matten *et al.*, 2003 and Wood and Logsdon, 2002 for corporate citizenship).

Furthermore, some theories combine different approaches and use the same terminology with different meanings. This problem is an old one. It was 30 years ago that Votaw wrote: "corporate social responsibility means something, but not always the same thing to everybody. To some it conveys the idea of legal responsibility or liability; to others, it means socially responsible behavior in the ethical sense; to still others, the meaning transmitted is that of 'responsible for' in a causal mode; many simply equate it with a charitable contribution; some take it to mean socially conscious; many of those who embrace it most fervently see it as a mere synonym for legitimacy in the context of belonging or being proper or valid; a few see a sort of fiduciary duty imposing higher standards of behavior on businessmen than on citizens at large" (Votaw, 1972, p.25). Nowadays the panorama is not much better. Carroll, one of the most prestigious scholars in this discipline, characterized the situation as "an eclectic field with loose boundaries, multiple memberships, and differing training/perspectives; broadly rather than focused, multidisciplinary; wide breadth; brings in a wider range of literature; and interdisciplinary" (Carroll, 1994, p. 14). Actually, as Carroll added (1994, p. 6), the map of the overall field is quite poor.

However, some attempts have been made to address this deficiency. Frederick (1987, 1998) outlined a classification based on a conceptual transition from the ethical–philosophical concept of CSR (what he calls CSR1), to the action-orientated managerial concept of social responsiveness (CSR2). He then included a normative element based on ethics and values (CSR3) and finally he introduced the cosmos as the basic normative reference for social issues in management and considered the role of science and religion in these issues (CSR 4). In a more systematic way, Heald (1988) and Carroll (1999) have offered a historical sequence of the main developments in how the responsibilities of business in society have been understood.

Other classifications have been suggested based on matters related to CSR, such as Issues Management (Wartick and Rude, 1986; Wood, 1991a) or the concept of Corporate Citizenship (Altman, 1998). An alternative approach is presented by Brummer (1991) who proposes a classification in four groups of theories based on six criteria (motive, relation to profits, group affected by decisions, type of act, type of effect, expressed or ideal interest). These classifications, in spite of their valuable contribution, are quite limited in scope and, what is more, the nature of the relationship between business and society is rarely situated at the center of their discussion. This vision could be questioned as CSR seems to be a consequence of how this relationship is understood (Jones, 1983; McMahon, 1986; Preston, 1975; Wood, 1991b).

In order to contribute to a clarification of the field of business and society, our aim here is to map the territory in which most relevant CSR theories and related approaches are situated. We will do so by considering each theory from the perspective of how the interaction phenomena between business and society are focused.

As the starting point for a proper classification, we assume as hypothesis that the most relevant CSR theories and related approaches are focused on one of the following aspects of social reality: economics, politics, social integration and ethics. The inspiration for this hypothesis is rooted in four aspects that, according to Parsons (1961), can be observed in any social system: adaptation to the environment (related to resources and economics), goal attainment (related to politics), social integration and pattern maintenance or latency (related to culture and values).[1] This hypothesis permits us to classify these theories in four groups:

1   A first group in which it is assumed that the corporation is an instrument for wealth creation and that this is its sole social responsibility. Only the economic aspect of the interactions between business and society is considered. So any supposed social activity is accepted if, and only if, it is consistent with wealth creation. This group of theories could be called *instrumental theories* because they understand CSR as a mere means to the end of profits.

2   A second group in which the social power of corporation is emphasized, specifically in its relationship with society and its responsibility in the political arena associated with this power. This leads the corporation to accept social duties and rights or participate in certain social cooperation. We will call this group *political theories*.

3   A third group includes theories which consider that business ought to integrate social demands. They usually argue that business depends on society for its continuity and growth and even for the existence of business itself. We can term this group *integrative theories*.

4   A fourth group of theories understands that the relationship between business and society is embedded with ethical values. This leads to a vision of CSR from an ethical perspective and as a consequence, firms ought to accept social responsibilities as an ethical obligation above any other consideration. We can term this group *ethical theories*.

Throughout this paper we will present the most relevant theories on CSR and related matters, trying to prove that they are all focused on one of the aforementioned aspects. We will not explain each theory in detail, only what is necessary to verify our hypothesis and, if necessary, some complementary information to clarify what each is about. At the same time, we will attempt to situate these theories and approaches within a general map describing the current panorama regarding the role of business in society.

Instrumental theories

In this group of theories CSR is seen only as a strategic tool to achieve economic objectives and, ultimately, wealth creation. Representative of this approach is the well-known Friedman view that "the only one responsibility of business towards society is the maximization of profits to the shareholders within the legal framework and the ethical custom of the country" (1970).[2]

Instrumental theories have a long tradition and have enjoyed a wide acceptance in business so far. As Windsor (2001) has pointed out recently, "a leitmotiv of wealth creation progressively dominates the managerial conception of responsibility" (Windsor, 2001, p. 226).

Concern for profits does not exclude taking into account the interests of all who have a stake in the firm (stakeholders). It has been argued that in certain conditions the satisfaction of these interests can contribute to maximizing the shareholder value (Mitchell *et al.*, 1997; Ogden and Watson, 1999). An adequate level of investment in philanthropy and social activities is also acceptable for the sake of profits (McWilliams and Siegel, 2001). We will return to these points afterwards.

In practice, a number of studies have been carried out to determine the correlation between CSR and corporate financial performance. Of these, an increasing number show a positive correlation between the social responsibility and financial performance of corporations in most cases (Frooman, 1997; Griffin and Mahon, 1997; Key and Popkin, 1998; Roman *et al.*, 1999; Waddock and Graves, 1997). However, these findings have to be read with caution since such correlation is difficult to measure (Griffin, 2000; Rowley and Berman, 2000).

Three main groups of instrumental theories can be identified, depending on the economic objective proposed. In the first group the objective is the maximization of shareholder value, measured by the share price. Frequently, this leads to a short-term profits orientation. The second group of theories focuses on the strategic goal of achieving competitive advantages, which would produce long-term profits. In both cases, CSR is only a question of enlightened self-interest (Keim, 1978) since CSRs are a mere instrument for profits. The third is related to cause-related marketing and is very close to the second. Let us examine briefly the philosophy and some variants of these groups.

Maximising the shareholder value

A well-known approach is that which takes the straightforward contribution to maximizing the shareholder value as the supreme criterion to evaluate specific corporate social activity. Any investment in social demands that would produce an increase of the shareholder value should be made, acting without deception and fraud. In contrast, if the social demands only impose a cost on the company they should be rejected. Friedman (1970) is clear, giving an example about investment in the local community: "It will be in the long run interest of a corporation that is a major employer in a small community to devote resources to providing amenities to that community or to improving its government. That makes it easier to attract desirable employees, it may reduce the wage bill or lessen losses from pilferage and sabotage or have other worthwhile effects." So, the socio-economic objectives are completely separate from the economic objectives.

Currently, this approach usually takes the shareholder value maximization as the supreme reference for corporate decision-making. The Agency Theory (Jensen and Meckling, 1976; Ross, 1973) is the most popular way to articulate this reference. However, today it is quite readily accepted that shareholder value maximization is not incompatible with satisfying certain interests of people with a stake in the firm (stakeholders). In this respect, Jensen (2000) has proposed what he calls "enlightened value maximization". This concept specifies long-term value maximization or value-seeking as the firm's objective. At the same time, this objective is employed as the criterion for making the requisite tradeoffs among its stakeholders.

Strategies for achieving competitive advantages

A second group of theories are focused on how to allocate resources in order to achieve long-term social objectives and create a competitive advantage (Husted and Allen, 2000). In this group three approaches can be included: (a) social investments in competitive context, (b) natural resource-based view of the firm and its dynamic capabilities and (c) strategies for the bottom of the economic pyramid.

(a) Social investments in a competitive context. Porter and Kramer (2002) have recently applied the well-known Porter model on competitive advantage (Porter, 1980) to consider investment in areas of what they call competitive context.[3] The authors argue that investing in philanthropic activities may be the only way to improve the context of competitive advantage of a firm and usually creates greater social value than individual donors or government can. The reason presented – the opposite of Friedman's position – is that the firm has the knowledge and resources for a better understanding of how to solve some problems related to its mission. As Burke and Logsdon (1996) pointed out, when philanthropic activities are closer to the company's mission, they create greater wealth than other kinds of donations. That is what happens, e.g., when a telecommunications company is teaching computer network administration to students of the local community.

Porter and Kramer conclude, "philanthropic investments by members of a cluster, either individually or collectively, can have a powerful effect on the cluster competitiveness and the performance of all its constituent companies" (2002, pp. 60–61).

(b) Natural resource-based view of the firm and dynamic capabilities. The resource-based view of the firm (Barney, 1991; Wernerfelt, 1984) maintains that the ability of a firm to perform better than its competitors depends on the unique interplay of human, organizational, and physical resources over time. Traditionally, resources that are most likely to lead to competitive advantage are those that meet four criteria: they should be valuable, rare, and inimitable, and the organization must be organized to deploy these resources effectively.

The "dynamic capabilities" approach presents the dynamic aspect of the resources; it is focused on the drivers behind the creation, evolution and recombination of the resources into new sources of competitive advantage (Teece *et al.*, 1997). So dynamic capabilities are organizational and strategic routines, by which managers acquire resources, modify them, integrate them, and recombine them to generate new value-creating strategies. Based on this perspective, some authors have identified social and ethical resources and capabilities which can be a source of competitive advantage, such as the process of moral decision-making (Petrick and Quinn, 2001), the process of perception, deliberation and responsiveness or capacity of adaptation (Litz, 1996) and the development of proper relationships with the primary stakeholders: employees, customers, suppliers, and communities (Harrison and St. John, 1996; Hillman and Keim, 2001).

A more complete model of the 'Resource-Based View of the Firm' has been presented by Hart (1995). It includes aspects of dynamic capabilities and a link with the external environment. Hart argues that the most important drivers for new resource and capabilities development will be constraints and challenges posed by the natural biophysical environment. Hart has developed his conceptual framework with three main interconnected strategic capabilities: pollution prevention, product stewardship and sustainable development. He considers as critical resources continuous improvement, stakeholder integration and shared vision.

(c) Strategies for the bottom of the economic pyramid. Traditionally most business strategies are focused on targeting products at upper- and middle-class people, but most of the world's population is poor or lower-middle class. At the bottom of the economic pyramid there may be some 4000 million people. On reflection, certain strategies can serve the poor and simultaneously make profits. Prahalad (2002), analyzing the India experience, has suggested some mind-set changes for converting the poor into active consumers. The first of these is seeing the poor as an opportunity to innovate rather than as a problem.

A specific means for attending to the bottom of the economic pyramid is disruptive innovation. Disruptive innovations (Christensen and Overdorf, 2000; Christensen *et al.*, 2001) are products or services that do not have the same capabilities and conditions as those being used by customers in the mainstream markets; as a result they can be introduced only for new or less demanding applications among non-traditional customers, with a low-cost production and adapted to the necessities of the population. For example a telecommunications company inventing a small cellular telephone system with lower costs but also with less service adapted to the base of the economic pyramid.

Disruptive innovations can improve the social and economic conditions at the "base of the pyramid" and at the same time they create a competitive advantage for the firms in telecommunications, consumer electronics and energy production and many other industries, especially in developing countries (Hart and Christensen, 2002; Prahalad and Hammond, 2002).

Cause-related marketing

Cause-related marketing has been defined as "the process of formulating and implementing marketing activities that are characterized by an offer from the firm to contribute a specified amount to a designated cause when customers engage in revenue-providing exchanges that satisfy organizational and individual objectives" (Varadarajan and Menon, 1988, p. 60). Its goal then is to enhance company revenues and sales or customer relationship by building the brand through the acquisition of, and association with the ethical dimension or social responsibility dimension (Murray and Montanari, 1986; Varadarajan and Menon, 1988). In a way, it seeks product differentiation by creating socially responsible attributes that affect company reputation (Smith and Higgins, 2000). As McWilliams and Siegel (2001, p.120) have pointed out: "support of cause related marketing creates a reputation that a firm is reliable and honest. Consumers typically assume that the products of a reliable and honest firm will be of high quality". For example, a pesticide-free or non-animal-tested ingredient can be perceived by some buyers as preferable to other attributes of competitors' products.

Other activities, which typically exploit cause-related marketing, are classical musical concerts, art exhibitions, golf tournaments or literary campaigns. All of these are a form of enlightened self-interest and a win–win situation as both the company and the charitable cause receive benefits: "The brand manager uses consumer concern for business responsibility as a means for securing competitive advantage. At the same time a charitable cause receives substantial financial benefits" (Smith and Higgins, 2000, p. 309).

Political Theories

A group of CSR theories and approaches focus on interactions and connections between business and society and on the power and position of business and its inherent responsibility. They include both political considerations and political analysis in the CSR debate. Although there are a variety of approaches, two major theories can be distinguished: Corporate Constitutionalism and Corporate Citizenship.

Corporate constitutionalism

Davis (1960) was one of the first to explore the role of power that business has in society and the social impact of this power.[4] In doing so, he introduces business power as a new element in the debate of CSR. He held that business is a social institution and it must use power responsibly. Additionally, Davis noted that the causes that generate the social power of the firm are not solely internal of the firm but also external. Their locus is unstable and constantly shifting, from the economic to the social forum and from there to the political forum and vice versa.

Davis attacked the assumption of the classical economic theory of perfect competition that precludes the involvement of the firm in society besides the creation of wealth. The firm has power to influence the equilibrium of the market and therefore the price is not a Pareto optimum reflecting the free will of participants with perfect knowledge of the market.

Davis formulated two principles that express how social power has to be managed: "the social power equation" and "the iron law of responsibility". The social power equation principle states that "social responsibilities of businessmen arise from the amount of social power that they have" (Davis, 1967, p. 48). The iron law of responsibility refers to the negative consequences of the absence of use of power. In his own words: "Whoever does not use his social power responsibly will lose it. In the long run those who do not use power in a manner which society considers responsible will tend to lose it because other groups eventually will step in to assume those responsibilities" (1960, p. 63). So if a firm does not use its social power, it will lose its position in society because other groups will occupy it, especially when society demands responsibility from business (Davis, 1960).

According to Davis, the equation of social power-responsibility has to be understood through the functional role of business and managers. In this respect, Davis rejects the idea of total responsibility of business as he rejected the radical free-market ideology of no responsibility of business. The limits of functional power come from the pressures of different constituency groups. This "restricts organizational power in the same way that a governmental constitution does." The constituency groups do not destroy power. Rather they define conditions for its responsible use. They channel organizational power in a supportive way and to protect other interests against unreasonable organizational power (Davis, 1967, p. 68). As a consequence, his theory is called "Corporate Constitutionalism".

Integrative social contract theory

Donaldson (1982) considered the business and society relationship from the social contract tradition, mainly from the philosophical thought of Locke. He assumed that a sort of implicit social contract between business and society exists. This social contract implies some indirect obligations of business towards society. This approach would overcome some limitations of deontological and teleological theories applied to business.

Afterwards, Donaldson and Dunfee (1994, 1999) extended this approach and proposed an "Integrative Social Contract Theory" (ISCT) in order to take into account the socio-cultural context and also to integrate empirical and normative aspects of management. Social responsibilities come from consent. These scholars assumed two levels of consent. Firstly a theoretical macrosocial contract appealing to all rational contractors, and secondly, a real microsocial contract by members of numerous localized communities. According to these authors, this theory offers a process in which the contracts among industries, departments and economic systems can be legitimate. In this process the participants will agree upon the ground rules defining the foundation of economics that will be acceptable to them.

The macrosocial contract provides rules for any social contracting. These rules are called the "hyper-norms"; they ought to take precedence over other contracts. These hyper-norms are so fundamental and basic that they "are discernible in a convergence of religious, political and philosophical thought" (Donaldson and Dunfee, 2000, p. 441). The microsocial contracts show explicit or implicit agreements that are binding within an identified community, whatever this may be: industry, companies or economic systems. These microsocial contracts, which generate "authentic norms", are based on the attitudes and behaviors of the members of the norm-generating community and, in order to be legitimate, have to accord with the hyper-norms.

Corporate citizenship

Although the idea of the firm as citizen is not new (Davis, 1973) a renewed interest in this concept among practitioners has appeared recently due to certain factors that have had an impact on the business and society relationship. Among these factors, especially worthy of note are the crisis of the Welfare State and the globalization phenomenon. These, together with the deregulation process and decreasing costs with technological improvements, have meant that some large multinational companies have greater economical and social power than some governments. The corporate citizenship framework looks to give an account of this new reality, as we will try to explain here.

In the 1980s the term "corporate citizenship" was introduced into the business and society relationship mainly through practitioners (Altman and Vidaver-Cohen, 2000). Since the late 1990s and early 21st century this term has become more and more popular in business and increasing academic work has been carried out (Andriof and McIntosh, 2001; Matten and Crane, 2005).

Although the academic reflection on the concept of "corporation citizenship", and on a similar one called "the business citizen", is quite recent (Matten *et al.*, 2003; Wood and Logsdon, 2002; among others), this notion has always connoted a sense of belonging to a community. Perhaps for this reason it has been so popular among managers and business people, because it is increasingly clear that business needs to take into account the community where it is operating.

The term "corporate citizenship" cannot have the same meaning for everybody. Matten *et al.* (2003) have distinguished three views of "corporate citizenship": (1) a limited view, (2) a view equivalent to CSR and (3) an extended view of corporate citizenship, which is held by them. In the limited view "corporate citizenship" is used in a sense quite close to corporate philanthropy, social investment or certain responsibilities assumed towards the local community. The equivalent to the CSR view is quite common. Carroll (1999) believes that "Corporate citizenship" seems a new conceptualisation of the role of business in society and depending on which way it is defined, this notion largely overlaps with other theories on the responsibility of business in society. Finally, in the extended view of corporate citizenship (Matten *et al.*, 2003; Matten and Crane, 2005), corporations enter the arena of citizenship at the point of government failure in the protection of citizenship. This view arises from the fact that some corporations have gradually come to replace the most powerful institution in the traditional concept of citizenship, namely government.

The term "citizenship", taken from political science, is at the core of the "corporate citizenship" notion. For Wood and Logsdon "business citizenship cannot be deemed equivalent to individual citizenship – instead it derives from and is secondary to individual citizenship" (2002, p. 86). Whether or not this view is accepted, theories and approaches on "corporate citizenship" are focused on rights, responsibilities and possible partnerships of business in society.

Some theories on corporate citizenship are based on a social contract theory (Dion, 2001) as developed by Donaldson and Dunfee (1994, 1999), although other approaches are also possible (Wood and Logsdon, 2002).

In spite of some noteworthy differences in corporate citizenship theories, most authors generally converge on some points, such as a strong sense of business responsibility towards the local community, partnerships, which are the specific ways of formalizing the willingness to improve the local community,[5] and for consideration for the environment.

The concern for local community has extended progressively to a global concern in great part due to the very intense protests against globalization, mainly since the end of the 1990s. This sense of global corporate citizenship led to the joint statement "Global Corporate Citizenship – the Leadership Challenge for CEOs and Boards", signed by 34 of the world's largest multinational corporations during the World Economic Forum in New York in January 2002. Subsequently, business with local responsibility and, at the same time, being a global actor that places emphasis on business responsibilities in a global context, have been considered as a key issue by some scholars (Tichy et al., 1997; Wood and Logsdon, 2002).

Integrative Theories

This group of theories looks at how business integrates social demands, arguing that business depends on society for its existence, continuity and growth. Social demands are generally considered to be the way in which society interacts with business and gives it a certain legitimacy and prestige. As a consequence, corporate management should take into account social demands, and integrate them in such a way that the business operates in accordance with social values.

So, the content of business responsibility is limited to the space and time of each situation depending on the values of society at that moment, and comes through the company's functional roles (Preston and Post, 1975). In other words, there is no specific action that management is responsible for performing throughout time and in each industry. Basically, the theories of this group are focused on the detection and scanning of, and response to, the social demands that achieve social legitimacy, greater social acceptance and prestige.

Issues management

Social responsiveness, or responsiveness in the face of social issues, and processes to manage them within the organization (Sethi, 1975) was an approach which arose in the 1970s. In this approach it is crucial to consider the gap between what the organization's relevant publics expect its performance to be and the organization's actual performance. These gaps are usually located in the zone that Ackerman (1973, p. 92) calls the "zone of discretion" (neither regulated nor illegal nor sanctioned) where the company receives some unclear signals from the environment. The firm should perceive the gap and choose a response in order to close it (Ackerman and Bauer, 1976).

Ackerman (1973), among other scholars, analysed the relevant factors regarding the internal structures of organizations and integration mechanisms to manage social issues within the organization. The way a social objective is spread and integrated across the organization, he termed "process of institutionalisation". According to Jones (1980, p. 65), "corporate behavior should not in most cases be judged by the decisions actually reached but by the process by which they are reached". Consequently, he emphasized the idea of process rather than principles as the appropriate approach to CSR issues.

Jones draws an analogy with the political process assessing that the appropriate process of CSR should be a fair process where all interests have had the opportunity to be heard. So Jones has shifted the criterion to the inputs in the decision-making process rather than the outcomes, and has focused more on the process of implementation of CSR activities than on the process of conceptualization.

The concept of "social responsiveness" was soon widened with the concept "Issues Management". The latter includes the former but emphasizes the process for making a corporate response to social issues. Issues management has been defined by Wartick and Rude (1986, p. 124) as the "processes by which the corporation can identify, evaluate and respond to those social and political issues which may impact significantly upon it". They add that issues management attempts to minimize "surprises" which accompany social and political change by serving as an early warning system for potential environmental threats and opportunities. Further, it prompts more systematic and effective responses to particular issues by serving as a coordinating and integrating force within the corporation. Issues management research has been influenced by the strategy field, since it has been seen as a special group of strategic issues (Greening and Gray, 1994), or a part of international studies (Brewer, 1992). That led to the study of topics related with issues (identification, evaluation and categorization), formalization of stages of social issues and management issue response. Other factors, which have been considered, include the corporate responses to media exposure, interest group pressures and business crises, as well as organizational size, top management commitment and other organizational factors.

The principle of public responsibility

Some authors have tried to give an appropriate content and substance to help and guide the firm's responsibility by limiting the scope of the corporate responsibility. Preston and Post (1975, 1981) criticized a responsiveness approach and the purely process approach (Jones, 1980) as insufficient. Instead, they proposed "the principle of public responsibility". They choose the term "public" rather than "social", to stress the importance of the public process, rather than personal-morality views of narrow interest groups defining the scope of responsibilities.

According to Preston and Post an appropriate guideline for a legitimate managerial behavior is found within the framework of relevant public policy.

They added that "public policy includes not only the literal text of law and regulation but also the broad pattern of social direction reflected in public opinion, emerging issues, formal legal requirements and enforcement or implementation practices" (Preston and Post, 1981, p. 57). This is the essence of the principle of public responsibility.

Preston and Post analyzed the scope of managerial responsibility in terms of the "primary" and "secondary" involvement of the firm in its social environment. Primary involvement includes the essential economic task of the firm, such as locating and establishing its facilities, procuring suppliers, engaging employees, carrying out its production functions and marketing products. It also includes legal requirements. Secondary involvements come as a consequence of the primary. They are, e.g., career and earning opportunities for some individuals, which come from the primary activity of selection and advancement of employees.

At the same time, these authors are in favor of business intervention in the public policy process especially with respect to areas in which specific public policy is not yet clearly established or it is in transition: "It is legitimate – and may be essential – that affected firms participate openly in the policy formation" (Preston and Post, 1981, p. 61).

In practice, discovering the content of the principle of public responsibility is a complex and difficult task and requires substantial management attention. As Preston and Post recognized, "the content of public policy is not necessarily obvious or easy to discover, nor is it invariable over time" (1981, p. 57). According to this view, if business adhered to the standards of performance in law and the existing public policy process, then it would be judged acceptably responsive in terms of social expectations.

The development of this approach was parallel to the study of the scope regarding business–government relationship (Vogel, 1986). These studies focused on government regulations – their formulation and implementation – as well as corporate strategies to influence these regulations, including campaign contributions, lobbying, coalition building, grass-roots organization, corporate public affairs and the role of public interest and other advocacy groups.

Stakeholder management

Instead of focusing on generic responsiveness, specific issues or on the public responsibility principle, the approach called "stakeholder management" is oriented towards "stakeholders" or people who affect or are affected by corporate policies and practices. Although the practice of stakeholder management is long-established, its academic development started only at the end of the 1970s (see, e.g., Sturdivant, 1979). In a seminal paper, Emshoff and Freeman (1978) presented two basic principles, which underpin stakeholder management. The first is that the central goal is to achieve maximum overall cooperation between the entire system of stakeholder groups and the objectives of the corporation. The second states that the most efficient strategies for managing stakeholder relations involve efforts, which simultaneously deal with issues affecting multiple stakeholders.

Stakeholder management tries to integrate groups with a stake in the firm into managerial decision-making. A great deal of empirical research has been done, guided by a sense of pragmatism. It includes topics such as how to determine the best practice in corporate stakeholder relations (Bendheim *et al.*, 1998), stakeholder salience to managers (Agle and Mitchell, 1999; Mitchell *et al.*, 1997), the impact of stakeholder management on financial performance (Berman *et al.*, 1999), the influence of stakeholder network structural relations (Rowley, 1997) and how managers can successfully balance the competing demands of various stakeholder groups (Ogden and Watson, 1999).

Stakeholder dialogue helps to address the question of responsiveness to the generally unclear signals received from the environment. In addition, this dialogue "not only enhances a company's sensitivity to its environment but also increases the environment's understanding of the dilemmas facing the organization" (Kaptein and Van Tulder, 2003 p. 208).

Corporate social performance

A set of theories attempts to integrate some of the previous theories. The corporate social performance (CSP) includes a search for social legitimacy, with processes for giving appropriate responses.

Carroll (1979), generally considered to have introduced this model, suggested a model of "corporate performance" with three elements: a basic definition of social responsibility, a listing of issues in which social responsibility exists and a specification of the philosophy of response to social issues. Carroll considered that a definition of social responsibility, which fully addresses the entire range of obligations business has to society, must embody the economic, legal, ethical, and discretionary categories of business performance. He later incorporated his four-part categorization into a "Pyramid of Corporate Social Responsibilities" (Carroll, 1991). Recently, Schwartz and Carroll (2003) have proposed an alternative approach based on three core domains (economic, legal and ethical responsibilities) and a Venn model framework. The Venn framework yields seven CSR categories resulting from the overlap of the three core domains.

Wartick and Cochran (1985) extended the Carroll approach suggesting that corporate social involvement rests on the principles of social responsibility, the process of social responsiveness and the policy of issues management. A new development came with Wood (1991b) who presented a model of corporate social performance composed of principles of CSR, processes of corporate social responsiveness and outcomes of corporate behavior.

The principles of CSR are understood to be analytical forms to be filled with value content that is operationalized. They include: principles of CSR, expressed on institutional, organizational and individual levels, processes of corporate social responsiveness, such as environmental assessment, stakeholder management and issues management, and outcomes of corporate behavior including social impacts, social programs and social policies.

Ethical Theories

A fourth group of theories or approaches focuses on the ethical requirements that cement the relationship between business and society. They are based on principles that express the right thing to do or the necessity to achieve a good society. As main approaches we can distinguish the following.

Normative stakeholder theory

Stakeholder management has been included within the integrative theories group because some authors consider that this form of management is a way to integrate social demands. However, stakeholder management has become an ethically based theory mainly since 1984 when Freeman wrote *Strategic Management: a Stakeholder Approach*. In this book, he took as starting point that "managers bear a fiduciary relationship to stakeholders" (Freeman, 1984, p. xx), instead of having exclusively fiduciary duties towards stockholders, as was held by the conventional view of the firm. He understood as stakeholders those groups who have a stake in or claim on the firm (suppliers, customers, employees, stockholders, and the local community). In a more precise way, Donaldson and Preston (1995, p. 67) held that the stakeholder theory has a normative core based on two major ideas: (1) stakeholders are persons or groups with legitimate interests in procedural and / or substantive aspects of corporate activity (stakeholders are identified by their interests in the corporation, whether or not the corporation has any corresponding functional interest in *them* and (2) the interests of all stakeholders are of *intrinsic value* (that is, each group of stakeholders merits consideration for its own sake and not merely because of its ability to further the interests of some other group, such as the shareowners).

Following this theory, a socially responsible firm requires simultaneous attention to the legitimate interests of all appropriate stakeholders and has to balance such a multiplicity of interests and not only the interests of the firm's stockholders. Supporters of normative stakeholder theory have attempted to justify it through arguments taken from Kantian capitalism (Bowie, 1991; Evan and Freeman, 1988), modern theories of property and distributive justice (Donaldson and Preston, 1995), and also Libertarian theories with its notions of freedom, rights and consent (Freeman and Philips, 2002).

A generic formulation of stakeholder theory is not sufficient. In order to point out how corporations have to be governed and how managers ought to act, a *normative core* of ethical principles is required (Freeman, 1994). To this end, different scholars have proposed differing normative ethical theories. Freeman and Evan (1990) introduced Rawlsian principles. Bowie (1998) proposed a combination of Kantian and Rawlsian grounds. Freeman (1994) proposed the doctrine of fair contracts and Phillips (1997, 2003) suggested introducing the fairness principle based on six of Rawls' characteristics of the principle of fair play: mutual benefit, justice, co-operation, sacrifice, free-rider possibility and voluntary acceptance of the benefits of cooperative schemes. Lately, Freeman and Phillips (2002) have presented six principles for the guidance of stakeholder theory by combining Libertarian concepts and the Fairness principle. Some scholars (Burton and Dunn, 1996; Wicks *et al.*, 1994) proposed instead using a "feminist ethics" approach. Donaldson and Dunfee (1999) hold their "Integrative Social Contract Theory". Argandoña (1998) suggested the common good notion and Wijnberg (2000) an Aristotelian approach. From a practical perspective, the normative core of which is risk management, The Clarkson Center for Business Ethics (1999) has published a set of *Principles of Stakeholder Management*.

Stakeholder normative theory has suffered critical distortions and friendly misinterpretations, which Freeman and co-workers are trying to clarify (Phillips *et al.*, 2003). In practice, this theory has been applied to a variety of business fields, including stakeholder management for the business and society relationship, in a number of textbooks. Some of these have been republished several times (Carroll and Buchholtz, 2002; Post *et al.*, 2002; Weiss, 2003; among others).

In short, stakeholder approach grounded in ethical theories presents a different perspective on CSR, in which ethics is central.

Universal rights

Human rights have been taken as a basis for CSR, especially in the global market place (Cassel, 2001). In recent years, some human-rights-based approaches for corporate responsibility have been proposed. One of them is the UN Global Compact, which includes nine principles in the areas of human rights, labor and the environment. It was first presented by the United Nations Secretary-General Kofi Annan in an address to The World Economic Forum in 1999. In 2000 the Global Compact's operational phase was launched at UN Headquarters in New York. Many companies have since adopted it. Another, previously presented and updated in 1999, is The Global Sullivan Principles, which has the objective of supporting economic, social and political justice by companies where they do business. The certification SA8000 (www.cepaa.org) for accreditation of social responsibility is also based on human and labor rights. Despite using different approaches, all are based on the Universal Declaration of Human Rights adopted by the United Nations general assembly in 1948 and on other intentional declarations of human rights, labor rights and environmental protection.

Although for many people universal rights are a question of mere consensus, they have a theoretical grounding, and some moral philosophy theories give them support (Donnelly, 1985). It is worth mentioning the Natural Law tradition (Simon, 1992), which defends the existence of natural human rights (Maritain, 1971).

Sustainable development

Another values-based concept, which has become popular, is "sustainable development". Although this approach was developed at macro level rather than corporate level, it demands a relevant corporate contribution. The term came into widespread use in 1987, when the World Commission on Environment and Development (United Nations) published a report known as "Brundtland Report". This report stated that "sustainable development" seeks to meet the needs of the present without compromising the ability to meet the future generation to meet their own needs (World Commission on Environment and Development, 1987, p. 8). Although this report originally only included the environmental factor, the concept of "sustainable development" has since expanded to include the consideration of the social dimension as being inseparable from development. In the words of the World Business Council for Sustainable Development (2000, p. 2), sustainable development "requires the integration of social, environmental, and economic considerations to make balanced judgments for the long term".

Numerous definitions have been proposed for sustainable development (see a review in Gladwin and Kennelly 1995, p. 877). In spite of which, content analysis of the main definitions suggests that sustainable development is "a process of achieving human development in an inclusive, connected, equiparable, prudent and secure manner" (Gladwin and Kennelly 1995, p. 876).

The problem comes when the corporation has to develop the processes and implement strategies to meet the corporate challenge of corporate sustainable development. As Wheeler et al. (2003, p. 17) have stated, sustainability is "an ideal toward which society and business can continually strive, the way we strive is by creating value, creating outcomes that are consistent with the ideal of sustainability along social environmental and economic dimensions".[6]

However, some suggestions have been proposed to achieve corporate ecological sustainability (Shrivastava, 1995; Stead and Stead, 2000; among others). A pragmatic proposal is to extend the traditional "bottom line" accounting, which shows overall net profitability, to a "triple bottom line" that would include economic, social and environmental aspects of corporation. Van Marrewijk and Werre (2003) maintain that corporate sustainability is a custom-made process and each organization should choose its own specific ambition and approach regarding corporate sustainability. This should meet the organization's aims and intentions, and be aligned with the organization strategy, as an appropriate response to the circumstances in which the organization operates.

The common good approach

This third group of approaches, less consolidated than the stakeholder approach but with potential, holds the common good of society as the referential value for CSR (Mahon and McGowan, 1991; Velasquez, 1992). The common good is a classical concept rooted in Aristotelian tradition (Smith, 1999), in Medieval Scholastics (Kempshall, 1999), developed philosophically (Maritain, 1966) and assumed into Catholic social thought (Carey, 2001) as a key reference for business ethics (Alford and Naughton, 2002; Melé, 2002; Pope John Paul II, 1991, #43). This approach maintains that business, as with any other social group or individual in society, has to contribute to the common good, because it is a part of society. In this respect, it has been argued that business is a mediating institution (Fort, 1996, 1999). Business should be neither harmful to nor a parasite on society, but purely a positive contributor to the well-being of the society.

Business contributes to the common good in different ways, such as creating wealth, providing goods and services in an efficient and fair way, at the same time respecting the dignity and the inalienable and fundamental rights of the individual. Furthermore, it contributes to social well-being and a harmonic way of living together in just, peaceful and friendly conditions, both in the present and in the future (Melé, 2002).

To some extent, this approach has a lot in common with both the stakeholder approach (Argandoña, 1998) and sustainable development, but the philosophical base is different. Although there are several ways of understanding the notion of common good (Sulmasy, 2001), the interpretation based on the knowledge of human nature and its fulfilment seems to us particularly convincing. It permits the circumnavigation of cultural relativism, which is frequently embedded in some definitions of sustainable development.

The common good notion is also very close to the Japanese concept of Kyosei (Goodpaster, 1999; Kaku, 1997; Yamaji, 1997), understood as "living and working together for the common good", which, together with the principle of human dignity, is one of the founding principles of the popular "The Caux Roundtable Principles for Business" (www.cauxroundtable.org).

Discussion

The preceding description, summed up on Table 1, leads to the conclusion that the hypothesis considered in the introduction about the four basic focal points employed by CSR theories and related approaches is adequate. Consequently, most of the current theories related to CSR could be broadly classified as instrumental, political, integrative and ethical theories.

Donati (1991), a contemporary sociologist, has reviewed many aspects of the work of Parsons. He suggests that adaptation, goal attainment, integration and latency presented by Parsons (1961) as rigid functions, have to be understood as four interconnected dimensions present in every social phenomenon. This suggests that the concept of business and society relationship must include these four aspects or dimensions and some connection among them must exist. This must be reflected in every theory. In some authors, such as Friedman, it is relatively easy to discover these dimensions and connections, in other theories it is not so easy.

In fact, although the main concern in the Friedman view (Friedman, 1970; Friedman and Friedman, 1962) is for wealth creation, as we have pointed out above, this concern is rooted in certain cultural values regarding the free market, private property and the fact that wealth creation is good for society. This shows us that certain values are present, even though they are frequently questioned. At the same time, he accepts the rules of the free market, laws and ethical customs in each place. Friedman and, above all, Jensen (2000) also accept the integration of some social demands into the company if it is profitable in the long-term. Regarding politics, underpinning the Friedman view there is a functional conception of the social with clear political consequences. Society is understood as a mechanism with mono-functional groups, each with a concrete purpose. Thus, the exclusive purpose of business organizations is the creation of wealth. It is held that business operating in a free market is the best way to allocate scarce resources because society can achieve an optimum situation in the sense of Pareto (Pareto Optimum). This means that the satisfaction of all people involved in the situation is the greatest possible or, at least, the situation satisfies most of them without being detrimental for others. However, in the presence of externalities, when decision-makers do not take into account secondary effects of their actions that burden or benefit others, the market is inefficient and the equilibrium is not a Pareto optimum. When externalities appear, another system of society, the political system, should act. The political system must confront these externalities through taxes, regulation and minimum package of rights. So, business contributes to the welfare of society through the market mechanism and in compliance with the law. Of course, outside business, the manager can spend any quantity of personal money on social activities according to his or her personal preferences. However, the social objectives and demands come under business consideration only through the law applied by the political system.

A contrasting theory, in which the four dimensions mentioned and their connections are not so easy to discover, is "the principle of public responsibility" of Preston and Post (1975). However, these dimensions are implicit. In fact, this theory presupposes a certain conception of society and values. The political dimension is clear, since public policy is assumed as a basic criterion. Regarding wealth creation, undoubtedly the application of this theory would have consequences for profit generation. Actually, these scholars recognize that what they call secondary relationships (related to secondary involvements) "as essential to effective management over the long term" (Preston and Post, 1981, p. 57).

It is not our aim to review all theories described, but what has been said regarding the four dimensions in the approaches of Friedman and Preston and Post, could probably be extended to other theories. If our intuition is correct, a proper concept of the business and society relationship should include these four aspects or dimensions, and some mode of integration of them. Although most theories studied do not make it explicit, one can appreciate a tendency to overcome this deficit.

In fact, in the last few years, some theories have been proposed in which two or even more of these dimensions and their interconnection have been considered. That is the case, e.g., of Wood's Corporate Social Performance model (1991b). This model basically focuses on integrating social demands, however, it also considers institutional legitimacy, accepting that "society grants legitimacy and power to business" (Davis, 1973, p. 314). In this manner, Wood introduces both political and integrative dimensions while economic and ethical dimensions are implicit. Regarding the latter, the stated principles of corporate responsibility assumed are based on social control rather than on prescriptive responsibility coming from ethics. This is precisely the criticism Swanson (1995) made of Wood's model. As an alternative, Swanson (1995, 1999) proposed a derived model in which she tried to include the ethical dimension explicitly, through a theory of values. Following Frederick (1992) she accepted that business organizations have responsibilities related to economizing and ecologizing. Furthermore executive decision-making should forgo power-seeking in favour of directing the firm to economize and ecologize.

More recently, Wood and Logsdon (2002), dealing with the corporate or business citizen model, have introduced the ethical dimension in their model. They focus on the political dimension but also incorporate universal rights into their vision of corporate behavior.

Theories on CSR, which take long-term profits as the main goal normally, use an empirical methodology and are descriptive, although explicitly they also present a conditional prescription. Their generic statement might take the form: "if you want to maximize profits you must assume CSR in the way proposed by this theory". In contrast, ethical theories are prescriptive and use a normative methodology. Integrating empirical and normative aspects of CSR, or economic and ethics, is a great challenge. Some authors

Table 1 Corporate social responsibilities theories and related approaches

Types of theory	Approaches	Short description	Some key references
Instrumental Theories (focusing on achieving economic objectives through social activities)	Maximization of shareholder value	Long-term value maximization	Friedman (1970), Jensen (2000)
	Strategies for competitive advantages	• Social investments in a competitive context	Porter and Kramer (2002)
		• Strategies based on the natural resource view of the firm and the dynamic capabilities of the firm	Hart (1995), Lizt (1996)
		• Strategies for the bottom of the economic pyramid	Prahalad and Hammond (2002), Hart and Christensen (2002), Prahalad (2003)
	Cause-related marketing	Altruistic activities socially recognized used as an instrument of marketing	Varadarajan and Menon (1988), Murray and Montanari (1986)
Political theories (focusing on a responsible use of business power in the political arena)	Corporate constitutionalism	Social responsibilities of businesses arise from the amount of social power that they have	Davis (1960, 1967)
	Integrative Social Contract Theory	Assumes that a social contract between business and society exists	Donaldson and Dunfee (1994, 1999)
	Corporate (or business) citizenship	The firm is understood as being like a citizen with certain involvement in the community	Wood and Logsdon (2002), Andriof and McIntosh (2001), Matten and Crane (2005)
Integrative theories (focusing on the integration of social demands)	Issues management	Corporate processes of response to those social and political issues which may impact significantly upon it	Sethi (1975), Ackerman (1973), Jones (1980), Vogel (1986), Wartick and Mahon (1994)
	Public responsibility	Law and the existing public policy process are taken as a reference for social performance	Preston and Post (1975, 1981)

Stakeholder management	Balances the interests of the stakeholders of the firm	Mitchell et al. (1997), Agle and Mitchell (1999), Rowley (1997)
Corporate social performance	Searches for social legitimacy and processes to give appropriate responses to social issues	Carroll (1979), Wartick and Cochran (1985), Wood (1991b) Swanson (1995)
Ethical theories (focusing on the right thing to achieve a good society)		
Stakeholder normative theory	Considers fiduciary duties towards stakeholders of the firm. Its application requires reference to some moral theory (Kantian, Utilitarianism, theories of justice, etc.)	Freeman (1984, 1994), Evan and Freeman (1988), Donaldson and Preston (1995), Freeman and Phillips (2002), Phillips et al. (2003)
Universal rights	Frameworks based on human rights, labor rights and respect for the environment	The Global Sullivan Principles (1999), UN Global Compact (1999)
Sustainable development	Aimed at achieving human development considering present and future generations	World Commission on Environment and Development (Brundtland Report) (1987), Gladwin and Kennelly (1995)
The common good	Oriented towards the common good of society	Alford and Naughton (2002), Melé (2002), Kaku (1997)

(Brandy, 1990; Etzioni, 1988; Quinn and Jones, 1995; and Swanson, 1999; Treviño and Weaver, 1994; among others) have considered this problem, but it is far from being resolved. This lack of integration has been denounced as the cause of the lack of a paradigm for the business and society field (Swanson, 1999).

Finally, the current situation presents many competing ethical theories. This very often produces confusion and scepticism. The problem is especially serious in the case of ethical theories, and even within each group of theories. Considering, for instance, the stakeholder normative theory. As we have explained above, this can be developed using a great number of different ethical theories. Although each of these theories states universal principles, in practice, the global effect is one of unabashed relativism: "If you are Utilitarian, you'll do this, if you are Kantian you'll do that" (Solomon, 1992, p. 318).

Conclusion

We can conclude that most current CSR theories are focused on four main aspects: (1) meeting objectives that produce long-term profits, (2) using business power in a responsible way, (3) integrating social demands and (4) contributing to a good society by doing what is ethically correct. This permits us to classify the most relevant theories on CSR and related concepts into four groups, which we have called instrumental, political, integrative and value theories. Most of the theories considered do not make explicit the implications of each specific approach for the aspects considered in other groups of theories.

Further research could analyze these four dimensions and their connection in the most relevant theories and consider their contributions and limitations. What seems more challenging, however, is to develop a new theory, which would overcome these limitations. This would require an accurate knowledge of reality and a sound ethical foundation.

Notes

1   Parsons considers the existence of four interconnected problems in any action system: (1) the problem mobilizing of resources from the environment and then distributing them throughout the system, which requires adaptation to environment; (2) the problem of establishing priorities among system goals and mobilizing system resources for the attainment of the goals; (3) the problem of coordinating and maintaining viable relationships among system units and (4) the problem of assuring that the actors in the social system display the appropriate values. This entails motivation and other characteristics (pattern maintenance) and dealing with the internal tensions and strain of the actors in the social system (tension management). That means preserving the basic structure of the system and adjusting to changing conditions within the framework that the basic structure provides. According to

Parsons these problems necessitate four requisites or imperatives for the maintenance of a social system: adaptation (A), goal attainment (G), integration (I) and pattern maintenance or latency (L).

2   Some years before, T. Levitt, a Harvard Business School professor, expressed this approach in an even more radical way: "Corporate welfare makes good sense if it makes good economic sense – and not infrequently it does. But if something does not make economic sense, sentiment or idealism ought not to let it in the door" (Levitt, 1958, p. 42).

3   According to Porter and Kramer (2002), a competitive context consists of four interrelated elements of the local business environment that shape potential productivity. The first element is the factor condition, which involves employee education, natural resources, high quality technological institutions and physical infrastructure. The second element is related to demand conditions: that is to say, how the firm can influence the quality and the size of local market by, for example, developing educated and demanding customers. The third, the context for strategy and rivalry involves how the firm can invest in incentives and norms that rule competition as for example all the efforts for reducing corruption, preventing the formation of cartels and opening markets. The last is the firm's investment in related and supporting industries, for example, strengthening the relationship with suppliers of services, components and machinery.

4   According to Davis, "markets leave business theoretically without any social power and hence, no social responsibility (balanced zero equation). This zero equation of no power and no responsibility is a proper theoretical model for pure competition, but it is theory only and it's inconsistent with the power realities of modern organizations. They possess such a great initiative, economic assets, and power in their actions do have social effects" (Davis, 1967, p. 49).

5   In fact, different models have been constructed in order to explain how and why partnerships are built and how to determine, measure, evaluate partnerships (Andriof, 2001; Zadek, 2001).

6   That is not the only problem. According to Gladwin and Kennelly (1995, p. 876), the concept of sustainable development is "fuzzy, elusive, contestable and/or ideologically controversial" and with multiple objectives and ingredients, complex interdependencies and considerable moral thickness. But, in spite of everything, the concept is becoming more and more popular and has introduced an important element to the CSR debate.

References

Ackerman, R. (1973) 'How Companies Respond to Social Demands', *Harvard University Review* 51(4): 88–98.

Ackerman, R. and Bauer, R. (1976) *Corporate Social Responsiveness*, Reston, Virginia.

Agle, B. and Mitchell, R. (1999) 'Who Matters to CEOs? An Investigation of Stakeholder Attributes and Salience, Corporate Performance and CEO Values', *Academy of Management Journal* 42(5): 507–526.

Alford, H. and Naughton, M. (2002) 'Beyond the Shareholder Model of the Firm: Working toward the Common Good of a Business', in S.A. Cortright and M. Naughton (eds) *Rethinking the Purpose of Business: Interdisciplinary Essays from the Catholic Social Tradition*, Notre Dame University Press, Notre Dame, pp. 27–47.

Altman, B. (1998) 'Corporate Community Relations in the 1990s: A Study in Transformation', *Business and Society* 37(2): 221–228.

Altman, B. and Vidaver-Cohen, D. (2000) 'Corporate Citizenship in the New Millennium: Foundation for an Architecture of Excellence', *Business and Society Review* 105(1): 145–169.

Andriof, J. and McIntosh, M. (eds) (2001), *Perspectives on Corporate Citizenship*, Greenleaf, Sheffield, UK.

Andriof, J. (2001) 'Patterns of Stakeholder Partnership Building', in J. Andriof and M. McIntosh, (eds) *Perspectives on Corporate Citizenship*, Greenleaf, Sheffield, UK, pp. 200–213.

Argandoña, A. (1998) 'The Stakeholder Theory and the Common Good', *Journal of Business Ethics* 17: 1093–1102.

Barney, J. (1991) 'Firm Resource and Sustained Competitive Advantage', *Journal of Management* 17: 99–120

Bendheim, C., Waddock, S. and Graves, S. (1998) 'Determining Best Practice in Corporate-Stakeholder Relations Using Data Envelopment Analysis', *Business and Society* 37(3): 306–339.

Berman, S., Wicks, A., Kotha, S. and Jones, T. (1999) 'Does Stakeholder Orientation Matter? The Relationship between Stakeholder Management Models and Firm Financial Performance', *Academy of Management Journal* 42(5): 488–509.

Bowen, H. (1953) *Social Responsibilities of the Businessman*, Harper & Row, New York.

Bowie, N. (1991) 'New Directions in Corporate Social Responsibility', *Business Horizons* 34(4): 56–66.

Bowie, N. (1998) 'A Kantian Theory of Capitalism', *Business Ethics Quarterly*, Ruffin Series, Special Issue, No. 1: 37–60.

Brandy, F. (1990) *Ethical Managing: Rules and Results*, Macmillan, London.

Brewer, T. (1992) 'An Issue Area Approach to the Analysis of MNE–Government Relations', *Journal of International Business Studies* 23: 295–309.

Brummer, J. (1991) *Corporate Responsibility and Legitimacy*, Greenwood Press, New York.

Burke, L. and Logsdon, J. (1996) 'How Corporate Social Responsibility Pays Off', *Long Range Planning* 29(4): 495–503.

Burton, B. and Dunn, C. (1996) 'Feminist Ethics as Moral Grounding for Stakeholder Theory', *Business Ethics Quarterly* 6(2): 133–147.

Carey, J. (2001) 'The Common Good in Catholic Social Thought', *St. John's Law Review* 75(2): 311–313.

Carroll, A. (1979), 'A Three-Dimensional Conceptual Model of Corporate Performance', *Academy of Management Review* 4(4): 497–505.

Carroll, A. (1991), 'The Pyramid of Corporate Social Responsibility: Towards the Moral Management of Organizational Stakeholders', *Business Horizons* (July/August): 39–48.

Carroll, A. (1994) 'Social Issues in Management Research', *Business and Society* 33(1): 5–25.

Carroll, A. (1999) 'Corporate Social Responsibility: Evolution of Definitional Construct', *Business and Society* 38(3): 268–295.

Carroll, A. and Buchholtz, A. (2002) *Business and Society: Ethics and Stakeholder Management*, 5th edn, South-Western, Cincinnati.

Cassel, D. (2001) 'Human Rights Business Responsibilities in the Global Marketplace', *Business Ethics Quarterly* 11(2): 261–274.

Christensen, C., Craig, T. and Hart, S. (2001) 'The Great Disruption', *Foreign Affairs* 80(2): 80–96.

Christensen, C. and Overdorf, M. (2000) 'Meeting the Challenge of Disruptive Change', *Harvard Business Review* 78(2): 66–75.

Davis, K. (1960) 'Can Business Afford to Ignore Corporate Social Responsibilities?', *California Management Review* 2: 70–76.

Davis, K. (1967) 'Understanding the Social Responsibility Puzzle', *Business Horizons* 10(4): 45–51.

Davis, K. (1973) 'The Case For and Against Business Assumption of Social Responsibilities', *Academy of Management Journal* 16: 312–322.

Dion, M. (2001) 'Corporate Citizenship and Ethics of Care: Corporate Values, Codes of Ethics and Global Governance', in J. Andriof and M. McIntosh (eds), *Perspectives on Corporate Citizenship* (Greenleaf, Sheffield, UK), pp. 118–138.

Donaldson, T. (1982) *Corporations and Morality*, Prentice-Hall, Englewood Cliffs, NJ.

Donaldson, T. and Dunfee, T. (1994) 'Towards a Unified Conception of Business Ethics: Integrative Social Contracts Theory', *Academy of Management Review* 19: 252–284.

Donaldson, T. and Dunfee, T. (1999) *Ties That Bind: A Social Contracts Approach to Business Ethics*, Harvard Business School, Boston.

Donaldson, T. and Dunfee, T. (2000) 'Précis for Ties that Bind', *Business and Society* 105 (Winter): 436–444.

Donaldson, T. and Preston, L. (1995) 'The Stakeholder Theory of the Corporation: Concepts, Evidence, and Implications', *Academy of Management Review* 20(1): 65–91.

Donati, P. (1991) *Teoria relazionale della società*, Franco Agnelli, Milano.

Donnelly, J. (1985) *The Concept of Human Rights*, Croom Helm, London.

Emshoff, J. and Freeman, R. (1978) 'Stakeholder Management', Working Paper from the Wharton Applied Research Center (July). Quoted by Sturdivant (1979).

Etzioni, A. (1988) *The Moral Dimension: Towards a New Economics*, The Free Press, New York.

Evan, W and Freeman, R. (1988) 'A Stakeholder Theory of the Modern Corporation: Kantian Capitalism', in T. Beauchamp and N. Bowie (eds) *Ethical Theory and Business*, Prentice Hall, Englewood Cliffs, pp. 75–93.

Fort, T. (1996) 'Business as Mediating Institutions', *Business Ethics Quarterly* 6(2): 149–164.

Fort, T. (1999) 'The First Man and the Company Man: The Common Good, Transcendence, and Mediating Institutions', *American Business Law Journal* 36(3): 391–435.

Frederick, W. (1987) 'Theories of Corporate Social Performance', in S. Sethi and C. Flabe (eds) *Business and Society: Dimensions of Conflict and Cooperation*, Lexington Books, New York, pp. 142–161.

Frederick, W. (1992) 'Anchoring Values in Nature: Towards a Theory of Business Values', *Business Ethics Quarterly* 2(3): 283–304.

Frederick, W. (1998) 'Moving to CSR 4', *Business and Society* 37(1): 40–60.

Freeman, R. (1984) *Strategic Management: A Stakeholder Approach*, Pitman, Boston.

Freeman, R. (1994) 'The Politics of Stakeholder Theory: Some Future Directions', *Business Ethics Quarterly* 4(4): 409–429.

Freeman, R. and Evan, W. (1990) 'Corporate Governance: A Stakeholder Interpretation', *Journal of Behavioral Economics* 19(4): 337–359.

Freeman, R. and Phillips, R. (2002) 'Stakeholder Theory: A Libertarian Defence', *Business Ethics Quarterly* 12(3): 331–349.

Friedman, M. (1970) 'The Social Responsibility of Business Is to Increase Its Profits', *New York Times Magazine*, September 13th: 32–33, 122, 126.

Friedman, M. and Friedman, R. (1962) *Capitalism and Freedom* University of Chicago Press, Chicago.

Frooman, J. (1997) 'Socially Irresponsible and Illegal Behavior and Shareholder Wealth', *Business and Society* 36(3): 221–250.

Gladwin, T. and Kennelly, J. (1995) 'Shifting Paradigms for Sustainable Development: Implications for Management Theory and Research', *Academy of Management Review* 20(4): 874–904.

Global Sullivan Principles, The (1999) http://globalsullivanprinciples.org (September 2003).

Goodpaster, K. (1999) 'Bridging East and West in Management Ethics: Kyosei and the Moral Point of View', in G. Enderle (ed.) *International Business Ethics: Challenges and Approaches*, University of Notre Dame Press, Notre Dame, pp. 151–159.

Greening, D. and Gray, B. (1994) 'Testing a Model of Organizational Response to Social and Political Issues', *Academy of Management Journal* 37: 467–498.

Griffin, J. (2000) 'Corporate Social Performance: Research Directions for the 21st Century', *Business and Society* 39(4): 479–493.

Griffin, J. and Mahon, J. (1997) 'The Corporate Social Performance and Corporate Financial Performance Debate: Twenty-five Years of Incomparable Research', *Business and Society* 36(1): 5–31.

Harrison, J. and St. John, C. (1996) 'Managing and Partnering with External Stakeholders', *Academy of Management Executive* 10(2): 46–61.

Hart, S. (1995) 'A Natural-Resource-Based View of the Firm', *Academy of Management Review* 20(4): 986–1012.

Hart, S. and Christensen, C. (2002) 'The Great Leap: Driving Innovation from the Base of the Pyramid', *MIT Sloan Management Review* 44(1): 51–57.

Heald, M. (1988) *The Social Responsibilities of Business: Company and Community, 1900–1960*, Transaction Books, New Brunswick.

Hillman, A. and Keim, G. (2001) 'Shareholder Value, Stakeholder Management, and Social Issues: What's the Bottom Line', *Strategic Management Journal* 22(2): 125–140.

Husted, B. and Allen, D. (2000) 'Is It Ethical to Use Ethics as Strategy?', *Journal of Business Ethics* 27(1–2): 21–32.

Jensen, M. (2000) 'Value Maximization, Stakeholder Theory, and the Corporate Objective Function', in M. Beer and N. Nohria (eds) *Breaking the Code of Change*, Harvard Business School Press, Boston, pp. 37–58. Reprinted (2002) as 'Value Maximization, Stakeholder Theory, and the Corporate Objective Function', *Business Ethics Quarterly* 12(2): 235–256.

Jensen, M. and Meckling, W. (1976) 'Theory of the Firm: Managerial Behavior, Agency Cost and Capital Structure', *Journal of Financial Economics* 3 (October): 305–360.

Jones, T. (1980) 'Corporate Social Responsibility Revisited, Redefined', *California Management Review* 22(2): 59–67.

Jones, T. (1983) 'An Integrating Framework for Research in Business and Society:

A Step Toward the Elusive Paradigm?' *Academy of Management Review* 8(4): 559–565.

Kaku, R. (1997) 'The Path of Kyosei', *Harvard Business Review* 75(4): 55–62.

Kaptein, M. and Van Tulder, R. (2003) 'Toward Effective Stakeholder Dialogue', *Business and Society Review* 108(Summer): 203–225.

Keim, G. (1978) 'Corporate Social Responsibility: An Assessment of the Enlightened Self-Interest Model', *Academy of Management Review* 3(1): 32–40.

Kempshall, M. (1999) *The Common Good in Late Medieval Political Thought*, Oxford University Press, Oxford.

Key, S. and Popkin, S. (1998) 'Integrating Ethics into the Strategic Management Process: Doing Well by Doing Good', *Management Decision* 36(5–6): 331–339.

Levitt, T. (1958) 'The Dangers of Social Responsibility', *Harvard Business Review* 36 (September–October): 41–50.

Litz, R. (1996) 'A Resource-Based View of the Socially Responsible Firm: Stakeholder Interdependence, Ethical Awareness, and Issue Responsiveness as Strategic Assets', *Journal of Business Ethics* 15: 1355–1363.

McMahon, T. (1986) 'Models of the Relationship of the Firm to Society', *Journal of Business Ethics* 5: 181–191.

McWilliams, A. and Siegel, D. (2001) 'Corporate Social Responsibility: A Theory of the Firm Perspective', *Academy of Management Review* 26(1): 117–127.

Mahon, J. and McGowan, R. (1991) 'Searching for the Common Good: A Process-Oriented Approach', *Business Horizons* 34(4): 79–87.

Maritain, J. (1966) *The Person and the Common Good*, Notre Dame University Press, Notre Dame.

Maritain, J. (1971 [c1943]) *The Rights of Man and Natural Law*, Gordian Press, New York.

Matten, D. and Crane, A. (2005) 'Corporate Citizenship: Toward an Extended Theoretical Conceptualization', *Academy of Management Review*, 30(1): 166–179.

Matten, D., Crane, A. and Chapple, W. (2003) 'Behind the Mask: Revealing the True Face of Corporate Citizenship', *Journal of Business Ethics* 45(1–2): 109–120.

Melé, D. (2002) *Not Only Stakeholder Interests: The Firm Oriented toward the Common Good*, University of Notre Dame Press, Notre Dame.

Mitchell, R., Agle, B., and Wood, D. (1997) 'Toward a Theory of Stakeholder Identification and Salience: Defining the Principle of Who and What Really Counts', *Academy of Management Review* 22(4): 853–886.

Murray, K. and Montanari, J. (1986) 'Strategic Management of the Socially Responsible Firm: Integrating Management and Marketing Theory', *Academy of Management Review* 11(4): 815–828.

Ogden, S. and Watson, R. (1999) 'Corporate Performance and Stakeholder Management: Balancing Shareholder and Customer Interests in the U.K. Privatized Water Industry', *Academy of Management Journal* 42(5): 526–538.

Parsons, T. (1961) 'An Outline of the Social System', in T. Parsons, E. Shils, K. Naegle and J. Pitts (eds) *Theories of Society*, Free Press, New York.

Petrick, J. and Quinn, J. (2001) 'The Challenge of Leadership Accountability for Integrity Capacity as a Strategic Asset', *Journal of Business Ethics* 34: 331–343.

Phillips, R. (1997) 'Stakeholder Theory and a Principle of Fairness', *Business Ethics Quarterly* 7(1): 51–66.

Phillips, R. (2003) 'Stakeholder Legitimacy', *Business Ethics Quarterly* 13(1): 25–41.

Phillips, R., Freeman, E. and Wicks, A. (2003) 'What Stakeholder Theory Is Not', *Business Ethics Quarterly* 13(1): 479–502.

Pope John Paul II (1991) *Encyclical 'Centesimus Annus'* (Catholic Truth Society, London) and www.vatican.va.

Porter, M. (1980) *Competitive Strategy: Techniques for Analyzing Industries and Competitors*, Free Press, New York.

Porter, M. and Kramer, M. (2002) 'The Competitive Advantage of Corporate Philanthropy', *Harvard Business Review* 80(12): 56–69.

Porter, M. and Van der Linde, C. (1995) 'Green and Competitive: Ending the Stalemate', *Harvard Business Review* 73(5): 120–133.

Post, J., Preston, L., Sauter-Sachs, S. and Sachs, S. (2002) *Redefining the Corporation: Stakeholder Management and Organizational Wealth*, Stanford University Press, Stanford.

Prahalad, C. (2002) 'Strategies for the Bottom of the Economic Pyramid: India as a Source of Innovation', *Reflections: The SOL Journal* 3(4): 6–18.

Prahalad, C. and Hammond, A. (2002) 'Serving the World's Poor, Profitably', *Harvard Business Review* 80(9): 48–58.

Preston, L. (1975) 'Corporation and Society: The Search for a Paradigm', *Journal of Economic Literature* 13(2): 434–454.

Preston, L. and Post, J. (1975) 'Private Management and Public Policy', *The Principle of Public Responsibility*, Prentice Hall, Englewood Cliffs, NJ.

Preston, L. and Post, J. (1981) 'Private Management and Public Policy', *California Management Review* 23(3): 56–63.

Quinn, D. and Jones, T. (1995) 'An Agent Morality View of Business Policy', *Academy of Management Review* 20(1): 22–42.

Roman, R., Hayibor, S. and Agle, B. (1999) 'The Relationship between Social Performance and Financial Performance', *Business and Society* 38(1): 109–125.

Ross, S. (1973) 'The Economy Theory of the Agency: The Principal's Problem', *American Economic Review* 63: 134–139.

Rowley, T. (1997) 'Moving Beyond Dyadic Ties: A Network Theory of Stakeholder Influences', *Academy of Management Review* 22(4): 887–911.

Rowley, T. and Berman, S. (2000) 'New Brand of Corporate Social Performance', *Business and Society* 39(4): 397–412.

Schwartz, M. and Carroll, A. (2003) 'Corporate Social Responsibility: A Three-Domain Approach', *Business Ethics Quarterly* 13(4): 503–530.

Sethi, S. (1975) 'Dimensions of Corporate Social Performance: An Analytical Framework', *California Management Review* 17(3): 58–65.

Shrivastava, P. (1995) 'The Role of Corporations in Achieving Ecological Sustainability', *Academy of Management Review* 20:936–960.

Simon, Y. (1992) (1965), in V. Kuic (ed.), *The Tradition of Natural Law: A Philosopher's Reflections*, Fordham University Press, New York.

Smith, T. (1999) 'Aristotle on the Conditions for and Limits of the Common Good', *American Political Science Review* 93(3): 625–637.

Smith, W. and Higgins, M. (2000) 'Cause-Related Marketing: Ethics and the Ecstatic', *Business and Society* 39(3): 304–322.

Solomon, R. (1992) 'Corporate Roles, Personal Virtues: An Aristotelian Approach to Business Ethics', *Business Ethics Quarterly* 2(3): 317–340.

Stead, J. and Stead, E. (2000) 'Eco-enterprise Strategy: Standing for Sustainability', *Journal of Business Ethics* 24(4): 313–330.

Sturdivant, F. (1979) 'Executives and Activists: Test of Stakeholder Management', *California Management Review* 22(Fall): 53–59.

Sulmasy, D. (2001) 'Four Basic Notions of the Common Good', *St. John's Law Review* 75(2): 303–311.

Swanson, D. (1995) 'Addressing a Theoretical Problem by Reorienting the Corporate Social Performance Model', *Academy of Management Review* 20(1): 43–64.

Swanson D. (1999) 'Toward an Integrative Theory of Business and Society: A Research Strategy for Corporate Social Performance', *Academy of Management Review* 24(3): 506–521.

Teece, D., Pisano, G. and Shuen, A. (1997) 'Dynamic Capabilities and Strategic Management', *Strategic Management Journal* 18(7): 509–533.

The Clarkson Center for Business Ethics: (1999) *Principles of Stakeholder Management* (Joseph L. Rotman School of Management, Toronto, Canada). Reprinted (2002) in *Business Ethics Quarterly* 12(4): 257–264.

Tichy, N., McGill, A. and St. Clair, L. (1997) *Corporate Global Citizenship*, The New Lexington Press, San Francisco.

Treviño, L. and Weaver, G. (1994) 'Normative and Empirical Business Ethics', *Business Ethics Quarterly* 4(2): 129–143.

United Nations (1999) Global Compact (www.unglobalcompact.org).

Van Marrewijk, M. (2003) 'Concept and Definitions of CSR and Corporate Sustainability: Between Agency and Communion', *Journal of Business Ethics* 44: 95–105.

Van Marrewijk, M. and Werre, M. (2003) 'Multiple Levels of Corporate Sustainability', *Journal of Business Ethics* 44(2/3): 107–120.

Varadarajan, P. and Menon, A. (1988) 'Cause-Related Marketing: A Coalignment of Marketing Strategy and Corporate Philanthropy', *Journal of Marketing* 52(3): 58–74.

Velasquez, M. (1992) 'International Business, Morality and the Common Good', *Business Ethics Quarterly* 2(1): 27–40.

Vogel, D (1986) 'The Study of Social Issues in Management: A Critical Appraisal', *California Management Review* 28(2): 142–152.

Votaw, D. (1972) 'Genius Became Rare: A Comment on the Doctrine of Social Responsibility Pt 1', *California Management Review* 15(2): 25–31.

Waddock, S. and Graves, S. (1997) 'The Corporate Social Performance–Financial Performance Link', *Strategic Management Journal* 18(4): 303–320.

Wartick, S. and Cochran, P. (1985) 'The Evolution of Corporate Social Performance Model', *Academy of Management Review* 10(4): 758–769.

Wartick, S. and Rude, R. (1986) 'Issues Management: Corporate Fad or Corporate Function?', *California Management Review* 29(1): 124–132.

Wartick, S. and Mahon, J. (1994) 'Towards a Substantive Definition of the Corporate Issue Construct: A Review and Synthesis of Literature', *Business and Society* 33(3): 293–311.

Weiss, J. (2003) *Business Ethics: A Stakeholder and Issues Management Approach*, 3rd edn, Thomson – South-Western. Ohio.

Wernerfelt, B. (1984) 'A Resource Based View of the Firm', *Strategic Management Review* 5: 171–180.

Wheeler, D., Colbert, B. and Freeman, R. (2003) 'Focusing on Value: Reconciling Corporate Social Responsibility, Sustainability and a Stakeholder Approach in a Network World', *Journal of General Management* 28(3): 1–29.

Wicks, A., Gilbert, Jr, D. and Freeman, R. (1994) 'A Feminist Reinterpretation of the Stakeholder Concept', *Business Ethics Quarterly* 4(4): 475–497.

Wijnberg, N. (2000) 'Normative Stakeholder Theory and Aristotle: The Link between Ethics and Politics', *Journal of Business Ethics* 25: 329–342.

Windsor, D. (2001) 'The Future of Corporate Social Responsibility', *International Journal of Organizational Analysis* 9(3): 225–256.

Wood, D. (1991a) 'Social Issues in Management: Theory and Research in Corporate Social Performance', *Journal of Management* 17(2): 383–406.

Wood, D. (1991b) 'Corporate Social Performance Revisited', *Academy of Management Review* 16(4): 691–718.

Wood, D. and Logsdon, J. (2002) 'Business Citizenship: From Individuals to Organizations', *Business Ethics Quarterly*, Ruffin Series, No. 3: 59–94.

World Business Council for Sustainable Development (2000) *Corporate Social Responsibility: Making Good Business Sense*, World Business Council for Sustainable Development, Geneva.

World Commission on Environment and Development (1987) *Our Common Future*, Oxford University Press, Oxford.

Yamaji, K. (1997) 'A Global Perspective of Ethics in Business', *Business Ethics Quarterly* 7(3): 55–71.

Zadek, S. (2001) 'Partnership Alchemy: Engagement, Innovation, and Governance', in J. Andriof and M. McIntosh (eds) *Perspectives on Corporate Citizenship*, Greenleaf, Sheffield, UK, pp. 200–212.

Chapter 4

Responsibilities to stakeholders

I N THIS CHAPTER WE WILL:

- Define and conceptualize the idea of what a stakeholder is.
- Understand the initial basic ideas of stakeholder theory.
- Examine the multifaceted aspects of stakeholder theory.
- Learn to distinguish between different levels of CSR.
- Discuss the relevance of stakeholder theory for the broader understanding and practice of CSR.

Introduction

So far in this book we have discussed the contested nature of CSR and assessed the key arguments in favour of corporations assuming some degree of responsibility for the wider interests of society. We have also analysed how we could characterize these responsibilities and gained an overview of the various theoretical perspectives which may help us to understand the interface between the corporation and society at large. As future practitioners of CSR, however, we might ask ourselves at this stage how we could possibly translate this fairly vague construct of 'society', towards which the corporation may have some kinds of responsibilities, into something concrete, something we can translate into an object of managerial attention and action.

This is exactly the point where the notion of stakeholders enters the picture. If a manager would think about what exactly his or her responsibilities are to this fairly abstract entity called 'society', considering them in terms of definable constituencies (i.e. 'stakeholders') is perhaps the answer. The father of stakeholder theory, R. Edward

Freeman, puts it plainly and simply in the foreword of the book whose third chapter is our first reading in this section (Freeman, 1984: vi): 'A stakeholder is any group or individual who can affect, or is affected by, the achievement of a corporation's purpose.'

In essence, then, stakeholder theory helps us to find a very pragmatic answer as to what the 'S' in CSR in a given situation actually is. As such, stakeholder theory is mainly a managerial tool: in a given situation, a company needs to work with selected individuals or groups in society in order to fulfil its aims, and every one of these 'stakeholders' that may have an influence on the company's goals has to be taken into account. This simple approach to make the broader abstract entity of 'society' concrete and tangible for the company is one of the reasons why stakeholder theory today is a core element in most basic introductions to strategic management.

The Moral Aspect of Stakeholder Theory

One aspect that makes stakeholder theory particularly interesting in the CSR context is the fact that it is not just an analytical tool to identify and manage crucial constituencies of the company. As Freeman reiterates two decades later, 'stakeholder theory is a theory of organizational management *and ethics*' (Phillips, Freeman and Wicks, 2003: 480; emphasis added). Stakeholder theory has always been a core CSR theory, since it argues that, if the company affects individuals or groups to reach its goals, these groups also have a legitimate interest in the corporation. So, depending on how the company affects them, and their relative power and influence, they have a more or less higher 'stake' in the corporation, thereby putting them in a position where the company should consider their interests (Mitchell, Agle and Wood, 1997). There are different normative approaches in business ethics to make these claims legitimate (Phillips *et al.*, 2003: 481), and there might be contestation about the degree of legitimacy of different stakes in a given situation. However, the central message of stakeholder theory is that corporations are not only strategically rational but arguably also morally right in considering the interests of the individuals or groups they affect and are affected by.

It is this normative element which sets the stakeholder model of the firm apart from the traditional managerial model of the firm (such as that espoused in the reading by Milton Friedman in Chapter 2), where only the interests of the owners are considered as legitimate. A good illustration of this difference is the often cited case of a company that produces a potentially unsafe product which occasionally leads to injury or even death of a small percentage of its customers. After a short cost–benefit analysis, the company may discover that, even though customers and their families can suffer, it is cheaper to pay damages than to redesign the product completely. While the Friedman model would suggest that shareholder interests come first and customer interests come second, a stakeholder model would argue that in such a situation the health of the customer represents a more legitimate stake than the financial stakes of the shareholders (for details on this case, see Gioia, 1992).

The Relevance of Stakeholder Theory

Stakeholder theory is arguably the single most influential theory in CSR. In its various forms it is used in most areas of CSR and has given rise to a large body of literature (see, for an overview, Andriof, Waddock, Husted and Sutherland Rahman, 2002, 2003). But also, beyond academia, corporations have adopted the language of stakeholders, and even governments frame their various relations in this language (Kelly, Kelly and Gamble, 1997). In a CSR context, the main implication of stakeholder thinking is a new role for management: rather than being 'agents' of shareholders only, managers find themselves in a role of assessing and balancing the interests of all stakeholders in running the firm. It has also given rise to new approaches to corporate governance: if the stakes of multiple stakeholders are legitimate, it is perhaps inappropriate if only the interests of shareholders are represented on the board – stakeholders should also, arguably, be allowed a fair share of influence on how 'their' corporation is run. In this context, there is an ongoing debate on how and to what degree such a 'stakeholder democracy' (Matten and Crane, 2005) is at all a desirable and realistic aspiration for the modern corporation.

Introducing the Readings

Similar to Chapter 3, the two readings in this chapter provide, first, an in-depth outline of the basic features of the theory, written by probably the single most influential author on the topic, and then we go on to an excellent overview and systematization of the theory which details different ways in which it has been applied and understood in the CSR literature.

Basic features of stakeholder theory

R. Edward Freeman is considered the main progenitor of stakeholder theory, and this selection is the third chapter from his seminal 1984 book on the topic. The chapter still very much breathes the initial context of stakeholder theory which is also reflected by the main title of the book: rather than being a CSR theory, the approach was designed to be a new approach to strategic management. Consequently, Freeman draws stakeholder theory, first, as an analytical (or 'rational', as he puts it) tool: it helps us to design 'maps' of all relevant groups or individuals in the context of the achievement of the company's goals. Second, on the 'process' level, stakeholder thinking helps us to consider which players will actually be influential in the process of achieving the company's goals. Third, Freeman fleshes out the 'transactional' level of stakeholder theory by analysing how the company reaches different goals by successfully managing its relationships with customers, employees, the press or analysts, to name just a few of the examples he provides.

It is interesting to see that the normative or ethical side of stakeholder theory, which came out much more clearly in other (mostly later) writings by Freeman, is still relatively absent in this initial outline of the theory. The only slight hint to normative questions is given away in the concluding section where the author makes 'a plea for voluntarism' in the application of the framework. The reasons he gives are interesting as well: not only, he argues, is voluntarism the only philosophy compatible with the American social fabric, but all other approaches, in his view, are not cost-effective. One might discuss the extent to which this makes stakeholder thinking just another largely US-centric idea – a feature that we have already discussed in relation to CSR itself.

Types of stakeholder theory

The article by Thomas Donaldson and Lee Preston, written a decade after Freeman's seminal book, takes stock of the main developments in stakeholder theory and disentangles the various aspects and levels of the approach. In fact, they argue that we can talk about four different types of stakeholder theory. First, there is descriptive stakeholder theory, which analyses what managers actually do and what groups are taken into account. Second, there is the instrumental aspect, as it explains the role which different individuals or groups play in reaching the company's goals. On a third level, stakeholder theory is normative, as it is predicated on the assumption that stakeholder interests are legitimate. Finally, stakeholder theory is a managerial theory, as it recommends practices, tools and structures to managers in order to manage stakeholder relations successfully. This reading is important because it makes clear that, as with much of the CSR debate, different people mean different things when they discuss stakeholder theory, and the authors help us to understand the various ways in which the theory may be interpreted.

Study Questions

1   What is a stakeholder of an organization? Why should even the most hard-core profit-driven manager bother about who the firm's stakeholders are?

2   Construct a normative (moral) and an instrumental (strategic) set of arguments suggesting why firms should or should not consider the interests of core stakeholders such as employees, consumers, suppliers and shareholders. Which is the most persuasive?

3   What are the core normative or ethical implications of stakeholder theory? Think of some unpopular corporate decisions, such as the closure of a plant in the USA or Europe and its relocation to Eastern Europe or China. What implications does stakeholder theory have for the social responsibilities of such a firm?

4   What are the key practical implications for managers from stakeholder theory? What tools, structures, processes or strategies would stakeholder theory suggest for firms seeking to be socially responsible?

5   To what extent is stakeholder theory a uniquely US concept? Answer the question by drawing on examples of how key stakeholders, such as owners, employees,

managers and local communities relate to companies in a Western European, Scandinavian, or Japanese context.

References

Andriof, J., Waddock, S., Husted, B. and Sutherland Rahman, S. (eds) (2002) *Unfolding Stakeholder Thinking 1: Theory, Responsibility and Engagement*, Sheffield: Greenleaf.

Andriof, J., Waddock, S., Husted, B. and Sutherland Rahman, S. (eds) (2003) *Unfolding Stakeholder Thinking 2: Relationships, Communication, Reporting and Performance*, Sheffield: Greenleaf.

Freeman, R. (1984) *Strategic Management: A Stakeholder Approach*, Marshfield, MA: Pitman Publishing Inc.

Gioia, D. (1992) 'Pinto Fires and Personal Ethics: A Script Analysis of Missed Opportunities'. *Journal of Business Ethics* 11(5/6): 379–389.

Kelly, G., Kelly, D. and Gamble, A. (eds) (1997) *Stakeholder Capitalism*. Basingstoke: Macmillan.

Matten, D. and Crane, A. (2005) 'What Is Stakeholder Democracy? Perspectives and Issues'. *Business Ethics: A European Review* 14(1): 6–13.

Mitchell, R., Agle, B. and Wood, D. (1997) 'Toward a Theory of Stakeholder Identification and Salience: Defining the Principle of Who and What Really Counts'. *Academy of Management Review* 22(4): 853–886.

Phillips, R., Freeman, R. and Wicks, A. (2003) 'What Stakeholder Theory Is Not'. *Business Ethics Quarterly* 13(4): 479–502.

STAKEHOLDER MANAGEMENT: FRAMEWORK AND PHILOSOPHY

R. Edward Freeman

Introduction

Organizations have stakeholders. That is, there are groups and individuals who can affect, or are affected by, the achievement of an organization's mission. I have shown that if business organizations are to be successful in the current and future environment then executives must take multiple stakeholder groups into account. The purpose of this chapter is to discuss how the stakeholder management framework can be used to better understand and manage both internal and external change, and how the management philosophy which accompanies this framework fits into our more customary way of thinking about organizations.[1]

The Stakeholder Framework

The literature yields a broad range of definitions of the stakeholder concept. From the standpoint of strategic management, or the achievement of organizational purpose, we need an inclusive definition. We must not leave out any group or individual who can affect or is affected by organizational purpose, because that group may prevent our accomplishments. Theoretically, therefore "stakeholder" must be able to capture a broad range of groups and individuals, even though when we put the concept to practical tests we must be willing to ignore certain groups who will have little or no impact on the corporation at this point in time. Such a broad notion of "stakeholders" will include a number of groups who may not be "legitimate" in the sense that they will have vastly different values and agendas for action from our own. Some groups may have as an objective simply to interfere with the smooth operations of our business. For instance, some corporations must count "terrorist groups" as stakeholders. As unsavoury as it is to admit that such "illegitimate" groups have a stake in our business, from the standpoint of strategic management, it must be done. Strategies must be put in place to deal with terrorists if they can substantially affect the operations of the business.

The stakeholder concept must capture specific groups and individuals as "stakeholders." As we move from a theory of strategic planning to a theory of strategic management, we must adopt an action orientation.[2] Therefore, if the stakeholder concept is to have practical significance, it must be capable of yielding concrete actions with specific groups and individuals. "Stakeholder Management" as a concept, refers to the necessity for an organization to manage the relationships with its specific stakeholder groups in an action-oriented way.

The very definition of "stakeholder" as "any group or individual who can affect or is affected by the achievement of an organization's purpose" gives rise to the need for processes and techniques to enhance the strategic management capability of the organization. There are at least three levels at which we must understand the processes which an organization uses to manage the relationships with its stakeholders.[3]

First of all, we must understand from a rational perspective, who are the stakeholders in the organization and what are the perceived stakes. Second, we must understand the organizational processes used to either implicitly or explicitly manage the organization's relationships with its stakeholders, and whether these processes "fit" with the rational "stakeholder map" of the organization. Finally, we must understand the set of transactions or bargains among the organization and its stakeholders and deduce whether these negotiations "fit" with the stakeholder map and the organizational processes for stakeholders.

We might define an organization's "Stakeholder Management Capability" in terms of its ability to put these three levels of analysis together.[4] For instance, an organization which understands its stakeholder map and the stakes of each group, which has organizational processes to take these groups and their stakes into account routinely as part of the standard operating procedures of the organization and which implements a set of transactions or bargains to balance the interests of these stakeholders to achieve the organization's purpose, would be said to have high (or superior) stakeholder management capability. On the other hand, an organization which does not understand who its stakeholders are, has no processes for dealing with their concerns and has no set of transactions for negotiating with stakeholders would be said to have low (or inferior) stakeholder management capability. Each of these levels of analysis needs to be discussed in more detail, if the stakeholder management framework is to become a useful managerial tool.

The Rational Level: Stakeholder Maps

Any framework which seeks to enhance an organization's stakeholder management capability must begin with an application of the basic definition. Who are those groups and individuals who can affect and are affected by the achievement of an organization's purpose? How can we construct a "stakeholder map" of an organization? What are the problems in constructing such a map?

The traditional picture of the firm consisting of customers, suppliers, employees and owners has had to change to encompass the emergence of environmentalists, consumer advocates, media, governments, global competitors, etc. I base this argument on an analysis of the changes in the business environment of the last twenty years. The resulting generic stakeholder map can serve as a starting point for the construction of a stakeholder map of a typical firm. Ideally the starting point for constructing a map for a particular business is an historical analysis of the environment of that particular firm.[5] In the absence of such an historical document, Exhibit 1 can serve as a checkpoint for an initial generic stakeholder map.

Exhibit 1 depicts a stakeholder map around one major strategic issue for one very large organization, the XYZ Company, based primarily in the U.S. The executives in this organization, however, believed that Exhibit 1 could be used as a starting point for almost any issue of importance to the company. Unfortunately, most attempts at "stakeholder analysis" end with the construction of Exhibit 1. As the literature suggests, the primary use of the stakeholder concept has been as a tool for gathering information about generic stakeholders. "Generic stakeholders" refers to "those categories of groups who can affect. . . ." While "Government" is a category, it is EPA, OSHA, FTC, Congress, etc. who can take actions to affect the achievement of an organization's purpose. Therefore, for stakeholder analysis to be meaningful Exhibit 1 must be taken one step further. Specific stakeholder groups must be identified. Exhibit 2 is a chart of specific stakeholders to

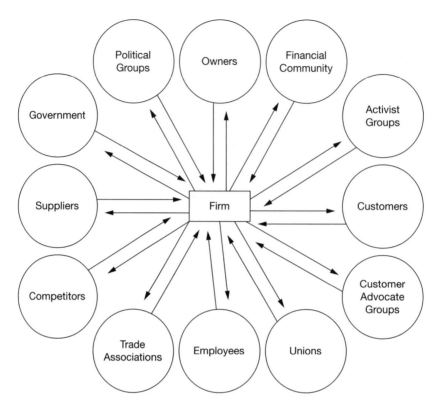

Exhibit 1 Stakeholder map of a very large organization

accompany Exhibit 1 for the XYZ Company. Even in Exhibit 2 some groups are aggregated, in order to disguise the identity of the company. Thus, "Investment Banks" would be replaced by the names of those investment banks actually used by XYZ.

Most very large organizations have a stakeholder map and accompanying stakeholder chart which is relatively similar to the above exhibits. There will be variations among industries, companies, and geographies at the specific stakeholder level, but the two exhibits can be used as a checklist of stakeholder groups. In the several industries analyzed in subsequent chapters there is little variation at the generic level.

Exhibit 3 is an analysis of the stakes of some of those specific stakeholder groups listed in the stakeholder chart (Exhibit 2). Thus the stake of Political Parties #1 and #2 is as a heavy user of XYZ's product, as being able to influence the regulatory process to mandate change in XYZ's operations and as being able to elevate XYZ to national attention via the political process. The stake of XYZ's owners varied among specific stakeholder groups. Those employees of XYZ, and the pension funds of XYZ's unions are concerned with long term growth of XYZ's stock, as their retirement income will depend on the ability of XYZ to earn returns during their retirement years. Other shareowner groups want current income, as XYZ has been known for

Owners	Financial Community	Activist Groups
Shareowners	Analysts	Safety and Health Groups
Bondholders	Investment Banks	Environmental Groups
Employees	Commercial Banks	"Big Business" Groups
	Federal Reserve	Single Issue Groups
Suppliers	Government	Political Groups
Firm #1	Congress	Political Party #1
Firm #2	Courts	Political Party #2
Firm #3	Cabinet Departments	National League of Cities
etc.	Agency #1	National Council of Mayors
	Agency #2	etc.
Customers	Customer Advocate Groups	Unions
Customer Segment #1	Consumer Federation of	Union of Workers #1
Customer Segment #2	America	Union of Workers #2
etc.	Consumer's Union	etc.
	Council of Consumers	Political Action Committees
	etc.	of Unions
Employees	Trade Associations	Competitors
Employee Segment #1	Business Roundtable	Domestic Competitor #1
Employee Segment #2	NAM	Domestic Competitor #2
etc.	Customer Trade Org. #1	etc.
	Customer Trade Org. #2	Foreign Competitor #1
	etc.	etc.

Exhibit 2 Specific stakeholders in a very large organization*

*The actual names of most stakeholder groups are disguised.

Customer Segment #1	Political Parties #1 and #2
High Users of Product	High Users of Product
Improvement of Product	Able to Influence Regulatory Process
	Able to Get Media Attention on a National Scale
Customer Segment #2	Customer Advocate #1
Low Users of Product	Effects of XYZ on the Elderly
No Available Substitute	
Employees	Consumer Advocate #2
Jobs and Job Security	Safety of XYZ's Products
Pension Benefits	
Owners	
Growth and Income	
Stability of Stock Price and Dividend	

Exhibit 3 'Stakes' of selected stakeholders in XYZ company

steady though modest growth over time. Customer Segment #1 used a lot of XYZ's product and was interested in how the product could be improved over time for a small incremental cost. Customer Segment #2 used only a small amount of XYZ's product, but that small amount was a critical ingredient for Customer Segment #2, and there were no readily available substitutes. Thus, the stakes of the different customer segment stakeholders differed. One customer advocate group was concerned about the effects of XYZ's product decisions on the elderly, who were for the most part highly dependent on XYZ's products. Another consumer advocate group was worried about other XYZ products in terms of safety.

As these three exhibits from the XYZ company show, the construction of a rational "stakeholder map" is not an easy task in terms of identifying specific groups and the stakes of each. The exhibits are enormously over-simplified, for they depict the stakeholders of XYZ as static, whereas in reality, they change over time, and their stakes change depending on the strategic issue under consideration. Similarly, the construction of an accurate portfolio is no easy task as the problems with measuring market share have shown.[6] The task becomes even harder when we consider several implications of these three exhibits.

The first implication is that just as Merton (1957) identified the role set for individuals in society, and Evan (1966) generalized this notion for organizations to the organization set, we might combine these notions into a "stakeholder role set," or the set of roles which an individual or group may play qua being a stakeholder in an organization. For example, an employee may be a customer for XYZ's products, may belong to a Union }of XYZ, may be an owner of XYZ, may be a member of Political Party #1 and may even be a member of a consumer advocate group. Many members of certain stakeholder groups are also members of other stakeholder groups, and *qua stakeholder in an organization* may have to balance (or not balance) conflicting and competing roles. Conflict within each person and among group members may result. The role set of a particular stakeholder may well generate different and conflicting expectations of corporate action. For certain organizations and stakeholder groups, a "stakeholder role set" analysis may be appropriate. Exhibit 4 is an example of the stakeholder role set of employees and a government official.

The second implication of Exhibits 1–3 is the interconnection of stakeholder groups, or the interorganizational relationships which exist, a phenomenon well studied in organizational theory.[7] XYZ Company found that one of their Unions was also a large contributor to an adversarial consumer advocate group who was pressuring a key government agency to more closely regulate XYZ. Networks of stakeholder groups easily emerge on a particular issue and endure over time. Coalitions of groups form to help or oppose a company on a particular issue. Also, some firms are quite adept at working indirectly, i.e. at influencing Stakeholder A to influence Stakeholder B, to influence Stakeholder C.[8]

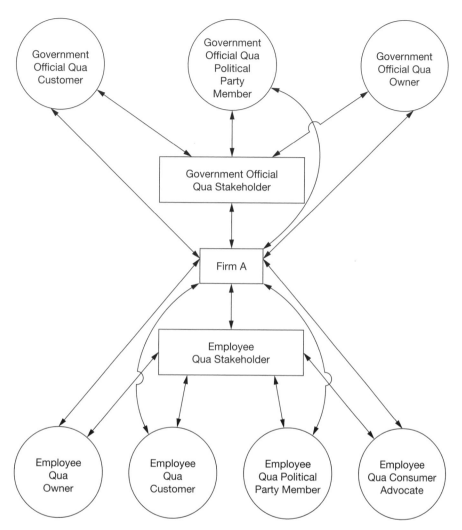

Exhibit 4 Possible stakeholder role set of employees and government officials

More traditional examples include the emergence of the courts as a key stakeholder in takeover bids. Marathon Oil successfully used the courts and the agencies involved in anti-trust to fend off a takeover bid from Mobil, while finding U.S. Steel to come to the rescue. AT&T recently marshalled the support of employees and stockholders to try and influence the Congress through a letter writing campaign. While there is some research on power and influence networks, little is known in the way of formulating strategies for utilizing such networks in a positive and proactive fashion. Little is known, prescriptively, about what range of alternatives is open to managers who want to utilize such an indirect approach to dealing with stakeholders. Exhibit 5 depicts several networks, and illustrates the necessity of thinking through the possible networks that can emerge or be created to accomplish organizational purposes.

Example #1: Marathon–U.S. Steel Merger

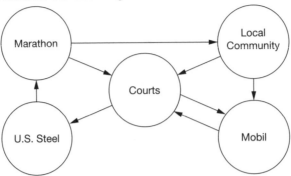

Example #2: AT&T and House Bill 5158

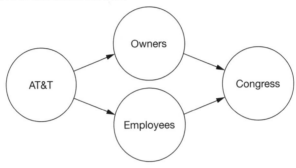

Exhibit 5 Typical indirect or coalition strategies

The courts and some government agencies play a special role as part of the process by which groups interact. They have a special kind of "stake," one of formal power. While they usually do not initiate action, they can serve as resolver of conflicts, or as guarantor of due process. If we generalize this notion we see that another implication of Exhibits 1–3 is the phenomenon of the differing kinds of stakes and the differing perceptions of stakes that various groups have. "Stake" is obviously multi-dimensional, and not measured solely in dollar terms. However, exactly what the dimensions are of "stake" is a more difficult question. Exhibit 3 ranges across a broad spectrum of phenomena from more traditional dollar returns to stockholders to a call for "voice" in running the affairs of XYZ (Hirschman, 1970). Clearly we need to understand "stake" in more detail.

One analytical device depicts an organization's stakeholders on a two-dimensional grid.[9] The first dimension categorizes stakeholders by "interest" or "stake." The idea is to look at the range of perceived stakes of multiple stakeholders. While there are no hard and fast criteria to apply here, one typical categorization is to classify "stake" from "having an equity interest in the firm" to "being an influencer" or in Dill's (1975) terms, "being a kibbitzer, or someone who has an interest in what the firm does because it affects them in some way, even if not directly in marketplace terms." We might place a middle category between equity and kibbitzer and call it having a "market" stake. These three categories of a continuum are meant to represent the more traditional theory of the firm's differing stakes of owners (equity stake), customers and suppliers (market stake) and government (kibbitzer).

The second dimension of this classificatory grid can be understood in terms of power, or loosely speaking, the ability to use resources to make an event actually happen.[10] The three points of interest on this continuum are voting power, economic power and political power. Owners can expend resources in terms of voting power, by voting for directors or voting to support management, or even "voting" their shares in the marketplace in a takeover battle. Customers and suppliers can expend resources in terms of economic power, measured by dollars invested in R&D, switching to another firm, raising price or withholding supply. Government can expend resources in terms of political power by passing legislation, writing new regulations or bringing suit in the courts.

Exhibit 6 represents this two dimensional grid, with owners being the textbook case of an equity stake and voting power; customers and suppliers having a market stake and economic power; and government having an influencer stake and political power. The diagonal of Exhibit 6 represents the development of classical management thought, and the prevailing "world-view" of the modern business firm. Management concepts and principles have evolved to treat the stakeholders along this diagonal. Managers learn how to handle stockholders and boards of directors via their ability to vote on certain key decisions, and conflicts are resolved by the procedures and processes written into the corporate charter or by methods which involve former legal parameters. Strategic planners, marketing managers, financial analysts and operations executives base their decisions on marketplace variables and a long tradition of wisdom and research based on an economic analysis of marketplace forces. Public relations and public affairs managers and lobbyists learn to deal in the political arena, to curry the favor of politicians and to learn to strategically use PACs, "perks" and the regulatory process.

As long as the "real world" approximately fits this diagonal case of Exhibit 6 there are few problems. Each set of managerial problems and issues has an established body of knowledge upon which to draw in times of change. Another way of further supporting the argument of chapter One is to say that the world can no longer be seen in terms of the diagonal of Exhibit 6.

For instance, in the auto industry one part of government has acquired formal power, the Chrysler Loan Guarantee Board, while in the steel industry some agencies have acquired economic power in terms of the imposition of import quotas or the trigger-price mechanism. The SEC might be viewed as a kibbitzer with formal power in terms of disclosure and accounting rules. Outside directors, now, do not necessarily have an equity stake. This is especially true of women, minority group members and academics who are

POWER STAKE	Formal or Voting	Economic	Political
Equity	Stockholders Directors Minority Interests		
Economic		Customers Competitors Suppliers Debt Holders Unions	Foreign Governments
Influencers			Consumer Advocates Government Nader's Raiders Sierra Club Trade Association

Exhibit 6 Classical stakeholder grid

becoming more normal for the boards of large corporations, even though it is far from certain that such directors are really effective and not merely symbolic. Some traditional kibbitzer groups are buying stock and acquiring an equity stake. While they also acquire formal power, the yearly demonstration at the stockholders meeting or the proxy fight over social issues is built on their political power base. Witness the marshalling of the political process by church groups in bringing up issues such as selling infant formula in the third world or investing in South Africa at the annual stockholders meeting. Unions are using political power as well as their equity stake in terms of pension fund investing, to influence management decisions. Customers are being organized by consumer advocates to exercise the voice option and to politicize the marketplace.

In short the nice neat orderly world of Exhibit 6 is no longer realistic. The real world looks more like Exhibit 7 which catalogs some of the differing stakes mentioned above. Of course, each individual organization will have its own separate grid, and given the complexity of the stakeholder role set, there may be groups which fall into more than one box on the grid. The "messiness" of Exhibit 7 lends credence to the search for alternative applications of more traditional management knowledge and processes. Getting the last two degrees of knowledge out of the diagonal of Exhibit 6 is simply no longer good enough. We must find innovative ways of understanding both the power and stakes of a variety of influential and interconnecting stakeholder groups. Thus MacMillan (1978) has argued that elements of strategic planning, traditionally reserved for market stakeholders with economic power, can be applied to the pure political case. While there is a long tradition

POWER / STAKE	Formal or Voting	Economic	Political
Equity	Stockholders Directors Minority Interests		Dissident Stockholders
Economic		Suppliers Debt Holders Customers Unions	Local Governments Foreign Governments Consumer Groups Unions
Influencers	Government SEC Outside Directors	EPA OSHA	Nader's Raiders Government Trade Associations

Exhibit 7 'Real world' stakeholder grid

of applying economic analysis to public policy questions, we are beginning to see the application of political concepts to economic questions, via recent discussions of co-determination and quality of work life.[11]

The second issue which a "power and stakes" analysis surfaces is the issue of congruent perceptions among the organization and its stakeholders. There may be differing perceptions of both power and stake depending on one's point of view. An organization may not understand that a particular union has political power, and may treat the union as a "purely economic entity," only to be surprised when the union gets a bill introduced in the legislature to prevent a proposed plant closing. The ABC Company completely misread the power and stake of a group of realtors who were upset over a proposed change in ABC's product. The legislature in the state where ABC operates was composed of a number of realtors, who easily introduced a bill to prevent the proposed product changes. It was only by some tough eleventh hour negotiations that ABC escaped some completely devastating legislation. The DEF Utility could not understand why a consumer advocate group was opposing them on a certain issue which had no economic effect on the group. Finally they spoke to a consumer leader who told them that the only reason that the group was opposing them was that they had not informed the group of the proposed rate change before the case was filed. In short the consumer group perceived that they had a different stake than that perceived by the management of DEF. DEF managers naturally believed that so long as the proposed rate change was in the economic interest of the consumer group and its constituency there would be no problem. The consumer group perceived things differently, that they had a vital role to play as influencer or kibbitzer.

Analyzing stakeholders in terms of the organization's perceptions of their power and stake is not enough. When these perceptions are out of line with the perceptions of the stakeholders, all the brilliant strategic thinking in the world will not work. The congruence problem is a real one in most companies for there are few organizational processes to check the assumptions that managers make every day about their stakeholders. The rational analysis proposed here in terms of stakeholder maps must be tempered by a thorough understanding of the workings of the organization through an analysis of its strategic and operational processes.

The "Process" Level: Environmental Scanning and the Like

Large complex organizations have many processes for accomplishing tasks. From routine applications of procedures and policies to the use of more sophisticated analytical tools, managers invent processes to accomplish routine tasks and to routinize complex tasks. To understand organizations and how they manage stakeholder relationships it is necessary to look at the "Standard Operating Procedures," "the way we do things around here," or the organizational processes that are used to achieve some kind of "fit" with the external environment. While there are many such processes, I shall concentrate on three well known and often used ones which purport to assist managers in the strategic management of corporations: Portfolio Analysis Processes, Strategic Review Processes and Environmental Scanning Processes. Variations of each of these strategic management processes are used in many large complex organizations. Each is usually inadequate in terms of taking complex stakeholder relationships into account and can be enriched by the stakeholder concept.

A good deal of research during the past twenty years has gone into understanding how a corporation can be seen as a set or portfolio of businesses.[12] Discrete business units are easier to manage and factors for success may well be easier to discern at the business level, than at the aggregated level of the corporation as a whole. The idea is to look at this set of businesses as stocks in a portfolio, with selection and nourishment given to winners and the door given to losers. Corporate planners and division managers (or Strategic Business Unit managers) plot the firm's set of businesses on a matrix which arrays an external against an internal dimension. The external dimension is usually labeled "Industry Attractiveness" and is usually measured by the growth rate of the industry under consideration. The internal dimension is usually labeled "Business Strengths" and is usually measured by market share. The corporate managers, after plotting the portfolio of businesses, seek to arrive at a balanced portfolio which maximizes returns (measured by Return on Equity or Earnings per Share or Return on Investment, etc.) and minimizes risks. Managers of particular businesses are then given a strategic mission based on their place in the portfolio and the potential of the business in question.

As an analytical tool and a management process, Portfolio Analysis can easily be out of touch with the stakeholder maps of most firms, as depicted in earlier exhibits. It simply looks at too narrow a range of stakeholders, and measures business performance on too narrow a dimension. While industry growth rate may be influenced by a number of non-marketplace stakeholders, to rely on it solely is to forgo opportunities to influence stakeholders which may determine the future growth rate of the industry. For example, in the auto industry foreign competitors and governments, U.S. government agencies, the Congress, the courts, Ralph Nader and the Center for Auto Safety, environmental groups, the United Auto Workers, etc. all have an influence on future growth rates in the industry. However, if market share is relied upon as the sole criterion to measure competitive strength, we will not necessarily invest resources to deal with all of the groups who can influence future market position. Market share is too broad a measure and an overreliance on it can be detrimental.

To illustrate, consider the fate of JKL Company after spending several million dollars in R&D to develop a new product which would serve as a substitute to a large established market. JKL believed that the product offered high growth potential, and in accordance with accepted theory, introduced the new product before getting approval from a key government agency which closely regulates the industry in which JKL would be competing. The product was later found to be carcinogenic and JKL took a large loss. Market share was not the sole indicator of success for JKL.

Or, consider Proctor and Gamble's experience with Rely tampons. P&G had entered a mature market with a new product and spent heavily to gain market share. When reports linking Rely with toxic shock syndrome surfaced, P&G voluntarily moved Rely from the market rather than jeopardize future products and its corporate reputation. Industry attractiveness was not the sole criterion for the success of Rely. The future attractiveness of the market together with the possibility of tarnishing P&G's excellent reputation, caused them to make a decision that was quite expensive. Even though it cannot be shown that use of Rely caused the disease, the mere possibility of a linkage was enough for P&G to recall the product.

Similarly, Johnson and Johnson acted quickly to recall the entire stock of Extra-Strength Tylenol after several deaths were reported as a result of criminal tampering with bottles of the product. Someone allegedly put cyanide capsules in bottles of the product after it was on retail store shelves. Johnson and Johnson's actions were lauded on "60 Minutes," a show sometimes critical of the actions of large corporations. They have reintroduced the product in "tamper proof" packages, and advertised heavily. Portfolio analysis simply cannot prepare the corporation to deal with issues such as those faced by these companies. Industry or market attractiveness analysis·is not sophisticated enough to yield practical conclusions in areas where economics, social and political forces and new technologies combine.

The point of this critique of portfolio analysis is not that managers must be certain of success before taking action, nor that since market share and industry attractiveness do not yield certainty they must be rejected. But, rather, that *the strategic processes that we use must, as a minimum, raise the right questions*. Portfolio analysis processes are enormously useful in helping managers understand some of the factors for success in a business, yet for the most part they ignore non-marketplace stakeholders who can often, though not always, determine the success or failure of a business.

A related issue is that to view the corporation as a portfolio of businesses to be managed like stocks in an investment portfolio runs the risk that managerial processes will become overly concerned with the financial performance of the corporation.[13] While financial performance is vital to the health of a business, it is but one criterion used by external stakeholders to judge the viability of the corporation over time. When interpreted too narrowly, portfolio processes are asking for more regulation of "externalities," more social critics and ultimately less productive work.

A second strategic management process, made famous by Harold Geneen at ITT, is the strategic review process (Pascale and Athos, 1981; Charan, 1982). The idea of this process is for the top executives in a corporation to periodically meet with division or Strategic Business Unit (SBU) managers in a formal review session. Progress towards the planned goal is reviewed and new strategies are sometimes formulated. Top executives are usually accompanied by staff experts who have unearthed hard questions for the reviewee to answer. These reviews are usually built into the strategic planning cycle and are used as methods of communicating expectations and evaluating both personal and business performance.

The major problem with strategic reviews, in terms of being in synch with the stakeholder map of an organization, is that they do not encourage and reward an external orientation or stakeholder thinking. The emphasis from the point of view of the divisional manager under review is to "look good" to the senior executives who are reviewing performance. The formality of most strategic review processes and the mixing of personal and business evaluation make it difficult for the division manager to pay attention to multiple stakeholder concerns, which may contradict established corporate wisdom about the factors for success in a particular business. The nature of the organizational beast is such that it doesn't like and doesn't reward bad news and can hardly tolerate innovation. (How else can we explain the state of U.S. business?) It is much easier to play "Blame the Stakeholder" after the fact. "What senior executive in his right mind can hold a division manager accountable for a regulation which accounts for lost profits?" While responsibility for profits has been decentralized in most large multi-business firms, the responsibility for managing non-marketplace stakeholders (and some marketplace stakeholders) has not. Corporate Public Relations and Public Affairs are for the most part responsible for ensuring a stable business climate for all the corporation's businesses. Division managers naturally perceive that they have a lack of control over critical stakeholder variables. During one seminar on stakeholder analysis with division managers the predominant response was "Great stuff, too bad my boss isn't here to hear it." Upon giving the same seminar to the top levels in the corporation the predominant response was "Great stuff, too bad our people (the division managers) weren't here to hear it." While too much should not be made of an isolated case, processes like the strategic review process can exacerbate the inability of the organization to ask the right questions.

A third strategic management process which explicitly tries to focus the organization externally is Environmental Scanning.[14] Adopting a metaphor of the radar technology, the idea is for corporate managers to "put up their antennae" and to scan the business horizon for key events, trends, etc. which will affect the business in the future. There are several versions of environmental scanning, each of which has strengths and weakness. Scenario building, whereby several key events and trends are linked together to form a possible future for the organization, is a favorite technique of some corporate planners and a product of several consulting firms. Another technique is trend analysis, whereby key variables, usually demographic and economic are monitored for change. And, futures research, which predicts the future, is yet another technique for helping managers scan the external environment.

While all of these processes are useful, most of them do not yield concrete action steps. It is hard to see how a 10 year forecast can help the SBU manager worried about how to overcome the latest regulation. Consequently, most corporate plans have an environmental scan in the front section of the plan, which states the environmental assumptions on which the plan is based. These assumptions are usually stated in terms of an econometric forecast of macro-economic variables such as inflation, unemployment, interest rates, etc. If the assumptions have not been forgotten by the time the plan produces concrete strategic programs, they surely will be by the time the results are reviewed. Then, no one is held accountable for using the wrong assumptions.

Focusing the strategic management processes in a corporation is a necessary condition for success in the current business environment. However, this external focus must be pervasive, from "front-end" analysis to control processes. Our portfolio analysis, strategic review and environmental scanning processes must get better and more sophisticated, yet this is not the whole story.

Organizational processes serve multiple purposes. One purpose is as a vehicle for communication, and as symbols for what the corporation stands for.[15,16] "The way we do things around here" depicts what activities are necessary for success in the organization. And, the activities necessary for success inside the organization must bear some relationship to the tasks that the external environment requires of the organization if it is to be a successful and ongoing concern. Therefore, if the external environment is a rich multi-stakeholder one, the strategic processes need not be baroque 25-step rigid analytical devices, but rather existing strategic processes which work reasonably well must be enriched with a concern for multiple stakeholders.

For instance, strategic management processes. . . . can easily be enriched by adding "who are our stakeholders" to a concern with corporate mission;

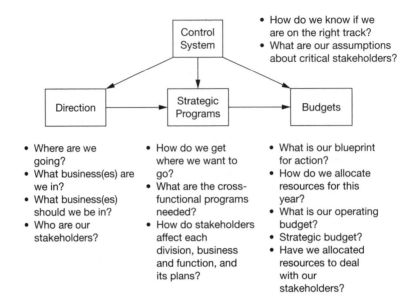

Exhibit 8 Typical strategic planning process schematic

Source: Lorange, 1980

"how do stakeholders affect each division, business and function, and its plans" to the formulation of strategic programs; "have we allocated resources to deal with our stakeholders" in the budget cycle; and "what are our critical assumptions about key stakeholders" to the control process. Exhibit 8 depicts a revised version of Lorange's schema for strategic management processes. Each of these questions which are added will be discussed in more detail in subsequent chapters. The point is that relatively simple ideas can be used to encourage managers to think through the external environments of their businesses, and that such ideas must be added to organizational processes if they are to continue to be useful and to "fit" the stakeholder picture of the firm that is emerging.

The "Transactional" Level: Interacting with Stakeholders

The bottom line for stakeholder management has to be the set of transactions that managers in organizations have with stakeholders. How do the organization and its managers interact with stakeholders? What resources are allocated to interact with which groups? There has been a lot of research in social psychology about the so called "transactional environment" of individuals and organizations, and I shall not attempt to recapitulate that research here.[17] Suffice it to say that the nature of the behavior of organizational members and the nature of the goods and services being exchanged are key ingredients in successful organizational transactions with stakeholders.

Corporations have many daily transactions with stakeholder groups, such as selling things to customers and buying things from suppliers. Other transactions are also fairly ordinary and unexciting, such as paying dividends to stockholders or negotiating a new contract with the union. Yet when we move from this relatively comfortable zone of transactions to dealing with some of the changes that have occurred in traditional marketplace stakeholders and the emergence of new stakeholder groups there is little wonder that transactions break down. The lack of "fit" of an organization's transactions with its processes and its processes with its stakeholder map becomes a real source of discontent.

The XAB Company is an interesting study in how this lack of fit can be dysfunctional. XAB understood its stakeholder map and had some organizational processes to formulate and implement strategies with important non-traditional stakeholder groups. However, XAB sent some top executives out to talk with several of these groups who had little empathy with the causes of these groups. Needless to say the company has made little progress with them. Perhaps the strategy and the processes are inappropriate given the objectives of the company. However, another interpretation is that the transactions between company and stakeholders have not given the strategy and processes a fair test.

New England Telephone adopted a stakeholder approach to implementing a plan for charging for Directory Assistance in Massachusetts (Emshoff and Freeman, 1979). The rational analysis of the stakeholder environment was sound and the planning process used to chart out an implementation scenario was successful. However, its transactions with several key stakeholders, most notably and ironically, its own union, as well as the State Legislature, were not successful. The union got a piece of legislation prohibiting the company's plan passed in the state legislature, and even though the company was successful in persuading the Governor of Massachusetts to veto the legislation, as there was no public support, the state legislature overrode the Governor's veto, at the cost of $20 million to the customers of New England Telephone.

Consumer complaints are an area where there is usually a noticeable breakdown in the organization's Stakeholder Management Capability. Many large corporations simply ignore consumer complaints and dismiss them as that 5 percent of the market which they had rather someone else serve. Not only are there few successful processes for dealing with consumer complaints, but the transactions involved are material for every stand-up comic who ever walked. Nothing is more frustrating to the consumer than being told "sorry, I wish I could help you, but it's company policy to do things this way." One consumer leader commented that being told it was company policy may well finish the incident for the manager, but it begins the incident for the consumer advocate.[18] Several successful companies seem to "overspend" on handling consumer complaints. IBM's commitment to service, P&G's consumer complaint department and the Sears philosophy of taking merchandising back with no questions asked, yield valuable lessons in understanding the nature of transactions with customers. These companies act as if consumer complaints yield an opportunity for understanding customer needs which ultimately translates into a good bottom line and satisfied stakeholders.

Other sets of transactions, which often get out of line with process and rational analysis, include the firm's relationships with the media, shareholder meetings, meetings with financial analysts, encounters with government officials and day to day interactions with employees and unions.

Many managers actively perspire during "60 Minutes" in fear of being before the sharp tongues of the reporters and the skilful editing of the news show producers. Some organizations have become proactive and given their senior executives special training on "How to Meet the Press."

Shareholder meetings have become rituals for most corporations, except for the occasional meaningful proxy fight à la Rockwell-SCM. Rather than carry out meaningful transactions with shareholders in accordance with a clearly thought out strategy and process, executives now treat stockholders to lunch and speeches (with the stockholders' money) and a round of abuse from corporate critics who have bought one share of stock in order to be heard.

Meetings with financial analysts are another opportunity for transactions which can be made consistent with a firm's strategy and processes. Many executives understand that U.S. firms have underinvested in modern plant and equipment relative to foreign competition, and that they have lost sight of the marketing prowess of some of their competitors. How U.S. corporations can regain their competitive edge is a source of much debate in managerial and academic circles. Yet to regain competitive position will be neither easy nor inexpensive. Many U.S. firms will have to "take a hit on earnings" for several years in a row to be truly competitive. Most financial analysts are by their nature short-term focused. If executives use meetings with analysts to tout earnings per share, which may be inflated in real terms, then analysts will continue to expect short-term results. Talk of an investment strategy to regain competitive edge will be just talk. The transactions which executives make with analysts must square with the strategy of the organization regardless of the pain. By taking a leadership position in this area perhaps the thoughtful company can change the expectations of financial analysts. Of course, there is a vicious "chicken–egg" cycle here, that illustrates the dilemma of attempting to change stakeholder expectations. If we are measured on short-term performance results, and such a system is reinforced by expectations from the financial community, then to break the cycle involves additional pain. If strategic investments really are necessary then we must bite the bullet, and work to change the expectations of analysts, stockholders, and even board members, even at substantial personal risk.

Transactions with government officials often take place under adversarial conditions. Because government is a source of trouble for many companies, their transactions with government show their discontent. One company is reported to have rented a truck and dumped the requested documentation on the doorstep of the government agency which requested it. When stakeholder relationships are viewed on both sides as adversarial it is a small wonder that anyone ever changes. The Business Roundtable, as a transactional organization for large businesses with the government, published a study decrying the cost of regulation and calling for regulatory reform. While it is clear that the regulatory process has gotten out of control in some areas, a more helpful transaction would have been to try and gain some formal input into the regulatory process. To gain such input would mean that a firm's transactions with the government could be made congruent with its organizational processes, and the firm could formulate strategies for influencing government in a positive way, breaking down the adversarial barriers of so many years and so many hard-fought battles.

Perhaps the most fruitful area for transactional analysis is with the employee stakeholder group. One large company announced that it was committing to "Quality of Work Life," and set up national and local committees to form a partnership with its employees for the long term. However, shortly thereafter the company announced that many employees were in fact "surplus," and offered incentive programs for early retirement. Its transactions were simply inconsistent with its stated future direction for this stakeholder group. Much has been written lately about Japan and Theory Z (Ouchi, 1981), and co-determination in Europe. However, before U.S. managers launch into different directions with employees, perhaps we should understand whether our current managerial principles can work. When processes are set up to treat employees one way, no matter how well-meaning or "humanistic" they may be, and day-to-day transactions treat them another, it is not lack of theory that is the problem. The real importance of the suggestion box in Japan, and Quality Circles that work, is the consistent message that they send to employees, that their ideas have some impact on the firm.

If corporate managers ignore certain stakeholder groups at the rational and process level, then there is little to be done at the transactional level. Encounters between corporation and stakeholder will be on the one hand brief, episodic and hostile, and on the other hand non-existent, if another firm can supply their needs. Successful transactions with stakeholders are built on understanding the "legitimacy" of the stakeholder and having processes to routinely surface their concerns. However the transactions themselves, must be executed by managers who understand the "currencies" in which the stakeholders are paid. There is simply no substitute for thinking through how a particular individual can "win" and how the organization can "win" at the same time.

Clearly, there must be some "fit" among the elements of an organization's Stakeholder Management Capability – defined as its understanding or conceptual map of its stakeholders, the processes for dealing with these stakeholders, and the transactions which it uses to carry out the achievement

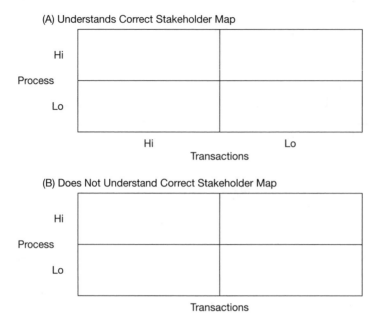

Exhibit 9 Stakeholder management capability = f (stakeholder map, organizational process, stakeholder transactions)

of organization purpose with stakeholders. Exhibit 9 illustrates how some criteria might be used to measure the Stakeholder Management Capability of an organization. Whether an organization falls into the "Understands Correct Stakeholder Map" or "Does Not Understand Correct Stakeholder Map" is a relatively easy test. If, over time, an organization is continually surprised and continually plays "Blame the Stakeholder" then something is amiss. Whether an organization's processes and transactions are in line with that stakeholder map is a more difficult problem, for as I have shown, we do not have an adequate understanding as to what processes are appropriate for the multitude of stakeholders which firms now have. I shall return to the issue of defining a firm's Stakeholder Management Capability, by way of suggesting several processes to be used to understand and manage stakeholder relationships. However, before attempting such a task it is necessary to be more explicit about the underlying philosophy which accompanies the Stakeholder Management model. How can the multitude of charts, graphs, and maps be integrated into the current managerial wisdom of running a successful business?

The Stakeholder Philosophy: A Plea for Voluntarism

While the temptation to play "Blame the Stakeholder" is a strong one, the major problem facing U.S. managers is really not an external one, but an internal one. Pogo's saying is once again applicable, "we have met the enemy and he is us." The challenge for us is to reorient our thinking and our managerial processes externally, in order to be responsive to stakeholders. There are three levels of analysis which must be consistent, rational, process and transactional. However, there are several common themes, or philosophical propositions, which can serve as "intellectual glue" to hold these ideas together. Such a philosophy of management is necessary if we are to undertake the rather considerable task of regaining managerial competence in the new business environment, without losing even more of our competitive position in the marketplace. We must learn to use our current knowledge and skill-base to respond quickly to the "stakeholder challenge" and to create some initial "win–win" situations, if meaningful change is to occur.

Such a philosophy of management must be based on the idea of voluntarism, if it is to be implemented in U.S. based companies. Not only is voluntarism the only philosophy which is consistent with our social fabric, but the costs of other approaches are simply too high. Voluntarism means that an organization must on its own will undertake to satisfy its key stakeholders. A situation where a solution to a stakeholder problem is imposed by a government agency or the courts must be seen as a managerial failure. Similarly, a situation where Firm A satisfies the needs of consumer advocates, government agency, etc. better than Firm B, must be seen as a competitive loss by Firm B. The driving force of an organization becomes, under a voluntarism philosophy of management, to satisfy the needs of as many stakeholders as possible.

Consider the current "Stakeholder Dilemma" in which many firms find themselves. The following story is a simplified illustration based on several real situations.

An Activist Group (AG) is worried about some aspect of the ABC Company's Product Y. AG believes that if ABC is allowed to continue to produce and sell the product as it now exists, harm will be done to the public and to some of AG's constituents. AG is a credible group in some circles, especially with a key government agency and the national media. While it has not always been successful in getting large corporations to be responsive to its claims, it has had some successes. AG does not have a large reservoir of resources, nevertheless, it can devote adequate resources to the pursual of this current case. ABC believes that there is nothing wrong with its product, and that they should be allowed to continue to sell it. ABC is a veteran of several campaigns against its products, and it has won some and lost some in the past, but each has been expensive to wage.

Let us assume that ABC has two major strategic responses. It can *Negotiate* with AG to reach a mutually agreeable solution with respect to Product Y by listening to the concerns of the leaders of AG, explaining the position of ABC on Product Y, exploring solutions to AG's concerns, voluntarily agreeing how AG and ABC are to proceed on this and future areas of mutual concern, involving other interested parties in the discussions, etc.

Or, it can *Play Hard Ball*, by ignoring AG's concern, perhaps disparaging AG and the cause that it stands for, respond when AG files a formal complaint, try to delay AG through countersuits, etc.

Of course, AG also has two very similar strategies. It can *Negotiate* with ABC by attending meetings with ABC managers and presenting the concerns of AG, attempting to understand the needs of other interested parties in Product Y, working with ABC to find a mutually acceptable solution, or a mutually acceptable process for finding a solution to the issue in a timely fashion, etc. AG can also *Play Hard Ball* by trying to make a splash in the media, bringing formal action in the Courts against ABC, complaining to government agencies which regulate ABC, tying ABC up on other issues unrelated to Product Y, introducing legislation prohibiting the sale of Product Y, etc.

Clearly if both parties negotiate, then an agreement which both find mutually satisfactory is the result.[19] Both parties may have to compromise, or at least be willing to compromise, if negotiation is to proceed in good faith, else *Negotiate* is an identical strategy to *Play Hard Ball*. If ABC negotiates and AG decides to play hard ball (perhaps after the first session, AG decides to double cross ABC), then ABC will be embarrassed and vulnerable to AG's formal challenges by having admitted that there may be some legitimacy to AG's claims about Product Y. AG members will have the feeling of having "beaten" ABC and may well be successful in their challenge to Product Y. Managers in ABC will not trust AG, and will respond in a "win–lose" way to AG's initiatives. On the other hand if AG tries to negotiate and ABC responds by playing hard ball, the same sorts of feelings arise for AG members as in the case where AG double-crossed ABC. If both parties Play Hard Ball, then the outcome is a long drawn out process with a solution imposed by the courts, government agencies and legislation – plus the cost of doing battle.

The most preferred outcome for ABC, in a cold and calculating sense, is for AG to negotiate and for ABC to double cross, since ABC then "beats" AG. The most preferred outcome for AG is for ABC to negotiate and for AG to double cross, thereby "beating" ABC. Yet when each plays its preferred strategy, *Play Hard Ball*, the result is far inferior to the result of playing the *Negotiate* strategy. In a real sense, by following the dictates of self-interest, both lose.

Exhibit 10 sets out the form of this stakeholder problem. Of course, it is identical in form with the so called "Prisoners' Dilemma Game" which illustrates the difficulty of achieving cooperative solutions under communication constraints.[20] In the classical form of the game, two suspects to a crime (which they actually committed) are caught, and interrogated separately. Each is told that if they confess a light sentence will be passed depending on whether or not the other confesses. If one prisoner turns state's evidence and the other does not, the book is thrown at the non-confessing prisoner. If both confess, then each gets a medium-length sentence, while if neither confess they are convicted of a much lesser charge. Neither confessing yields a preferred outcome to both confessing, but self-interest dictates confessing. The payoff structure is identical to Exhibit 10 with "Negotiate" replacing "Don't Confess" and "Play Hard Ball" replacing "Confess." If the prisoners could communicate they would form an agreement not to confess, or agree to get revenge if the other double-crossed. The lack of communication and the ability to form binding agreements dooms the prisoners to a heavy sentence.

The striking fact about the Stakeholder Dilemma version of this game is that there are absolutely no such communication constraints upon ABC and AG, and there are no constraints which prevent binding agreements. The managerial processes of both groups simply do not include considering communication and responsiveness as normal managerial activities. The status quo imposes similar Prisoners' Dilemma-like constraints on ABC and AG.

The "Stakeholder Dilemma" game is one which is played out in some form in many organizations.[21] The only way out is to *voluntarily* adopt a posture of negotiation with stakeholder groups. Why negotiate voluntarily? Because, there is no other way to keep from having a solution imposed upon the organization from outside. And, to accept such an imposition of a solution to a problem is to give up the managerial role. Additionally, there seems to be no reason to pay the enforcement costs of adversarial proceedings. How

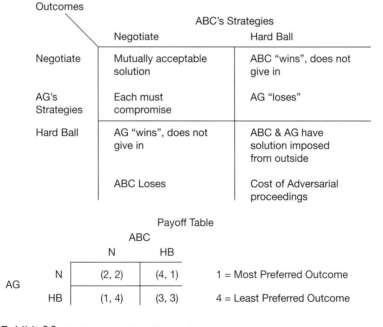

Exhibit 10 The 'stakeholder dilemma' game

many managers, lawyers and other professionals in large organizations spend most of their time in some sort of adversarial proceedings with stakeholders? Could not these resources be put to work more productively?

Our managerial processes must make managers "Free to Cooperate," rather than forcing them to play the Stakeholder Dilemma Game. Negotiation must become accepted practice, rather than conflict escalation through formal channels. The "try it, fix it, do it" mentality (Peters and Waterman, 1982) which many companies have used successfully with customers, must be applied to other stakeholder groups. This implies that voluntarism as a basic managerial value must permeate the organization which is successful in managing its relationships with multiple stakeholders.

This philosophy of voluntarism can be summarized in several pre-scriptive propositions which build on successful managerial theories and techniques. These propositions should be taken as tentative statements of a theory which needs much more elaboration, but which are hopefully practical suggestions.

Organizations with high Stakeholder Management Capability design and implement communication processes with multiple stakeholders.

An example of a communication process is the recent formation by some utilities, of Consumer Advisory Panels, whereby the company brings issues which are usually settled in the formal regulatory process to the attention of leaders of consumer advocate groups well in advance of actually filing the rate case. Company executives and consumer leaders can negotiate on the issues of mutual concern and avoid the costly adversarial proceedings of the rate case on a number of issues.

Organizations with high Stakeholder Management Capability explicitly negotiate with stakeholders on critical issues and seek voluntary agreements.

An example of explicit negotiation is AT&T's convening an industry-wide conference of telecommunications executives, academics and consumer leaders over the issue of how to reprice local telephone service to bring it in line with its true costs. The outcomes of such a meeting are multiple and not all have been successful. However, the tenor of negotiation was set, and at least some of the local telephone companies have begun to explicitly follow up and negotiate on issues before the rate case proceedings.

Organizations with high Stakeholder Management Capability generalize the marketing approach to serve multiple stakeholders. Specifically, they overspend on understanding stakeholder needs, use marketing techniques to segment stakeholders to provide a better understanding of their individual needs and use marketing research tools to understand, viz., the multi-attribute nature of most stakeholder groups.

We might define "overspending" as paying extra attention, beyond that warranted by considerations of efficiency, to those groups who are critical for the long term success of the firm. Overspending on stakeholders without whose support the company would fail can make sense in a number of instances. For instance P&G overspends on customers, interviewing several thousand customers a year. AT&T overspends on the attention it pays to the regulatory process, which was for a long time, its major source of revenue. Oil companies should, likewise, consider adopting a conscious policy of overspending on OPEC and government and stakeholder who can convey a positive image to the public. Chemical companies have not overspent on environmentalists, for the most part, with the results being onerous regulations and reputations as "spoilers of the environment."

Organizations with high Stakeholder Management Capability integrate boundary spanners into the strategic formulation processes in the organization.

Many organizations have public relations and public affairs managers who have a good working knowledge of stakeholder concerns, and marketing and production managers who have expertise in the needs of customers and suppliers. However, these managers are not always a part of the strategic planning process. Hence, their expertise is lost. The assumption is that those managers who are rewarded to be sensitive to stakeholder needs are in the best position to represent their interests inside the organization. For this representation to occur successfully, those boundary spanners must have some credibility and some meaningful role to play in the organizational processes.

Organizations with high Stakeholder Management Capability are proactive. They anticipate stakeholder concerns and try to influence the stakeholder environment.

The micro-computer industry is full of firms who practice anticipation as a way of life. These firms, some of them quite small, spend resource trying to "guess" what will best serve the customer in the future and where the market will be. Similarly, large computer manufacturers, should be "guessing" that issues such as "privacy" and "individual freedom" and "computer literacy" will be major concerns as we move to technologies where "1984" is a distinct possibility. Several utilities try to anticipate the concerns of intervenors in their rate cases, and actively seek out those groups which will be critical to try and influence their views.

Organizations with high Stakeholder Management Capability allocate resources in a manner consistent with stakeholder concerns.

Emshoff (1980) tells of analyzing the stakeholders in a large international firm and ranking the stakeholders in order of importance. A rough check was also made of how the firm's resources were allocated to deal with those groups who would be most important in the future. The results of his investigation were that almost no resources were being allocated to deal with those groups felt to be absolutely critical to the future success of the company. Many executives are not reticent to play "Blame the Stakeholder," yet are not willing to devote resources to changing a particular stakeholder's point of view.

> *Managers in organizations with high Stakeholder Management Capability think in "stakeholder-serving" terms.*

Just as many successful companies think in terms of "how to serve the customer" or "how to serve the employees," it is possible to generalize this philosophy to "how to serve my stakeholders." The "reason for being" for most organizations is that they serve some need in their external environment. When an organization loses its sense of purpose and mission, when it focuses itself internally on the needs of its managers, it is in danger of becoming irrelevant. Someone else (if competition is possible) will serve the environmental need better. The more we can begin to think in terms of how to better serve stakeholders, the more likely we will be to survive and prosper over time.

Summary

The purpose of this chapter has been to explicate the stakeholder management framework and philosophy in general terms. I have shown that the three levels of analysis, rational, process and transactional must be consistent if the stakeholder concept is to make a difference in the way that organizations are managed. I have offered a brief sketch of the principles of voluntarism which I believe must go hand in hand with the application of the stakeholder concept to strategic management processes.

Notes

1   The ideas presented in this chapter form part of a paper, "Managing Stakeholders: One Key to Successful Adaptation", presented to the Academy of Management National Meeting in August 1982. I wish to thank the participants in the symposium on managing adaptation, and its chairperson, Professor Bala Chakravarthy, for many helpful comments. In addition, several Faculty members at the University of Pittsburgh's Graduate School of Management and Rutgers University's Department of Management have made helpful comments. In particular Barry Mitnick and Aubrey Mendelow have been encouraging over the past year.

2   See Schendel and Hofer (1979) for a collection of essays that catalog the development of strategic management. Freeman (1983) is an overview of how the stakeholder concept fits into the development of strategic management theory, as well as a conceptual history of the term, "stakeholder."

3   My use of "rational," "process" and "transactional" parallels Graham Allison's (1971) three levels of organizational analysis. However, the three levels are not mutually exclusive as is often interpreted from Allison's account. Each level of analysis offers a different "lens" for viewing the organization and offers different kinds of explanation for some underlying phenomena broadly called "organization behavior." While the explanations at each level need not be identical, they do need to be consistent. Hence, the concept of "fit" among the three levels. The application of this three-leveled conceptual scheme is not unique to the stakeholder concept, as it is conceivable that we could define the process and transactional levels to complement a "portfolio approach" to strategic management.

4   Chakravarthy (1981) defines a similar concept of the adaptive capabilities of an organization using "management capability" and "organization capability."

5   For instance, as in a clinical case study, viz., Emshoff and Freeman's (1981) analysis of the brewing industry around the issue of beverage container legislation or an in-depth historical study as per Miles (1982) of tobacco companies.

6   The point here is that any theory must explicitly define the range of entities over which the propositions in the theory range. Sometimes it is convenient to speak of "stakeholders" as referring to categories, or sets, of specific groups. But, I insist that, strictly speaking, it is specific groups and individuals which are real, and hence, which can be strictly said to "hold stakes." For a philosophical treatment of the rather nominalistic position taken here see Nelson Goodman (1955).

7   The literature on interorganizational relations is quite enormous and is rich in insights for strategic management. Evan (1976), Negandhi (1975), Nystrom and Starbuck (1981) are excellent collections of articles, each of which contains review articles which summarize the state of the art.

8   See Miles' (1982) analysis of the tobacco industry, and Wilson (1981) for analyses of coalitions among interest groups.

9   For a discussion of this grid in the context of corporate governance see Freeman and Reed (1983).

10   The approach to "power" outlined here is quite simplistic, and should be viewed as illustrative rather than definitive. Pfeffer (1981) is suggestive of a more comprehensive analysis of the concept which could be applied to the "power and stakes" grid.

11   For an interesting distinction between economic and political explanations see the work of Hirschman (1970; 1981).

12   For a more complete discussion of portfolio theory see Abell (1980), Rothschild (1976), Lorange (1980), and the literature referenced in these works.

13   The critique of portfolio theory surfaced here is quite general in that it applies equally well to "misuses" of other processes. The point is that the processes must be capable of "fitting" with the other levels of analysis. They must describe the world as it is, and must prescribe transactions that are consistent with such a description.

14   See Schendel and Hofer (1979) for several review articles on the state of the art in environmental scanning.

15   Lorange (1980) explores the communications aspects of strategic management, and recommends a 3×3 matrix to diagram such processes.

16   See Freeman (1983) for an analysis of "what do we stand for" and the relationship of enterprise-level strategy to the stakeholder concept and managerial values.

17   Emery and Trist (1965), Pfeffer and Salancik (1978) and many others have looked at the transactional level of organizations. Van de Ven, Emmett and Koenig (1975) describe several different models of transactions.

18   Interview with Professor Currin Shields, University of Arizona, and past President of the Conference of Consumer Organizations, a national consortium of local consumer advocate organizations.

19   The structure of the payoffs of the game outlined here presupposes that the issue is vague enough for there not to be a "clearly optimal" solution, but that a solution which is mutually acceptable is possible, and further that this mutually acceptable

solution is preferable by both parties to a solution which is imposed by external parties, such as government.

20   There is a vast literature on the Prisoners' Dilemma, however, a clear discussion of the game can be found in Luce and Raiffa (1957). The game described here is similar to the plight of wheat farmers that is taught in every introductory economics class and chronicled by Garrett Hardin in the "Tragedy of the Commons."

21   I am not claiming that every game that a corporation plays with stakeholders is a Prisoners' Dilemma game, but only that some interactions are Prisoners' Dilemmas. The use of game theory in strategic management, as an explanatory tool, is a long-neglected research issue. McDonald (1977) is one source. Recent work in applying game theory at the conceptual level can be found in Brams (1981) and Muzzio (1982). Both of these works by political scientists yield interesting insights into the workings of individuals in organizations.

References

Abell, D. (1980) *Defining the Business*, Englewood Cliffs: Prentice Hall, Inc.

Allison, G. (1971) *Essence of Decision*, Boston: Little Brown.

Brams, S. (1981) *Biblical Games*, Cambridge: MIT Press.

Chakravarthy, B. (1981) *Managing Coal*, Albany: SUNY Press.

Charan, R. (1982) 'The Strategic Review Process', *The Journal of Business Strategy* 2(4): 50–60.

Dill, W. (1975) 'Public Participation in Corporate Planning: Strategic Management in a Kibitzer's World', *Long Range Planning* 8(1): 57–63.

Emery, F. and Trist, E. (1965) 'The Causal Texture of Organizational Environments', *Human Relations* 18: 21–31.

Emshoff, J. (1980) *Managerial Breakthroughs*, New York: AMACOM.

Emshoff, J. and Freeman, E. (1979) 'Who's Butting Into Your Business', *The Wharton Magazine* 1: 44–48, 58–59.

Emshoff, J. and Freeman, E. (1981) 'Stakeholder Management: A Case Study of the U.S. Brewers and the Container Issue', *Applications of Management Science*, Volume 1, 57–90.

Evan, W. (1966) 'The Organization Set: Toward a Theory of Inter-Organizational Relations', In Thompson, J. (ed.) *Approaches to Organizational Design*, Pittsburgh: University of Pittsburgh Press, pp. 175–190; also in W. Evan, (1976) *Organization Theory: Structures, Systems, and Environments*, New York: John Wiley & Sons.

Evan, W. (1976) *Organization Theory: Structures, Systems, and Environments*, New York: John Wiley & Sons.

Freeman, R. (1983) 'Strategic Management: A Stakeholder Approach', in R. Lamb (ed.) *Advances in Strategic Management*, Vol. 1, Greenwich: JAI Press, pp. 31–60.

Freeman, R. and Reed, D. (1983) 'Stockholders and Stakeholders: A New Perspective on Corporate Governance', in C. Huizinga (ed.) *Corporate Governance: A Definitive Exploration of the Issues*, Los Angeles: University Press.

Goodman, N. (1955) *Fact, Fiction, and Forecast*, New York: Bobbs Merrill Co.

Hirschman, A. (1970) *Exit, Voice and Loyalty*, Cambridge, MA: Harvard University Press.

Hirschman, A. (1981) *Essays in Trespassing*, Cambridge: Cambridge University Press.

Lorange, P. (1980) *Corporate Planning: An Executive Viewpoint*, Englewood Cliffs: Prentice Hall, Inc.

Luce, D. and Raiffa, H. (1957) *Games and Decisions*, New York: John Wiley & Sons.

McDonald, J. (1977) *The Game of Business*, New York: Anchor Press.

MacMillan, I. (1978) *Strategy Formulation: Political Concepts*, St Paul: West Publishing Co.

Merton, R. (1957) *Social Theory and Social Structure*, Glencoe: The Free Press.

Miles, R. (1982) *Coffin Nails and Corporate Strategies*, Englewood Cliffs: Prentice Hall Inc.

Muzzio, D. (1982) *Watergate Games*, New York: New York University Press.

Negandhi, A. (ed.) (1975) *Interorganization Theory*, Canton: The Kent State University Press.

Nystrom, P. and Starbuck, W. (eds) (1981) *Handbook of Organizational Design*, Volumes 1 and 2 New York: Oxford University Press.

Ouchi, W. (1981) *Theory Z*, Reading: Addison Wesley.

Pascale, R. and Athos, A. (1981) *The Art of Japanese Management*, New York: Simon & Schuster.

Peters, T. and Waterman, R. (1982) *Searching for Excellence*, New York: Harper & Row.

Pfeffer, J. (1981) *Power in Organizations*, Marshfield: Pitman Publishing Inc.

Pfeffer, J. and Salancik, G. (1978) *The External Control of Organizations*, New York: Harper & Row.

Rothschild, W. (1976) *Putting It All Together*, New York: AMACOM.

Schendel, D. and Hofer, C. (eds) (1979) *Strategic Management: A New View of Business Policy and Planning*, Boston: Little, Brown.

Van de Ven, A., Emmett, D. and Koenig, R. (1975) 'Frameworks for Interorganizational Analysis', in A. Negandhi, *Interorganization Theory*, pp. 19–38, Canton: The Kent State University Press.

Wilson, G. (1981) *Interest Groups in the United States*, New York: Oxford University Press.

THE STAKEHOLDER THEORY OF THE CORPORATION: CONCEPTS, EVIDENCE, AND IMPLICATIONS

Thomas Donaldson and Lee Preston

The idea that corporations have *stakeholders* has now become commonplace in the management literature, both academic and professional. Since the publication of Freeman's landmark book, *Strategic Management: A Stakeholder Approach* (1984), about a dozen books and more than 100 articles with primary emphasis on the stakeholder concept have appeared. (Significant recent examples include books by Alkhafaji, 1989; Anderson, 1989; and Brummer, 1991; and articles by Brenner & Cochran, 1991; Clarkson, 1991; Goodpaster, 1991; Hill & Jones, 1992; and Wood, 1991a,b; plus numerous papers by Freeman and various collaborators, individually cited.) *Stakeholder management* is the central theme of at least one important recent business and society text (Carroll, 1989), and a diagram purporting to represent the *stakeholder model* has become a standard element of "Introduction to Management" lectures and writings.

Unfortunately, anyone looking into this large and evolving literature with a critical eye will observe that the concepts *stakeholder*, *stakeholder model*, *stakeholder management*, and *stakeholder theory* are explained and used by various authors in very different ways and supported (or critiqued) with diverse and often contradictory evidence and arguments. Moreover, this diversity and its implications are rarely discussed – and possibly not even recognized. (The blurred character of the stakeholder concept is also emphasized by Brummer, 1991.) The purpose of this article is to point out some of the more important distinctions, problems, and implications associated with the stakeholder concept, as well as to clarify and justify its essential content and significance.

In the following section we contrast the stakeholder model of the corporation with the conventional input–output model of the firm and summarize our central thesis. We next present the three aspects of stakeholder theory – descriptive/empirical, instrumental, and normative – found in the literature and clarify the critical differences among them. We then raise the issue of justification: Why would anyone accept the stakeholder theory over alternative conceptions of the corporation? In subsequent sections, we present and evaluate the underlying evidence and arguments justifying the theory from the perspective of descriptive, instrumental, and normative justifications. We conclude that the three approaches to stakeholder theory, although quite different, are mutually supportive and that the *normative* base serves as the critical underpinning for the theory in all its forms.

The Central Theses

We summarize our central theses here:

> *Thesis 1: The stakeholder theory is unarguably **descriptive**.* It presents a model describing what the corporation is. It describes the corporation as a constellation of cooperative and competitive interests possessing intrinsic value. Aspects of this model may be tested for descriptive accuracy: Is this model more descriptively accurate than

The development of this article benefited greatly from discussions held at the Conference on Stakeholder Theory at the University of Toronto, May 1993, and from the specific comments of many people, including Professors Aupperle, Carroll, Clarkson, Halal, Freeman, Jones, and Sethi.

rival models? Moreover, do observers and participants, in fact, see the corporation this way? The model can also serve as a framework for testing any empirical claims, including instrumental predictions, relevant to the stakeholder concept (but not for testing the concept's normative base).

Thesis 2: The stakeholder theory is also **instrumental**. It establishes a framework for examining the connections, if any, between the practice of stakeholder management and the achievement of various corporate performance goals. The principal focus of interest here has been the proposition that corporations practicing stakeholder management will, other things being equal, be relatively successful in conventional performance terms (profitability, stability, growth, etc.).

Thesis 3: Although Theses 1 and 2 are significant aspects of the stakeholder theory, its fundamental basis is **normative** *and involves acceptance of the following ideas:*

(a) Stakeholders are persons or groups with legitimate interests in procedural and/or substantive aspects of corporate activity. Stakeholders are identified by *their* interests in the corporation, whether the corporation has any corresponding functional interest in *them*.

(b) The interests of all stakeholders are of *intrinsic value*. That is, each group of stakeholders merits consideration for its own sake and not merely because of its ability to further the interests of some other group, such as the shareowners.

Thesis 4: The stakeholder theory is **managerial** *in the broad sense of that term. It does not simply describe existing situations or predict cause–effect relationships; it also recommends attitudes, structures, and practices that, taken together, constitute stakeholder management. Stakeholder management requires, as its key attribute, simultaneous attention to the legitimate interests of all appropriate stakeholders, both in the establishment of organizational structures and general policies and in case-by-case decision making. This requirement holds for anyone managing or affecting corporate policies, including not only professional managers, but shareowners, the government, and others. Stakeholder theory does not necessarily presume that managers are the only rightful locus of corporate control and governance. Nor does the requirement of simultaneous attention to stakeholder interests resolve the long-standing problem of identifying stakeholders and evaluating their legitimate "stakes" in the corporation. The theory does not imply that all stakeholders* (however they may be identified) should be equally involved in all processes and decisions.

The distinction between a stakeholder conception of the corporation and a conventional input–output perspective is highlighted by the contrasting models displayed in Figures 1 and 2. In Figure 1, investors, employees, and suppliers are depicted as contributing inputs, which the "black box" of the firm transforms into outputs for the benefit of customers. To be sure, each contributor of inputs expects to receive appropriate compensation, but the liberal economics, or "Adam Smith" interpretation, of this model in long-run equilibrium is that input contributors, at the margin, receive only "normal" or "market competitive" benefits (i.e., the benefits that they would obtain from some alternative use of their resources and time). Individual contributors who are particularly advantaged, such as possessors of scarce locations or skills, will, of course, receive "rents," but the rewards of the marginal contributors will only be "normal." As a result of competition throughout the system, the bulk of the benefits will go to the customers. (There is, of course, a Marxist–capitalist version of this model in which both the consumer and the investor arrows are reversed, and the object of the game is merely to produce benefits for the investors. This interpretation now seems to be confined almost exclusively to the field of finance.) The stakeholder model (Figure 2) contrasts explicitly with the input–output model in all its variations. Stakeholder analysts argue that *all* persons or groups with legitimate interests participating in an enterprise do so to obtain benefits and that there is no prima facie priority of one set of interests and benefits over another. Hence, the arrows between the firm and its stakeholder constituents run in both directions. All stakeholder relationships are depicted in the same size and shape and are equidistant from the "black box" of the firm in the center. The distinctive features of this conception, as contrasted with conventional input–output conceptions, will become apparent as our analysis proceeds.

This summary of the stakeholder theory and our discussion throughout this article refer specifically to the theory's application to the investor-owned corporation. Although stakeholder concepts have been applied in other settings (e.g., government agencies and social programs), these situations are fundamentally different, and simultaneous discussion of a variety of possible stakeholder relationships leads, in our view, to confusion rather than clarification. The critical corporate stakeholder issues, both in theory and in practice, involve evidentiary considerations and conceptual issues (e.g., the meaning of property rights) unique to the corporate setting.

It is also worth noting at the outset that the extent to which the stakeholder theory is understood to represent a controversial or challenging approach to conventional views varies greatly among market capitalist economies. These differences are highlighted in a recent issue of *The Economist* (1993: 52):

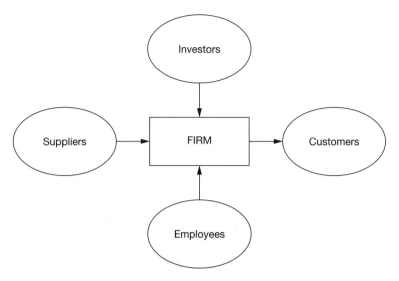

Figure 1 Contrasting models of the corporation: input–output model

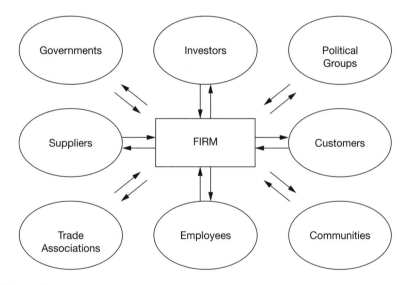

Figure 2 Contrasting models of the corporation: the stakeholder model

In America, for instance, shareholders have a comparatively big say in the running of the enterprises they own; workers . . . have much less influence. In many European countries, shareholders have less say and workers more . . . [I]n Japan . . . managers have been left alone to run their companies as they see fit – namely for the benefit of employees and of allied companies, as much as for the share-holders.

Alternative Aspects of Stakeholder Theory:
Descriptive/Empirical, Instrumental, and Normative

One of the central problems in the evolution of stakeholder theory has been confusion about its nature and purpose. For example, stakeholder theory has been used, either explicitly or implicitly, for descriptive purposes. Brenner and Cochran (1991: 452) offered a "stakeholder theory of the firm" for "two purposes: to describe how organizations operate and to help predict organizational behavior." They contrasted this "theory," which they developed only in outline form, with other "theories of the firm," but they did not ask whether the various theories cited have comparable purposes.

In fact, different theories have different purposes and therefore different validity criteria and different implications. For example, according to Cyert and March (1963), the neoclassical theory of the firm attempts to explain the economic principles governing production, investment, and pricing decisions of established firms operating in competitive markets. In contrast, their behavioral theory of the firm attempts to explain the process of decision making in the modern firm in terms of goals, expectations, and choice-making procedures. Aoki's (1984) cooperative game theory of the firm attempts to explain internal governance, particularly the balance between owners' and workers' interests. In contrast to all of these contributions, transaction cost theory attempts to explain why firms exist (i.e., why economic activities are coordinated through formal organizations rather than simply through market contacts) (Coase, 1937; Williamson & Winter, 1991). (Although all of these theories are put forward as "positive" or "scientific" conceptions, there is a tendency for them to be used for normative purposes as well.)

The stakeholder theory differs from these and other "theories of the firm" in fundamental ways. The stakeholder theory is intended both to explain and to guide the structure and operation of the established corporation (the "going concern" in John R. Commons' famous phrase). Toward that end it views the corporation as an organizational entity through which numerous and diverse participants accomplish multiple, and not always entirely congruent, purposes. The stakeholder theory is general and comprehensive, but it is not empty; it goes well beyond the descriptive observation that "organizations have stakeholders." Unfortunately, much of what passes for stakeholder theory in the literature is implicit rather than explicit, which is one reason why diverse and sometimes confusing uses of the stakeholder concept have not attracted more attention.

The stakeholder theory can be, and has been, presented and used in a number of ways that are quite distinct and involve very different methodologies, types of evidence, and criteria of appraisal. Three types of uses are critical to our analysis.

Descriptive/empirical

The theory is used to describe, and sometimes to explain, specific corporate characteristics and behaviors. For example, stakeholder theory has been used to describe (a) the nature of the firm (Brenner & Cochran, 1991), (b) the way managers think about managing (Brenner & Molander, 1977), (c) how board members think about the interests of corporate constituencies (Wang & Dewhirst, 1992), and (d) how some corporations are actually managed (Clarkson, 1991; Halal, 1990; Kreiner & Bhambri, 1991).

Instrumental

The theory, in conjunction with descriptive/empirical data where available, is used to identify the connections, or lack of connections, between stakeholder management and the achievement of traditional corporate objectives (e.g., profitability, growth). Many recent instrumental studies of corporate social responsibility, all of which make explicit or implicit reference to stakeholder perspectives, use conventional statistical methodologies (Aupperle, Carroll, & Hatfield, 1985; Barton, Hill, & Sundaram, 1989; Cochran & Wood, 1984; Cornell & Shapiro, 1987; McGuire, Sundgren & Schneeweis, 1988; Preston & Sapienza, 1990; Preston, Sapienza & Miller, 1991). Other studies are based on direct observation and interviews (Kotter & Heskett, 1992; O'Toole, 1985; see also, O'Toole, 1991). Whatever their methodologies, these studies have tended to generate "implications" suggesting that adherence to stakeholder principles and practices achieves conventional corporate performance objectives as well or better than rival approaches. Kotter and Heskett (1992) specifically observed that such highly successful companies as Hewlett-Packard, Wal-Mart, and Dayton Hudson – although very diverse in other ways – share a stakeholder perspective. Kotter and Heskett (1992: 59) wrote that "[a]lmost all [their] managers care strongly about people who have a stake in the business – customers, employees, stockholders, suppliers, etc."

Normative

The theory is used to interpret the function of the corporation, including the identification of moral or philosophical guidelines for the operation and management of corporations. Normative concerns dominated the classic stakeholder theory statements from the beginning (Dodd, 1932), and this tradition has been continued in the most recent versions (Carroll, 1989; Kuhn & Shriver, 1991; Marcus, 1993). Even Friedman's (1970) famous attack on the concept of corporate social responsibility was cast in normative terms.

Contrasting/combining approaches

Each of these uses of stakeholder theory is of some value, but the values differ in each use. The *descriptive* aspect of stakeholder theory reflects and explains past, present, and future states of affairs of corporations and their stakeholders. Simple description is common and desirable in the exploration of new areas and usually expands to generate explanatory and predictive propositions. (All such activities shall be called *descriptive* for our purposes.) *Instrumental* uses of stakeholder theory make a connection between stakeholder approaches and commonly desired objectives such as profitability. Instrumental uses usually stop short of exploring specific links between cause (i.e., stakeholder management) and effect (i.e., corporate performance) in detail, but such linkage is certainly implicit. The much-quoted Stanford Research Institute's (SRI) definition of stakeholders as "those groups without whose support the organization would cease to exist" (SRI, 1963; quoted in Freeman, 1984: 31) clearly implies that corporate managers must induce constructive contributions from their stakeholders to accomplish their own desired results (e.g., perpetuation of the organization, profitability, stability, growth).

In *normative* uses, the correspondence between the theory and the observed facts of corporate life is not a significant issue, nor is the association between stakeholder management and conventional performance measures a critical test. Instead, a normative theory attempts to interpret the function of, and offer guidance about, the investor-owned corporation on the basis of some underlying moral or philosophical principles. Although both normative and instrumental analyses may be "prescriptive" (i.e., they may express or imply more or less appropriate choices on the part of decision makers), they rest on entirely different bases. An instrumental approach is essentially hypothetical; it says, in effect, "If you want to achieve (avoid) results X, Y, or Z, then adopt (don't adopt) principles and practices A, B, or C." The normative approach, in contrast, is not hypothetical but categorical; it says, in effect, "Do (Don't do) this because it is the right (wrong) thing to do." Much of the stakeholder literature, including the contributions of both proponents and critics, is clearly normative, although the fundamental normative principles involved are often unexamined.

A striking characteristic of the stakeholder literature is that diverse theoretical approaches are often combined without acknowledgement. Indeed, the temptation to seek a three-in-one theory – or at least to slide easily from one theoretical base to another – is strong. Clarkson (1991: 349), for example, asserted an explicit connection among all three when he concluded that his stakeholder management model represents a new framework for "describing, evaluating, and managing corporate social performance."

All three types of theory are also found in the work of Freeman, whom many regard as the leading contributor to the stakeholder literature. In his original treatise, he asserted that changing events create a descriptive fit for the theory:

> Just as the separation of the owner-manager-employee required a rethinking of the concept of control and private property as analysed by Berle and Means (1932), so does the emergence of numerous stakeholder groups and new strategic issues require a rethinking of our traditional picture of the firm . . . We must redraw the picture in a way that accounts for the changes. (1984: 24)

At the same time, he also endorsed the theory's *instrumental basis*. We should, he noted, "explore the logic of this concept in practical terms, i.e., in terms of how organizations can succeed in the current and future business environment" (1984: 25). Instrumental concerns are also reflected in Freeman's extensive discussion of stakeholder management implementation techniques, both in his 1984 treatise and in other papers (Freeman & Gilbert, 1987; Freeman & Reed, 1983). In a later work, however, Evan and Freeman (1988: 97) justified stakeholder theory on normative grounds, specifically its power to satisfy the moral rights of individuals. They asserted that the theory of the firm must be reconceptualized "along essentially Kantian lines." This means each stakeholder group has a right to be treated as an end in itself, and not as means to some other end, "and therefore must participate in determining the future direction of the firm in which [it has] a stake."

The muddling of theoretical bases and objectives, although often understandable, has led to less rigorous thinking and analysis than the stakeholder concept requires. To see the significance of the distinctions among descriptive, instrumental, and normative uses of the stakeholder concept, consider the current controversy over the special privileges of top managers in large corporations, particularly in connection with mergers and acquisitions. There is considerable evidence that in the burst of large corporate takeovers during the 1980s, share values typically rose for acquired firms and fell for acquiring firms. Many observers have speculated that self-serving managerial activity accounts for both results (Jensen, 1989; Weidenbaum & Vogt, 1987). The acquired firms gain in value because, prior to the takeover, they were burdened by inefficient, self-serving managers, and the acquiring firms lose in value because the impetus for the acquisition was not return on investment for owners but ego gratification and career advancement for their top managers. If this analysis is accurate, and if managers' nests are often feathered in other ways (e.g., salaries, bonuses) at the expense of shareowners, then it is descriptively true that managers' interests have priority over those of other stakeholders, including shareowners. But we cannot move directly from an *is* claim – the de facto priority of managers' interests – to an *ought* claim in either instrumental or normative contexts. Moreover, even if it were true that higher paid managers did, in fact, achieve higher levels of profitability (thus meeting instrumental criteria), it would still not follow that higher pay/profit results were normatively justifiable. (Witness the near-universal condemnation of the income/profit achievements of the 19th-century robber barons.)

The Problem of Justification

The underlying epistemological issue in the stakeholder literature is the problem of justification: Why should the stakeholder theory be accepted or preferred over alternative conceptions? Until this question is addressed, the distinctions among empirical, instrumental, and normative approaches can be papered over. Moreover, the answer to this question must be related to the distinct purpose that the theory is intended to serve. That is, reasons to accept the stakeholder theory as a descriptive account of how managers behave, or of how the business world is constituted, are different from reasons to accept the stakeholder theory as a guide for managerial behavior, and so on.

The stakeholder theory is justified in the literature, explicitly or implicitly, in ways that correspond directly to the three approaches to the theory set out in the previous section: descriptive, instrumental, and normative. Descriptive justifications attempt to show that the concepts embedded in the theory correspond to observed reality. Instrumental justifications point to evidence of the connection between stakeholder management and corporate performance. Normative justifications appeal to underlying concepts such as individual or group "rights," "social contract," or utilitarianism. (Brummer's recent survey of this literature ignores descriptive issues but emphasizes "power and performance," i.e., instrumental, and "deontological," i.e., normative, arguments; cf. Brummer, 1991.)

In our view, the three aspects of the stakeholder theory are nested within each other, as suggested by Figure 3. The external shell of the theory is its descriptive aspect; the theory presents and explains relationships that are observed in the external world. The theory's descriptive accuracy is supported, at the second level, by its instrumental and predictive value; *if* certain practices are carried out, *then* certain results will be obtained. The central core of the theory is, however, normative. The descriptive accuracy of the theory presumes that managers and other agents act *as if* all stakeholders' interests have intrinsic value. In turn, recognition of these ultimate moral values and obligations gives stakeholder management its fundamental normative base. In the following sections, we survey the evidence and argument involved in each of these approaches to the justification of the stakeholder theory.

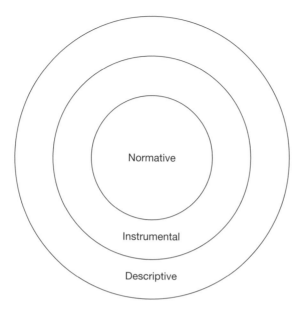

Figure 3 Three aspects of stakeholder theory

Descriptive Justifications

There is ample descriptive evidence, some of which has already been cited, that many managers believe themselves, or are believed by others, to be practicing stakeholder management. Indeed, as early as the mid-1960s, Raymond Baumhart's (1968) survey of upper-level managers revealed that about 80 percent regarded it as unethical management behavior to focus solely in the interest of shareowners and not in the interest of employees and customers. Since then, other surveys asking similar questions about the stakeholder sensitivity of managers have returned similar results (Brenner & Molander, 1977; Posner & Schmidt, 1984). Ongoing empirical studies by both Clarkson (1991) and Halal (1990) attempt to distinguish firms that practice stakeholder management from those that do not, and both investigators found significant numbers of firms in the first category. Managers may not make explicit reference to "stakeholder theory," but the vast majority of them apparently adhere in practice to one of the central tenets of the stakeholder theory, namely, that their role is to satisfy a wider set of stakeholders, not simply the shareowners. (Note, however, that the 171 managers surveyed by Alkhafaji, 1989, did not believe that the corporate governance roles of any stakeholders, including shareowners, should be increased. Perhaps not surprisingly, they strongly favored increased dominance of corporate governance by management.)

Another kind of descriptive justification for the stakeholder theory stems from the role it plays as the implicit basis for existing practices and institutions, including legal opinion and statutory law. Recent court decisions and new legislation have weakened the so-called "business judgement rule," which vests management with exclusive authority over the conduct of a company's affairs only on the condition that the financial welfare of stockholders is single-mindedly pursued (Chirelstein, 1974: 60). At last count, at least 29 states have adopted statutes that extend the range of permissible concern by boards of directors to a host of non-shareowner constituencies, including employees, creditors, suppliers, customers, and local communities (Orts, 1992). Furthermore, courts have tended to support these statutes. For example, the well-known Delaware Supreme Court decision in Unocal, although requiring corporate directors to show that a "reasonable" threat exists before fighting hostile takeover offers, nonetheless allowed a number of concerns to affect the determination of such "reasonableness," including "the impact [of the takeover] on 'constituencies' other than shareholders (i.e., creditors, customers, employees, and perhaps even the community generally)" (*Unocal Corp. v. Mesa Petroleum Co.*, 1985). In a more recent Delaware case, *Paramount Communications, Inc. v. Time, Inc.* (1990), the Unocal rationale was expanded to allow directors to include factors such as long-range business plans and a corporation's "culture." In one of the most dramatic challenges to the ownership rights of hostile acquirers, the Supreme Court of the United States upheld an Indiana statute that in the Court's own words "condition[s] acquisition of control of a corporation on approval of a majority of the *pre-existing* disinterested shareholders" (emphasis added) (*CTS Corp. v. Dynamics Corp. of America*, 1987).

As Orts noted, this trend toward stakeholder law is not solely a U.S. phenomenon and is reflected in the existing and emerging laws of many developed countries. The so-called codetermination laws of Germany require employee representation on second-tier boards of directors. The Companies Act of Great Britain mandates that company directors shall include the interests of employees in their decision making (*Companies Act*, 1980). The new "harmonization" laws of the European Community (EC) will, when approved, include provisions permitting corporations to take into account the interests of creditors, customers, potential investors, and employees (Orts, 1992). Finally, the well-known corporate governance model in Japan – through both law and custom – presumes that Japanese corporations exist within a tightly connected and interrelated set of stakeholders, including suppliers, customers, lending institutions, and friendly corporations.

Another series of legal developments in the U.S. asserts the interests of third-party stakeholders – specifically, unsuccessful job applicants – in business operations. Title VII of the Civil Rights Act of 1964 explicitly makes it a violation of law for an employer "to fail or refuse to hire . . . any individual" on the basis of discriminatory criteria (42 U.S.C. §§ 2000e-2a(1) & (2), 1982). This legislation has become the focus of numerous legal complaints and some substantial settlements. In a class action suit involving Potomac Electric Power Co., Washington, DC, complainants charged that the company had hired far fewer Blacks from its applicant pool than would have been expected on statistical grounds. The judge certified a "class" of more than 7,000 unsuccessful Black applicants, most of whom will be eligible for compensation out of a $38.4 million settlement pool (which is also available to employees experiencing discrimination) (*The Washington Post*, 21 February 1993).

Both of these sets of legal developments reinforce our initial statement that stakeholders are defined by *their* legitimate interest in the corporation, rather than simply by the corporation's interest in *them*. But neither the legal developments nor the management survey results provide definitive episte-mological justification for the stakeholder theory. Managers adopting the stakeholder approach may be relieved to learn that they are not alone, and indeed that they are conforming to the latest management or legal trends, but both the survey results and legal developments are, at bottom, simply facts. They do not constitute the basis for the stakeholder (or any other) theory of management. Indeed, even if the stakeholder concept is implicit in current legal trends (a proposition that is not universally accepted), one cannot derive a stakeholder theory of management from a stakeholder theory of law any more than one can derive a "tort" theory of management from the tort theory of law.

The hazards of using purely descriptive data, whether jurisprudential or otherwise, as justification for a broad theory are well known. There is the problem of the so-called "naturalistic fallacy," moving from *is* to *ought* or from *describe* to *evaluate*, without the necessary intervening analysis and explanation (Moore, 1959/1903: 15–16). Then, again, there is the simple problem of hasty generalization. By the logic of descriptive justification, if new surveys showed that managers were abandoning stakeholder orientations, or if the legal support for broad stakeholder interests were to weaken, the theory would be invalidated. But this observation offers a significant clue about the nature of the theory itself, because few if any of its adherents would be likely to abandon it, even if current legal or managerial trends were to shift. This suggests that the descriptive support for the stakeholder theory, as well as the critiques of this support to be found in the literature, are of limited significance and that the most important issues for stakeholder theory lie elsewhere.

Instrumental Justifications

Because the descriptive approach to grounding a stakeholder theory is inade-quate, justifications based on a connection between stakeholder strategies and organizational performance should be examined. Consider, for example, the simple hypothesis that corporations whose managers adopt stakeholder principles and practices will perform better financially than those that do not. This hypothesis has never been tested directly, and its testing involves some formidable challenges. (Clarkson's ongoing work is the only significant effort of this type known to us; cf. Clarkson, Deck & Shiner, 1992.) The view that stakeholder management and favorable performance go hand in hand has, however, become commonplace in the management literature, both professional and academic. The earliest direct statement is probably that of General Robert E. Wood, then-CEO of Sears, in 1950: "All I can say is that if the other three parties named above [customers, employees, community] are properly taken care of, the stockholder will benefit in the long pull" (quoted in Worthy, 1984: 64). A recent effort to introduce practicing managers to the stakeholder concept and to improve their ability to implement stakeholder management practices is the work by Savage, Nix, Whitehead, and Blair (1991). Brummer (1991) cited not only Freeman (1989) but also Ackoff; Manning; Maslow; Peters and Waterman; Starling; Sturdivant; and others in support of stakeholder theory's instrumental base.

Unfortunately, the large body of literature dealing with the connections, if any, between various aspects of corporate social performance or ethics, on one hand, and conventional financial and market performance indicators, on the other, does not translate easily into a stakeholder theory context. Whatever value the social/financial performance studies may have on their own merits, most of them do not include reliable indicators of the stakeholder management (i.e., the independent variable) side of the relationship. There is some evidence, based on analysis of the *Fortune* corporate reputation surveys, that the satisfaction of multiple stakeholders need not be a zero sum game (i.e., that benefits to one stakeholder group need not come entirely at the expense of another) (Preston & Sapienza, 1990). As previously noted, Kotter and Heskett's (1992) case studies of a small number of high-performance companies indicated that the managers of those companies tend to emphasize the interests of all major stakeholder groups in their decision making. However, there is as yet no compelling empirical evidence that the optimal strategy for maximizing a firm's conventional financial and market performance is stakeholder management.

Analytical arguments

Even without empirical verification, however, stakeholder management can be linked to conventional concepts of organizational success through analytical argument. The main focus of this effort in the recent literature builds on established concepts of principal–agent relations (Jensen & Meckling, 1976) and the firm as a nexus of contracts (Williamson & Winter, 1991). Agency theory and firm-as-contract theory, although arising from different sources, are closely related and share a common emphasis: efficiency. (They also share the terminology and methodology of the new transaction cost literature; cf. Williamson, 1985). Agency theorists argue that corporations are structured to minimize the costs of getting some participants (the agents) to do what other participants (the principals) desire. Firm-as-contract theorists argue that participants agree to cooperate with each other within organizations (i.e., through contracts), rather than simply deal with each other through the market, to minimize the costs of search, coordination, insecurity, etc.

Hill and Jones (1992: 132, 134) are responsible for the most ambitious attempt to integrate the stakeholder concept with agency theory (see also, Sharplin & Phelps, 1989). These authors enlarged the standard principal–agent paradigm of financial economics, which emphasizes the relationship between shareowners and managers, to create "stakeholder–agency theory," which constitutes, in their view, "a generalized theory of agency." According to this conception, managers "can be seen as the agents of [all] other stakeholders." They noted that stakeholders differ among themselves with respect to (a) the *importance* (to them) of their stake in the firm and (b) their *power* vis-à-vis the managers. They also noted that there is considerable friction within the stakeholder–agent negotiation process – some of it because of some participants' ability to retard equilibrating adjustments that are unfavorable to themselves. They therefore argued that there is no reason to assume that stakeholder–agent relationships are in equilibrium at any particular time. (This contrasts sharply with the "perfect markets" hypothesis favored in the finance literature.) In their view, the process, direction, and speed of adaptation in stakeholder–agent relationships, rather than the equilibrium set of contributions and rewards, should be the primary focus of analysis. This brief summary cannot do justice to their rich conception, but the key point for current purposes is that the stakeholders are drawn into relationships with the managers to accomplish organizational tasks as efficiently as possible; hence, the stakeholder model is linked instrumentally to organizational performance.

A similar theme emerges from the firm-as-contract analysis of Freeman and Evan (1990; see also Evan & Freeman, 1988). They recommended integrating the stakeholder concept with the Coasian view of the firm-as-contract and a Williamson-style analysis of transaction costs to "conceptualize the firm as a set of multilateral contracts over time." According to Freeman and Evan,

> Managers administer contracts among employees, owners, suppliers, customers, and the community. Since each of these groups can invest in asset specific transactions which affect the other groups, methods of conflict resolution, or safeguards must be found. (1990: 352)

They emphasized that all parties have an equal right to bargain and, therefore, that a minimal condition for the acceptance of such multipartite arrangements by each contracting party is a notion of "fair contract," i.e., governance rules that "ensure that the interests of all parties are at least taken into consideration" (1990: 352). Once again, the stakeholder model (and its implementation through a set of acceptable implicit contracts) is seen as essential to successful organizational performance.

The stakeholder interpretations of both agency theory and firm-as-contract theory give special attention to the differential position and special role of managers vis-à-vis all other stakeholders. Hill and Jones (1992: 140) emphasized "information asymmetry" between managers and other stakeholders and contrasted the concentration of resource control by managers with the diffusion of control within stakeholder groups in which there may be no mechanism to gain command over a significant portion of the group's total resources. Evan and Freeman (1993: 102–103) asserted that "management has a duty of safeguarding the welfare of the abstract entity that is the corporation" and of balancing the conflicting claims of multiple stakeholders to achieve this goal. They further declared:

> A stakeholder theory of the firm must redefine the purpose of the firm . . . The very purpose of the firm is, in our view, to serve as a vehicle for coordinating stakeholder interests. (102–103)

According to this perspective, success in satisfying multiple stakeholder interests – rather than in meeting conventional economic and financial criteria – would constitute the ultimate test of corporate performance.

But how will multiple and diverse stakeholders be assured that their interests are being coordinated in ways that lead to the most favourable possible results for themselves (i.e., the most favourable results consistent with the requirements of other stakeholders)? Hill and Jones (1992: 140–143) stressed the importance of (a) monitoring devices that have the effect of reducing information asymmetry (e.g., public reporting requirements) and (b) enforcement mechanisms, including law, "exit" (the possibility, or credible threat, of withdrawal from the relationship), and "voice." Freeman and Evan (1993) emphasized the notion of fairness. Going beyond the notion of "fair contracting," they recommended that the criterion of "fairness" in stakeholder bargains be a Rawlsian "veil of ignorance." Under a "veil of ignorance," parties to a bargain agree upon a set of possible outcomes prior to determining which outcome will be received by which party (e.g., one person cuts the cake, another takes the first slice) (Rawls, 1971, cited in Freeman & Evan, 1990: 352–353).

Both pairs of analysts, Hill and Jones and Freeman and Evan, placed greater emphasis on the process of multiple-stakeholder coordination than on the specific agreements/bargains. Both groups stressed that mutual and voluntary acceptability of bargains by all contracting stakeholders is the necessary criterion for efficient contracts. Both neglected the roles of potential stakeholders not conspicuously involved in explicit or implicit contracts with the firm. The two pairs of authors differed slightly in one respect: Hill and Jones saw the network of relationships as consisting of separate implicit contracts between each stakeholder group and "management" (as a central node), whereas Freeman and Evan ultimately viewed the firm "as a series of multilateral contracts among [all] stakeholders" (1990: 354).

Weaknesses of instrumental justifications

Perhaps the most important similarity between these two independent attempts to justify the stakeholder model lies in the fact that although they draw initially on the conceptual apparatus of instrumental or efficiency-based theories (i.e., principal–agent relations and "firm-as-contract" theory), they ultimately rely upon noninstrumental or normative arguments. This shift is less conspicuous in the case of Hill and Jones, who implied that monitoring and enforcement mechanisms will be sufficient to curb opportunistic behavior by managers at the expense of other stakeholders. The authors would no doubt agree, however, that the ultimate success of stakeholder–agency theory would require a fundamental shift in managerial objectives away from shareowners and toward the interests of all stakeholders; such a shift would necessarily involve normative, rather than purely instrumental, considerations. Freeman and Evan's recourse to a Rawlsian concept of "fairness" as the ultimate criterion for stakeholder bargains is an overt elevation of normative criteria over instrumental ones. No theorist, including Rawls, has ever maintained that bargains reached on the basis of a "veil of ignorance" would maximize efficiency. By elevating the fairness principle to a central role, Freeman and Evan shifted their attention from ordinary economic contracts of the sort envisaged by Coase, Williamson, and the mainstream agency theorists, which are governed by individual efficiency considerations. Instead, they emphasized what have been called "heuristic" or "social" contracts that rest upon broad normative principles governing human conduct (Donaldson & Dunfee, In press, 1994).

It should come as no surprise that stakeholder theory cannot be fully justified by instrumental considerations. The empirical evidence is inadequate, and the analytical arguments, although of considerable substance, ultimately rest on more than purely instrumental grounds. This conclusion carries an important implication: Although those who use the stakeholder concept often cite its consistency with the pursuit of conventional corporate performance objectives (and there is no notable evidence of its inconsistency), few of them would abandon the concept if it turned out to be only as *equally* efficacious as other conceptions. O'Toole (1991: 18–19), for example, examined a case in which the economic consequences of stakeholder versus conventional management "ended up neutral"; he stressed that "it is the *moral consequences* that are at issue" and described stakeholder analysis as "the sine quo non of business virtue" (emphasis in the original).

Normative Justifications

The normative basis for stakeholder theory involves its connection with more fundamental and better-accepted philosophical concepts. The normative assumptions of traditional economic theory are too feeble to support stakeholder theory, and the concept of a free market populated with free and rational preference seekers, however correct and important, is compatible with both stakeholder and nonstakeholder perspectives. Of course, the two normative propositions stated at the beginning of this article – that stakeholders are identified by *their* interests in the affairs of the corporation and that the interests of all stakeholders have intrinsic value – can be viewed as axiomatic principles that require no further justification. Unfortunately, this approach provides no basis for responding to critics who reject these propositions out of hand.

One way to construct a normative foundation for the stakeholder model is to examine its principal competitor, the model of *management* control in the interests of shareowners, as represented by the business judgement rule. As noted in previous sections, there is considerable criticism of this model on descriptive grounds. Pejovich (1990: 58) noted that in the modern corporation (as opposed to the owner-managed firm) the rights of shareowners are "attenuated" by the dispersion of ownership and by high agency costs; he stressed that "the *economic system*," not "the *legal system*," is responsible for this "attenuation of the right of ownership" (emphasis in original). Many direct observers (e.g., Geneen & Moscow, 1984; Pickens, 1987) have questioned managers' devotion to shareowner welfare, and survey results such as those of Alkhafaji (1989) and Posner and Schmidt (1992) provide statistical support for these perceptions.

But the management serving the shareowners model (i.e., the principal–agent model in its standard financial economics form) is not only descriptively inaccurate; careful analysis reveals that it is normatively unacceptable as well. Changes in state incorporation laws to reflect a "constituency" perspective have been mentioned. The normative basis for these changes in current mainstream legal thinking is articulated in the recent American Law Institute report, *Principles of Corporate Governance* (1992). The relevant portion of this document begins by affirming the central corporate objective of "enhancing corporate profit and shareholder gain," but it immediately introduces qualifications: "Even if corporate profit and shareholder gain are not thereby enhanced," the corporation *must* abide by law and *may* "take into account ethical considerations" and engage in philanthropy (Sec. 2.01(a)(b); 1992: 69). The accompanying commentary explicitly affirmed the stakeholder concept:

> The modern corporation by its nature creates interdependencies with a variety of groups with whom the corporation has a legitimate concern, such as employees, customers, suppliers, and members of the communities in which the corporation operates. (1992: 72)

The commentary further noted that response to social and ethical considerations is often consistent with long-run (if not short-run) increases in profit and value, but it continues:

Nevertheless, observation suggests that corporate decisions are not infrequently made on the basis of ethical consideration even when doing so would not enhance corporate profit or shareholder gain. *Such behavior is not only appropriate, but desirable. Corporate officials are not less morally obliged than any other citizens to take ethical considerations into account, and it would be unwise social policy to preclude them from doing so* . . . [The text] does not impose a legal obligation to take ethical considerations into account. However, the absence of a legal obligation to follow ethical principles does not mean that corporate decisionmakers are not subject to the same ethical considerations as other members of society. (American Law Institute, 1992: 80–82, emphasis added)

Formal Analysis: Theory of Property

To go beyond this practical rejection of the "management serving the share-owners" model, more formal normative justifications of stakeholder theory might be based either on broad theories of philosophical ethics, such as utilitarianism, or on narrower "middle-level" theories derived from the notion that a "social contract" exists between corporations and society. A comprehensive survey of this terrain would go far beyond the scope of this article, and much of it has been recently traversed by others (Brummer, 1991; Freeman, 1991; see also, Donaldson, 1982). Here, we offer a brief sketch of a normative basis for the stakeholder theory that combines several different philosophical approaches and that is, we believe, original in the literature. We argue that the stakeholder theory can be normatively based on the evolving theory of property.

There is a subtle irony in proposing that the stakeholder model can be justified on the basis of the theory of property, because the traditional view has been that a focus on property rights justifies the dominance of share-owners' interests. Indeed, the fact that property rights are the critical base for conventional shareowner-dominance views makes it all the more significant that the current trend of thinking with respect to the philosophy of property runs in the opposite direction. In fact, this trend – as presented in the now-classic contributions of Coase (1960) and Honore (1961) and in more recent works by Becker (1978, 1992a,b,c) and Munzer (1992) – runs strongly counter to the conception that private property exclusively enshrines the interests of owners.

Considerable agreement now exists as to the theoretical definition of property as a "bundle" of many rights, some of which may be limited. More than 30 years ago, Coase (1960: 44) chided economists for adhering to a simplistic concept of ownership:

We may speak of a person owning land . . . but what the land-owner in fact possesses is the right to carry out a circumscribed list of actions. The rights of a land-owner are not unlimited . . . [This] would be true under any system of law. A system in which the rights of individuals were unlimited would be one in which there were no rights to acquire.

Honore (1961) specifically included the notion of restrictions against harmful uses within the definition of property itself. Pejovich (1990: 27–28), probably the most conservative economic theorist working in this area, emphasized that "property rights are relations between individuals" and thus "it is wrong to separate human rights from property rights"; he further noted that "the right of ownership is not an unrestricted right."

The notion that property rights are embedded in human rights and that restrictions against harmful uses are intrinsic to the property rights concept clearly brings the interests of others (i.e., of non-owner stakeholders) into the picture. Of course, *which* uses of property should be restricted and *which* persons should count as stakeholders remain unspecified. Simply bringing nonowner stakeholders into the conception of property does not provide by itself justification for stakeholder arguments assigning managerial responsibilities toward specific groups, such as employees and customers. The important point, however, is that the contemporary theoretical concept of private property clearly does not ascribe unlimited rights to owners and hence does not support the popular claim that the responsibility of managers is to act solely as agents for the shareowners. (The necessary compromise between individual property rights and other considerations is highlighted in the "takings" issue – i.e., modified to protect the interests of others or society in general. For a survey of current views on this complex matter, see Mercuro, 1992.)

These comments examine the scope of property rights, but it is also relevant to examine their source (i.e., What basic principles determine *who* should get [and be allowed to keep] *what* in society?). Unless property rights are regarded as simple, self-evident moral conceptions, they must be based on more fundamental ideas of distributive justice. The main contending theories of distributive justice include Utilitarianism, Libertarianism, and social contract theory (Becker, 1992). The battle among competing theories of distributive justice is most often a battle over which characteristics highlighted by the theories – such as need, ability, effort, and mutual agreement – are most relevant for determining fair distributions of wealth, income, etc. (The role of theories of justice within organizations is attracting considerable current attention; cf. Greenberg, 1987.)

For example, when the characteristic of *need* (a feature highlighted by Utilitarianism) is the criterion, the resulting theory of property places formidable demands upon property owners to mitigate their self-interest in favor of enhancing the interests (i.e., meeting the needs) of others. When *ability* or *effort* (features highlighted by Libertarianism) is the criterion, the resulting theory leaves property owners freer to use their resources (acquired, it is assumed, as a result of ability and effort) as they see fit. Social contract theory places primary emphasis on expressed or implied understandings among individuals and groups as to appropriate distributions and uses of property.

Many of the most respected contemporary analysts of property rights reject the notion that any *single* theory of distributive justice is universally applicable. Indeed, it seems counterintuitive that any one principle could account for all aspects of the complex bundle of rights and responsibilities that constitutes "property." Beginning with Becker's (1978) analysis, the trend is toward theories that are pluralistic, allowing more than one fundamental principle to play a role (Becker, 1992a; see also, Munzer, 1992). But if a pluralistic theory of property rights is accepted, then the connection between the theory of property and the stakeholder theory becomes explicit. All critical characteristics underlying the classic theories of distributive justice are present among the stakeholders of a corporation, as they are conventionally conceived and presented in contemporary stakeholder theory. For example, the "stake" of long-term employees who have worked to build and maintain a successful business operation is essentially based on effort. The stake of people living in the surrounding community may be based on their need, say, for clean air or the maintenance of their civic infrastructure. Customer stakes are based on the satisfaction and protections implicitly promised in the market offer, and so on. One need not make the more radical assertion that such stakes constitute formal or legal property rights, although some forceful critics of current corporate governance arrangements appear to hold this view (Nader & Green, 1973). All that is necessary is to show that such characteristics, which are the same as those giving rise to fundamental concepts of property rights, give various groups a moral interest, commonly referred to as a "stake," in the affairs of the corporation. Thus, the normative principles that underlie the contemporary pluralistic theory of property rights also provide the foundation for the stakeholder theory as well.

Managerial Implications

A full discussion of the managerial implications of this analysis would require much more discussion. As a summary, the two points we emphasize are (a) the recognition of specific stakeholders and their stakes by managers and other stakeholders and (b) the role of managers and the *managerial function*, as distinct from the *persons* involved, within the stakeholder model. These two issues are intimately intertwined.

It is the responsibility of managers, and the management function, to select activities and direct resources to obtain benefits for legitimate stakeholders. The question is, Who are the legitimate stakeholders? Some answers in the literature are, in our view, too narrow; others are too broad. The firm-as-contract view holds that legitimate stakeholders are identified by the existence of a contract, expressed or implied, between them and the firm. Direct input contributors are included, but environmental interests such as communities are also believed to have at least loose quasi-contracts (and, of course, sometimes very specific ones) with their business constituents.

We believe that the firm-as-contract perspective, although correct, is incomplete as a description of the corporation. For example, many business relationships with "communities" are so vague as to pass beyond even the broadest conception of "contract." The plant-closing controversy of the last couple of decades clearly shows that some communities had come to expect – and sometimes were able to enforce – stakeholder claims that some firms clearly did not recognize. As another example, potential job applicants, unknown to the firm, nevertheless have a stake in being considered for a job (but not necessarily to *get* a job). Lacking any connection to the firm, these potential employees are difficult to view as participating in the firm by reason of a *contract*, either implied or explicit. (We do not mean, however, to rule out possible relevance of so-called social contracts to such situations; cf. Donaldson & Dunfee, 1994b.) Stakeholders are identified through the actual or potential harms and benefits that they experience or anticipate experiencing as a result of the firm's actions or inactions. In practice, and in addition to legal requirements, appraisal of the legitimacy of such expectations is an important function of management, often in concert with other already recognized stakeholders.

Excessive breadth in the identification of stakeholders has arisen from a tendency to adopt definitions such as "anything influencing or influenced by" the firm (Freeman, 1984, quoting with approval Thompson, 1967). This definition opens the stakeholder set to actors that form part of the firm's environment – and that, indeed, may have some impact on its activities – but that have no specific stake in the firm itself. That is, they stand to gain no particular benefit from the firm's successful operation. The two types of interests that have cropped up most frequently in this connection are (a) competitors and (b) the media. Competitors were introduced as factors that have "an influence on managerial autonomy" in Dill's (1958) article, which is appropriately cited in the literature as a precursor of stakeholder analysis. However, neither the term *stakeholder* nor the notion of a *stake* (i.e., potential benefit) was explicitly introduced in Dill's analysis. In any event, in the normal course of events, competitors do not seek benefits from the focal firm's success; on the contrary, they may stand to lose whatever the focal firm gains. Competitive firms may, of course, join in common collaborative activities (e.g., through trade associations), but here the shared (noncompetitive) interests account for the stakeholder relationship. The notion that the media should be routinely recognized as stakeholders was originally introduced by Freeman (1984), but it seems to have been eliminated (without explicit explanation) from his later writings. It is essential to draw a clear distinction between influencers and stakeholders: some actors in the enterprise (e.g., large investors) may be both, but some recognizable stakeholders (e.g., the job applicants) have no influence, and some influencers (e.g., the media) have no stakes.

The role of managers within the stakeholder framework described in the literature is also contradictory. Aoki (1984), for example, recognized only investors and employees as significant stakeholders and saw managers as essentially "referees" between these two stakeholder groups. He acknowledged neither (a) the essential role of management in the identification of stakeholders nor (b) the fact that managers are, themselves, stakeholders – and, indeed, a very privileged class of stakeholders – in the enterprise. Williamson (1985) is almost alone among academic analysts in emphasizing the fact that the managers of a firm are one of its most important and powerful constituencies and that – wittingly or unwittingly – they are extremely likely to practice opportunistic and self-aggrandizing behavior.

This last point is absolutely critical for our argument, and recognition of it confirms our most important proposition: that the stakeholder theory is fundamentally normative. We observed at the close of our discussion of instrumental justifications that the instrumental case for stakeholder management cannot be satisfactorily proved. Here we restate that observation and add that the ultimate managerial implication of the stakeholder theory is that managers *should* acknowledge the validity of diverse stakeholder interests and *should* attempt to respond to them within a mutually supportive framework, because that is a moral requirement for the legitimacy of the management function.

It is feared by some that a shift from the traditional shareowner orientation to a stakeholder orientation will make it more difficult to detect and discipline self-serving behavior by managers, who may always claim to be serving some broad set of stakeholder interests while they increase their powers and emoluments. Indeed, Orts (1992: 123) saw this as the "greatest danger" of the new "constituency statutes" for corporate governance, although he nevertheless supported the constituency approach.

Our response to this fear is twofold: First, the conventional model of the corporation, in both legal and managerial forms, has failed to discipline self-serving managerial behavior. In this era of multimillion dollar CEO compensation packages that continue to increase even when profits and wages decline (Bok, 1993), it is difficult to conceive of managers having greater scope for self-serving behavior than they have already. Second, the stakeholder model we have advanced here entails comprehensive restrictions on such behavior. Indeed, its very foundation prohibits any undue attention to the interests of any single constituency. To be sure, it remains to implement in law the sanctions, rules, and precedents that support the stakeholder conception of the corporation; in short, it remains to develop the legal version of the stakeholder model. (See, for example, Eisenberg's [1976] attempt to restructure the legal model of the corporation.) Yet over time, statutory and common law are almost certainly capable of achieving arrangements that encourage a broader, stakeholder conception of management – one which eschews single-minded subservience to shareowners' interests – while at the same time restraining the moral hazard of self-serving managers.

Conclusion

We have argued that the stakeholder theory is "managerial" and recommends the attitudes, structures, and practices that, taken together, constitute a *stakeholder* management philosophy. The theory goes beyond the purely descriptive observation that "organizations have stakeholders," which, although true, carries no direct managerial implications. Furthermore, the notion that stakeholder management contributes to successful economic performance, although widely believed (and not patently inaccurate), is insufficient to stand alone as a basis for the stakeholder theory. Indeed, the most thoughtful analyses of why stakeholder management might be casually related to corporate performance ultimately resort to normative arguments in support of their views. For these reasons, we believe that the ultimate justification for the stakeholder theory is to be found in its normative base. The plain truth is that the most prominent alternative to the stakeholder theory (i.e., the "management serving the shareowners" theory) is morally untenable. The theory of property rights, which is commonly supposed to support the conventional view, in fact – in its modern and pluralistic form – supports the stakeholder theory instead.

References

Alkhafaji, A. (1989) *A Stakeholder Approach to Corporate Governance: Managing in a Dynamic Environment*, New York: Quorum Books.

American Law Institute (1992) *Principles of Corporate Governance: Analysis and Recommendations*. (Proposed final draft, March 31, 1992), Philadelphia, PA: Author.

Anderson, J. Jr (1989) *Corporate Social Responsibility*, New York: Quorum Books.

Aoki, M. (1984) *The Co-operative Game Theory of the Firm*, Oxford: Clarendon Press.

Aupperle, K., Carroll, A.and Hatfield, J. (1985) 'An Empirical Examination of the Relationship Between Corporate Social Responsibility and Profitability', *Academy of Management Journal* 28(2): 446–463.

Barton, S., Hill, N. and Sundaram, S. (1989) 'An Empirical Test of Stakeholder Theory Predictions of Capital Structure', *Financial Management* 18(1): 36–44.

Baumhart, R. (1968) *An Honest Profit: What Businessmen Say About Ethics in Business*, New York: Holt, Rinehart & Winston.

Becker, L. (1978) *Property Rights*, London: Routledge & Kegan Paul.

Becker, L. (1992a) 'Property', in L. Becker and C. Becker (eds) *Encyclopedia of Ethics*, vol. 2: 1023–1027, New York: Garland.

Becker, L. (1992b) 'Places for Pluralism', *Ethics* 102: 707–719.

Becker, L. (1992c) 'Too Much Property', *Philosophy and Public Affairs* 21: 196–206.

Berle, A. and Means, G. (1932) *Private Property and the Modern Corporation*, New York: Macmillan.

Bok, D. (1993) *The Cost of Talent: How Executives and Professionals are Paid and How It Affects America*, New York: Free Press.

Brenner, S. and Cochran, P. (1991) *The Stakeholder Theory of the Firm: Implications for Business and Society Theory and Research*, Paper presented at the annual meeting of the International Association for Business and Society, Sundance, UT.

Brenner, S. and Molander, E. (1977) 'Is the Ethics of Business Changing?' *Harvard Business Review* 58(1): 54–65.

Brummer, J. (1991) *Corporate Responsibility and Legitimacy: An Interdisciplinary Analysis*, New York: Greenwood Press.

Carroll, A. (1989) *Business and Society: Ethics and Stakeholder Management*, Cincinnati, OH: South-Western.

Chirelstein, M. (1974) 'Corporate Law Reform', in J. McKie (ed.) *Social Responsibility and the Business Predicament* 41–78, Washington, DC: The Brookings Institution.

Civil Rights Act, Title VII: 42 USC §§ 2000e-2a(1) & (2), 1982.

Clarkson, M. (1991) 'Defining, Evaluating, and Managing Corporate Social Performance: A Stakeholder Management Model', in J. Post (ed.) *Research in Corporate Social Performance and Policy*, pp. 331–358, Greenwich, CT: JAI Press.

Clarkson, M., Deck, M. and Shiner, N. (1992) *The Stakeholder Management Model in Practice*, Paper presented at the annual meeting of the Academy of Management, Las Vegas, NV.

Coase, R. (1937) 'The Nature of the Firm', in O. Williamson and S. Winter (eds) *The Nature of the Firm: Origins, Evolution, and Development*, pp. 18–33, New York: Oxford University Press.

Coase, R. (1960) 'The Problem of Social Cost', *Journal of Law and Economics* 3: 1–44.

Cochran, P. and Wood, R. (1984) 'Corporate Social Responsibility and Financial Performance', *Academy of Management Journal* 27(1): 42–56.

Companies Act (1980) Great Britain.

Cornell, B. and Shapiro, A. (1987) 'Corporate Stakeholders and Corporate Finance', *Financial Management* 16: 5–14.

CTS Corp. v. Dynamics Corp. of America (1987) U.S. Supr., 481, 69, 87.

Cyert, R. and March, J. (1963) *A Behavioral Theory of the Firm*, Englewood Cliffs, NJ: Prentice Hall.

Dill, W. (1958) 'Environment as an Influence on Managerial Autonomy' *Administrative Science Quarterly* 2: 409–443.

Dodd, E. Jr. (1932) 'For Whom Are Corporate Managers Trustees?' *Harvard Law Review* 45: 1145–1163.

Donaldson, T. (1982) *Corporations and Morality*, Englewood Cliffs, NJ: Prentice Hall.

Donaldson, T. and Dunfee, T. (1994) 'Towards a Unified Conception of Business Ethics: Integrative Social Contracts Theory', *Academy of Management Review* 19: 252–284.

Donaldson, T. and Dunfee, T. (in press), 'Integrative Social Contracts Theory: A Communitarian Conception of Economic Ethics', *Economics and Philosophy*.

The Economist (1992) [Corporate governance special section] September 11: 52–62.

Eisenberg, M. (1976) *The Structure of the Corporation: A Legal Analysis*, Toronto: Little, Brown.

Evan, W. and Freeman, R. (1988) 'A Stakeholder Theory of the Modern Corporation: Kantian Capitalism', in T. Beauchamp and N. Bowie (eds) *Ethical Theory and Business*, pp. 75–93, Englewood Cliffs, NJ: Prentice Hall.

Freeman, R. (1984) *Strategic Management: A Stakeholder Approach*, Boston: Pitman.

Freeman, R. (ed.) (1991) *Business Ethics: The State of the Art*, New York: Oxford University Press.

Freeman, R. and Evan, W (1990) 'Corporate Governance: A Stakeholder Interpretation', *The Journal of Behavioral Economics* 19(4): 337–359.

Freeman, R. and Gilbert, D. Jr. (1987) 'Managing Stakeholder Relationships', in S. Sethi and C. Falbe (eds) *Business and Society*, pp. 397–423, Lexington, MA: Lexington Books.

Freeman, R. and Reed, D. (1983) 'Stockholders and Stakeholders: A New Perspective on Corporate Governance', *California Management Review*, 25(3): 88–106.

Friedman, M. (1970) 'The Social Responsibility of Business Is to Increase Its Profits', *New York Times Magazine*, September 13: 32–33, 122, 126.

Geneen, H. and Moscow, A. (1984) *Managing*, Garden City, NY: Doubleday.

Goodpaster, K. (1991) 'Business Ethics and Stakeholder Analysis', *Business Ethics Quarterly* 1(1): 53–73.

Greenberg, J. (1987) 'A Taxonomy of Organizational Justice Theories', *Academy of Management Review* 12: 9–22.

Halal, W. (1990) 'The New Management: Business and Social Institutions in the Information Age', *Business in the Contemporary World* 2(2): 41–54.

Hill, C. and Jones, T. (1992) 'Stakeholder–Agency Theory', *Journal of Management Studies* 29: 131–154.

Honore, A. (1961) 'Ownership', in A. Guest (ed.) *Oxford Essays in Jurisprudence*, pp. 107–147. Oxford: Clarendon Press.

Jensen, M. (1989) 'Eclipse of the Public Corporation', *Harvard Business Review* 67(5): 61–74.

Jensen, M. and Meckling, W. (1976) 'Theory of the Firm: Managerial Behavior, Agency Costs, and Capital Structure', *Journal of Financial Economics* 3 (October): 305–360.

Kotter, J. and Heskett, J. (1992) *Corporate Culture and Performance*, New York: Free Press.

Kreiner, P. and Bhambri, A. (1991) 'Influence and Information in Organization–Stakeholder Relationships', in J. Post (ed.) *Research in Corporate Social Performance and Policy*, vol. 12: 3–36, Greenwich, CT: JAI Press.

Kuhn, J. and Shriver, D. Jr. (1991) *Beyond Success: Corporations and Their Critics in the 1990s*, New York: Oxford University Press.

Marcus, A. (1993) *Business and Society: Ethics, Government and the World Economy*, Homewood, IL: Irwin.

McGuire, J., Sundgren, A. and Schneeweis, T. (1988) 'Corporate Social Responsibility and Firm Financial Performance', *Academy of Management Journal* 31: 354–372.

Mercuro, N. (ed.) (1992), *Taking Property and Just Compensation*, Boston: Kluwer.

Moore, G. (1959) *Principia Ethica*, Cambridge: Cambridge University Press, (original work published 1903).

Munzer, S. (1992) *A Theory of Property*, New York: Cambridge University Press.

Nader, R. and Green, M.(eds)(1973) *Corporate Power in America*, New York: Grossman.

Orts, E. (1992) 'Beyond Shareholders: Interpreting Corporate Consistency Statutes', *The George Washington Law Review* 61(1): 14–135.

O'Toole, J. (1985) *Vanguard Management*, Garden City, NY: Doubleday.

O'Toole, J. (1991) 'Do Good, Do Well: The Business Enterprise Trust Awards', *California Management Review* 33(3): 9–24.

Paramount Communications, Inc. v. Time, Inc. (1990) Del. Supr., 571 A. 2d 1140.

Pejovich, S. (1990) *The Economics of Property Rights: Towards a Theory of Comparative Systems*, Dordrecht, The Netherlands: Kluwer Academic.

Pickens, T. (1987) *Boone*, Boston: Houghton Mifflin.

Posner, B. and Schmidt, W. (1984) 'Values and the American Manager', *California Management Review* 26(3): 202–216.

Preston, L. and Sapienza, H. (1990) 'Stakeholder Management and Corporate Performance', *Journal of Behavioral Economics* 19: 361–375.

Preston, L., Sapienza, H. and Miller, R. (1991) 'Stakeholders, Shareholders, Managers: Who Gains What from Corporate Performance?' in A. Etzioni and P. Lawrence (eds) *Socio-economics: Toward a New Synthesis*, pp. 149–165, Armonk, NY: M. Sharpe.

Rawls, J. (1971) *A Theory of Justice*, Cambridge, MA: Harvard University Press.

Savage, G., Nix, T., Whitehead C. and Blair, J. (1991) 'Strategy for Assessing and Managing Organizational Stakeholders', *Academy of Management Executive*, 5(2): 61–75.

Sharplin, A. and Phelps, L. (1989) 'A Stakeholder Apologetic for Management', *Business and Professional Ethics Journal*, 8(2): 41–53.

Thompson, J. (1967) *Organizations in Action*, New York: McGraw-Hill.

Unocal Corp. v. Mesa Petroleum Co. (1985) Del. Supr., 493 A. 2d 946.

Wang, J. and Dewhirst, H. (1992) 'Boards of Directors and Stakeholder Orientation', *Journal of Business Ethics* 11: 115–123.

Washington Post (1993) 'Pepco Bias Suit Heads for 38 Million Settlement', February 21: A1.

Weidenbaum, M. and Vogt, S. (1987) 'Takeovers and Stockholders: Winners and Losers', *California Management Review*, 29(4): 157–168.

Williamson, O. (1985) *The Economic Institutions of Capitalism*, New York: Free Press.

Williamson, O. and Winter, S. (eds) (1991) *The Nature of the Firm: Origins, Evolution and Development*, New York: Oxford University Press.

Wood, D. (1991a) 'Corporate Social Performance Revisited', *Academy of Management Review* 16: 691–718.

Wood, D. (1991b) 'Social Issues in Management: Theory and Research in Corporate Social Performance', *Journal of Management* 17: 383–405.

Worthy, J. (1984) *Shaping an American Institution: Robert E. Wood and Sears, Roebuck*, Urbana: University of Illinois.

Vodafone: Africa calling

Introduction

In this case study, we see Vodafone, one of the world's largest mobile phone groups, and one with fairly good CSR credentials in its sector, operating in a global economy with varying concerns and needs. In the developed world, particularly Europe and North America, there are various social considerations that mobile phone companies need to take account of. These include: the potential dangers of radio frequency technology used in mobile phones on biological bodily systems; the accessing of inappropriate adult content through mobile phones by children; concerns about individualism, isolation and excessive consumerism among the 'mobile generation'; and the use of components procured from unsustainable sources. The developing world, represented in this case study by South Africa, still has to build its own internal economy and overcome basic social and other inequalities. Mobile telephones are being promoted by research funded by Vodafone as a way of positively contributing to fundamental needs in developed countries, with very little reference to the social concerns raised in the global North. This raises the question of what corporate social responsibility is, or should be, in different contexts, and also of where multinational companies should draw the line in terms of defining their social responsibilities and obligations in a complex multiple-stakeholder world.

CSR in Africa

The past decade has been a time of change in Africa, with a combination of sustained conflict, poverty, disease and dictatorship existing alongside emerging democracy and economic growth. There are very real social concerns around literacy, life expectancy (including high levels of child mortality), hunger and HIV/AIDS. The colonial history of the continent, combined with more recent socio-political developments, has left an environment in which social responsibility in business appears to be a low priority, but one with considerable potential for contributing to social and economic development.

In the worst cases, corporations have been complicit in political corruption, environmental destruction and labour exploitation. They have been found to be involved in unethical behaviour such as discrimination on the basis of race, gender and people with HIV/AIDS, employee intimidation, nepotism and neglect of safety. Nevertheless, corporations are well placed to lead in the continent in terms of investment, job creation, training and skills transfer, development of infrastructure, knowledge sharing, working against environmental degradation, and in using CSR to help address social and environmental issues.[1] To date, much of the attention to CSR in Africa has focused on philanthropy and community programmes, with relatively few companies actually seeking to examine their broader impacts on social and economic development.

Focus on South Africa

Corporations operating in South Africa in times of apartheid (which ended with the first free democratic elections in 1994) were bound to have an economic and political interest in the country, but the transition to democracy has also brought much new investment into the country. The ending of apartheid also enabled the formerly isolated South African companies entry into the global economy (including the listing of South African companies on international stock exchanges). Moreover, a more professional and systematic approach to CSR has developed, prompted partly by the need for compliance with global standards and clearer accountability, as well as by a recognition that business could play a part in the successful development of the country. Other influences include legislation and stakeholder pressure (largely through community groups). The 1996 Bill of Rights and a wave of new legislative reform relating to socio-economic development, the environment, health and safety, labour, governance and ethics have been put into place.[2]

None the less, having legislation in place is of little value unless it is backed up by enforcement, and this is a problem which still pervades South Africa. It is also important to note that, while the political system of apartheid has gone, economic apartheid remains, with whites continuing to have by far the best access to the best education and careers. Affirmative action programmes and investment in decent housing and education for all South Africa's citizens are helping to rectify the situation, but it will take a generation at least to integrate the people of the 'rainbow nation' fully.

A special mention is needed regarding HIV/AIDS. Prevalence of the disease in South Africa is at extremely worrying levels, with over half of the 40 million people living with HIV/AIDS in 2004 coming from sub-Saharan Africa. From a business perspective, at the most fundamental level, the prevalence of HIV/AIDS in South Africa causes labour-supply problems as employees hit by the disease are lost and need replacing. Apart from the direct costs of absenteeism, recruitment, retraining, health benefits and insurance, there are hidden impacts on profitability such as strained labour relations, declining employee morale, and distrust between employee and employer. A study published in the *Harvard Business Review* in 2003 estimated that the 'AIDS tax' on companies in South Africa could be more than 5 per cent of annual wage costs or as much as $12 million annually.[3] Moreover, the disease is particularly dangerous for the most disadvantaged groups in terms of education, economic stability and access to health, increasing still further the problems of the underprivileged. While corporations have made some initial efforts to engage with this extremely serious problem, barriers to involvement include high financial costs, the fear that governments will not get involved if business is seen as leading the way, the need for long-term commitment, and problems of stigma, ignorance and fear.

Vodafone

Vodafone is the world's largest mobile phone company. Originally formed in 1984, the Vodafone Group has grown rapidly through mergers and acquisitions involving Racal Telecom, Cable and Wireless, Mannesmann, and many others. After 20 years of growth, most developed markets have reached, or are reaching, saturation point in terms of phone ownership. The competitive situation is also threatened by increased regulation and competition from internet-based telephony. Key growth markets for Vodafone in the twenty-first century are therefore Africa and South East Asia, made possible in part by the liberalization of telecommunications markets.

Vodafone in South Africa: Vodacom

Penetration rates of mobile phones are among the highest in South Africa compared with other African countries, at over 36 mobile phones per 100 people. Vodafone has made major investments in emerging markets, including increasing to 50 per cent their stake in Vodacom, which operates in South Africa, Tanzania, Lesotho, Mozambique and the Democratic Republic of the Congo.

Like Vodafone, Vodacom takes a clear position on social issues, stating on its website that 'The existence of the digital divide means that a company such as Vodacom has a moral obligation to use the funds generated from its revenue to assist in addressing social backlogs'. Primary areas of involvement are education, health and welfare, and safety and security. Secondary areas are arts and culture, sports development and the environment. Their activities in this area take the form of bursaries to students in tertiary education in subjects relevant to Vodacom, and the Vodacom Foundation. The Foundation makes straight donations but also takes a proactive approach in identifying areas of need and seeking out partners for longer-term collaboration. Many of their projects focus on empowering women, young people and people living with disabilities.

A Two-worlds Anomaly?

Somewhat of a conundrum in the mobile phone industry are the different levels of concern in the developing and developed worlds about the various social implications of mobile phone technologies. A striking example of this is the debate over health effects. While in developed countries there is a recurring wave of fear that radio frequency exposure may cause serious long-term health problems, in developing countries these concerns are not widely raised. Instead, the focus is often on the economic and even health *advantages* of access to mobile phones. This difference in perspective is addressed in different ways by Vodafone.

The developed world perspective: the negative health effects of mobile phone technology

An area of concern for Vodafone to address in Europe and the USA concerns public fears that mobile phone technology may have negative health implications. In the UK, the Stewart Report published in 2000 recommended that a precautionary approach should be taken to mobile phone technologies until more scientific evidence on the health effects was available. Evidence is still lacking, but areas of concern include the interference of radio frequency fields with biological systems, the impact of long-term use on epidemiology, brain function, genetic predisposition of some groups to the impact of electromagnetic field exposure, the vulnerability of children and their developing nervous systems, and the impact of base stations on well-being.

In response to worries about health effects from the radio frequency (RF) fields emitted by handsets and base stations, Vodafone notes in its Corporate Responsibility report 2006 that the company is addressing this by:

- Engaging with local communities as part of our responsible network deployment process.
- Offering guidance to those who are concerned about how best to limit their RF field exposure from handsets.
- Providing easy-to-understand information through a variety of channels including websites and brochures to help people reach informed views.
- A commitment to inform customers and the general public of significant new developments in published research. We advocate the publication of scientific research in peer-reviewed journals.
- Supporting independent research at arm's length so that areas identified by the World Health Organisation as priorities are properly funded.
- The handsets we sell and our network of base stations comply with international standards for limiting human exposure to RF fields.

Vodafone is also continuing, along with various other carriers and mobile phone manufacturers, to defend four legal cases in the USA alleging personal injury, including brain cancer, from mobile phone use. The threat from legal action for this and other reasons is sufficiently serious for 'Contingent Liability' for Legal Proceedings to be included in the Vodafone financial statements and reported in the 2006 Annual Report (p. 117).

While Vodacom in South Africa acknowledges the potential health impacts of mobile phone technology, it does not give the issue such import as Vodafone, deferring any concerns to Vodafone's research. On the website it says:

> Even though the weight of evidence does not suggest any adverse affects, Vodacom supports independently conducted research because our technology has rapidly spread and is now used by one in six people around the world. Since 1991, Vodafone has globally committed more than six million pounds to an eight year programme of research projects.[4]

In fact, concerns about health issues related to use of mobile phones are very low key in South Africa. Rather, mobile phones are being heralded as important aids in promoting health in the country, and as a means of tackling the digital divide and opening up economic opportunities in a democratic way.

Developing world perspective: the positive health effects of mobile phones in South Africa

Africa, despite often being left behind in some of the economic advancements made in the rest of the world, has seen the world's most rapid growth in mobile phone penetration, albeit from a low starting point. The explosion of use of mobile phones in Africa has not been matched by awareness of concern for their potential health implications and other negative social impacts. Rather, the emphasis has been on the benefits of the spread of mobile voice telephony, including social issues such as maintaining social capital, stimulating a sense of well-being, improving income opportunities, and providing advantages in terms of personal security. At the most optimistic is the hope that mobile phones may be used to help offer services directly targeted at helping the poor, including health-related areas such as HIV/AIDS (for example, doctors monitoring their patients in remote regions). Clearly, this requires that the poorest in society have access to mobile phones. It is difficult to determine the current extent of access, since in rural districts phones will tend to be shared, but access to the facilities is possible without ownership of a mobile phone.

Vodafone has funded policy research, including a focus on the impact of mobile phones in Africa.[5] In the foreword to the 2005 report, the International Institutions Director for Vodafone Group claims that the reason for investing in the project was to contribute to systematic research on the economic and social impacts of a mobile phone. The report noted that mobile telephones are used and owned differently in developing countries from the developed world. For example, the value of a mobile phone to the individual is greater because other forms of communication are often poor. Mobiles provide a point of contact and enable users to participate in the economic system. Many people who cannot afford to own a mobile themselves can access mobile services through informal sharing with family and friends or through community phone shops. Furthermore, use of text messaging in rural communities is much lower due to illiteracy and the many indigenous languages, which act as a barrier to the adoption of other technologies that use the written word, such as the internet.

The report funded by Vodafone found that mobiles can have a positive and significant impact on economic growth and social stability, emphasizing that:

- A developing country with an extra 10 phones per 100 people between 1996 and 2003 would have had GDP growth 0.59 per cent higher than an otherwise identical country.
- Fixed and mobile communications networks (in addition to the openness of the economy, the level of GDP and other infrastructure) are positively linked with foreign direct investment. The impact of mobile telecommunications has grown in recent years.
- Many of the small businesses surveyed use mobiles as their only means of communication. The proportion is highest for black-owned businesses in South Africa.
- Sixty-two per cent of the small businesses surveyed in South Africa said they had increased profits as a result of mobile phones, in spite of increased call costs.
- Mobiles are used as a community amenity. Most mobile owners surveyed in South Africa allow family members to use their handset free, and a third do the same for friends.
- Seventy-nine per cent of those surveyed in South Africa said they had more contact and better relationships with family and friends as a result of mobile phones. This is particularly pertinent in rural areas, which are often not served by normal telecommunication services.

Other findings include the suggestion that mobile phones are accessible to the poorest members of the community, and normal barriers to accessing technology (gender, age, education levels) are not generally so much of a problem.

Conclusions

Vodafone has highlighted different areas of social concern in developing and developed countries in relation to mobile telephone use. While the potential health and social problems associated with using mobile phones represent important planks in the firm's approach to CSR in the global North, not only are these sidelined in the global South, but also social responsibility is represented as more a matter of extending phone use and ownership in order to help enable development to take place. It could well be argued that these differences are appropriate, given the very different social contexts represented by, for example, the UK and South Africa. However, there is also the question of whether stakeholders in one region should expect the same degree of social responsibility from a company as stakeholders elsewhere. Ultimately, the case also highlights the problem of how a multinational might determine if it has social responsibilities at all beyond making a profit, producing products, employing people and obeying the law. This became a particularly pertinent question for Vodafone in 2006, when the company announced the biggest annual losses ever by a European company. This led to the sale of Vodafone Sweden and Vodafone Japan, a massive reorganization of the company, and increasingly strident calls from investors for the removal of Chief Executive Officer Arun Sarin.

Study Questions

1   Consider the case for CSR as illustrated by Vodaphone. Is Milton Friedman right in advocating attention solely to economic issues? Or do you agree with Henry Mintzberg that an ethical approach to CSR is necessary in the mobile phone industry? Where would these two different views suggest that Vodafone should draw the line in terms of defining its social obligations?

2   James Stewart at Edinburgh University has coined the phrase "Mobile phones: cigarettes for the twenty-first century". Can you draw any parallels with the mobile telephone industry's response to public concerns about health problems arising from radio frequency exposure, and the tobacco industry's response to concerns about nicotine's addictive and carcinogenic nature in the latter half of the twentieth century? Which types of responsibility as depicted in Carroll's CSR pyramid is Vodafone exhibiting and how do these compare to those of the tobacco industry?

3   Vodafone is a part owner (50 per cent) of Vodacom in South Africa. To what extent might we expect the influence of the larger company, Vodafone, to dictate corporate social responsibility concerns to the smaller Vodacom? What impact should local knowledge of the South African situation play? Use stakeholder theory, as presented by Ed Freeman (Reading 5, Chapter 4), to address the question of how Vodacom should develop its CSR strategy.

4   South Africa is thriving on the introduction of mobile phones. Would you expect health risk concerns in a developing country with significant economic needs to be less pronounced than in developed countries? Why? Answer using one or more of the arguments presented in Section A.

Notes

1   See Rossouw (2002).
2   Details presented here drawn largely from Visser (2005). See his work for further information on corporate citizenship in Africa.
3   See Rosen *et al.* (2003).
4   www.vodacom.com.za.
5   See Coyle (2005).

References

Coyle, D. (ed.) (2005) *Africa: The Impact of Mobile Phones, Moving the Debate Forward*, The Vodafone Policy Paper Series No. 3.

Gillwald, A. (ed.) (2005) *Towards an African e-Index: Household and Individual ICT Access and Usage Across 10 African Countries*, Link Centre, University of Witwatersrand, Johannesburg, South Africa.

NRPB (National Radiological Protection Board) (2004) *Mobile Phones and Health* 15(5), Oxfordshire.

Rosen, S., Simon, J., Vincent, J., MacLeod, W., Fox, M. and Thea, D. (2003) 'Aids Is Your Business', *Harvard Business Review* (February): 81–87.

Rossouw, D. (2002) *Business Ethics in Africa* (2nd edn), Oxford University Press Southern Africa, Cape Town.

Scott, N., Batchelor, S., Ridley, J. and Jorgensen, B. (2004) *The Impact of Mobile Phones in Africa*, Commission for Africa, CNTR 026.

Visser, W. (2005) 'Corporate Citizenship in South Africa: A Review of Progress Since Democracy', *Journal of Corporate Citizenship* 18 (Summer): 29–38.

Visser, W., McIntosh, M. and Middleton, C. (2006) *Corporate Citizenship in Africa: Lessons from the Past; Paths to the Future*, Greenleaf Publishing, Sheffield, UK.

Visser, W., Middleton, C. and McIntosh, M. (2005) Corporate Citizenship in Africa, Special Issue, *Journal of Corporate Citizenship* 18 (Summer).

Vodafone Group PLC (2006) *Expanding the Power of Mobile Communication*, Annual Report, 2005/2006.

Vodafone Group PLC (2006) *We Said, We Have, We Will*, Corporate Responsibility Report 2005/2006.

Sources of Further Information

www.researchictafrica.net – Website of the Link Centre, University of Witwatersrand, South Africa.

www.vodacom.com.za – Vodacom, Vodafone's partner in South Africa.

www.vodafone.com – Vodafone's corporate website.

www.hpa.org.uk/radiation – Website of the Health Protection Agency in the UK, which merged with the National Radiological Protection Board in 2005.

SECTION B

Applying corporate social responsibility

Having now discussed what CSR is, elaborated on some of its basic underlying principles and key theories, and considered the arguments for and against the adoption of responsible business practices above and beyond the legal minimum, we now move on to the question of how these issues can be applied to specific business activities. This is an incredibly important aspect of the debate around CSR, most notably because, whether or not we agree about the significance or relevance of CSR for the modern corporation, it is, in essence, a real management process that takes place in thousands of businesses across the globe.

Let us make no mistake about it: CSR – or something that goes under the banner of CSR or one of its many counterparts – is now practised in most large corporations in Europe and the USA, as well as in parts of Asia, and has been taken up by corporations from many major developing countries such as Brazil, India, and increasingly China. The CSR practices of huge multinationals such as BP, Carrefour, McDonald's, Microsoft, Nestlé, Shell, Toyota, Unilever and Wal-Mart affect millions, perhaps billions of people across the world, whether through the products they supply, the people they employ, the communities in which they locate, or the natural environments they affect.

Therefore, the question of *how* corporations actually implement their social responsibilities could not be a more important one. It is one thing to talk in the abstract about the social role and responsibilities of the corporation, but it is quite another to consider how the corporation can apply those responsibilities to tangible business activities.

In this section, we consider the responsibilities of the corporation in four key arenas,[1] followed by an integrative case study that deals with all four:

● CSR in the marketplace

- CSR in the workplace
- CSR in the community
- CSR in the ecological environment
- ABN AMRO Brazil case study

These four arenas, we would suggest, capture the main areas of business where the philosophy and practice of CSR can be meaningfully applied. They also represent specific arenas of practice in which the interests of particular stakeholder groups can be usefully considered; i.e. under CSR in the marketplace we will consider consumers and (to a lesser extent) suppliers, under CSR in the workplace we will consider employees, and so on.

The purpose of breaking the application of CSR down into four specific arenas is twofold. First, it helps to provide some issue-specific focus for some of the key debates in the CSR literature. For instance, when we ask whether CSR pays off for the firm, we might consider this question in more detail by asking: Does CSR involvement in the community pay off, or do customers respond positively to CSR initiatives? In this sense, the distinct arenas provide greater *specificity* and *simplification* – i.e. sometimes CSR is too broad and overarching to be able to address important questions meaningfully. Second, it makes sense from the perspective of business practice. While many firms will seek to integrate their CSR initiatives, they also need to consider how to suffuse responsibility throughout the different functions. If a responsible firm must know how to market its products responsibly, manage its environmental impacts and protect the human rights of its employees, it will need to engender responsibility in its marketing team, its production units and in its human resource department. Therefore, by breaking the subject down in this way, we are providing an *applied perspective* that offers greater potential for understanding CSR practice.

At the end of Section B, we extend this applied perspective to consider the different arenas of CSR in the context of the real-world experiences of ABN AMRO Bank in Brazil. This case study explores the challenges posed to the Dutch bank in designing an integrated CSR strategy in the developing world.

Note

1   This categorization was inspired by the core CSR areas distinguished by the UK's leading CSR member organization, Business in the Community. See www.bitc.org.uk.

Chapter 5

CSR in the marketplace

IN THIS CHAPTER WE WILL:

- Explain some of the core corporate responsibilities in the marketplace.
- Distinguish between different marketplaces in which corporations might encounter CSR.
- Evaluate the argument that market demands offer a substantial imperative for corporations to engage in social responsibility.
- Explore how corporations might respond to demands from consumers for greater responsibility.
- Examine the meaning of key concepts such as ethical branding, cause-related marketing and reputational risk management.

Introduction

The marketplace is frequently portrayed as one of the most important arenas for considering CSR. For many, the marketplace is seen as one of the main areas where business *ir*responsibility is exposed. For example, in controversial industries such as alcohol, tobacco or, increasingly, fast food, firms are responsible for their products and marketing, and the impact of their activities on consumers dominates the CSR agenda. Should McDonald's provide only 'unhealthy' food or should it also offer salads, fruit and other healthier alternatives? Should Carlsberg help alcoholics and other problem drinkers to reduce consumption of their products? Is British American Tobacco being responsible if they advertise their products in some countries, while others impose bans in the name of public health? These are just some of the market-place responsibility issues facing controversial industries, but similar considerations confront all corporations in some way or another, whether they sell cars, chewing-gum or financial services. The responsible design and marketing of products and services is one of the core responsibilities of the corporation.

The marketplace is crucial for another reason, too – demands from consumers and other stakeholders of products and services are said to act as a key driver for CSR activities more generally. The basic argument here is that CSR is essentially a market preference expressed by consumers. In one of the best-known expressions of this view, McWilliams and Siegel (2001: 119) state:

> One way to assess investment in CSR is as a mechanism for product differ-entiation. In this context, there are CSR "resources" and "outputs." A firm can create a certain level of CSR by embodying its products with CSR attributes (such as pesticide-free fruit) or by using CSR-related resources in its production process (such as naturally occurring insect inhibitors and organic fertilizers). As such, it seems natural to consider the nature of the markets for CSR attributes and CSR-related resources.

Another way of looking at this is to say that the market can act as a social control of business (Smith, 1990) – namely, that consumers can use the market to ensure that corporations act sufficiently responsibly. If firms do not, consumers can retract their purchase dollars or even boycott the company; if, however, they do act responsibly, they will gain the approval of consumers with 'ethical' preferences and (at least in theory) flourish in the marketplace. Of course, this also means that if sufficient numbers of consumers do not express any market preferences for CSR, or if they are not willing to pay for them, then it may well be rational for firms to desist from additional investment in CSR from this perspective.

What we have, then, are two main types of responsibility in the marketplace: on the one hand, we have what Garriga and Melé (pp. 76–107) or Donaldson and Preston (pp. 140–66) might call a *normative* type, namely, that firms have a social respon-sibility to ensure that their marketplace activities offer appropriate benefits to consumers; on the other hand, we have a more *instrumental* type, which suggests that firms should offer social responsibility to the extent that it is expressed as a market preference. Having made this important distinction, let us now go on to look at the sorts of market in which these considerations might be raised.

Understanding the Marketplaces of CSR

When considering CSR in the marketplace, we are referring to a range of business practices including sourcing, buying, marketing, advertising, pricing, and selling of products and services. This occurs in a range of different marketplaces, the most important of which are as follows:

● *Consumer markets* – These are markets in which firms will be marketing directly to end consumers such as you or us. Here, issues such as responsible marketing and the development of CSR brands and communications to consumers are the main considerations.

- *Financial markets* – These are markets for stocks, shares, bonds and other financial products. Here, consumers may still be individual end consumers who might, for example, invest their money in the shares of companies they deem to be socially responsible. More importantly, though, the consumer here may be a pension fund or other institutional investor that can screen out irresponsible firms (or screen in responsible ones) on behalf of end consumers, or that can use its consolidated power as a shareholder to encourage firms to be more responsible. This is a particular case of the market preference for CSR, discussed above, known as *socially responsible investment* (SRI).

- *Business-to-business markets* – These are markets that operate between firms for the supply of goods and services. Here the 'consumer' is essentially another firm. In some cases this can mean that the corporate 'consumer' has significantly more power than an individual consumer would have to influence the behaviour of firms in its supply chain. For example, in Case 3 on Nike in this book (pp. 492–93), we can see how Nike has used its buying power in global supply chains to improve the conditions of workers in its contractors' factories in developing countries.

In this chapter, we mainly focus on the first category, with some discussion of the other two – but most of the issues raised may be applied to any type of market. We will also deal in more detail with supply chain issues in Section C of the book when we come on to discuss codes of conduct (Chapter 10) and global responsibilities (Chapter 11).

Introducing the Readings

The two readings that follow offer a good introduction to marketplace issues, dealing in turn with the questions of the extent of the market for CSR, and then how firms should respond to market preferences for CSR.

The market for CSR

David Vogel's article 'Is there a market for virtue?' considers the business case for CSR in terms of the market imperatives for responsible business. This issue is perhaps the one most frequently raised in relation to CSR, especially on the part of practitioners, namely: does CSR pay? This question is at the heart of the instrumental perspective on CSR which, as we first saw in Chapter 2, suggests that firms should invest in social responsibility when it is in their own 'enlightened' self-interest. While we saw there that Milton Friedman regarded this as the only context in which firms should invest in CSR, Henry Mintzberg countered that this was an insufficient rationale for engaging in responsible practices.

Vogel's article offers a refreshingly clear-sighted examination of the evidence for a substantial market for CSR. His conclusions are unusually candid, however, regarding the limited significance of this market:

> Unfortunately, there is no evidence that behaving more virtuously makes firms more profitable. This finding is important because, unless there is a clear business case for CSR, firms will have fewer incentives to act more responsibly. Conversely, the fact that CSR also does not make firms less profitable means that it is possible for a firm to commit resources to CSR without becoming less competitive. In brief, there is a place in the business system for responsible firms, but the market for virtue is not sufficiently important to make it in the interest of all firms to behave more responsibly.
>
> (pp. 181–210)

Vogel's case is persuasive, but it is important to note that it contradicts the findings of a large swathe of studies which provide support for the relationship between social responsibility and business success (see e.g. Orlitzky, Schmidt and Rynes, 2003). However, Vogel is correct in insisting that market imperatives are present only for some firms in some instances. This is a theme also taken up in the second reading.

Responding to market preferences for CSR

Andrew Crane's article complements Vogel's in that it asks what firms can do when they are among those that perceive a market preference for CSR. Focusing his attention on the response of firms to 'ethical consumers', Crane considers in particular the strategies that firms may implement to appeal to ethical consumers, both in the well-defined 'ethical niches' targeted by companies such as Ecover and the Co-operative Bank, and in mainstream markets targeted by major multinationals. In so doing, he discusses various marketing strategies such as 'ethical branding', cause-related marketing and reputational risk management. Ultimately, he argues that many niche companies have increasingly moved to mainstream positioning, while approaches to CSR have tended towards more cautious risk management rather than explicit ethical branding. While Crane talks mainly about consumer markets, his analysis may also be applied to financial markets, where evidence suggests that SRI has been undergoing similar processes of mainstreaming and risk management in recent years (Friedman and Miles, 2001; Sparkes and Cowton, 2004).

Study Questions

1   Do firms have a responsibility for their products and services, over and above ensuring that they comply with safety legislation and are promoted honestly?

2   To what extent can consumers act as a social control of corporations? In which

of the three marketplace contexts – consumer, financial and business-to-business markets – is this control likely to be the most extensive?

3   In which industries is the market for virtue likely to be the least important? Why is this, and what are the alternatives for promoting social responsibility in these industries?

4   What is an ethical brand, and what are the advantages and disadvantages of developing one? Nominate a firm that you would say has developed an ethical brand, giving reasons for your nomination.

5   'Reputational risk management is not about CSR – it's simply good management.' Discuss.

References

Friedman, A. and Miles, S. (2001) 'Socially Responsible Investment and Corporate Social and Environmental Reporting in the UK: An Exploratory Study', *The British Accounting Review* 33: 523–548.

McWilliams, A. and Siegel, D. (2001) 'Corporate Social Responsibility: A Theory of the Firm Perspective', *Academy of Management Review* 26(1): 117–127.

Orlitzky, M., Schmidt, F. and Rynes, S. (2003) 'Corporate Social and Financial Performance: A Meta-analysis', *Organization Studies* 24(3): 403–411.

Smith, N. (1990) *Morality and the Market: Consumer Pressure for Corporate Accountability*, London: Routledge.

Sparkes, R. and Cowton, C. (2004) 'The Maturing of Socially Responsible Investment: A Review of the Developing Link with Corporate Social Responsibility', *Journal of Business Ethics* 52(1): 45–57.

IS THERE A MARKET FOR VIRTUE? THE BUSINESS CASE FOR CORPORATE SOCIAL RESPONSIBILITY

David Vogel

It is impossible to exaggerate the significance of the contemporary claim that there is a business case for corporate responsibility, business ethics, corporate citizenship, environmental stewardship, pollution control, sustainable development, and the like. To be sure, improving the bottom line is not the only possible reason for CSR. Many executives genuinely care about conducting their business in ways that are more environmentally sustainable, that respect human rights, and that foster economic development. Self-regulation can

Adapted from *The Market for Virtue: The Potential and Limits of Corporate Social Responsibility* by David J. Vogel, Brookings Institution Press, ©2005. By permission of the publisher.

also reduce the likelihood of more government regulation or place a firm in a better competitive position if and when new regulations emerge. Some of the benefits of CSR to a firm, such as higher employee morale or a better reputation, never appear on a balance sheet. For profitable firms, CSR can represent a civic-minded allocation of discretionary resources. But while profitability may not be the only reason corporations will or should behave virtuously, it has become the most influential.

According to the business case for CSR, firms will increasingly behave more responsibly not because managers have become more public-spirited – though some may have – but because more managers now believe that being a better corporate citizen is a source of competitive advantage. A more responsibly managed firm will face fewer business risks than its less virtuous competitors: it will be more likely to avoid consumer boycotts, be better able to obtain capital at a lower cost, and be in a better position to attract and retain committed employees and loyal customers. Correspondingly, firms that are unable or unwilling to recognize this new competitive reality will find themselves disadvantaged in the marketplace: both "responsible" and "sophisticated" investors will regard their shares as too risky; the value of their brands and thus their sales will decline as a result of media exposure, public protests, and boycotts; and the morale of their employees will suffer.

Unfortunately, there is no evidence that behaving more virtuously makes firms more profitable. This finding is important because, unless there is a clear business case for CSR, firms will have fewer incentives to act more responsibly. Conversely, the fact that CSR also does not make firms *less* profitable means that it is possible for a firm to commit resources to CSR without becoming less competitive. In brief, there is a place in the business system for responsible firms, but the market for virtue is not sufficiently important to make it in the interest of all firms to behave more responsibly.

Old-style Corporate Responsibility: Doing Good to Do Good

The business case for corporate responsibility is not new, though its current emphasis is. Historically, the relationship between virtue and profits was understood to be more indirect. The 1954 U.S. court case that legitimated corporate philanthropy was brought by a shareholder who complained that Standard Oil of New Jersey had misused "his" funds by making a contribution to the engineering school of Princeton University. This gift came to typify much corporate philanthropy. It was not unrelated to the purposes of the company: Standard Oil needed well-trained engineers, and its gift to Princeton could be expected to increase their number. But in one sense the shareholder who sued the firm's managers was probably right: this gift was unlikely to make Standard Oil more profitable, since those engineers could just as easily work for its competitors. In effect, Standard Oil was providing a collective good. Nonetheless, the court held that the allocation of such a gift was within the scope of management discretion.

Many firms took advantage of this ruling. By the 1960s, corporate philanthropy had become part of the widely accepted definition of being a good corporate citizen. Allocating some portion of pretax profits, typically via a corporate foundation, had become the expected and common practice of large firms. However, the link between these gifts and the interest of shareholders was indirect, in many cases much more so than that between Standard Oil's shareholders and Princeton University. Corporate philanthropy went well beyond higher education, supporting civic institutions in communities where the firms had employees (often through United Way) and cultural activities in the firm's headquarters community. Many of these expenditures reflected the firm's "enlightened" self-interest as it was broadly understood; only infrequently did these gifts reflect a strategy to increase shareholder value.

The importance attached to corporate philanthropy as an expression of corporate citizenship during the 1960s and 1970s is suggested by the emergence of a "5 percent club," so named because its members donated at least 5 percent of their pretax earnings. Many of the firms widely regarded as the leaders in corporate responsibility during this period – such as Levi Strauss, Dayton Hudson, Cummins Engine, Atlantic Richfield, and Control Data – were members. Many cities established similar clubs, requiring minimum donations to philanthropy of 2 to 5 percent of pretax earnings. While there was substantial peer pressure among corporations to become more philanthropic, no one claimed that such firms were likely to be more profitable than their less generous competitors. And it certainly did not occur to any management scholar that correlating a firm's membership in any of these "clubs" with its financial performance would demonstrate that corporate philanthropy "pays."

According to a study of businesses' urban affairs programs between 1967 and 1970, the most important motivation for their establishment was "enlightened self-interest." David Rockefeller, the chairman of Chase Manhattan Bank, whose firm was a local and national leader in these programs, stated, "Our urban affairs work is good for Chase Manhattan in a strictly business sense. Our efforts are aimed at creating a healthy economic and social environment that is vital to the existence of any corporation." Other executives explained their participation on the grounds that business required both skilled manpower and social stability in order to survive. In light of the ghetto riots that were then sweeping so many American cities, "it was only common sense to try to solve social problems that could threaten their future."[1]

But the benefits generated by these urban programs went to the business community or to society as a whole rather than to the firms that had committed resources to them. These programs reflected, in the words of the Committee for Economic Development, a "broad recognition that corporate self-interest is inexorably involved in the well-being of the society of which business is an integral part."[2] For all his rhetoric about the interests of "business," Rockefeller did not believe that Chase's extensive urban initiatives would improve its earnings compared to those of other NYC banks. Significantly, only one-eighth of the 201 executives surveyed around 1970 viewed their urban affairs programs as a potential source of profits.[3] Indeed, it is precisely these kinds of enlightened expenditures that prompted Milton Friedman to write the now classic 1970 *New York Times* article in which he argued that the only responsibility of managers was to increase shareholder value.[4] Friedman had no quarrel with corporate social policies or programs that benefited shareholders – a category in which he included contributions to the community where the firm's employees resided. What he objected to were expenditures that benefited "society." And in the late 1960s there was no shortage of business initiatives that appeared to violate his criteria.

The New World of CSR: Doing Good to Do Well

Were Friedman now to revisit this subject, he would find much less to concern him. Virtually all contemporary writing on CSR emphasizes its links to corporate profitability. The typical business book on CSR consists either of examples of companies that have behaved more responsibly and thus have also been financially successful, or it advises managers how to make their firms both responsible and profitable. Many of their titles and dust jackets tout the responsibility–profitability connection. Thus *Cause for Success* describes "10 companies that have put profit second and come in first." The experience of these firms, its dust jacket says, illustrates "how solving the world's problems improves corporate health, growth, and competitive edge." The subtitle of *The Sustainability Advantage* is "several business case benefits of a triple bottom line," and *Walking the Talk* is subtitled "the business case for sustainable development." *Corporate Citizenship* presents "successful strategies for responsible companies," and *The Bottom Line of Green Is Black* puts forward "strategies for creating profitable and environmentally sound businesses." For its part, *Profits with Principles* offers "several strategies for delivering value with values."[5]

The message of Chris Laszlo's *The Sustainable Company* is that "an integrated economic, social, and environmental approach leads to more enduring shareholder value . . . It is a long-term strategy, uniquely relevant to the twenty-first century, in which responsible social change can become a source of innovation and profits rather than added cost." A widely used textbook on CSR, Sandra Waddock's *Leading Corporate Citizens*, analyzes "responsible practices and the associated bottom line benefits." *Companies with a Conscience*, now in its third edition, describes twelve companies whose experiences "prove" that "caring capitalism . . . is not only decent, it is also profitable." *Building Reputational Capital* presents "strategies for integrity and fair play that improve the bottom line." According to *Faith and Fortune: The Quiet Revolution to Reform American Business*, "the business case for doing the right things has become so compelling that companies that do good will also do well."[6]

Writing about corporate environmental policies in the *Harvard Business Review*, Stuart Hart argues that "the more we learn about the challenges of sustainability, the clearer it is that we are poised at the threshold of an historic moment in which many of the world's industries may be transformed." He criticizes managers for looking at their environmental policies in too narrow terms: "Greening has been framed in terms of risk reduction, reengineering or cost cutting. Rarely is greening linked to strategy or technical development, and as a result, most companies fail to recognize opportunities of *potentially staggering proportions*" (italics added). Hart concludes: "The responsibility for ensuring a sustainable world falls largely on the shoulders of the world's enterprises," and that, "in the final analysis, it makes good business sense to pursue strategies for a sustainable world."[7] In another influential *HBR* article, Amory Lovins, L. Hunter Lovins, and Paul Hawken predict that "the companies that first make [the change to environmentally responsible practices] will have a competitive edge." The authors add, "Those that don't make that effort won't be a problem because ultimately they won't be around."[8]

The business case for CSR is also widely accepted by many corporate executives. According to a 2002 survey by PricewaterhouseCoopers, "70 percent of global chief executives believe that CSR is vital to their companies' profitability."[9] Another survey reports that 91 percent of CEOs believe CSR management creates shareholder value.[10] As one corporate report put it in 2004, "If we aren't good corporate citizens as reflected in a Triple Bottom Line that takes into account social and environmental responsibilities along with financial ones – eventually our stock price, our profits and our entire business could suffer."[11] According to a KPMG study of 350 firms, "More big multinational firms are seeing the benefits of improving their environmental performance. . . . Firms are saving money and boosting share performance by taking a close look at how their operations impact the environment. . . . Companies see that they can make money as well."[12]

Trends in corporate philanthropy illustrate the extent to which "doing well" and "doing good" have become more closely linked. Michael Porter has urged companies to connect their philanthropic expenditures "to areas that improve their long-term competitive potential."[13] In fact, U.S. corporations are increasingly "adopting strategic philanthropy" by linking their philanthropy to their business missions.[14] A Council on Foundations study based on interviews with 225 corporate chief executives and 100 "next-generation" CEOs reports that, "seventy-one percent felt that a company must determine the benefits to the business of each cause it supports."[15]

The popularity of cause-related marketing is another illustration of the growing links between corporate social and financial objectives. Such marketing typically features promotions in which a portion of the purchase price of a product or service is donated to a social cause: it essentially links marketing and corporate philanthropy. Besides the obvious public relations benefits, one of the most important measures of its success is increased sales. One of the first cause-related marketing efforts was initiated by American Express in 1983 in connection with the restoration of the Statue of Liberty. The firm promised that over a three-month period it would contribute to this civic enterprise a portion of the amount customers charged to their American Express cards. The result of the campaign made marketing history. AmEx card use increased 28 percent, new card applications rose 17 percent, and $1.7 million dollars was raised for the Statue of Liberty and Ellis Island.[16] Cause-related marketing has since grown significantly, from $125 million in 1990 to an estimated $828 million in 2002. In 2004 this figure increased to $991 million.[17]

The change in the rationale for and focus of socially responsible investing (SRI) also reflects the increased links between profits and corporate responsibility. When the concept of socially responsible investing first emerged, its purpose was to enable individuals or organizations opposed to particular kinds of businesses or business activities on moral or political grounds to avoid purchasing shares in these companies. For example, some religious institutions and organizations established policies that excluded investing in firms that produced or sold liquor, tobacco, and in some cases military weapons.

Social investment first became politicized during the late 1960s, but its purposes initially remained the same: to enable investors to reconcile their portfolios with their consciences. In 1971, the Pax World Fund was formed as an investment vehicle to register public and investor opposition to the war in Vietnam by avoiding shares in defense firms. Subsequently, activists seeking to end racial segregation in the Republic of South Africa as well as Portuguese control of Angola and Mozambique waged a determined and in many cases successful effort to pressure universities, public sector pension funds, churches, and foundations to divest themselves of their shares of companies with investments in southern Africa. The Calvert Social Investment Fund, established in 1982, excluded shares in companies that "made money out of environmental degradation . . . that failed to respect human rights (and that) trampled on the rights of indigenous peoples around the world."[18]

But these initial efforts to politicize share selection did not assume that a more "responsible" portfolio would perform better or even as well as a less responsibly managed one. The students who demanded that their universities sell their holdings in firms with investments in South Africa or firms with defense contracts did not believe that this investment strategy would financially benefit their institutions. Rather, they sharply *attacked* their universities for financially benefiting from their "unethical" holdings in firms that made weapons and had investments in South Africa. Nor did those who excluded defense stocks from their portfolios to protest the war in Vietnam believe that this strategy would make their investments perform better.

Advocates of social investment now claim that it makes financial as well as moral sense. According to the director of research for Calvert Asset Management, "We believe that a company that pollutes the environment or mistreats its workers can get away with it for a while. But eventually it's going to come back to haunt them."[19] One purpose of promoting greater transparency in business conduct is precisely to enable investors to take advantage of the positive relationship between corporate social performance and financial success. Judy Henderson, a member of the directorate of the Global Reporting Initiative, states that a transparent reporting framework provides a competitive advantage "because discerning investors now recognize that a company managed according to interests broader than those of only shareholders is more likely to profit over the long term." She adds, "Corporations with a stakeholder focus have been shown to enjoy greater sales and value growth than companies with narrow shareholder focus."[20] In that same vein, the title of a report by the Global Compact on "connecting financial markets to a changing world" confidently asserts that companies that care will come out on top: *Who Cares Wins*.[21]

The strategy of many social investment funds has changed to reflect this more businesslike approach to SRI. While most ethical funds continue to exclude investing in some firms on the basis of their core business, virtually all also seek to identify and then invest in the firms with the best CSR practices. The increased use of positive screening has an economic as well as a political purpose: positive screening reflects the belief that more responsible firms are also likely to have superior financial performance.[22]

A belief in the business benefits of CSR is particularly influential in Europe. Influenced by the work of Michael Porter, who argues that more stringent environmental standards can improve the competitiveness of a nation's businesses, the European Union has repeatedly stressed the business benefits of CSR.[23] The business case for CSR informs the European Union's influential White Paper on Corporate Social Responsibility. It also is a central motif in conferences sponsored by the EU and its affiliates, where presentations emphasize the benefits of CSR to both investors and companies.[24] Advocates of social and environmental disclosure requirements for companies in Europe believe that they will help the capital markets identify more responsible firms and help predict which firms are likely to be more competitive.

Academic studies have also taken an interest in the relationship between ethics and profits. The first such study was published in 1972; there are currently more than 120 and new ones keep appearing.[25] The rationale for many of these studies is clear: to legitimate a broader conception of the firm's role and responsibilities by integrating it with a narrower financial conception. As Margolis and Walsh insightfully observe:

> Empirical evidence of a positive causal relationship moving from social performance to financial performance also promises, for some,

> a solution to endless debate about the social role and responsibilities of the firm. . . . Those who construe a narrow economic role for the firm would embrace a financial rationality for socially responsible practices, and those with a broader conception of the firm's responsibilities would not need to appeal to an alternative construal of the firm's purpose to justify expansive responsibilities.[26]

Such a "solution" clearly appeals to those who study and teach business and society and business ethics at business schools: it places what they teach and study much closer to the mainstream of business education and practice.

The influence of the business case for CSR also has affected the strategies of some NGOs. While many NGOs remain indifferent or hostile to the financial objectives of business, some have developed more cooperative relationships with firms, often helping companies to reconcile their business missions with other objectives, notably environmental quality.[27] They frequently urge firms to behave more responsibly on the grounds that doing so is also good business. The antiwar activists who, during the 1960s, pressured Dow Chemical to stop producing napalm, framed their argument exclusively in moral terms: they neither knew or cared whether producing napalm would affect Dow's earnings. In contrast, the contemporary environmental activists who are working with Dow to reduce its carbon emissions argue that doing so will make Dow more profitable by lowering its costs. Many socially oriented investors articulate their interest in sustainable environmental practices or human rights issues in similar terms: they ask corporations to act more responsibly on the grounds that doing so is in the best interests of their shareholders, in part by reducing business risk.

The New Business Environment

Never before has the claim that corporate virtue can and should be profitable enjoyed so much currency or influence. Two factors help account for this development: One has to do with a change in the structure of the business system, another with changes in attitudes toward business. Both are particularly influential in the United States, but their influence is apparent in Europe as well.

The changing nature of the firm

The view that corporate responsibility reflected the enlightened self-interest of business or its obligations to society rather than its contribution to profits was associated with a distinctive structure of industrial organization. Such a firm was typically large and professionally managed, and its shares were widely held. It enjoyed a reasonably secure or very secure market position

– often an oligopolistic one – and faced little if any foreign competition, at least in its domestic market. Importantly, neither the compensation nor the tenure of its managers was directly linked to its earnings or share price.

The emergence of the modern doctrine of corporate responsibility in the United States is linked to the managerial revolution that occurred around the turn of the century. George Perkins of U.S. Steel, the professional manager of the world's first billion-dollar corporation, wrote in 1908:

> The larger the corporation becomes, the greater become its respon-
> sibilities to the entire community. The corporations of the future
> must be those that are semi-public servants, serving the public, with
> ownership widespread among the public, and with labor so fairly
> treated that it will look upon the corporation as its friend.[28]

In the view of many observers, it was the separation of ownership and control – first noted at the turn of the twentieth century and subsequently documented by Berle and Means in 1932 – that made it both possible and necessary for business leaders to behave more responsibly. As Walter Lippmann put it in his 1914 book *Drift and Mastery*, "The cultural basis of property is radically altered . . . The men connected with these essential properties cannot escape the fact that they are expected to act increasingly like public officials . . . Big businessmen who are at all intelligent recognize this. They are talking more and more about their 'responsibilities,' their 'stewardship.'"[29]

This change in the pattern of corporate ownership meant that professional managers and owners had different priorities. Unlike owners, managers were in a position "to balance the claims of the firm's stockholders, consumers and the public in general."[30] Freed from the pressure to earn as much money as possible for their shareholders, managers could use corporate resources to pursue a variety of goals – essentially making companies into "multipurpose social institutions."[31]

This firm, popularly depicted in Galbraith's *New Industrial State*, could "afford" to engage or support programs or policies that were unrelated or only tangentially linked to its business objectives since its market position was relatively stable, and equally important, its shareholders were relatively passive. Its managers might not always, or even often, have acted like "public officials," judiciously and responsibly balancing the claims of the firm's many stakeholders, only one of whom was its shareholders, but in principle they were in a position to do so. And in fact, many adopted highly paternalistic labor policies, provided job security for their white-collar employees and generous benefits for their blue-collar employees, and made substantial philanthropic contributions.

For better or worse, the world in which these corporations existed has disappeared in the U.S. and increasingly in Europe as well. Thanks to increased domestic and international competition, threats of hostile takeovers, the concentration of ownership in the hands of institutional investors, and changes in the basis of executive compensation, the creation of shareholder value has become a central objective of managers. Their personal wealth and continued employment as well as the survival of their firms now depend on their ability to shape and meet the expectations of financial markets. Accordingly, "the freedom of top executives to pursue corporate goals unrelated to the bottom line has been circumscribed. . . . Managerial capitalism tolerated a host of company objectives besides shareholder value. Investor capitalism does not."[32] In a sense, managers now have little choice but to follow Friedman's dictum: they *must* strive to maximize shareholder value.

Ironically, one might have thought that these changes in both management incentives and the competitive environment would have led to the conclusion that it has become much *more* difficult for firms to act responsibly. Instead it has led to a shift in the rationale for corporate sensibility. Now the main justification for corporate responsibility *is* its contribution to the bottom line. While criticizing Friedman's article remains de rigueur in virtually every book and article on corporate responsibility, many contemporary advocates of CSR have implicitly accepted Friedman's position that the primary responsibility of companies is to create wealth for their shareholders. But they have added a twist: in order for companies to do so, they must now act virtuously.

The new embrace of money and morals

The contemporary importance of the business case for CSR is linked to a second development: the popular embrace of business and the values of money-making. The movement for corporate responsibility of the 1960s and 1970s took place during a period of considerable hostility to business. Indeed, companies began to talk more about their social responsibilities during the late 1960s and early 1970s in part as a response to the disenchantment expressed by many college students and graduates with business values. *Fortune* noted in 1966 that "the prejudice against business is undeniable, and permeates the country's highest-ranking colleges."[33] A student at the Harvard Business School admitted, "If people are really interested in tackling social problems, they will have nothing to do with business."[34] A 1967 survey of college students reported that 61 percent found "their fellow students to be indifferent or hostile toward working in industry."[35] During the second half of the 1960s, enrollment in business schools increased only one-third as fast as total college enrollment.[36]

The current revival of interest in corporate responsibility began in a somewhat different cultural and social context. While surveys continue to report widespread hostility to and suspicion of business, the 1990s were also a decade when many of America's and Europe's "best and brightest" became attracted to business careers. Successful entrepreneurs became admired and respected, and the growth of Silicon Valley became a focus of national pride in the United States and envy in other countries. "Making money" became more respectable, popular interest in business grew, and not coincidentally, business school enrollment soared in both the United States and Europe.

Still, some of the people who enrolled in business schools or began to work for or start companies also cared about social and environmental concerns. And many were highly critical of corporate social and environmental practices. How could their interest in business – and making money – and their social values be reconciled? The business case for corporate responsibility provided an answer. Like investors in socially responsible mutual funds, they did not have to abandon their values to become prosperous. On the contrary: they could simultaneously become financially secure *and* make the world a better place. Indeed, they could now become prosperous *by* making the world a better place.

One strain of the contemporary movement for corporate responsibility links the "counterculture" values of the 1960s with those of the "decade of greed," as the 1980s came to be known. This vision appeals not only to those who were influenced by the values revolution of the 1960s and 1970s, in some cases belatedly. Many of the latter individuals now hold positions of leadership in corporations. They too want to believe that there is a business case for corporate responsibility since it enables them to link their personal values with their responsibility as managers. And it is the baby-boomer generation, many of whose members have become relatively affluent but still hold liberal social values, who are the major individual investors in socially responsible mutual funds.[37] These investors care about social values, but they also want to protect the value of their savings.

The emergence of "companies with a conscience" represents a particularly vivid expression of the contemporary reconciliation of social values and the business system. These are companies whose vision of social responsibility was integral to their business strategies from the outset. They were formed by individuals with strong personal social commitments who regarded their businesses both as vehicles to make money and as a means to improve society. Among those that became widely known and celebrated are the Body Shop, Seventh Generation, Domini, Esprit, Celestial Seasonings, Stonyfield Farm, Tom's of Maine, Ben and Jerry's, and Patagonia. As Ben Cohen, one of the founders of Ben and Jerry's put it: "We are in the process of creating . . . a business climate in which the right way to go about solving social problems is by founding and maintaining and sustaining a socially responsible business." Anita Roddick, the founder of the Body Shop, acknowledged, "I think a lot of us would have slit our wrists if we ever thought we'd be part of corporate America or England." Likewise, many of the individuals who established socially responsible funds and research services, such as Peter Kinder and Amy Domini, had political as well as financial motivations:

they wanted to use SRI to bring about social change by improving business practices, as well as create successful businesses.[38]

In 2000, Goldman Sachs began funding a national – subsequently international – business competition in which business students and recent MBAs develop business plans that are judged on how well they meet *both* social and financial criteria. The most promising plans are often funded. Many business schools now offer courses in social entrepreneurship – in effect teaching MBA students how to form and secure funding for future Ben and Jerry's. One of the largest American MBA student organizations is Net Impact. Its well-attended annual conventions feature inspirational speeches by business leaders – entrepreneurs and professional managers – who personify both the financial benefits of corporate responsibility and the social contributions of successful firms. In Britain, First Tuesday, which formerly functioned as a "dating agency" for dot.com entrepreneurs and venture capitalists, now hosts meetings that bring together entrepreneurs with sustainable ideas and investors with environmental concerns, with the goal of building a "global sustainability business network."[39]

In short, the increasing influence of the business case for CSR reflects changes in the nature of business competition and changes in beliefs about the potential social role of business. It is both widely believed and influential. But what is the evidence that such a business case exists?

Putting the Business Case to the Test

An extensive body of academic research examines the relationship between corporate responsibility and profitability.[40] Its central conclusion can be easily summarized: at best, it is inconclusive.

What the studies show

While many studies report a positive relationship between ethics and profits, some find a negative relationship, and still others find the relationship to be either neutral or mixed. These results hold both for those studies that use financial performance to explain social performance and for those in which the causal relationship is reversed. Equivocal results also characterize those studies that assess a wide variety of measures of corporate social responsibility as well as those that focus on specific areas such as environmental performance, corporate philanthropy, and community relations.

In the area of environmental performance, one study found a moderate positive relationship between levels of emissions reduction between 1988 and 1989 and the financial performance for firms involved in manufacturing, mining, and production, though the direction of causality was not clear.[41] Another study reports a strong positive relationship between the financial performance of large manufacturing and mining firms and their adherence to relatively stringent uniform global environmental standards, though such firms may perform better just because they are better managed.[42] A third study reports a positive relationship between financial performance and various dimensions of environmental performance based on ratings by the Franklin Research and Development Corporation. This relationship was especially strong for firms in high-growth industries.[43] But reviews of a broader range of research suggest that environmentally responsible behavior does not raise performance:

> Researchers have yet to demonstrate that environmental expenditures improve firm profitability in a structural way, and that is it not a matter of reverse causality, where profitable firms can afford to invest in environmental performance. A more likely explanation of the research to date [which demonstrates a positive relationship between environmental and financial performance] is that various omitted variables affecting both environmental and financial performance are responsible for the apparent statistical relationship.[44]

Research that relates measures of corporate environmental performance to measures of financial performance suffers from several shortcomings. Few studies attempt to explain how better environmental strategies have changed financial analysts' views of a firm's future earnings. Among those studies that compare the portfolios of environmental leaders and laggards, virtually none correct for differences in risk other than environmental performance. These studies also do not address the issue of causation. It is as likely that more profitable firms are able to devote more resources to environmental protection as it is that such firms are more profitable *because* they have adopted better environmental practices.[45] It is also possible that good environmental performance is a proxy for management quality.

It is hard to draw broad conclusions about the relationship between CSR and profits because the studies often measure different things. In the ninety-five studies summarized by Margolis and Walsh, financial performance is measured in seventy different ways: these studies employ forty-nine different accounting measures, twelve different market measures, five measures that mix accounting and market indicators, and four other measures of outcome performance.[46] Accounting measures are usually used as indications of prior financial performance for studies that seek to explain the impact of CSR on financial performance, while market measures are usually employed to assess future performance when financial performance is used to explain CSR.[47]

Measurements of corporate social performance also vary widely.[48] In ninety-five studies, twenty-seven different data sources were used. These range from multidimensional screening criteria, surveys, conduct in South Africa (which has since become irrelevant), organizational programs and

practices, disclosure, money spent, environmental performance and reputation. The most frequently used are environmental practices, followed by
omnibus measures such as the *Fortune* reputation rankings and the indexes of
Kinder Lyderberg Domini (KLD) Research & Analytics.

Not only does the diversity of these measures make drawing conclusions
from this literature difficult, but there is considerable debate about the
validity of some of them. For example, one of the most commonly employed
measures of CSR is based on *Fortune*'s annual reputational survey of America's
most admired corporations. One of the attributes rated by *Fortune* is a "company's responsibility to the community and the environment." However, its
raw scores appear to be heavily influenced by a company's previous financial
performance, which means that any relationship between it and corporate
profitability is tautological. In addition, the surveys on which the rankings
are based poll only industry executives and market analysts.[49]

The most exhaustive and widely used measure of CSR is KLD's extensive
database of 400 mainly U.S. companies. KLD evaluates five different measures of corporate performance: community relations, diversity, employee
relations, natural environment, and product safety and quality. The rankings
rely on publicly available data such as information supplied to tax and
regulatory agencies, newspapers, and magazines, and on company reports,
supplemented by surveys of the 400 firms. Companies also have the opportunity to review KLD's assessments before they are released. However, KLD
does not reveal its basis for weighing each screening category in determining
a firm's overall CSR ranking. Many of its rankings are subjective; few are
based on quantitative measures. In many instances the data on which ratings
are based are incomplete, particularly with respect to the non-U.S. operations of the companies in its database.

Studies that employ a narrower range of criteria capture only some of
the policies usually associated with corporate responsibility, while those that
employ a broader range are unable to identify which policies might be
affecting financial performance. And it is not uncommon for firms to exhibit
more virtuous performance in some areas than in others. Even within a
relatively narrow category such as environmental performance, measures
can be inconsistent with one another. Thus how should a firm's environmental
responsibilities be assessed if it has relatively low emissions, but a poor
record of compliance and a weak environmental management system?[50]
Virtually every measure employed has been subject to substantial criticism:
no consensus has emerged as to how either environmental responsibility or
corporate responsibility more generally can or should be measured.

Any effort to explain a firm's financial performance must also control
for other antecedent factors. But not all studies adequately do so. For example, McWilliams and Siegel, in re-examining the conclusions of a study that
strongly linked corporate social and financial performance, found that "when
R&D intensity is included in the equation, CSP (corporate social performance) is shown to have a neutral effect on profitability," since firms that

actively engage in CSR also tend to make strategic investments in R&D.[51] Some studies employ no control variables, which means that any relationship they find may be spurious. In all, nearly fifty different control variables have been used by different scholars. Industry, size, and risk are employed most frequently, but most control variables have been used only once. This also increases the difficulty of identifying the relative contribution of social performance to financial performance.[52]

Equally important, correlations drawn from surveys and other cross-sectional data cannot establish the direction of causality. It is just as likely that more successful firms are more responsible than others as it is that more responsible firms are more successful than others. For example, if firms identified as "good places to work" are more profitable, this may be because they can afford to treat their employees well, not because their labor policies increase shareholder value. Moreover, correlations between social and financial performance may reflect the fact that well-managed firms are also better at managing CSR, making it difficult to discern whether or to what extent they are more profitable because they are more responsible.

The dozen literature reviews published between 1979 and 1999 identify nearly fifty shortcomings of the broader body of research. They agree that the connection between CSR and financial performance has not been established and that neither academics nor practitioners should rely on the research results because they are incomparable.[53] Summarizing both their own analysis and these studies, Margolis and Walsh concur:

> The clear signal that emerges from thirty years of academic research – indicating that a positive relationship exists between social performance and financial performance – must be treated with caution. Serious methodological concerns have been raised about many of the studies and about efforts to aggregate results . . . Questions arise about the connection between the underlying CSP [corporate social performance] construct and efforts to measure it; the validity of the measures used to assess social performance; the diversity of measures used to assess financial performance; and the direction and mechanisms of causation; given the heavy reliance on correlation analyses and contemporaneous financial and social performance data.[54]

It is thus difficult to know what to make of the claim that "those hoping for a positive or neutral impact of social performance on financial performance can feel some satisfaction, because the vast majority of studies support the idea that, at the very least, good social performance does not lead to poor financial performance."[55] If this is true, it might reflect the fact that corporate responsibility is not sufficiently costly to affect earnings. Or it might be attributable to the fact that many corporate CSR expenditures are discretionary and therefore more likely to be made by more profitable firms. But although CSR may not make firms any less profitable, it is possible that some more responsible firms might be even more profitable if they were less responsible.

Putting CSR in its place

Studies of the links between social responsibility and profitability continue to be published and are becoming increasingly sophisticated. It is possible that future research will confirm the validity of the several studies that have posited positive causal relationships between the two. However, the effort to demonstrate through statistical analyses that corporate responsibility pays may be not only fruitless, but also pointless and unnecessary, because such studies purport to hold corporate responsibility to a standard to which no other business activity is subject. For example, it is highly unlikely that there is a positive correlation between advertising expenditures and corporate profitability; some profitable firms spend little on advertising, and many advertising expenditures produce disappointing results. Yet no one would dispute that there is a business case for advertising.

But just as firms that spend more on marketing are not necessarily more profitable than those that spend less, there is no reason to expect more responsible firms to outperform less responsible ones. In other words, the risks associated with CSR are no different than those associated with any other business strategy; sometimes investments in CSR makes business sense and sometimes they do not. Why should we expect investments in CSR to consistently create shareholder value when virtually no other business investments or strategies do so?

It is not necessary to find a positive statistical relationship between CSR and profits to claim that some firms may benefit financially from being more responsible or suffer from being irresponsible. This is certainly true. Such a claim, however, does not satisfy CSR advocates. The reason they have placed so much importance on "proving" that CSR pays is because they want to demonstrate, first, that behaving more responsibly is in the self-interest of *all* firms, and second, that CSR *always* makes business sense. Were they able to satisfactorily do either or both, then presumably all firms would begin to behave more responsibly so that they too could become more profitable.[56]

But even if it were possible to convincingly demonstrate a positive causal link between CSR and business financial performance, it is unclear what this would prove. If some firms are actually more profitable *because* they are more responsible, it does not necessarily follow that their less responsible competitors would be more profitable if they were more responsible. It is equally possible that the market niche for relatively responsible firms is limited and that they would be better off continuing to pursue a less responsible strategy. And a link between responsibility and profitability does not necessarily mean that firms would be even more profitable if they were more responsible, since there may be declining returns for behaving more responsibly. In fact, if all firms behaved responsibly – which presumably is the goal of the CSR movement – then at least some of the advantages a firm receives from being *more* responsible than its competitors would disappear, and thus, ironically, future studies of the links between CSR and profits would find no statistical significant relationship.

Moreover, if CSR were actually a significant source of competitive advantage, then it might logically be in the interest of more responsible firms to discourage their competitors from following their example. After all, a firm that has developed a profitable new product does not want its competitors to imitate it, or even learn from its example. But in the case of CSR the opposite is true: rather than seek to protect their "first mover" advantages, these firms frequently encourage their less responsible competitors to emulate their behavior.[57] Hence the popularity of industry codes of conduct in business sectors that are under public pressure to improve their social performance. This suggests that more virtuous firms are frequently not able to capture the financial benefits of their more responsible behavior.

Instead of being defined as a necessary condition for business success, corporate responsibility is better understood as one dimension of corporate strategy. Corporations pursue a wide variety of strategies: some are highly diversified, others are specialized; some invest heavily in research and development, others focus on marketing; some pay relatively high wages, others pay close to the minimum wage; some are global, others focus on national or local markets. CSR is no different: firms have chosen and will continue to choose different levels of corporate responsibility, depending upon the risks and opportunities they face. There is no reason to expect a convergence of CSR strategies, any more than companies can be expected to converge on any other strategy. That said, it is of course possible that the baseline or benchmark for corporate behavior could steadily improve. But correlations of responsibility and profitability will not tell us whether this is occurring.

Taking a Second Look at CSR: Socially Responsible Investment

The validity of the business case for virtue can also be explored through the financial performance of socially responsible mutual funds. The results of this analysis reveal that socially responsible funds and indexes perform no better or worse than those of any other kind of fund or stock index. The three most widely used ethical fund indexes are the Domini 400 Social Index, which is based on the research of KLD discussed above; the Dow Jones Sustainability World Index (DJSWI); and the FTSE4Good Index. In addition to using positive screens, the Domini uses negative screens based on military contracting, the manufacture of alcohol or tobacco products, revenues from gaming products or services, and the ownership of nuclear power plants. DJSWI, which was established in 1999 by the Sustainability Asset Management Group, a Swiss company, in cooperation with Dow Jones Indexes, tracks the performance of the top 10 percent of leading sustainability firms in each industry group. The FTSE4Good Index includes firms that meet its criteria on social, environmental, and human rights issues and excludes tobacco, arms manufacturers, and firms that produce nuclear power or uranium.

The performance of socially responsible funds

Between May 1, 1990, and June 30, 2004, KLD's Domini 400 Social Index, which is used as the basis for selecting the Domini Social Equity Fund (the fourth largest social fund with $1.2 billion under management), returned $5.40 for each dollar invested, while the S&P 500 returned $4.60. But this difference is largely attributable to the industries in which the fund invested; there was no evidence of a "social" factor.[58] For its part, the FTSE4Good has closely tracked the performance of the FTSE All Share Index since 2000.

The DJSWI has performed more poorly than the benchmark Dow Jones Global Index since its inception in 1999, but much of this difference can be traced to the relative size of the two indexes. The DJSWI consists of only 250 companies, while the DJ Global comprises 5,029, making the former much less diversified and therefore more susceptible to changes in the market valuation of any one firm. It is also overweighted in large-capitalization stocks and growth companies, and it adds and deletes companies more frequently than do most indexes: in 2002, it replaced more than seventy companies, nearly one-quarter of its portfolio. Although the performance of the DJWSI Index is often taken as evidence for or against the financial case for SRI, the lack of comparability between it and the DJ Global Index renders any such assessment problematic. Alois Flatz, its former research director, cautions: "It is premature to draw definitive conclusions regarding the business case for sustainability. . . . A much longer time frame is needed to attribute index or fund performance to particular sustainability criteria or strategies.[59]

As in the case of the Domini Social 400 and DJSWI, much of the relative performance of SRI mutual funds and indexes is affected by the performance of the industries in which their investments are concentrated.[60] For this reason, in some years they have outperformed their mainstream counterparts and in other years have lagged behind them. For example, during the latter part of the 1990s, many social funds showed relatively strong returns due to their heavy exposure in financials, "clean" technology, health care, media, and communications. But their performance was then negatively affected when the value of many of these firms declined.

In addition, social investors are not free from the fads that affect all other investors.[61] In Britain during the late 1980s, there was considerable excitement about the financial prospects of "green" companies, and a "green index" of thirty companies involved in environmental services increased in value from 100 to 147 in just five months. This green euphoria, however, could not be sustained, and over the next five years the index steadily underperformed the FTSE All Share Index. A similar development occurred in the United States, where the fifty worst mutual funds listed by the *Wall Street Journal* in 1993 contained a number of environmental funds, most of them involved in environmental remediation.

While there continues to be debate over whether the use of negative screens by virtually all SRI funds increases risk or lowers returns (or both), or alternatively, whether socially screened investments are less volatile and result in higher returns, the consensus of the more than 100 studies of social investment funds and their strategies is that the risk-adjusted returns of a carefully constructed socially screened portfolio is zero.[62] In other words, share returns are neither harmed nor helped by including social criteria in stock selection. This explains why SRI investment vehicles have recently grown in popularity in both the United States and Europe; there appears to be little cost associated with making such investments. But it also undermines the frequent claim that more responsible firms, at least as assessed by SRI fund managers and researchers, perform better. It also explains why the funds that manage 98 percent of investments in mutual funds in the United States continue to pursue other investment strategies, none of which is necessarily any better or worse.

Ironically, if more socially responsible firms did systematically perform better, we would expect all fund managers to heavily weigh their portfolios with those firms' securities. This would both erase all differences in financial performance between socially responsible and "normal" funds and raise the price of the shares of more responsible firms so as to reduce the return from future purchases of them. Still, if the financial markets undervalue corporate social performance, then more responsible investors might in principle be able to earn higher returns when the financial consequences of responsible or irresponsible behavior eventually affected earnings. But there is no persuasive evidence that the market does so.

Some advocates of SRI continue to claim that socially informed investment funds will perform better because their managers are more aware of the significance of corporate social and environmental policies on long-term financial performance.[63] As one environmental foundation writes: "We believe that we are once again on the cusp of redefining the responsibilities of a prudent fiduciary – this time to recognize that improving environmental performance is a primary pathway to increasing shareholder value."[64] Its claim is that, as an environmentally conscious investor, it possesses insights into the long-term financial benefits of corporate environmental efforts, which more conventional investors have overlooked.

That such claims have not yet been validated does not mean that they never will be. But there is reason to be skeptical. For this claim cannot rest on an investor's ability to accurately measure current corporate environmental practices, or more precisely, the relationships between current and future corporate environmental practices and between those practices and current and future environmental pressures and opportunities. But how can anyone know which environmental issues will become politically salient or whether a firm that has successfully addressed environmental issues in the past will also manage them well in the future? Such uncertainties about future financial performance are no different from those that confront any investment strategy.

In this context it is worth recalling that the social investment community was no more able than any other investors to identify the failures of corporate governance that created such massive shareholder losses at the beginning of the twenty-first century. Enron, WorldCom, Adelphia, and Healthcare were all widely held by SRI funds. Enron was widely respected for its CSR: it was ranked one of the 100 best companies to work for; received several environmental awards; issued a triple-bottom-line report; established a social responsibility task force; developed codes of conduct covering security, corruption, and human rights; supported progressive climate change policies; and was known for its generous philanthropic contributions. These practices, which led a number of SRI funds to include Enron in their portfolios, did not make Enron a sound investment. And Shell, whose environmental and human rights initiatives led it to be included in many SRI portfolios, also did not turn out to be a prudent investment when in 2004 it was revealed to have falsified the amount of its oil reserves.

The dubious claims for socially responsible investing

Implicit in the very existence of SRI is the claim that it is possible to identify which firms are more or less responsible. Not only is this claim questionable, but the selection criteria employed by SRI fund managers and researchers can be criticized on several grounds.

First, questions have been raised about both the information that fund managers rely on to make investment decisions and the consistency of the criteria they employ. According to a study of eight of the most prominent funds, "Sources of social information used varied widely from fund to fund with data provided by firms themselves being the most frequently used."[65] While all investors depend heavily on corporate self-reporting, the shortcomings of corporate financial reporting pale when compared with those of corporate voluntary disclosures of nonfinancial performance, in part because, with one rare exception, there have been no legal penalties for providing incomplete or misleading information. Another common source of data, articles in the business and popular press, may reflect the effectiveness of a firm's public relations, or that of its critics, rather than its actual behavior. Moreover, many SRI fund managers use screening methodologies that are proprietary and thus they cannot reveal why a particular firm is excluded or included.

A second criticism focuses on the criteria employed by SRI funds to determine corporate "irresponsibility."[66] Tobacco and alcohol are the two negative screens American funds use most often. The reasons for the former are relatively straightforward, but the latter is more problematic: why should a firm automatically be considered irresponsible because it produces or distributes wine, a product that shareholders in ethical mutual funds are as likely to enjoy as any other group of investors? More substantively, many funds restrict or prohibit investments in firms that produce military equipment or nuclear power. But should such firms be considered "irresponsible" in light of the fact that the former may contribute to legitimate national security needs and the latter may contribute to reducing carbon emissions? Despite all their claims to be on the cutting edge of changing public expectations of business, no fund has relaxed its exclusion of military contractors since September 11.

SRI has also been criticized for being *too* inclusive. According to a survey of more than 600 SRI funds, by Paul Hawken, more than 90 percent of *Fortune 500* companies are included in at least one SRI portfolio. Hawken argues that the selection criteria employed by many social funds allows virtually any publicly held firm to be considered responsible. The most widely held firm by socially responsible investment funds is Microsoft, a firm that Hawken criticizes for "its ruthless, take-no-prisoners management tactics," as well as for antitrust violations in both the United States and Europe. (According to Calvert, "aside from its [Microsoft's] legal troubles, the company has a number of exemplary practices with respect to workplace issues, international operations and human rights.")[67] Hawken is also critical of the social and ethical practices of other firms that feature prominently in SRI portfolios, including Wal-Mart (held by thirty-three SRI funds), Halliburton (held by twenty-three funds), and ExxonMobil (held by forty funds).

Finally, the emphasis many funds place on competitive rates of return renders problematic a critical raison d'être of social investment, namely that social responsibility pays. These funds typically apply their social attributes or yardsticks only *after* firms have been screened by normal financial criteria. The result may be the exclusion of investments in firms whose social performance is outstanding or highly innovative, but whose financial prospects are uncertain or modest. An innovative or pioneering firm that has chosen to sacrifice short-term profits in the pursuit of social goals thus might not be owned by many socially responsible funds. This may be counterproductive from the perspective of promoting more responsible corporate behavior, and it also calls into question the popular claim that being more responsible can and should make a firm a better investment.

These criticisms suggest that even if SRI funds were to consistently outperform nonsocially screened portfolios (which there is little evidence that they do), it is unclear what this would prove about the relationship between corporate responsibility and profitability.

Are Virtuous Firms Built to Last?

CSR advocates assert that while CSR may not affect short-term earnings or share performance, *in the long run* the more responsible firms will perform better. One way of investigating this assertion is to examine the social performance of companies that have performed extremely well financially over an extended period of time.

Consider, for example, the U.S.-based firms included in the 1994 bestseller *Built to Last* on the basis of their having attained "extraordinary long-term performance." According to its authors James Collins and Jerry Porras, these firms are "more than successful. They are more than enduring. In most cases, they are the best of the best in their industries, and have been that way for decades."[68] The firms that meet their criteria are 3M, American Express, Boeing, Citicorp, Ford, General Electric, Hewlett-Packard, IBM, Johnson & Johnson, Marriott, Merck, Motorola, Nordstrom, Philip Morris, Procter & Gamble, Sony, Wal-Mart, and Walt Disney. To this list of distinguished financial performers we can add the companies featured in the sequel *Good to Great* published in 2001, whose cumulative stock return was 6.9 times that of the market as a whole. These firms are Abbott, Circuit City, Fannie Mae, Gillette, Kimberly-Clark, Kroger, Nucor, Philip Morris, Pitney Bowes, Walgreens, and Wells Fargo.

Some of these twenty-eight firms do enjoy reputations for exhibiting above average levels of CSR on some dimensions, including American Express, 3M, Hewlett-Packard, IBM, Johnson & Johnson, Citicorp, and Merck. And it is possible that their social responsibility has contributed to their above average financial performance during the time frame considered in the two best-sellers, though it is unlikely to have been critical to it. But no one would confuse all or even most of these companies with firms that are also leaders on many dimensions of CSR. (Note that the only company featured in both books is Philip Morris.) It is true that these firms have been built around values, visions, and goals other than profit maximization, and, according to Collins and Porras, these factors have contributed to their financial success. But only in a few instances do these values have anything to do with social responsibility.

Social responsibility and irresponsibility may well matter, but their impact on the long-term financial performance of companies is typically dwarfed by a host of other factors. Particular firms succeed or fail for many reasons, but exemplary or irresponsible social or environmental performance is rarely among them. And there is no evidence that the relative importance of CSR to financial success is increasing for most or even many companies. For all the claims that being responsible is a necessary condition for long-term business success, what is striking is how few responsible firms have been "built to last." There are certainly firms that have been both relatively profitable and responsible over more than one or two decades, but the list is not long. More important, it does not appear to be growing. It is of course possible that in ten years the number of financially successful "responsible" companies will be much larger. But the historical record to date gives few grounds for such optimism.

During the 1970s, lists of the most socially responsible firms would have included Atlantic Richfield, Control Data, Cummins Engine, Dayton-Hudson, Levi Strauss, and Polaroid.[69] Polaroid filed for bankruptcy in 2001. In 1992, Control Data, faced with losses that at one point totalled more than $1 billion, was divided into two companies; its CSR practices are no longer distinctive. Dayton-Hudson barely survived a hostile takeover in the 1980s, and Levi Strauss's sales have been declining since the mid-1990s, forcing it to abandon its prior commitment to source some of its products from domestic manufacturers. Cummins Engine has survived – and prospered – but competitive pressures have forced it to abandon many of its highly paternalistic employment policies and the community contributions that made it socially distinctive. In 1999, Atlantic Richfield was acquired by British Petroleum as part of a general consolidation of the oil industry.

Merck, a firm widely recognized for its decision in the 1980s to develop and distribute without charge a drug for river blindness and more recently for its work with the Gates Foundation to make AIDS drugs available in Botswana, began experiencing declining profits and an underperforming stock price after 2000, leading some analysts to question the continued validity of George Merck's celebrated 1950 credo: "Medicine is for the people. It is not for the profits. The profits follow."[70] (The firm's financial difficulties predated but were exacerbated by its withdrawal of the painkiller Vioxx from the market in late 2004.)

The retailer Marks & Spencer (M&S) has long enjoyed a reputation as one of Britain's most virtuous companies. It has been a highly benevolent employer and for many years had a policy of selling only British made goods. In July 2004, Business in the Community, a prominent British NGO, named M&S company of the year for putting responsible business practices at the heart of its strategy and for producing "measurable, outstanding positive impacts on society."[71] The Dow Jones Sustainability World Index rated M&S "the most sustainable retailer in the world" in 2002 and 2003, and a survey of worldwide labor standards carried out by Insight Investments and Accountability gave the firm its top ranking.[72] But in the same month it received its CSR award, M&S attracted a hostile takeover bid made possible by the firm's recent poor earnings and poorly performing share price.[73] Although the investor attempting to take over M&S had promised to continue the firm's progressive policies, and the takeover bid was ultimately unsuccessful, the juxtaposition of these two events prompted a column in the *FT* which noted:

> The battle for CSR has to be won in an environment more hostile than many of its proponents appreciate . . . CSR is best seen as the management of risk, as the avoidance of damages to the company's

reputation. But it is no substitute for the avoidance of the larger risk: that consumers may go elsewhere because the company's offering is not good enough. As models we need companies whose risk management has made them commercially successful. CSR is only as sustainable as the companies that practice it.[74]

Another journalist concluded that M&S showed that "being a good corporate citizen has nothing to do with being profitable," an appraisal apparently confirmed by a contemporary survey of London financial analysts, which found "that they placed most corporate responsibility issues well down their list of company concerns."[75] Competitive pressures have also forced M&S to abandon its "buy British" policy.

During the late 1990s, Chiquita Brands International (an outgrowth of the United Fruit Company), which produces a quarter of the world's bananas and is the largest agricultural employer in Latin America, implemented a highly innovative program aimed at improving the environmental practices of its growers in Central America; more than 79 percent of its independent suppliers have been certified by the Rainforest Alliance. The funds spent by the company to bring its farms up to the Rainbow Alliance's environmental standards have resulted in considerable cost savings by reducing pesticide use and recycling the wooden pallets used to transport the fruit. Nonetheless the firm was forced to declare bankruptcy in November 2001.[76]

Some of the recent generation of ethical business "icons" have not fared any better. Both the Body Shop International and Ben & Jerry's had strong financial results for several years. Yet both began to experience financial difficulties in the late 1990s. Pressures from investors relegated founder Anita Roddick to an advisory nonexecutive role at the Body Shop, and in 2000, Ben and Jerry's, faced with a highly undervalued share price and declining profits due to a series of management failures, was taken over by Unilever. The carpet manufacturer Interface, whose chief executive, Ray Anderson, was called "the green CEO" and whose environmental practices have been described as "leading the way to the next frontier of industrial ecology," has been unprofitable since 2000.[77] In 2001, it consolidated its services operations, exited the broadloom market in Europe, and cut about 10 percent of its workforce, making further cuts the following two years. Notwithstanding Hewlett-Packard's widely applauded CSR initiatives under CEO Carly Fiorina, the firm's disappointing financial performance forced her resignation in 2004.

The more responsible firms, no less than the less responsible ones, must survive in highly competitive markets. Consumers can choose to purchase pharmaceutical products, household products, ice cream, herbal tea, clothes, jeans, computers, or body care products from many companies. Socially responsible firms, like all other firms, are subject to the vagaries of shifting consumer preferences and poor management. And when such firms find themselves in financial difficulty, many of their distinctive CSR practices can become more difficult to sustain.

The less-than-strong financial performance of many firms with strong CSR reputations hardly suggests that such firms represent the wave of the future. Rather it says that while the business system has a place for socially responsible firms, this place is at least as precarious and unstable as for any other kinds of firm. The market for social responsibility is dynamic. Some companies with strong CSR reputations are prospering (for example, Patagonia, Seventh Generation, Starbucks, Stonyfield Farm, Ikea, BP), while others are not (Levi Strauss, Merck, M&S, HP, Interface, Shell); still others perform well financially but have become less socially distinctive (Cummins Engine). At the same time, new relatively responsible firms continue to emerge, some of which will be financially successful and some of which will not.

Proponents of CSR tend to view the dynamics of responsible business in evolutionary terms. Since they assume that only the most responsible firms can or will survive in the long run, they believe that over time there will be more responsible firms and fewer irresponsible ones – a kind of survival of the virtuous. However the dynamics of corporate responsibility are better understood in ecological terms. There *is* a market or ecological niche for the relatively responsible firms. But there is also a market or ecological niche for less-virtuous ones. And the size of the former does not appear to be increasing relative to the latter.

Conclusion

The belief that corporate virtue pays is both attractive and influential. It appeals to those who wish to encourage firms to become more responsible as well as to those who want to manage, and work and invest in, virtuous enterprises. It is also an important component of the business model of the SRI industry and informs much popular and academic writing on CSR. And it reflects the business reality that firms are under pressure to satisfy the financial markets by producing strong earnings.

Unfortunately, a review of the evidence, including academic studies of the relationship between profitability and responsibility and the relative performance of SRI, finds little support for the claim that more responsible firms are more profitable. But this does not mean that there is no business case for virtue. It is rather to suggest that any such claim must be more nuanced. CSR does make business sense for some firms in specific circumstances.

Notes

1   See Jules Cohn, *The Conscience of the Corporation: Business and Urban Affairs, 1967–1970* (Johns Hopkins University Press, 1971), p. 4.
2   See James W. McKie, "Changing Views," in *Social Responsibility and the Business Predicament*, edited by James W. McKie (Brookings, 1974), p. 32.

3   Cohn, *The Conscience of the Corporation*, p. 7.
4   Milton Friedman, "The Social Responsibility of Business Is to Increase Profits," *New York Times Magazine*, September 13, 1970, pp. 32–33.
5   Christine Arena, *Cause for Success: Ten Companies That Have Put Profits Second and Come in First* (Novato, Calif.: New World Library, 2004); Bob Willard, *The Sustainability Advantage: Seven Business Case Benefits of a Triple Bottom Line* (Gabriola Island, B.C.: New Society, 2002; Charles O. Holliday Jr., Stephan Schmidheiny, and Philip Watts, *Walking the Talk: The Business Case for Sustainable Development* (Sheffield, England: Greenleaf, 2002); Malcolm McIntosh, Deborah Leipziger, Keith Jones, and Gill Coleman, *Corporate Citizenship: Successful Strategies for Responsible Companies* (London: Financial Times, 1998); Tedd Saunders and Loretta McGovern, *The Bottom Line of Green Is Black: Strategies for Creating Profitable and Environmentally Sound Businesses* (HarperSanFrancisco, 1993); and Ira Jackson and Jane Nelson, *Profits with Principles: Seven Strategies for Delivering Value with Values* (New York: Currency/Doubleday, 2004).
6   Chris Laszlo, *The Sustainable Company: How to Create Lasting Value through Social and Environmental Performance* (Washington: Island Press, 2003), p. xxiii; Sandra Waddock, *Leading Corporate Citizens: Vision, Values, Value-Added* (New York: McGraw-Hill, 2002), p. xvii. Mary Scott and Howard Rothman, *Companies with a Conscience: Intimate Portraits of the Twelve Firms That Make a Difference* (New York: Citadel, 1992); Kevin T. Jackson, *Building Reputational Capital: Strategies for Integrity and Fair Play That Improve the Bottom Line* (Oxford University Press, 2004); Mark Gunther, *Faith and Fortune: The Quiet Revolution to Reform American Business*, p. 43.
7   Stuart Hart, "Beyond Greening: Strategies for a Sustainable World," *Harvard Business Review* (January-February, 1997): 67–68, 76.
8   Amory Lovins, L. Hunter Lovins, and Paul Hawken, "A Road Map for Natural Capitalism," *Harvard Business Review* (May 1999): 158.
9   Jane Simms, "Business: Corporate Social Responsibility – You Know It Makes Sense," *Accountancy*, 130, no. 1311 (2002): 48–50.
10   Stan Friedman, "Corporate America's Social Conscience," *Fortune*, Special Advertising Section, May 16, 2003.
11   Wayne Norman and Chris MacDonald, "Getting to the Bottom of 'Triple Bottom Line,'" *Business Ethics Quarterly*, 14, no. 2 (2004): 245.
12   See Willard, *The Sustainability Advantage*, p. 3.
13   Michael Porter and Mark Kramer, "The Competitive Advantage of Corporate Philanthropy," *Harvard Business Review* (December 2002): 67.
14   Craig Smith, "The New Corporate Philanthropy," *Harvard Business Review* (May–June 1994): 106.
15   See Richard Steckel, Robin Simons, Jeffrey Simons, and Norman Tanen, *Making Money While Making a Difference* (Homewood, Ill.: High Tide Press, 1999), p. 105.
16   Ibid., p. 5.
17   Porter and Kramer, "The Competitive Advantage of Corporate Philanthropy," p. 57.
18   Hollender and Fenichell, *What Matters Most*, p. 6.
19   Quoted in Gunther, *Faith and Fortune*, p. 42.
20   Quoted in Hollender and Fenichell, *What Matters Most*, p. 163.
21   <www.Unglobalcompact.org/content/NewsDocs/WhoCaresWins>.
22   The presumed financial benefits of ethical investing are also reflected in many book titles; see, for example, Amy Domini, *Socially Responsible Investing: Making a Difference and Making Money* (Chicago: Dearborn Trade, 2001); and Peter Kinder, Steven Lyderberg, and Amy Domini, *Investing for Good: Making Money While Being Socially Responsible* (New York: Harper-Business, 1993). Other examples are Hall Brill, Jack A. Brill, and Cliff Feigenbaum, *Investing with Your Values: Making Money and Making a Difference* (Gabriola Island, B.C.: New Society, 2000), which "shows you how to put your money to work to support your ethical beliefs while earning returns that are as

good or better than those earned by traditional investments." It "explains . . . how to unlock the power of investments to accomplish the dual goal of growing a nest egg and improving the world" (first page of book, n.p.); Peter Camejo's *The SRI Advantage* is subtitled *Why Socially Responsible Investing Has Outperformed Financially* (Gabriola Island, B.C.: New Society, 2002); and Amy Domini with Peter Kinder, *Ethical Investing: How to Make Profitable Investments without Sacrificing Your Principles* (Reading, Mass.: Addison-Wesley, 1986).

23   Michael Porter and Claas van der Linde, "Green and Competitive: Ending the Stalemate," *Harvard Business Review* (October 1995): 120–34.

24   One of those was the Seminar on the Business Case for CSR, European Commission, Enterprise Directorate-General, Brussels, June 17, 2004.

25   See Joshua Daniel Margolis and James Patrick Walsh, *People and Profits? The Search for a Link between a Company's Social and Financial Performance* (Mahwah, N.J.: Lawrence Erlbaum, 2001), for the most comprehensive list of these studies.

26   Ibid., pp. 4–5.

27   For descriptions and analyses of relationships between firms and NGOs, see Dennis Rondinelli and Ted London, "How Corporations and Environmental Groups Cooperate: Assessing Cross-Sector Alliances and Collaborations," *Academy of Management Executive*, 17, no. 1 (2003): 61–76; and Michael Yaziji, "Turning Gadflies into Allies," *Harvard Business Review* (February 2004): 112–15.

28   Quoted in Leonard Silk and David Vogel, *Ethics and Profits: The Crisis of Confidence in American Business* (New York: Simon & Schuster, 1976), p. 145.

29   Walter Lippmann, *Drift and Mastery* (Englewood Cliffs, N.J.: Prentice-Hall, 1961), pp. 22, 23.

30   A Standard Oil executive speaking in the early 1960s, ibid., p. 134.

31   Marina v. N. Whitman, *New World, New Rules: The Changing Role of the American Corporation* (Boston: Harvard Business School Press, 1999), p. 7.

32   Ibid., p. 11.

33   Duncan Norton-Taylor, "The Private World of the Class of '66," *Fortune*, February 1966, p. 13D.

34   "Why Business Faces Campus Ire," *Business Week*, August 9, 1967, p. 74.

35   Gordon Fich, "Students in Business: What Do They Think about It? Why?" *Vital Issues*, March 1969, p. 1.

36   David Vogel, *Fluctuating Fortunes: The Political Power of Business in America* (New York: Basic Books, 1989), pp. 54–55.

37   According to a British study, the average SRI investor was middle-aged and worked in a managerial or professional occupation. His or her income and education were higher than those of the public as a whole. Russell Sparkes, *Socially Responsible Investment* (New York: John Wiley, 2002), p. 77.

38   Cohen quoted in Hollender and Fenichell, *What Matters Most*, p. 263; see also Carmel McConnell, *Change Activist: How to Make Big Things Happen* (New York: Prentice Hall, 2001). Its author, formerly a radical activist, is now a management consultant. The theme of her book is that you can make good money and still stay true to your values. Roddick quoted in McConnell, *Change Activist*, p. 12. And see, for example, Peter Kinder, "Values and Money," KLD Research & Analytics (<www.kld.com/resources/papers/values> [2004]).

39   Roger Cowe, "From First Tuesday to Green Tuesday," *Financial Times*, May 20, 2004, p. 8.

40   See Margolis and Walsh, *People and Profits?* for a list and summary of twelve "reviews of reviews," pp. 20–24.

41   Stuart Hart and Gautam Ahuja, "Does It Pay to Be Green?" *Business Strategy and the Environment*, 5, no. 1 (1996): 30–37.

42   Glen Dowell, Stuart Hart, and Bernard Young, "Do Corporate Global Environmental Standards Create or Destroy Market Value?" *Management Science*, 46, no. 8 (1999): 1059–74.

43 Michael Russo and Paul Fouts, "A Resource-Based Perspective on Corporate Environmental Performance," *Academy of Management Journal*, 40, no. 3 (1997): 534–59.

44 Dinah Koehler, "Capital Markets and Corporate Environmental Performance – Research in the United States", INSEAD, Fontainebleau, France, p. 11. See also Khaled Elsayed and David Paton, "The Impact of Environmental Performance on Firm Performance: Static and Dynamic Panel Date Evidence," Nottingham University Business School, October 2003.

45 Donald Reed, *Green Shareholder Value: Hype or Hit?* (Washington: World Resources Institute, 1998).

46 Margolis and Walsh, *People and Profits?* p. 8.

47 For a comprehensive and thoughtful assessment of the literature on the financial impact of environmental performance that reaches a different conclusion, namely that environmental leaders tend to outperform the stock market, see Frank Dixon, "Financial Markets and Corporate Environmental Results," in *Environmental Performance Measurement*, edited by Daniel Esty and Peter K. Cornelius (Oxford University Press, 2002), pp. 54–65.

48 Margolis and Walsh, *People and Profits?* p. 8.

49 See Brad Brown, "Do Stock Market Investors Reward Companies with Reputations for Social Performance?" *Corporate Reputation Review*, 1, no. 2 (1996): 275–76; and Alan Richardson, Michael Welker, and Ian Hutchison, "Managing Capital Market Reactions to Corporate Social Responsibility," *IJMR* (March 1999): 38, for critical analyses of this measure. For a debate on its usefulness, see Research Forum, *Business and Society Review*, 34, no. 2 (August 1995): 197–240.

50 See Anne Ilinitch, Naomi Soderstrom, and Tom Thomas, "Measuring Corporate Environmental Performance," *Journal of Accounting and Public Policy*, 17 (1998): 383–408.

51 Abigail McWilliams and Donald Siegel, "Corporate Social Responsibility and Financial Performance: Correlations for Misspecification," *Strategic Management Journal*, 21, no. 8 (2000): 608. The study they critique is Sandra Waddock and S. Graves, "The Corporate Social Performance–Financial Performance Link," *Strategic Management Journal*, 18, no. 4 (1997): 305–8.

52 Jennifer J. Griffen and John Mahon, "The Corporate Social Performance and Corporate Financial Performance Debate: Twenty-five Years of Incomparable Research," *Business and Society* (March 1997): 12.

53 See Ibid., pp. 7, 20–24; and John Mahon and Jennifer J. Griffen, "Painting a Portrait," *Business and Society* (March 1999): p. 130.

54 Margolis and Walsh, *People and Profits?* p. 13.

55 Ronald Roman, Sefa Hayibor, and Bradley Agle, "The Relationship between Social and Financial Performance," *Business and Society*, 38, no. 1 (March 1999): 121.

56 As one recent scholarly article put it after an extensive literature review, "As findings about the positive relationships between CFP (corporate financial performance) and CSR become more widely known, managers may be more likely to pursue CSR as part of their strategy for attaining high CFP." Mark Orlitzky, Frank Schmidt, and Sara Rynes, "Corporate Social and Financial Performance: A Meta-analysis" *Organization Studies*, 24, no. 2 (2003): 426.

57 Every book written by an executive whose firm is widely recognized for its CSR initiatives urges other managers to follow his company's example. See, for example, Ray C. Anderson, *Mid-Course Correction: Toward a Sustainable Enterprise* (White River Junction, Vt.: Chelsea Green 1998); Charles Holliday, Stephan Schmidheiny, and Philip Watts, *Walking the Talk: The Business Case for Sustainable Development*; and Hollender and Fenichell, *What Matters Most.*

58 Dan diBartolomeo and Lloyd Kurtz, "Managing Risk Exposures of Socially Screened Portfolios," Northfield Information Services, September 9, 1999 (<www.northinfo.com>), p. 8. Another study notes that the DSI also had different macroeconomic

exposures than the S&P 500. Lloyd Kurtz and Dan diBartolomeo, "Socially Screened Portfolios: An Attribution Analysis of Relative Performance," *Journal of Investing* (Fall 1996): 35–41.

59 For a detailed discussion of the composition of this index and its performance, see Alois Flatz, "Corporate Sustainability and Financial Indexes," in *Environmental Performance Measurement*, edited by Daniel Esty and Peter K. Cornelius (Oxford University Press, 2002), pp. 66–81.

60 See, for example, Alan Gregory, John Matatko, and Robert Luther, "Ethical Unit Trust Financial Performance: Small Company Size Effects and Fund Size Effects," *Journal of Business Finance & Accounting* (June 1997): 705–23, which found that the most important reason why a group of British unit trusts (mutual funds) outperformed matched pairs of funds was that the former were most heavily invested in smaller firms, which performed better during the time period of their analysis. Similarly, an unpublished paper by Kelly Young and Dennis Proffitt, "Socially Responsible Funds: Recent Performance and Other Issues Relating to Portfolio Choice" (dproffitt@grand-canyon.edu) reports that while the returns of most SRI funds were comparable to traditional funds of the same type, all size categories of growth funds had significantly lower returns, largely because the "typical SRI fund is over invested in high-tech industry" (p. 17).

61 Russell Sparkes, *Socially Responsible Investment* (New York: John Wiley & Sons, 2002), p. 270.

62 See, for example, Kelly Young and Dennis Proffitt, "Socially Responsible Mutual Funds: Recent Performance and Other Issues Relating to Portfolio Choice," Grand Canyon University, College of Business and Professional Studies, p. 17; Alicia Munnell and Annika Sunden, "Social Investing: Pension Plans Should Just Say 'No,'" paper prepared for the conference "Cost and Benefits: 'Socially Responsible' Investing and Pension Funds," Washington: American Enterprise Institute, June 7, 2004, p. 7. This is also the conclusion of the two studies considered by the Socially Responsible Investment Forum to represent "the most rigorous and insights quantitative studies of socially screened funds' performance" (2003 Report on Socially Responsible Investing Trends in the U.S., Social Investment Forum, p. 44); Bernell Stone, John Guerard Jr., Mustafa Gultekin, and Greg Adams, "Socially Responsible Investment Screening: Strong Evidence of No Significant Cost for Activity Managed Portfolios," *Journal of Investing* (forthcoming); and Rob Bauer, Kees Koedijk, and Roger Otten, "International Evidence on Ethical Mutual Fund Performance and Investment Style," Discussion Paper (London: Centre for Economic Policy Research, January 2002). For a list of the extensive literature on this subject, see Appendix 3 of the 2003 Report on Socially Responsible Investing Trends.

63 See, for example, Camejo, *The SRI Advantage*; and Jeroen Derwall, Nadja Gunster, Rob Bauer, and Kees Koedijk, "The Eco-Efficiency Premium Puzzle" (<www.erim. eir.ni>).

64 Susannah Goodman, Jonas Kron, and Tim Little, *The Environmental Fiduciary* (Oakland, Calif.: Rose Foundation for Communities and the Environment), p. 2.

65 Joanne Rickness and Paul Williams, "A Descriptive Study of Social Responsibility Mutual Funds," *Accounting Organizations and Society*, 13, no. 4 (1998): 397.

66 For this criticism, as well as a series of more wide-ranging criticisms of SRI, see Jon Entine, "The Myth of Social Investing," *Organization & Environment* (September 2003): 1–17.

67 Paul Hawken and the Natural Capital Institute, *Socially Responsible Investing* <www. natural-capital.org/images/NCI> [October 2004]; the quotes are from p. 17.

68 James C. Collins and Jerry I. Porras, *Built to Last: Successful Habits of Visionary Companies* (New York: Harper Business, 1994), pp. 2, 3.

69 For a list of the most socially responsible firms of the 1970s, see the corporations included in Thornton Bradshaw and David Vogel, eds., *Corporations and Their*

Critics: Issues and Answers to the Problems of Corporate Social Responsibility (New York: McGraw-Hill, 1981).

70 Peter Landers and Joann Lublin, "Merck's Big Bet on Research by Its Scientists Comes Up Short," *Wall Street Journal*, November 28, 1993, p. 1; see also "Face Value: The Acceptable Face of Capitalism," *Economist*, December 14, 2002, p. 61.

71 Alison Maitland, "Winner's New Leaders Face a 'Healthy Challenge,'" *Financial Times*, July 8, 2004, p. 1.

72 Jonathon Porritt, "Does Philip Green Understand?" (letter to the editor), *Financial Times*, July 9, 2004, p. 14.

73 Simon Zadek, "Doing Good and Doing Well: Making the Business Case for Corporate Citizenship" (New York: Conference Board, 2000), p. 19.

74 Michael Skapinker, "Why Corporate Laggards Should Not Win Ethics Awards," *Financial Times*, July 21, 2004, p. 8.

75 Martin Dickson, "Good, Not Great," *Financial Times*, July 7, 2004, p. 20.

76 Sara Silver, "How to Grow a Good Name on Green Bananas," *Financial Times*, November 26, 2004, p. 8. See also J. Gary Taylor and Patricia Scharlin, *Smart Alliance* (Yale University Press, 2004).

77 Rogelio Oliva and James Quinn, "Interface's Evergreen Services Agreement," Harvard Business School case 9–603–112, July 4, 2003, p. 5.

MEETING THE ETHICAL GAZE: CHALLENGES FOR ORIENTING TO THE ETHICAL MARKET

Andrew Crane

Introduction

We have seen thus far that the ethical gaze cast by consumers onto businesses and their practices can be questioning and frequently critical. But for the firms concerned it can also seem inconsistent, ebbing and flowing with personal conscience, determination, and the pull of a good anti-corporate exposé – not to mention the ever-present trade-offs with price, quality and convenience. Nevertheless, the message now seems to be getting through to many organizations that their consumers and other stakeholders increasingly have ethical expectations that they wish to see addressed in one way or another. The question, of course, is how do organisations respond to these expectations? . . .

In this chapter, I shall take these discussions forward into the specific realm of marketing and strategy, focusing in particular on how organisations might orient themselves in order to appeal to the ethical demands of consumers. This is an important area to consider, not least because it starts us thinking about how (or even whether) ethical concerns might be translated into tangible products and services. But perhaps more importantly, it also starts to focus our attentions on the myriad challenges that ethical consumers might pose for organisations, and in particular, on the difficulties inherent in turning their demands into a viable and sustainable business proposition.

I will begin by establishing the type and range of organisation that might be within the field of vision for ethically concerned consumers – and then put this into the context of other constituencies likely to be casting their ethical gaze at the organisation. I will then go on to look at specific strategic positions that might be adopted, primarily with a view to delineating strategies appropriate to 'ethical niche' and 'mainstream' organisations, before proceeding to outline the challenges and tensions that these postures typically raise. Once I have set out these broad strategic orientations, I will look closer at the types of products, brands, images and programmes that organisations might produce to appeal to ethically concerned consumers, and how we might conceptualise them as 'augmentations' to the basic value proposition but crucially, augmentations that typically have implications well beyond the purview of the marketing department. This will lead us into a consideration of the deeper issues around organisational culture that the ethical gaze might raise for companies, and so in the final section, I will summarise some recent debates about how managers interpret the ethical gaze *within* their organisations. I will conclude with a summary of the main points and a few brief comments on the state of current theory and practice plus prospects for the future.

The Ethical Gaze: Locating the Horizon

Responding to the ethical demands of consumers is something that all sorts of companies might need to do at some stage – from companies that have been expressly established to pursue particular social goals, such as those in the co-operative or fair trade movements, to huge multinational corporations dedicated to maximising shareholder value, such as Monsanto or BP. Therefore, just as ethical consumers might be from all different walks of life, so too are the companies that might seek to meet (or avoid) their gaze. The horizon, we might say, is an expansive one.

In examining how companies seek to appeal positively to these consumers, it is not unusual to think primarily of those companies at either end of the spectrum, that is, those most in the 'firing line' of boycotters (at one end), or those seeking to capitalise on an explicitly 'ethical' selling proposition (at the other). But even a good deal of those occupying more of a middle ground will need to exercise some kind of strategic decision making, perhaps because they recognise that the firing line isn't fixed, or because they cherish a reputation for being 'good citizens'.

Now, although certain companies might wish to respond to ethically concerned consumers, it needs to be said that there are many companies that do not, and probably even *need* not, consider ethical consumers at all. Although I am not going to discuss these companies here, it is worth remembering that those which do seek to respond to ethical consumers are by no means necessarily in the majority. And, as we shall see, even for many of these, ethical considerations are not always at the heart of their operations.

The first substantive issue to note here is that it is almost impossible to separate out the impact of ethically concerned consumers on organisations from the host of other 'ethical' forces that might confront them. This includes pressure from the media, government, civil society, competitors, or any other relevant constituency. In part, this inability to separate out the impact of ethical consumers is due to lack of research – indeed, I can think of no single study that has as its main focus the impact of consumers' ethical preferences or actions on organisational decision making. But there is also a largely unexamined assumption prevalent in much of the debate around ethical consumption that firms will automatically respond to the demands of consumers – the 'accepted sequence' (Galbraith, 1974) of *consumer sovereignty*. Notwithstanding the theoretical limitations of this assumption, there are also a number of conditions that might influence this purported cause-and-effect relationship. Most notably, this includes the amount of concentrated power wielded by consumers, and the vulnerability and visibility of the corporate brand in the market-place.

The relative influence of ethically concerned customers on firms compared with other 'ethical forces' is not, however, just a matter of establishing empirical fact. There is an extremely important normative question here that is frequently eclipsed by the assumption that firms *will* respond to consumers, namely whether firms *should* respond to the ethical demands of consumers. Now to many advocates of ethical consumption, this probably sounds perverse. But from a normative standpoint, there seems to be no prima facie reason why a firm – even supposing it wanted to act in the best interests of society – should privilege the views of one particular group of consumers, or one particular preference expressed by consumers, however well meaning those consumers might appear to be. Although marketers often assume the primacy of consumer interests, a multi-stakeholder view of the firm would typically regard this as problematic (Jackson, 2001). Moreover, who is to say that answering the demands of ethical consumers is really in the best interests of society? Of course it may be, but then again, it may not. Indeed, determining the 'right thing to do' is inevitably fraught with complexity and uncertainty, especially when firms have a whole range of stakeholders to satisfy. Listening to, and attempting to appeal to, ethically concerned consumers is one possible approach, but there are clearly other approaches that can also be considered (see Crane and Desmond, 2002).

For example, many firms often held up as exemplars of successful social responsibility, such as Ben & Jerry's, Tom's of Maine, and the Body Shop claim to have followed the instincts and drives of their leaders in determining their ethical stance, rather than taking a customer-led approach (see Chappell, 1993; Lager, 1994; Roddick, 1992). This kind of internal drive could be seen as a more stable (though arguably less 'democratic') foundation for responsible business than one that relies on changing market preferences. Similarly, it could be argued that government and civil society organisations have a more legitimate mandate to act in society's best interests than individual consumers, and so companies should primarily determine their ethical priorities in consultation with these parties rather than conducting customer opinion surveys. These propositions are most certainly contestable, but that does not deflect from the issue that the appropriate status of ethical consumers' demands is an often-overlooked issue that almost certainly warrants further debate in the literature. At the very least, I think it is worth considering ethical consumers as just one part of the 'ethical gaze' confronting corporations, albeit one that may well be influential in how firms orient themselves to the 'ethical market'. Let us now turn our attention to the types of strategies that firms may adopt in establishing this orientation.

Strategies for Orienting Towards the Ethical Market: Mainstreaming or Ethical Niche?

In recent years, there has been a growing number of commentators extolling firms to listen and respond to the ethical demands of consumers, to 'sell corporate social responsibility' (Cobb, 2002), to build 'ethical brands' (Mitchell, 1997), and to capitalise on the growing ethical market. The notion of an ethical market is perhaps a rather nebulous one, but what I mean by it here is essentially a demand, either implicit or explicit, for corporate actions, communications, or other artefacts that have a positive and identifiable ethical component to those outside the company. This can mean products with ethical features of one kind or another, such as fair trade or recycled products; it can mean cause-related marketing programmes, employee welfare programmes, or the development of an ethical code; in fact, it can mean a whole host of corporate endeavours that consumers and other stakeholders might demand from corporations for supposedly ethical reasons.

Probably the most straightforward way of thinking about how firms orient towards this ethical market is to conceive of a continuum of focus, from a narrow specialisation in an 'ethical niche' towards an attempt to address ethical concerns within a more 'mainstream' market. Basically, all I'm saying here is that some firms focus exclusively or mainly on promoting their ethical credentials (ethical niche), whilst others primarily stress alternative factors, yet still articulate their ethical credentials as a secondary or additional factor (mainstreaming).

One obvious way of conceptualising this distinction is to consider niche and mainstreaming strategies as the two main manifestations of Porter's (1985) 'differentiation' strategies, whereby firms seek to position themselves as offering superior qualities either across the whole market or in a specific market niche (see Figure 1 for a simple depiction). Why should we consider ethical considerations as a 'differentiation'? Well, this is a slightly tricky one, since for many people the whole idea of using ethics or social responsibility

Orientation

	Low cost	Differentiation
Broad	Cost leadership	Mainstream ethical orientation
Narrow	Cost focus	Ethical niche

Figure 1 Orientations to the ethical market

to strategically promote firms and products is in fact questionable in itself (for a discussion, see Husted and Allen, 2000). Again, such thinking starts to raise another of the fundamental paradoxes in much of our thinking about firms in relation to ethical consumers. On the one hand, we want firms to *genuinely* and *actively* embrace social responsibility, but at the same time, we extol them to listen and respond to ethical consumers, which suggests a more *instrumental* and *reactive* approach.

Putting such tensions aside for one moment though (we will return to them later), the mere fact that some, perhaps many, consumers are likely to be attracted to firms they perceive to be socially responsible suggests that ethical considerations are a means by which consumers differentiate between firms and their offerings. In this sense, firms promoting their ethical credentials may be seen as supplying 'augmentations' to the basic product offering (Crane, 2001). It is not just a bank account, but a bank account from a 'caring' bank; not just a bar of chocolate, but a bar of chocolate that ensures growers a decent standard of living; not just a trip to the supermarket, but going to a supermarket that gives some of the money you spend back to local schools. There will certainly be other augmentations too, but ethical qualities are part of the bundle of benefits through which firms seek to differentiate themselves in the mind of the consumer.

There are, I should add, considerable limitations to the usefulness of Porter's (1985) model for understanding strategic positioning (see for example, Miller and Dess, 1993). However, as long as we use this model simply to identify the basic approaches evident in the ethical market, it seems to be a reasonable conceptualisation, and in so far as it is widely understood and used in strategy theory and practice, it seems to be a useful starting point for thinking about how firms respond to ethical consumers. Let us look now in a little more detail at these main differentiating orientations.

Ethical niche orientation

Firms targeting the ethical niche will see their customers as having strong ethical preferences which drive their product selections and other consumer decisions such as where and how to shop. Hence, such companies will typically position their products as ethical alternatives to conventional competitive offerings. According to marketing logic, these companies' products should therefore offer unique ethical features above and beyond industry standards, and communications should generally concentrate on emphasising these benefits rather than other attributes of the product or firm. Again, conventional marketing logic would tend to dictate that this type of differentiation should provide added value to consumers, and so should command a premium price. Firms occupying the ethical niche might also ordinarily have social, ethical, or environmental goals as an integral part of their espoused mission, coupled with a public commitment to certain principles or practices.

Typical examples of firms targeting the 'ethical niche' include Triodos, the Dutch 'ethical bank', which aims to enable 'money to work for positive social, environmental and cultural change' and markets its corporate banking services to charities and 'social businesses'. Similarly, the UK-based Co-operative Bank has sought to target an ethical niche, as has the Ethical Clothing Company, set up by trade union groups to provide 'sweatshop-free' merchandise for the music industry. Given their commitment to ensuring growers a premium price, many companies marketing certified fair trade products (such as Max Havelaar products in the Netherlands or TransFair in the USA) have also typically targeted a niche of concerned consumers, as have green firms offering more environmentally benign products, such as the Belgium cleaning products company Ecover, or the US toiletries firm Tom's of Maine. The key point is that ethical niche firms see their aims best achieved by satisfying a relatively small group of concerned customers, and as a result, are mainly small specialist firms.

Mainstream orientation

In contrast, a mainstreaming orientation towards the ethical market includes a range of various types of firm with potentially very different values. The ethical considerations of consumers are still important here, and mainstreaming firms may well have ethical codes, or be part of ethical sourcing programmes such as SA8000, or use labels such as eco-labels to certify their credentials. But these will not be the main selling proposition of the products and services on offer, the primary focus of differentiation. This means that it could be that ethical credentials are seen as a fundamental part of doing business, or simply an 'added extra' or even a passing fad, but either way these firms will not principally position their products on this basis.

The reasons why these firms do not seek to invoke ethical criteria as the main selling proposition for their products might stem from a range of factors, including a perceived scepticism or 'backlash' amongst consumers against corporate 'greenwash', and doubts over consumers' willingness to pay a premium for ethical attributes (Crane, 2000). I think it is reasonable to assume though that the basic underlying assumption here is that firms believe that most of their consumers' ethical concerns are secondary to other considerations such as price, quality and convenience – or at least are secondary for more of the time than they are primary. Mainstream firms typically target a larger market than niche firms, and it would appear that there are few if any markets where differentiation primarily on the basis of ethics is a sustainable business proposition beyond a narrow niche. This is not to say that firms will ignore the ethical considerations of their consumers in this context, since we are very much concerned with those firms that do attempt to differentiate at least partly on the basis of ethics. Such ethical differentiation though is typically just one element in a portfolio of differentiating factors that are necessary to gain significant market share in mainstream markets.

This is a relatively broad definition, so naturally there are numerous examples of firms in this category, from those such as the UK home improvements company B&Q which pioneered the use of the Forest Stewardship Council sustainable timber accreditation programme in the UK, to the oil company BP, which in 2001 rolled out an ambitious high profile $100m ethical rebranding campaign complete with a new name, 'Beyond Petroleum', and a new green logo. The key point though is that mainstream firms see their aims best achieved by satisfying a relatively large group of customers who are concerned about ethical factors, but are unwilling to sacrifice the other aspects they value for those concerns.

A low-cost ethical orientation?

If it then seems reasonable to suggest that firms orienting towards the ethical market have adopted some form of differentiating strategy, we might similarly conjecture that firms adopting Porter's (1985) other main strategic posture – a low-cost strategy – would probably not seek to orient at all towards the ethical market. Indeed, given that attention to ethical considerations and the concomitant needs to certify and communicate ethical credentials are inevitably a costly business, it would seem fairly unlikely that a firm seeking to maintain a strong cost advantage over its competitors would desire, or be able, to appeal very successfully to ethical consumers. For example, in 2003 when the UK clothing retailer Littlewoods experienced a change in ownership, and a reinvigoration of its low-cost strategy, the firm shut down its entire ten-person ethical trading team and pulled out of the flagship Ethical Trading Initiative, despite having been a founding member of the programme (Bowers and Finch, 2003).

Conversely, in the specific area of environmental marketing, a low-cost strategy has been identified as a possible alternative (for example, Peattie, 1995: 146). This might be because firms have opportunities for reducing resource inputs (Peattie, 1995: 146), and/or establishing cost leadership by pre-empting legislative burdens (Porter and van der Linde, 1995). For example, the UK energy supplier Ecotricity offers to match its competitors' prices at the same time as claiming to have 'the greenest tariff in the UK' due to its commitment to wind power.

Whilst issues such as resource utilisation and reuse appear to be particular to environmental considerations, the pre-emptive argument could also be extended perhaps to other 'ethical' issues that are potentially open to legislative change, such as employee rights or social reporting. For instance, moves to implement mandatory social reporting in France may confer cost advantages on those companies that had already advanced along the learning curve and established efficient procedures for auditing and reporting prior to the introduction of legislation. Still, it takes considerable foresight and commitment to be an early adopter of ethical approaches for reasons of cost leadership rather than differentiation, and it is hard to imagine many situations or issues that have clear potential to beget such outcomes. Overall, I would suggest that whilst a low-cost orientation to the ethical market remains a possibility, it is far less common than our two main differentiation approaches.

Opportunities and Tensions in Ethical Market Orientations

Both differentiation approaches offer certain opportunities as well as raising significant tensions for firms choosing to orient to the ethical market. In the case of niche firms, it might be said to be reasonably straightforward to maintain an ethical focus whilst marketing to a fairly committed group of consumers. However, there are often intense competitive pressures from mainstream firms who choose to orient towards the ethical market, and who may be able to replicate (or at least approximate) certain ethical attributes, at the same time as enjoying cost advantages and superior marketing budgets. For instance, many of the groundbreaking green products produced by ethical niche firms in the early 1990s, had by the end of the decade either left the market or been absorbed or copied by mainstream competitors (Crane, 2000; Peattie, 1999). Similarly, many niche firms focusing on organic products now face intense competitive threats from powerful retail multiples who have rapidly expanded their ranges in recent years (Mintel, 2003).

In other instances, ethical niche firms may actually find themselves dissatisfied with miniscule market shares and effectively 'preaching to the converted'. The drive for more mass-market success, firm growth, and a larger audience for the ethical message have therefore led many ethical niche firms to seek opportunities for expansion beyond their existing niche. As

Meyer (1999) suggests, this often requires firms to think more in terms of Hamel and Prahalad's (1991) 'expeditionary marketing' approach and 'envision' appropriate mass markets. This means looking towards shaping future markets and going beyond typical niche assumptions and practices that may restrict growth – such as depending on specialist distribution channels and relying on conventional 'ethical' marketing practices.

For instance, many fair trade companies in the UK such as Cafédirect, Day Chocolate, and Traidcraft have moved away from the movement's traditional 'solidarity' approach towards a more market-oriented model in a bid to appeal to a more mainstream market (Davies and Crane, 2003; Nicholls, 2002). This has led to a change in emphasis in product advertising towards product quality and other aspects of consumer self-interest rather than the typical fair trade message that emphasises producer poverty. As Wright (2003) argues, Cafédirect's groundbreaking success in seizing over 8 per cent of the UK roast and ground coffee market by 2002 coincided with a definite shift in communications strategy, from a 'bleeding hearts' message to one reinforcing the 'pleasures of consumerism'. Thus, 'emphasis is placed on the gratification available to the consumers, who can realise their self-worth and display their distinction through treating themselves to a superior coffee' (Wright, 2003: 21).

Such moves, as one might imagine, almost inevitably raise tensions between the need to increase competitiveness and attract more customers whilst at the same time honouring corporate values and maintaining ethical integrity. For example, some ethical nichers seeking to go mainstream may have to face the thorny question of whether they should risk dilution of their ethical values and reputation by either sourcing from, or supplying to, key mainstream companies. For example, major retailers might open the doors to larger markets, but potentially not share the same values as an ethical niche company. Research at the UK fair trade firm Day Chocolate Company, for instance, suggested that the acceptability of various types of relationships with companies such as Sainsbury's, Shell, Body Shop and McDonald's was a matter of quite complex rationalisation and renegotiation amongst managers about who was or was not 'acceptable' to work with (Davies and Crane, 2003). Similarly, ethical nichers risk alienating existing customers and staff alike if the move to the mainstream marks too much of a break with established traditions (Dey, 2002).

At the extreme, ethical nichers may even be purchased by mainstream firms, as was the case with Ben & Jerry's ice cream which was bought by Unilever, and the organic seed supplier Seeds of Change which was bought by the Mars Corporation. Competitive pressures, as well as intense scrutiny from the media and other stakeholders, can challenge the ability of mainstream firms to sustain a convincing ethical differentiation. For example, the Body Shop and Marks & Spencer have found that their attempts to offer 'ethical' differentiation have sometimes been seized upon and condemned by critics, whilst firms such as McDonald's and Nike have struggled even more to convince a sceptical and often hostile public of their ethical credentials.

What these tensions and conflicts suggest is that efforts to target the mainstream with an ethical message have considerable potential to engender strategic confusion or even what we might regard as *dis*orientation towards the ethical market. By this, I mean that firms may well run the risk of either failing to communicate successfully with their stakeholders, or even simply encountering problems in finding the right balance of ethical and other differentiating values to offer their customers. These are significant challenges for all firms faced with some degree of ethical consumption in their markets, and so in the next section I will go on to look closer at the brand building exercises that might be involved in orienting towards the ethical market and to explore the kind of contribution they might make to the overall strategies identified above.

Reflections of the Ethical Gaze: Building the Ethical Image Through Campaigns and Brands

Ethical differentiation or augmentation is essentially a process of creating an 'ethical image', a 'good reputation', or what marketers typically refer to as a 'socially responsible' or 'ethical' brand. The challenge of creating such a brand has given rise to considerable discussion across the business and research communities, especially given growing concerns about falling levels of trust in corporations to behave in an ethical manner (Handy, 2002), coupled with efforts by corporations to use their social responsibility pro-grammes more strategically in order to enhance brand value (Middlemiss, 2003; Mitchell, 1997).

'Ethical' branding in context

Many brands are argued to communicate social or ethical elements of one sort or another, especially values such as trust and honesty, but also increasingly qualities such as 'good citizenship', 'social responsibility' and 'environmental concern' (Lane Keller, 2000). Of course, most firms would like to build brands that customers trust; however, for the most part, what we mean here by trust is typically conceptualised in fairly limited terms, such as trusting the brand to be truthful about its ingredients, deliver consistent quality, or offer value-for-money. Trusting a company to be ethical goes considerably further than this, and it is evident that many brands are facing something of a trust deficit in terms of the public's faith in their commitment to 'doing the right thing'. For example, Wootliff and Deri's (2001) survey shows that rather than businesses, it is non-governmental organisations (NGOs) such as Amnesty International and WWF who are the new 'super brands', particularly in Europe where NGOs apparently enjoy a much higher degree of trust (48 per cent) than either government (36 per cent) or business (32 per cent).

Such problems with the ethical image of corporations are of course something faced mainly by large multinationals, especially as it is typically multinationals that have borne the brunt of the major scandals, media exposés, and boycotts that have accelerated the public's loss of trust. To some extent, the ethical nichers identified in the previous section may have found themselves somewhat insulated from (and possibly even benefiting from) this growing trust deficit of big business. However, it has to be said that the more people distrust business – whether large or small, 'ethical' or otherwise – the more scrutiny business is subjected to, and the harder it becomes for any firm to maintain trust and legitimacy.

In fact, this is likely to impact upon firms seeking to respond in a positive way to the ethical gaze perhaps even more than the others. After all, differentiating on the basis of ethics or social responsibility, even when this is only a minor element in the overall bundle of attributes offered, is somewhat different to many other forms of differentiation. Most notably, in order to be credible 'ethical' differentiation requires a whole company effort (Crane, 2001). Compare, for example, the difference involved in backing up a claim that a company is more 'socially responsible' than a competitor or a product 'more ethical', with the rather more straightforward task of claiming that a sofa is more comfortable, a drink better tasting, or a manufacturer better at designing stylish automotives. Whilst the latter claims can be ascertained by consumers simply by sitting on, tasting, or looking at the products on offer, the former are far more difficult to determine since such claims assume numerous contingencies deep within the operations of the firm and even beyond its boundaries to include the operations of suppliers, advertisers, investors, and so on.

In part, this is because most evaluations of ethical claims, even when very product specific, are likely to involve some broader evaluation of the reputation of the company. After all, any attempt to differentiate a product as an ethical alternative may be assessed by consumers against a backdrop of knowledge about how the company treats its workforce, its environmental record, which companies it has bought from or sold to in the past, and all kinds of other possible factors. Consumers may not always be very consistent themselves in their purchasing, but they are often quick to denounce a 'cynical' or 'hypocritical' corporation for any observable gap between the socially responsible image projected in advertising campaigns and the 'reality' perceived in the stores and through the media.

Probably the key issue here is one of consistency. I am not sure how realistic it is for firms to attempt to always be completely consistent, not least because they often have such conflicting demands and will project different impressions, identities, even different 'realities' to their various stakeholders (Crane and Livesey, 2003). Nonetheless, marketers often seek to emphasise that in the marketing game 'perception *is* reality', so it is not so much whether firms are consistent that matters, but whether they appear to be. Such a view is popular with brand managers and other advocates of corporate branding, since much of their *raison d'être* is to find and deliver a stable and consistent image of the firm. However, as Cheney and Christensen (2000) argue, there is great potential for self-delusion and self-seduction in such beliefs. In a fragmented and volatile business environment, where corporations are ever more complex, and where some degree of consumer cynicism can be almost taken for granted, the search for a shared understanding about a corporation's values may often be a hopelessly idealistic one.

Indeed, many of the high profile campaigns waged by pressure groups against corporations have involved a hijacking of the carefully nurtured brand image of companies such as Exxon, McDonald's and Nike, in order to take advantage of the brands' immense global leverage to promulgate a radically different message to that intended by the companies. The corporate image, insofar as it is a response to, or reflection of, the ethical gaze of consumers, is open to contestation by those same customers.

A New Approach to 'Ethical' Branding?

So what can corporations do when faced with such a business environment, where many consumers and other stakeholders seem to be demanding more in ethical terms, but at the same time, are extremely quick to contest the brand image and denounce any efforts they deem to be hypocritical or insufficient? One way to respond could be through better communication to stakeholders. I think it is fair to say that the most risible attempts at corporate 'greenwash' are probably behind us now. The late 1980s and early 1990s were often characterised by researchers and corporate critics as a time when the communications environment was awash with misleading and over-hyped claims about ethical credentials and in particular about purported environmental concerns and benefits (Davis, 1992; National Consumer Council, 1996).

Firms appear to have now backed away from such an approach, not least because of the cynicism and 'backlash' that it engendered amongst consumers and other stakeholders (Crane, 2000). Although there are of course exceptions, corporations now seem to be more reserved and cautious about the types of claims that they make. As even Robert Wilson, the Chairman of Rio Tinto (a company no stranger to criticism) said on the dangers of not 'walking the talk': 'It's pretty important to get the policies and implementation right before you start spending too much time on the external communications' (Middlemiss, 2003: 358).

For some this has meant taking a more defensive or 'muted' approach (Crane, 2000), whereby specific 'ethical' claims are relegated behind other brand attributes. As we saw earlier, this is consistent with a more mainstream approach to the ethical market, but it also means that social responsibility becomes more of a background quality that isn't necessarily vigorously promoted, but is embedded as part of a broader programme of *reputational risk management* (Middlemiss, 2003). Increasingly, it would appear, the key factor for many companies when orienting towards the mainstream ethical market is not so much the lure of increasing sales, but rather an attempt to prevent their brand being attacked and suffering a similar fate as befell Nike, Shell and others. Here, for example, is David Rice, a BP executive, talking about why he considers it important for firms to address human rights issues: 'In business terms, mitigation of risk is a key component of sound business development. To ignore human rights today in the era of globalisation is to significantly increase the risk of doing business – risk to our markets, risk to the value of our assets, as well as risk to our reputation' (Rice, 2002: 135).

Companies such as Rio Tinto and BP are now all too aware of the dangers inherent in attempting to maintain legitimacy in the face of an ethical gaze by consumers, NGO's, and other potential critics. Therefore, it is perhaps not too surprising that many firms have invested in more defensive approaches to communicating their responsibility, such as social and sustainability reports. Similarly, many such companies have also increasingly claimed to have moved from a one-way model of communicating their social responsibility towards a dialoguing model that actually consults with stakeholders to determine their expectations and priorities (Crane and Livesey, 2003).

This is perhaps best encapsulated in the much discussed changearound at Shell following the Brent Spar controversy in the mid-1990s. In the words of its 1998 report, the company decided it had to move from a 'trust me' world to a 'show me' world, meaning that the firm had to learn how to listen before acting. The transformation in its decision processes, the company claimed, went from DAD – decide, announce, deliver – to DDD – dialogue, decide, deliver (Livesey, 2002). It is debatable how many multinationals have actually succeeded in this endeavour, or how far they have actually progressed (or intend to progress) down this path. However, it is fairly clear that the conventional wisdom now is that rather than just undertaking a 'charm offensive' in the foreground of the market-place through advertising and PR, the most effective way to build an ethical brand is to adopt a more holistic, long-term, and some might say conservative, approach that focuses more on communicating with key reality definers in the relative background of the CSR industry.

Of course, this is not to deny that many firms are actively promoting a growing range of ostensibly 'ethical' products to consumers, such as fair trade or organic produce, energy efficient washing machines, and the like. But as we have seen, ethical claims have decreased in emphasis whilst the whole bureaucratic process of backing up and certifying claims, as well as the emphasis on reputational risk management, have rapidly escalated in importance. Similarly, other popular ways of appealing directly to ethical consumers, such as *cause-related marketing*, tend to be rather cautious in their approach to brand building. By cause-related marketing, I mean where consumer purchases are linked to corporate contributions to good causes – essentially a co-alignment of marketing goals with corporate philanthropy (Varadarajan and Menon, 1988). For example, in Tesco's Computers for Schools Campaign (in the UK) customers collect vouchers for every £10 they spend in the supermarket and then local schools redeem them for computer equipment.

Such programmes have become increasingly popular with corporations and charities alike (Cobb, 2002; Lewis, 2003). And as far as ethical branding is concerned, although cause-related marketing is one of the most visible aspects of a company's social responsibility programme (Lewis, 2003), it has a relatively narrow remit that tends to focus attention on the specific project rather than the company's broader social role and impacts. As a result, such campaigns are likely to contribute only gradually to the 'ethical' brand image (and for some consumers, arguably not at all) given that the motivations for such 'win–win' initiatives will always be questioned to some extent. Perhaps though, as Cobb (2002: 26) argues, 'even the disillusioned will concede that actions which benefit society are still worthy, whatever the motive'. Hence, providing the project and the partnering are right, cause-related marketing is probably a relatively safe option for companies seeking to 'look good' in the ethical market.

The question of motive that has arisen here in relation to cause-related marketing is something that I raised earlier in the chapter. This is an important issue that in many ways goes to the heart of what exactly consumers expect from corporations in ethical terms – do they just want action that benefits society, or do they also desire firms to be ethical in a deeper sense, perhaps to be motivated by some degree of altruism, or guided by a mission to do good? I will not seek to provide a definitive answer to this question, since my aim in this chapter is not to examine consumers' preferences but to explore how firms respond to them. Therefore, in the final section, I will look more closely at how ethical preferences from consumers are interpreted and made meaningful inside companies – and in so doing, start to unpack the whole motives issue somewhat further.

Refocusing the Ethical Gaze? Accommodating Ethical Concerns In and Around the Organisation

So far in this chapter I have spoken of companies as if they were essentially 'black boxes' that responded in certain ways to certain kinds of stimulus from consumers and other stakeholders. This is helpful in some senses, but also somewhat limiting in others. In particular, it seems to me that the ethical gaze on corporations at times begs certain questions about the motives of corporations, and about what we might call the 'ethical essence' of the company – is its commitment to social responsibility genuine, do its managers really believe in what they are doing, is it in the final analysis an 'ethical company'? These are not really questions that it is particularly easy to answer, and many of them rest on fairly shaky anthropomorphic assumptions that a company 'thinks', 'feels', or 'believes' in anything in the first place. But at the very least, they start us thinking about organisational processes that translate the actions or commitments of ethical consumers into tangible products, campaigns, and other corporate artefacts.

I think the first thing to say here is that most companies probably don't have a very clear idea of their consumers' ethical beliefs and values in the first place. Companies such as the UK's Co-operative Bank and the Co-operative Group may have preceded ethical branding initiatives in the mid-1990s with extensive customer surveys ascertaining views on various issues such as animal welfare, the environment, fair trade, and the supply of weapons (CWS, 1995; Kitson, 1996), but these remain the exception. Certainly many ethical niche companies do not tend to go in for (or cannot afford) formal market research. And amongst mainstream firms, the whole idea of canvassing the ethical opinions of the customer base has still not received a wide uptake. Most companies would appear to rely on evidence from more general surveys and market intelligence such as the Ethical Purchase Index (Brock *et al.*, 2001), or MORI polls (see for example, MORI, 2000), as well as the occasional question or two that might make it onto their usual market research instruments.

Regardless though of the factuality of customers' ethical demands, there is little doubt that some sense of the ethical gaze is perceived within companies. Of course, this doesn't necessarily mean that the ethical gaze experienced inside corporations is necessarily recognisable as the same thing that the customer expresses (or intends to express) outside. The corporate decision making process itself often obscures or reconstructs the moral identities of ethical consumers. For a start, most organisations interface with consumers at something of a distance – they canvass opinions through agencies, and with mailshot questionnaires; if they interact with consumers, it is often only at the point of sale; and those making decisions in production, marketing or finance remain physically and psychologically distant from the end consumer. Similarly, because of the bureaucratic nature of most organisations, customers' ethical thoughts and feelings often need to be labelled, aggregated, quantified, and fed into the productive process as inputs and outputs, targets and projections, as objects or units to be plotted onto a chart (Desmond and Crane, 2004). Even if these processes do then lead to 'ethical' corporate behaviour, the paradox is that the moral 'face' of the consumer tends to get removed (Bauman, 1993).

By this, I mean that within the rational decision making process of organisations, the satisfaction of the desires or interests of ethical consumers is often not treated as morally meaningful, or an end in itself, but as the means to an end – namely whatever goals the corporation may have set for itself. Ethical consumers, therefore, can enter this process as moral persons but leave it in pieces, reduced to a series of abstract preferences, variables and averages (Desmond and Crane, 2004). You and I, the thinking feeling moral person becomes simply 'the consumer', or worse, a preference on a questionnaire, a number in a database.

It is probably fair to say that this construction of 'moral indifference' in organisations, and in marketing especially, is not specific to ethical consumers (see Desmond, 1998). However, the paradox is probably more striking in such a context, given that ethical consumers may be hoping to impress a distinctly moralised discourse upon companies from the outside in. Of course, it would probably be misguided to argue that this process happened in the same way, and to the same extent, in all companies. It might also be suggested that I am being a little too pessimistic in my interpretation of the corporate terrain. Some companies may well be more than able to accommodate and sustain some sense of a meaningful moral identity for consumers – especially in smaller, more niche-oriented firms. But I still doubt whether ethical consumers would recognise themselves in how they are constructed within organisations. And as we have seen, the image of themselves that is increasingly reflected back on ethical consumers by advertisers is that of a self-interested indulgent hedonist rather than a concerned citizen troubled by the plight of workers and the environment (Wright, 2003).

Perhaps the most intriguing situation in this respect is when the whole idea of there being ethical consumers 'out there' is surfaced within a firm in order to drive the development of some kind of ethical policy or social responsibility programme. Customer-focused firms consistently invoke 'consumer pressure' as one of the main driving forces behind their attention to social responsibility – a relationship also vigorously supported by many contributors to this book. Regardless of the truth of this claim, or the beneficial outcomes this may ultimately have, the point is that it essentially instrumentalises the consumer to construct a convincing motive of corporate self-interest. In most cases, I would suggest that there are a whole host of reasons and motives used by managers to explain and rationalise social programmes, but the potency of the concept of the 'ethical consumer' is in its power to suggest that failure to act in an ethical manner may bring upon the firm dire reputational consequences. Perhaps in the long run this instrumentalisation doesn't really matter, providing of course that the firm does good deeds and contributes positively to society. But it does give us a clearer conception of the fascinating and at times bewildering paradoxes that surround the whole notion of ethical consumerism when it comes to seeing how exactly it might actually impact upon corporations and managers. Sometimes it seems that the more we try and understand the ethical gaze, the cloudier the picture becomes.

Conclusion

The purpose of this chapter was to provide an overview of the issues and challenges for organisations involved in responding to ethical consumers. I first discussed the range of different companies likely to be confronted by such pressure, as well as the strategic postures they might choose to adopt in the face of them – primarily focusing on differentiation strategies of ethical niche versus mainstream orientations. A predominant trend identified here was a move to the mainstream by certain ethical niche firms, although as we saw, such a reorientation raised a number of challenges and tensions. I then reviewed current thinking about ethical 'branding', and in particular, the apparent shift away from explicit ethical branding towards a more conservative reputational risk management approach, as well as narrower, and safer, cause-related marketing initiatives. I then finished with an analysis of what ethical consumerism could or might mean once it had been 'processed' by companies.

Overall, I would say that there is evidence of growing interest in the corporate response to ethical consumers, particularly in terms of how social responsibility issues can be incorporated into organisational practices such as branding, cause-related marketing, and reputational risk management. Of course, consumers are not the only reason that researchers and practitioners are interested in such things, but they are certainly implicated in various ways. That said, there is still a lot of scope for much closer attention to the specific influence of consumers' ethical preferences and values on corporations; it seems to me that too often a simplistic cause-and-effect relation between the two is just automatically assumed rather than rigorously examined. More in-depth in-company research would probably bring to the surface some extremely valuable insights that may well challenge some of our conventional thinking on the subject.

This lack of co-ordination and integration of organisational research with consumer research is part of a broader problem in business research – the two sides too often simply fail to speak to each other. But there is no real reason why this should be replicated by those interested in ethics and business. Indeed, there is potential for a closer-knit field of enquiry that isn't just interested in ethical consumers in the abstract, but also in the diverse and complex yet ultimately fascinating relations that they have with corporations and their members.

References

Bauman, Z. (1993) *Postmodern Ethics*, London: Blackwell.

Bowers, S. and Finch, J. (2003) 'Littlewoods Drops Ethical Code', *The Guardian*, 1 February: 25.

Brock, G., Clavin, B. and Doane, D. (2001) *Ethical Purchasing Index 2001*, Manchester: Co-operative Bank.

Chappell, T. (1993) *The Soul of a Business: Managing for Profit and the Common Good*, New York: Bantam.

Cheney, G. and Christensen, L. (2000) 'Self-absorption and Self-seduction in the Corporate Identity Game', in M. Schultz, M. Hatch and M. Larsen (eds) *The Expressive Organization: Linking Identity, Reputation, and the Corporate Brand*, Oxford: Oxford University Press, pp. 246–270.

Cobb, R. (2002) 'Selling Responsibility', *Marketing Business* June: 25–27.

Crane, A. (2000) 'Facing the Backlash: Green Marketing and Strategic Reorientation in the 1990s', *Journal of Strategic Marketing* 8 (3): 277–296.

Crane, A. (2001) 'Unpacking the Ethical Product', *Journal of Business Ethics*, 30: 361–373.

Crane, A. and Desmond, J. (2002) 'Social Marketing and Morality', *European Journal of Marketing*, 36 (5/6): 548–569.

Crane, A. and Livesey, S. (2003) 'Are You Talking to Me? Stakeholder Communication and the Risks and Rewards of Dialogue', in J. Andriof, S. Rahman, S. Waddock and B. Husted (eds) *Unfolding Stakeholder Thinking 2: Relationships, Communication, Reporting and Performance*, Sheffield: Greenleaf, pp. 39–52.

CWS (1995) *Responsible Retailing*, Manchester: CWS Ltd.

Davies, I. and Crane, A. (2003) 'Ethical Decision-making in Fair Trade Companies', *Journal of Business Ethics* 45 (1/2): 79–92.

Davis, J. (1992) 'Ethics and Environmental Marketing', *Journal of Business Ethics* 11: 81–87.

Desmond, J. (1998) 'Marketing and Moral Indifference', in M. Parker (ed.), *Ethics and Organizations*. London: Sage.

Desmond, J. and Crane, A. (2004) 'Morality and the Consequences of Marketing Action', *Journal of Business Research*, 57: 1222–1230.

Dey, C. (2002) 'Social Bookkeeping at Traidcraft plc: An Ethnographic Study of a Struggle for the Meaning of Fair Trade', Paper presented at 12th CSEAR Research Summer School, Dundee.

Galbraith, J. (1974) *The New Industrial State* (2nd edn), Harmondsworth: Penguin.

Hamel, G. and Prahalad, C. (1991) 'Corporate Imagination and Expeditionary Marketing', *Harvard Business Review*, 69 (July/Aug.): 81–92.

Handy, C. (2002) 'What's a Business For?', *Harvard Business Review*, 80 (Dec.): 49–55.

Husted, B. and Allen, D. (2000) 'Is It Ethical to Use Ethics as Strategy?', *Journal of Business Ethics* 27 (1/2): 21–31.

Jackson, J. (2001) 'Prioritising Customers and Other Stakeholders Using the AHP', *European Journal of Marketing* 35 (7/8): 858–871.

Kitson, A. (1996) 'Taking the Pulse: Ethics and the British Co-operative Bank', *Journal of Business Ethics* 15 (9): 1021–1031.

Lager, F. (1994) *Ben and Jerry's: The Inside Scoop*, New York: Crown.

Lane Keller, K. (2000) 'Building and Managing Corporate Brand Equity', in M. Schultz, M. Hatch and M. Holten Larsen (eds) *The Expressive Organization: Linking Identity, Reputation, and the Corporate Brand*, Oxford: Oxford University Press, pp. 115–137.

Lewis, E. (2003) 'Why Giving Is Good for You', *Brand Strategy* 170 (Apr.): 26–28.

Livesey, S. (2002) 'The Discourse of the Middle Ground: Citizen Shell Commits to

Sustainable Development', *Management Communication Quarterly* 15 (3): 313–349.

Meyer, A. (1999) 'Green and Competitive Beyond the Niche: Reflections on Green Positioning Strategies', Paper presented at Business Strategy and the Environment Conference, University of Leeds.

Middlemiss, N. (2003) 'Authentic Not Cosmetic: CSR as Brand Enhancement', *Journal of Brand Management* 10 (4/5): 353–361.

Miller, A. and Dess, G. (1993) 'Assessing Porter's (1980) Model in Terms of Its Generalizability, Accuracy and Simplicity', *Journal of Management Studies* 30 (4): 553–585.

Mintel (2003) 'Organic Foods – UK – November 2003', Intelligence report, London: Mintel.

Mitchell, A. (1997) 'The Power of Ethical Branding', *Marketing Week* 22: 26–27.

MORI (2000) *The First Ever European Survey of Consumers' Attitudes Towards Corporate Social Responsibility and Country Profiles*, London: MORI and CSR Europe.

National Consumer Council (1996) *Green Claims: A Consumer Investigation into Marketing Claims About the Environment*, London: NCC.

Nicholls, A. (2002) 'Strategic Options in Fair Trade Retailing', *International Journal of Retail and Distribution Management* 30 (1): 6–17.

Peattie, K. (1995) *Environmental Marketing Management: Meeting the Green Challenge*, London: Pitman.

Peattie, K. (1999) 'Trappings Versus Substance in the Greening of Marketing Planning', *Journal of Strategic Marketing*, 7: 131–148.

Porter, M. (1985) *Competitive Advantage: Creating and Sustaining Superior Performance*, New York: Free Press.

Porter, M. and van der Linde, C. (1995) 'Green and Competitive', *Harvard Business Review* September–October: 120–134.

Rice, D. (2002) 'Human Rights Strategies for Corporations', *Business Ethics: A European Review* 11 (2): 134–136.

Roddick, A. (1992) *Body and Soul*, London: Vermilion.

Varadarajan, P. and Menon, A. (1988) 'Cause-related Marketing: A Coalignment of Marketing Strategy and Corporate Philanthropy', *Journal of Marketing* 52 (July): 58–74.

Wootliff, J. and Deri, C. (2001) 'NGOs: The New Super Brands', *Corporate Reputation Review* 4 (2): 157–165.

Wright, C. (2003) 'Consuming Lives, Consuming Landscapes: Interpreting Advertisements for Cafédirect Coffees', Paper presented at British Sociological Association Annual Conference, University of York, UK.

Chapter 6

CSR in the workplace

N THIS CHAPTER WE WILL:

- Explain some of the core corporate responsibilities in the workplace.
- Discuss the different types of workplace where CSR might be relevant.
- Examine the meaning of key concepts such as human rights, employee participation and corporate democracy.
- Establish the significance of human rights responsibilities for multinationals.
- Explore the questions of whether and how employees should be involved in CSR programmes.

Introduction

Today, the reputation of many companies appears to rest to some extent on their treatment of employees. Major brands such as McDonald's, Wal-Mart and others have been threatened by accusations of poor labour relations at home, while there is no end of firms that have been caught in the spotlight of media scrutiny for their working conditions in developing countries, including accusations of child labour, forced overtime and abuse of human rights. On the other hand, it has become clear that a reputation for social responsibility can, in some circumstances, help to attract skilled knowledge workers to firms, and thereby boost their performance (Greening and Turban, 2000). Thus, whichever way we look at it, if we want to understand and apply CSR better, we cannot avoid undertaking a thorough examination of workplace issues.

Responsibilities in the workplace were in fact among the first elements of social responsibility recognized and taken up by corporations. Enlightened industrialists of the nineteenth century, such as the Cadbury, Lever and Boot families in the UK, recognized that the working and housing conditions of their employees needed improving – and that attention to employee welfare could in turn bring benefits to the firm (Cannon, 1994). Model communities built at Port Sunlight and Bournville in the late nineteenth century in the UK, for example, offered factory workers decent, affordable housing, recreational and health facilities, along with enhanced working conditions in order to help employees out of poverty and provide them with a chance to improve themselves. Such schemes were, of course, what we would now refer to as highly paternalistic, in that the founding fathers expected the workers living in the model villages to lead lives of piety and sobriety, and to repay the debt to their benefactors with high commitment, reliability and hard work. Nevertheless, such approaches to CSR clearly offered benefits to workers and employers alike, and have been replicated in various ways in countries across the globe, including the Indian subcontinent and parts of Africa.

Over time, corporate responsibilities towards employees have seen significant shifts, especially with the rise and fall of unionization over the past hundred years or so, and the institutionalization of labour laws in most parts of the world. In much of continental Europe, for instance, corporations have tended not to consider workplace issues as a major facet of CSR because the legal protection of employees is so well developed and comprehensive, and because labour unions have traditionally been strong (Matten and Moon, 2004). This leaves little scope for 'voluntary' CSR initiatives in the workplace beyond the legal minimum. In other countries, however, corporations may at times have been expected to take on responsibility for providing good working conditions, equality of opportunity, health and safety in the workplace and so on, owing to the absence of effective legal protection or enforcement.

Today, with ageing and diversifying populations in many Western countries, wide-scale restructuring in industry, the rise of the multinational, and the mounting significance of outsourcing through global supply chains, CSR in the workplace has become a major issue for companies everywhere. Whether this pertains to the provision of employee pension schemes in the USA, the offshoring of the workforce to low-cost countries such as China and India, or the problems of protecting employees from HIV/AIDS in Africa, workplace issues are now central to CSR. The point is, though, that the relevant social responsibilities will vary according to the particular workplace we are considering.

Understanding the Workplaces of CSR

Workplace issues in CSR will vary according to whether we are considering highly regulated or unregulated workplaces, or whether we are considering in-house or outsourced workplaces.

● *Regulated workplaces* – These are typically found in developed countries where legislation largely takes care of most of the main problems of employee protection. Here, then, CSR is likely to focus on ensuring that the firm lives up to the spirit as well as the letter of the law, and goes beyond legislation by attending to issues of diversity, work–life balance, training and employability, pension provision, anti-harassment, and so on.

- *Less regulated workplaces* – These are typically found in developing countries, because employee protection legislation is either absent or poorly enforced. Hence CSR issues here will tend to include such concerns as working conditions, pay, unionization, health and safety, equal opportunity, and so on. It is important to note that less regulated workplaces can also occur in developed countries, for example, when the workplace is part of the informal economy.
- *In-house workplaces* – Corporations are obviously directly responsible for their own in-house workers. However, where the willingness or the ability to provide responsible workplace practices is limited, other actors such as major customers or NGOs might become involved in CSR programmes aimed at improving these practices.
- *Outsourced workplaces* – Various producers of branded products have also at times been expected to take on some responsibility for the workplaces of their suppliers. This is not to say that the supplier is absolved from CSR in the workplace, but the nature of its responsibilities may change; for example, because the purchasing company begins to act as a quasi-regulator. Relevant outsourced workplaces can go beyond immediate first-tier suppliers to encompass a sphere of responsibility that stretches throughout the supply chain, both upstream and downstream.

What we can see, then, is that CSR in the workplace is quite a complex arena, with different contexts, issues and responsibilities arising for the corporation in different situations. However, corporations can be guided as to their responsibilities by a variety of different codes and guidelines. Some of the most important of these include the OECD guidelines for multinationals, the ILO global labour standards and the UN global compact. There are also a range of different initiatives in place that have been developed to tackle workplace responsibility issues, such as codes of conduct and social auditing systems (which we will discuss in Part C of this book).

Introducing the Readings

The two readings that follow offer a good introduction to workplace issues, dealing in turn with the questions of multinational companies' responsibilities for human rights, and the participation of employees in CSR programmes and policies.

Responsibilities for human rights

The issue of human rights has increasingly been entering the CSR debate, especially in the context of multinational corporations and their responsibilities towards workers in developing countries. Peter Muchlinski's article discusses this development, and provides us with a compelling argument for why human rights are an important obligation for corporations to shoulder, rather than simply being a matter for governments to deal with. He then describes the nature of the rights that are at stake, the types of corporation that may be affected, and how corporate responsibilities for human rights might be implemented.

Muchlinski's argument is that, as corporations take on these obligations, they begin to act as a 'soft law'. This points to a broader political role of corporations in societal governance, and the involvement of private enterprises in the provision, protection and enabling of basic rights and entitlements (Matten and Crane, 2005a; Scherer, Palazzo and Baumann, 2006). This, as Garriga and Melé (pp. 76–107) discussed earlier in Chapter 3, represents a political theory of CSR, and as such suggests that CSR in the workplace can be considered both at a micro-level of the firm as well as at a macro-level of global rules and governance.

Involving employees in CSR programmes

Patrick Maclagan's article takes a rather different view of CSR in the workplace. While, for many, CSR is something that corporations do to achieve certain outcomes, Maclagan focuses us on the individuals involved in the CSR programmes, and on the degree of involvement employees have in the CSR decision-making processes. This is part of a broader endeavour undertaken by Maclagan and others to orient discussions of business ethics and CSR around individual actors and managerial discretion (e.g. Hemingway and Maclagan, 2004; Maclagan, 1998).

Such a perspective is relatively rarely proposed in the CSR literature – individuals are more usually identified as recipients of CSR rather than as participants. However, as Maclagan suggests, with corporations being pressed to be more open, accountable and democratic, the issue of whether employee (and other stakeholder) views are genuinely incorporated within CSR programmes represents an important dimension of the debate (see e.g. Harrison and Freeman, 2004; Matten and Crane, 2005b). As we will see in Chapter 9, the involvement of stakeholders is a key criterion for social accountability, and Maclagan offers a normative argument for why this should be so.

Study Questions

1   What social responsibilities does a firm have in the workplace? Outline a business case for these responsibilities.
2   To what extent should firms be expected to extend their workplace responsibilities to employees in their supply chain?
3   'The protection of human rights is the responsibility of governments. Multinational corporations have neither the mandate, nor the ability to do so.' Discuss, using examples.
4   What are the advantages and disadvantages of involving employees in CSR policies and programmes?
5   Can and should CSR be a democratic workplace practice?

References

Cannon, T. (1994) *Corporate Responsibility*, London: Pearson.

Greening, D. and Turban, D. (2000) 'Corporate Social Performance as a Competitive Advantage in Attracting a Quality Workforce', *Business and Society* 39(3): 254–280.

Harrison, J. and Freeman, R. (2004) 'Is Organizational Democracy Worth the Effort?', *Academy of Management Executive* 18(3): 49–53.

Hemingway, C. and Maclagan, P. (2004) 'Managers' Personal Values as Drivers of Corporate Social Responsibility', *Journal of Business Ethics* 50(1): 33–44.

Maclagan, P. (1998) *Management and Morality*, London: Sage.

Matten, D. and Crane, A. (2005a) 'Corporate Citizenship: Towards an Extended Theoretical Conceptualization', *Academy of Management Review* 30(1): 166–179.

Matten, D. and Crane, A. (2005b) 'What Is Stakeholder Democracy? Perspectives and Issues', *Business Ethics: A European Review* 14(1): 6–13.

Matten, D. and Moon, J. (2004) '"Implicit" and "Explicit" CSR: A Conceptual Framework for Understanding CSR in Europe', *ICCSR Research Paper Series*, Nottingham University (29–2004).

Scherer, A., Palazzo, G. and Baumann, D. (2006) 'Global Rules and Private Actors – Towards a New Role of the TNC in Global Governance', *Business Ethics Quarterly* 16(3): 505–532.

THE DEVELOPMENT OF HUMAN RIGHTS RESPONSIBILITIES FOR MULTINATIONAL ENTERPRISES

Peter Muchlinski

The issue of whether, and how far, multinational enterprises (MNEs), or transnational corporations (TNCs) in UN parlance,[1] should be required to observe fundamental human rights standards and, possibly, to be liable for their violation, has been the subject of much discussion in recent times. This may be attributed to a number of factors including increased unease at the seemingly unaccountable operations of private capital in a globalising economy, the perception that the ability of the nation-state to act in the public interest has been weakened by the effects of economic globalisation, and the greater ease of communicating cases of corporate misconduct through the media, wherever this may occur. In addition, the increased vigilance of non-governmental organisations (NGOs) that are concerned with such misconduct has led to greater awareness of this issue (see further Muchlinski 2001a: 33–35; UN Sub-Commission on Human Rights 2002a: 2–4; International Council on Human Rights Policy 2002: 1–2). Whether corporations are, in fact, behaving worse now than before is not the real question. The fact that they are perceived as having to conform to certain standards of public conduct, hitherto exclusively required of the state and its public agencies, is.

This chapter discusses the developing legal consequences of this increased awareness, specifically the evolution of the debate concerning the extent to which MNEs and other business enterprises should observe, and be bound by, human rights standards. The chapter is divided into three main parts. The first is a discussion of the wider context of the debate on corporate social responsibility (CSR) and, in particular, the extension of human rights responsibilities to corporate actors. This provides an essential conceptual and policy background to the current debate. The second part discusses the major substantive principles that may be said to form the foundations of MNE human rights responsibilities, and offers a guide to the most important international instruments in this field. In addition it refers to the continuing debates within the UN Sub-Commission on Human Rights concerning the drafting of a new UN instrument in this field, the most recent draft text of which is now referred to as the 'Draft Norms of Responsibilities of Transnational Corporations and Other Business Enterprises with Regard to Human Rights' (hereafter referred to as the Draft Norms). This continues to be discussed by the Working Group of the Sub-Commission set up for this purpose (UN Sub-Commission on Human Rights 2002b; see Weissbrodt 2000 for a discussion of the background to the development of the Draft Norms). The third part examines the practical issues of monitoring and implementation of corporate human rights performance, including both the major practical legal issues that arise in the context of national litigation and the possible role of intergovernmental organisations (IGOs) in the supervision of MNE adherence with human rights norms.

The Context: The Debate on Corporate Social Responsibility and the Extension of Human Rights Standards to Corporate Actors

There are at least three principal sets of issues that need to be considered in this connection: first, how should the 'social dimension' and 'social responsibility' be defined for the purposes of developing new international standards; second, following from this general issue, on what basis should human rights responsibilities extend to corporations; and, third, what are the sources of substantive standards from which a new international code of corporate social responsibility can be drawn?

Defining the 'social dimension' and 'social responsibility'

The phrase 'corporate social responsibility' can mean many different things and the obligations of firms in this matter can be drawn rather widely. For example, the Draft UN Code of Conduct for Transnational Corporations contained obligations ranging from respect for the sovereignty and political system of the host state, respect for human rights, abstention from corrupt practices, full disclosure or observance of tax and competition laws, to obligations on TNCs not to abuse their economic power in a manner damaging to the economic well-being of the countries in which they operate (UNCTAD 2001a: 5). Equally, the revised OECD Guidelines for Multinational Enterprises contain an extensive range of social obligations for MNEs including, *inter alia*, duties to contribute to the sustainable development of the countries in which they operate, to respect human rights, to encourage local capacity-building, and to refrain from seeking or accepting exemptions to local regulatory frameworks in the areas of environment, health and safety, labour, taxation, financial incentives or other issues (OECD 2000). In contrast, the UN Global Compact[2] focuses on just three issue areas on which world business should act by upholding the major international instruments in each field:

1.   Respect for human rights as defined in the Universal Declaration of Human Rights.
2.   The International Labour Organisation (ILO)'s Declaration on Fundamental Principles and Rights at Work, which requires respect for freedom of association, recognition of collective bargaining, elimination of all forms of forced and compulsory labour, the effective abolition of child labour and elimination of discrimination in respect of employment and occupation.
3.   The Rio Declaration of the UN Conference on Environment and Development, which requires support for a precautionary approach to environmental challenges, the undertaking of initiatives to promote greater environmental responsibility and the encouragement of the development and diffusion of environmentally friendly technologies.

The question of what the list of social responsibility standards should contain is, of course, a question of choice bounded by ideological considerations (Muchlinski 2000a: 373–74). However, it is clear that the list can cover potentially all aspects of corporate conduct, and that the matter may assume economic, social, political and ethical dimensions (UNCTAD 2001a: II). It is equally clear that certain basic standards of ethical behaviour can no longer be seen as outside the responsibilities of corporate actors, even if, traditionally, such standards were, in the first instance, applicable to public bodies alone. This is particularly so when the reasons for extending human rights responsibilities to private non-state actors are considered.

The basis of human rights obligations for non-state actors

The use of human rights standards to assess the conduct of corporations is replete with conceptual difficulties. Indeed, there are a number of strong arguments against the extension of human rights responsibilities to TNCs.[3] First, TNCs and other business enterprises are in business. Their only social responsibility is to make profits for their shareholders. It is not for them to act as moral arbiters in relation to the wider issues arising in the communities in which they operate. Indeed to do so may be seen as unwarranted interference in the internal affairs of those communities, something that TNCs have, in the past, been urged not to do.[4] Second, private non-state actors do not have any positive duty to observe human rights. Their only duty is to obey the law. Thus it is for the state to regulate on matters of social importance and for such actors to observe the law. It follows also that TNCs and other business enterprises, as private actors, can only be beneficiaries of human rights protection and not human rights protectors themselves. Third, which human rights are TNCs and other business enterprises to observe? They may have some influence over social and economic matters – for example, by ensuring the proper treatment of their workers – but they can do nothing to protect civil and political rights. Only states have the power and the ability to do that. Fourth, the extension of human rights obligations to corporate actors will create a 'free-rider' problem (Vernon 1999: 49). It is predictable that not all states and not all firms will take the same care to observe fundamental human rights. Thus the more conscientious corporations that invest time and money into observing human rights and making themselves accountable for their record in this field, will be at a competitive disadvantage in relation to more unscrupulous corporations that do not undertake such responsibilities. They may also lose business opportunities in countries with poor human rights records, as the host government may prefer not to do business with ethically driven corporations. Fifth, unfairness may be exacerbated by the selective and politically driven activities of NGOs, whose principal concern may be to maintain a high profile for their particular campaigns rather than to ensure that all corporations are held equally to account.

Such arguments can, however, be answered. First, as regards the extension of social responsibility standards to corporations, it should be noted that TNCs have been expected to observe socially responsible standards of behaviour for a long time (UNCTAD 1999a, 1999b: ch. XII). This expectation has been expressed in national and regional laws and in numerous codes of conduct drawn up by intergovernmental organisations, as will be discussed more fully below. Indeed, TNCs themselves appear to be rejecting a purely non-social role for themselves through the adoption of corporate and industry-based codes of conduct (for examples, see UNCTAD 1994: ch. VIII; 1999a: 31–42). Second, observance of human rights is increasingly being seen by TNCs as 'good for business'. It is argued that business cannot flourish in an environment where fundamental human rights are not respected – what firm would be happy with the disappearance or imprisonment without trial of employees for their political opinions? In addition, businesses themselves may justify the adoption of human rights policies by reference to good reputation (see, for example, Williams 1999; Harvard Law School Human Rights Program 1999: 19–22). The benefit to be reaped from espousing a pro human rights stance is seen as outweighing any free-rider problem, which, in any case, may be exaggerated (Muchlinski 2001a: 38–39).

Third, the private legal status of TNCs and other business enterprises may be seen as irrelevant to the extension of human rights responsibilities to such entities. As Andrew Clapham has forcefully argued, changes in the nature and location of power in the contemporary international system, including an increase in the power of private non-state actors such as TNCs (which may allow them to bypass traditional state-centred systems of governance) have forced a reconsideration of the boundaries between the private and public spheres. This, in turn, has brought into question the traditional notion of the corporation as a private entity with no social or public obligations, with the consequence that such actors, including TNCs, may in principle be subjected to human rights obligations (Clapham 1993: 137–38). This position coincides with the fear that these powerful entities may disregard human rights and, thereby, violate human dignity. It follows that corporations, including, in particular, TNCs, should be subjected to human rights responsibilities, notwithstanding their status as creatures of private law, because human dignity must be protected in every circumstance (Clapham 1993: 147). Fourth, in response to the view that TNCs cannot be subjected to human rights designed to direct state action, it may be said that, to the contrary, TNCs can affect the economic welfare of the communities in which they operate. Given the indivisibility of human rights, this means that they have a direct impact on the extent that economic and social rights, especially labour rights in the workplace, can be enjoyed.

Although it is true that TNCs may not have direct control over matters arising outside the workplace, they may nonetheless exercise important influence in this regard. Thus, TNCs may seek to defend the human rights of their employees outside the workplace, set standards for their subcontractors and refuse to accept the benefits of governmental measures that seek to improve the business climate at the expense of fundamental human rights. Equally, where firms operate in unstable environments they should ensure that their security arrangements comply with fundamental human rights standards. Moreover, where companies have no direct means of influence they should avoid, at the very least, making statements or engaging in actions that appear to condone human rights violations. This may include silence in the face of such violations. Furthermore, all firms should develop an internal human rights policy that ensures that such concerns are taken into account in management decision-making, and which may find expression in a corporate code of conduct. Fifth, the argument that MNEs may find expression in a corporate code of conduct. Fifth, the argument that MNEs may be subjected to arbitrary and selective targeting by NGOs should not be overstated. While it is true that such behaviour can arise out of what Upendra Baxi (1998) has termed 'the market for human rights', in which NGOs strive for support from a consuming public in a manner not dissimilar to that of a service industry, TNCs and other major business enterprises are big enough to take care of themselves.

Despite the convincing arguments for extending responsibility for human rights violations to TNCs, the legal responsibility of TNCs for such violations remains uncertain. Thus, much of the literature on this issue suggests ways to reform and develop the law towards full legal responsibility, rather than documenting actual juridical findings of human rights violations by TNCs, or, indeed, other non-state actors (see, for example Kamminga 1999; Joseph 2000; Amnesty International [The Netherlands] and Pax Christi 2000; Muchlinski 2001a). We are yet to see such an event in the courts of the world, although it should be remembered that findings of human rights violations concerning slave labour practices have been made against individual German industrialists at the end of the Second World War (Clapham 2000: 166–171). Against this background, the activities of the Sub-Commission and its Working Group may be seen, first, as an acceptance of the *principle* that TNCs and other business enterprises can be responsible for the observance of human rights standards and, second, as a move towards the *clarification of the rules and norms* by which TNCs and other business entities should be made subject to human rights responsibilities. In relation to the latter, the next important issue concerns the sources of such responsibilities.

The sources of substantive provisions

At the outset, it must be stressed that, traditionally, international agreements regulating international business have not covered social issues, or at least not directly or expressly. In the area of foreign direct investment (FDI) the main category of treaty, the bilateral investment treaty (BIT), usually covers: non-discrimination, based on most-favoured-nation and national treatment standards; investment guarantees against expropriation or civil unrest and in support of free transfer of funds; and dispute settlement (UNCTAD 1998). Indeed, even the failed Multilateral Agreement on Investment (MAI), as originally conceived, contained no references to labour or environmental standards, only provisions, echoing BITs, for the promotion and protection of investors and their investments coupled with new standards guaranteeing entry and establishment of investors and their investments, based on US and Canadian BIT practice, and on NAFTA (for further analysis see Picciotto 1998; Henderson 1999; Muchlinski 2000b).

The vast bulk of social responsibility standards for the conduct of international business can be found in instruments outside the field of international business regulation, even, indeed, outside the sphere of work covered by IGOs. These sources are, for the most part, non-binding voluntary codes or declarations. They are 'soft law' instruments, offering little more than moral force, in that the major method of enforcement is through the shame of non-adherence. They include: codes of conduct developed by individual companies or industry sectors (see, further, UNCTAD 2001a);[5] NGO codes (see, for example, Amnesty International [UK] 1998; UNCTAD 2000a); and codes drawn up by governments[6] or IGOs of which the codes of conduct developed by the International Labour Organisation (ILO) are of special importance.[7] On the other hand, some sources are legally binding as they take the form of binding conventions on specific issues. The 1997 OECD Convention on Combating Bribery of Foreign Officials in International Business Transactions is the most prominent example[8] – similarly, the numerous ILO Conventions on labour standards. Such international standard-setting conventions acquire the force of binding international treaties among the membership of the sponsoring IGO, or among the signatory states, if membership of the convention is permitted to any country including non-members of the sponsoring IGO.

The Major Substantive Human Rights Obligations of MNEs

The basis of obligation

Given that, historically, the observance of human rights standards has been an obligation of the state alone, the first element in the evolution of substantive standards is the assertion of a direct link between the obligations of states and of non-state actors to promote universal respect for, and observance of, human rights and fundamental freedoms. An express reference to such a link can be found in the Universal Declaration of Human Rights. This instrument is addressed both to governments and to 'other organs of society'. Following this provision, the Preamble to the UN Draft Norms recognises that:

> even though States have the primary responsibility to promote and protect human rights, transnational corporations and other business enterprises, *as organs of society*, are also responsible for promoting and securing the human rights set forth in the Universal Declaration of Human Rights [emphasis added].

This is a clear acceptance of the view that corporate entities do have human rights responsibilities on the basis of their social existence. Although the first concern of the Draft Norms is to address the obligations of TNCs and other business enterprises in respect of human rights, this instrument continues to address the obligations of governments as well. Thus, the Draft Norms also contain the following general statement:

States have the primary responsibility to respect, ensure respect for, prevent abuses of, and promote human rights recognised in international as well as national law, including assuring that transnational corporations and other business enterprises respect human rights. Within their respective spheres of activity and influence, transnational corporations and other business enterprises have the obligation to respect, ensure respect for, prevent abuses of, and promote human rights recognised in international as well as national law.

This provision places states over TNCs and other business enterprises as the principal regulators of human rights observance. In addition, it recognises that states and businesses operate in different fields and so each has a specific set of responsibilities in its particular field of operations, thereby obviating the possibility that business enterprises could supplant the state in its obligations to uphold and observe human rights.

The kinds of enterprises covered by human rights obligations

The discussions over the Draft Norms in the UN Sub-Commission reflect a desire to see human rights obligations being applied to all business entities and not merely to TNCs. This avoids an otherwise unjustifiable distinction between TNCs and national firms as regards responsibilities to observe fundamental human rights standards. The focus of the debate on international CSR has tended to be towards TNCs, given the transnational character of their operations. However, the underlying issues of principle would apply *mutatis mutandis* to national firms as the applicability of human rights standards to private corporate actors does not depend on the mere fact that their business operations cross borders. Such a geographically based justification for applying human rights standards to one class of corporations, rather than another, would be unprincipled.

The focus on TNCs can perhaps be explained as a pragmatic choice, evolving out of their visibility in certain widely publicised cases of mass violations of human rights and from the perception that TNCs, unlike purely national firms, can take advantage of more lax legal regimes in foreign host countries. These regimes pay scant regard to social welfare concerns, allowing unscrupulous firms to turn this to their commercial advantage (UN Sub-Commission on Human Rights 2002a: paragraphs 22–26). On the other hand, it should be noted that TNCs are more likely than local firms, in countries where social welfare issues are either un-or deregulated, to observe good practices in this arena. Thus, the real problem may be a lack of proper regulation in the host country of local businesses and institutions for which TNCs may not be responsible. Therefore, any programme of responsibility must take into account the relationship between local and transnational practices and the influence of TNCs thereon. In addition the reference to both TNCs and other business enterprises avoids the risk that an inadequate definition could allow companies to use financial and other structures to conceal their transnational nature and to appear as a domestic company thereby avoiding responsibility under the Draft Norms.

The principal substantive obligations

The discussions concerning the Draft Norms have given rise to a re-examination of the range of sources from which human rights responsibilities for TNCs and other business enterprises can be drawn, making these discussions a useful stocktaking exercise concerning the current state of possible substantive obligations in this field. From the existing instruments dealing with corporate social responsibility and human rights, as synthesised into the substantive contents of the Draft Norms, at least five different types of provisions can be identified.

First, there are those that cover 'traditional' civil and political human rights issues, namely:

- The right to equal treatment (see also OECD 2000)
- The right of security of persons as concerns business engagement in, or benefit from, 'war crimes, crimes against humanity, genocide, torture, forced disappearance, forced or compulsory labour, hostage-taking, other violations of humanitarian law and other international crimes against the human person as defined by international law'
- Rights of workers dealing, in particular, with those rights listed in Article 2 of the ILO Declaration on Fundamental Principles and Rights at Work 1998, namely: the prohibition on forced or compulsory labour, the rights of children to be protected against economic exploitation,[9] and freedom of association
- Respect for other civil and political rights, such as freedom of movement, freedom of thought, conscience and religion, and freedom of opinion and expression

Second, following the contents, in the main, of the ILO Tripartite Declaration of Principles Concerning Multinational Enterprises and Social Policy,[10] the UN Draft Norms contain provisions reflecting the main economic, social and cultural rights including:

- The provision of a safe and healthy working environment
- Compensation of workers with remuneration that ensures 'an adequate standard of living for them and their families'
- Protection of collective bargaining
- Respect for the social, economic and cultural policies of the countries in which companies operate[11]

- Respect for the rights of health, adequate food and adequate housing and other economic, social and cultural rights such as rights to 'adequate food and drinking water; the highest attainable standard of physical and mental health; adequate housing; education . . . and refrain from actions which obstruct the realisation of those rights'.

No distinction is made in the Draft Norms between the importance of these so-called 'first'- and 'second'-generation human rights. Indeed, as the Preamble explains, the Draft Norms are based on the 'universality, indivisibility, interdependence and interrelatedness of human rights including the right to development'. This approach also covers the so-called 'third-generation' rights of collective solidarity, as expressed through the inclusion, in the Draft Norms, of the right of development and other community-based rights such as respect for the rights of local communities and of indigenous peoples.

A fourth group of provisions can be said to deal with the special problems created by the operations of MNEs for the realisation of the types of rights listed above. Thus, the Draft Norms deal with a specific issue that has arisen in a number of cases: namely, the operation of security arrangements for companies. Such arrangements must 'observe international human rights norms as well as the laws and professional standards of the country or countries in which they operate'. This general principle is further elaborated in the attached Commentary, which requires companies to observe the emerging best practices evolving in this field through various codes of conduct, particularly the UN Principles on the Use of Force and Firearms and the UN Code of Conduct for Law Enforcement Officers; and the UN Convention against Torture and the Rome Statute on the International Criminal Court. Business enterprises and TNCs are further urged not to supplant the state military and law enforcement services but only provide for their own preventative or defensive services and not to hire individuals known to have been responsible for human rights or humanitarian law violations. Other provisions that can be added to this category are: the duty to recognise and respect applicable norms of international law, national laws, regulations, administrative practices and the rule of law,[12] and the final saving provision which makes clear that

> nothing in these Human Rights Responsibilities shall be construed as diminishing, restricting, or adversely affecting the human rights obligations of States under national or international law. Nor shall they be construed as diminishing, or adversely affecting more protective human rights norms.

Not only does this provision offer a rule of interpretation favourable to the effective protection of human rights but it also emphasises that the operations of business enterprises can observe higher standards than the minimum standards required by the Draft Norms.

A fifth, and final, group of substantive provisions go beyond a conventional human rights-based agenda and belong more to a general corporate social responsibility code. This reflects the fact that many of the sources, referred to as contributing to the Draft Norms, constitute more general codes of business ethics, which, by their nature, deal with social issues not usually described as human rights issues. Thus, for example, the Draft Norms require that TNCs and other business enterprises shall act

> in accordance with fair business, marketing and advertising practices and shall take all necessary steps to ensure the safety and quality of the goods and services they provide. Nor shall they produce, distribute, market or advertise potentially harmful or harmful products for use by consumers.

This introduces general consumer protection standards into the instrument. Other such social responsibility provisions include a prohibition against bribery and obligations with regard to environmental protection. Whether these are truly 'human rights' issues is open to debate. On the other hand, as the Preamble to the Draft Norms notes,

> new human rights issues and concerns are continually emerging and that transnational corporations and other business enterprises often are related to these issues and concerns, such that further standard-setting and implementation are required at this time and in the future.

It may well be that consumer and environmental protection are emergent human rights issues. It has been argued, for example, that a right to a clean and healthy environment is a human right, though this has been disputed (see, generally, Fitzmaurice 1996: 909–14). Whether consumer protection is a human right seems rather more tenuous, as it is hard to see how elevating such issues to the status of quasi-constitutional rights makes such protection more effective. In any case, other established human rights could be sufficient. For example, death or serious injury caused by unsafe products or processes could come within the right to life and the right to personal security under Article 3 of the Universal Declaration on Human Rights (UDHR) and Articles 6 and 9 of the International Covenant on Civil and Political Rights. Loss of livelihood due to disability could be covered by Article 25 of the UDHR. As for bribery, who are the victims? What do they suffer? Surely, this is an area in which the wider social undesirability of such practices is in issue, rather than any significant adverse effects on any one individual.

Monitoring and Enforcement

The third part of this paper deals with the question of how to ensure that the substantive human rights obligations of MNEs and other business enterprises are actually upheld. This involves a mix of national and international legal approaches. At the national level both standard setting, through new laws and regulations, and public interest litigation, taken against firms alleged to have broken their human rights obligations, may be used. At the international level there arises the possibility that IGOs could have a monitoring role that would supplement such national initiatives. In particular, they could require states to comply with certain obligations to ensure that their domestic regulatory structures adequately reflect the emergent norms in this area, and they could provide adequate and effective remedies for those who allege to have been harmed by the failure of firms to observe fundamental international human rights standards.

At the national level, there has, to date, been relatively little progress on standard setting through new laws or regulations embodying human rights standards. The most significant examples in this regard may be the US and EU initiatives to link labour rights protection to the extension of trade preferences (see, further, Trebilcock and Howse 1999: 458–60), or the UK Ethical Trading Initiative. However, specialised legislation on MNEs and human rights is virtually non-existent. One example of what might be possible arose in Australia where the draft Corporate Code of Conduct Bill contained a provision that subjected the overseas subsidiaries of Australian companies to a general obligation to observe human rights and the principle of non-discrimination.[13] That Bill was never adopted.

On the other hand there are early signs at the level of US national law that a degree of direct responsibility for human rights violations on the part of MNEs is being recognised. Thus in the United States District Court case of *Doe v. Unocal*[14] it was held, for the first time, that MNEs could, in principle, be directly liable for violations of human rights under the Alien Tort Claims Act (ATCA).[15] However, on 31 August 2000, the US District Court awarded a summary judgment to Unocal on the grounds that, although there was evidence that Unocal knew about, and benefited from, forced labour on the pipeline project in Burma (Myanmar) in which it was a joint venture partner, it was not directly involved in the alleged abuses. These were the responsibility of the Burma authorities alone. Giving the Court's judgment, Judge Ronald Lew followed a series of decisions by US Military Tribunals after the Second World War, involving the prosecution of German industrialists for their participation in the Third Reich's slave labour policies.[16] These established that, in order to be liable, the defendant industrialists had to take active steps in co-operating or participating in the forced labour practices. Mere knowledge that someone else would commit abuses was insufficient. By analogy with these cases, Unocal could not be held liable as a matter of international law and so the claim under the Alien Tort Statute failed.[17]

However, the principle that a private non-state actor can be sued before the US courts for alleged violations of human rights was not questioned.[18]

The summary judgment was overturned in part on appeal to the United States Court of Appeal (USCA) for the Ninth Circuit.[19] The USCA held that there were genuine issues of material fact to be determined as regards the possible liability of Unocal for the alleged acts of forced labour, for aiding and abetting the Burma military in subjecting the plaintiffs to forced labour and for aiding and abetting the Burma military in subjecting the plaintiffs to murder and rape occurring in furtherance of forced labour. On the other hand, there were insufficient facts to justify an examination of the allegations of liability on the part of Unocal for torture. Of particular importance in this judgment is the reaffirmation of the principle that, under ATCA, private actors may be directly liable for alleged violations of fundamental human rights norms that constitute *jus cogens* and to which individual liability applies. In this context, forced labour was seen by the USCA as a modern variant of slavery, one of the crimes to which international law attributes individual liability. The incidents of rape and murder that occurred in relation to the forced labour practices of the Burma military were also of this type as they arose directly out of the furtherance of forced labour.

A second notable element in the judgment is the affirmation of the applicability of the law relating to aiding and abetting an offence to crimes or torts involving alleged violations of fundamental human rights under ATCA.[20] This allows for a finding that a corporation may be liable even if it has not directly taken part in the alleged violations, but has given practical assistance and encouragement to the commission of the crime or tort in question (the *actus reus* of aiding and abetting) and has actual or constructive knowledge that its actions will assist the perpetrator in the commission of the crime or tort (the *mens rea* of aiding and abetting). Thus the District Judge was wrong to give the weight that he had done to the 'active participation' standard used in the Nuremberg Military Tribunal cases that he had relied on. In those cases this standard had been used in response to the defendant's 'necessity defence'. No such defence was invoked, nor could be invoked, by Unocal in the present case.

Furthermore, in the case of *Wiwa v. Royal Dutch Petroleum Company and Shell Transport and Trading Company plc*[21] the US Court of Appeal held that the US interest in pursuing claims for torture under the ATCA and the more recent Torture Victim Prevention Act[22] was a significant factor to be taken into account when determining whether an action brought on such grounds before a US court against a foreign MNE should be removed to a foreign jurisdiction on the basis that it was a more suitable forum for the litigation. On the facts, the USCA held that an action brought against the defendant corporation, for allegedly supporting the Nigerian state in its repression of the Ogoni people through *inter alia* the supply of money, weapons and logistical support to the Nigerian military which carried out the alleged abuses, could be heard in the United States. Thus the US courts have set themselves up as a forum in which allegations of complicity in torture made against private corporations can be heard.

However, this case was brought by US resident plaintiffs. It is not certain that US jurisdiction will be so readily accepted where the plaintiffs are from outside the US. Indeed, in *Aguinda et al. v. Texaco* the USCA Second Circuit upheld the decision and the reasoning of the District Court for the Southern District of New York that rejected US jurisdiction over a claim under ATCA, brought by Ecuadorian and Peruvian citizens against Texaco, alleging that the company had polluted rainforests and rivers in those two countries causing environmental damage and personal injuries.[23] The District Court had reviewed the *Wiwa* decision and concluded that it did not introduce a different test of jurisdiction under ATCA from that generally applicable to cases where the issue of whether the US, or a foreign forum, was more appropriate as the place in which the claim should be heard (the *forum non conveniens* doctrine). Given that the balance of the private- and public-interest factors used to determine the appropriate forum pointed overwhelmingly to Ecuador, the District Court held that this claim should be heard there. In any case, the corporate links between the US parent and the Ecuadorian operating affiliate were of a kind of which it could not be said that any wrong had been committed by the parent in the US such as would justify a claim under ATCA. Thus it may be difficult for a foreign claimant to assert the jurisdiction of the US courts over US-based MNEs for alleged violations of human rights where there exists an appropriate alternative forum in the host country and where there is little evidence of direct involvement by the parent in the acts leading to the alleged harm. The only possible exception may be where the plaintiff is claiming to be a victim of torture, though, even in such cases, the choice of US forum will not be decisive under the *forum non conveniens* doctrine.

Although a finding of direct responsibility for human rights violations is, as yet, unprecedented, there is some support for establishing the indirect responsibility of MNEs for human rights violations. Here the state may be held liable for the conduct of non-state actors that amounts to a violation of the human rights of a third person. Such a responsibility could be established by international convention (Kamminga 1999: 559, 569). No such responsibility has ever been expressly provided for. Instead there is some evidence from the case-law under the European Convention on Human Rights (ECHR) that the state may be under an obligation to 'secure' the rights of third persons against interference by a non-state actor. Failure to do so may result in a violation of the Convention.[24] However, this case-law is uncertain in its scope and too much cannot be read into it. At most, it is clear that the state cannot absolve itself of its direct human rights responsibilities by hiving them off to a privatised entity.[25]

Turning to the role of IGOs in monitoring and enforcement, two sets of issues arise. First, what should the legal status of any standard-setting instruments be and, second, what kinds of procedure for monitoring and enforcement could be put in place? The discussions over the UN Draft Norms are instructive as these very questions have had to be faced by the Working Group. It was mentioned above that the legal status of the Draft Norms is yet to be settled. Much here depends on the goodwill of states. There are arguments in favour of, and against, a binding code. The main advantage of a voluntary instrument is that it could be used in conjunction with existing voluntary corporate codes of conduct to develop a more comprehensive system of internal values to be observed by the company. This would need to be supplemented by an effective system of accountability within the company.[26]

While the discussions on the Draft Norms have tended to favour a binding instrument, the Working Group has recognised that, given the uncertainties around the precise legal status of companies and other non-state actors, some form of 'soft law' exercise is a necessary starting point. This has been the normal pattern of operation in relation to the adoption of other binding human rights instruments. Hence, in the absence of state opinion to the contrary (perhaps an unlikely eventuality), some transition from 'soft' to 'hard' law is more likely to occur, with the Draft Norms as the first step in the process. On the other hand, as David Weissbrodt pointed out at the 54th Session of the Sub-Commission, the Draft Norms are binding to the extent that they apply human rights law under ratified conventions to activities of TNCs and other business enterprises. Moreover, the language of the document emphasises binding responsibilities through the use of the term 'shall' rather than 'should' and through the inclusion, in more recent drafts, of more comprehensive implementation measures (UN Sub-Commission on Human Rights 2002a: 6).

Connected with this issue is the question of how to give the Draft Norms 'teeth' through effective implementation and monitoring procedures. In this regard the Draft Norms require TNCs and other business enterprises to adopt, disseminate and implement internal rules of operation in com-pliance with the Norms. In addition, they must incorporate the principles contained in the Draft Norms in their contracts or other arrangements and dealings with contractors, subcontractors, suppliers and licensees in order to ensure their implementation and respect. This represents a significant advance on the earlier drafts, which did not contain express provisions on the use of such legal measures to give force to their contents, though such measures were recommended in commentaries on those earlier drafts. The Draft Norms also require that TNCs and other business enter-prises shall monitor and verify their compliance in an independent and transparent manner, which includes input from relevant stakeholders. This monitoring and verification may be done by national, international, govern-mental and/or non-governmental mechanisms in addition to internal review procedures.

The original text of the Principles/Guidelines focused on corporate implementation. However, the current Draft Norms suggest that their contents could be used by other actors to assess business practice and performance in the area of human rights responsibilities. For example:

- They could form the basis of industry-wide codes.
- Unions could use them as a benchmark for their expectations of company conduct.
- IGOs outside the UN could apply them to develop their own standard-setting instruments.
- Governments could use the Draft Norms as a model for legislation or administrative rules as part of the internal regulatory structure applicable to companies with a statutory seat in the country, or to help interpret legal standards.
- The UN's human rights treaty bodies could apply the Draft Norms to create additional reporting requirements about corporate compliance.

The Draft Norms include a provision requiring TNCs and other business enterprises to 'provide prompt, effective and adequate reparation to those persons, entities, and communities who have been adversely affected by failures to comply with these Responsibilities through, inter alia, reparations, restitution, compensation and rehabilitation for any damage done or property taken'. The Draft Norms state further (in paragraph 17) that: 'In connection with determining damages and in all other respects, these Responsibilities shall be enforced by national courts.' By taking this approach, the Draft Norms envisage a binding enforcement mechanism, centred on national courts, which offers directly effective rights of reparation for the individuals or groups affected as a consequence of a violation of the instrument. This presupposes a legally binding document that is effective within the national laws of the UN Member States that adopt it. Such an effect could not be presumed from a non-binding declaration or recommendation of the UN, neither of which normally has the force of positive international law nor are they sources of directly effective individual rights that can be invoked before national tribunals.

Arguably, the Draft Norms, as an instrument that contains many binding norms of international human rights law, may be enforceable by that fact alone. However, as argued above, not all the norms contained in its provisions are uncontroversial in this respect. Some of the rights that are included may not have such a legal status. Therefore, if the reparation mechanism is to be real and effective, it requires the adoption of an instrument that has the force of law within the legal orders of the signatory states, and recognises the legal effectiveness of all the norms that it contains. This would need to be something akin to an international convention, which contains an obligation to implement its contents and enforcement mechanisms into the municipal law of the signatory state. This is a far cry from a 'soft law' instrument of the kind, as discussed above, usually adopted in this field. Equally, it is unlikely that a UN framework could enforce binding rules and norms relating to the activities of TNCs (see, for example, the views of Mr Alfonso Martinez [a member of the Working Group] in UN Sub-Commission on Human Rights 2002a: 7). In the light of these matters, there is a significant need for further clarification of what legal form this enforcement mechanism will take and how it is expected to work.[27]

A further issue that requires some comment and clarification is the identification of the precise forum before which any claim for reparations under paragraph 17 can be brought. As it stands paragraph 17 is silent on this matter. It could, therefore, be presumed that the question of forum remains to be determined by the national laws of the jurisdiction or jurisdictions in which a claim is brought. If so, then claims brought under the Draft Norms may be embroiled in lengthy and unhelpful disputes over jurisdiction, particularly in common law jurisdictions where the doctrine of *forum non conveniens* continues to apply. In such jurisdictions it may be possible for the respondent corporation – particularly if it is a TNC and the *locus* of the alleged violation of the UN Norms is in another jurisdiction – to challenge the appropriateness of the forum chosen by the claimants and, thereby, to gain a procedural advantage either by vacating the case to another forum more sympathetic to the corporation's defence, or simply by causing delay while this issue is litigated (Muchlinski 2001b; Anderson 2002; Blumberg 2002). In that process the claimants may suffer significant delay in access to justice, not to mention financial loss that might undermine their ability to continue with their claim. Some legal systems are becoming sensitive to such issues[28] but others are not (see, for example, Blumberg 2002). Thus, the Draft Norms may need to establish certain basic rules of jurisdiction so that such legal techniques are not allowed to undermine legitimate claims.

One solution would be to make available the jurisdiction of any state that adheres to the UN Norms on the basis of either the *locus* of the alleged violation, or the domicile of the corporation alleged to be responsible, with the claimant having the choice of forum. Equally, it might be necessary to ensure that the corporate (or contractual) separation between affiliates in a TNC group (or network)[29] is not allowed to act as a barrier to jurisdiction against related (or cooperating) entities located outside the jurisdiction where the harm is alleged to have been suffered, but which are seen as complicit in a violation of the Draft Norms on the basis of their relationship with the affiliate (or network partner) located in that jurisdiction. This may prove to be rather controversial as it challenges long-accepted notions of separate corporate personality (and, in the case of transnational networks or alliances, freedom of contract) as the basis for attributing liability to legal persons. However, in the absence of some clarification of this matter, national laws may well come to be used to insulate discrete entities, involved in a TNC or in a transnational network enterprise, production or retailing chain that leads to a violation of human rights, from full responsibility.

Conclusions

The preceding discussion illustrates the challenges ahead for any IGO that wishes to develop a new social responsibility agenda for TNCs and other business entities. The first point to note is that the process is a slow one and is probably more likely to create 'soft law' obligations. That does not imply that the Draft Norms, or any other international corporate social responsibility instrument, are doomed to complete legal ineffectiveness if they are not legally binding. At the international level 'soft law' can 'harden' into positive law, where it is seen as evidence of emergent new standards of international law. For these purposes the origin of the legal principle in a 'soft law' instrument, such as a voluntary code of conduct or a non-binding resolution of an international organisation, is of little consequence if a consensus develops that the principle in question should be viewed as an obligatory standard by reason of subsequent practice (see, for example, Elias and Lim 1998: 230–232). Given that many of the most important international expressions of welfare values tend to be in such form (Elias and Lim 1998), the 'hardening process' may be of especial importance here. Indeed, as the debate over the social content of the MAI shows, the demand for 'hard law' in this field might be difficult to resist. On the other hand, it should not be forgotten that, even in 'hard law' agreements, provisions concerning controversial social issues have been put into very general, and probably meaningless, hortatory language, simply to show that something has been done, where there is little intention to see these provisions having any real legal effect (see, for example, Waelde 1998, 1999). It is to be hoped that such a fate will not befall the contents of the Draft Norms should it become a legally binding document.

A second significant issue concerns the effect of international instruments at the level of national law. It is arguable that, even if the Draft Norms were to be adopted as a non-binding voluntary instrument, without direct effect on individual rights under national law, they could conceivably acquire legal force in private law. Private law suits can be brought against any firm or organisation that holds itself out as adopting a voluntary code such as, for example, the UN Norms, by other firms or organisations, consumers or other members of the community. Such claims may allege that a failure to comply with the Draft Norms, or other international corporate social responsibility instruments adopted by a company, is evidence that the firm or organisation in question is not meeting standards of conduct that may represent accepted general principles and is, therefore, not exercising reasonable care or due diligence. Moreover, failure to follow the terms of such instruments could be evidence of a breach of contract, where adherence is an express or implied term of the agreement, or of an actionable misrepresentation, where a firm alleges that its adherence to the instrument in question entitles it to be regarded as qualifying for a governmental standard-setting mark of approval, but where in fact it fails to meet these standards.

In such cases, consumers can bring an action if they claim to have been attracted to purchasing the firm's products or services in the light of such assertions of good conduct. Also the relevant government agency might bring an action for abuse of its certification scheme (Government of Canada 1998: 27; Webb 1999).

Therefore, to dismiss voluntary sources of international or national corporate social responsibility standards as irrelevant seems to fail to appreciate how formal rules and principles of law emerge. The very fact that an increasing number of non-binding codes is being drafted and adopted in this area suggests a growing interest among important groups and organisations – corporations, industry associations, NGOs, governments and IGOs – and is leading to the establishment of a rich set of sources from which new binding standards can emerge. Indeed, it is noteworthy that the Draft Norms make use of already existing standards produced by other IGOs. A kind of 'collective law of IGOs' seems to be developing, in which various organisations working in the field of corporate social responsibility cross-fertilise one another's initiatives by reference to one another's instruments.

No doubt this process can be, and is being, criticised as one in which corporate interests are trying to capture the agenda through code making and lobbying before international forums and organisations. It is fair to say that non-business NGOs are attempting the same with their codes. The real issue is when and how will all this 'codification' turn into detailed legal standards that can act as fully binding benchmarks for the control of unacceptable lapses in corporate conduct at the international and national levels. That is, of course, an issue of ideological contest, but one that seems to be veering slowly towards an acceptance of some kind of articulated set of minimum international standards for corporate social responsibility, as a trade-off for greater corporate freedom in the market. The Draft Norms represent a very important contribution to this process – one that may possibly turn out to be legally binding.

Notes

1   The terms 'transnational corporation' and 'multinational enterprise' are essentially interchangeable and are so used in this chapter (see further Muchlinski 1999: 12–15; 2002: 169–170).
2   www.unglobalcompact.org (last accessed 17 March 2003).
3   This section of the chapter draws on Muchlinski 2001a: 35–44.
4   See, for example, the UN Draft Code of Conduct for Transnational Corporations paragraphs 15–16 (reprinted in UNCTAD 1996: 165).
5   See esp. 37–40. See also UNCTAD 2000b; Muchlinski 2000a: 386–388 n. 14 and sources cited therein. For a full inventory of corporate codes of conduct, see OECD 1999.
6   For example the UK Ethical Trading Initiative: www.ethicaltrade.org (last accessed 17 March 2003).
7   See, for an overview, UNCTAD 2000b: n. 33 and the ILO website at www.ilo.org (last accessed 17 March 2003).

8   This Convention entered into force on 15 February 1999. See OECD Doc DAFFE/ IME/BR(97)20, 8 April 1998, or see www.imf.org/external/np/gov/2001/eng/ 091801.htm.

9   'Draft Norms', paragraph 6. This formulation in the text, introduced by the 'Draft Principles', replaces an earlier formulation of the 'Draft Norms' which stated that 'Companies shall not use child labour and shall contribute to its abolition.' Thus the prohibition in the earlier draft has been modified so that child labour conducted in a non-exploitative manner can be used. This reflects concern that, in some developing countries, the denial of access to labour for children might actually worsen their economic situation and that of their families. In such cases the issue is to make child labour non-abusive. To that end the 'Draft Principles' laid down a basic framework for the control of abuses of child labour. Equally, business enterprises that use child labour must create and implement a plan to eliminate this ('Draft Commentary' at page 8). By comparison, the 1998 ILO Declaration requires 'the effective abolition of child labour' without qualification.

10   ILO Tripartite Declaration on Multinational Enterprises and Social Policy 1977 as amended at the 279th Session of the ILO, Geneva, 17 November 2000: 41 ILM 186 (2002).

11   These include transparency, accountability and prohibition of corruption.

12   This principle is echoed in the OECD Guidelines and the ILO Tripartite Declaration.

13   *Corporate Code of Conduct Bill 2000*, The Parliament of the Commonwealth of Australia draft of 28 August 2000, clause 10.

14   As noted in *American Journal of International Law* 92 (1998): 309. See also *Wiwa v. Royal Dutch Petroleum Company* 226 Federal Supplement 2nd series 88 (US Court of Appeal Second Circuit 2000).

15   28 United States Code S.1350.

16   *US v. Flick* (Trials of War Criminals Before the Nuremberg Military Tribunals under Control Council Law No. 10 [1952]); *US v. Carl Krauch, ibid.* Vol. 8; *US v. Alfred Krupp, ibid.* Vol. 9; *Flick v. Johnson* 174 Federal Reporter 2nd Series 983 (Court of Appeals for District of Columbia 1949).

17   *DOE v. Unocal*, US District Court for the Central District of California, 31 August 2000, 2000 US District Court Report on LEXIS at 13327. See also Branigin 2000.

18   See too in this regard *Kadic v. Karadzic* 70 Federal Reporter 3rd Series 232 (US Court of Appeal 2nd Circuit 1995) where it was held that the Alien Tort Statute reaches the conduct of private parties provided that their conduct is undertaken under the colour of state authority or violates a norm of international law that is recognised as extending to the conduct of private parties.

19   *DOE v. Unocal Corp.* Judgment of 18 September 2002 (2002) *International Legal Materials* 41: 1,367 (2002).

20   For this purpose the USCA held that the distinction between the aiding and abetting of a crime and a tort was not significant, in that similar principles applied in each situation.

21   US Court of Appeal 2nd Circuit, 14 September 2000: 2000 US Appeal Court Report on LEXIS at 23274.

22   28 United States Code S.1350 (1991).

23   945 Federal Supplement 625 (2001) upheld on appeal 303 Federal Reporter 3rd Series. 470 (US Court of Appeal 2nd Circuit, 16 August 2002).

24   See e.g. *Young James and Webster v. UK* (1981) European Court of Human Rights Ct.HR Series A, Vol. 44; *X and Y v. The Netherlands* (1985) European Court of Human Rights Ct.HR Series A, Vol. 91; *Arzte fur das Leben* (1988) European Court of Human Rights E.Ct.HR Series A, Vol. 139; Drzemczewski 1983: ch. 8; Clapham 1993: ch. 7.

25   *Costello-Roberts v. UK* (1993) European Court of Human Rights E.Ct.HR (1993) Series A, Vol. 247.

26   Indeed, a business representative at the 54th Session stressed the need for a voluntary

27   approach and that businesses themselves should develop the draft (UN Sub-
      Commission on Human Rights 2002a: 12).

27   In this connection a number of possible approaches were canvassed by the Working
      Group. These at the 54th Session include: a follow-up mechanism, composed of a
      group of experts, that would be incorporated into the draft; annual reporting on the
      activities of TNCs; the UN could ensure that respect for the Draft Norms was
      included in the contracts it concluded with private-sector entities for the pro-
      curement of services; the appointment of a special rapporteur on TNCs (UN Sub-
      Commission on Human Rights 2002a: 9–10 at paras 28–29).

28   See e.g. the UK House of Lords decision in *Lubbe et al. v. Cape plc* (2000) 2 *Lloyds
      Reports* 2: 383; (2000) 4 *All England Reports* 4: P 268.

29   It is necessary to make a distinction between equity-based linkages between affiliates
      in a corporate group and contractual linkages between co-operating enterprises in a
      network enterprise or alliance for the purposes of liability. In the former case the
      issue of group liability involves the lifting of the corporate veil between the affiliates,
      whereas in the latter it involves disregarding any contractual warranties or exclusion
      clauses that seek to limit the liability of some or all of the participating enterprises
      (see, further, Muchlinski 1999: chs. 5, 9).

References

Amnesty International (The Netherlands) and Pax Christi International (2000)
      Multinational Enterprises and Human Rights, Utrecht, Netherlands: Amnesty
      International (The Netherlands) and Pax Christi International.

Anderson, M. (2002) 'Transnational Corporations and Environmental Damage: Is
      Tort Law the Answer?', *Washburn Law Journal* 41: 399–425.

Baxi, U. (1998) 'Voices of Suffering and the Future of Human Rights', *Transnational
      Law and Contemporary Problems* 8: 125–175.

Blumberg, P. (2002) 'Asserting Human Rights Against Multinational Corporations
      under United States Law: Conceptual and Procedural Problems', *American
      Journal of Comparative Law* 50: 493–529.

Branigin, W. (2000) 'Claim Against Unocal Rejected: Judge Cites Evidence of Abuses
      in Burma but No Jurisdiction', *Washington Post*, 8 September 2000: E10.

Clapham, A. (1993) *Human Rights in the Private Sphere*, Oxford, UK: Clarendon
      Press.

Clapham, A. (2000) 'The Question of Jurisdiction under International Criminal
      Law over Legal Persons', in M. Kamminga and S. Zia-Zarifi (eds.) *Liability of
      Multinational Corporations under International Law*, The Hague: Kluwer Law
      International: 139–195.

Drzemczewski, A. (1983) *European Human Rights Convention in Domestic Law*, Oxford:
      Oxford University Press.

Elias, O., and Lim, C. (1998) *The Paradox of Consensualism in International Law*, The
      Hague: Kluwer Law International.

Fitzmaurice, M. (1996) 'The Contribution of Environmental Law to the
      Development of Modern International Law', in J. Makarczyk (ed.) *The Theory
      of International Law at the Threshold of the 21st Century*, The Hague: Kluwer Law
      International: 909–925.

Government of Canada (1998) *Voluntary Codes: A Guide for Their Development and Use*,
      Ottawa: Government of Canada.

Harvard Law School Human Rights Program (1999) *Business and Human Rights*, Cambridge, MA: Harvard Law School Human Rights Program.

Henderson, D. (1999) *The MAI Affair: A Story and Its Lessons*, London: Royal Institute of International Affairs.

International Council on Human Rights Policy (2002) *Beyond Voluntarism: Human Rights and the Developing International Legal Obligations of Companies*, Versoix, Switzerland: International Council on Human Rights Policy.

Joseph, S. (2000) 'An Overview of the Human Rights Accountability of Multinational Enterprises' in M. Kamminga and S. Zia-Zarifi (eds) *Liability of Multinational Corporations under International Law*, The Hague: Kluwer Law International: 75–93.

Kamminga, M. (1999) 'Holding Multinational Corporations Accountable for Human Rights Abuses: A Challenge for the EC', in P. Alston (ed.) *The EU and Human Rights*, Oxford: Oxford University Press: 553–569.

Muchlinski, P. (1999) *Multinational Enterprises and the Law*, Oxford, UK: Blackwell Publishers, rev. pbk edn.

Muchlinski, P. (2000a) 'The Social Dimension of International Investment Agreements', in J. Faundez, M. Footer and J. Norton (eds) *Governance Development and Globalization*, London: Blackstone Press: 373–396.

Muchlinski, P. (2000b) 'The Rise and Fall of the Multilateral Agreement on Investment: Where Now', *International Lawyer* 34: 1,033–1,053.

Muchlinski, P. (2001a) 'Human Rights and Multinationals: Is There a Problem?' *International Affairs* 77.1: 31–49.

Muchlinski, P. (2001b) 'Corporations in International Litigation: Problems of Jurisdiction and the United Kingdom Asbestos Case', *International and Comparative Law Quarterly* 50: 1–25.

Muchlinski, P. (2002) 'Holding Multinationals to Account: Recent Developments in English Litigation and the Company Law Review', *Company Lawyer* 23.6: 168–179.

OECD (2000) *OECD Guidelines for Multinational Enterprises*, Paris: OECD.

Picciotto, S. (1998) 'Linkages in International Investment Regulation: The Antinomies of the Draft Multilateral Agreement on Investment', *University of Philadelphia Journal of International Economic Law* 19: 731–768.

UNCTAD (UN Conference on Trade and Development) (1994) *World Investment Report 1994*, Geneva: UNCTAD.

UNCTAD (1998) *Bilateral Investment Treaties in the Mid-1990s*, Geneva: UNCTAD.

UNCTAD (1999a) *The Social Responsibility of Transnational Corporations*, Geneva: UNCTAD.

UNCTAD (1999b) *World Investment Report 1999*, Geneva: UNCTAD.

UNCTAD (2000a) *International Investment Agreements: A Compendium*, Geneva: UNCTAD.

UNCTAD (2001a) *Social Responsibility*, Issues in International Investment Agreements, Geneva: UNCTAD.

UNCTAD (2001b) *Statistical Profiles of the Least Developed Countries*, Geneva: UNCTAD.

UN Sub-Commission on Human Rights (Working Group on the Working Methods and Activities of Transnational Corporations) (2002a) *Human Rights Principles and Responsibilities for Transnational Corporations and Other Business Enterprises: Introduction* (UN Doc.E/CN.4/Sub.2/2002/WG.2/WP.1/Add.1).

UN (2002b) 'Draft Norms on Responsibilities of Transnational Corporations and Other Business Enterprises with Regard to Human Rights' (UN Doc.E/ CN.4/Sub.2/2002/13, www.umn.edu/humanrts/links/tncreport-2002. html, 15 August 2002), accessed 17 March 2003.

Vernon, R. (1999) Intervention in discussion in Harvard Law School *Business and Human Rights*, Cambridge, MA: Harvard Law School Human Rights Program: 49.

Waelde, T. (1998) 'Sustainable Development and the 1994 Energy Charter Treaty: Between Pseudo-Action and the Management of Environmental Investment Risk', in F. Weiss, E. Denters and P. de Waart (eds) *International Economic Law with a Human Face*, The Hague: Kluwer Law International: 223–270.

Waelde, T. (1999) 'Non-conventional Views on "Effectiveness": The Holy Grail of Modern International Lawyers: The New Paradigm? A Chimera? Or a Brave New World in the Global Economy?', *Austrian Review of International and European Law* 4: 164–203.

Weissbrodt, D. (2000) 'The Beginning of a Sessional Working Group on Transnational Corporations within the UN Sub-Commission on Prevention of Discrimination and Protection of Minorities', in M. Kamminga and S. Zia-Zarifi (eds) *Liability of Multinational Corporations under International Law*, The Hague: Kluwer Law International: 119–138.

Williams, S. (1999) 'How Principles Benefit the Bottom Line: The Experience of the Cooperative Bank', in M. Addo (ed.) *Human Rights Standards and the Responsibility of Transnational Corporations*, The Hague/London: Kluwer Law International: 63–68.

CORPORATE SOCIAL RESPONSIBILITY AS A PARTICIPATIVE PROCESS

Patrick Maclagan

Introduction

There is a vast literature, spanning many decades, on employee participation in organisations. As was noted by Dachler and Wilpert (1978), this literature includes a variety of theoretical perspectives or paradigms, each with its characteristic underlying value-assumptions and concerns. Four different traditions identified in Dachler and Wilpert are: *Democratic Theory* (concerning the potential contribution which individual members can make to the governance of institutions), *Socialistic Theory* (a Marxist position, concerning the ultimate goal of persons' control over their work through ownership of the enterprise, and consequent countering of alienation), *Human Growth and Development* (concerning the redesign of organisation and work so as to facilitate self-actualisation and employees' mental health), and *Productivity and Efficiency* (in which the primary explicit concern is the improvement to organisational performance which is assumed to follow participative management approaches). Each of these perspectives is relevant to the theme of this paper, although socialistic theory will not be addressed explicitly.

Regarding corporate social responsibility (CSR) it is assumed here that this calls for institutional *governance*, and that it is not served by a narrowly defined concept of management in which the public relations function of 'ethical business' is used as a means to 'selfish' organisational ends. As Selznick has said, 'To govern [as opposed to manage] is to accept responsibility for *the whole life* of the institution . . . Governance takes account of all the interests that affect the viability, competence and moral character of an enterprise' (1992: 290). Following this, a second assumption is that the social processes involved in such governance should be participative. These processes could of course involve many stakeholder groups (Wheeler and Sillanpaa 1997) but the focus in this paper is on those who work in organisations, the employees. This is a cue for democratic theory as a perspective on participation (e.g. Pateman 1970), and for a view of organisations as 'moral communities' (Warren 1996, Maclagan 1998) where people would 'learn and practise responsibility' (Warren 1996: 91) and develop morally as a result.

Defining Corporate Social Responsibility

The idea that employees might participate in a process leading to more socially responsible organisational conduct invites closer scrutiny of what this might mean for our understanding of CSR. So let us consider two positions, one *outcome-oriented*, and the other *process-oriented*. On the one hand CSR may be construed in terms of specific desired consequences of action, such as reduced environmental pollution or greater consumer protection, and analysed in terms of the substantive ethical dilemmas and decision-outcomes involved when pursuing such aims in actuality. On the other hand one could focus on the structures and decision making processes which such management activity (or governance) entails. It is this second perspective which provides the defining framework for the present discussion.

(i) CSR as a process

If one is concerned with a generally applicable normative theory of CSR, then one is not going to do this by looking at broadly defined issues and decision outcomes alone. That is, one cannot usefully say that socially responsible action consists of trading with acceptable political regimes only, or stopping pollution, or providing employment, and so on, in such general terms. These may be *prima facie* moral obligations for organisations, but in any actual case one may not be able to meet all of these responsibilities in full. It will depend on the circumstances; stopping pollution may not be possible without closing down a manufacturing facility and losing jobs. As Jones observed, 'it is virtually impossible to define social responsibility in terms of specific decisions' (1980: 65). His argument was that one rarely has consensus on the morally right substantive course of action to be followed in such real situations. As in the second position offered in the previous paragraph, Jones argued that we should instead concentrate on generally accepted notions of 'fair process', whereby attention would be paid to the interests and concerns of various stakeholders liable to be affected by organisational activity.

(ii) A process involving people

A focus on processes, involving individual members of organisations, is a reminder that the very idea of corporate *responsibility* strongly suggests a need to consider the values, motives and choices of those real people who are involved in formulating policy and taking decisions. Responsibility suggests that one can attribute blame or praise to the moral agent, but while it has been claimed by writers such as Goodpaster and Matthews (1982) that one *can* treat organisations, as systems, in this manner, there are powerful counter-arguments against that position (e.g. Downie 1971, chs. 3–4, Velasquez 1983). Of course, in a limited sense, we may say that particular events are the outcome of organisational activity. We may even engage in *consequentialist* moral evaluation of this systemic behaviour, which we can do without understanding the underlying motives or freely chosen actions of those behind the events in question. But unless we possess that understanding we cannot judge the individuals involved (or anyone else) from a deontological moral standpoint.

This indicates the distinction between what Maclagan (1998) calls the 'ethically acceptable (or unacceptable) organisation' and the organisation as a 'moral community'. In the former, we are confronted with a 'black box'; we think we know what the organisation is doing to, or for, society, but we do not necessarily know why. We do not understand the internal workings of the organisational system. Now, for many commentators and concerned parties this lack of understanding does not seem important, so long as they can feel reassured that things are satisfactory, or can identify grounds for criticising or attacking the organisation. So why does the distinction matter?

One reason why it matters is that what are perceived as the socially or environmentally acceptable consequences of organisational behaviour may be due to chance, or have been brought about by external pressures such as consumer boycotts or the threat of government intervention. But this in itself is no guarantee that the satisfactory situation will continue. It would be much more reassuring to know that the real people who populate the organisation, most obviously those in authority, consciously value, intend and support such outcomes. This is not to deny the effectiveness of pressure groups' influence over organisations, but such influence, in itself, does not necessarily address the question of responsibility, which requires from management, and others in the organisation, a conscious awareness of, and concern for, the substantive issues in question.

To summarise so far, there is a pragmatic argument that while tax-onomies of issues, and of the associated stakeholders, are valuable, any normative and *practically applicable* theory of CSR must focus on the social processes involved (including possible approaches to ethical policy and decision-making) rather than attempt to legislate in advance for ideal solu-tions to hypothetical dilemmas. And this is supported by a further argument; that unless one brings real people as moral agents into the picture, as the focus on processes does, one cannot talk sensibly of 'responsibility' at all.

However, a third reason for focusing on organisational processes is that it is only by doing so that we can discuss the potential contribution of employ-ees (and other stakeholders) to the essentially ethical debates involved. This is important because it would seem inconsistent, if not hypocritical, to discuss CSR without at the same time considering the moral claims of those who wish to have a say on matters of concern to them.

Arguments for Employee Participation

The dominant paradigm for employee participation in management theory and practice represents a concern for 'productivity and efficiency' (Coch and French 1948). This includes a variety of contemporary practices such as quality circles, team-working and 'empowerment'. Such approaches share theoretical underpinnings with the 'human growth and development' school (McGregor 1960, Argyris 1964), and indeed such writers have been accused of 'trying to serve two masters, seeing no incompatibility between their humanistic concerns and those of efficient management (Maclagan 1998: 82).

In the context of the present discussion, what is noticeable about such managerial writing, past and present, is that discussion of terms like motiva-tion and commitment, which people are presumed to demonstrate following their involvement in participative processes, typically implies that employees subscribe to officially recognised organisational values. Seldom if ever is it suggested explicitly that such personnel might harbour a *critical moral* view on the implications of their work and employment; on the way in which organisational activity affects society, the public or the environment (although of course it may be recognised that employees are likely to have views on the ethics of how they themselves are being treated).

Were one to recognise such possibilities, and also the right of employ-ees to express their views, this could have profound implications for the organisational processes relating to CSR. It would suggest that employees generally, not just senior managers, could have something to offer in the formulation of CSR policy. This is important for a number of reasons. First, from a Kantian ethical standpoint (and reflecting democratic theory), it would suggest a moral imperative for the facilitation of employee participation in this arena. Second, there is a case for democratic systems of governance in those corporations which can escape from, or counter, the restrictions of legal controls. And, third, it can be argued that the alignment of individual and organisational values which could result would lead to higher performing organisations, although here particularly there is a need to guard against the manipulative tendencies which are often associated with employee participation in the management process (Hart 1988).

(i) Respect for persons

On the first point, it is quite clear that people do subscribe to moral values, and can have views regarding the ethics of that organisational activity in which they are implicated as employees. Apart from whistleblowers' concerns regarding illicit conduct, such subjective moral evaluation can express itself in different ways, from collective dissent against corporate policy (Coates 1978) to individuals' personal sense of alienation (e.g. Steinbeck 1951, ch. 5) or modes of identification with work and its implications (Klein 1963).

The Kantian argument is that such personally held values should be respected by others. Moral management would therefore recognise and attend to employees' concerns regarding their organisation's ethics (Bowie 1990). This would represent the idea of governance outlined in the introduction, and indeed Selznick adopts an explicitly Kantian position when he states that '[t]he claims of purpose and efficiency are strong, but they cannot justify practices that reduce human beings to "means only" ' (1992: 319).

(ii) Corporations and democracy

In both the international arena, through their ability to transcend local political controls, and in their capacity to influence national governments, large business corporations have for years provoked concern amongst those worried about the fate of democratic processes. This general issue is as real now as it was in past decades, although the terms of the debate may have changed somewhat. Today, as Sampson (1995) notes, the size of corporations may not be so critical; but the power exercised by top management is, as is the influence of other players in the global capitalist system, such as fund managers. Thus, as David Matthew, Director of the New Academy of Business (1998) has observed, the 'political, democratic, control of organisations' is the number one issue. Employee involvement, on a wider range of issues than in the past, is essential.

(iii) Employee commitment and motivation

Devotees of Human Relations theory, job enrichment, participative leadership, and related schools of management thought, have always assumed that by involving employees in decisions one could engender their identification with corporate values and goals and thus stimulate their commitment to the organisation. But, as suggested earlier, virtually all such work, from its earliest beginnings around 1930, has been conducted from a control or performance oriented stance (even if only implicitly) with a blind spot when it comes to recognition of individuals' potential for critical moral judgment (Perrow 1979: 114, Maclagan 1983, Nord et al. 1990: 288).

However, the seeds of a more widely accepted shift in perspective are discernible. There is recognition that employees face a plurality of commitments: to professional values, trade unions, customers and others, as well as to managerially defined goals (Reichers 1986, Iles et al. 1990). The moral dimension of such situations is clear, most obviously where whistleblowing is called for, as noted earlier. What is less obvious, but equally important for the present argument, is that persons' *positive* orientations to their work can have a moral dimension (Klein 1963, Maclagan 1998). The point is that if an organisation is *really* doing something useful for society, if it is socially responsible, then one would think, as does Bowie (1990), that morally aware employees would feel motivated to contribute high quality performance. It would make sense, therefore, for organisations to involve such people in policy-making processes which facilitate an alignment between corporate values and those moral values harboured by society at large.

CSR as a Participative Process

Ideally, a participatory process aimed at enhanced CSR would require mechanisms to ensure adherence to the Kantian principle of respect for persons. This is where much that has been written on the subject is suspect, because it reveals an ambiguous conflation of genuine concern for social responsibility on the one hand, and deference to the dominant productivity and efficiency paradigm on the other. For example, while Clutterbuck et al. recognise that employees wish to be associated with ethical companies, 'demanding a greater say in policy making', these authors then add that management seeks 'greater employee involvement' so as to harness their 'commitment and creativity' (1992: 17).

(i) The danger of manipulation

From the Kantian standpoint (and from the perspectives of both democratic theory and human development) one might accept employee commitment as a beneficial spin-off, but not as a *deciding factor* in whether or not to invite participation. The possibility that conflict rather than commitment might emerge in participative arenas must be recognised, and it is important to avoid the hierarchical control and manipulation which is often associated with direct participation in teams and other workplace initiatives. Such manipulation is more likely if employee commitment to predetermined values and policies is a primary managerial concern. Davis and Donaldson, in a recent book on management as a cooperative activity, stress 'individual autonomy' as a principle, meaning that people in organisations should have 'equality of access to the information on which proposals or actions are based' (1998: xix) and that in so far as this condition is met, people share in the responsibility for organisational actions. But Davis and Donaldson also note that 'the freedom to be oneself' is critical (1998: 95).

In the context of CSR, what we are concerned with is the accommodation of various stakeholders' interests in a process of organisational governance. This calls for an approach to *the identification of issues* and to *the resolution of moral dilemmas* which emerge as a result. Wheeler and Sillanpaa spell out a way of creating 'inclusive relationships with stakeholders' through their participation in focus groups. In these, people would not feel inhibited or have their views distorted unreasonably. So, for example, 'focus groups of employees should not include their supervisors or managers' (Wheeler and Sillanpaa 1997: 171).

(ii) Conflict, dialogue and responsible action

Through such means one can identify issues, establishing what concerns different stakeholders have. But where Wheeler and Sillanpaa are rather less specific, and many other writers on CSR are unconvincing, is when stakeholders' varying demands and moral claims are in conflict. To resolve such dilemmas a 'dialogic mode' is needed in the process leading to CSR, so that such concerns may be articulated and addressed (Maclagan 1998: 45–50; Wheeler and Sillanpaa 1997: 213). This takes us beyond engagement with the interests of single stakeholder groups. Now we are discussing 'governmental' processes in organisations, and in keeping with the spirit of this paper it is maintained that such processes would involve employees at least, even if not other interested parties. On this, Wheeler and Sillanpaa assert that ethical outcomes are arrived at through 'genuine involvement of the entire workforce in discussing and agreeing what represents best practice and then education programs to help make the shared values stick' (1997: 214). The role of 'education' in this context merits further comment. Dialogue in such situations will call for 'moral assertiveness' if individuals are to realise their potential for autonomous ethical judgment (Snell 1993: 9). So programmes of training and development in appropriate personal and interpersonal skills are required for all, not just for managers as has tended to be assumed in the past.

There are numerous methodologies which could be of value in all of this (e.g. Schein 1988, Nielsen 1990, Flood and Romm 1996). But one approach which seems to provide a useful connection for present purposes is Open Systems Planning (OSP) (Jayaram 1976). In essence, OSP is conducted by a 'planning group' – a 'community of trust' – which seeks to understand the internal workings and external context of the focal organisation and the relationships between these. This group aims to identify and clarify the *expectations* held of the organisation by its own members and by parties in its environment. The group then assesses 'idealistic' and 'realistic' future scenarios and the variance between these, identifying and discussing points of agreement and disagreement, including value-conflicts.

The expectations revealed through OSP can be equated with the concerns of all the various stakeholders, and can indicate *prima facie* moral obligations for the organisation which are 'apprehended' (Ross 1930) by members of the planning group, or whoever is involved in the process. These *prima facie* obligations must be weighed up against each other in particular cases, taking account of what Dancy (1993) calls the 'ethical shape' of the situation, so that even those which are less pressing may still be recognised in the overall policy or course of action decided upon (Maclagan 1998, ch. 4). Thus broad CSR policy is interpreted in specific contexts, in a participative process.

Conclusion

Taxonomies of CSR issues, and of the associated social or environmental impact of corporate activity, must of necessity be fairly general. It is of more practical value to focus on social processes, including the methods by which issues are identified and ethical dilemmas resolved in concrete situations. In any case, to talk of corporate responsibility without due attention to processes which involve actual people whose beliefs and values are expressed in corporate action, both entails a logical category mistake and fails to do justice to the moral and work-related potential of employees.

In keeping with an ethos of ethical responsibility, this process of CSR should involve employees and others. Such participation should be non-manipulative and should encourage open communication between those involved. In this paper there has only been a very limited discussion of the variety of forms which such participation might take, and questions relating to, for example, the difference between direct and indirect participation and the practical and ethical implications of this distinction, would require more extensive and detailed examination.

References

Argyris, C. (1964) *Integrating the Individual and the Organization*, New York: John Wiley.

Bowie, N. (1990) 'Empowering People as an End for Business', in G. Enderle, B. Almond and A. Argandona (eds) *People in Corporations: Ethical Responsibilities and Corporate Effectiveness*: 105–112, Dordrecht: Kluwer.

Clutterbuck, D., Dearlove, D. and Snow, D. (1992) *Actions Speak Louder: A Management Guide to Corporate Social Responsibility*, London: Kogan Page.

Coates, K. (ed.) (1978) *The Right to 'Useful' Work*, Nottingham: Institute for Workers' Control/Spokesman Books.

Coch, L. and French, Jr. P. (1948) 'Overcoming Resistance to Change', *Human Relations*, 1(4): 512–532.

Dachler, H. and Wilpert, B. (1978) 'Conceptual Dimensions and Boundaries of Participation in Organisations: A Critical Evaluation', *Administrative Science Quarterly* 23: 1–39.

Dancy, J. (1993) *Moral Reasons*, Oxford: Blackwell.

Davis, P. and Donaldson, J. (1998) *Co-operative Management: A Philosophy for Business*, Cheltenham: New Harmony Press.

Downie, R. (1971) *Roles and Values: An Introduction to Social Ethics*, London: Methuen.

Flood, R. and Romm, N. (eds) (1996) *Critical Systems Thinking: Current Research and Practice*, London: Plenum.

Goodpaster, K. and Matthews, J. (1982) 'Can a Corporation Have a Conscience?', *Harvard Business Review* 60: Jan/Feb: 132–141.

Hart, D. (1988) 'Management and Benevolence: The Fatal Flaw in Theory Y', in K. Kolenda (ed.) *Organizations and Ethical Individualism*: 73–105, New York: Praeger.

Iles, P., Mabey, C. and Robertson, I. (1990) 'HRM Practices and Employee Commitment: Possibilities, Pitfalls and Paradoxes', *British Journal of Management*, 1(3): 147–157.

Jayaram, G. (1976) 'Open Systems Planning', in W. Bennis, K. Benne, R. Chin, and K. Corey (eds) *The Planning of Change*, 3rd edn: 275–283, New York: Holt, Rinehart & Winston.

Jones, T. (1980) 'Corporate Social Responsibility Revisited, Redefined', *California Management Review*, 22(2): 59–67.

Klein, L. (1963) 'The Meaning of Work', *Fabian Tract 349*, London: Fabian International Bureau.

McGregor, D. (1960) *The Human Side of Enterprise*, New York: McGraw-Hill.

Maclagan, P. (1983) 'The Concept of Responsibility: Some Implications for Organisational Behaviour and Development', *Journal of Management Studies*, 20(4): 411–423.

Maclagan, P. (1998) *Management and Morality: A Developmental Perspective*, London: Sage.

Matthew, D. (1998) 'Re-visioning Business Leadership', Keynote address, EBEN-UK Conference, University of Salford, 15 April.

Nielsen, R. (1990) 'Dialogic Leadership as Ethics (Praxis) Method', *Journal of Business Ethics*, 9(10): 765–783.

Nord, W., Brief, A., Atieh, J. and Doherty, E. (1990) 'Work Values and the Conduct of Organizational Behavior', in B. Staw and L. Cummings (eds) *Work in Organizations*: 255–296, Greenwich, Conn.: JAI Press.

Pateman, C. (1970) *Participation and Democratic Theory*, Cambridge: Cambridge University Press.

Perrow, C. (1979) *Complex Organizations: A Critical Essay*, 2nd edn, Glenview, Ill.: Scott, Foresman.

Reichers, A. (1986) 'Conflict and Organizational Commitments', *Journal of Applied Psychology*, 71(3): 508–514.

Ross, W. (1930) *The Right and the Good*, Oxford: Clarendon Press.

Sampson, A. (1995) *Company Man: The Rise and Fall of Corporate Life*, London: HarperCollins.

Schein, E. (1988) *Process Consultation: Its Role in Organization Development*, Vol 1, 2nd edn, Reading, Mass.: Addison-Wesley.

Selznick, P. (1992) *The Moral Commonwealth: Social Theory and the Promise of Community*, Berkeley: University of California Press.

Snell, R. (1993) *Developing Skills for Ethical Management*, London: Chapman & Hall.

Steinbeck, J. (1951) *The Grapes of Wrath*, Harmondsworth: Penguin.

Velasquez, M. (1983) 'Why Corporations Are Not Morally Responsible for Anything They Do', *Business and Professional Ethics Journal*, 2(3): 1–17.

Warren, R. (1996) 'Business as a Community of Purpose', *Business Ethics: A European Review*, 5(2): 87–96.

Wheeler, D. and Sillanpaa, M. (1997) *The Stakeholder Corporation*, London: Pitman.

Chapter 7

CSR in the community

I N THIS CHAPTER WE WILL:

- Explain some of the core corporate responsibilities in the community.
- Show how community responsibilities vary according to different cultural and temporal contexts.
- Examine the meaning of key concepts such as corporate philanthropy, strategic philanthropy and corporate community involvement.
- Establish the significance of corporate community initiatives that are linked to a firm's core competencies.
- Examine how social and economic objectives can potentially be aligned through community investments in the firm's competitive context.

Introduction

Some years ago, it would have been quite common for many people to equate CSR with community responsibilities such as donations to good causes and involvement in local development initiatives. While we would argue that this is too narrow a perspective to capture the full possibilities of the CSR concept, there are good reasons for such a view. To begin with, philanthropic donations to local community initiatives were among the first corporate activities to go under the banner of CSR, especially in the USA where the term was first coined (Carroll, 1999). Second, even today, community initiatives are typically the first manifestation of CSR to become evident in countries and cultures relatively new to CSR. For example, Chapple and Moon (2005) show that firms in Asian countries including India, Thailand, Singapore, Malaysia and the Philippines report far more on their community initiatives than they do on marketplace and workplace CSR issues. Finally, community programmes are probably the most obvious manifestation of the voluntary and discretionary elements that are often seen to be central to CSR. While treating your employees or customers well can very readily be seen as simply good business (or even a matter of legal compliance), donating money to charity or helping out in the local community is more often regarded as a matter of corporate largesse. It is, then, perhaps no surprise that it was exactly this kind of CSR that Milton Friedman so vehemently attacked in the reading in Chapter 2 and, indeed, why Archie Carroll may have elevated such good deeds to the top of his CSR pyramid as a desirable form of 'good citizenship' where firms put something back into the local communities of which they are a part.

Community responsibilities may come in many shapes and forms. The most obvious and well known would be philanthropic donations from the firm to deserving causes, including community groups, educational initiatives, sporting associations, youth groups, health programmes, the arts and so on. For example, the Japanese car maker Toyota claims that it 'works to actively promote corporate social contribution activities using its technology and expertise in response to societal needs in areas such as the arts and culture, and achieving a harmonious society' (www.toyota.co.jp). Such philanthropy may be in the form of financial donations as well as contributions in terms of free products and employee time. In the UK, the drugs company GlaxoSmithKline is the largest single donor according to the annual 'charity trends' corporate giving index, including its donations of cash and drugs to good causes.[1] In Africa, the mining company Anglo-American distributes some $10 million a year through its Chairman's Fund, more than half of which goes to education (Visser, 2006).

Such corporate giving is particularly prevalent in the USA (though in decline), while in much of Europe the traditional assumption is that such funds would be provided by public bodies out of tax revenues. In parts of Asia, such as India or Pakistan, corporate giving is arguably less widespread than personal giving from wealthy industrialist patrons, although companies such as the Indian conglomerate Tata have long invested a substantial proportion of their profits in community programmes. Africa has long been a recipient of foreign aid, creating an 'ingrained culture of philanthropy' which, coupled with unusually high socio-economic needs, means that giving is an 'expected norm' in business (Visser, 2006).

Philanthropy towards the communities in which corporations operate clearly remains a significant element of CSR in some contexts. However, the past few decades have also seen various important criticisms raised against straightforward corporate giving, either because it is viewed as too paternal, or merely a public relations device that raises cynicism because it adds little of value to the cause, or even because it provides little real benefit to the firm. These criticisms are elaborated on in more detail in the two readings collated in this chapter. What we have seen, then, is a shift towards more 'built-in' responsibilities rather than simple 'bolt-on' approaches that leave most of the firm largely unaffected (Grayson and Hodges, 2004). These new approaches to community responsibility typically go under the label of 'strategic philanthropy' or 'corporate community investment' (or involvement).

The Shift to Strategic Philanthropy

Since the 1980s corporate philanthropy has undergone a major makeover. What was once seen as a simple act of charity has now evolved into a strategic corporate process that, at least in principle, seeks to add value both to the cause and to the corporation. Such strategic philanthropy has seen a whole host of innovations in the area of community relations. These include:

- Linking employee volunteering to human resource strategies. Increasingly employees are extolled to go beyond simply donating their time and effort to local community projects, and are encouraged to select projects that will enhance their skills and competences in ways that are of benefit to their employer.
- Linking charitable giving to marketing and branding strategies through cause-related marketing and sponsorship. Donations are increasingly expected to provide tangible benefits to the firm in terms of increased sales, brand recognition, or brand identification among consumers.
- Establishing cross-sector partnerships with community groups to build reputation and legitimacy with the public, as well as specific competence in managing social issues. Working with NGOs is widely touted to be a 'win–win' strategy for businesses facing a trust deficit in the community and charities facing a skills or resource deficit.

This transformation of community responsibility into a more strategic approach suggests that firms can readily 'do well by doing good' – a philosophy that has many advocates (though not always such convincing evidence), as we saw in Chapter 5. None the less, it is clear that, in a broader sense, enlightened companies probably realize that they cannot succeed in communities that fail – or as the UK retailer Marks & Spencer puts it: 'we have long believed that healthy high streets need healthy back streets. We also believe that business has a vital role to play in creating those healthy back streets through innovative, sustained and appropriate investment of its skills, time and money.'[2] Many firms in just about every nation on the globe engage in some form of community initiatives that seek to do just that: whether it is HIV/AIDS prevention in South African townships, education programmes in Brazilian favelas, or provision of aid to hurricane victims in New Orleans, they seek to enhance the social fabric of the societies in which they do business.

Introducing the Readings

The two readings in this chapter both address the more strategic approach to community responsibility, dealing, first, with its drivers and design – i.e. why has it happened and what does it look like – and, second, with the links between philanthropic projects and improvements in the competitive context of business – i.e. how to create the 'healthy backstreets' in ways that provide a strategic advantage to the firm.

Drivers and design of corporate community involvement

The first article, by David Hess, Nikolai Rogovsky and Thomas Dunfee, looks at the evolution of corporate community involvement, from 'relatively passive, after-profit direct cash donations' to 'more complex forms with ever-broadening impact'. They examine the drivers for this shift over the past few decades, and then go on to describe the main features of community outreach programmes that specifically link with the long-term strategic priorities of the firm. In particular, they focus on initiatives that relate to the development of the firm's 'core competencies', i.e. areas of specialization within an organization that enable it to out-compete its rivals in strategically signif-icant ways (Hamel and Prahalad, 1990). In this sense, Hess *et al.* focus mainly on linking community programmes to a *resource-based* view of strategy, as in a view of strategy that is primarily concerned with identifying the types of internal resources a firm has (or can access) that enable it to create value and generate 'excess rents' (Barney, 1991, 2001). This is typically distinguished from a view of strategy that is more concerned with the *positioning* of the firm within the environment, most notably associated with the Harvard Business School strategy guru Michael Porter, who is one of the authors of the second reading.

Enhancing the competitive context through community involvement

The second article takes up a similar theme to the first in that it is concerned with how to make philanthropy more strategically purposeful for the firm while also ensur-ing that tangible benefits are provided for the community – in the authors' words, 'bringing social and economic goals into alignment'. Michael Porter and Mark Kramer, however, focus their attention on improvements in the *competitive context* in which firms operate rather than on the unique capabilities of the firm itself. This reflects a long-standing emphasis in Porter's work on industry structure and firm positioning within the competitive environment, as demonstrated, for example, by his widely cited works on the 'five forces' and 'generic strategies' (Porter, 1980, 1985).

For many people, the publishing of this paper in the *Harvard Business Review* (HBR) signalled the increasing attention to CSR among mainstream business acad-emics, especially coming as it did after Porter's earlier contribution to environmental strategies (Porter and van der Linde, 1995). Indeed, this was followed by the once unlikely spectacle of Porter appearing as a keynote speaker in CSR conferences and then another HBR publication on CSR by the two authors in 2006 (Porter and Kramer, 2006). Although many therefore saw this development as a further sign that CSR was now much more central to core strategy thinking, others also pointed to the way that Porter and other strategy theorists were as much squeezing CSR into their existing ideas as they were expanding our understanding of CSR. Certainly it is clear from the two readings collated here that community responsibilities are no longer seen as simply minor add-ons to the 'real' business of corporations, but it is also important to realize that this has mainly happened by finding ways of making community relationships pay off for the firm in ways that even Milton Friedman might applaud.

Study Questions

1 'Corporate responsibilities to the community are the least important of the firm's social responsibilities. Marketplace and workplace responsibilities are much more important because they relate to core stakeholders for the firm.' Critically evaluate this statement.

2 To what extent are corporate community initiatives likely to vary across national contexts? Support your answer with examples of community programmes from a multinational operating in several different continents.

3 What is the difference between philanthropy and strategic philanthropy? Provide examples of each from current business practice.

4 Why have firms sought to make their community programmes more strategic? What are the main advantages and disadvantages of such a development?

5 What is the difference between strategic community programmes based on enhancing core competences and those that focus on improving the competitive context? Are there any reasons for suggesting that one might be more preferable than the other?

Notes

1 Charities Aid Foundation (2006) *Charity Trends 2006,* London: Caritas Data.
2 http://www2.marksandspencer.com/thecompany/ourcommitmenttosociety/community/news/sieff_award_2006.shtml.

References

Barney, J. (1991) 'Firm Resources and Sustained Competitive Advantage', *Journal of Management* 17(1): 99–120.

Barney, J. (2001) 'Is the Resource-based Theory a Useful Perspective for Strategic Management Research? Yes', *Academy of Management Review* 26(1): 41–56.

Carroll, A. (1999) 'Corporate Social Responsibility – Evolution of a Definitional Construct', *Business and Society* 38(3): 268–295.

Chapple, W. and Moon, J. (2005) 'Corporate Social Responsibility in Asia: A Seven Country Study of CSR Website Reporting', *Business and Society* 44(4): 415–441.

Grayson, D. and Hodges, A. (2004) *Corporate Social Opportunity: Seven Steps to Make Corporate Social Responsibility Work for Your Business,* Sheffield: Greenleaf.

Hamel, G. and Prahalad, C. (1990) 'The Core Competence of the Corporation', *Harvard Business Review* 68 (May–June): 79–93.

Porter, M. (1980) *Competitive Strategy: Techniques for Analysing Industries and Competitors,* New York: Free Press.

Porter, M. (1985) *Competitive Advantage: Creating and Sustaining Superior Performance,* New York: Free Press.

Porter, M. and Kramer, M. (2006) 'Strategy and Society: The Link Between Competitive Advantage and Corporate Social Responsibility', *Harvard Business Review*, December.

Porter, M. and van der Linde, C. (1995) 'Green and Competitive', *Harvard Business Review* (September–October): 120–134.

Visser, W. (2006) 'Revisiting Carroll's CSR Pyramid: An African Perspective', in E. R. Pedersen and M. Huniche (eds) *Corporate Citizenship in Developing Countries: New Partnership Perspectives*, Copenhagen: Copenhagen Business School Press.

THE NEXT WAVE OF CORPORATE COMMUNITY INVOLVEMENT: CORPORATE SOCIAL INITIATIVES

David Hess, Nikolai Rogovsky and Thomas Dunfee

Within hours of the terrorist attack on New York and Washington, major corporations were donating money and services to help the victims. The services were directly connected to immediate needs: metal cutters and spreaders to aid the search for survivors, work boots, coffee, energy bars, and even aspirin. The sums donated were substantial – General Electric, Microsoft, Pfizer, and Daimler Chrysler each pledged $10 million while AOL Time Warner, Cisco, duPont, and Merck pledged at least $5 million.[1]

While the social initiatives, significant though they were, seemed appropriate and natural, they should not be viewed in isolation. Instead, they are part of a broader movement toward more community involvement, a phenomenon explored in this article.

Increasingly, many leading U.S. and global firms are devoting significant time and resources in support of community involvement projects. These projects encompass a variety of forms and points of focus, ranging from corporate support for training and educating adults and youth in local communities, to nationwide programs helping welfare recipients get jobs, to globally focused efforts providing aid to developing countries.

Many of these new corporate social initiatives are taking on aspects more commonly associated with corporate strategy than community relations; they are grounded in the core competencies of the firm and related to the firm's long-term strategy. Moreover, many firms are becoming key providers of aid to civil society. For example, United Parcel Service (UPS) has used its existing resources to become an important actor in the delivery of humanitarian aid on an as-needed basis. In 1999, this aid included assisting the Red Cross in providing food to Kosovo refugee camps in Albania and Macedonia. UPS collected food donated throughout France, stored and packaged the goods at a UPS distribution center, and then airlifted them (estimated at 500 tons of food parcels) to the areas in need.[2] UPS consistently steps forward to assist in a variety of similar situations, such as delivering thousands of pounds of food and water to the hurricane-stricken Dominican Republic or bringing supplies to victims of tornadoes in Kentucky.

Other examples include the transfer of knowledge and direct support for education. Intel employees provide science education to elementary and high school students in the Philippines and other developing countries. Combined with Intel-donated computers, the provision of tutors enables these children to understand and appreciate technology. These experiences allow the students to attain jobs and higher education that would not otherwise be possible.[3] Similarly, IBM's Reinventing Education and Wired for Learning programs use company technology and the time of its researchers to help public schools develop solutions to problems ranging from assessing student progress consistently to improving communication among teachers, students, and parents.[4]

The innovative programs of Intel and IBM have clear antecedents. Over the past half century, corporate community outreach has evolved into more complex forms with ever-broadening impact. Initially, the most common form of corporate philanthropy was relatively passive, after-profit direct cash donations. Over time philanthropy became more directly related to firm strategy and marketing. In the 1980s, corporations developed and refined the notion of "strategic philanthropy." Based on the idea that "competing on price and corporate citizenship is smarter than competing on price alone," firms developed giving plans that were linked to the firm's overall strategy.[5] For example, book and newspaper publishers began promoting causes to increase literacy. To improve its image as an innovator and to attract upscale customers, AT&T developed a giving program in support of creative new artists.[6] With American Express's plan to support the restoration of the Statue of Liberty (donating one cent to the cause every time someone used their credit card), "cause-related marketing" was born and is used today by many countries to associate their image with popular social endeavors.[7]

Today, corporate philanthropy has evolved into a new form with the business-like description of "corporate community involvement." A recent Ford Foundation Report describes corporate investment in community development as a new paradigm likely to "result in a healthier economy and positive business outcomes."[8] Rosabeth Moss Kanter has identified numerous companies in the vanguard of this new paradigm. Such firms "view community needs as opportunities to develop ideas and demonstrate business technologies, to find and serve new markets, and to solve long-standing business problems."[9] Structured volunteer programs for corporate employees are a widespread example of this new phenomenon demonstrating the mutually beneficial nature of such programs. While the community benefits from the donation of the employee's time and talent, the company benefits from more loyal employees, aid in recruiting, and the teaching of teamwork skills to employees.[10]

This article focuses on corporate community involvement that entails a significant use of firm resources related to the organization's core competencies. We term these programs "corporate social initiatives" (CSI). Several characteristics of existing corporate social initiatives are starting to emerge that, in combination, distinguish them from their predecessors. First, CSI programs are connected to the core values of the firm. By their nature, they also reflect corporate recognition of specific community problems or needs as expressed by relevant stakeholder groups. McDonald's has expressed a commitment to developing entry-level employees, which reflects the needs of communities in which it operates. The training and support programs McDonald's uses have resulted in over half of their executives and a third of their franchisees being alumni of entry-level jobs in their fast food outlets.[11] Insurance provider State Farm has an alliance with a nonprofit organization in Chicago that sponsors inspections of homes in low-income neighborhoods for potential safety hazards and provides funding for necessary repairs.[12] Second, CSI programs are linked with the core competencies of the firm. In the UPS example, the company is utilizing its physical resources (e.g., airplanes, delivery trucks, warehouses), human capital (e.g., experienced and knowledgeable managers, drivers), and organizational capital (e.g., the ability to track packages and efficiently route them to their destination) to collect and deliver necessary supplies to those in need.[13] Programs such as these are actively initiated and guided by top management who incorporate them into strategic planning.[14] This distinguishes them from programs delegated to community relations personnel not necessarily knowledgeable about the core businesses of the corporation.

Third, CSI programs are systematically evaluated, assessed, and communicated to stakeholders. Firms such as Shell provide information on their social activities in reports that are audited by major accounting firms, in Shell's case jointly by KPMG and PricewaterhouseCoopers. In its report for calendar year 2000, Shell described its involvement in such projects as helping Mexican villages use renewable energy to reduce dependence on firewood as well as for running road safety education programs in Asia that are designed to help children and the general public avoid road accidents.[15]

Drivers of the New Forms of Corporate Social Initiatives

What can explain the shift in corporate philanthropic activities and the emergence of this new phenomenon of corporate social involvement?[16] We identify three broadly-defined categories of drivers behind CSI programs:

- The Competitive Advantage Factor
- The New Moral Marketplace Factor
- The Comparative Advantage Factor

The competitive advantage factor

Trade liberalization and the rapid growth of Internet technology have made traditional sources of competitive advantage (such as financial capital, technology, and location) more accessible and, therefore, less significant as a source of competitive advantage. In response, senior management is searching for new, hard-to-imitate, less-tangible sources of competitive advantage. These "soft sources" may include the benefits achieved through the successful implementation of corporate social initiatives. Better corporate image and reputation are arguably the most important of these benefits.

Building reputation assets

Corporate social initiatives provide a greater benefit to corporate reputation assets than traditional corporate philanthropy. While widespread, the appropriateness of corporations' philanthropic contributions remains controversial.[17] Contributions clearly provide benefits to the recipient, but shareholders and others often worry that such grants are tainted by conflicts of interest (e.g., large grants of corporate money to pet charities of the chief executive officer) or are simply motivated by tax considerations. These concerns have led to legislative bills and shareholder proposals to expand the disclosure of corporate giving practices or even the complete cession of the practice.[18] The donation of corporate time and talent, on the other hand, is less subject to these concerns. Stakeholders are less likely to view such contributions as self-serving.[19] In addition, the argument by shareholders that they can give their money to a charity if they choose (and not have the firm make a donation for them) may not apply. Social programs based on a firm's core competencies means that it may be one of only a few firms (or perhaps the only firm) capable of providing such aid. This mitigates conflicts of interest problems.

Long-lasting community involvement programs are more likely to improve the image of the corporation than after-profit cash contributions. This is a reflection of the basic sentiment that people need help solving their problems, not just money.[20] In a survey of 1000 Americans asking which philanthropic activity is "most impressive," 43 percent of respondents said "donating products and services," 37 percent said "volunteering employees to help," and only 12 percent said "giving a large sum of money."[21] Activities that demonstrate a real commitment to the community affect the perceptions of not only a firm's customers, but also stakeholders as employees, suppliers, the community, and opinion leaders.[22] A strong reputation with these stakeholders is necessary for the long-term success of the firm.

In times of crisis, reputation assets that have been carefully built up over time may pay large dividends. A dramatic example of this is the case of McDonald's during the 1992 South Central Los Angeles riots. The company's efforts in developing community relations through its Ronald McDonald's houses and its involvement in developing employee opportunities gave the company such a strong reputation, McDonald's executives stated, that rioters refused to harm their outlets. While vandalism caused tremendous damages to businesses in the area, all sixty of McDonald's franchises were spared harm.[23]

International expansion

Reputation is also an important source of competitive advantage when a firm chooses to operate in a foreign environment. As firms enter new, unfamiliar markets, community involvement programs in those countries can help the expansion succeed. These programs can develop reputation assets in the new market, strengthen marketing and branding initiatives, improve relations with local governments, and assist in the understanding of local cultural norms of appropriate behavior.[24] For example, AT&T has established a presence in several Latin American countries by using its communications technology to assist in linking rural hospitals to national medical centers. Such involvement is extremely valuable for establishing relationships with important customers and business partners in the new markets, as well as developing a favorable reputation.[25] Immediately after the end of World War II, Merck brought antibiotics to Japan to treat tuberculosis. This initial act developed a tremendous amount of goodwill for Merck and helps explain their subsequent success in the Japanese market.[26]

In some cases, community involvement is not an option but a requirement to operate effectively in the international market. In the petroleum industry, oil and gas companies with operations in Asia, Latin America, and Africa are facing demands from the local community to provide education and health care.[27] These communities want a share of the benefits that the firm receives from operating there. By establishing such programs early on and working with the demands of the community, firms find less resistance to their operations not only from the local community, but from environmental and human rights special interest groups as well. Importantly, these programs are not "give-aways" but rather involve training and working with community members to allow them to plan for meeting their own needs in the future.[28]

The new moral marketplace factor

A firm's performance depends on its capacity to anticipate and adjust not only to competition and rapid technological transformation, but also to changes in the attitudes of consumers, employees, governments, investors, and other stakeholders. Moral desires expressed by stakeholders are embodied in capital, consumer, and labor markets. Marketplace participants make trade-offs between their moral desires and desires for lower-priced goods, better investment returns, and so on. The aggregate product of participants' moral desires in their choices as consumers, investors, and employees represents "morality in markets" and has the potential to affect the outcome of the commercial marketplace.[29] Examples of marketplace morality include investors choosing socially screened investment funds, consumers boycotting Shell Oil because of its decision to sink the Brent Spar oil rig, and employees' desires to work for socially responsible firms.

Based on a social contracts analysis, Thomas Dunfee has argued that the existence of morality within markets creates certain obligations for corporate management.[30] While managers have a basic duty to undertake actions to maximize shareholder value, they also have an obligation to respond to and anticipate existing and changing marketplace morality relevant to the firm. A failure to do so may have a significant negative impact on shareholder wealth. Furthermore, a clear signal from the relevant stakeholder groups will justify corporate involvement even if a direct link to shareholder wealth cannot be shown.[31]

There appears to be significant public support and high expectations for CSI programs. The recent "Millennium Poll" of over 25,000 persons in 23 countries conducted by Environics International Ltd. showed that in almost all countries, and strongly in the United States and Great Britain, the public believes corporations should go beyond simply making a profit and creating jobs and should "help build a better society for us all."[32] Moral pressures in the market place may be enhanced through credible reporting of social activities by firms and may be directly influenced by peer pressure.

Social reporting

The influence of morality in markets is enhanced through disclosure and dissemination of information. Increasingly, pressure is building on firms to provide information on the social impact of all of their activities – regardless of whether or not the firm is undertaking significant community involvement programs. This pressure results from the recent revival of the social reporting movement.

In both the United States and Europe, corporate social auditing, accounting, and reporting (SAAR) is gaining increasing attention. SAAR is a means of measuring a firm's social performance, communicating its performance to stakeholders, and taking into account feedback from stakeholders. Two major attempts to improve the quality and quantity of social reports are the Global Reporting Initiative (GRI)[33] and the Institute of Social and Ethical AccountAbility (ISEA).[34] The GRI is a major collaborative effort of large accounting firms, non-governmental organizations, corporations, and universities, which seeks to establish a common framework for corporate social reporting worldwide. The ISEA, through initiatives such as AccountAbility 1000, is not only developing reporting standards, but also auditing standards and an accreditation path for accountants and auditors in SAAR.[35]

As more firms comply with social reporting standards, stakeholders will gain a better understanding of the community involvement programs undertaken by firms and their competitors. By including within such reports audited accounts of a firm's community involvement programs, stating the costs and benefits (as best as they can be measured), the firm can make considerable strides toward establishing a credible reputation and furthering its competitive advantage.

Peer pressure

In 1999, Pfizer and SmithKline Beecham donated drugs to alleviate medical conditions existing primarily in the developing world. Pfizer donated $60 million worth of an oral antibiotic to help eliminate trachoma, the world's leading cause of preventable blindness. In an effort to help eliminate the disease lymphatic filariasis, more commonly known as elephantiasis, SmithKline Beecham donated the drug albendazole. While these programs provided a significant boost to Pfizer's and SmithKline Beecham's reputations, they also may be viewed as a competitive response to each other.

In developing reputation assets through CSI programs, as with most aspects of business, a firm must keep pace with the actions of its peers. In a highly publicized action, Merck developed Mectizan, a drug responsive to a disease known as "river blindness" that was widespread in certain impoverished regions of Africa. Because those afflicted by the disease were unable to pay for the drug, Merck decided to donate the drug and even assisted in its distribution. These decisions established a benchmark for Merck's competitors. The leadership of Merck placed pressure on Pfizer and SmithKline Beecham to act likewise when faced with a similar situation. We expect peer pressure to become an important driving force for social initiatives in many industries and geographic locations.

The comparative advantage of private firms

A final factor putting pressure on firms to enact corporate social initiatives is the potential comparative advantage of business over governments or nonprofits to provide assistance in solving certain social problems. This advantage is most readily seen in the developing world,[36] but it also exists in developed nations. Comparing the public sector (including NGOs and nonprofit corporations) and the private sector under a resource-based perspective provides the explanation of this comparative advantage. Through intense marketplace competition, firms have developed unique competencies that provide them not only a competitive advantage over other firms in the marketplace, but also a comparative advantage over governments in being able to respond to certain problems.[37] In general, businesses are adept problem solvers with knowledge bases and stocks of resources that may far exceed those of governments or non-profits in addressing a particular problem. The UPS example is instructive. UPS has the warehouses, transportation vehicles, and other capital assets necessary for a relief operation. Further, they have experience in dealing with corrupt environments. British Petroleum had cost and technical advantages over local governments when they provided solar-powered refrigerators to store anti-malaria vaccines in Zambia. Firms can play critical complementary roles to government and NGOs when they exercise a core competency in responding to a social need.[38]

Precautionary Factors

Management implementation of CSIs should always be sensitive to potential criticisms. Some shareholders may object on the grounds that the programs are a cost that they do not wish to bear out of potential dividends and earnings. Others, however, will recognize the value CSI programs provide the company when properly aligned with corporate strategy. In addition, as social investment funds develop more sophisticated, positive screens – that is, screening companies based on a demonstrated record of social responsibility – shareholders will recognize the value in getting the company's stock included in those funds.

Some stakeholders may object to the choice of the social cause and even object that it is inappropriate, or even illegitimate, for corporations to engage in such actions. Although a few vocal critics may object on these grounds, there appears to be wide acceptance of corporate actions in this area. It is hard to imagine today serious calls that McDonald's abandon the Ronald McDonald houses, or that (then) Bell Atlantic acted inappropriately in their Project Explorer which supported a technical school for inner city youth in Union City, New Jersey.[39] In response to those who take the position that it is illegitimate for business to engage in these types of endeavors, Jeanne Logsdon and Donna Wood counter that the legitimacy of business will be questioned if it fails to act as a global citizen. They argue that "corporate social responsibility and citizenship of both types – individual and business – exist to guard against the undesirable consequences of power imbalances in social structures." They extend their analysis to argue that "business citizenship is a necessity for the survival and health of the business institution" noting that it "represents a pathway to the public good."[40]

The implementation of CSIs may require difficult judgments. For example, it may be very difficult to judge accurately consumer desires and their likely impact in the marketplace. Firms expecting immediate market returns from CSIs should be careful in their assessment of consumer preferences and in their assumptions about market impact. Star-Kist conducted internal market surveys that indicated that about one-half of their customer base would pay more for dolphin-safe tuna. The other half were presumably indifferent to the fate of dolphins and wanted the cheapest tuna they could buy. Even so, partly in response to consumer boycotts, they adopted a costly policy of dolphin-safe tuna that was immediately matched by Van Camp and Bumble Bee. In the long term, they did not gain any market share.[41]

Designing Corporate Social Initiatives

As relatively new phenomena, CSIs are going through an experimental phase in which the learning curve is steep. As firms gain more experience, they will identify and employ more efficient strategies. It is probable that strategies will often be unique to particular firms. In the interim, there are certain core factors likely to be critical to success.

Connection to the firm's core values

The success of a corporate social initiative may be critically dependent on whether the program is based on the corporation's values, which in turn reflect the values and beliefs of the firm's managers and other employees. Mission statements and credos form the basis of the firm's core values and culture. These statements guide firm management in times of crisis. For example, in the early 1980s, when several people died from taking Tylenol that had been tampered with, Johnson & Johnson was faced with the difficult decision of whether or not to recall bottles of Tylenol across the nation – a very expensive proposition. Johnson & Johnson's Credo contained a clear statement of responsibility to those who used their products, which made it clear to CEO James Burke that he should recall Tylenol. Such statements form an organization's culture and make difficult ethical decisions easier and more consistent at all levels of the firm. Likewise, established values guide firms in using their resources effectively in a Corporate Social Initiative. Furthermore, active involvement in such programs may help companies bridge the "rhetoric–reality gap" that often occurs when a company's mission statement is disconnected from the day-to-day activities of the firm.[42] Linking such initiatives with firm values also demonstrates long-term commitment to the initiative, which improves credibility with firm stakeholders.

AT&T's contributions to Planned Parenthood represent an example of a firm encountering difficulty because its actions were not clearly connected to the firm's core values. AT&T was a long-time donor to Planned Parenthood until 1990 when groups opposed to Planned Parenthood's position on abortion placed pressure on the company to stop its support. Presumably, AT&T yielded to pressure in part because they did not have a clearly articulated position concerning why they were supporting Planned Parenthood. AT&T's concession to pro-life pressure led to counter pressure from pro-choice groups. By appearing to be responding to whatever pressure was exerted, AT&T was criticized for making everyone angry.[43]

A CSI program should have top management actively involved in its formulation, implementation, and evaluation. Although the operational management of CSI programs can still be carried out by the community relations unit of the firm, top management should make strategic decisions related to such programs. The support of the CEO and top management is imperative. It shows commitment and expresses the firm's values to both the members of the organization and to its stakeholders.

Response to moral pressures

Increasingly, managers must be in tune with marketplace expectations of social responsibility or risk losing value-increasing opportunities at a minimum, and severe damage to their reputation at the worst. Certain demands may be expected of most firms, such as employee volunteer programs, but others may be more specific to the industry, community, or even individual firms. Appropriately reading market demands is the challenge for management. In 1999, Monsanto initiated a program to teach Thai farmers new technologies, such as the use of herbicides, conservation tillage, and "improved quality" seeds.[44] To many, this social initiative appeared to match the competencies of Monsanto with the demands of Thai farmers for better rice farming techniques. However, local Thai interest groups who questioned Monsanto's motives quickly challenged this initiative. Challengers feared that Monsanto was developing the program only to get Thai farmers to become dependent on Monsanto products and to improve a reputation that was damaged by the ongoing genetically modified seeds controversy. Thus, Monsanto's failure to accurately read the market led to a social initiative that may have actually harmed the firm's reputation.

In England, animal rights groups sent drug testing company Huntingdon Life Sciences into a financial crisis by not only directly pressuring the company, but also by exerting secondary pressures on Huntingdon's lenders, securities firms, and those who made a market in Huntingdon's stock.[45] While clearly not the only company conducting animal testing, Huntingdon has been singled out by animal rights activists. Had Huntingdon perceived the significance of moral pressures concerning testing products on animals and in response sought to develop better community relations and communicated more effectively concerning their work and values, they may have found more allies when confronted by a group whose stated mission was to shut them down. In contrast, McDonald's – a common target by activists of all shapes, including animal rights interest groups – has been able to weather such controversies. Again relying on a "reservoir of goodwill"[46] developed from its significant community practices, McDonald's was able to withstand an attack on the treatment of animals used in its food products while it formulated its position on the matter, apparently taking into account moral pressures in the process, and McDonald's eventually emerged as an industry leader on animal welfare.[47]

Through corporate social initiatives, firms can take a proactive role in shaping their reputations and demonstrate commitment to their espoused values. To do so requires that the firm look to the expectations of the consumer, labor, and capital markets, and most importantly, of the entire local community. Being responsive to these expectations is key to the success of any corporate social initiative. Obvious budgetary constraints dictate the necessity to invest only in programs that are most beneficial to the community and the firm. When making a choice among various types of community programs, it is advisable that the firm gets direct input from community leaders and other stakeholders. Such an approach would take into account both community concerns and the firm's business objectives and values. At Home Depot, for example, the community affairs department spends half of its operating budget developing its community involvement strategy, which includes identifying important community organizations and non-profits in the new markets it enters and conducting research with national groups such as the United Way.[48] This significant investment of resources allows the company to find the best opportunities to meet local community needs and recognize emerging trends while also maintaining a unified theme to its CSI programs.

Connection to the core competencies of the firm

One of the most important features of corporate social initiatives is reflected in the link between these programs and the core competencies and key resources of the firm. Management's strategic objective should be to link firm capabilities with the opportunities presented in the external environment.[49] For CSIs, management should scan the external environment to determine where its resources can provide the greatest benefit to the community. As stated above, in its analysis of the environment, the firm should also consider the opinion of community and other stakeholders on what kind of programs are of the most value for the potential program recipients.

The programs firms have implemented based on their competencies are extremely diverse and broad in scope. For example, Home Depot – a home improvement retailer – has structured volunteer programs that capitalize on their employees' knowledge of construction skills and firm resources to focus on affordable living and at-risk youth initiatives.[50] Over one-third of Home Depot's employees are involved in a program called YouthBuild which teaches construction skills to youth who have dropped out of school.

In the process, this program rehabilitates houses for low-income families and builds playgrounds across the U.S.

The donations of drugs by companies such as Merck, Pfizer, and SmithKline Beecham to alleviate medical conditions that exist primarily in the developing world are key examples of firms using their resources to work for the community. Due to their drug patent ownerships, these were the only firms capable of providing this type of assistance. While these companies were not developing the drugs specifically with the diseases of the developing world in mind, after the potential benefits of these drugs became known, they acted responsibly in assisting in the distribution to the communities in need.

A dramatic example involves Coca-Cola's recent commitment to the global fight against AIDS. Coca-Cola, the largest employer in Africa, plans to use its core competencies in advertising and distribution to assist with awareness and medical campaigns against the plague of AIDS. In Nigeria, Coca-Cola plans to use its trucks to deliver AIDS testing kits to hospitals. In Kenya, Coca-Cola will make 30 billboards available for an awareness campaign their marketing specialists helped to develop. It is even speculated that Coca-Cola trucks will deliver condoms to areas where they are needed.[51]

Marriott International combines its social program aimed at developing skills of less-fortunate community members with its innovative human resources practices.[52] This internationally recognized hotel chain introduced Pathways to Independence, a training and orientation program aimed at welfare recipients. This labor market group is of critical importance for hotel chains, where a significant number of employment needs require very basic skills and do not pay well. Turnover is one of the major problems in this business. Marriott introduced a very sensitive program that hones the job skills, life skills, and work habits of welfare recipients, and the company guarantees participants a job offer when they complete the program. In addition to creating new jobs in the community, this program has brought tangible benefits to the company: after one year, approximately 70 per cent of the program's graduates continued to be employed by Marriott, while only 45 per cent of similar hires not in the program were still with the firm.[53] Moreover, this program helped Marriott to better understand the values and needs of its employees and make its human resources management policies and practices more efficient.

Bell Atlantic has combined their research and development with their social initiative Project Explorer. To try out new technological know-how, Bell Atlantic provided inner city schools with equipment and software for free in return for a testing site. This project helped Bell Atlantic to create one of the first-ever models for using computer networks in schools.[54] This case shows that corporate social and business needs can coincide. It was clearly a mainstream business project that was funded out of operating and technology-development budgets. As an outcome of this project, Bell Atlantic created a valuable revenue stream selling network services to educational organizations.

Companies such as Alcoa, a leading aluminum manufacturer, are transferring their workplace knowledge to the community. In furtherance of the company value to "work safely in a manner that promotes the health and well-being of the individual and the environment," Alcoa's A Way of Life program transfers its commitment to employee safety to the employee's homes and communities. Throughout the world, Alcoa assists communities in obtaining necessary emergency relief equipment and provides training on a variety of safety issues.[55]

Setting clear objectives and means of measurement

A significant lesson from the shift towards strategic philanthropy is the need to establish objectives for community involvement projects and standards for measuring their success. The revival of the social auditing, accounting, and reporting movement is also pushing firms to measure and disclose all aspects of their social performance. Social audits provide accountability to stakeholders, but more importantly assist firms in evaluating and understanding their own performance and the impact of their programs.

This is an area where firms must now place more emphasis. Corporate social initiatives cannot be successfully implemented without a full understanding of the costs and benefits of the program. Just as any effective corporate strategy requires clear goals, an effective use of key resources, and successful implementation, so must a corporate social initiative. In either situation, the basic goal is to create long-term value, which can only be achieved if management has a clear record of where its resources have been invested and what return the firm has achieved on those resources. To accomplish this, management will have to develop new definitions and indicators of successful social initiatives.

Currently, many corporations are attempting to measure the effectiveness of their contributions programs, but few are satisfied with the results.[56] This reflects the significant challenges in measuring the social impact of CSI programs. Organizations such as Walker Information, the Council on Foundations,[57] and the London Benchmarking Group[58] are working to develop indicators that will provide management with information on the benefits to business (such as strengthened relationships with stakeholders) as well as the benefits to community (such as jobs created and the overall positive economic impact). With this information, business can provide the most value to the community.

Conclusion

The practice of corporate philanthropy has evolved significantly over the past several decades to a point where it is becoming an important part of corporate strategy. Firms are increasingly devoting more resources to their social initiatives and making them a key factor in establishing a competitive advantage. At the same time, the communities in which corporations operate, both at home and abroad, are demanding a share of the benefits that a firm receives by operating in their community. As this "moral" market becomes more sophisticated, establishing successful corporate social initiatives becomes more imperative.

Notes

1   T. Brady and A. Wood, "Firms Donate Millions in Money and Services," *The Philadelphia Inquirer*, September 15, 2001, p. A18.

2   A. Freudmann, "Relief Logistics: Antidote to Strife," *Journal of Commerce*, April 16, 1999, p. 1A.

3   T. Dunfee and D. Hess, "The Legitimacy of Direct Corporate Humanitarian Investment," *Business Ethics Quarterly*, 10/1 (January 2000): 95–109.

4   IBM Homepage, <http://www.ibm.com/ibm/ibmgives/grant/education/programs/reinventing/>.

5   C. Smith, "The New Corporate Philanthropy," *Harvard Business Review*, 72/3 (May/June 1994): 105–116, at 110.

6   Smith, op. cit.

7   M. Drumwright, "Company Advertising with a Social Dimension: The Role of Noneconomic Buying Criteria," *Journal of Marketing*, 60/4 (October 1996): 71–87; P. Varadarajan and A. Menon, "Cause-Related Marketing: A Co-Alignment of Marketing Strategy and Corporate Philanthropy," *Journal of Marketing*, 52/3 (July 1988): 58–74.

8   "The Double Bottom Line: Competitive Advantage Through Community Investment," The Ford Foundation, New York, NY, 2001, p. 2.

9   R. Kanter, "From Spare Change to Real Change: The Social Sector as Beta Site for Business Innovation," *Harvard Business Review*, 77/3 (May/June 1999): 122–132.

10   C. Wild, "Corporate Volunteer Programs: Benefits to Business," Conference Board Report # 1029, 1993.

11   "The Double Bottom Line," op. cit. p. 12.

12   "The Double Bottom Line," op. cit. p. 7.

13   These are the three types of firm resources discussed in J. Barney, "Firm Resources and Sustained Competitive Advantage," *Journal of Management*, 17/1 (March 1991): 99–120. For a complete discussion on the resources firms use to establish a competitive advantage, see R. Grant, "Resource-Based Theory of Competitive Advantage: Implications for Strategy Formulation," *California Management Review*, 33/3 (Spring 1991): 114–135.

14   S. Waddock and M. Boyle, "The Dynamics of Change in Corporate Community Relations," *California Management Review*, 37/4 (Summer 1995): 125–140.

15   "People, Planet and Profits," Royal Dutch/Shell Group, 2001.

16   Other commentators have considered the expanding role of corporate community relations. Waddock and Boyle [op. cit.] identified several external and internal pressures that are transforming corporate community relations practices. Among the external factors they identify are the process of globalization and the development of more alliances between firms. These factors increase the number of communities in which corporations operate and for whom they are responsible for their actions. Likewise, Marsden and Mohan found that 39 percent of firms became involved in social programs for internal needs (such as employee motivation and recruitment, and marketing opportunities), 38 percent identified external social stimuli (such as

threat of legislation or concern about a social issue), and 23 percent were responding to both. C. Marsden and A. Mohan, "'I whistle all the way to work and all the way home': Research on 500 Business Best Practices," CSR Europe Research Paper, 1999, <http://www.csreurope.org/csr_europe/Activities/Communications/Publications/chrismarsden1.html>.

17   See H. Butler and F. McChesneney, "Why They Give at the Office: Shareholder Welfare and Corporate Philanthropy in the Contractual Theory of the Corporation," *Cornell Law Review*, 84 (1999): 1195–1226; F. Stevelman Kahn, "Pandora's Box: Managerial Discretion and the Problem of Corporate Philanthropy," *UCLA Law Review*, 44 (1997): 579; "Corporate Philanthropy Symposium," *Stetson Law Review*, 28 (1998).

18   In the late 1990s, Representative Paul Gillmor pushed for legislation requiring full disclosure of charitable giving and allowing greater shareholder participation in selecting donees. In 1997 and 1998, shareholders submitted proposals at American Express and Aluminium Co. of America (ALCO) to end charitable giving.

19   Wild, op. cit.

20   M. Alperson, "Giving Strategies that Add Business Value," Conference Board Report # 1126, 1995.

21   "Money Can't Buy Love, According to New Survey," *PR Newswire*, September 8 1998.

22   F. Simon, "Global Corporate Philanthropy: A Strategic Framework," *International Marketing Review*, 12/4 (1995): 20–37.

23   G. Smith and R. Stodghill, "Are Good Causes Good Marketing," *Business Week*, March 21, 1994, p. 64.

24   Business for Social Responsibility web site (last visited February 17, 2000), <www.bsr.org>.

25   Ibid.

26   D. Bollier, *Case: Merck and Co., Inc.*, Business Enterprise Trust, 1991.

27   R. Wasserstrom and S. Reider, "Petroleum Companies Crossing New Threshold in Community Relations," *Oil and Gas Journal* 96 (1998): 24–27.

28   Ibid.

29   T. Dunfee, "The Marketplace of Morality: First Steps Toward a Theory of Moral Choice," *Business Ethics Quarterly*, 8/1 (January 1998): 127–145.

30   T. Dunfee, "Corporate Governance in a Market with Morality," *Law and Contemporary Problems*, 62 (1999): 129. The obligations are expressed as follows: (1) There is a presumption that all corporate actions must be undertaken to maximise shareholder wealth; (2) Managers must respond to and anticipate existing and changing marketplace morality relevant to the firm that may have a negative impact on shareholder wealth; (3) The presumption in Principle One may be rebutted where clear and convincing evidence exists that marketplace morality relevant to the firm would justify a decision that cannot be shown to maximize shareholder wealth directly; and (4) Managers must act consistently with hypernorms (manifest universal norms and principles).

31   Ibid. (see Principle 3).

32   Environics International Ltd., *The Millennium Poll on Corporate Social Responsibility: Executive Briefing*, 1999.

33   *Sustainability Reporting Guidelines: Exposure Draft for Public Comment and Pilot Testing*, March 1999, <http://www.globalreporting.org>.

34   See Institute for Social and Ethical AccountAbility web site, <http://www.accountability.org.uk>.

35   See Institute for Social and Ethical AccountAbility, *AccountAbility1000 (AA1000): Overview of standard and its applications*, 1999.

36   Dunfee and Hess, op. cit.

37   D. Hess and T. Dunfee, "The Private Sector Role in Alleviating Human Misery," in World Bank, *A Guide to Developing Agricultural Markets and Agro-enterprises* (forthcoming).

38   Dunfee and Hess, op. cit.

39   Kanter, op. cit.

40   J. Logsdon and D. Wood, "Business Citizenship: From Domestic to Global Level of Analysis," *Business Ethics Quarterly* (in press).

41   See H. Schachter, "How Companies Can Profit by Going Green," *The Toronto Globe and Mail*, August 9, 2000, p. M1.

42   S. Waddock and N. Smith, "Corporate Responsibility Audits: Doing Well by Doing Good," *Sloan Management Review*, 41/2 (Winter 2000): 75–83.

43   P. Gillmor and C. Bremer, "Corporate Governance Symposium: Disclosure of Corporate Charitable Contributions as a Matter of Shareholder Accountability," *The Business Lawyer*, 54 (1999): 1007.

44   P. Daorueng, "Rice Project Plants Seeds of Controversy," *Interpress Service*, April 28, 1999 (available in LEXIS-NEXIS Academic Universe World News file).

45   See G. Naik, "Tooth and Nail: A U.K. Lab Company is Besieged by Protests Against Animal Testing," *Wall Street Journal*, April 27, 2001, p. A1; F. Guerrera and J. Pickard, "Stockbroker Cuts Links with Huntingdon," *Financial Times*, April 17, 2001, p. 1; G. Malkani and P. Jenkins, "Schwab Severs Links with Huntingdon Life Sciences," *Financial Times*, April 11, 2001, p. 1; F. Guerrera and G. Malkani, "Broker Quits HLS as Protests Increase," *Financial Times*, March 28, 2001, p. 1.

46   C. Fombrun, "Mastering Management: The Value To Be Found in Corporate Reputation," *Financial Times*, December 4, 2000, Survey, p. 2.

47   See Joby Warrick, "Big Mac's Big Voice in Meat Plants; McDonald's Becomes a Force in Pressing to Improve Conditions," *Washington Post*, April 10, 2001, p. A11; Tony Perry, "Egg Producers Are McMiffed: Industry Balks at McDonald's Tough Rules on Hen Treatment," *L.A. Times*, September 7, 2000, p. C1.

48   M. Alperson, "Measuring Corporate Community Involvement," Conference Board Report # 1169, 1996.

49   David Collis and Cynthia Montgomery, "Competing on Resources: Strategy in the 1990s," *Harvard Business Review*, 73/4 (July/August 1995): 118–128.

50   "Home Depot Ups Charitable Giving," *National Home Center News*, May 24, 1999, p. 11.

51   See B. McKay, "Coca-Cola, Gates Help Step Up Assault on AIDS," *Wall Street Journal*, June 20, 2001, p. B1.

52   Kanter, op. cit.; "The Double Bottom Line," op. cit.

53   Kanter, op. cit.

54   Ibid.

55   The Ron Brown Award for Corporate Leadership Homepage, <http://www.ron-brown-award.org/>.

56   A Conference Board study in 1996 found that 44 percent of the 177 respondents to their survey (sent to all members of the *Fortune 1000*) were attempting to evaluate their community relations programs or contributions. M. Alperson, "Measuring Corporate Community Involvement," Conference Board Report # 1169, 1996.

57   Walker Information and the Council on Foundations have teamed together to form MeasuringPhilanthropy.com, to measure the impact of philanthropy on corporate performance.

58   Formed by the Corporate Citizenship Company, the London Benchmarking Group is comprised of officers from leading London-based corporations and is working to better measure the effectiveness of community involvement programs. For additional information, see <http://www.corporate-citizenship.co.uk/community/lbg.asp#1bg>.

THE COMPETITIVE ADVANTAGE OF
CORPORATE PHILANTHROPY

Michael E. Porter and Mark R. Kramer

Corporate Philanthropy is in decline. Charitable contributions by U.S. companies fell 14.5% in real dollars last year, and over the last 15 years, corporate giving as a percentage of profits has dropped by 50%. The reasons are not hard to understand. Executives increasingly see themselves in a no-win situation, caught between critics demanding ever higher levels of "corporate social responsibility" and investors applying relentless pressure to maximize short-term profits. Giving more does not satisfy the critics – the more companies donate, the more is expected of them. And executives find it hard, if not impossible, to justify charitable expenditures in terms of bottom-line benefit.

This dilemma has led many companies to seek to be more strategic in their philanthropy. But what passes for "strategic philanthropy" today is almost never truly strategic, and often isn't even particularly effective as philanthropy. Increasingly, philanthropy is used as a form of public relations or advertising, promoting a company's image or brand through cause-related marketing or other high-profile sponsorships. Although it still represents only a small proportion of overall corporate charitable expenditures, U.S. corporate spending on cause-related marketing jumped from $125 million in 1990 to an estimated $828 million in 2002. Arts sponsorships are growing, too – they accounted for an additional $589 million in 2001. While these campaigns do provide much-needed support to worthy causes, they are intended as much to increase company visibility and improve employee morale as to create social impact. Tobacco giant Philip Morris, for example, spent $75 million on its charitable contributions in 1999 and then launched a $100 million advertising campaign to publicize them. Not surprisingly, there are genuine doubts about whether such approaches actually work or just breed public cynicism about company motives. (See the box "The Myth of Strategic Philanthropy.")

Given the current haziness surrounding corporate philanthropy, this seems an appropriate time to revisit the most basic of questions: Should corporations engage in philanthropy at all? The economist Milton Friedman laid down the gauntlet decades ago, arguing in a 1970 *New York Times Magazine* article that the only "social responsibility of business" is to "increase its profits." "The corporation," he wrote in his book *Capitalism and Freedom*, "is an instrument of the stockholders who own it. If the corporation makes a contribution, it prevents the individual stockholder from himself deciding how he should dispose of his funds." If charitable contributions are to be made, Friedman concluded, they should be made by individual stockholders – or, by extension, individual employees – and not by the corporation.

The way most corporate philanthropy is practiced today, Friedman is right. The majority of corporate contribution programs are diffuse and unfocused. Most consist of numerous small cash donations given to aid local civic causes or provide general operating support to universities and national charities in the hope of generating goodwill among employees, customers, and the local community. Rather than being tied to well-thought-out social or business objectives, the contributions often reflect the personal beliefs and values of executives or employees. Indeed, one of the most popular approaches – employee matching grants – explicitly leaves the choice of charity to the individual worker. Although aimed at enhancing morale, the same effect might be gained from an equal increase in wages that employees could then choose to donate to charity on a tax-deductible basis. It does indeed seem that many of the giving decisions companies make today would be better made by individuals donating their own money.

What about the programs that are at least superficially tied to business goals, such as cause-related marketing? Even the successful ones are hard to justify as charitable initiatives. Since all reasonable corporate expenditures are deductible, companies get no special tax advantage for spending on philanthropy as opposed to other corporate purposes. If cause-related marketing is good marketing, it is already deductible and does not benefit from being designated as charitable.

But does Friedman's argument always hold? Underlying it are two implicit assumptions. The first is that social and economic objectives are separate and distinct, so that a corporation's social spending comes at the expense of its economic results. The second is the assumption that corporations, when they address social objectives, provide no greater benefit than is provided by individual donors.

These assumptions hold true when corporate contributions are unfocused and piecemeal, as is typically the case today. But there is another, more truly strategic way to think about philanthropy. Corporations can use their charitable efforts to improve their *competitive context* – the quality of the business environment in the location or locations where they operate. Using philanthropy to enhance context brings social and economic goals in to alignment and improves a company's long-term business prospects – thus contradicting Friedman's first assumption. In addition, addressing context enables a company not only to give money but also to leverage its capabilities and relationships in support of charitable causes. That produces social benefits far exceeding those provided by individual donors, foundations, or even governments. Context-focused giving thus contradicts Friedman's second assumption as well.

A handful of companies have begun to use context-focused philanthropy to achieve both social and economic gains. Cisco Systems, to take one example, has invested in an ambitious educational program – the Cisco Networking Academy – to train computer network administrators, thus alleviating a potential constraint on its growth while providing attractive job

The Myth of Strategic Philanthropy

Few phrases are as overused and poorly defined as "strategic philanthropy." The term is used to cover virtually any kind of charitable activity that has some definable theme, goal, approach, or focus. In the corporate context, it generally means that there is some connection, however vague or tenuous, between the charitable contribution and the company's business. Often this connection is only semantic, enabling the company to rationalize its contributions in public reports and press releases. In fact, most corporate giving programs have nothing to do with a company's strategy. They are primarily aimed at generating goodwill and positive publicity and boosting employee morale.

Cause-related marketing, through which a company concentrates its giving on a single cause or admired organization, was one of the earliest practices cited as "strategic philanthropy," and it is a step above diffuse corporate contributions. At its most sophisticated, cause-related marketing can improve the reputation of a company by linking its identity with the admired qualities of a chosen non-profit partner or a popular cause. Companies that sponsor the Olympics, for example, gain not only wide exposure but also an association with the pursuit of excellence. And by concentrating funding through a deliberate selection process, cause-related marketing has the potential to create more impact than unfocused giving would provide.

However, cause-related marketing falls far short of truly strategic philanthropy. Its emphasis remains on publicity rather than social impact. The desired benefit is enhanced goodwill, not improvement in a company's ability to compete. True strategic giving, by contrast, addresses important social and economic goals simultaneously, targeting areas of competitive context where the company and society both benefit because the firm brings unique assets and expertise.

---

opportunities to high school graduates. By focusing on social needs that affect its corporate context and utilizing its unique attributes as a corporation to address them, Cisco has begun to demonstrate the unrealized potential of corporate philanthropy. Taking this new direction, however, requires fundamental changes in the way companies approach their contribution programs. Corporations need to rethink both *where* they focus their philanthropy and *how* they go about their giving.

Where to Focus

It is true that economic and social objectives have long been seen as distinct and often competing. But this is a false dichotomy; it represents an increasingly obsolete perspective in a world of open, knowledge-based competition. Companies do not function in isolation from the society around them. In fact, their ability to compete depends heavily on the circumstances of the locations where they operate. Improving education, for example, is generally seen as a social issue, but the educational level of the local workforce substantially affects a company's potential competitiveness. The more a social improvement relates to a company's business, the more it leads to economic benefits as well. In establishing its Networking Academy, for example, Cisco focused not on the educational system overall, but on the training needed to produce network administrators – the particular kind of education that made the most difference to Cisco's competitive context. (For a more detailed look at that program, see the box "The Cisco Networking Academy.")

In the long run, then, social and economic goals are not inherently conflicting but integrally connected. Competitiveness today depends on the productivity with which companies can use labor, capital, and natural resources to produce high-quality goods and services. Productivity depends on having workers who are educated, safe, healthy, decently housed, and motivated by a sense of opportunity. Preserving the environment benefits not only society but companies too, because reducing pollution and waste can lead to a more productive use of resources and help produce goods that consumers value. Boosting social and economic conditions in developing countries can create more productive locations for a company's operations as well as new markets for its products. Indeed, we are learning that the most effective method of addressing many of the world's pressing problems is often to mobilize the corporate sector in ways that benefit both society and companies.

That does not mean that every corporate expenditure will bring a social benefit or that every social benefit will improve competitiveness. Most corporate expenditures produce benefits only for the business, and charitable contributions unrelated to the business generate only social benefits. It is only where corporate expenditures produce simultaneous social and economic gains that corporate philanthropy and shareholder interests converge, as illustrated in Exhibit 1, "A Convergence of Interests." The highlighted area shows where corporate philanthropy has an important influence on a company's competitive context. It is here that philanthropy is truly strategic.

Competitive context has always been important to strategy. The availability of skilled and motivated employees; the efficiency of the local infrastructure, including roads and telecommunications; the size and sophistication of the local market; the extent of governmental regulations – such contextual variables have always influenced companies' ability to compete. But competitive context has become even more critical as the basis of

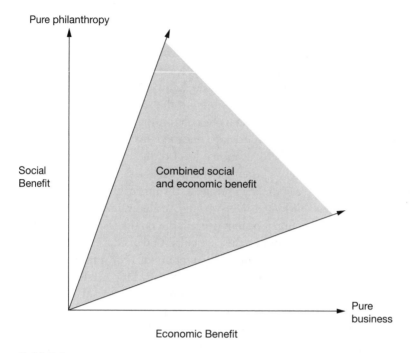

Exhibit 1 A convergence of interests

competition has moved from cheap inputs to superior productivity. For one thing, modern knowledge- and technology-based competition hinges more and more on worker capabilities. For another, companies today depend more on local partnerships: They rely on outsourcing and collaboration with local suppliers and institutions rather than on vertical integration; they work more closely with customers; and they draw more on local universities and research institutes to conduct research and development. Finally, navigating increasingly complex local regulations and reducing approval times for new projects and products are becoming increasingly important to competition. As a result of these trends, companies' success has become more tightly intertwined with local institutions and other contextual conditions. And the globalization of production and marketing means that context is often more important for a company not just in its home market but in multiple countries.

A company's competitive context consists of four interrelated elements of the local business environment that shape potential productivity: factor conditions, or the available inputs of production; demand conditions; the context for strategy and rivalry; and related and supporting industries. This framework is summarized in Exhibit 2, "The Four Elements of Competitive Context", and described in detail in Michael E. Porter's *The Competitive Advantage of Nations*. Weakness in any part of this context can erode the competitiveness of a nation or region as a business location.

Some aspects of the business environment, such as road systems, corporate tax rates, and corporate laws, have effects that cut across all industries. These general conditions can be crucial to competitiveness in developing countries, and improving them through corporate philanthropy can bring enormous social gains to the world's poorest nations. But often just as decisive, if not more, are aspects of context that are specific to a particular *cluster* – a geographic concentration of interconnected companies, suppliers, related industries, and specialized institutions in a particular field, such as high-performance cars in Germany or software in India. Clusters arise through the combined influence of all four elements of context. They are often prominent features of a region's economic landscape, and building them is essential to its development, allowing constituent firms to be more productive, making innovation easier, and fostering the formation of new businesses.

Philanthropic investments by members of a cluster, either individually or collectively, can have a powerful effect on the cluster's competitiveness and the performance of all of its constituent companies. Philanthropy can often be the most cost-effective way – and sometimes the only way – to improve competitive context. It enables companies to leverage not only their own resources but also the existing efforts and infrastructure of nonprofits and other institutions. Contributing to a university, for example, may be a far less expensive way to strengthen a local base of advanced skills in a company's field than developing training in-house. And philanthropy is amenable to collective corporate action, enabling costs to be spread over multiple

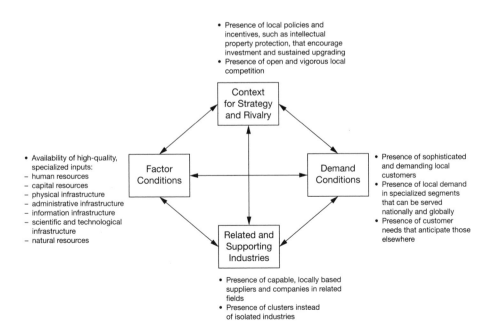

Exhibit 2 The four elements of competitive context

companies. Finally, because of philanthropy's wide social benefits, companies are often able to forge partnerships with nonprofit organizations and governments that would be wary of collaborating on efforts that solely benefited a particular company.

Influencing Competitive Context

By carefully analyzing the elements of competitive context, a company can identify the areas of overlap between social and economic value that will most enhance its own and its cluster's competitiveness. Consider each of the four elements of context and how companies have influenced them through philanthropy in ways that have improved their long-term economic prospects.

Factor Conditions. Achieving high levels of productivity depends on the presence of trained workers, high-quality scientific and technological institutions, adequate physical infrastructure, transparent and efficient administrative processes (such as company registration or permit requirements), and available natural resources. All are areas that philanthropy can influence.

Charitable giving can, for example, improve education and training. DreamWorks SKG, the film production company, recently created a program to train low-income students in Los Angeles in skills needed to work in the entertainment industry. Each of the company's six divisions is working with the Los Angeles Community College District, local high schools, and after-school programs to create a specialized curriculum that combines classroom instruction with internships and mentoring. The social benefit is an improved educational system and better employment opportunities for low-income residents. The economic benefit is greater availability of specially trained graduates. Even though relatively few of them will join DreamWorks itself, the company also gains by strengthening the entertainment cluster it depends on.

Philanthropic initiatives can also improve the local quality of life, which benefits all citizens but is increasingly necessary to attract mobile employees with specialized talents. In 1996, SC Johnson, a manufacturer of cleaning and home-storage products, launched "Sustainable Racine," a project to make its home city in Wisconsin a better place in which to live and work. In partnership with local organizations, government, and residents, the company created a communitywide coalition focused on enhancing the local economy and the environment. One project, an agreement among four municipalities to coordinate water and sewer treatment, resulted in savings for residents and businesses while reducing pollution. Another project involved opening the community's first charter school, targeting at-risk students. Other efforts focused on economic revitalization: Commercial vacancy rates in downtown Racine have fallen from 46% to 18% as polluted sites have been reclaimed and jobs have returned for local residents.

Philanthropy can also improve inputs other than labor, through enhancements in, say, the quality of local research and development institutions, the effectiveness of administrative institutions such as the legal system, the quality of the physical infrastructure, or the sustainable development of natural resources. Exxon Mobil, for example, has devoted substantial resources to improving basic conditions such as roads and the rule of law in the developing countries where it operates.

Demand Conditions. Demand conditions in a nation or region include the size of the local market, the appropriateness of product standards, and the sophistication of local customers. Sophisticated local customers enhance the region's competitiveness by providing companies with insight into emerging customer needs and applying pressure for innovation. For example, the advanced state of medical practice in Boston has triggered a stream of innovation in Boston-based medical device companies.

Philanthropy can influence both the size and quality of the local market. The Cisco Networking Academy, for instance, improved demand conditions by helping customers obtain well-trained network administrators. In doing so, it increased the size of the market and the sophistication of users – and hence users' interest in more advanced solutions. Apple Computer has long donated computers to schools as a means of introducing its products to young people. This provides a clear social benefit to the schools while expanding Apple's potential market and turning students and teachers into more sophisticated purchasers. Safeco, an insurance and financial services firm, is working in partnership with nonprofits to expand affordable housing and enhance public safety. As home ownership and public safety increased in its four test markets, insurance sales did too, in some cases by up to 40%.

Context for Strategy and Rivalry. The rules, incentives, and norms governing competition in a nation or region have a fundamental influence on productivity. Policies that encourage investment, protect intellectual property, open local markets to trade, break up or prevent the formation of cartels and monopolies, and reduce corruption make a location a more attractive place to do business.

Philanthropy can have a strong influence on creating a more productive and transparent environment for competition. For example, 26 U.S. corporations and 38 corporations from other countries have joined to support Transparency International in its work to disclose and deter corruption around the world. By measuring and focusing public attention on corruption, the organization helps to create an environment that rewards fair competition and enhances productivity. This benefits local citizens while providing sponsoring companies improved access to markets.

Another example is the International Corporate Governance Network (ICGN), a nonprofit organization formed by major institutional investors, including the College Retirement Equities Fund (TIAA-CREF) and the California Public Employees Retirement System, known as CalPERS, to promote improved standards of corporate governance and disclosures, especially in developing countries. ICGN encourages uniform global accounting standards and equitable shareholder voting procedures. Developing countries and their citizens benefit as improved governance and disclosure enhance local corporate practices, expose unscrupulous local competitors, and make regions more attractive for foreign investment. The institutional investors that support this project also gain better and fairer capital markets in which to invest.

Related and Supporting Industries. A company's productivity can be greatly enhanced by having high-quality supporting industries and services nearby. While outsourcing from distant suppliers is possible, it is not as efficient as using capable local suppliers of services, components, and machinery. Proximity enhances responsiveness, exchange of information, and innovation, in addition to lowering transportation and inventory costs.

Philanthropy can foster the development of clusters and strengthen supporting industries. American Express, for example, depends on travel-related spending for a large share of its credit card and travel agency revenues. Hence, it is part of the travel cluster in each of the countries in which it operates, and it depends on the success of these clusters in improving the quality of tourism and attracting travelers. Since 1986, American Express has funded Travel and Tourism Academies in secondary schools, training students not for the credit card business, its core business, nor for its own travel services, but for careers in other travel agencies as well as airlines, hotels, and

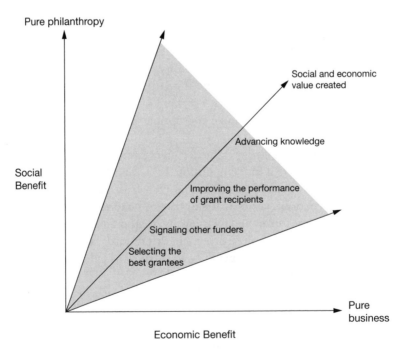

Exhibit 3 Maximizing philanthropy's value

restaurants. The program, which includes teacher training, curriculum support, summer internships, and industry mentors, now operates in ten countries and more than 3,000 schools, with more than 120,000 students enrolled. It provides the major social benefits of improved educational and job opportunities for local citizens. Within the United States, 80% of students in the program go on to college, and 25% take jobs in the travel industry after graduation. The economic gains are also substantial, as local travel clusters become more competitive and better able to grow. That translates into important benefits for American Express.

The Free Rider Problem

When corporate philanthropy improves competitive context, other companies in the cluster or region, including direct competitors, often share the benefits. That raises an important question: Does the ability of other companies to be free riders negate the strategic value of context-focused philanthropy? The answer is *no*. The competitive benefits reaped by the donor company remain substantial, for five reasons:

- Improving context mainly benefits companies based in a given location. Not all competitors will be based in the same area, so the company will still gain an edge over the competition in general.
- Corporate philanthropy is ripe for collective activity. By sharing the costs with other companies in its cluster, including competitors, a company can greatly diminish the free rider problem.
- Leading companies will be best positioned to make substantial contributions and will in turn reap a major share of the benefits. Cisco, for example, with a leading market share in networking equipment, will benefit most from a larger, more rapidly growing market.
- Not all contextual advantages are of equal value to all competitors. The more tightly corporate philanthropy is aligned with a company's unique strategy – increasing skills, technology, or infrastructure on which the firm is especially reliant, say, or increasing demand within a specialized segment where the company is strongest – the more disproportionately the company will benefit through enhancing the context.
- The company that initiates corporate philanthropy in a particular area will often get disproportionate benefits because of the superior reputation and relationships it builds. In its campaign to fight malaria in African countries, for example, Exxon Mobil not only improves public health. It also improves the health of its workers and contractors and builds strong relationships with local governments and nonprofits, advancing its goal of becoming the preferred resource-development partner.

A good example of how a company can gain an edge even when its contributions also benefit competitors is provided by Grand Circle Travel. Grand Circle, the leading direct marketer of international travel for older Americans, has a strategy based on offering rich cultural and educational experiences for its customers. Since 1992, its corporate foundation has given more than $12 million to historical preservation projects in locations that its customers like to visit, such as the Foundation of Friends of the Museum and Ruins of Ephesus in Turkey and the State Museum of Auschwitz-Birkenau in Poland. Other tours travel the same routes and so benefit from Grand Circle's donations. Through its philanthropy, however, Grand Circle has built close relationships with the organizations that maintain these sites and can provide its travellers with special opportunities to visit and learn about them. Grand Circle thus gains a unique competitive advantage that distinguishes it from other travel providers.

How to Contribute

Understanding the links between philanthropy and competitive context helps companies identify *where* they should focus their corporate giving. Understanding the ways in which philanthropy creates value highlights *how* they can achieve the greatest social and economic impact through their contributions. As we will see, the where and the how are mutually reinforcing.

In "Philanthropy's New Agenda: Creating Value" (HBR November–December 1999), we outlined four ways in which charitable foundations can create social value: selecting the best grantees, signalling other funders, improving the performance of grant recipients, and advancing knowledge and practice in the field. These efforts build on one another: Increasingly greater value is generated as a donor moves up the ladder from selecting the right grantees to advancing knowledge. (See Exhibit 3, "Maximizing Philanthropy's Value.") The same principles apply to corporate giving, pointing the way to how corporate philanthropy can be most effective in enhancing competitive context. Focusing on the four principles also ensures that corporate donations have greater impact than donations of the same magnitude by individuals.

Selecting the Best Grantees. Most philanthropic activity involves giving money to other organizations that actually deliver the social benefits. The impact achieved by a donor, then, is largely determined by the effectiveness of the recipient. Selecting a more effective grantee or partner organization will lead to more social impact per dollar expended.

Selecting the most effective grantees in a given field is never easy. It may be obvious which nonprofit organizations raise the most money, have the greatest prestige, or manage the best development campaigns, but such factors may have little to do with how well the grantees use contributions.

Extensive and disciplined research is usually required to select those recipients that will achieve the greatest social impact.

Individual donors rarely have the time or expertise to undertake such serious due diligence. Foundations are far more expert than individuals, but they have limited staff. Corporations, on the other hand, are well positioned to undertake such research if their philanthropy is connected to their business and they can tap into their internal capabilities, particularly the financial, managerial, and technical expertise of employees. Whether through their own operations or those of their suppliers and customers, corporations also often have a presence in many communities across a country or around the world. This can provide significant local knowledge and the ability to examine and compare the operation of nonprofits firsthand.

In some cases, a company can introduce and support a particularly effective nonprofit organization or program in many of the locations in which it operates. Grand Circle Travel, for example, uses its 15 overseas offices to identify historical preservation projects to fund. FleetBoston Financial assembles teams of employees with diverse management and financial skills to examine the inner-city economic development organizations that its foundation supports. The teams visit each nonprofit, interview management, review policies and procedures, and report to the corporate foundation on whether support should be continued and, if so, where it should be directed. This level of attention and expertise is substantially greater than most individual donors, foundations, or even government agencies can muster.

Signaling Other Funders. A donor can publicize the most effective nonprofit organizations and promote them to other donors, attracting greater funding and thus creating a more effective allocation of overall philanthropic spending.

Corporations bring uniquely valuable assets to this task. First, their reputations often command respect, becoming imprimaturs of credibility for grantees. Second, they are often able to influence a vast network of entities in their cluster, including customers, suppliers, and other partners. This gives them far greater reach than individual donors or even most nonprofits and foundations. Third, they often have access to communication channels and expertise that can be used to disseminate information widely, swiftly, and persuasively to other donors.

Signaling other funders is especially important in corporate philanthropy because it mitigates the free rider problem. Collective social investment by participants in a cluster can improve the context for all players, while reducing the cost borne by each one. By leveraging its relationships and brand identity to initiate social projects that are also funded by others, a corporation improves the cost–benefit ratio. The Cisco Networking Academy draws support from numerous technology companies in Cisco's cluster as well as educational systems and governments throughout the world, all of which benefit from the graduates' success. American Express's Travel and Tourism Academies depend on the help of more than 750 travel cluster partners who

The Cisco Networking Academy

Cisco Systems' Networking Academy exemplifies the powerful links that exist between a company's philanthropic strategy, its competitive context, and social benefits. Cisco, the leading producer of networking equipment and routers used to connect computers to the internet, grew rapidly over the past decade. But as Internet use expanded, customers around the world encountered a chronic shortage of qualified network administrators, which became a limiting factor in Cisco's – and the entire IT industry's – continued growth. By one estimate, well over 1 million information technology jobs remained unfilled worldwide in the late 1990s. While Cisco was well aware of this constraint in its competitive context, it was only through philanthropy that the company found a way to address it.

The project began as a typical example of goodwill-based giving: Cisco contributed networking equipment to a high school near its headquarters, then expanded the program to other schools in the region. A Cisco engineer working with the schools realized, however, that the teachers and administrators lacked the training to manage the networks once they were installed. He and several other Cisco engineers volunteered to develop a program that would not only donate equipment but also train teachers how to build, design, and maintain computer networks. Students began attending these courses and were able to absorb the information successfully. As Cisco expanded the program, company executives began to realize that they could develop a Web-based distance-learning curriculum to train and certify secondary- and postsecondary-school students in network administration, a program that might have a much broader social and economic impact. The Networking Academy was born.

Because the social goal of the program was tightly linked to Cisco's specialized expertise, the company was able to create a high-quality curriculum rapidly and cost-effectively, creating far more social and economic value than if it had merely contributed cash and equipment to a worthy cause. At the suggestion of the U.S. Department of Education, the company began to target schools in "empowerment zones," designated by the federal government as among the most economically challenged communities in the country. The company also began to include community colleges and mid-career training in the program. More recently, it has worked with the United Nations to expand the effort to developing countries, where job opportunities are particularly scarce and networking skills particularly limited. Cisco has also organized a worldwide database of employment opportunities for academy graduates, creating a more efficient job market that benefits its cluster as well as the graduates and the regions in which they live.

Cisco has used its unique assets and expertise, along with its worldwide presence, to create a program that no other educational institution, government agency, foundation or corporate donor could have designed as well or expanded as rapidly. And it has amplified the impact by signalling other corporations on its cluster. Other companies supplemented Cisco's contributions by donating or discounting products and services of their own, such as Internet access and computer hardware and software. Several leading technology companies also began to recognize the value of the global infrastructure Cisco had created, and, rather than create their own Web-based learning programs, they partnered with Cisco. Companies such as Sun Microsystems, Hewlett-Packard, Adobe Systems, and Panduit expanded the academy curriculum by sponsoring courses in programming, IT essentials, Web design, and cabling. Because the project was linked to Cisco's business, it could gain the support of other companies in its cluster and use their contributions effectively.

Although the program is only five years old, it now operates 9,900 academies in secondary schools, community colleges, and community-based organizations in all 50 states and in 147 countries. The social and economic value that has been created is enormous. Cisco estimates that it has invested a total of $150 million since the program began. With that investment, it has brought the possibility of technology careers, and the technology itself, to men and women in some of the most economically depressed regions in the United States and around the world. More than 115,000 students have already graduated from the two-year program, and 263,000 students are currently enrolled, half of them outside the United States. The program continues to expand rapidly, with 50 to 100 new academies opening every week. Cisco estimates that 50% of academy graduates have found jobs in the IT industry, where the average salary for a network administrator in the United States is $67,000. Over the span of their careers, the incremental earnings potential of those who have already joined the workforce may approach several billion dollars.

To be sure, the program has benefited many free riders – employers around the world who gain access to highly skilled academy graduates and even direct competitors. But as the market-leading provider of routers, Cisco stands to benefit the most from this improvement in the competitive context. Through actively engaging others, Cisco has not had to bear the full cost of the program. Not only has Cisco enlarged its market and strengthened its cluster, but it has increased the sophistication of its customers. Through these tangible improvements in competitive context, and not just by the act of giving, Cisco has attracted international recognition for this program, generating justified pride and enthusiasm among company employees, goodwill among its partners, and a reputation for leadership in philanthropy.

bear part of the cost and reap part of the benefit. Different companies will bring different strengths to a given philanthropic initiative. By tapping each company's distinctive expertise, the collective investment can be far more effective than a donation by any one company.

Improving the Performance of Grant Recipients. By improving the effectiveness of nonprofits, corporations create value for society, increasing the social impact achieved per dollar expended. While selecting the right grantee improves society's return on a single contribution, and signalling other funders improves the return on multiple contributions, improving grantee performance can increase the return on the grantee's total budget.

Unlike many other donors, corporations have the ability to work directly with nonprofits and other partners to help them become more effective. They bring unique assets and expertise that individuals and foundations lack, enabling them to provide a wide range of nonmonetary assistance that is less costly and more sophisticated than the services most grantees could purchase for themselves. And because they typically make long-term commitments to the communities in which they operate, corporations can work closely with local nonprofits over the extended periods of time needed for meaningful organizational improvement. By operating in multiple geographical areas, moreover, companies are able to facilitate the transfer of knowledge and operational improvements among nonprofits in different regions or countries. Contextual issues within a particular industry or cluster will often be similar across different locations, increasing a company's ability to add and derive value in multiple regions.

By tying corporate philanthropy to its business and strategy, a company can create even greater social value in improving grantee performance than other donors. Its specialized assets and expertise, after all, will be most useful in addressing problems related to its particular field. DreamWorks' film production expertise helped it design the educational curriculum necessary to help inner-city students in Los Angeles get jobs in the entertainment industry. The Cisco Networking Academy utilized the special expertise of Cisco employees.

FleetBoston Financial took similar advantage of its corporate expertise in launching its Community Renaissance Initiative. Recognizing that its major markets were in older East Coast cities, Fleet decided to focus on inner-city economic revitalization as perhaps the most important way to improve its context. Fleet combined its philanthropic contributions with its expertise in financial services, such as small business services, inner-city lending, home mortgages, and venture capital. The bank's foundation identified six communities where the bank had a presence, the economic need was great, and strong community-based organizations could be identified as reliable partners: Brooklyn and Buffalo, New York; Lawrence, Massachusetts; New Haven, Connecticut; and Camden and Jersey City, New Jersey. The foundation committed $725,000 to each city, building a coalition of local community, business, and government organizations to work on a set of issues identified by the community as central to its revitalization. Bank personnel provided technical advice and small business financing packages to local companies as well as home mortgages and home-buyer education programs. The foundation also attracted $6 million from private and municipal sources, greatly amplifying its own $4.5 million investment.

Another example is America Online, which has unique capabilities in managing Internet access and content. Working closely with educators, AOL developed AOL@School, a free, easy-to-use, non-commercial site tailored by grade level to students, administrators, and teachers. This service improves the classroom experience for hundreds of thousands of students nationally by giving them access to enrichment and reference tools while providing lesson plans and reference materials for teachers. Through this program, AOL has been able to leverage its specialized expertise, more than just its donations, to assist in improving secondary school performance more rapidly and cost-effectively than could most other organizations. In the process, it has improved both the long-term demand for its services and the talent needed to provide them.

Advancing Knowledge and Practice. Innovation drives productivity in the nonprofit sector as well as in the commercial sector. The greatest advances come not from incremental improvements in efficiency but from new and better approaches. The most powerful way to create social value, therefore, is by developing new means to address social problems and putting them into widespread practice.

The expertise, research capacity, and reach that companies bring to philanthropy can help nonprofits create new solutions that they could never afford to develop on their own. Since 1994, IBM has committed a total of $70 million to its Reinventing Education program, which now reaches 65,000 teachers and 6 million students. Working in partnership with urban school districts, state education departments, and colleges of education, IBM researched and developed a Web-based platform to support new instructional practices and strategies. The new curriculum is intended to redefine how teachers master their profession; it bridges the gap between teacher preparation and the classroom experience by providing a common platform that is used in the teachers' college courses and also supports their first years of teaching. Neither the colleges of education nor the school districts had the expertise or financial resources to develop such a program on their own. An independent evaluation in 2001 found that teachers in the Reinventing Education program were registering substantial gains in student performance.

Pfizer developed a cost-effective treatment for the prevention of trachoma, the leading cause of preventable blindness in developing countries. In addition to donating the drugs, Pfizer worked with the Edna McConnell Clark Foundation and world health organizations to create the infrastructure needed to prescribe and distribute them to populations that previously had little access to health care, much less modern pharmaceuticals. Within one year, the incidence of trachoma was reduced by 50% among target populations in Morocco and Tanzania. The program has since expanded aggressively, adding the Bill & Melinda Gates Foundation and the British government as partners, with the aim of reaching 30 million people worldwide. In addition to providing an important social benefit, Pfizer has enhanced its own long-term business prospects by helping build the infrastructure required to expand its markets.

Just as important as the creation of new knowledge is its adoption in practice. The know-how of corporate leaders, their clout and connections, and their presence in communities around the world create powerful networks for the dissemination of new ideas for addressing social problems. Corporations can facilitate global knowledge transfer and coordinated multisite implementation of new social initiatives with a proficiency that is unequaled by most other donors.

A Whole New Approach

When corporations support the right causes in the right ways – when they get the *where* and the *how* right – they set in motion a virtuous cycle. By focusing on the contextual conditions most important to their industries and strategies, companies ensure that their corporate capabilities will be particularly well suited to helping grantees create greater value. And by enhancing the value produced by philanthropic efforts in their fields, the companies gain a greater improvement in competitive context. Both the corporations and the causes they support reap important benefits.

Adopting a context-focused approach, however, goes against the grain of current philanthropic practice. Many companies actively distance their philanthropy from the business, believing this will lead to greater goodwill in local communities. While it is true that a growing number of companies aim to make their giving "strategic," few have connected giving to areas that improve their long-term competitive potential. And even fewer systematically apply their distinctive strengths to maximize the social and economic value created by their philanthropy. Instead, companies are often distracted by the desire to publicize how much money and effort they are contributing in order to foster an image of social responsibility and caring. Avon Products, for example, recently mobilized its 400,000 independent sales representatives in a high-profile door-to-door campaign to raise more than $32 million to fund breast cancer prevention. Fighting breast cancer is a worthy cause and one that is very meaningful to Avon's target market of female consumers. It is not, however, a material factor in Avon's competitive context or an area in which Avon has any inherent expertise. As a result, Avon may have greatly augmented its own cash contribution through effective fundraising – and generated favorable publicity – but it failed to realize the full potential of its philanthropy to create social and economic value. Avon has done much good, but it could do even better. As long as companies remain focused on the public relations benefit of their contributions instead of the impact achieved, they will sacrifice opportunities to create social value.

This does not mean that corporations cannot also gain goodwill and enhance their reputations through philanthropy. But goodwill alone is not a sufficient motivation. Given public scepticism about the ethics of business – scepticism that has intensified in the wake of the string of corporate scandals this year – corporations that can demonstrate a significant impact on a social problem will gain more credibility than those that are merely big givers. The acid test of good corporate philanthropy is whether the desired social change is so beneficial to the company that the organization would pursue the change even if no one ever knew about it. Cisco, for example, has achieved wide recognition for its good works, but it would have had sufficient reason to develop the Networking Academy even if no goodwill had been created.

Moving to context-focused philanthropy will require a far more rigorous approach than is prevalent today. It will mean tightly integrating the management of philanthropy with other company activities. Rather than delegating philanthropy entirely to a public relations department or the staff of a corporate foundation, the CEO must lead the entire management team through a disciplined process to identify and implement a corporate giving strategy focused on improving context. Business units, in particular, must play central roles in identifying areas for contextual investments.

The new process would involve five steps:

Examine the competitive context in each of the company's important geographic locations. Where could social investment improve the company's or cluster's competitive potential? What are the key constraints that limit productivity, innovation, growth, and competitiveness? A company should pay special attention to the particular constraints that have a disproportionate effect on its strategy relative to competitors; improvements in these areas of context will potentially reinforce competitive advantage. The more specifically a contextual initiative is defined, the more likely the company is to create value and achieve its objectives. A broad initiative such as Avon's efforts to improve the health of all women will not necessarily deliver contextual benefits, even if it helps some employees or customers. And a tightly targeted objective does not necessarily diminish the scale of impact. Narrowly focused initiatives, like Pfizer's trachoma program, IBM's Reinventing Education, or Cisco's Networking Academy, can potentially benefit millions of people or strengthen the global market for an entire industry.

Review the existing philanthropic portfolio to see how it fits this new paradigm. Current programs will likely fall into three categories:

- Communal obligation: support of civic, welfare and educational organizations, motivated by the company's desire to be a good citizen.
- Goodwill building: contributions to support causes favored by

employees, customers, or community leaders, often necessitated by
the quid pro quo of business and the desire to improve the company's
relationships.

- Strategic giving: philanthropy focused on enhancing competitive context, as outlined here.

Most corporate giving falls into the first two categories. While a certain
percentage of giving in these categories may be necessary and desirable, the
goal is to shift, as much as possible, a company's philanthropy into the third
category. As for cause-related marketing, it is marketing, not philanthropy,
and it must stand on its own merits.

*Assess existing and potential corporate giving initiatives against the four forms
of value creation.* How can the company leverage its assets and expertise to
select the most effective grantees, signal other funders, improve grantees'
performance, and advance knowledge and practice? Given its strategy, where
can the company create the greatest value through giving in ways that no
other company could match?

Seek opportunities for collective action within a cluster and with other partners.
Collective action will often be more effective than a solo effort in addressing
context and enhancing the value created, and it helps mitigate the free rider
problem by distributing costs broadly. Few companies today work together
to achieve social objectives. This may be the result of a general reluctance to
work with competitors, but clusters encompass many related partners and
industries that do not compete directly. More likely, the tendency to view
philanthropy as a form of public relations leads companies to invent their
own contributions campaigns, which are branded with their own identities
and therefore discourage partners. Focusing on the social change to be
achieved, rather than the publicity to be gained, will expand the potential
for partnerships and collective action.

Once a company has identified opportunities to improve the competitive
context and determined the ways in which it can contribute by adding unique
value, the search for partners becomes straightforward: Who else stands to
benefit from this change in competitive context? And who has complementary expertise or resources? Conversely, what philanthropic initiatives by
others are worth joining? Where can the company be a good partner to others
by contributing in ways that will enhance value?

Rigorously track and evaluate results. Monitoring achievements is essential
to continually improving the philanthropic strategy and its implementation.
As with any other corporate activity, consistent improvement over time
brings the greatest value. The most successful programs will not be short-
term campaigns but long-term commitments that continue to grow in scale
and sophistication.

The context-focused approach to philanthropy is not simple. One size
does not fit all. Companies will differ in their comfort levels and time
horizons for philanthropic activity, and individual firms will make different

choices about how to implement our ideas. Philanthropy will never become an exact science – it is inherently an act of judgment and faith in the pursuit of long-term goals. However, the perspective and tools presented here will help any company make its philanthropic activities far more effective.

Were this approach to be widely adopted, the pattern of corporate contributions would shift significantly. The overall level of contributions would likely increase, and the social and economic value would go up even more sharply. Companies would be more confident about the value of their philanthropy and more committed to it. They would be able to communicate their philanthropic strategies more effectively to the communities in which they operate. Their choices of areas to support would be clearly understandable and would not seem unpredictable or idiosyncratic. Finally, there would be a better division of labor between corporate givers and other types of funders, with corporations tackling the areas where they are uniquely able to create value.

Charities too would benefit. They would see an increased and more predictable flow of corporate resources into the nonprofit sector. Just as important, they would develop close, long-term corporate partnerships that would better apply the expertise and assets of the for-profit sector to achieve social objectives. Just as companies can build on the nonprofit infrastructure to achieve their objectives more cost-effectively, nonprofits can benefit from using the commercial infrastructure.

To some corporate leaders, this new approach might seem too self-serving. They might argue that philanthropy is purely a matter of conscience and should not be adulterated by business objectives. In some industries, particularly those like petrochemicals and pharmaceuticals that are prone to public controversy, this view is so entrenched that many companies establish independent charitable foundations and entirely segregate giving from the business. In doing so, however, they give up tremendous opportunities to create greater value for society and themselves. Context-focused philanthropy does not just address a company's self-interest, it benefits many through broad social change. If a company's philanthropy only involved its own interests, after all, it would not qualify as a charitable deduction, and it might well threaten the company's reputation.

There is no inherent contradiction between improving competitive context and making a sincere commitment to bettering society. Indeed, as we've seen, the more closely a company's philanthropy is linked to its competitive context, the greater the company's contribution to society will be. Other areas, where the company neither creates added value nor derives benefit, should appropriately be left – as Friedman asserts – to individual donors following their own charitable impulses. If systematically pursued in a way that maximizes the value created, context-focused philanthropy can offer companies a new set of competitive tools that well justifies the investment or resources. At the same time, it can unlock a vastly more powerful way to make the world a better place.

Chapter 8

CSR in the ecological environment

I N THIS CHAPTER WE WILL:

- Discuss the growing attention to ecological responsibilities in corporations.
- Examine the meaning of sustainability in relation to CSR.
- Explain some of the core corporate responsibilities in the ecological environment.
- Examine how ecological responsibilities can be integrated into corporate strategy.
- Elaborate on the political dimension of ecological responsibilities.

Introduction

The current wave of interest in CSR essentially emerged from growing attention to ecological issues in business in the late 1980s and early 1990s. This transformation of ecological responsibilities 'from heresy to dogma' (Hoffman, 2001) brought with it a growing recognition among corporations that effective management of their ecological environment was a necessary part of doing business. To begin with, such responsibilities were mainly couched in terms of pollution prevention, waste minimization, energy conservation and recycling. They have since grown to incorporate deeper elements of sustainability, including major challenges such as climate change, biodiversity and resource security.

There are a number of factors driving the increasing attention to ecological problems, including spiralling consumption and resource use in developed countries, major growth in industrialization in Asia and Latin America, the increasing power of NGOs to galvanize public opinion around the issues, and sustained attention from regulators. As a result, while firms now have a range of environmental management tools and techniques at their disposal to deal with ecological responsibilities – such as environmental management systems, life-cycle analysis, ISO standards – they also have to face increasing expectations that require them to go beyond their existing technologies.

It is clear, then, that not only are the ecological responsibilities facing corporations not going away, but they are also becoming ever larger, more complex and challenging to solve. It is one thing to institute a recycling programme in the office, or to introduce 'end-of-pipe' technologies to reduce pollution from the manufacturing plant; it is quite another to consider how to change an entire industrial model to end a reliance on fossil fuels or to innovate a sustainable system of product recapture and reuse that prevents the need for endless supplies of non-renewable resources in the first place.

From a CSR perspective, ecological issues may be seen either as a separate arena of responsibility from workplace, marketplace and community issues – or as an issue that cuts through these and other areas. Indeed, there are few CSR issues that do not have some kind of ecological dimension, especially when considering the types of trade-off between social, ecological and economic factors that are captured in the notion of sustainability. As we saw in Chapter 3, the label of sustainability is even sometimes used synonymously with CSR in business circles, making clear-cut distinctions between the different areas of responsibility rather difficult to make. For the purposes of our discussion, though, responsibilities for the ecological environment are concerned with business impacts specifically on the sustainability of the natural environment, the core features of which we will now introduce.

Core features of ecological responsibility

Sustainability of the natural environment is essentially about the long-term maintenance of the earth's natural ability to sustain itself. Human progress, and industrialization in particular, are widely thought to pose a severe challenge for the continued sustainability of our society given expectations about increasing demands and limits to carrying capacity. Some have suggested that living sustainably is like making an investment and living on the interest, not on the capital (Savitz and Weber, 2006). For corporations, this presents a number of critical responsibilities in that it is business as much as any other institution that extracts resources, creates pollution through its processes and products, and generates waste that has to be absorbed by the earth in some way.

To implement these responsibilities, various authors (Bradbury and Clair, 1999; Hart, 1997; Menon and Menon, 1997; Stead and Stead, 2004) have suggested a number of actions that firms can take, including:

● *Using natural resources efficiently and minimizing waste.* The earth has limited resources and finite capacity for absorbing waste. Corporations have a role to play in ensuring that non-renewable resources such as fossil fuels are preserved and renewable resources such as soft woods are managed sustainably.

- *Pollution prevention.* Corporations, especially those in manufacturing, can be major polluters, giving rise to responsibilities to minimize pollution (end-of-pipe technologies) and the causes of pollution (clean technologies).
- *Establishing product stewardship.* Adopting a 'cradle-to-grave' approach to product management means that corporations can take responsibility for a product's ecological impacts from resource extraction right through to disposal and reuse.
- *Innovation in products, processes and services.* Progress to sustainability will require radical transformation in the kinds of things that corporations do and produce. In order to achieve these changes they need to innovate for the future.
- *Managing climate change.* The production of greenhouse gases by industrial processes and products poses a serious challenge to the livelihood of the planet. It is increasingly recognized that firms have a responsibility to manage their 'carbon footprint' by steadily reducing their reliance on fossil fuels and moving to 'carbon-neutral' products and processes.
- *Ensuring resource security and resource justice.* Finally, sustainability is not just about whether there are sufficient natural resources, but also about who owns them and who is able to access them. Corporations may be expected increasingly to play a role in ensuring that scarce essential resources such as water, oil and food are available to those who need them.

In all of these areas, corporations can play a significant role. However, because of their nature, the ecological responsibilities of corporations (like so many social responsibilities) are not necessarily individualized responsibilities that firms have to take on alone, but may also sometimes be collective responsibilities that they share with others. In the ecological arena, partnerships with NGOs and participation in regulatory initiatives with governments have been common forms of CSR for corporations (Bendell, 2000; Cashore, 2002), and many initiatives require collaboration with other firms in the product supply chain.

Introducing the Readings

The two readings offer very different, but ultimately complimentary, views on the issue of corporate responsibilities in the ecological environment. While the first is concerned with how ecological responsibility can be integrated into corporate strategy to generate revenue for the firm, the second considers the political role that corporations can take in the realm of environmental regulation.

Integrating ecological responsibilities into corporate strategy

The first reading is a classic – and, indeed, one of the first articles in *Harvard Business Review* to deal with environmental issues in business. Written by Stuart Hart, a business school professor at Cornell University, the article focuses on describing the ecological problems faced by business and society today, and then spelling out how management of these problems can be successfully integrated within the core strategy of the firm. In this sense, the article has much in common with the two articles that appeared in the previous chapter on community responsibilities – they, too, were about linking a particular element of CSR with corporate strategy. As such, this very much reflects an instrumental view of CSR, which sees the solution of social or ecological problems as an opportunity for business to make money rather than just as a problem that needs to be avoided or fixed. As Hart makes clear in the final sentence of the article: 'In the final analysis, it makes good business sense to pursue strategies for a sustainable world.'

Despite this avowedly instrumental stance, Hart also suggests other reasons why corporations should be involved in solving environmental problems – basically, that they are the only ones that can. As he puts it: 'Corporations are the only organizations with the resources, the technology, the global reach, and ultimately, the motivation to achieve sustainability' and therefore, 'like it or not, the responsibility for ensuring a sustainable world falls largely on the shoulders of the world's enterprises'. Therefore, in urging corporations to 'lead the way' in solving ecological problems by influencing governments and consumers, we see some echoes of the more political role that corporations can take by engaging in CSR. This idea, that corporations may play a role in shaping public policy on ecological problems, is taken up explicitly in the article that follows.

Political dimensions of ecological responsibilities

The second reading in this chapter, by David Levy and Daniel Egan, looks at the role of corporations in national and international policy-making around climate change. In recent years, climate change has become perhaps the single most important issue in the environmental arena of CSR. As a result, a number of multinationals have suggested that business has no choice but to develop a response that takes climate change seriously. For instance, while BP claims that 'we can play a major part in finding and implementing solutions to one of the greatest challenges of this century',[1] the Ford Motor Group published a stand-alone report on climate change and business in 2005 which suggested that

> concerns about climate change – along with growing constraints on the use and availability of carbon-based fuels – affect our operations, our customers, our investors and our communities. The issue warrants precautionary, prudent and early actions to enhance our competitiveness and protect our profitability in an increasingly carbon-constrained economy.[2]

Levy and Egan examine the different types of influence corporations can and have had on the development of climate change policy. Their evidence suggests that corporations are active players in the political game and can play a significant role in shaping the institutions that govern environmental protection, especially at the national level. These are important findings, but in some respects it could actually be said that this is not really an article about CSR at all – the term 'Corporate Social Responsibility' does not even appear in the text. However, a broad view of CSR requires its inclusion. This is because it demonstrates that corporate engagement on 'CSR issues' such as the environment do not actually always happen under the banner of CSR. Lobbying activities and other political deal-making by corporations have crucial impacts on the future of the ecological environment, but may never appear in firms' glossy CSR reports, and until recently have not even been widely discussed by CSR academics. This is now beginning to change with a growing interest emerging in 'responsible lobbying' (e.g. AccountAbility, 2005), and much closer attention being given to the political dimensions of CSR (Matten and Crane, 2005; Scherer and Palazzo, 2007). As such, Levy and Egan's article provides an illuminating account of how corporate responsibilities for the ecological environment encompass political as well as economic actions by firms.

Study Questions

1   'To be responsible, corporations have to be sustainable.' Critically evaluate this statement in the light of current business approaches to the ecological environment.
2   What are the core features of corporate ecological responsibility? To what extent have these responsibilities changed over time?
3   Do ecological problems present threats or opportunities to corporations? Provide a critical review based on the articles by Hart, and Levy and Egan.
4   How can a firm integrate its ecological responsibilities into its core strategies?
5   What are the different ways that firms can influence environmental policy-making at the national and international levels? What would constitute a responsible approach to this practice?

Notes

1   http://www.bp.com/subsection.do?categoryId=9007561&contentId= 7014605. Downloaded on 9 February 2007.
2   Ford report on the business impact of climate change, 2005.

References

AccountAbility (2005) *Towards Responsible Lobbying: Leadership and Public Policy*, London: AccountAbility.
Bendell, J. (ed.) (2000) *Terms for Endearment: Business, NGOs and Sustainable Development*, Sheffield: Greenleaf.

Bradbury, H. and Clair, J. A. (1999) 'Promoting Sustainable Organizations with Sweden's Natural Step', *Academy of Management Executive* 13(4): 63–74.

Cashore, B. (2002) 'Legitimacy and the Privatization of Environmental Governance: How Non-state Market-driven (NSMD) Governance Systems Gain Rule-making Authority', *Governance* 15(4): 503–529.

Hart, S. (1997) 'Beyond Greening: Strategies for a Sustainable World', *Harvard Business Review* (January–February): 67–76.

Hoffman, A. (2001) *From Heresy to Dogma: An Institutional History of Corporate Environmentalism* (expanded edn), Palo Alto, CA: Stanford University Press.

Matten, D. and Crane, A. (2005) 'Corporate Citizenship: Towards an Extended Theoretical Conceptualization', *Academy of Management Review* 30(1): 166–179.

Menon, A. and Menon, A. (1997) 'Enviropreneurial Marketing Strategy: The Emergence of Corporate Environmentalism as Market Strategy', *Journal of Marketing* 61(1): 51–67.

Savitz, A. and Weber, K. (2006) *The Triple Bottom Line: How Today's Best-run Companies are Achieving Economic, Social and Environmental Success – and How You Can Too*, New York: Jossey-Bass.

Scherer, A. and Palazzo, G. (2007) 'Toward a Political Conception of Corporate Responsibility: Business and Society Seen from a Habermasian Perspective', *Academy of Management Review* 32(4): in press.

Stead, W. and Stead, J. (2004) *Sustainable Strategic Management*, London: M. Sharpe.

BEYOND GREENING:
STRATEGIES FOR A SUSTAINABLE WORLD

Stuart Hart

The environmental revolution has been almost three decades in the making, and it has changed forever how companies do business. In the 1960s and 1970s, corporations were in a state of denial regarding their impact on the environment. Then a series of highly visible ecological problems created a groundswell of support for strict government regulation. In the United States, Lake Erie was dead. In Europe, the Rhine was on fire. In Japan, people were dying of mercury poisoning.

Today many companies have accepted their responsibility to do no harm to the environment. Products and production processes are becoming cleaner, and where such change is under way, the environment is on the mend. In the industrialized nations, more and more companies are "going green" as they realize that they can reduce pollution and increase profits simultaneously. We have come a long way.

But the distance we've traveled will seem small when, in 30 years, we look back at the 1990s. Beyond greening lies an enormous challenge – and an enormous opportunity. The challenge is to develop a *sustainable global economy*: an economy that the planet is capable of supporting indefinitely. Although we may be approaching ecological recovery in the developed world, the planet as a whole remains on an unsustainable course. Those who think that sustainability is only a matter of pollution control are missing the bigger picture. Even if all the companies in the developed world were to achieve zero emissions by the year 2000, the earth would still be stressed beyond what biologists refer to as its carrying capacity. Increasingly, the scourges of the late twentieth century – depleted farmland, fisheries, and forests; choking urban pollution; poverty; infectious disease; and migration – are spilling over geopolitical borders. The simple fact is this: in meeting our needs, we are destroying the ability of future generations to meet theirs.

The roots of the problem – explosive population growth and rapid economic development in the emerging economies – are political and social issues that exceed the mandate and the capabilities of any corporation. At the same time, corporations are the only organizations with the resources, the technology, the global reach, and, ultimately, the motivation to achieve sustainability.

It is easy to state the case in the negative: faced with impoverished customers, degraded environments, failing political systems, and unraveling societies, it will be increasingly difficult for corporations to do business. But the positive case is even more powerful. The more we learn about the challenges of sustainability, the clearer it is that we are poised at the threshold of a historic moment in which many of the world's industries may be transformed.

To date, the business logic for greening has been largely operational or technical: bottom-up pollution-prevention programs have saved companies billions of dollars. However, few executives realize that environmental opportunities might actually become a major source of *revenue growth*. Greening has been framed in terms of risk reduction, reengineering, or cost cutting. Rarely is greening linked to strategy or technology development, and as a result, most companies fail to recognize opportunities of potentially staggering proportions.

Worlds in Collision

The achievement of sustainability will mean billions of dollars in products, services, and technologies that barely exist today. Whereas yesterday's businesses were often oblivious to their negative impact on the environment and today's responsible businesses strive for zero impact, tomorrow's businesses must learn to make a positive impact. Increasingly, companies will be selling solutions to the world's environmental problems.

Envisioning tomorrow's businesses, therefore, requires a clear under-standing of those problems. To move beyond greening to sustainability, we must first unravel a complex set of global interdependencies. In fact, the global economy is really three different, overlapping economies.

The *market economy* is the familiar world of commerce comprising both the developed nations and the emerging economies.[1] About a billion people – one-sixth of the world's population – live in the developed countries of the market economy. Those affluent societies account for more than 75 percent of the world's energy and resource consumption and create the bulk of industrial, toxic, and consumer waste. The developed economies thus leave large ecological *footprints* – defined as the amount of land required to meet a typical consumer's needs. (See Exhibit 1, "Ecological footprints.")

Despite such intense use of energy and materials, however, levels of pollution are relatively low in the developed economies. Three factors account for this seeming paradox: stringent environmental regulations, the greening of industry, and the relocation of the most polluting activities (such as commodity processing and heavy manufacturing) to the emerging market economies. Thus to some extent the greening of the developed world has been at the expense of the environments in emerging economies. Given the much larger population base in those countries, their rapid industrialization could easily offset the environmental gains made in the developed economies. Consider, for example, that the emerging economies in Asia and Latin America (and now Eastern Europe and the former Soviet Union) have added nearly 2 billion people to the market economy over the past 40 years.

With economic growth comes urbanization. Today one of every three people in the world lives in a city. By 2025, it will be two out of three. Demographers predict that by that year there will be well over 30 megacities with populations exceeding 8 million and more than 500 cities with popu-lations exceeding 1 million. Urbanization on this scale presents enormous infrastructural and environmental challenges.

Because industrialization has focused initially on commodities and heavy manufacturing, cities in many emerging economies suffer from oppressive

United States   The Netherlands   India

In the United States, it takes 12.2 acres to supply the average person's basic needs; in the Netherlands, 8 acres; in India, 1 acre. The Dutch ecological footprint covers 15 times the area of the Netherlands, whereas India's footprint exceeds its area by only about 35 percent. Most strikingly, if the entire world lived like North Americans, it would take three planet Earths to support the present world population

Source: Donella Meadows, "Our 'Footprints' Are Treading Too Much Earth," *Charleston (S.C.) Gazette*, April 1, 1996.

Exhibit 1 Ecological footprints

levels of pollution. Acid rain is a growing problem, especially in places where coal combustion is unregulated. The World Bank estimates that by 2010 there will be more than 1 billion motor vehicles in the world. Concentrated in cities, they will double current levels of energy use, smog precursors, and emissions of greenhouse gas.

The second economy is the *survival economy*: the traditional, village-based way of life found in the rural parts of most developing countries. It is made up of 3 billion people, mainly Africans, Indians, and Chinese who are subsistence oriented and meet their basic needs directly from nature. Demographers generally agree that the world's population, currently growing by about 90 million people per year, will roughly double over the next 40 years. The developing nations will account for 90 percent of that growth, and most of it will occur in the survival economy.

Owing in part to the rapid expansion of the market economy, existence in the survival economy is becoming increasingly precarious. Extractive industries and infrastructure development have, in many cases, degraded the ecosystems upon which the survival economy depends. Rural populations are driven further into poverty as they compete for scarce natural resources. Women and children now spend on average four to six hours per day searching for fuelwood and four to six hours per day drawing and carrying water. Ironically, those conditions encourage high fertility rates because, in the short run, children help the family to garner needed resources. But in the long run, population growth in the survival economy only reinforces a vicious cycle of resource depletion and poverty.

Short-term survival pressures often force these rapidly growing rural populations into practices that cause long-term damage to forests, soil, and water. When wood becomes scarce, people burn dung for fuel, one of the greatest – and least well-known – environmental hazards in the world today. Contaminated drinking water is an equally grave problem. The World Health Organization estimates that burning dung and drinking contaminated water together cause 8 million deaths per year.

As it becomes more and more difficult to live off the land, millions of desperate people migrate to already overcrowded cities. In China, for example, an estimated 120 million people now roam from city to city, landless and jobless, driven from their villages by deforestation, soil erosion, floods, or droughts. Worldwide, the number of such "environmental refugees" from the survival economy may be as high as 500 million people, and the figure is growing.

The third economy is *nature's economy*, which consists of the natural systems and resources that support the market and the survival economies. Nonrenewable resources, such as oil, metals, and other minerals, are finite. Renewable resources, such as soils and forests, will replenish themselves – as long as their use does not exceed critical thresholds.

Technological innovations have created substitutes for many commonly used non-renewable resources, for example, optical fiber now replaces copper wire. And in the developed economies, demand for some virgin materials may actually diminish in the decades ahead because of reuse and recycling. Ironically, the greatest threat to sustainable development today is depletion of the world's *renewable* resources.

Forests, soils, water, and fisheries are all being pushed beyond their limits by human population growth and rapid industrial development. Insufficient fresh water may prove to be the most vexing problem in the developing world over the next decade, as agricultural, commercial, and residential uses increase. Water tables are being drawn down at an alarming rate, especially in the most heavily populated nations, such as China and India.

Soil is another resource at risk. More than 10 percent of the world's topsoil has been seriously eroded. Available cropland and rangeland are shrinking. Existing crop varieties are no longer responding to increased use of fertilizer. As a consequence, per capita world production of both grain and meat peaked and began to decline during the 1980s. Meanwhile, the world's 18 major oceanic fisheries have now reached or actually exceeded their maximum sustainable yields.

By some estimates, humankind now uses more than 40 percent of the planet's net primary productivity. If, as projected, the population doubles over the next 40 years, we may outcompete most other animal species for food, driving many to extinction. In short, human activity now exceeds sustainability on a global scale. (See Exhibit 2, "Major challenges to sustainability.")

As we approach the twenty-first century, the interdependence of the three economic spheres is increasingly evident. In fact, the three economies have become worlds in collision, creating the major social and environmental challenges facing the planet: climate change, pollution, resource depletion, poverty, and inequality.

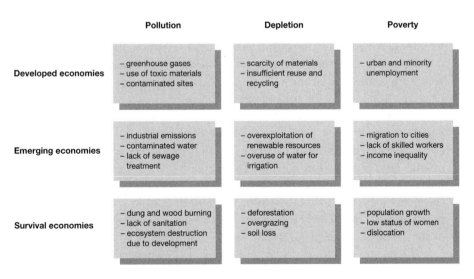

	Pollution	Depletion	Poverty
Developed economies	– greenhouse gases – use of toxic materials – contaminated sites	– scarcity of materials – insufficient reuse and recycling	– urban and minority unemployment
Emerging economies	– industrial emissions – contaminated water – lack of sewage treatment	– overexploitation of renewable resources – overuse of water for irrigation	– migration to cities – lack of skilled workers – income inequality
Survival economies	– dung and wood burning – lack of sanitation – ecosystem destruction due to development	– deforestation – overgrazing – soil loss	– population growth – low status of women – dislocation

Exhibit 2 Major challenges to sustainability

Consider, for example, that the average American today consumes 17 times more than his or her Mexican counterpart (emerging economy) and hundreds of times more than the average Ethiopian (survival economy). The levels of material and energy consumption in the United States require large quantities of raw materials and commodities, sourced increasingly from the survival economy and produced in emerging economies.

In the survival economy, massive infrastructure development (for example, dams, irrigation projects, highways, mining operations, and power generation projects), often aided by agencies, banks, and corporations in the developed countries, has provided access to raw materials. Unfortunately, such development has often had devastating consequences for nature's economy and has tended to strengthen existing political and economic elites, with little benefit to those in the survival economy.

At the same time, infrastructure development projects have contributed to a global glut of raw materials and hence to a long-term fall in commodity prices. And as commodity prices have fallen relative to the prices of manufactured goods, the currencies of developing countries have weakened and their terms of trade have become less favorable. Their purchasing power declines while their already substantial debt load becomes even larger. The net effect of this dynamic has been the transfer of vast amounts of wealth (estimated at $40 billion per year since 1985) from developing to developed countries, producing a vicious cycle of resource exploitation and pollution to service mounting debt. Today developing nations have a combined debt of more than $1.2 trillion, equal to nearly half of their collective gross national product.

Strategies for a Sustainable World

Nearly three decades ago, environmentalists such as Paul Ehrlich and Barry Commoner made this simple but powerful observation about sustainable development: the total environmental burden (EB) created by human activity is a function of three factors. They are population (P); affluence (A), which is a proxy for consumption; and technology (T), which is how wealth is created. The product of these three factors determines the total environmental burden. It can be expressed as a formula: $EB = P \times A \times T$.

Achieving sustainability will require stabilizing or reducing the environmental burden. That can be done by decreasing the human population, lowering the level of affluence (consumption), or changing fundamentally the technology used to create wealth. The first option, lowering the human population, does not appear feasible short of draconian political measures or the occurrence of a major public-health crisis that causes mass mortality.

The second option, decreasing the level of affluence, would only make the problem worse, because poverty and population growth go hand in hand: demographers have long known that birth rates are inversely correlated with level of education and standard of living. Thus stabilizing the human population will require improving the education and economic standing of the world's poor, particularly women of childbearing age. That can be accomplished only by creating wealth on a massive scale. Indeed, it may be necessary to grow the world economy as much as tenfold just to provide basic amenities to a population of 8 billion to 10 billion.

That leaves the third option: changing the technology used to create the goods and services that constitute the world's wealth. Although population and consumption may be societal issues, technology is the business of business.

If economic activity must increase tenfold over what it is today just to provide the bare essentials to a population double its current size, then technology will have to improve twentyfold merely to keep the planet at its current levels of environmental burden. Those who believe that ecological disaster will somehow be averted must also appreciate the commercial implications of such a belief: over the next decade or so, sustainable development will constitute one of the biggest opportunities in the history of commerce.

Nevertheless, as of today few companies have incorporated sustainability into their strategic thinking. Instead, environmental strategy consists largely of piecemeal projects aimed at controlling or preventing pollution. Focusing on sustainability requires putting business strategies to a new test. Taking the entire planet as the context in which they do business, companies must ask whether they are part of the solution to social and environmental problems or part of the problem. Only when a company thinks in those terms can it begin to develop a vision of sustainability – a shaping logic that goes beyond today's internal, operational focus on greening to a more external, strategic focus on sustainable development. Such a vision is needed to guide companies through three stages of environmental strategy.

Stage One: Pollution Prevention. The first step for most companies is to make the shift from pollution control to pollution prevention. Pollution control means cleaning up waste after it has been created. Pollution prevention focuses on minimizing or eliminating waste before it is created. Much like total quality management, pollution prevention strategies depend on continuous improvement efforts to reduce waste and energy use. This transformation is driven by a compelling logic: pollution prevention pays. Emerging global standards for environmental management systems (ISO 14,000, for example) also have created strong incentives for companies to develop such capabilities.

Over the past decade, companies have sought to avoid colliding with nature's economy (and incurring the associated added costs) through greening and prevention strategies. Aeroquip Corporation, a $2.5 billion manufacturer of hoses, fittings, and couplings, saw an opportunity here. Like most industrial suppliers, Aeroquip never thought of itself as a provider of environmental solutions. But in 1990, its executives realized that the company's products might be especially valuable in meeting the need to reduce waste and prevent pollution. Aeroquip has generated a $250 million business by focusing its attention on developing products that reduce emissions. As companies in emerging economies realize the competitive benefits of using raw materials and resources more productively, businesses like Aeroquip's will continue to grow.

The emerging economies cannot afford to repeat all the environmental mistakes of Western development. With the sustainability imperative in mind, BASF, the German chemical giant, is helping to design and build chemical industries in China, India, Indonesia, and Malaysia that are less polluting than in the past. By colocating facilities that in the West have been geographically dispersed, BASF is able to create industrial ecosystems in which the waste from one process becomes the raw material for another. Colocation solves a problem common in the West, where recycling waste is often infeasible because transporting it from one site to another is dangerous and costly.

Stage Two: Product Stewardship. Product stewardship focuses on minimizing not only pollution from manufacturing but also all environmental impacts associated with the full life cycle of a product. As companies in stage one move closer to zero emissions, reducing the use of materials and production of waste requires fundamental changes in underlying product and process design.

Design for environment (DFE), a tool for creating products that are easier to recover, reuse, or recycle, is becoming increasingly important. With DFE, all the effects that a product could have on the environment are examined during its design phase. Cradle-to-grave analysis begins and ends outside the boundaries of a company's operations – it includes a full assessment of all inputs to the product and examines how customers use and dispose of it. DFE thus captures a broad range of external perspectives by including technical staff, environmental experts, end customers, and even community representatives in the process. Dow Chemical Company has pioneered the use of a board-level advisory panel of environmental experts and external representatives to aid its product-stewardship efforts.

By reducing materials and energy consumption, DFE can be highly profitable. Consider Xerox Corporation's Asset Recycle Management (ARM) program, which uses leased Xerox copiers as sources of high-quality, low-cost parts and components for new machines. A well-developed infrastructure for taking back leased copiers combined with a sophisticated remanufacturing process allows parts and components to be reconditioned, tested, and then reassembled into "new" machines. Xerox estimates that ARM savings in raw materials, labor, and waste disposal in 1995 alone were in the $300-million to $400-million range. In taking recycling to this level, Xerox has reconceptualized its business. By redefining the product-in-use as part of the company's asset base, Xerox has discovered a way to add value and

Aracruz Celulose: A Strategy for the Survival Economy

"Poverty is one of the world's leading polluters," notes Erling Lorentzen, founder and chairman of Aracruz Celulose. The $2 billion Brazilian company is the world's largest producer of eucalyptus pulp. "You can't expect people who don't eat a proper meal to be concerned about the environment."[1]

From the very start, Aracruz has been built around a vision of sustainable development. Lorentzen understood that building a viable forest-products business in Brazil's impoverished and deforested state of Espirito Santo would require the simultaneous improvement of nature's economy and the survival economy.

First, to restore nature's economy, the company took advantage of a tax incentive for tree planting in the late 1960s and began buying and reforesting cut-over land. By 1992, the company had acquired over 200,000 hectares and planted 130,000 hectares with managed eucalyptus; the rest was restored as conservation land. By reforesting what had become highly degraded land, unsuitable for agriculture, the company addressed a fundamental environmental problem. At the same time, it created a first-rate source of fiber for its pulping operations. Aracruz's forest practices and its ability to clone seedlings have given the company advantages in both cost and quality.

Aracruz has tackled the problem of poverty head-on. Every year, the company gives away millions of eucalyptus seedlings to local farmers. It is a preemptive strategy, aimed at reducing the farmers' need to deplete the natural forests for fuel or lumber. Aracruz also has a long-term commitment to capability building. In the early years, Aracruz was able to hire local people for very low wages because of their desperate situation. But instead of simply exploiting the abundant supply of cheap labor, the company embarked on an aggressive social-investment strategy, spending $125 million to support the creation of hospitals, schools, housing, and a training center for employees. In fact, until recently, Aracruz spent more on its social investments than it did on wages (about $1.20 for every $1 in wages). Since that time, the standard of living has improved dramatically, as has productivity. The company no longer needs to invest so heavily in social infrastructure.

1 Marguerite Rigoglioso, "Stewards of the Seventh Generation," *Harvard Business School Bulletin*, April 1996, p. 55.

lower costs. It can continually provide its lease customers with the latest product upgrades, giving them state-of-the-art functionality with minimal environmental impact.

Product stewardship is thus one way to reduce consumption in the developed economies. It may also aid the quest for sustainability because developing nations often try to emulate what they see happening in the developed nations. Properly executed, product stewardship also offers the potential for revenue growth through product differentiation. For example, Dunlop Tire Corporation and Akzo Nobel recently announced a new radial tire that makes use of an aramid fiber belt rather than the conventional steel belt. The new design makes recycling easier because it eliminates the expensive cryogenic crushing required to separate the steel belts from the tire's other materials. Because the new fiber-belt tire is 30 percent lighter, it dramatically improves gas mileage. Moreover, it is a safer tire because it improves the traction control of antilock braking systems.

The evolution from pollution prevention to product stewardship is now happening in multinational companies such as Dow, DuPont, Monsanto, Xerox, ABB, Philips, and Sony. For example, as part of a larger sustainability strategy dubbed A Growing Partnership with Nature, DuPont's agricultural products business developed a new type of herbicide that has helped farmers around the world reduce their annual use of chemicals by more than 45 million pounds. The new Sulfonylurea herbicides have also led to a 1-billion-pound reduction in the amount of chemical waste produced in the manufacture of agricultural chemicals. These herbicides are effective at 1 percent to 5 percent of the application rates of traditional chemicals, are non-toxic to animals and nontarget species, and biodegrade in the soil, leaving virtually no residue on crops. Because they require so much less material in their manufacture, they are also highly profitable.

Stage Three: Clean Technology. Companies with their eye on the future can begin to plan for and invest in tomorrow's technologies. The simple fact is that the existing technology base in many industries is not environmentally sustainable. The chemical industry, for example, while having made substantial headway over the past decade in pollution prevention and product stewardship, is still limited by its dependence on the chlorine molecule. (Many organochlorides are toxic or persistent or bioaccumulative.) As long as the industry relies on its historical competencies in chlorine chemistry, it will have trouble making major progress toward sustainability.

Monsanto is one company that is consciously developing new competencies. It is shifting the technology base for its agriculture business from bulk chemicals to biotechnology. It is betting that the bioengineering of crops rather than the application of chemical pesticides or fertilizers represents a sustainable path to increased agricultural yields.

Clean technologies are desperately needed in the emerging economies of Asia. Urban pollution there has reached oppressive levels. But precisely because manufacturing growth is so high – capital stock doubles every six years – there is an unprecedented opportunity to replace current product and process technologies with new, cleaner ones.

Japan's Research Institute for Innovative Technology for the Earth is one of several new research and technology consortia focusing on the development and commercialisation of clean technologies for the developing world. Having been provided with funding and staff by the Japanese government and more than 40 corporations, RITE has set forth an ambitious 100-year plan to create the next generation of power technology, which will eliminate or neutralize greenhouse gas emissions.

Sustainability Vision

Pollution prevention, product stewardship, and clean technology all move a company toward sustainability. But without a framework to give direction to those activities, their impact will dissipate. A vision of sustainability for an industry or a company is like a road map to the future, showing the way products and services must evolve and what new competencies will be needed to get there. Few companies today have such a road map. Ironically, chemical companies, regarded only a decade ago as the worst environmental villains, are among the few large corporations to have engaged the challenge of sustainable development seriously.

Companies can begin by taking stock of each component of what I call their *sustainability portfolio*. (See Exhibit 3, "The Sustainability Portfolio.") Is there an overarching vision of sustainability that gives direction to the company's activities? To what extent has the company progressed through the three stages of environmental strategy – from pollution prevention to product stewardship to clean technology?

Consider the auto industry. During the 1970s, government regulation of tailpipe emissions forced the industry to focus on pollution control. In the 1980s, the industry began to tackle pollution prevention. Initiatives such as the Corporate Average Fuel Efficiency requirement and the Toxic Release Inventory led auto companies to examine their product designs and manufacturing processes in order to improve fuel economy and lower emissions from their plants.

The 1990s are witnessing the first signs of product stewardship. In Germany, the 1990 "take-back" law required auto manufacturers to take responsibility for their vehicles at the end of their useful lives. Innovators such as BMW have influenced the design of new cars with their *design for disassembly* efforts. Industry-level consortia such as the Partnership for a New Generation of Vehicles are driven largely by the product stewardship logic of lowering the environmental impact of automobiles throughout their life cycle.

Early attempts to promote clean technology include such initiatives as California's zero-emission vehicle law and the U.N. Climate Change

	internal	external
tomorrow	**Clean technology** Is the environmental performance of our products limited by our existing competency base? Is there potential to realize major improvements through new technology?	**Sustainability vision** Does our corporate vision direct us toward the solution of social and environmental problems? Does our vision guide the development of new technologies, markets, products, and processes?
today	**Pollution prevention** Where are the most significant waste and emission streams from our current operations? Can we lower costs and risks by eliminating waste of the source or by using it as useful input?	**Product stewardship** What are the implications for product design and development if we assume responsibility for a product's entire life cycle? Can we add value or lower costs while simultaneously reducing the impact of our products?

This simple diagnostic tool can help any company determine whether its strategy is consistent with sustainability. First, assess your company's capability in each of the four quadrants by answering the questions in each box. Then rate yourself on the following scale for each quadrant: 1–nonexistent; 2–emerging; 3–established; or 4–institutionalized.

Most companies will be heavily skewed toward the lower left-hand quadrant, reflecting investment in pollution prevention. However, without investments in future technologies and markets (the upper half of the portfolio), the company's environmental strategy will not meet evolving needs.

Unbalanced portfolios spell trouble: a bottom-heavy portfolio suggests a good position today but future vulnerability. A top-heavy portfolio indicates a vision of sustainability without the operational or analytical skills needed to implement it. A portfolio skewed to the left side of the chart indicates a preoccupation with handling the environmental challenge through internal process improvements and technology-development initiatives. Finally, a portfolio skewed to the right side, although highly open and public, runs the risk of being labeled a "greenwash" because the underlying plant operations and core technology still cause significant environmental harm.

Exhibit 3 The sustainability portfolio

Convention, which ultimately will limit greenhouse gases on a global scale. But early efforts by industry incumbents have been either incremental – for example, natural-gas vehicles – or defensive in nature. Electric-vehicle programs, for instance, have been used to demonstrate the infeasibility of this technology rather than to lead the industry to a fundamentally cleaner technology.

Although the auto industry has made progress, it falls far short of sustainability. For the vast majority of auto companies, pollution prevention and product stewardship are the end of the road. Most auto executives assume that if they close the loop in both production and design, they will have accomplished all the necessary environmental objectives.

But step back and try to imagine a sustainable vision for the industry. Growth in the emerging markets will generate massive transportation needs in the coming decades. Already the rush is on to stake out positions in China, India, and Latin America. But what form will this opportunity take?

Consider the potential impact of automobiles on China alone. Today there are fewer than 1 million cars on the road in China. However, with a population of more than 1 billion, it would take less than 30 percent market penetration to equal the current size of the U.S. car market (12 million to

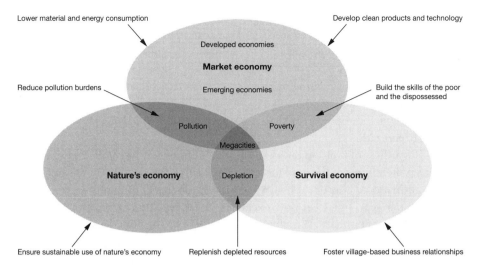

Lower material and energy consumption

Develop clean products and technology

Developed economies

Market economy

Emerging economies

Reduce pollution burdens

Build the skills of the poor
and the dispossessed

Pollution

Poverty

Megacities

Nature's economy

Depletion

Survival economy

Ensure sustainable use of nature's economy

Replenish depleted resources

Foster village-based business relationships

Exhibit 4 Building sustainable business strategies

15 million units sold per year). Ultimately, China might demand 50 million or more units annually. Because China's energy and transportation infrastructures are still being defined, there is an opportunity to develop a clean technology yielding important environmental and competitive benefits.

Amory Lovins of the Rocky Mountain Institute has demonstrated the feasibility of building *hypercars* – vehicles that are fully recyclable, 20 times more energy efficient, 100 times cleaner, and cheaper than existing cars. These vehicles retain the safety and performance of conventional cars but achieve radical simplification through the use of lightweight, composite materials, fewer parts, virtual prototyping, regenerative braking, and very small, hybrid engines. Hypercars, which are more akin to computers on wheels than to cars with microchips, may render obsolete most of the competencies associated with today's auto manufacturing – for example, metal stamping, tool and die making, and the internal combustion engine.

Assume for a minute that clean technology like the hypercar or Mazda's soon-to-be-released hydrogen rotary engine can be developed for a market such as China's. Now try to envision a transportation infrastructure capable of accommodating so many cars. How long will it take before gridlock and traffic jams force the auto industry to a halt? Sustainability will require new transportation solutions for the needs of emerging economies with huge populations. Will the giants in the auto industry be prepared for such radical change, or will they leave the field to new ventures that are not encumbered by the competencies of the past?

A clear and fully integrated environmental strategy should not only guide competency development, it should also shape the company's relationship to customers, suppliers, other companies, policymakers, and all its stakeholders. Companies can and must change the way customers think by creating preferences for products and services consistent with sustainability. Companies must become educators rather than mere marketers of products. (See Exhibit 4, "Building sustainable business strategies.")

For senior executives, embracing the quest for sustainability may well require a leap of faith. Some may feel that the risks associated with investing in unstable and unfamiliar markets outweigh the potential benefits. Others will recognize the power of such a positive mission to galvanize people in their organizations.

Regardless of their opinions on sustainability, executives will not be able to keep their heads in the sand for long. Since 1980, foreign direct investment by multinational corporations has increased from $500 billion to nearly $3 trillion per year. In fact, it now exceeds official development-assistance aid in developing countries. With free trade on the rise, the next decade may see the figure increase by another order of magnitude. The challenges presented by emerging markets in Asia and Latin America demand a new way of conceptualizing business opportunities. The rapid growth in emerging economies cannot be sustained in the face of mounting environmental deterioration, poverty, and resource depletion. In the coming decade, companies will be challenged to develop clean technologies and to implement strategies that drastically reduce the environmental burden in the developing world while simultaneously increasing its wealth and standard of living.

Like it or not, the responsibility for ensuring a sustainable world falls largely on the shoulders of the world's enterprises, the economic engines of the future. Clearly, public policy innovations (at both the national and international levels) and changes in individual consumption patterns will be needed to move toward sustainability. But corporations can and should lead the way, helping to shape public policy and driving change in consumers' behavior. In the final analysis, it makes good business sense to pursue strategies for a sustainable world.

Note

1   The terms *market economy, survival economy*, and *nature's economy* were suggested to me by Vandana Shiva, *Ecology and the Policies of Survival* (New Delhi: United Nations University Press, 1991).

CORPORATE POLITICAL ACTION IN THE GLOBAL POLITY: NATIONAL AND TRANSNATIONAL STRATEGIES IN THE CLIMATE CHANGE NEGOTIATIONS

David Levy and Daniel Egan

Climate change is a global environmental problem of potentially devastating proportions. Caused by the build-up of greenhouse gases, particularly carbon dioxide and methane, in the earth's atmosphere, climate change is a global commons issue requiring a coordinated international response. Because greenhouse gases are predominantly produced through activities associated with contemporary industrial economies, however, such a response is constrained by powerful economic and political forces which are unlikely to question the fundamental relationship between capitalism and ecological degradation. As capitalism and its ecological consequences become more universal, 'a *global* analysis of the power of capital is essential' (Gill and Law 1993: 102). Such a global analysis of the power of capital is essential for understanding the possibilities for and limits to international efforts to address global environmental issues such as climate change.

A major component of such an analysis is an understanding of how capital operates in the political arena. In the context of accelerating international economic integration and the growth of international institutions such as the World Trade Organisation, there has been growing concern that multinational capital has begun to turn to international fora to circumvent constraints from governments and social movements at the national state level. If the national state has historically been a site where the power of capital could be contested, the increased mobility of capital and interdependence of national economies within a system of international institutions defined by market rather than democratic values has, it is argued, eroded the autonomy and power of the national state and outmanoeuvred nationally-based social movements (Barnet and Cavanagh 1994; Korten 1995; Reich 1991; Strange 1996). The subsequent weakening of the national state's ability to manage national economies and construct nationally-defined social contracts, as well as the diffusion of state responsibilities to a variety of private and non-state actors, has resulted in 'a tendential "hollowing out" of the national state' (Jessop 1994: 251). The globalisation thesis sees the national state as 'look[ing] more and more like an institution of a bygone age' (Barnet and Cavanagh 1994: 19), as 'victims of the market economy' (Strange 1996: 14).

While this debate has focused on the ways in which the tripartite relationship among business, the state, and social forces is being reshaped at the national level, relatively little attention has been paid to the relationship between capital and international institutions. Proponents of the globalisation thesis generally assume that capital prefers to operate at the international level to avoid national regulation. In contrast to this monolithic under-standing, we distinguish two major types of international institutions. *Enabling* institutions are those that provide the infrastructure of a neo-liberal world trade and investment regime and in which multinational capital is highly influential and supportive; *regulatory* institutions are those respon-sible for negotiating and promulgating social, labour and environmental policies. We argue in this paper that capital is far from uncontested in these arenas. More specifically, based on a case study of the climate change negotiations, we argue that many large companies fear the emergence of an international environmental regulatory structure beyond the channels of influence to which they are accustomed at the national level. This sug-gests that, in contrast to the globalisation thesis, capital is undertaking a contingent, multi-dimensional strategy relative to the national state and international institutions.

The growth of international regimes to address global environmental problems has been analysed extensively in the burgeoning literature on regime theory (Haas, Keohane and Levy 1993; Haggard and Simmons 1987; Young 1994). This literature, even in its more institutionalist variety, tends to focus on states as the primary actors in the international polity and neglects the role of corporate and social interests (Paterson 1996; Strange 1988). Perhaps more relevant and fruitful for the present question has been the emergence of transnational historical materialism (THM) (Cox 1993; Gill 1990 and 1993). Grounded in the Gramscian theory of hegemony (Gramsci 1971), THM posits the emergence of a transnational historic bloc, comprising a coalition of businesses, intellectuals, and state managers that transcends any one class and is bound together through common identities and interests by material and ideological structures. This process serves the interests of an emergent and newly conscious international elite which depends for its prosperity upon the continuation and extension of a secure international neo-liberal trade and investment regime. In this conception, 'international organization functions as the process through which the institutions of hegemony and its ideology are developed' (Cox 1993: 62). In contrast to the globalisation approach, capital's hegemony is not uncontested in the international sphere; rather, it secures legitimacy and consent through a process of compromise and accommodation that reflects specific historical conditions.

Although the THM school emphasises the role of capital in the emerging global polity, the national state plays a major mediating role in the con-struction of world hegemony. Van der Pijl (1989: 19), for example, points to the national state as 'support[ing] the existence of ruling classes in their particularity' and argues that capitalist internationalisation can take place only if capital 'succeed[s] in synthesizing their international perspective with a national one' (Van der Pijl 1989: 12). Cox, as well as Gill and Law, see internationalisation as a contradictory process, one which is not mono-lithic and absolute but rather one which provides opportunities for the development of a counter-hegemonic alternative. The emergence of such an alternative is 'likely to be traceable to some fundamental change in social relations and in the *national* political orders which correspond to *national* structures of social relations' (Cox 1993: 64). THM, in contrast to the globalisation thesis, thus accords the national state a more active role in the construction, reproduction, and possible subversion of internationalised capital.

While we believe that the Gramscian roots of THM offer a sophisticated theory of the material and ideological bases of the capitalist state (Boggs 1976; Showstack-Sassoon 1987), we also believe that THM would benefit from making more explicit the specific mechanisms and channels of capital's power relative to the state and international institutions. Thus, while our analysis of the role of capital in the international climate change negotiations is broadly located in the THM framework, we seek to integrate critical theories of the state with this framework. More specifically, our analysis is based on power elite or intrumentalist theories (Mills 1967; Domhoff 1990; Miliband 1969), structural dependence theories (Block 1987; Offe 1984; Poulantzas 1978), and cultural/discursive theories of the state (Foucault 1977; Habermas 1984; Hall *et al.* 1978). These theories are relevant to the question at hand because, in their fundamentals, they seek to explain how business influences politics within a capitalist system.

Although international institutions such as the UN are clearly not true states in that they are not sovereign supranational entities, Shaw (1994: 650) has observed that 'a *de facto* complex of global state institutions is coming into existence through the fusion of Western state power and the legitimisation framework of the United Nations'. Our analysis of the climate change negotiations suggests that it might prove fruitful to reconstruct critical state theory to take account of the rise of extra-national bases of political power. We argue that international institutions are not mere epiphenomena created by dominant states, nor are they simply tools of international capital; rather, they possess significant resources, expertise, and regulatory initiative which they are able to deploy with some degree of organisational autonomy. In this context, critical theories of the state suggest a rich array of mechanisms by which capital might exert influence over these negotiations.

The increasing presence of social forces in the international arena has received growing attention in the literature on global civil society. Shaw (1994: 650) argues that 'civil society can be said to have become globalised to the extent that society increasingly represents itself globally, across nation-state boundaries, through the formation of global institutions'. The social movements engaged in such representation efforts are typically defined in terms of their common identity and interests, and their use of mass mobilisation as a prime form of sanction and power, though Peterson (1992) notes that international civil organisations tend to be decentralised, loose networks which typically lack coherence and common vision or goals. Wapner (1995) refers to the phenomenon of networks of associations actively working in international rather than national forums as 'world civic politics'. The relationships among civil society, social movements, the state and international institutions are subject to some debate. For Peterson (1992), civil society is autonomously organised public activity outside of the state. Shaw (1994: 648) articulates the Gramscian perspective in which civil society is both the 'outer earthworks of the state' and an arena in which social groups organise to contest state power. Some writers locate environmental organisations within the phenomenon of 'new social movements', which, it is argued, transcend class lines and are more concerned with personal identity than political conflict (Larana, Johnston, and Gusfield 1994). The climate change negotiations afford us an opportunity to witness the operation of global civil society.

Our extension of critical state theory to the international level will contribute to the development of the transnational historical materialist analysis of the relationship between capital, states, international institutions, and social forces. Where the globalisation thesis sees the withering and growing irrelevance of the state, we contend that developments in the international sphere serve to shift the ensemble of *national* relations in complex ways. If international economic integration erodes the access of nationally-based social movements to decision-making at the national level (Panitch 1994) and creates pressure for states to maintain 'economic competitiveness' by adopting measures favourable to mobile capital (Carnoy 1993; Picciotto 1991), this is likely to increase the political leverage of capital *within* the national state; indeed, it is the very division of the world into competing national states which provides global capital with its structural power (Gill and Law 1993). As a result, it is possible that the development of an international institutional infrastructure for a world neo-liberal economic order may contribute to a new relevance for the national state as capital's preferred arena for regulating social, labour, and environmental issues (Hirst and Thompson 1996). At the same time, social forces might attempt to coordinate internationally and press for the standardisation of environmental regulation through international governance structures. These preferences are the reverse of those for market-enabling institutions, where capital tends to prefer the international arena and social forces the national level. The international system is thus not supplanting or eclipsing the national state and its relations to national capital and social forces. Instead, these two spheres mediate and condition each other in a dialectical relationship. Our analysis of the development of international environmental policy on climate change illustrates this process.

The contention that business is running to the international arena in order to escape national social constraints is predicated on a more pluralist view of the relationship between business and the national state. Pluralists argue that sectoral divisions prevent business from acting in a unified way, and that the state can maintain neutrality and independence in mediating conflicting claims (Epstein 1969). By contrast, critical theories assert that the state actively serves business interests at the national level. Three major variants of these theories point to different sources of power that business wields over the state, despite the formal trappings of democratic and independent state institutions. The power-elite or instrumentalist perspective emphasises the ability of business to act cohesively in the political arena through a dense network of relationships between business and the state. Structural dependence theories acknowledge that the state enjoys a degree of autonomy from business power, but argue that in a market system, the state is structurally dependent on private sector profitability. State managers depend on popular support and legitimacy, which is a function of jobs and prosperity in the private sector and their ability to fund government programmes with tax revenue. These structural relationships cause state managers to act on behalf of, rather than at the behest of, business; indeed, the state needs to maintain its autonomy from any one business sector in order to resolve inter-sectoral conflicts and secure the system as a whole. Cultural or discursive theories emphasise the ideological and symbolic aspects of power. This loose collection of approaches has been applied to understand the state's relationship to business. Unlike power-elite theorists, who view cultural institutions such as schools and the media as subservient to business interests, discursive theories of the state see this sector as a relatively independent site of political struggle.

Corporate Influence on the Climate Change Process

Instrumentalist forms of power

The 1992 United Nations Conference on Environment and Development in Rio de Janeiro provided a setting for business to exert a very powerful influence over the direction of international environmental policy. Maurice Strong, head of the Canadian electric utility Ontario Hydro, was appointed to the position of Secretary-General of the conference; in turn, Strong appointed as his principal adviser the Swiss industrialist and multi-millionaire Stephan Schmidheiny, who organised the Business Council for Sustainable Development (BCSD), a group of industrialists representing forty-eight of the world's largest multinational corporations. Several scholars have argued that the conference structure gave companies special status and coherence that environmental NGOs lacked (Finger 1994; Kolk 1997). Despite the BCSD's professed commitment to achieving environmental goals through market measures such as green taxes (Schmidheiny 1992), it used its influence to help ensure that the Framework Convention on Climate Change (FCCC) agreed at the conference contained little commitment to concrete action (Mintzer and Leonard 1994; Hecht and Tirpak 1995). This example illustrates that when business does exert its power in international negotiations, it is often to keep regulation at the national level. Schmidheiny

(1992: 24) expressed his reasons for this quite candidly: 'Business has favored [national] regulation in the past because it also is more familiar with this approach, and feels it can influence it through negotiation. In addition, in many countries regulations are passed but rarely enforced.'

One important channel of influence at the domestic level in the US is the network of contacts maintained by large companies and their industry associations. For example, the Global Climate Coalition (GCC), the largest industry group active on the climate change issue, benefits from the personal connections of its director, John Schlaes, and of its member companies. Schlaes held a senior position in the executive office of the White House as director of communications under John Sununu, and still appears to exert significant influence on the Republican side of Congress. Financial donations to politicians represent a second channel of influence at the national level in the US. The oil industry alone provided $15.5 million in campaign contributions during the 1995–96 US election cycle, of which Republicans received about 80 per cent (Abramson 1997). Not surprisingly, recipients of this money tend to be people who are in a position to influence climate change policy (Makinson 1995). Industry associations opposing mandatory limitations on greenhouse gas emissions have been successful in securing the support of a key group of Republican Congresspeople in the 1994–6 House. The oil and automobile industries, which are major sources of greenhouse gases, are particularly powerful actors in the US domestic arena. A modest fuel tax proposed by the Clinton administration in 1992 was quickly dropped in the face of pressure from these industries. In more recent multi-party discussions sponsored by the White House on limiting emissions in the automobile sector, dubbed Car Talk, these industries appeared to be able to exert an effective veto. According to a representative of the Climate Action Network (CAN), an umbrella environmental organisation working on the climate issue, 'car companies would not discuss CAFE standards and oil companies would not entertain a gas tax. Without consensus, the process is dead.'[1]

In contrast to these points of leverage at the national level, industry's direct influence at the international negotiations since Rio has been more limited. Although groups such as the GCC have established good relationships with some national delegations, especially those from Canada, Australia, and oil exporting countries, these ties tend to be based on a congruence of interests rather than personal or financial links. The international negotiations involve more than 100 countries, with whom the US-dominated industry associations share few social ties and whose politicians are beyond the reach of Political Action Committee (PAC) money. Most of the national delegations are drawn from the ranks of career civil servants and staff within each country's equivalent to departments of state, environment, energy, and commerce. Industry has not enjoyed the direct top-level influence provided at Rio through the Schmidheiny–Strong channel. Industry associations also have limited influence over less developed countries' (LDC) policies regarding climate change. The major industry associations active in climate change represent mainly larger multinational corporations based in North America and to a lesser extent, Europe. Despite the potential leverage provided by their substantial investments in LDCs, the evidence suggests that industry has had little success in working with LDC delegations. Corporate managers report a degree of mistrust and suspicion, particularly from India and Latin America, which is partly a legacy of LDC hostility toward multinationals during the latter 1970s, and partly a function of the North–South divisions over climate change.

Industry groups have little direct influence over the UN environmental bureaucracy. Although the Conference of the Parties (COP), comprising delegates from more than 150 countries that are signatories to the Framework Convention, is formally the supreme decision-making body for the Climate Convention process, a number of UN-related bodies are more removed from national delegations susceptible to industry pressure. In January 1996 a permanent Convention Secretariat was established in Bonn, Germany. The Secretariat is based on a professional staff rather than country delegates, and, though it has no executive power, plays an important agenda setting role. Observers expect that the Secretariat will enjoy solid support from the host government, which is one of the leading advocates of a strong emissions treaty.

The COP process has a number of affiliated organisations that are widely regarded as relatively independent and committed to the process. The Conference Bureau, which organises the COP meetings, is staffed by a small group of country delegates who tend to be environmental professionals and staff from national environment ministries. The Ad-hoc Group on the Berlin Mandate (AGBM), with representatives from all the parties to the convention, is the main body that works between formal COP sessions to establish objectives for a protocol, study various options, and prepare recommendations for the next COP to adopt. Under the leadership of chairman Raul Estrada Oyuela of Argentina, the AGBM has steadily pushed towards a mandatory protocol. At AGBM-3, in March 1996, Estrada expressed his determination not to let oil producing countries delay AGBM activities, and 'declared that he would not tolerate obstruction from delegates who had tried to slow negotiations before' (ENB 1996: 19).

The convention process has been guided by the scientific and technical input provided by the IPCC, an international group of more than 2,000 respected scientists operating under the auspices of the World Meteorological Organisation and the United Nations Environmental Programme (UNEP). Despite efforts by the GCC to impugn the integrity of the IPCC process, the consensus reached in the IPCC's Second Assessment Report (1995) concerning the likelihood of greenhouse gas-induced climatic change has gained broad legitimacy and has been widely accepted by most national delegations and even centrist industry groups. Despite the vast resources available to business groups, most observers concur that their influence has not overwhelmed the voice of environmental NGOs at the international negotiations. Environmental NGOs have also been well organised. Indeed, according to Chris Flavin of the Worldwatch Institute, Washington D.C., 'the NGOs ran circles around the Global Climate Coalition in Berlin'.[2] The Climate Action Network has published an influential daily newsletter at post-Rio meetings that is distributed to delegates and around the world via e-mail and the web.

Critics of the instrumentalist position point to the diversity of industry interests as a source of weakness that prevents business from acting as a cohesive, conscious bloc. The climate change case is characterised by a plethora of industry associations representing different perspectives (Levy 1997a). Although pluralist theory suggests that this disunity would weaken the power of business in the negotiation process, it appears that the US administration is anxious to obtain the consent of *all* major affected sectors and to avoid steps that would be economically harmful to them (Wirth 1996). The desire for consensus in the face of these sectoral divisions provides the more intransigent industry associations such as the GCC with considerable leverage; it has been resolute in refusing to join the position of a more moderate industry group, the International Climate Change Partnership (ICCP), precisely because that could form the basis for a compromise agreement.

While this evidence suggests that industry associations are currently much more influential at the national than the international level, they are actively organising to broaden their geographic reach. Both the GCC and the ICCP are aggressively seeking more European, Asian, and developing country members. The International Chamber of Commerce has played a role in trying to coordinate international business responses to the climate change negotiations, although inter-sectoral differences have hindered its efforts. The International Chamber of Commerce, whose membership is primarily drawn from OECD countries, has a very active working party on climate change which met in London in January 1996 to plan strategy for the COP-2 negotiating session in Geneva in July 1996. Maurice Strong, having left Ontario Hydro in 1996, was appointed Deputy Secretary-General of the UN, and the UN is examining ways to formalise corporate input into its decision-making process.[3]

Structural dependency

Climate change has the potential to generate significant structural pressures on policy-makers because of the economic impact of measures to curb greenhouse gas emissions. Dependable access to cheap energy is often viewed by policy-makers as central to economic growth and prosperity, and a key strategic state objective (Newell 1997; Yergin 1991). Controls on emissions of carbon dioxide would affect not just the producers and refiners of oil and coal, but would significantly raise the price of these fuels for electric utilities and the transportation sector. Higher energy costs would also affect energy intense industries downstream on the value chain, such as chemicals, steel, glass, aluminium, cement, and paper. The GCC has been quick to point out the potential impact on growth and employment of curbing greenhouse gas emissions (WEFA 1996), and US officials have expressed concern about the sensitivity of American voters to fuel prices. In July 1997 the US Senate voted unanimously for the Byrd–Hagel resolution, which objected to any treaty measures that could hurt US competitiveness and employment. The US is not, of course, the lone champion of capital in international fora. European governments are extremely sensitive to the issue of unemployment, which has averaged more than ten per cent in the EU in recent years compared to around six per cent in the US. Structural dependence also extends to less developed countries, which have become increasingly eager to attract new inflows of private capital.

By contrast, the international institutions involved in the climate change negotiations are relatively insulated from structural pressures. The UN is not directly dependent for revenues on healthy national economies, nor does it have to compete with other entities to offer an attractive business climate. Indeed, the very lack of democratic accountability within international institutions that worries some observers also serves to insulate them from popular concerns about jobs and fuel prices. If curbing greenhouse gas emissions means higher fossil fuel prices, the UN might well be able to take actions that appear politically impossible in the US.

Those countries whose economic structures are most dependent on fossil fuels are the natural allies of industry groups opposed to emission limitations. The Climate Council is known to have close links to Kuwait, Saudi Arabia, and other members of the OPEC. The Global Climate Coalition has tried to exert its influence primarily with the JUSCANZ bloc of industrialised countries opposing strong measures.[4] This loose coalition shares economic interests that could be harmed by greenhouse gas controls. The US possesses substantial reserves of coal and oil, the value of which would decline if demand were curbed or substitutes developed. Perhaps more importantly, the US is home to five of the seven oil majors, and is also the home to large multinationals in energy intense user industries, such as automobiles, steel, and chemicals. The US relies heavily on fossil fuels for its energy needs; its carbon emissions are the highest in the world, both in total and in per capita terms (Brown 1996). The imposition of carbon taxes at approximately uniform rates across the world would cause much more serious adjustment effects in the US where energy taxes are very low. Canada and Australia, also major consumers and exporters of fossil fuels, have strongly opposed specific emissions limits.

An examination of the positions of various European countries also supports the structural dependence position, as they appear closely attuned to each country's specific economic and industrial structure. France has been relatively supportive of emission controls because it already obtains more than 60 per cent of its electricity from nuclear plants, and stands to gain export markets for its nuclear technology. Although Germany, the strongest European advocate of controls, relied on coal for about one-third of its primary energy needs in 1990, dependence on coal was already being reduced due to concern about acid rain and the cost of coal subsidies, which exceeded $4 billion a year. Germany has been able to reduce emissions through the closure of inefficient plants in the former East Germany, and is in the forefront of pollution prevention and renewable energy technologies. The UK, heavily dependent on coal, had followed the US position against controls until the early 1990s. The UK reversed its stance following the decision to end subsidies to the coal mining industry and close most of the coal pits (Boehmer-Christiansen 1995).

Much of the developing world has opposed any international agreement to limit emissions on the grounds that climate change is a rich country problem and that cheap energy is needed to fuel growth. China, with one-third of the world's proven reserves of coal, relies on coal for around 80 per cent of its energy needs, and in 1995 was already the world's third largest emitter of carbon dioxide. China planned to expand its coal production fivefold to three billion tons a year by 2020, which would increase global carbon dioxide emissions nearly 50 per cent (Grubb 1990). Brazil, Indonesia, and Malaysia, which are home to much of the world's tropical rain forest, have expressed concern that a treaty might limit their ability to log and export timber, or to clear the land for agricultural use.

Although the broad correspondence between a country's negotiating position and its economic interests suggests that structural economic dependence is a powerful factor in the formation of policy, it does not illuminate which specific channels of influence are at work. Structural dependence can be translated into policy through instrumentalist mechanisms exerted by affected sectors, as discussed earlier, or discursively through the construction of 'competitiveness' as a primary goal of national policy. US government publications and interviews with US government officials reveal that US competitiveness is considered a high-priority issue of legitimate concern throughout government. A few government respondents expressed fear of the voters and the need to accommodate business concerns, but none gave any hint that dependence on tax revenues played any role. Rather, it was simply taken for granted that government policy-making should promote economic growth and avoid economic disruption to major sectors. This vision of the 'competition state' has been internalised as part of the construction of the public official and has been institutionalised on policy-making processes. The three forms of influence thus appear to be inherently intertwined and interdependent.

Discursive influence

If environmental policy formation is, at least in part, a struggle for discursive hegemony (Hajer 1995) it is important to examine corporate efforts to influence the discourse around climate change. In the US, corporate interests likely to be affected by climate change have made significant efforts to influence discourse over the issue. Fossil fuel interests have engaged in substantial public relations campaigns in the US, targeted to the public in general as well as policy-makers, to highlight scientific uncertainties concerning global warming and emphasise the high economic costs of curbing emissions. More broadly, they have attempted to construct global warming as the invention of anti-business environmental extremists, while the UN is often depicted as a threat to American freedom and prosperity. These themes find fertile ground because they resonate with existing discourses in American society, reflected in the growth of the Wise Use movement, a suspicion of federal, let alone international, authorities and a particular concept of freedom that is highly individualistic and symbolically related to automobiles (Rowell 1996).

Advertising and education are two channels through which industry associations have tried to influence public opinion. Western Fuels, a US utility association and member of the GCC, ran an advertisement in 1993 titled 'Repeal Rio' calling climate change a 'controversial theory' with 'no support in observations', and made the claim that 'CO_2 fertilization of the atmosphere helps produce more food for people and wildlife.' The association also spent around $250,000 to produce a video in 1991 called *The Greening of Planet Earth*, which carried the same message and was apparently influential in the Bush administration. One industry tactic has been to establish 'front groups' to mask the corporate interests involved. Coal, oil, and utility interests in the US established a group called The Information Council for the Environment in 1991, whose purpose, as stated in internal documents, was to 'reposition global warming as theory, not fact' (*Ozone Action* 1996). ICE developed a sophisticated print and radio media campaign directed at 'older, less educated men' and 'young, low income women', and set up a Science Advisory Panel which included three 'climate sceptics,' Robert Balling, Patrick Michaels and S. Fred Singer, all of whom have received funding from fossil fuel industries.

The GCC and its member organisations have engaged in a much more targeted effort to convince business leaders and policy-makers that measures to curb greenhouse gas emissions 'are premature and are not justified by the state of scientific knowledge or the economic risks they create' (GCC 1995). The GCC commissioned a series of economic studies that suggest that the US might suffer economic losses in the region of 3 to 5 per cent of GDP annually if it follows proposals to cut emissions 20 per cent below 1990 levels by 2005 (Montgomery and Charles River Associates 1995; WEFA 1996). In a September 1996 press release, the GCC warned that measures to curb emissions by 20 per cent 'could reduce the US gross domestic product by 4 per cent and cost Americans up to 1.1 million jobs annually.' As a result of these efforts, industry's concerns have permeated governmental discourse, in some cases almost literally; respondents at the Department of Energy talked in terms of the need to avoid 'premature retirement of capital', a term frequently used by fossil fuel and utility interests. Fossil fuel interests have also attempted to convince opinion leaders and policy-makers that the science of climate change is dubious at best. The Western Fuels Association has funded the publication and distribution of a monthly newspaper called the *World Climate Review*. Edited by Patrick Michaels of the University of Virginia, the newsletter is dedicated to debunking climate change science and is mailed to all the members of the Society of Environmental Journalists.

Despite the resources invested in influencing the scientific and policy debates, it is evident that the fossil fuel industry's point of view has not achieved hegemonic status, even within the US. The ICE programme was halted following a number of embarrassing media stories, and few familiar with the issue are as sanguine about climate change as the Western Fuels advertisements. Nevertheless, the 'climate sceptics' have succeeded in turning climate change into an apparently balanced 'debate' in the media. Moreover, they have played a key role in a number of state and Congressional hearings by providing some cover for politicians who, because of their ideological inclination or allegiance to certain business interests, want to delay any action on greenhouse gas emissions (Gelbspan 1997).

Industry associations have enjoyed much less influence over the scientific and policy discourse in the international negotiations. Although international networks of media ownership and distribution have expanded in recent years, the sophisticated public relations campaigns waged in the US are not easily duplicated in other countries, where corporate public relations departments are less experienced and more restrictions exist on commercial activities in educational institutions. An industry effort to challenge the integrity of the Intergovernmental Panel on Climate Change Second Assessment Report illustrates the difficulty faced by industry in affecting the scientific discourse within the UN process. The GCC and the Climate Council claimed that Benjamin Santer and Tom Wigley, two of the lead authors, had deleted passages that dissented or expressed uncertainty (ECO 1996). These accusations were quickly picked up by the mass media, including the *Wall Street Journal* (Seitz 1996) and the *New York Times* (Stevens 1996), but the allegations had little impact on the international negotiations, where officials were quick to express their support for the peer review process that resulted in the changes.

The primary reason for the failure of the GCC viewpoint to gain hegemony in the US is the emerging challenge from a competing discursive paradigm, that of ecological modernisation (Hajer 1995). The lure of this approach lies in the core assumption that being 'green' can also be good for business, and that addressing environmental problems can be a positive sum game (Levy 1995, 1997b; Russo and Fouts 1997). To generate these 'win–win' situations, ecological modernisation puts its faith in the technological, organisational, and financial resources of the private sector, voluntary partnerships between government agencies and business, flexible market-based measures, and the application of environmental management techniques (Cairncross 1991; Schmidheiny 1992). In the climate change context, this view has been embraced by industry associations representing companies in the renewable energy, gas, and energy efficiency sectors, by a number of major environmental organisations, especially the World Resources Institute and the Environmental Defense Fund (Dudek 1996), and increasingly by other sectors of industry, including members of the ICCP. The Clinton Administration's approach to Climate Change bears the clear imprint of this paradigm. The US Climate Change Action Plan (1993: 2) states that 'returning US greenhouse gas emissions to their 1990 levels by the year 2000 is an ambitious but achievable goal that can be attained while enhancing prospects for market growth and job creation, and positioning our country to compete and win in the global market'. The joint EPA/Department of Energy Climate Wise programme describes itself as 'a unique partnership that can help you turn energy efficiency and environmental performance into a corporate asset' (US DoE 1996).

This discourse has also permeated the international climate negotiations, partly due to the powerful position of the US and partly to the influence of Schmidheiny and the World Business Council for Sustainable Development. To coincide with the 1992 UN Conference on Environment and Development conference, Stephan Schmidheiny published the influential book *Changing Course* (1992), which championed the role of private capital and free markets in achieving 'sustainable development', while downplaying any possible contradictions between vigorous economic growth and environmental protection. The primacy of markets and private capital in addressing climate change is also reflected in the Second Assessment Report of the IPCC, particularly the section by Working Group III, which addressed social and economic policies.

Conclusions

Overall, the evidence does not support the notion that the international arena offers capital a safe haven from environmental regulations. For the case of a regulatory international regime such as climate change, business appears to prefer the well-charted and predictable waters of the national political economy. Indeed, the correspondence between national negotiating stances and economic interests provides testimony to the hegemony of corporate influence over national policy. The case study suggests that instrumentalist forms of power operate more effectively at the national level, and that international institutions are relatively insulated from these sources of pressure.

US-based companies and industry associations have limited leverage over the climate policies of other countries, which tend to pursue what they perceive to be their own economic interests. In addition, the potential for greenhouse gas controls to cause substantial economic dislocation generates structural pressures at the national level, particularly in those countries most dependent on fossil fuels. International institutions themselves are removed from these pressures. Finally, business efforts to influence the science and policy discourse have also been much more prevalent and effective at the national than the international level. Even at the national level, the views advocated by the fossil fuel industry serve more to create the appearance of controversy than a hegemonic consensus. The more blatant attempts to discredit climate change science have fallen flat in the UN. Although a broad consensus has emerged about the central role of corporate solutions guided by market incentives in a future regulatory regime, the hegemonic nature of this discourse cannot be directly attributed to specific industry efforts; rather, it is related to the broader dissemination of the related discourses of neo-liberalism and ecological modernism.

The case highlights the importance of our distinction between regulatory institutions, such as those governing international environmental policy, and market-enabling institutions that provide the infrastructure for governance of global trade, investment, and financial flows. While capital might be highly supportive of international enabling institutions at the expense of national states, there is reason to be sceptical of the globalisation thesis in the case of regulatory institutions. This study suggests that capital does operate at the international level in an effort to influence emerging regulatory institutions, but that such action in this arena, rather than eclipsing the national state, is largely channelled through it, and is frequently directed toward blocking strong transnational action. In short, there are strong reservations against the claim of the neo-liberal global discourse that transnational capital would gain authority at the expense of states due to globalisation.

Hirst and Thompson's argument that non-governmental organisations are more inclined to be transnational actors than are corporations is supported by the climate change case; environmental NGOs advocate for international regulation of greenhouse gas emissions because they recognise that many countries would not take strong action in the absence of an international agreement due to corporate pressures and the high cost of unilateral action. Moreover, they recognise the high status and influence of the international scientific community within UN-based institutions and the relative weakness of corporate pressures. This is the complete reverse of the case for international market enabling institutions such as the World Trade Organisation from which international civil society is largely excluded.

While our analysis provides support for the continued relevance of the national state within an internationalised capitalism, it also points to the changing relationship between capital, the state, international institutions, and social forces. Multinationals are developing more sophisticated transnational political capacities and are learning to coordinate their activities at the national and international level. As nation states lose some autonomy over economic policies and cede some responsibility for environmental regulation to international institutions, they are increasingly important as conduits of business power and as sites for the formulation and implementation of social, labour, and environmental policies. The international arena can thus be understood as a contested political field of increasing significance that interrelates with and modifies relations in the national domain. Hegemony must be secured, but can also be contested, at both levels, opening up new possibilities for resistance.

Notes

The authors gratefully acknowledge funding for this research from the University of Massachusetts, Boston. This research is based on a series of interviews with representatives of industry associations, corporations, US government agencies, and environmental organizations, as well as extensive analysis of documentary and secondary materials.

1   Interview with Jennifer Morgan, 10 January 1996.
2   Interview with Chris Flavin, 11 January 1996.
3   On 24 June 1997, ten CEOs of transnational corporations, mostly members of the BCSD, met with fifteen government representatives, including three heads of state, the Secretary-General of the UN, and the Administrator of UNDP, to establish terms of reference for business sector participation in the policy setting process of the UN and partnering in the uses of UN development assistance funds (source: letter from David Korten, http://iisd1.iisd.ca/pcdf).
4   JUSCANZ comprises Japan, the US, Canada, and New Zealand.

References

Abramson, D. (1997) *The Oil Daily*, 24 February, 47(36): 1.
Barnet, R. and Cavanagh, J. (1994) *Global Dreams: Imperial Corporations and the New World Order*, New York: Simon & Schuster.
Block, F. (1987) *Revising State Theory*, Philadelphia: Temple University Press.
Boehmer-Christiansen, S. (1995) 'Britain and the international panel on climate change: the impacts of scientific advice on global warming, part II: the domestic story of the British response to climate change', *Environmental Politics* 4(2): 175–96.
Boggs, C. (1976) *Gramsci's Marxism*, London: Pluto Press.
Brown, L. (1996) *State of the World, 1996*, Washington, D.C.: Norton/Worldwatch Institute.
Cairncross, F. (1991) *Costing the Earth*, Boston, Mass.: Harvard Business School Press.
Carnoy, M. (1993) 'Multinationals in the changing world economy: whither the nation-state?', in M. Carnoy, M. Castells, S. Cohen, and F. Cardoso (eds) *The New Global Economy in the Information Age*, University Park: Pennsylvania State University Press: 45–96.

Climate Change Action Plan (1993) Washington, D.C.: US White House.

Cox, R. (1993) 'Gramsci, Hegemony and International Relations: An Essay in Method' in S. Gill (ed.) *Gramsci, Historical Materialism and International Relations*. Cambridge: Cambridge University Press: 49–66.

Domhoff, G. (1990) The Power Elite and the State: How Policy is Made in America, New York: Aldine de Gruyter.

Dudek, D. (1996) *Emission Budgets: Creating Rewards, Lowering Costs and Ensuring Results*, New York: Environmental Defense Fund.

ECO (1996) *ECO Newsletter*, COP-2, Geneva, Issue no.1, 8 July.

ENB (1996) *Earth Negotiations Bulletin* 12(27), 11 March.

Epstein, E. (1969) *The Corporation in American Politics*, Englewood Cliffs, N.J.: Prentice Hall.

Finger, M. (1994) 'NGOs and transformation: beyond social movement theory', in T. Princen and M. Finger (eds) *Environmental NGOs in World Politics*, New York: Routledge: 48–66.

Foucault, M. (1977) *Discipline and Punish* (A. Sheridan, trans.), New York: Random House.

GCC (1995) *Global Climate Coalition press release*, February 9.

Gelbspan, R. (1997) *The Heat is On*, Reading, Mass.: Addison-Wesley.

Gill, S. (1990) *American Hegemony and the Trilateral Commission*, Cambridge: Cambridge University Press.

—— (1993) 'Gramsci and global politics: towards a post-hegemonic research agenda', in S. Gill (ed.) *Gramsci, Historical Materialism and International Relations*, Cambridge: Cambridge University Press: 1–18.

Gill, S., and Law, D. (1993) 'Global Hegemony and the Structural Power of Capital', in S. Gill (ed.) *Gramsci, Historical Materialism and International Relations*, Cambridge: Cambridge University Press: 93–124.

Gramsci, A. (1971) *Selections from the Prison Notebooks* (Q. Hoare and G. Nowell-Smith, trans.), New York: International Publishers.

Grubb, M. (1990) 'The greenhouse effect: negotiating targets', *International Affairs* 66(1): 67–89.

Haas, P., R. Keohane and M. Levy (eds) (1993) *Institutionss for the Earth: Sources of Effective International Environmental Protection*, Cambridge, Mass.: MIT Press.

Habermas, J. (1984) *The Theory of Communicative Action*, Cambridge: Polity Press.

Haggard, S., and B. Simmons (1987) 'Theories of international regimes', *International Organization* 41: 491–517.

Hajer, M. (1995) *The Politics of Environmental Discourse: Ecological Modernization and the Policy Process*, Oxford: Clarendon Press.

Hall, S., C. Critcher, T. Jefferson, J. Clarke and B. Roberts (1978) *Policing the Crisis: Mugging, the State, and Law and Order*, London: Macmillan.

Hecht, A. and D. Tirpak (1995) 'Framework agreement on climate change: a scientific and policy history', *Climatic Change* 29: 371–402.

Hirst, P. and Thompson, G. (1996) *Globalization in Question*, Cambridge: Polity Press.

IPCC (1995) *Second Assessment Report of the Intergovernmental Panel on Climate Change*, Cambridge: Cambridge University Press.

Jessop, R. (1994) 'Post-Fordism and the State', in A. Amin (ed.) *Post-Fordism*, Cambridge: Blackwell: 251–79.

Kolk, A. (1997) *Forests in International Environmental Politics*, Atlanta: International Books.

Korten, D. (1995) *When Corporations Rule the World*, West Hartford, Conn.: Kumarian Press.

Larana, E., H. Johnston and J. Gusfield (eds.) (1994) *New Social Movements: From Ideology to Identity*, Philadelphia: Temple University Press.

Levy, D. (1995) 'The environmental practices and performance of transnational corporations', *Transnational Corporations* 4(1): 44–68.

—— (1997a) 'Business and international environmental treaties: ozone depletion and climate change', *California Management Review* 39(3): 54–71.

—— (1997b) 'Environmental management as political sustainability', *Organization and Environment* 10(2): 126–47.

Makinson, L. (1995) *The Price of Admission: Campaign Spending in the 1994 Elections*, Washington, D.C.: Center for Responsive Politics.

Miliband, R. (1969) *The State in Capitalist Society*, New York: Basic Books.

Mills, C. (1967) *The Power Elite*, New York: Oxford University Press.

Mintzer, I. and J. Leonard (eds.) (1994) *Negotiating Climate Change: the Inside Story of the Rio Convention*, Cambridge: Cambridge University Press.

Montgomery, D. and Charles River Associates (1995) *Toward an Economically Rational Response to the Berlin Mandate*, prepared on behalf of GCC, Washington, D.C.: Charles River Associates.

Newell, P. (1997) *The International Politics of Global Warming: A Non-Governmental Account*, doctoral thesis, University of Keele, England.

Offe, C. (1984) 'Theses on the theory of the state', in J. Keane (ed.) *Contradictions of the Welfare State*, Cambridge: MIT Press: 119–29.

Ozone Action (1996) *Distorting the Debate: a Case Study of Corporate Greenwashing*, Washington, D.C.: Ozone Action.

Panitch, L. (1994) 'Globalization and the State', in R. Miliband and L. Panitch (eds) *Socialist Register 1994: Between Globalism and Nationalism*, London: Merlin Press: 60–93.

Paterson, M. (1996) 'IR theory: neorealism, neoinstitutionalism and the Climate Change Convention', in J. Vogler and M. Imber (eds) *The Environment and International Relations*, London: Routledge: 59–76.

Peterson, M. (1992) 'Transnational activity, international society and world politics', *Millennium* 21(3): 371–88.

Picciotto, S. (1991) 'The internationalization of the state', *Capital and Class* 43: 43–63.

Poulantzas, N. (1978) *Political Power and Social Classes*, London: Verso.

Reich, R. (1991) *The Work of Nations*, New York: Vintage Books.

Rowell, A. (1996) *Green Backlash: Global Subversion of the Environmental Movement*, London: Routledge.

Russo, M. and P. Fouts (1997) 'A resource-based perspective on corporate environmental performance and profitability', *Academy of Management Journal* 40(3): 534.

Schmidheiny, S. (1992) *Changing Course*, Cambridge, Mass.: MIT Press.

Seitz, F. (1996) A major deception on 'Global Warming', *Wall Street Journal*, 6 June: A16.

Shaw, M. (1994) 'Civil society and global politics: beyond a social movements approach', *Millennium* 23(3): 648–55.

Showstack-Sassoon, A. (1987) *Gramsci's Politics*, London: Hutchinson.

Stevens, W. (1996) 'UN climate report was improperly altered, underplaying uncertainties, critics say', *New York Times*, 17 June: B6.

Strange, S. (1988) *States and Markets: an Introduction to International Political Economy*, New York: Blackwell.

—— (1996) *The Retreat of the State*, New York: Cambridge University Press.

US DoE (1996) *Climate Wise* DOE/EE-0071, EPA 230-K-95–003, Washington, D.C.: US Department of Energy.

US Office of the White House (1993) *US Climate Change Action Plan*, Washington, D.C.: US White House.

Van der Pijl, K. (1989) 'Ruling classes, hegemony, and the state system', *International Journal of Political Economy* 19: 7–35.

Wapner P. (1995) 'Politics beyond the state: environmental activism and world civic politics', *World Politics* 47, April: 311–40.

WEFA Group and H. Zinder and Associates (1996) *A Review of the Economic Impacts of AOSIS-type Proposals to Limit Carbon Dioxide Emissions* (prepared for Global Climate Coalition), Eddystone, Pa.: WEFA Group.

Wirth, T. (1996) Statement by Timothy E. Wirth, Under Secretary for Global Affairs, on behalf of the USA, at the Convention on Climate Change, second Conference of the Parties, July 17. Geneva, Switzerland: US Mission, Office of Public Affairs.

Yergin, D. (1991) *The Prize*, New York: Simon and Schuster.

Young, O. (1994) *International Governance: Protecting the Environment in a Stateless Society*, Ithaca: N.Y.: Cornell University Press.

ABN AMRO Bank: banking on Brazil

Introduction

As a service industry which mainly employs white-collar workers, the banking sector does not always attract the same high levels of attention to its social impacts as do manufacturing industries with obvious environmentally damaging practices or poor labour standards. However, as a service provider to other organizations, the financial services industry has an important role to play in taking responsibility for its support and facilitation of responsible (or irresponsible) practices on the part of its customers. A number of banks have built their entire business around the strength of their ethical stance and social responsibility portfolio, such as the Dutch Triodos Bank and the UK's Co-operative Bank. However, mainstream leaders in the banking sector are now also demonstrating an awareness of the power they have to influence improvements in CSR through their policies. One such bank is the large Dutch group, ABN AMRO, which has long been involved in CSR in Europe, but has also, as we see in this case, developed a range of CSR practices in Latin America, and in Brazil in particular. These practices help us to see the range of CSR initiatives and challenges that multinationals may put in place across their operations, focusing in the main here on marketplace, community and environmental responsibilities.

CSR in Latin America

Challenges facing businesses in Latin America include free-trade treaties, corporate downsizing, offshore manufacturing, and the demand to be more socially and environmentally responsible. Particular areas of concern here include deforestation and environmental degradation, unemployment, income inequality, corruption, and crime.

CSR has emerged alongside wider social, political and economic changes since the 1980s in the region, including increased foreign investment and exports, privatization, democratization, and shifts in economic and political systems. The past decade or so has also witnessed increasing pressures from governments, non-governmental organizations, the media and local communities to encourage firms in Latin America to be more responsible, and to contribute positively to social and economic development. However, the social values and philanthropic approaches common to CSR are not new to Latin America, but rather have been embedded in the prevalent Catholic tradition. None the less, the level of engagement with CSR varies across Latin American countries, with Brazil, Chile and Mexico being the most advanced in terms of developing their own approaches to the phenomenon (de Oliveira, 2006).

Focus on Brazil

Brazil has the largest economy in South America and the ninth largest in the world. Paradoxically, it is a rich country with a poor population – a legacy of sixteenth-century Portuguese colonial rule which has seen its inequalities entrenched by an authoritarian culture of military rule and centuries of slavery. Despite the recent democratization process, the richest 10 per cent of Brazilians receive 50 per cent of the nation's income, the poorest 10 per cent receiving less than 1 per cent. Power and assets (including land) are similarly inequitably distributed. In addition to social injustice, problems experienced by the poor include malnutrition, disease, illiteracy and abject poverty. As a result of inequality, high levels of violence exist in Brazil's cities.

From an environmental perspective, Brazil has an important global role, being home to 30 per cent of the remaining tropical rainforest in the form of the Amazon, and 10 per cent of plant and animal species. Cattle ranching, subsistence farming and commercial agriculture cause major deforestation in a country which is itself a significant energy consumer. Perhaps for these reasons, Brazil has long been associated with sustainable development: hosting the first Earth Summit in 1992 and convening the first World Social Forum in 2001.

From the point of view of business, investing in improving poverty is a contribution to expanding markets as well as an issue of social responsibility. CSR activities have tended to focus on education as a means of contributing to the improvement of the social context, despite the rather more immediate problems of hunger, sickness, poverty and lack of opportunity. Wider pressure internationally has encouraged a focus on the environment and sustainability issues, while the establishment of CSR think-tanks, and high-profile initiatives from leading corporations have helped to make Brazil probably Latin America's leading country in terms of CSR practice.[1]

ABN AMRO Bank

ABN AMRO Bank operates in the financial services industry with a history going back to 1824. Since the merger in 1991 between Algemene Bank Nederland (ABN) and

Amsterdamsche-Rotterdamsche Bank (AMRO), it has been the largest bank in the Netherlands, the eleventh largest in Europe and twentieth in the world. It has a presence in sixty countries, although the four home markets are the Netherlands, the USA, Italy and Brazil. The firm has been active in CSR for a number of years and in 2006 was highly commended in the UK *Financial Times* Sustainable Bank of the Year Awards, coming second only to HSBC. ABN AMRO was commended for 'global excellence in environmental and social risk management'. The Dutch banking group was applauded for being a leading adopter of the Equator Principles (a financial industry benchmark for determining, assessing and managing social and environmental risk in project financing),[2] and has a long-standing commitment to using sustainability as a driver for business growth and asset quality.

ABN AMRO in Brazil: Banco ABN AMRO Real

ABN AMRO began operations in Brazil in 1927, acquiring Banco Real in 1998. The resulting merged institution, Banco ABN AMRO Real, is currently the fifth largest privately owned bank in the country and the second largest foreign bank. It employs over 28,500 employees across 5,400 branches, and services 9.7 million retail clients and over 3,500 corporate clients, including 400 of the largest corporations in Brazil. ABN AMRO's Brazilian subsidiary is therefore a major player in the country, and Brazil represents a key market for the Dutch company.

The firm's approach to CSR is significant in that it is linked to the bank's core business of providing financial services rather than just a bolt-on approach to philanthropy. The firm was identified as a best-practice exponent in Sustainability consultancy's recent country study of Brazil.[3] This identified that ABN AMRO Real's approach integrated responsibility issues throughout its business activities, including in particular the following:

- Evaluation of its loan portfolio based on social and environmental risk for virtually all corporate clients (in partnership with the Eco-finance Project, an initiative of Friends of the Earth-Amazonia). This incorporates an extensive training programme for 1,100 branch and middle managers across Brazil.
- Training of more than 1,800 relationship managers around opportunities arising from sustainability.
- Creation of an environmental and social business development department tasked with developing profitable products with direct social and environmental impacts.
- Creation of the first Ethical Fund in Latin America: FIA ABN AMRO Ethical–Brazilian Equities).
- Development of a supplier relationship department to address social and environmental issues – a process involving extensive engagement of the company's major suppliers. The ABN AMRO Sustainability Report 2005 notes the recruitment of suppliers in Brazil to follow through the bank's commitment to sustainability further up the supply chain. This takes the form of a Suppliers'

Forum, a supplier website as a medium of exchange on sustainability issues and an e-sourcing system which automatically incorporates standard sustainable development selection criteria.

● Annual reporting based on the Global Reporting Initiative guidelines.
● The only bank in Brazil to be recipients of International Finance Corporation money (a total of US$98 million) with which to finance social, environmental and corporate governance projects.

One of the most striking aspects of the bank's engagement with CSR is its Real Microcrédito programme. This is a major microcredit initiative launched by the bank in 2002. Real Microcrédito is a for-profit micro-lending subsidiary of the bank that offers small loans to growing businesses that lack access to conventional forms of credit. Through the provision of microcredit, the bank contributes to the economic and social development of its borrowers, and more broadly promotes Brazil's economic growth. Accion (an international non-profit organization that fights poverty through microfinance) is a minority (20 per cent) shareholder in the venture.

By 2005, Real Microcrédito had over 8,000 active clients – namely, individuals or small enterprises, 95 per cent of which work in the informal sector, and which therefore do not have facilities to gain access to credit through the usual financial institutions that support small businesses. Loans are typically between US$89 and US$8,900, and are often made to entrepreneurs in the favelas (slums) of São Paulo and Rio de Janeiro. The operational organization of Real Microcrédito is designed to build a relationship between the bank's agent and the client, with initial contact likely to be through door-to-door sales calls. The timescale from application to approval/refusal is forty-eight hours, with the agent visiting the client for an assessment. Once approved, the agent returns to the business shortly before a repayment is due, seeking further to establish bonds.[4] Interestingly, despite the social aims of the programme, ABN AMRO states in its 2005 Sustainability report that it is involved in offering microcredit 'for profit, not for philanthropy'.

Conclusion

ABN AMRO Real is clearly seeking to be a CSR leader in both its industry and its region. The bank was awarded the 'Emerging Markets Sustainable Bank of the Year' Award for having shown outstanding leadership in sustainable banking, and applying world-class standards to the integration of social and environmental objectives as a business driver throughout the institution. As such, the bank has helped set best-practice standards in sustainable banking for other Latin American banks. It played a leading role in the development of the BOVESPA sustainability index and launched Brazil's first carbon credit fund. As many as 4,280 socio-environmental deals were approved in 2005. In the same year they were also awarded the Good Corporate Citizen Best Practice by Brazil's business magazine, *EXAME*.

However, the bank's approach is not, of course, without its problems. Some customers, for example, take their stance as being a sign that they are not prioritizing business objectives. In the parent company ABN AMRO's 2005 Sustainability report, the following is cited from a company that no longer banked with them:

> Our company together with some of our peers, have the impression that ABN AMRO's business practices are too much influenced by the opinion of NGO's. Policies on restricting international transfers for certain countries should be set by the government, and not by our banker.
>
> (Worldwood, the Netherlands)

For others, the bank is still seen as not doing enough, and it has been accused of hypocrisy for perceived inconsistencies in its international commitments. A coalition of environmental NGOs marked the occasion of another environmental award being presented to the Dutch parent company in 2006 with a full-page advert (reprinted on p. 348)[5] in the *Washington Post* denouncing the company as a hypocrite due to its bid to finance the controversial Sakhalin II oil and gas project in eastern Russia. While one of the NGOs placing the ad suggested that 'Sakhalin II's radical resource extraction is exactly the type of project that the Equator Principles were designed to prevent', another claimed that 'ABN Amro giving money to Sakhalin II is the same as giving money for extinction of whales and the destruction of salmon runs'; 'ABN Amro should be a real environmental leader and reject financing for oil drilling in Sakhalin', it concluded.

Finally, some of the bank's many employees might also feel that the company's priorities need rethinking following the announcement in April 2006 of an extension to its cost-cutting scheme that saw thousands of job losses in the mid-2000s. The cuts, primarily in the Netherlands, the US, the UK and Brazil, were partially offset by new hires in lower-wage countries, principally India, although the net losses amounted to more than 5,000 staff. Hence, while the firm is clearly a leader in much of its CSR activities in Brazil and elsewhere, the experiences of ABN AMRO also starkly illustrate the challenges CSR brings to large multinational companies given the tremendous scope of activities that CSR encompasses.

Study Questions

1   Set out the CSR issues and initiatives faced by the Brazilian subsidiary of ABN AMRO in the marketplace, workplace, community and environment. How aligned are its activities in these arenas? Do you think ABN AMRO's credibility as a global bank is strengthened or undermined by its CSR activities in Brazil?

2   Can or should a bank be responsible for what its customers use its products and services for? Consider the implications of your answer for firms and their customers in the following industries: (a) automotives; (b) armaments; (c) internet service provision. Explain any similarities or differences.

3   Is it consistent that ABN AMRO undertake a social project like Real Microcrédito, then claim that they do so for financial rather than philanthropic reasons? Consider your argument in the light of David Vogel's discussions about the market for virtue and Porter and Kramer's assertions regarding the competitive advantage of corporate philanthropy.

And the award for

OUTSTANDING ENVIRONMENTAL HYPOCRISY

goes to...

ABN Amro has a decision to make.

Global banking leader ABN Amro promotes itself as an environmental leader for having led the 2003 implementation of the Equator Principles, the first-ever transition away from destructive capital investment and towards an ecologically and socially responsible financial system.

Now, this same bank is considering financing the world's most controversial oil and gas project.

Half a world away, Far East Russia's Sakhalin Island is home to both a thriving fishing community and the only feeding ground for the world's last 100 Western Gray whales. Unfortunately, a consortium led by Royal Dutch Shell seems determined to retrieve oil buried under the seabed of this global treasure. Just underway, the Sakhalin II oil and gas drilling project has already led to a 200-ton oil slick, the construction of oil platforms that interfere with the whales' feeding habitat, and damage to more than 100 local salmon spawning beds. And the "exploration" has only just begun.

Tomorrow, ABN Amro will be presented an award for its commitment to the environment. ABN has a choice to make: the company should either withdraw their consideration for financing Sakhalin II, or decline the award and admit to violating their commitment to the Equator Principles.

Anything else is environmental hypocrisy.

Workers in Kholmsk clean up after a Sakhalin II oil spill. The graffiti reads, "Thank you for not littering!"

 PACIFIC ENVIRONMENT
PacificEnvironment.org

 RAINFOREST ACTION NETWORK
RAN.org

 Sakhalin Environment Watch
Sakhalin.Environment.ru

4   Review ABN AMRO's current Sustainability report. To what extent is the bank developing a tailored approach to sustainability in Brazil compared with its operations elsewhere? Does the maxim 'think global, act local' suit the company, or do some sustainability activities require global action as well?

Notes

1   For further information, see www.sustainability.com and Wanderley (2004), from where much of the information in this section was drawn.
2   For more information, see the Equator Principles website (www.Equator-Principles.com). ABN AMRO led the initial drafting and adoption of the Principles in 2003 and immediately adopted a revised, strengthened version of the Principles in 2006.
3   www.sustainability.com. Sustainability is an independent think-tank. Some of the details presented here are from their *Country Study: Brazil*, March 2006.
4   Some information in this section is drawn from Mugica and Moura (2004). See their work for a more detailed case study.
5   With thanks to the Rainforest Action Network for permission to reprint the advertisement 'An award for Outstanding Environmental Hypocrisy'.

References

Finextra (2006) 'ABN Amro Cuts 1500 Back Office Jobs; Offshores 900', www.finextra.com, 26 April.

International Herald Tribune (2006) 'Profit Up, ABN AMRO Will Cut Jobs', www.iht.com, 26 April.

Mugica, Y. and Moura, F. (2004) ABN AMRO's Real Microcreditor: A Multinational Bank's Entry into the Micro-credit Market. Kenan-Flagler Business School. Available from www.wbcsd.org, World Business Council for Sustainable Development.

Oliveira, J. de (2006) Corporate Citizenship in Latin America: New Challenges for Business. Special Issue, *Journal of Corporate Citizenship*, 21 (Spring).

Wanderley, L. Outtes (2004) *Corporate Social Responsibility in Brazil: Actions and Perceptions in Large Corporations*. Unpublished Ph.D. thesis, University of Cambridge, Judge Institute of Management.

Additional sources of information

www.abnamro.com – ABN AMRO website. See the 2005 Sustainability report for further details on issues discussed here.

www.accion.org – The not-for-profit group which is a partner in the *Real Microcrédito* venture.

www.bancoreal.com.br – ABN AMRO subsidiary in Brazil, Banco Real.

www.ft.com – for information on the 2006 Sustainable Banking Awards.

SECTION C

Managing corporate social responsibility

The final section of this book seeks to examine in more depth the management issues associated with CSR. Of course, this is not, by any means, the first time that we have come across CSR management issues in the text. Each of the four CSR contexts discussed in Section B posed its own unique management challenges, and even basic CSR theory often includes management considerations, such as how to balance stakeholder responsibilities effectively. However, in Section C we will focus much more closely on the practical management side of CSR. After all, discussing CSR in the abstract is not really much use unless it is put into practice by real managers, in real companies, and with real effects on societies.

A focus in this final section on managing CSR does not, however, mean that we will be providing a 'how-to' guide for CSR managers. The purpose of an academic investigation into managing CSR in a global context is more to explore the challenges associated with putting CSR into practice, and to enable a more informed assessment of the different ways in which CSR can be managed and implemented. In so doing, we will certainly cast some light on the strengths and weaknesses of particular CSR management tools and techniques, but we will also be exploring the broader social and political significance of CSR management.

To this end, the final chapters focus on three key aspects, followed by an integrative case study that provides us with the opportunity to explore these issues in a real-life situation:

● CSR reporting and auditing
● CSR strategy and implementation
● CSR in a global context
● Nike case study

In discussing these different aspects of CSR management, we do not hope to cover every single aspect of management practice that might pertain to CSR. After all, as we will make clear, social responsibility is not something that can be easily disentangled from the rest of a company's operations, nor can it be neatly tucked away into a CSR department so that people in other parts of the organization never need to go near it. While many large companies do indeed now have CSR managers or departments, these cannot ever expect to manage every aspect of responsibility in the firm, since CSR issues pervade the organization from top to bottom and right across the global span of operations.

That said, we do hope to introduce the key issues that matter in terms of CSR management in the chapters that follow, such as what makes for a good CSR strategy, and how can CSR audits, reports and codes of conduct contribute to the effective management of CSR. Significantly, we also seek to show that even such 'practical' tools have significant social and political ramifications in terms of social accountability, international governance, and global justice and poverty. By concluding with the Nike case study, we take the opportunity to explore these practical/political issues in perhaps the best-known case of CSR management (or, to some, mismanagement!), demonstrating that, whatever else it is, CSR management is both a huge challenge for companies and a major potential avenue for social and organizational change.

Chapter 9

CSR reporting and auditing

IN THIS CHAPTER WE WILL:

- Explain the basic features of CSR reporting.
- Understand the main reasons why companies become involved in CSR reporting.
- Explore the role of CSR reporting in the broader social accounting process.
- Distinguish key prerequisites of social accounting.
- Discuss key features of good CSR reporting and auditing.

Introduction

A socially responsible company might be expected to respond to the expectations of society – and we have discussed in Section B of the book various ways that managers can address these demands with regard to key stakeholders and issues. A crucial step in this process, however, is how stakeholders actually find out about whether the company has acted responsibly or not. Somehow, a socially responsible company has to prove to its stakeholders that it is actually 'doing the right thing'. This is the point at which CSR reporting and auditing enter the picture.

Companies have long been required to audit and report on their performance, albeit with regard to a very limited range of issues and to just one main stakeholder. The annual report – mandatory for large businesses in most industrialized countries – reports on the financial performance of the firm, and is primarily prepared for the purposes of shareholders and, to a lesser degree, governments (for tax purposes). With the growth of CSR, however, we have seen a rise in *non-financial reporting* by many companies throughout the world, informing various stakeholders about their performance with regard to social and environmental issues. In a recent survey, 90 per cent of the top 100 companies in Europe reported annually about their social performance in some way, mostly in the form of a written report. In the USA the practice appears to be somewhat lower (59 per cent), while in the rest of the world some 61 per cent of the top 100 companies were active in CSR-related reporting (Context, 2006).

CSR Reporting and Auditing: Reasons and Types

If we look at why companies audit and report on their social performance, we can use the typology presented by Garriga and Melé in Chapter 3 (pp. 76–107):

- *Instrumental/economic reasons*. Social and environmental issues might pose a threat to the company's financial performance. In order to manage these risks, companies need to know about them and monitor these risks across time. If a company wants to avoid boycotts from consumers because of its employment practices in the developing world, it has to establish a system that keeps track of employment conditions across its global operations. For example, many companies in the clothing and retail industries conduct *social audits* of their suppliers' factories.
- *Political reasons*. Large multinational corporations are perceived as increasingly powerful institutions in society. This increased power might call for more transparency and accountability to the public in terms of how the corporation has impacted on society (in the same way that a government might report on its social impacts).
- *Integrating demand from stakeholders*. CSR reporting helps companies to improve their interaction with stakeholders. If a company wants to live up to the demands of stakeholders, it has to communicate in detail to these groups about its expectations and the company's performance with respect to these expectations. CSR auditing and reporting might then, ideally, be part of a broader process of dialogue and engagement with stakeholders.
- *Ethical reasons/responding to external pressure*. Companies face growing pressures from governments, investors, customers and competitors to live up to ethical standards. CSR reporting is a tool by which a company can communicate about its ethical values and how well they have performed against these goals. Typical situations are the interactions with large pension funds which increasingly want to know how well a company performs on the social and ethical indicators the fund uses in deciding which shares to add to its portfolio.

Currently, in most countries CSR reporting is still voluntary. There is, therefore, a wide variety in the language and content of CSR reporting. Most companies that publish a CSR report (or 'corporate responsibility' report, or 'corporate citizenship' report – we will regard these as synonymous) tend to inform their readers rather generally about the social performance of the company. Some companies may also choose to publish a 'Sustainability report' which will also tend to include environmental (and sometimes economic) issues and is a more popular way of couching CSR in Europe.

CSR reports are normally a result of a larger process of 'social accounting' within the company. A key element of this process is the 'social audit' which normally describes the actual measurement or checking exercise of the various indicators of social performance, such as pollution levels or number of injuries in the plants. Good CSR reports – analogous to financial reports – would also include some form of 'verification' resulting in an 'assurance' statement providing the addressees of the report with some indication about how accurate the CSR report actually is (Owen and O'Dwyer, 2008).

Current Trends in CSR Reporting

CSR reporting has often been criticized as nothing more than glossy public relations statements which make the company look good but have nothing do to with the actual social performance of the organization (Laufer, 2003). Being a voluntary exercise, the chief problem seems to be that it is mainly up to the individual company to decide what to put into the report, how to measure social performance, and how to verify and audit the report. This heterogeneity in approach makes it not only rather difficult for stakeholders to assess the actual quality of a company's CSR; it also prevents the reader from comparing different companies with regard to their CSR performance. These problems have led to a number of fairly recent initiatives to standardize CSR reporting and to provide mechanisms for enhancing the credibility of CSR reports.

The most prominent effort to standardize CSR reporting is the guidelines of the 'Global Reporting Initiative' (GRI), published for the first time in 2000.[1] The GRI is a multi-stakeholder initiative of NGOs, industry associations and many large (and some small) businesses, working together to develop a framework for sustainability reports. By 2006, there were nearly 900 organizations using the GRI guidelines in developing their reports, and more than 150 organizations across thirty-three countries publishing reports recognized as 'in accordance' with the GRI guidelines. The GRI guidelines are developed for different sectors and are continually updated, the most recent set being released in 2006. While the GRI is an important effort to harmonize CSR reporting, some critics argue that in attempting to be inclusive and consultative its requisites tend to be negotiated down to facilitate compromise (Laufer, 2003).

Another problem of CSR reports is the lack of assurance with, for instance, only three out of the top 100 US companies using external assurance for their CSR report (Context, 2006). To address this credibility gap, AccountAbility, the London-based CSR non-profit organization headed by Simon Zadek (see below), launched in 2002 the 'AA1000S Assurance Standard', which aims to provide a coherent framework for assessing the processes underlying a CSR report.[2] Its adoption by industry has been rather limited so far with just fifty-eight companies worldwide using the standard in 2006. While many of these standardization efforts are still work-in-progress, it may be expected that this is an ongoing area of concern and will result in future activities. The next landmark in this debate is certainly the new ISO 26000 standard on CSR which is due to be launched in 2008 (Sandberg, 2006).

Introducing the Readings

The readings in this chapter emerge from an influential group of CSR accounting scholars and practitioners who have been instrumental in pioneering CSR auditing and reporting in Europe. They provide an overview of the system of accounting underlying CSR reporting and also provide some concrete insights into the actual process of generating a CSR report.

Social accounting as the basis of CSR reports

The paper by Rob Gray, Colin Dey, David Owen, Richard Evans and Simon Zadek was published at a time when CSR reporting was about to become a practice no longer adopted only by CSR pioneers such as Body Shop or Ben and Jerry's but a standard feature of large mainstream companies around the globe. It provides a comprehensive overview of the definitions, concepts and contestations in social accounting, and highlights three major elements which help us to understand what effective CSR reporting actually is. They explain, first of all, the need to orient CSR reporting towards specific stakeholders. Second, they introduce the principle of accountability, which characterizes key features of effective accounting. And, third, more on a theoretical note, they embed CSR reporting in the context of the idea of 'polyvocal citizenship'. While the latter is probably a more challenging academic read, it nevertheless makes clear that CSR reporting is not just a new 'tool' but actually reflects fairly far-reaching changes in modern society with major implications for companies. Written by both academics (Dey, Gray, Owens) and practitioners (Evans, Zadek), the paper closes with a case study adding practical clout to the theoretical argument.

What makes for successful CSR reporting?

The paper by Simon Zadek, Peter Pruzan and Richard Evans provides more insight into the practicalities of what they refer to as 'social and ethical accounting, auditing and reporting (SEAAR)'. The article provides a brief overview of the history of the field, demonstrating that it was foremost a European initiative developed in Denmark and the UK. The 'quality principles' put together on the basis of their practical work and theoretical analysis represent an essential guide to the key criteria for good CSR reporting and auditing.

Study Questions

1   How would you convince a CEO of a large public company of the benefits of pub-
    lishing a CSR report? Which arguments might he or she find most compelling?
2   What is a CSR report and how is it related to stakeholder management in an
    organization?
3   What are the processes involved in preparing for the development of a CSR
    report? How important are these processes in determining the quality of the final
    report?
4   What do you think are the main reasons that the standardization efforts of CSR
    reporting are still more or less in their infancy? What are the main drawbacks
    for such initiatives and how could they be addressed?
5   Select a CSR report of a company of your choice on the internet. Try to assess
    its quality by using the 'quality principles' as outlined in the paper by Zadek
    et al.

Notes

1   http://www.globalreporting.org.
2   http://www.accountability21.net/.

References

Context (2006) *Global Corporate Responsibility Reporting Trends 2006*, London:
    Context Consulting.
Laufer, W. (2003) 'Social Accountability and Corporate Greenwashing', *Journal of
    Business Ethics* 43(3): 253–261.
Owen, D. and O'Dwyer, B. (2008) 'Corporate Social Responsibility: The Reporting
    and Assurance Dimension', in A. Crane, A. McWilliams, D. Matten, J. Moon
    and D. Siegel (eds) *The Oxford Handbook of Corporate Social Responsibility*
    (forthcoming), Oxford: Oxford University Press.
Sandberg, K. (2006) 'Groundwork Laid for ISO 26000', *Business and the
    Environment* 17(1): 14.

STRUGGLING WITH THE PRAXIS
OF SOCIAL ACCOUNTING: STAKEHOLDERS,
ACCOUNTABILITY, AUDITS AND PROCEDURES

Rob Gray, Colin Dey, Dave Owen, Richard Evans and Simon Zadek

Introduction

Social accounting, after its brief heyday in the early to mid-1970s (see, for example, AICPA, 1977; Estes, 1976; Gray, Owen and Maunders, 1987; Gray, Owen and Adams, 1996b), had disappeared almost entirely from both the language of practice and the orthodoxy of conventional accounting by the late 1970s. It returned to its previous obscurity even in accounting academe (see, for example, Gray *et al.*, 1987, 1991; Parker, 1986). The re-emergence of environmental accounting in the late 1980s and early 1990s (in so far as environmental accounting can, perhaps, be conceived of as one part of the social accounting concern)[1] appears to have been at least one of the reasons behind a current resurgence of interest in social accounting.[2] By the mid-1990s, not only was there an increase in the academic attention given to the area but, more importantly for this paper, there was a notable re-emergence of practice in the field. Indeed, social accounting is attracting an almost unprecedented level of interest at the present time. Recent social accounts issued by Traidcraft plc, Shared Earth, The New Economics Foundation and The Body Shop in the UK, and the SbN Bank in Denmark and Ben and Jerry's in the USA, for example, have all attracted widespread publicity. The Royal Society of Arts in the UK has published *An Inquiry into Tomorrow's Company* which recommends the development, use and disclosure of social performance indicators.[3] These and related developments, together with the recent formation of the Institute of Social and Ethical Accountability (ISEA),[4] have made the technical problems of social accounting a matter of some urgency if social accounting now is to develop in any systematic way and neither fizzle

We gratefully acknowledge the assistance provided by many individuals and organizations in developing this paper. We are grateful for the financial support received from the ESRC, The Carnegie Trust and the ACCA who have funded – or are continuing to fund – elements of this research project. We wish to express our thanks to the staff at Traidcraft plc and Traidcraft Exchange (especially Murdoch Gatwood) who have been so supportive and patient throughout the (continuing) research process. Jan Bebbington, David Collison, Emily Dick-Forde, Reza Kouhy, Ken McPhail and Noel Tagoe of the University of Dundee, and Sue Llewellyn of Edinburgh University were especially helpful in helping us to try to clarify the theoretical issues raised by the paper. We also acknowledge the very helpful comments on earlier drafts of this paper from Nabil Baydoun, Jan Bebbington, Jane Broadbent, Penny Ciancanelli, John Grinyer, Jim Haslam, John Innes, Richard Laughlin, Alasdair Lonie, Peter Raynard and colleagues who attended presentations at the CSEAR Summer School and at the Universities of Glasgow and Dundee.

out through lack of direction nor be captured and trivialized by powerful organizations.

This emergence of practice has brought both an increase in the examples from which researchers could learn about social accounting practice as well as an urgency to the question "how does one do social accounting?" How to do social accounting should not be a trivial question. If organizations are permitted to develop methods of social accounting without any critical assessment of their activities, then any emerging "best practice" can be expected to be partial, *ad hoc*, immanent and legitimising – thereby falling foul of the Marxian, deep green and feminist critiques of social accounting (see e.g., Cooper, 1992; Maunders and Burritt, 1991; Puxty, 1991; Tinker, Lehman and Neimark, 1991). Therefore, what might a "good" or even an "ideal type" of social accounting look like? Once we have an idea what it might look like, we must consider how it might be developed as an applied practice. Such questions, in turn, raise two fundamental problems:

1   What is social accounting?
2   What is the theoretical, political and ethical framework within which one's answers are to be framed?

Not only is there the tautological concern that assessing "good" social accounting needs a yardstick against which it might be judged, but the justification for deriving a practice must lie in the values and emancipatory moment which underpin the suggestions for practice.

Social accounting academics have long found themselves in this difficult and relatively under-populated area – lying between sophisticated critiques of current practice, imagining new (and "ideal") accounting systems and actively engaging with (hopefully emancipatory) practice.[5] The need to resolve the tensions that result from this separation of the "academic" and the "practical" is an increasingly important theme in the accounting literature (see, for example, Gray, 1992; Gray *et al.*, 1996b, 1988, 1991; Mitchell, Puxty, Sikka and Willmott, 1991; Sikka, 1987; Sikka, Willmott and Lowe, 1989, 1991; Tinker *et al*, 1991).[6] It is for this reason that we use the term *praxis* in the new title of this paper. While the theoretical critiques of accounting and new accountings must, in the interests of scholarship, be fully engaged with, this is not enough. Practice must be encouraged and we must find ways to encourage that practice to develop in a manner which is potentially emancipatory – not repressive.[7]

It is these tensions that this paper seeks to address. The paper is, therefore, very – perhaps overly – ambitious. To theorize a social accounting, to deduce lessons of best practice and to begin to derive standards for social accounting practice – while remaining cognizant of the radical critiques of social accounting – are clearly more than a single paper could hope to achieve. At the same time, the practice of social accounting is developing rapidly. New methods of accounting are being derived, new institutional arrangements are being developed and practitioners are meeting new difficulties. The paper is therefore explicitly exploratory and excuses its thinness in places in its attempts to bring *some* system to developing practice as a matter of some urgency. If the paper, then, can act as a catalyst, research agenda and starting-point for further refinement, it will have been more than successful.

This paper belongs to a continuing series in which we seek to develop our understanding of the theoretical and practical issues of social accounting (see, e.g. Dey, Evans and Gray, 1995; Evans, 1991; Gray *et al.*, 1988, 1996b; Harte and Owen, 1987; Raynard, 1995; Zadek and Evans, 1993; Zadek and Raynard, 1995). In line with those other papers, the present discussion is based on a belief in the primacy of democracy;[8] the importance and power of accountability in the development and discharge of democracy; and is empirically grounded in the experience arising from the production of the social accounts mentioned above.[9]

The paper itself seeks a synthesis of the different approaches to social accounting and then explores how the resulting theoretical structure can be employed in the systematic production of "auditable" social accounts.[10] This exploration is undertaken through an illustration of two cases based on the UK Traidcraft experience. This process, we believe, takes us towards a "portable" social accounting methodology that allows us (to use conventional accounting terminology) to begin a process of iteration towards a conceptual framework for social accounting and the derivation of generally accepted social accounting principles and basic social accounting standards.[11]

The paper is structured as follows. The second section introduces some of the underlying themes on which this paper draws. Rather than analysing these themes, this section simply attempts to locate the discussion in the wider theoretical literature. The third section then looks at terminology and outlines some different approaches to social accounting. The fourth and fifth sections examine three of the theoretical perspectives which can be taken on the organization–society relationships and which, thus, can be employed to guide the form of any subsequent social account. A broad synthesis of these three perspectives is offered in the sixth section. Sections seven and eight report the experiences of, respectively, Traidcraft plc and Traidcraft Exchange in their development of their own social accounts. Lessons about constructing the (social) accounting entity are drawn from the first case. The second case is used to illustrate how "three layers of information" can bring us towards a more complete social account. This case also flags up the role of auditing. Section nine is a short report of the key elements that our experiences have led us to believe are the backbone of a systematic social accounting practice and might, thus, form a basis for the emergence of social accounting standards.

Locating the Discussion: Some Initial Theoretical Reflections

It would be inappropriate – if only for reasons of space – to attempt to revisit all aspects of the social accounting debate here (but see Gray *et al.*, 1996b, for an introduction to some of the issues). This section will, therefore, seek to identify – in very general terms – the principal theoretical themes which will underpin the later analysis and discussion.

In the first place, social accounting is conceived of as the universe of all possible accountings. From a conventional accounting perspective, it is what happens if the constraining principles of conventional accounting (i.e. an accounting entity, a focus on economic events, financial description of those events and an assumption of [predominantly financial] users; see Gray, Laughlin and Bebbington, 1996b) are relaxed. This universe is, probably, infinite and, consequently, beyond our scope here. So we initially restrict our discussion to *formal accounts* from *accounting entities*. (These issues are discussed in more detail below.) We thus exclude – most obviously – informal (verbal and non-verbal accounts) between individuals and groups.

Similarly we restrict ourselves to a concern with the production of *single* periodic accounts. We should, however, stress that such single accounts do not assume a single point of view. That is, the social accounts are assumed to be, at least potentially, both *polyvocal* and *multiple* (see e.g. Zadek and Evans, 1993). This restriction to a single, formal account may well open the resulting social accounting to criticisms from feminist – and perhaps post-modern – critiques. That is, our approach to the social account may be masculine-gendered and modern. We have not addressed this formally, but the later discussion does, we suggest, acknowledge these charges and may go some way towards meeting the criticisms.

Furthermore, there are both political and social issues embedded in the social accounting which we have not explicitly explored. For example, almost any system of social accounting of which one can conceive will involve transfers of power, either through the democratisation of organizations and of capital or through the capture and manipulation of social issues by organizations and by capital. Similarly, there is a wide range of concerns over such matters as the role of accounts in reifying, constructing, reinforcing and trivializing organizations and relationships, both within and between those organizations (see e.g. Francis, 1990; Hines, 1988, 1989, 1991b, 1992; Lavoie, 1987; Meyer, 1986). How successfully such critiques can be levelled at this project – and perhaps undermine it – are matters dealt with only tangentially in this paper.

Next, social accounting is conceived of here as being both hermeneutic and emancipatory. It is hermeneutic in the sense of a "hermeneutic dialectic process" (Laughlin and Broadbent, 1996) which seeks out a means that might lead us towards reflexive mutual understanding between the organization and its stakeholders. These understandings will relate to both organizational activity and the accountability(ies) – see later – attaching to those activities. In this sense, the social accounting practice must be continuing and evolving. It is emancipatory in that its aim is to redress power asymmetries between organizations and their stakeholders through the reporting of information. This emancipatory moment lies beyond the accountability itself and, rather, underpins the project and provides its motivation. The project seeks to enhance the democratic virtues of transparency and accountability. It seeks this through (admittedly under-specified) assumptions that an informed demos is thereby empowered in its decision making and action to seek more benign organizational activity. Similarly, the production of social accounts is assumed to have an information inductance effect on the part of organizational managers that will encourage more ethically desirable forms of activity.

However, the specific focus employed here is rather less dependent on the optimism (and utility) which would justify a social accounting by reference to outcomes flowing from that accounting information, but is rather more concerned with deontological and intrinsic motivations. That is, the fulcrum of social accounting employed here is the discharge of organizational accountability. Accountability is conceived of as relating to the rights to information of a participatory democratic society which, for the sake of this project, is conceived of as neo-pluralist in structure.[12] Such choices have two implications: first, the choice of a neo-pluralist democratic accountability defines a "problem space" within which all parties can debate. It is reminiscent of – though in no sense synonymous with – Habermas' ideal speech situation. That is, Western practice and Western critique can all engage in this space because the conception does not necessarily deny the legitimacy of organizational practice, but brings to it critiques drawn from pristine liberal economic democracy, Marxism, deep green and feminist positions. While social accounting exists in a space critiqued by each of these positions – whether the critique from practice or the radical critique from academe – there remains a hermeneutic engagement, which a priori we find valuable, even essential.[13] The second implication of our choice is that, in a strict interpretation of accountability, action and decisions as a consequence of the discharged accountability are not necessarily part of the story. A participatory demos may well have rights to information, but once informed may choose not to act on that information. The assumptions of action and decision lie prior to the concern with accountability itself.

With this outline of the prior concerns which attempt to link this project with the wider theoretical literature, we can turn now to the body of the paper and explore the issue of terminology and definition, before moving into an exploration of the conceptual frameworks for an applied social accounting.

Social? Ethical? Accounting? Auditing?

A wide variety of terms have been employed in social accounting. Historically, the terms "social audit", "social responsibility accounting" and "corporate social reporting" have, from time to time, been popular (see e.g. Mathews, 1993), while more recently social accounts have appeared under the titles, *inter alia*, "social audits" (the early Traidcraft reports, for example), "ethical statements" (SbN Bank), "values report" and "social statement" (Body Shop). Further analogues can be found – "ethical audits" is a term favoured by some individuals.[14] The confusion generated by the diversity of terms is partly illusory, but also partly real. All the discussion and the practice hold a number of central ideas in common but, through the use of a diverse terminology, feature these central ideas with different degrees of exactitude. Indeed, the different conceptions permit undefined terms to encourage agreement and also, perhaps, to avoid historical baggage attached to terms which some parties may prefer to avoid.[15]

Nevertheless, we stay with *social accounting* as the generic term because it is the longest established and the simplest term (and construct) with which to work. Furthermore, as we shall see, we find its resonances of conventional accounting especially useful when defining the elements of a social accounting process.[16]

All social accounting (regardless of its actual title) relates to the presentation of information about organizational activity.[17] The resulting *account* (whatever the form it takes) is presented to someone – even if it is only the organization itself (see below). The social account, as with any other account, presupposes some defined *accounting entity* (there has to be something about which to account), although, as we shall see, the relationship is reflexive. Equally, there is an implication of complexity and size in the relationship between the accounting entity and those to whom the account is presented. This last point arises because we tend to find that *formal* accounts are only necessary in complex situations in which personal communication, trust and intimacy (what Rawls calls "closeness") are threatened or have disappeared. (For more detail see e.g. Lehman, 1995.) In personal and usually relatively simple situations involving only a small number of parties and/or activities, an *informal* account will suffice. The precise point at which an informal accounting in or by (for example) families breaks down and leads to the need for a formal account in or by (for example) multinational companies is quite unclear but deserving of further research. Finally, implicit in the notion of an account there is some intended or actual recipient to whom the account is (informally, perhaps) addressed. In the neo-pluralist accountability framework employed here, the *stakeholders* are those with rights to the account and it is for them that the account is prepared. Whether or not they use it, and if so for what, and whether or not other parties see and/or use the account, are largely irrelevant.[18] So, beyond the identification, prioritisation and needs of stakeholders (see below), it is possible to leave any conception of the recipient's decision making about or choice of action implicit in the discussion.

These three elements – the *accounting entity*, the *account* and the *intended recipient* (or group of recipients) *of the account* – are not sufficient in themselves to define social accounting. Figure 1 provides a collection of possible accounting processes which involve these three elements. The possible groupings of social accounts are initially defined by reference to who prepares and who receives the account.

We are going to restrict ourselves to the formal account and, furthermore, to the formal account which is *prepared by* (or on behalf of – see below) *the accounting entity* and (externally) *reported* or *disclosed* parties other than the directors/controllers of the reporting organization (although this does not preclude such parties from receiving – and, indeed, using – such an account). (This restriction places us in the shaded box in Figure 1.) The reasons for these restrictions, we believe, are not trivial. The restriction to the formal account arises from the complexity of the organizations about which the questions of social accounting most obviously arise.[19] The restriction to externally disclosed reports is driven by the commitment to accountability – of which more later (see e.g. Medawar, 1976). The matter of who prepares the report is really a matter of pragmatic and economic concern.[20] For example, while the first Traidcraft report (social audit 1992/93) was prepared with considerable external input from NEF, it was ultimately published by – and thus "owned by" – the reporting entity. This ownership is important

Report for the consumption of ...	Report compiled by ...	
	Internal participants	External participants

Internal participants	• Social accounts;
	• Programme evaluation;
	• Attitudes audit;
	• Performance indicators;
	• Compliance audit;
	• Environmental audit and accounting
		• Quanto reports, e.g.:
		  – Health and safety;
		  – Equal opportunities;
		  – EPA;
		• Environmental consultants;
		• Waste and energy audits

External participants	• Social accounts;
	• Social reports:
	  – narrative;
	  – quantitative;
	  – qualitative;
	  – financial;
	• Compliance audit;
	• Mission statements;
	• Environmental report;
	• Employee reports
		• Social Audit Ltd;
		• Counter Information Services;
		• New Consumer;
		• Consumers' Association;
		• Friends of the Earth;
		• Greenpeace;
		• Journalists;
		• Ethical investment/EIRIS;
		• External "social audits"

Figure 1 Examples of different approaches to social accounting

Source: Adapted from Gray, 1991, p.3

because the organization must thus stand by the contents of the report – it was, after all, the duty of the organization to be accountable that had driven the account in the first place. But there are other pragmatic reasons – most especially that:

- externally prepared reports typically experience problems in gaining access to the appropriate levels of data; and
- the economics of the regular production of social accounts will effectively preclude any systematic mechanism other than self-reporting by the organization involved (see e.g. Gray *et al.*, 1987, 1996b; Medawar, 1976). Furthermore, the analogue of relating social accounting to conventional financial accounting naturally leads us to assume the preparation of the report by the accounting entity.[21]

These restrictions, while placing us in the shaded box in Figure 1, still do not, of themselves, produce a full definition of the social account. As Figure 1 might suggest, a wide range of fairly basic examples – as well as the more developed examples to which we have already referred – would still be encompassed by our terms. Indeed, most large companies produce a range of social and environmental information which, if collated, might pass as a social account (see e.g. Gray, 1997).

Consequently, it might be helpful if a further schema, refining slightly the elements of Figure 1, were to be presented at this point. The following provides a classification of approaches to social accounting based on the complexity and system of the approaches and, more pertinently, their likely desirability to a conventional business organization:[22]

(1) *Company preferred:*

- existing corporate reporting of both voluntary and mandatory data;
- existing corporate public relations and advertising/education data;
- collation of the above into a single "social accounting" document – the "silent account";
- "one-off" experiments with approaches to social accounting.

(2) *Systematic corporate social accounts:*

- stakeholder reporting;
- describing the characteristics of the stakeholder relationship(s);
- accountability reporting;
- reporting of the voices of the stakeholders.

(3) *External "social audits":*

- single issue reporting (e.g. consumers, environmentalists etc.);
- systematic social audits;
- one-off reporting (e.g. investigative journalism).

The terms will be discussed and developed as the paper progresses. It is the second group – the systematic social accounts – that is of concern to us in this paper.

To refine our definition further we need to address the matter of theory and, in particular, the place and interpretation of accountability in the derivation of a social account.

Accountability and Stakeholder Perspectives

Our experience with social accounting plus our reading of the literature lead us to conclude that there are three dominant ways of theorizing[23] the (accountability) relationship between an accounting entity and its "outside world".[24] We want to conceive of these theoretical perspectives as a series of (overlapping) layers which can be synthesized and built up into a rich conception of the organization–society interaction. These three perspectives are a *stakeholder* perspective, an *accountability* perspective, and what we shall call a *polyvocal citizenship* perspective (PCP).[25] These three conceptions build up from the "harder", more functional organization-centred stakeholder, perspective, through the slightly "softer", society-centred accountability, perspective to (perhaps) the "softest", stakeholder-centred polyvocal citizenship perspective. (We will discuss the first two below, and then examine PCP in more detail in the next section.)

Stakeholder perspective

The stakeholder approach to analysis is well-established in the management (and accounting) literature (see e.g. Donaldson, 1988; Nasi, 1995; Roberts, 1992; Ullmann, 1985). Its essence is the definition of all those groups or parties[26] who are influenced by and/or who influence the organization (or accounting entity). From this point on, stakeholder theory struggles to maintain anything other than an organization-centred legitimacy because while the groups may be defined with a fair degree of objectivity, who (other than the organization) is left to define the priorities among the stakeholders and the information that should be disclosed to each one? Stakeholder theory, therefore, is concerned typically with how the organization *manages* its stakeholders. Thus, information disclosed to the stakeholders may be assumed more properly by the organization to be part of a legitimacy and/or social construction process. Stakeholder theory is relatively silent on how the organization does – if at all – monitor and respond to the *needs* of the stakeholders. It will do so, generally speaking, when it is in the organization's traditional interests (profit-seeking, for example) to do so. Therefore a social account based on the stakeholder perspective has social value only if we assume the beneficence of the organization and further assume that the stakeholders' needs can be subsumed morally with those of the organiza-tion.[27] If we assume this, then "market forces" will generally produce the sort of social accounting which is in the organization's best interests. We might reasonably assume that it is this thinking which produces the sort of voluntary social and environmental disclosure we currently see.

Despite its serious limitations, stakeholder theory *does* help us. It defines the influencing/influenced groups for us and explicitly defines what *account-ability* the organization itself is willing to recognize and discharge.[28] To deny the organization any role in a definition of a social account seems inappro-priate and largely indefensible. This, therefore provides our first layer – the stakeholder analysis in which the organization defines the accountability. To this we now add the accountability perspective – society's views.

Accountability perspective

Accountability and its role in social accounting has been discussed widely. It is concerned with the relationships between groups, individuals, organiza-tions and the *rights* to information that such relationships entail. Simply stated, accountability is the duty to provide an account of the actions for which one is held responsible. (For more detail see, e.g. Gray *et al.*, 1986, 1987, 1988, 1991, 1996b). The nature of the relationships – and the attendant rights to information – are contextually determined by the society in which the relationship occurs.

It is definitionally true that some sort of relationship will exist between an organization and each of its stakeholders. As we saw above with stake-holder theory, part of these relationships may be economic in nature and the terms determined by the parties – as reflecting their relative power in the relationships. The information flowing through the relationship will be determined by the power of the parties to demand it (a power which, where it exists, could arise from either the intrinsic abilities and power of the groups concerned or from the legislative processes of the society) and/or the will-ingness/desire of the organization to provide it. Society as a whole reflects (what might be thought of as) a concern that all such relationships and their attendant information rights should not be left entirely to the parties. The most obvious manifestation of this is statute law (e.g. companies' acts, equal opportunities legislation) and standards established by statutory bodies (e.g. an environmental protection agency, health and safety at work inspectorate). Additionally, other mechanisms (such as, voluntary codes of practice) will from time to time enter the public domain as an agreed or, at least, negotiated part of the stakeholder relationship. These "empirical, beyond-law" deter-minants of accountability have been referred as "quasi-law" (see, e.g. Gray *et al.*, 1987, 1988, 1991, 1996b). The extant law plus this "quasi-law" will therefore represent the first (and major) element in the construction of society's views on the accountability of organizations (see e.g. Stone, 1975).

It is, of course, naïve to assume a simple one-to-one mapping of a "society's" beliefs about the nature of relationships and the attendant information rights and extant law – even with the addition of "quasi-law". On the one hand, rights to information must reflect asymmetries of power and essential lags between a society's views and the enactment of law (see especially Dowling and Pfeffer, 1975; Epstein and Votaw, 1978; Stone, 1975). On the other hand, such rights to information can be argued to comprise both "positive" (legal) and "normative" (moral) rights (see e.g. Likierman, 1986; Likierman and Creasey, 1985). Empirical determination of the moral rights is clearly contestable. These moral rights must, in some manner, be added to the positive rights to reflect current views of accountability. Some of these rights will be accepted by organizations – through, for example, mission and/or ethical statements – and, to this extent at least, there will be a convenient overlap between the information rights determined by stakeholder theory and those determined by accountability theory.[29] But there are moral rights that will not be so accepted. Here one must resort, within an accountability framework, to other expressions of society's values. Malachowski (1990) for example argues for a recognition of media concern as an approximation of new emerging issues of society's concern. Broadly, this may be a plausible basis. For illustration, health and safety concern over accidents rose as a major issue in the UK in the 1980s while environmental issues clearly claimed a place in society's conception of the organization–society relationship in the early 1990s (see e.g. Gray et al., 1995b). Less obvious issues which are not governed by extant law – for example fair trade and impact on developing countries – are more clearly a matter for negotiation.

The second strand of social disclosure would derive therefore from the established accountability relationships and seek to provide information to which the stakeholders have a right.[30]

There is a danger, however, that a social accounting founded on a combination of stakeholder and accountability perspectives would be too inert and only slowly responsive to changing stakeholder needs. More particularly, the *modern* basis of these perspectives leave them open to challenge from perspectives arising out of critiques informed by more fluid and, perhaps, more "post-modern" conceptions. It is concerns such as these that have encouraged many of the newer social accounts to adopt the *polyvocal citizenship* perspective. It is to this that we now turn.

New Conceptions of the Organization–Society Dialogue: A Challenge

Many of the more recent social accounts, especially those influenced by NEF and Traidcraft, have adopted an approach to social accounting which has not previously been discussed in the social mainstream accounting literature (but see e.g. Raynard, 1995; Zadek and Evans, 1993; Zadek and Raynard, 1995).

This polyvocal citizenship perspective (PCP) draws broadly on Habermasian discourse ethics and directly from Guba and Lincoln's (1989) *Fourth Generation Evaluation*[31] and then applies the ideas in a social accounting setting. In its novelty, its explicitly hermeneutic concern and its emphasis on privileging the voices of stakeholders, the PCP offers an alternative conception of social accounting.[32]

The approach is built around *stakeholder dialogue* and its essence lies in providing each of the stakeholders with a "voice" in the organization. Focus groups are held with each stakeholder group, from which key issues are identified, and a wider constituency of the stakeholder group is consulted to collate their views on these and other issues. The social account comprises predominantly (but not exclusively) a reporting of the voices of the stakeholders. PCP thereby constitutes a different way of seeing the organization. Thus, if we were to take this to extremes (and thus attempt to typify the PCP approach as a post-modern "straw man"), the terms of the organization–society/group relationship are established, not by the organization or the society, but by the stakeholders themselves. More precisely, though, PCP is a form of symbolic interactionism (Guba and Lincoln, 1989) in which (to borrow the words of Innes, Nixon and Tagoe, 1996, p. 6), "the organizational stakeholders are seen as constituting and sustaining their own reality – and that of the organization – both socially and symbolically". The PCP social account aims to give voice to these actors so that their systems of interpretation and meanings and processes of structuring and organizing are revealed.[33]

The PCP, in drawing from Guba and Lincoln, is clearly working at the boundary of the modern and the post-modern.[34] The most important element of this is the way in which the organization is conceived. Again, taking this to extremes, the PCP might be typified as assuming that the organization has no existence prior to or independent of the stakeholders. That is, the stakeholders in a social constructivist sense *create* the organization. Such a view is central to Guba and Lincoln's analysis which ontologically denies the existence of an objective reality and assumes that epistemologically understanding (in this case represented by the social account) emerges from the interaction between observer and observed (Guba and Lincoln, 1989, p. 44). Therefore, while the stakeholders are privileged in the construction of the organization and the social account, the approach is hermeneutic and iterative with refined and developed understandings emerging over several cycles of the social accounting process.[35]

The NEF/Traidcraft approach does not stop here, though. First, at least in the early attempts at (what were referred to as) "social audits", the "social auditor" was cast in the role of Guba and Lincoln's *evaluator* whose job it is to encourage and engage with the dialogue process towards a *responsive constructivist evaluation* (in our case, a social account rather than an "evaluation" as such). Thus, there is no role for an external objective audit or attestation because, quite simply, such "externality" and "objectivity" cannot exist in the model. Second, the NEF/Traidcraft approach placed the "core values" of the organization at the heart of the dialogue (and thus at the heart of the account). These core values – which may emerge from the social accounting process or may be enshrined in mission statements or statements of ethics or principles – become that thing which the social accounting process is "evaluating" and negotiating and, hopefully, changing as a consequence of the stakeholder dialogue.[36] Consequently, the resulting social account will contain data reflective of the "core values" of the organization and which, inevitably, must overlap with the information we would expect to flow into a social account from the stakeholder and accountability perspectives itemized above.

Hopefully it is apparent from the brief outline above that the NEF/ Traidcraft version of PCP (more usually called the "stakeholder dialogue" approach) is concerned with *praxis*. In its concern to evolve an active practice, it has clearly moved away from the *solipsism* (see e.g. Laughlin and Broadbent, 1996) of the "pure" Guba and Lincoln approach and similarly edged away from the post-modern conceptions of organizational interactions, towards something which begins to look more like Habermas "ideal speech situation" (Habermas, 1978).

Thus, in the context of social accounting, it seems that in the PCP "social auditing" process three things are happening simultaneously:

1   the stakeholders are being encouraged to voice the terms of the accountability relationship, both as they see it currently and how they would wish it to be. That is, the stakeholders are defining the terms of accountability;
2   the stakeholders are active in defining the accounting entity itself;
3   the voices of the stakeholders provide an essential element of the basis for the social account of the organization.

Each of these matters needs to be further explored.

Synthesizing the Perspectives?

The first of the above points – that the stakeholders define their own terms of accountability – fits well with the discussion so far. Allowing through the voices of the stakeholders provides a systematic solution to the hitherto unaddressed problem of how to deal with the inevitable limits that an empirical accountability imposes on the social account.[37] So, in terms of this paper, PCP provides our third (and final) "layer" of the accountability relationships which comprise the social account: organization-, society- and stakeholder-determined terms of accountability.

The second point – how one is to conceive of and practically determine the definition of the accounting entity – is a subtle and important matter that is all too easily ignored in the stakeholder and accountability perspectives. We will examine this point more fully in a later section.

The third of the points – that it is the stakeholders who (in effect) provide the social account – produces both a significant synergy *and* a significant conflict with other forms of social accounting (as restricted above). The synergy arises from the type of information that PCP generates. This information includes such matters as employees' levels of satisfaction and motivation, customers' levels of satisfaction, environmentalists' anxieties about the organization. This sort of information, while it might be thought of loosely as accountability information, is, indeed, both an expression of the stakeholders' voices and management information of the sort that any organization needs if it is to manage its stakeholders – as suggested by stakeholder theory. In this way, information generated by PCP is both an important addition to the potential discharge of accountability *and* information which management can use under the stakeholder perspective.[38]

On the other hand, the conflict arises between PCP and more conventional approaches for several reasons:

1   Under "conventional" forms of social accounting, the organization provides the social account, whereas in PCP the stakeholders provide it (although the account is actually published and distributed by the organization itself). This latter point places the PCP within the more conventional interpretations of social accounting (see e.g. Gray *et al.*, 1996b) as a hybrid of self-reporting (the shaded quadrant in Figure 1) and the independent social reporting pioneered by units such as Social Audit Ltd (see the bottom right-hand quadrant of Figure 1).

2   Under the extreme version of PCP the account exists *only* as a social construction of the organization – the organization and its relationships do not exist without that construction. The stakeholder-accountability approaches assume an underlying reality which is *reconstructed* by the social account. That is, the latter suggests that the relationships and rights exist prior to the social accounting. Under PCP the relationships and rights do not so exist and are constructed through the account.

3   While the conventional forms of social accounting have been accused of being conservative (see e.g. Tinker *et al.*, 1991), they do have potential for change and evolution (see e.g. Gallhofer and Haslam, 1995; Gray *et al.*, 1996a; Lehman, 1995; Power, 1994). They offer this potential by reference to a wider set of societal values that, it is normally assumed, will challenge the organization's existence. On the face of it, PCP appears to do the same but may well have more conservative – albeit democratic – tendencies. That is, as a consequence of its genesis in the work of Guba and Lincoln, it may – we emphasize *may* – be less likely to assume, seek out and expose conflict between organizational

legitimacy and stakeholder views. This is, however, a practical, rather than a theoretical problem and relates to the final potential source of conflict with more conventional versions of social accounting.

4   There is a potential difficulty in that stakeholders, while their right to a voice is not, to our mind, contestable, may not be informed in a manner which permits the expression of their voice to challenge the essential problems of organizational legitimacy. Unlike the "external social audits" which raise and extend the boundaries of accountability (see example, Gray *et al.*, 1988; Harte and Owen, 1987) the voices may be heard only internally and offer comment only in the terms already set for them by the organizational hegemony.[39]

But these are problems only of degree – all forms of social accounting are susceptible to these problems (see, e.g. Puxty, 1986, 1991). Rather, PCP may, in offering greater synergy with other forms of social accounting, go some way towards muting the criticisms of the social accounting project.

Can the "conventional" stewardship-accountability approaches to social accounting be synthesized with the PCP approach? The answer is probably that they cannot be *fully* synthesized – but only because they draw from a fundamentally different ontology. While all three approaches to social accounting can be thought of as essentially social constructionist, it is the way in which PCP constructs the organization that raises the essential conflict. Yet it is apparent that both are motivated by similar principal concerns – that is to develop social accounting and thereby extend accountability and democracy. The two approaches, although ontologically incompatible, are not necessarily mutually exclusive – but rather it seems to us that they represent alternative perspectives on the organization and are, therefore, mutually reinforcing. There is little question in our minds that the PCP brings an important additional dimension to the processes of social accounting. It adds the (hitherto silent), voices of the stakeholders to the specification and construction of accountability and, as we will see in the next section, helps crystallize the way in which the accounting entity is conceptualized. These, in our judgement, are important developments in the conceptualization and application of accountability. But, for predominantly practical (even pragmatic) reasons, we believe the systematic development of social accounting requires that the organization be the reporting body. As such, it is the business of the reporting organization to construct the social account; and such a social account, to be complete, must, we infer, recognize the voices of the stakeholders. Under the continuing assumption that the organization constructs the account, then the organization needs to report:

● that the stakeholders have (or have not) been given a voice; and
● what those voices had to say about the terms of the organization's accountability.

This does not require that the organization reports the full detail of those voices (as we see in, e.g. *The Body Shop Values Report*, 1996). Should the organization choose to report the detailed findings from the consultations with stakeholders, that then goes beyond the *essential* requirements of an accountability report. In this way, although we stay grounded in the somewhat more realist ontology of the stakeholder-accountability perspective we open up that perspective in a way which can recognize challenges to that ontology.

Whatever the remaining theoretical conflicts, for reasons of practicability and political expedience, some synthesis needs to be found.[40] The further issues that arise in this reconciliation will become clearer, we suggest, when we examine, first, the construction of the accounting entity and, second, the information which must be contained in the channels of accountability. These follow in subsequent sections.

To try to ground the discussion thus far, we turn now to two examples of social accounting produced by Traidcraft plc and Traidcraft Exchange. We will discuss the Traidcraft plc case to illustrate the issues arising when we seek to define the accounting entity and their implications for the accountability information produced. We then discuss Traidcraft Exchange as an illustration of how the three layers of social accounting information can be used to work together.

The Traidcraft plc Case

This section provides a very brief outline of one experience of identifying the organizational stakeholders and defining-negotiating the accounting entity. More detail on the Traidcraft plc experience can be found in Dey *et al.* (1995); Evans (1991); Zadek and Evans (1993), and the published social accounts from the company.[41]

Traidcraft plc (sometimes referred to as "the plc", hereafter), a small "values-based" UK company working with the New Economics Foundation, produced its first comprehensive "social audit" in the UK in 1993.[42] This was the first example of a systematic self-generated and reported social account by a UK company and was a remarkable phenomenon for that alone. But the plc went further, publishing a booklet explaining their underlying thinking (Zadek and Evans, 1993) and committed the company to developing regular systematic social accounts of the company in future years.

Traidcraft plc has a called up share capital of £1.8 million and an annual turnover of nearly £7 million. The company's share capital consists of widely-held – but non-voting – "B" shares, a single "guardian share" which prevents the takeover or control of the company against the principles of the company, and a body of voting "A" shares which are held by the Traidcraft Foundation Trustees. Traidcraft plc's description of itself is given in Appendix 1 which is an extract from the 1994–95 social audit document.[43]

The company has about 150 employees and has reported modest profits in most of the last few years. While the company operates in a financial climate and must be economically viable, the relationships it has with its employees and directors (all of whom accept relatively low salaries), its representatives, agents and shareholders all ensure that the company is not subject to the full blast of the rigours of the late-twentieth century market economy.

The company exists to encourage "fair trade" between the so-called developed and developing countries. Most especially, profit and cash-flow are means to that end and not, as in conventional economic and accounting theory, vice versa. It was not appropriate therefore that the company should examine the extent to which it was living by its principles – especially as the company has always prided itself on its sensitivity to criticism from constituents.

The 1993 social audit was a joint effort by Traidcraft and NEF with a member of NEF working in the company on the development of the principles of the audit and the collation of the appropriate data (see Zadek and Evans, 1993). The audit was subject to a degree of independent attestation from an advisory board established by NEF, and the report was published in late 1993.[44] The 1993 experience had highlighted two major factors:

1   There was confusion of roles over accounting and auditing.
2   It was apparent that producing a systematic and transparent account of the company's activities was more difficult – technically and spiritually – than had been anticipated.

The 1994 and 1995 "social audits" were conducted with less involvement from NEF but were still subject to the audit process from the audit advisory board. Traidcraft plc, at the time of writing, have just completed their 1996 social accounts.

In the development of the 1995 social account (as it is now called), the plc and the audit advisory board met a real practical difficulty in conceiving of the organization and its social audit.[45] A systematic heuristic was needed to allow an explicit specification of the elements of the organization–society–constituents relationship that was practical enough to be applicable to a functioning company *and* which could be articulated in a way that recognizes the societal and political assumptions of the approach in a way sufficiently specific to resonate with the theoretical literature on organizations and accountability.[46]

Defining the accounting entity

Prior to the inception of the project of which this paper is a part, there was no established method for defining a social accounting system. Equally, there is little likelihood that it is possible to derive any one, unique, social account of any organization.[47] One of the many characteristics that makes Traidcraft's social accounting unique is its "semiotic nature" – in the sense that the whole process is designed to elicit a shared meaning or expression of the entity known as "Traidcraft". While power asymmetries are inevitable, all parties who are active in the Traidcraft plc enterprise are given a voice. By this means, a shared account of the organization begins to emerge. This is not to deny that other interpretations of the account are possible (or even desirable) but rather to suggest that the widely shared expression of the account is essentially an expression of communitarian accountability (see e.g. Pallot, 1987, 1991). The process is one in which all active parties, including the widely drawn social audit advisory board, the researcher-advisors of the New Economics Foundation (NEF) and the present researchers construct the organization.

The organization and its accountability

Traidcraft is conceived of as an organization with a transparent permeable membrane, the organizational boundary of which is constantly negotiated (Llewellyn, 1994). It is then conceived of as lying at the centre of a nexus of social relationships which are articulated in a manner akin to a stakeholder model located in a neo-pluralist conception of society. The key here is the notion of relationship. The "best" social accounts are those which, presumably, seem best to express the essence of those relationships. This conceptual model is illustrated – with a significant degree of simplification – in Figure 2.[48]

The relationships are, inevitably, of unequal importance and strength. They are, to a large degree, prioritized by Traidcraft's own mission statement.[49] The strength – or, indeed, the closeness (Gray, 1992) – of the relationships is also part of the defined organization. The "closer relationships" – with employees, the producer communities and even the representatives/agents – are negotiated so that these groups actually become part of "Traidcraft". That is, the organizational boundary membrane is especially thin at these points and is managed to accommodate all, or part of, these additional parties. This could be shown in a development of Figure 2 (see Figure 3 which is a basic attempt at a move towards this) in which, for example, the dominance of the relationship could be shown by the thickness of the line suggesting that relationship and a new "fuzzy" Traidcraft organizational boundary shown by the shaded area (some of this is shown in Figure 3).

The accountability of Traidcraft is an imposed accountability only in the case of any government reporting, any especial demands from the voting shareholders and the existing financial accountability of all UK companies. All other accountability is assumed because of the moral rights of the accountee parties and/or because of the value-based nature of the organization and

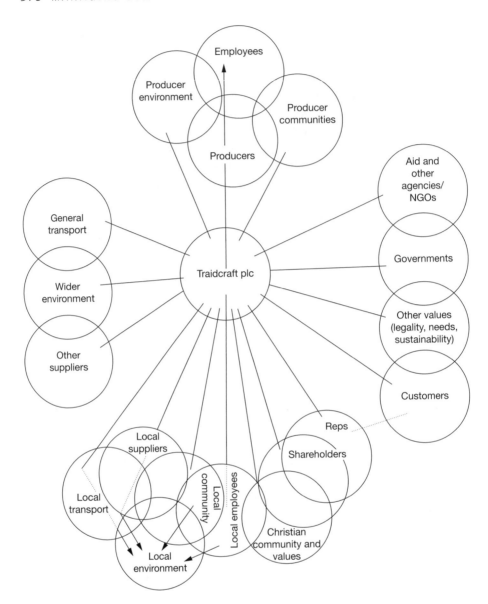

Figure 2 A simple depiction of Traidcraft's relationships

its desire to be accountable (Zadek and Evans, 1993). This principle is then extended via consultation with the stakeholders to give them an explicit voice – one element of which tells the organization (and the auditors) whether their initial perception of the relative strengths and "closeness" of the organizational relationships are adequately represented in the conception of the organizational boundary.

The organizational boundary – the "accounting entity" – is thus defined by the organization's, society's and the stakeholders' negotiations of closeness. Those stakeholders who come into the "entity" are then part of the

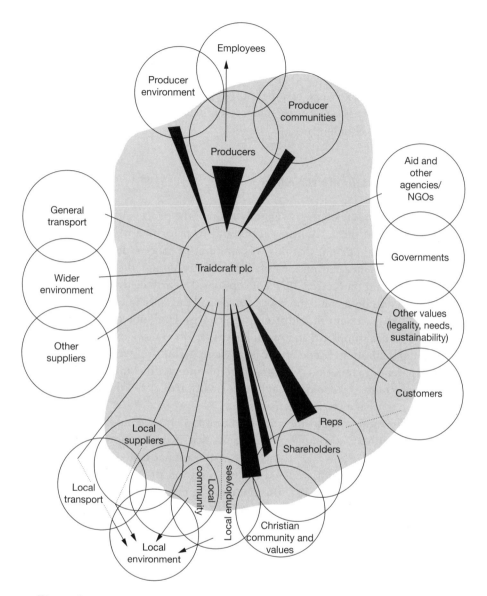

Figure 3 Prioritizing the stakeholder relationships

entity and need, consequently, to be included in the account. In this way, what the account is *of*, and who the account is *to* are clarified.[50] Additionally, some initial prioritization of stakeholder relationships is *explicitly* undertaken.

Traidcraft's relationships and the definition of the accounting entity

The 19 broadly prioritized relationships (shown in Figures 2 and 3) now have to be defined in somewhat greater detail. To provide a full social account, each of the 19 social relationships need to be accounted for: for completeness, the stakeholder, accountability and PCP information needs to be collated, synthesized and reported. However, at the time the Traidcraft social accounts were being prepared these were still unclear. This issue is explicated in the Traidcraft Exchange case below. (Appendix 2 contains an outline of some of the processes that were undertaken in the plc experience with one of its major stakeholders.)

Discussion of defining the entity

The foregoing has tried to give an indication of the process that was used to begin to define the accounting entity and to prioritize its stakeholders. Hopefully, it is apparent that this was an iterative process driven by a convergence between a conventional stakeholder conception, the accountability perspective and the "softer" PCP conceptions. The articulation of the entity is then used to determine the relationships and the consequent information that the social account should attempt to convey. Undoubtedly, the process was a great deal simpler than it would have been for a more explicitly profit-centred organization. Traidcraft plc is explicitly "values-centred", is by nature a transparent organization (with considerable interactions and shared values with many of its stakeholders) and has formally articulated these principles in very extensive mission statements.

Furthermore, ideally, the conception of the entity would be explicitly discussed with all stakeholders to ensure that it has semiotic validity. It seems inevitable, however, that such organizational conceptions will be (often implicitly) negotiated and the organization itself, as the dominant stakeholder, is likely to have a disproportionate influence on the final determination of the entity and, consequently, on the terms of reference offered to the stakeholders in which to express their voices. It is difficult to know at this stage how serious a limitation on social accounting this will prove to be.

The Traidcraft Exchange Case

This section reports a later experiment with the plc's sister organization – the Traidcraft Exchange – in which a systematic social account was sought employing the three layers of accountability information discussed above. The results of this have been published in the Exchange social accounts for 1995–1996.

Traidcraft Exchange (referred to as TX hereafter) is a small charitable company (limited by guarantee) involved in a range of activities concerned primarily with encouraging fair trade. TX has an annual income of a little under £1 million (derived through fundraising, grants and contracts) and a staff of 15–20 people, some of whom are "shared" with the plc. It is, thus, a very small organization. In 1995, TX decided to try to produce its own social account. This would be novel in a number of ways:

1   The organization is so small that while data therefore would be easier to capture, it would not be practicable to try and systematize the process through a social bookkeeping system.
2   The definition of the accounting entity would be even more problematic in that the edges of TX and the plc blur at times and, while this did not seem to be material for the plc, the relative size made it more important for TX; and voluntary organizations frequently have much less formal organizational interactions and the "membrane" was therefore likely to be thinner, fuzzier and more likely to float back and forth.
3   The experience of the plc showed that despite the dominance of the PCP approach, the final social accounts had to contain other data which did not emerge from the voices. These, it seemed in discussions, increased the importance of "completeness" that is central to constructing the social account.
4   It was judged to be a good time to try and discover whether it was possible to derive a "portable" social accounting process. To this end it was decided that the social accounting process should not rely on NEF, should be undertaken by a member of TX with no previous experience of social accounting (although consultancy advice was available from the authors) and, perhaps most dramatically, the *statutory financial auditors* would be requested to publish an audit opinion on the social accounts.

This final point – the statutory financial auditors expressing an opinion – became a touchstone for much else that followed. From discussions with the auditors[51] it became clear that the whole process would have to be documented, social accounting principles derived and stated and the accounting standards of information disclosure would have to be applied. A version of the standard long-form audit report – possibly with heavy qualifications – would be appended to the social accounts. Convincing the firm of accountants to take on this responsibility was not simple and they required a great deal of "comfort" from TX. This, in turn, had a remarkably "tightening-up" effect on the whole process and certainly introduced a higher degree of independence into the process.

The auditors had to be convinced by the definition of the stakeholders. This was achieved by following the same procedure described above for the plc. TX used its (very detailed) mission statement to categorize and prioritize its stakeholders to the satisfaction of the auditors.[52] Then three levels of information were collected about each relationship with each stakeholder. The stakeholder information – in the sense of an organization seeking to manage its stakeholders – was not strictly appropriate because of TX's highly transparent culture and the existence of the detailed mission statement which acts as an effective contract between the organization and its constituents. Information descriptive of the relationships was, however, essential and this was referred to as the "stakeholder data". The legal (identified by reference to statute law) and moral rights (as expressed in the TX mission statement) were then identified and information designed to discharge the resultant accountability was collated for each. Finally, arrangements were made, where possible through (relatively independent) third parties to seek out and collect the voices of the stakeholders. Throughout the process an audit trail was maintained whenever possible and specific notes were kept of all decisions, value judgements and missing information that (inevitably) arose during the process.

The resultant social account then comprised: a section outlining the process used; the auditors' report; and the social account itself, covering the six groups of stakeholders which was finally agreed as covering most of the material stakeholders.[53] Each stakeholder section provided the three layers of information: the descriptions of the relationship, the accountability information and the "voices" of the stakeholders. Although not all information was collected for all aspects of each of the stakeholder groups – completeness, it seems, will always be a problem – the result was a relatively transparent and replicable account. It seriously engaged the auditors and it looks highly likely that the method could be applied to any organization.

The TX social accounting process, then, has two distinctive elements:

1   the relatively programmed approach to the collection and reporting of information; and
2   the "true and fair" report from the statutory financial auditors.

The relatively programmed approach has clearly forced the active participants in the social accounting process towards a more specific explication of the processes and judgements made. That is, although the TX experience, drawing heavily from the plc experience, was an explicitly programmed process, it was not simply mechanical. Too many of the data and relationships were "soft" and required judgement by the social accountant. Such judgement was equally required by the auditors. The auditors' involvement forced a much more explicit process on the accounting process and threw into relief the absence of any accounting standards or GAAP for social accounting. While *generally accepted* auditing principles were found to be helpful in the attestation process, it was an absence of anything with which to define the account that caused problems. (This is a subject for the final section of the paper.) We could usefully express the view that, in our opinions, there never could be – nor, indeed, should be – a completely unqualified audit report on a social account. As a process designed primarily to enhance transparency and accountability, judgement will be essential and one should not expect an independent view to reach – or even agree with – such social judgements. As long as this is clear, the qualification of a "true and fair" report seems a desirable attribute,[54] though it is less easy to be prescriptive about the form that a PCP/evaluator's audit report should take.

In the next section we attempt to synthesize the present experience in order to move towards some social accounting standards.

Towards Social Accounting Standards

It is clear that Traidcraft plc and Exchange are very unusual organizations – in their orientation, values-based transparent cultures and in their size. It would be inappropriate therefore, to generalize their experience as applicable to all organizations. However, subsequent experience with different organizations (many of which are less willing to allow themselves and their inner secrets to be discussed with the same openness and freedom as Traidcraft has permitted)[55] suggests that the basic experience derived from the Traidcraft cases provides an especially useful basis on which to move towards identification of some key elements in the social accounting process. That is what this (final) section will attempt to do – but succinctly, leaving more detailed discussion of theoretical coherence of key social accounting principles to future papers.

There is not, nor is there ever likely to be, a single type of social account. The range of approaches and experiments increases all the time. We consider this healthy and desirable – not least because many different organizations in different social contexts will have different conceptions of the elements discussed here. (The range discussed in Zadek and Raynard [1995] and the emerging NGO community-based social accounts with their own special concerns speak eloquently of this.) Furthermore, as Tinker *et al.* (1991) have shown, no account of organization–society interactions can be static through time – issues, concerns and accountabilities change. This is inevitable.

However, an alternative approach which responds to the increasing requests for guidance on "how to do a social account" with a statement like "any way you want" is not helpful and does not necessarily advance the cause of accountability reporting in any productive way. The recent formation of the Institute for Social and Ethical Accountability (ISEA) was predicated on the need to guide organizations seeking to develop social accounting and to try to deduce best practice in the field where this is possible. This is not a simple task – nor one which can be accomplished quickly. This paper is an early attempt to begin the process of articulating some of the key matters which bodies such as ISEA will need to address.

What, then, do we believe are the key elements in an approach to an "ideal type" of social account that seem to have emerged from the experiences discussed above?

The following is an attempt to synthesize the messages that appear to emerge from the foregoing discussion and from the experiences of social accounting to date:

1 *Conceptual prerequisites for an accounting:*

- an accounting entity;
- an accounting/account.

2 *Definitions derived for:*

- social accounting;
- the recognition and boundaries of the accounting entity – via stakeholder analysis;
- the nature of the account and its completeness.

3 *Assumed:*

- a neo-pluralist context;
- that a stakeholder relationship conception of an organization reflects a neo-pluralist assumption;
- desirability of democracy;
- accountability as a democratic mechanism;
- organizational self-reporting (as opposed to "social audits");
- information should possess the characteristics of completeness, reliability, verifiability, consistency, comparability, understandability;
- the account socially re-constructs an organization which pre-exists the account;
- the reconstruction should be a reflexive and complex series of views from all stakeholders.

4 *Deduced:*

- groups and individuals have rights to information;
- these are resolved informally in smaller non-complex situations;
- formal accounts are needed for accountability in complex situations;
- organizations need to produce accountability accounts;
- rights to information determined by the organization, society, the stakeholders;
- the three layers of information – plus the descriptors of the relationships must be a "complete" account of information provided to assess the extent of the incompleteness;
- independent judgement – preferably without experience in social accounting – is essential to assess completeness and reliability.

5   *Asserted:*

- social accounting is a dynamic and developing process: nothing here should limit further development and experimentation;
- the social accounting is a continuous process of iteration and negotiation.

In time, each of these elements will either prove to be sound – and be expanded on – or will be rejected and replaced. At the present time, they appear to be key useful factors that social accounting needs to consider.

The conceptual framework above accommodates a fairly high degree of synthesis between the TX "accounting-style" approach, which incorporates the stakeholder dialogue voices; and the NEF–Traidcraft approach, in which the voices are paramount and the stakeholder and accountability information are incorporated: nevertheless there still remains a tension about the emphasis given to these two sides of the story.

This tension is perhaps best expressed in the role attributed to the auditor or even the "social auditor". Two alternative approaches have been mentioned above. The first was the use of a completely independent auditor (in the case of TX, the statutory financial auditor) who has no involvement with the construction of the account and simply expresses a (perhaps detailed) opinion on the account's "truth and fairness". The second approach to "auditing" was the far more active involvement of an organization like NEF which helps to construct the social account, oversees the collection of data and responses from stakeholders and relies, in its turn, on an "audit advisory body" to suggest some degree of impartiality in the assessment of the account. We remain split on this issue, but hope – indeed anticipate – some further synthesis of thinking on this matter as experience develops. Our current thinking suggests that we may, indeed, have two – probably similar and complementary – constructs. The first such construct – that with which this paper is primarily concerned – is a formal "social account" whose primary purpose is to construct a social image of the organization. The second construct is the "social audit" (which may or may not produce a social account) whose principal purpose is to encourage a negotiation for change between the organization and its stakeholders. The precise dividing line, if indeed there is one, needs further definition.

A final matter which still needs detailed specification is the way in which the stakeholders' voices are "heard" and collated. These voices are not making a single statement. They are making statements about:

- things about which the accounting organization wishes to know;
- information which each stakeholder would like to receive; and
- their views (e.g. complaints) on the organization and its activities plus the activities and issues the stakeholders would like the organization to address.

The first of these seems to relate to the stakeholder perspective and be useful for organizational management. The second seems to relate to accountability and the stakeholders determining the terms of accountability that they would wish. In both of these cases, it seems likely that the data could be collected by, *inter alia*, questionnaires. Confidentiality does not appear to be so important here. The third type of information does, however, require to be collected and collated – and reported? – by an entirely independent unit which the stakeholder can trust. (Otherwise are, for example, employees going to say things which might incur the wrath of management?) This is an emerging issue on which more work is required.

The social accounting agenda has opened out as never before. Certainly, for the first time in more than 20 years there is an active and dynamic process with which researchers and teachers need to engage. Academic engagement with the environmental accounting and reporting process has been fairly successful. Drawing from that, academe now needs to help bodies like ISEA set a new foundation for the formal accountability of organizations. It is an important, exciting and very urgent challenge.

Notes

1   The issue of sustainability makes this a contestable suggestion. That is, if social (and environmental) accounting are reconceived within the concept of sustainability, then broad (deep-green) conceptions of the environment will provide an over-arching framework for the conceptions of social accounting (to deal with justice issues) and environmental accounting (to deal with resource and physical environmental issues). The project suggested by such a reconception is still in a very early stage of development. It is perhaps also worth emphasizing that if sustainability is to become the central policy principle guiding future economic development – and accounting can play any role in this – social accounting may well be able to act for eco-justice as environmental accounting is acting for eco-efficiency. See, for example, Owen (forthcoming).

2   Convincing histories which explain the rise of environmental accounting and, more recently, of social accounting, have yet to be written.

3   British Telecom, one of Britain's largest companies, has publicly stated its commitment to produce and publish a social account. Other large companies are actively exploring these possibilities themselves – but in a less public manner.

4   Contact any of the authors for more information about the Institute. Address for correspondence: Professor R. Gray, The Centre for Social and Environmental Accounting Research, Department of Accountancy and Business Finance, University of Dundee, Dundee, Scotland, DD1 4HN.

5   There is a frequently voiced concern that academic accounting fails to engage sufficiently with the practice of accounting. This concern, which we accept as being broadly legitimate, is not, however, the product of a single voice. Practitioners express concerns that they neither understand – nor can see the applicability of – much accounting research (see e.g. Grinyer, 1996; Tomkins, Grinyer, McAulay, Osborne and Walker, 1996). Accounting policymakers – themselves often academics – bemoan the lack of useful guidance offered by the research community (see e.g. Baxter, 1988; Beresford and Johnson, 1995; Lee, 1989; Sterling, 1973; Whittington, 1995). Radical researchers accuse academics of failing to challenge practice and to exercise their political and ethical duty to seek to change practice (see e.g. Sikka,

1987; Sikka, Willmott and Puxty, 1995). Indeed, many radical researchers, in their criticisms of practice, could be thought to be suggesting that much practice is fundamentally flawed and, consequently, that seeking to engage with an agenda already controlled by practice – and corporate capitalism – is largely a waste of time. This last criticism, while well-founded, offers little scope for praxis.

6   The relationship between research and practice is clearly not an ideal one. The relationship is, however, a complex one (see e.g. Gray, 1996; Hopwood, 1983), in which different sections of the practice and academic communities hold significantly different objectives for the practice of accounting and make significantly different judgements about the responsibility of practitioner and academic to seek change. But part of this complexity arises from matters of practicability and pragmatism. As a backdrop to this paper, imagine that all accounting practices were abolished overnight and the academic community was asked to start with a clean sheet and redesign a full accounting practice from scratch. There is virtually nothing in the literature which addresses systematically how one might construct a "utopian" accounting. The suspicion must be that: accounting academics themselves would find such a challenge "unrealistic"; such analysis might fail to satisfy the current output measurement system and hierarchical pecking order which govern academe these days; and any such attempt would be heavily influenced by current practice anyway. So, in a very general sense, we can see academe as an implicitly negotiated balance between current practice, pragmatic opportunities and "more desirable" – but practicable – areas of change.

7   This is the sense in which *praxis* is used here.

8   As we will discuss below, the democracy referred to here is participatory democracy in a neo-pluralist conception (see e.g. Gray, 1989; Held, 1987; Macpherson, 1973, 1977). We should stress that we are aware of the potential cultural specificity of this basis and, therefore, our discussion relates principally to European and Anglo-American countries, plus those nations strongly influenced by those cultures. We will stress below that we see accounting and social accounting as culturally specific and contextually determined.

9   All the authors have been involved, to varying degrees, in the production of the UK social accounts, in the RSA enquiry and in the development of the ISEA.

10 There are other important developments in social accounting which are not addressed here. The most significant relates, in the UK at least (but see also Zadek and Raynard, 1995), to producing social accounts for "community enterprises" or "third sector". Here, the exigencies and motivations are somewhat different from the commercial sector. Nevertheless, the social accounting models are developing with a useful degree of overlap with the commercial sector. See for example Pearce (1993) and Pearce's new book (1996) on social accounting practice and social bookkeeping systems which is published by the New Economics Foundation. The exclusion of these works from our discussion is simply expedient and cautious. We see very strong sympathies and synergies between these two areas of social accounting development and ultimately would like to see social accounting as universal for all organizations.

11 We are explicitly conscious of the ambitiousness of this. Two thousand years of conventional accounting have failed to produce a (universally accepted) conceptual framework. It is somewhat unlikely that a single paper (or even series of papers) will succeed in this endeavour for the more complex case of social accounting. However, it is appropriate to note that social accounting, unlike conventional accounting, does not yet have a wide legislative basis from which to build, and that the derivation of a social accounting from the foundations of conventional accounting thinking may be misguided. These issues have not been explored in this paper.

12 For further detail see, for example, Gray (1989); Gray *et al.* (1996a), Held (1987); Macpherson (1973; 1977).

13 These views and assumptions are informed, in the very broadest terms, by the works of, *inter alia*, Dewey, Habermas, Rawls and Rorty. In the accounting literature, we would refer the reader to the works of Arrington (1990), Laughlin and Broadbent

(1996) and Lehman (1995). For a different conception of related issues, see e.g. Gallhofer and Haslam (1993).

14   See Zadek and Raynard (1995) who present a range of recent examples of social accounting which, while broadly similar in orientation, employ quite different terminology.

15   For example, personal experience suggests that the radical socialist overtones of "social accounting" in the 1970s (see e.g. Gray et al., 1996a), the radical activism of the "social audits" of the 1980s (see for example, Geddes, 1991; Harte and Owen, 1987) and the widespread British distaste for matters social (e.g. regarding the Social Chapter) have led to a significant distrust of anything with "social" in the title among major pockets of British political and industrial power. Similarly, the language of accounting does not always appeal to social accounting practitioners. Experience suggests that the analogue with, especially, independent audit (see below) has negative connotations for many business people because of their less than overwhelming enthusiasm for the accounting profession and their negative experiences with the (far from) independent audit process.

16   Implicit in this reasoning is a recognition that while a considerable amount of conventional accounting is problematic, many of its central functions and tenets are well established, highly theorized and practicable. (If, that is, one has accepted the need for any form of formal accounting at all.) We are seeking here to employ the "best" from conventional accounting and throw away the rest – which would comprise, almost certainly, much of the detail of conventional financial accounting.

17   "Organizational" is used here as a generic term. While we wish to restrict our engagement here, predominantly, to large organizations, we do not necessarily wish to exclude, for example, families and individuals. The term "organization" in a systems context can be taken to embrace all "units". (For more detail, see Gray et al., 1996a.)

18   This point, as we saw earlier, is taken as axiomatic in the present conception of accountability.

19   This paper will not be examining the pros and cons of social accounting. This has been extensively covered elsewhere. See Gray et al. (1996b) for a summary.

20   The use of the term "pragmatism" in this paper is the normal usage of the term and is related in only the most tenuous way to the work of, for example, Dewey and his colleagues.

21   And, indeed, to the development of independent reporting under the European EMAS environmental reporting scheme.

22   Not because we consider business views on desirability as the dominant criterion, but rather to highlight where the conflict from social accounting is more likely to arise.

23   It should be apparent that the issue of why an organization is undertaking social accounting is not discussed here. In addition to the problems that inferring motivation brings, we are working generally in a normative vein in which it is assumed that the motive should be the discharge of accountability. It is the nature of that accountability that is the issue.

24   We should emphasize that additional theories can be found and, in particular, those theories informed by Marxian thinking would largely challenge our approach here. We do not wish to dispute the Marxian approach, but in attempting to develop a systematic mechanism for social accounting by the entity itself, a conception which challenged the entity's very right of existence is unlikely to seem fruitful to the organization concerned. We are, therefore, choosing to work in a neo-pluralist conception of the organization–society interface (see e.g. Held, 1987; Gray et al., 1991; 1996a) with all the attendant problems that attracts from a critical perspective (see e.g. Tinker et al., 1991, but see also Lehman, 1995). For the sake of completeness we should mention that the broad accounting literature does contain very many other theoretical perspectives in which an organization–society relationship is often implied. The "economic-based" theories (see e.g. Gray, Kouhy and Lavers, 1995b) such as agency theory, decision-usefulness and information

economics theory, assume a narrower conception of the relationship, the motives of the parties and the "society" involved. They respond more to economic power than to rights and wider notions of justice and accountability (see e.g. Lehman, 1995). Other theories, for example, legitimacy theory and political economy theory, seem to be more appropriate for the analysis of existing practices than as normative bases from which to deduce "proper" accountability relationships (see, again, Gray et al., 1995b).

25 As far as we are aware, this approach has yet to enter management thinking – at least in the form in which it is employed here – in any systematic way. Hence the (somewhat clumsy) coined phrase.

26 This focus on groups will be continued throughout the paper and helps explain our attachment to neo-pluralist thinking.

27 We would like to acknowledge the work of David Woodward in this field. His papers and the conversations we have held have been most helpful in guiding us towards a clearer idea of the elements of active stakeholder thinking. See also Nasi (1995).

28 This point is also made by Tricker (1983) in his arguments that *real* accountability is *positive* accountability – that is, if an accountee cannot enforce an accountability disclosure then there is no real accountability relationship.

29 Indeed, an important part of the social accounting approach taken by Traidcraft and the New Economics Foundation – of which, more below – is the establishment of the organization's *core values*, how the organization performs against those core values and the views of the stakeholders on those values and the performance.

30 "Good" information is typically assumed to have a number of qualitative characteristics such as reliability, completeness and so on (see e.g. ASSC. 1975). To satisfy these characteristics (to which we return in the closing section of the paper) it seems practically necessary to also provide data which can be thought of as describing the terms of the relationship between the organization and its stakeholders. This descriptive data on, for example, numbers and types of employees, sources and types of suppliers, nature of the organization's interactions with the natural environment and so on, seems to be a necessary element of the information disclosure to provide context for the accountability information so reported.

31 See Laughlin and Broadbent (1996) for an especially clear critique of Guba and Lincoln in which that work is contrasted with the insights of Habermas (1978) and a Habermasian development and synthesis is attempted.

32 While this alternative conception may come in various forms (see, e.g. Zadek and Raynard, 1995) and has a significant overlap with aspects of the (characterization of) the stakeholder and accountability perspectives offered above (as we shall see), its differences are important.

33 The problem of how to give "silent" stakeholders – typically the unborn/future generations, the environment and, if one is to avoid anthropocentrism, non-human life – a voice is still unresolved.

34 We are grateful to Ken McPhail for his help on this issue. Ken argues that the value of the post-modern project lies, not in the existence of a "post-modern" epistemology so much as in the tension and critique of modernism offered by that project. Therefore we might see that, to varying degrees, the projects of Habermas, Foucauld and Guba and Lincoln work at the point of this tension.

35 What we see, therefore, is a more fluid construction of an accounting entity which explicitly recognizes parties other than the managers of the organization in the construction of the organization. In this, it is somewhat akin to Llewellyn's (1994) construction of the "post-modern" accounting entity. Second, in the privileging of the stakeholders' voices, we have a reversal of the traditional stakeholder theory which, as we have seen, privileges the organization's voice. Finally, we see that the process is hermeneutic, dynamic and iterative.

36 Guba and Lincoln's requirement that evaluation leads to action is also central to the PCP approach outlined here.

37   The limits of an empirical accountability lie, *inter alia*, in the extent to which *positive rights* – i.e. those which are demonstrable – successfully reflect a wider democratic awareness or, more likely, reflect undemocratic power structures (see e.g. Stone, 1975, for an excellent discussion of this and related issues). This role – of extending beyond the empirical accountability – was previously ascribed to the "external social audits" (see Figure 1; Geddes, 1988; Gray *et al.*, 1988; Harte and Owen, 1987); a role which we can see social audits continuing to play as a complement to the present social accounts.

38   This echoes a common concern that arises when constructing social accounts with the cooperation of the organization. That is, any organization, it seems, will want information for *control* purposes, while the principal objective of the social account is *accountability* purposes. While the information will usually be seen (see e.g. Roberts and Scapens, 1985) as comprising two overlapping sets, there will be many occasions when the demands for control information will conflict with the demand for accountability information.

39   Like conventional social accounting, there is a danger that the process will be captured by capital. But, unlike the more conventional approaches, the reader of such an account would have no external yardstick against which to assess the degree of that capture. This *may* be a role for the "social auditor" – a matter to which we return later.

40   One essential issue which has yet to be addressed by the PCP approach is that of the "completeness" of the resulting report. This and related matters are dealt with later in the paper, but we can see at this stage that should an organization find itself recording many seriously dissatisfied voices it may very reasonably be disinclined to continue with the accounting on the grounds that it is not an essential part of accountability and that it is difficult for an organization to justify expenditure in reporting all views expressed by its critics. While in a perfectly transparent world we may well desire such a situation, pragmatism and the recognition of current organizational constraints suggest that at present such ambitions lie beyond practicality.

41   Copies of the Traidcraft social audits can be consulted in CSEAR's library and are available from Richard Evans, Traidcraft Exchange, Kingsway North, Gateshead, Tyne and Wear, NE11 0NE, UK.

42   This was published following a document in 1992, "Towards a social audit", in which the early ideas and principles were discussed.

43   See also Adams (1989) and Hutchins (1987) for more historical expressions of the company's position.

44   The 1993 report was sent to all of the UK's Top 100 companies asking for comments and enquiring of each whether the company might not like to undertake a similar exercise.

45   There was confusion, for example, over whose point of view was to be taken (the company's or society's) and how this was to be established. There was also confusion over how the parameters of the conception were to be determined. In this, Traidcraft's experience echoes that of the early social accounting experiments (see, for example, Gray *et al.*, 1987). The discussion earlier in this paper is both motivated and informed by the process of resolving this confusion.

46   Other issues had also arisen. In particular, the advisory board had recognized the need for a systematic system of "social bookkeeping" – a term it had adopted to relate to the data which fed into a specified social account (but see Lazarsfeld, 1971, for an earlier use of the term). A discussion and exploration of this is presented in Dey *et al.* (1995). Furthermore, a growing literature was examining, not just how accountability works and can be conceived of (see, Gray *et al.*, 1987, 1988, 1991; Pallot, 1991; Roberts, 1991; Roberts and Scapens, 1985; Tinker *et al.*, 1991; Williams, 1987), but what changing forms of accountability means to the organization and its participants (see Gray, Bebbington, Walters and Thompson, 1995b;

Llewellyn, 1994; Laughlin, 1991). These latter issues are the subject of continuing research by one of the present authors.

47 Therefore, any attempt at social accounting is derived inevitably from first principles and almost certainly will have to evolve iteratively as the weaknesses, omissions and biases in the account are identified and refined. Because of this, the basis on which the social accounting is developed would be, ideally, as transparent as possible with the (inevitable) political, sociological and construction biases exposed as clearly as possible.

48 The simplification arises for a number of reasons. A simple Venn diagram would have to work in a number of dimensions to capture the overlap and interdependencies in the relationships. Also, the diagram implies a series of static relationships when, in practice, they are continually fluid.

49 This is justified politically by recognition that all active parties in the organization effectively "contract" with the organization and the basic terms of that social contract are the explicit elements of the mission statement.

50 Of some importance are the two dimensions:

1 the formal–informal dichotomy in each relationship; and
2 the extent to which an account is an account *to* the party and the extent to which the account is an account *of* the relationship.

Each of these will need further thought than we can give them here but, it seems currently plausible that the social account is a *formal* account – the organization and the parties will be informally accounting to each other continually and this will not be formalized. It will, however (relating to dichotomy) be necessary to account *for* both the formal and informal aspects *of* the relationship. And, it seems at this stage, this is best done through an account of the relationships. Whether correct or not, the discussion that follows proceeds on the basis of *formal* accounts *of* the relationships.

51 Rainbow Gillespie and Co., Gateshead, is a small local firm of accountants which has long audited the financial statements of the Traidcraft organizations but has had no previous involvement with social accounting.

52 The TX process here drew heavily from the plc experience described above. This was the first TX social account and was innovative in a number of ways. It seemed apposite therefore to simplify the definition of the accounting entity and let this iterate over subsequent social accounting cycles.

53 There is still further discussion to be held about *completeness* and *materiality*.

54 The issue of whether or not the "true and fair" audit report is the most suitable for the attestation of the social account needs further exploration. This form was used here in order to explore the extent to which conventional accounting experience could be used as a template for the social accounting and auditing process.

55 Simon Zadek, at the time of writing, is spending an increasing amount of his time simply discussing and undertaking various roles in the social accounting processes, and Richard Evans has been made director for social accounting at Traidcraft with intention of acting as consultants to organizations seeking to develop their own social accounts. They both – together with Rob Gray and others – were instrumental in the formation and development of (the Institute for Social and Ethical Accountability) ISEA.

56 There is a significant pragmatic economic limit on this consultation. Travel overseas involves significant funds and time.

References

ASSC (1975) *The Corporate Report*, Accounting Standards (Steering) Committee, ICAEW, London.

Adams, R. (1989) *Who Profits?*, Lion Books, Oxford.

AICPA (1977) *The Measurement of Corporate Social Performance*, American Institute of Certified Public Accountants, New York, NY.

Arrington, E. (1990) 'Intellectual Tyranny and the Public Interest: The Quest for the Holy Grail and the Quality of Life', *Advances in Public Interest Accounting*, 3: 1–16.

Baxter, W. (1988) *Academic Research: Academic Trends Versus Professional Needs*, ICAS, Edinburgh.

Beresford, D. and Johnson, L. (1995), 'Interactions Between the FASB and the Academic Community', *Accounting Horizons*, 9: 108–117.

Cooper, C. (1992) 'The Non and Nom of Accounting for (M)other Nature', *Accounting, Auditing & Accountability Journal*, 5: 16–39.

Dey, C., Evans, R. and Gray, R. (1995) 'Towards Social Information Systems and Bookkeeping: A Note on Developing the Mechanisms for Social Accounting and Audit', *Journal of Applied Accounting Research*, 2 (3).

Donaldson, J. (1988) *Key Issues in Business Ethics*, Academic Press, London.

Dowling, J. and Pfeffer, J. (1975) 'Organizational Legitimacy: Social Values and Organizational Behavior', *Pacific Sociological Review*, January, pp. 122–136.

Epstein E. and Votaw, D. (1978) (eds) *Rationality, Legitimacy, Responsibility: Search for New Directions in Business and Society*, Goodyear, California.

Estes, R. (1976) *Corporate Social Accounting*, Wiley, New York, NY.

Evans, R. (1991) 'Business Ethics and Changes in Society', *Journal of Business Ethics*, 10: 871–976.

Francis, J. (1990), 'After Virtue? Accounting as a Moral and Discursive Practice'. *Accounting, Auditing & Accountability Journal*, 3(3): 5–17.

Gallhofer, S. and Haslam, J. (1993) 'Approaching Corporate Accountability: Fragments from the Past', *Accounting and Business Research*, 23 (91a): 320–330.

Gallhofer, S. and Haslam, J. (1995) 'Worrying about Environmental Auditing', *Accounting Forum*, 19 (2/3): 205–218.

Geddes, M. (1988) *Social Audits and Social Accounting: An Annotated Bibliography and Commentary*, School of Applied Economics and Social Studies, South Bank Polytechnic, London.

Geddes, M. (1991) 'The Social Audit Movement', in Owen, D. (ed.) *Green Reporting*, Chapman & Hall, London, pp. 215–241.

Gray, R. (1989) 'Accounting and Democracy', *Accounting, Auditing & Accountability Journal*, 2 (3): 52–56.

Gray, R. (1991) *Trends in Corporate Social and Environmental Accounting*, British Institute of Management, London.

Gray, R. (1992) 'Accounting and Environmentalism: An Exploration of the Challenge of Gently Accounting for Accountability, Transparency and Sustainability', *Accounting, Organizations and Society*, 17 (5) July, pp. 399–426.

Gray, R. (1996) 'The Interesting Relationship Between Accounting Research and Accounting Practice: A Personal Reply to Professor Whittington', *Journal of Applied Accounting Research*, March.

Gray, R. (1997) 'The Practice of Silent Accounting', in S. Zadek, R. Evans, and P. Pruzan (eds) *Building Corporate Accountability: Emerging Practice in Social and Ethical Accounting and Auditing*, Earthscan, London.

Gray, R., Kouhy, R. and Lavers, S. (1995a) 'Corporate Social and Environmental Reporting: A Review of the Literature and a Longitudinal Study of UK Disclosure', *Accounting, Auditing & Accountability Journal*, 8 (2): 47–77.

Gray, R., Bebbington, K., Walters, D. and Thompson, I. (1995b) 'The Greening of Enterprise: An Exploration of the (Non) Role of Environmental Accounting and Environmental Accountants in Organizational Change', *Critical Perspectives on Accounting*, 6 (3): 211–239.

Gray, R., Laughlin, R. and Bebbington, K. (1996a) *Financial Accounting: Method and Meaning*, International Thomson Publishing Company, London.

Gray, R., Owen, D. and Adams, C. (1996b) *Accounting and Accountability: Changes and Challenges in Corporate Social and Environmental Reporting*, Prentice Hall, London.

Gray, R., Owen, D. and Maunders, K. (1986) 'Corporate Social Reporting: The Way Forward?', *Accountancy*, December, pp. 6–8.

Gray, R., Owen, D. and Maunders, K. (1987) *Corporate Social Reporting: Accounting and Accountability*, Prentice Hall, Hemel Hempstead.

Gray, R., Owen, D. and Maunders, K. (1988) 'Corporate Social Reporting: Emerging Trends in Accountability and the Social Contract', *Accounting, Auditing & Accountability Journal*, 1 (1): 6–20.

Gray, R., Owen, D. and Maunders, K. (1991) 'Accountability, Corporate Social Reporting and the External Social Audits', *Advances in Public Interest Accounting*, 5: 1–21.

Grinyer, J. (1996) 'Perceptions of Financial Managers Concerning their Role and the Relevance of Research', in C. Tomkins, J. Grinyer, L. McAulay, P. Osborne, and M. Walker (eds) *In Search of Relevance for Financial Management Research*, British Accounting Association Monograph, BAA, London, pp. 19–33.

Guba, E. and Lincoln, Y. (1989) *Fourth Generation Evaluation*, Sage Publications, Newbury Park, CA.

Habermas, J. (1978) *Knowledge and Human Interests*, Heinemann, London.

Harte, G. and Owen, D. (1987) 'Fighting De-industrialisation: The Role of Local Government Social Audits', *Accounting, Organizations and Society*, 12 (2): 123–142.

Held, D. (1987) *Models of Democracy*, Polity Press, Oxford.

Hines, R. (1988) 'Financial Accounting: In Communicating Reality, We Construct Reality', *Accounting, Organizations and Society*, 13 (3): 251–261.

Hines, R. (1989) 'The Sociopolitical Paradigm in Financial Accounting Research', *Accounting, Auditing & Accountability Journal*, 2 (1): 52–76.

Hines, R. (1991a) 'Accounting for Nature', *Accounting, Auditing & Accountability Journal*, 4 (3): 27–29.

Hines, R. (1991b) 'The FASB's Conceptual Framework, Financial Accounting and the Maintenance of the Social World', *Accounting, Organizations & Society*, 16 (4): 313–332.

Hines, R. (1992) 'Accounting: Filling the Negative Space', *Accounting, Organizations and Society*, 17 (3/4): 313–342.

Hopwood, A. (1983) 'Accounting Research and Accounting Practice: The Ambiguous Relationship Between the Two', Deloitte Haskins & Sells Accounting Lectures, UCW Aberystwyth.

Hutchins, B. (1987) 'A Day's Work', *Accountancy Age*, August, p. 48.

Innes, J., Nixon, W and Tagoe, N. (1996) 'Accounting and Strategic Processes – a Case Study', University of Dundee Discussion Paper ACC/9601.

Laughlin, R. (1991) 'Environmental Disturbances and Organizational Transitions and Transformations: Some Alternative Models', *Organization Studies*, 12 (2): 209–232.

Laughlin, R. and Broadbent, J. (1996) 'Redesigning Fourth Generation Evaluation: An Evaluation Model for the Public Sector Reforms in the UK?' *Evaluation*, 2 (4): 431–451.

Lavoie, D. (1987) 'The Accounting of Interpretations and the Integration of Accounts: The Communication Function of the Language of Business', *Accounting, Organizations and Society*, 12 (6): 579–604.

Lazarsfeld, P. (1971) 'Accounting and Social Bookkeeping', in R. Sterling and W. Bentz (eds), *Accounting in Perspective*, Scholars Books, Houston, TX, pp. 88–101.

Lee, T. (1989) 'Education, Practice and Research in Accounting: Gaps, Closed Loops, Bridges and Magic Accounting', *Accounting and Business Research*, Summer, pp. 237–254.

Lehman, G. (1995) 'A Legitimate Concern for Environmental Accounting', *Critical Perspectives on Accounting*, 6 (6): 393–412.

Likierman, A. (1986) *Rights and Obligations in Public Information*, University College Cardiff Press, Cardiff.

Likierman, A. and Creasey, P. (1985) 'Objectives and Entitlements to Rights in Government Financial Information', *Financial Accountability and Management*, 1 (1): 33–50.

Llewellyn, S. (1994) 'Managing the Boundary: How Accounting Is Implicated in Maintaining the Organization', *Accounting Auditing & Accountability Journal*, 7 (4): 4–23.

Macpherson, C. (1973) *Democratic Theory: Essays in Retrieval*, Oxford University Press, Oxford.

Macpherson, C. (1977) *The Life and Times of Liberal Democracy*, Oxford University Press, Oxford.

Malachowski, A. (1990) 'Business Ethics 1980–2000: An Interim Forecast', *Managerial Auditing Journal*, 5 (2): 22–27.

Matthews, M. (1993) *Socially Responsible Accounting*, Chapman & Hall, London.

Maunders, K. and Burritt, R. (1991) 'Accounting and Ecological Crisis', *Accounting, Auditing & Accountability Journal*, 4 (3): 9–26.

Medawar, C. (1976) 'The Social Audit: A Political View', *Accounting, Organizations and Society*, 1 (4): 389–94.

Meyer, J. (1986) 'Social Environments and Organizational Accounting', *Accounting, Organizations and Society*, 11 (4/5): 345–356.

Mitchell A., Puxty, A., Sikka, P. and Willmott, H. (1991), *Accounting for Change: Proposals for Reform of Audit and Accounting*, Fabian Society, London.

Nasi, J. (ed.) (1995) *Understanding Stakeholder Thinking*, LSR Publications, Helsinki.

Owen, D. (forthcoming) 'Social and Environmental Accounting and Sustainability: Keynote Speech to the EMAA Conference', *Proceedings of the EMAA Conference*, Limperg Instituut, Amsterdam.

Pallot, J. (1987) 'Infrastructure Assets as a Concept in Governmental Accounting', paper given to AAANZ, Canberra.

Pallot, J. (1991) 'The Legitimate Concern with Fairness: A Comment', *Accounting, Organizations and Society*, 16 (2): 201–208.

Parker, L. (1986) 'Polemical Themes in Social Accounting: A Scenario for Standard Setting', *Advances in Public Interest Accounting*, 1: 67–93.

Pearce, J. (1993) *At the Heart of the Community: Community Enterprise in a Changing Society*, Caloustie Gulbenkian Foundation, London.

Pearce, J. (1996) *Measuring Social Wealth: A Study of Social Audit Practice for Community and Cooperative Enterprises*, New Economics Foundation, London.

Power, M. (1994) 'Constructing the Responsible Organization: Accounting and Environmental Representation', in G. Teubner, L. Farmer and D. Murphy (eds), *Environmental Law and Ecological Responsibility: The Concept and Practice of Ecological Self-organization*, John Wiley, London, pp. 370–392.

Puxty, A. (1986) 'Social Accounting as Immanent Legitimation: A Critique of a Technist Ideology', *Advances in Public Interest Accounting*, 1: 95–112.

Puxty, A. (1991) 'Social Accountability and Universal Pragmatics', *Advances in Public Interest Accounting*, 4: 35–46.

Raynard, P. (1995) 'The New Economics Foundation's Social Audit: Auditing the Auditors?' *Social and Environmental Accounting*, 15 (1): 7–10.

Roberts, J. (1991) 'The Possibilities of Accountability', *Accounting, Organizations and Society*, 16 (4): 355–370.

Roberts, J. and Scapens, R. (1985) 'Accounting Systems and Systems of Accountability', *Accounting, Organizations and Society*, 10 (4): 443–456.

Roberts, R. (1992) 'Determinants of Corporate Social Responsibility Disclosure', *Accounting, Organizations and Society*, 17 (6): 595–612.

Sikka, P. (1987) 'Professional Education and Auditing Books: A Review Article', *British Accounting Review*, 19 (3), December: 291–304.

Sikka, P., Willmott, H. and Lowe, E. (1989) 'Guardians of Knowledge and the Public Interest: Evidence and Issues of Accountability in the UK Accountancy Profession', *Accounting, Auditing & Accountability Journal*, 2 (2): 47–71.

Sikka, P., Willmott, H. and Lowe, E. (1991) 'Guardians of Knowledge and the Public Interest: A Reply to Our Critics', *Accounting, Auditing & Accountability Journal*, 4 (4): 14–22.

Sikka, P., Willmott, H. and Puxty, T. (1995) 'The Mountains Are Still There: Accounting Academics and the Bearings of Intellectuals', *Accounting, Auditing & Accountability Journal*, 8 (3): 113–140.

Sterling, R. (1973) 'Accounting Research, Education and Practice', *Journal of Accountancy*, September: 44–52.

Stone, C. (1975) *Where the Law Ends*, Harper & Row, New York, NY.

Tinker, A., Lehman, C. and Neimark, M. (1991) 'Corporate Social Reporting: Falling Down the Hole in the Middle of the Road', *Accounting, Auditing & Accountability Journal* 4 (1): 28–54.

Tomkins, C., Grinyer, J., McAulay, L., Osborne, P. and Walker, M. (eds) (1996) *In Search of Relevance for Financial Management Research*, British Accounting Association Monograph.

Tricker, R. (1983) 'Corporate Responsibility, Institutional Governance and the Roles of Accounting Standards', in M. Bromwich, A. Hopwood (eds) *Accounting Standards Setting – An International Perspective*, Pitman, London.

Ullmann, A. (1985) 'Data in Search of a Theory: A Critical Examination of the Relationships Among Social Performance, Social Disclosure and Economic Performance of US Firms', *Academy of Management Review* 10 (3): 540–557.

Whittington, G. (1995) 'Is Accounting Becoming Too Interesting?', Sir Julian Hodge Lecture, UCW, Aberystwyth.

Williams, P. (1987) 'The Legitimate Concern with Fairness', *Accounting, Organizations and Society*, 12 (2): 169–189.

Zadek, S. (1993) 'The Social Audit of Traidcraft plc', *Social and Environmental Accounting*, 13 (2): 5–6.

Zadek, S. and Evans, R. (1993) *Auditing the Market: A Practical Approach to Social Accounting*, New Economics Foundation, London.

Zadek, S., Pruzan, P. and Evans, R. (1997) *Building Corporate Accountability: Emerging Practice in Social and Ethical Accounting and Auditing*, Earthscan, London.

Zadek, S. and Raynard, P. (1995) 'Social Auditing, Transparency and Accountability', *Accounting Forum* 19 (2/3) September/December.

Appendix 1. Extract from Traidcraft plc's 1994–95 Social Audit Document

Contents

Social accounting is based on the perceptions and evaluation of the company's performance made by its stakeholders, and comparative benchmarks established by the company. The structure of the Social Accounts follows this principle.

These accounts have been independently audited by The New Economics Foundation. Readers are advised to refer to the Auditor's Report on p. 22 before reading the accounts themselves.

Traidcraft's 94–95 Social Accounts are published by the directors of Traidcraft plc and have been prepared by Richard Evans, Director of Social Accounting with Traidcraft Exchange, and with the cooperation of the staff and directors of Traidcraft plc.

Traidcraft plc's stakeholders

Stakeholders are key groups who are affected by, or can affect, the activities of the company. Traidcraft is committed to accountability to its stakeholders by its Foundation Principles, which state that in seeking to *establish a just trading system which expresses the principles of love and justice fundamental to the Christian faith* it will foster . . . *an inclusive community of purpose and relationships* . . .

One of the principles of social accounting (see back cover) is that representatives of each class of stakeholder are consulted to ascertain which aspects of the company's performance are most relevant for them, what measures are to be used and what method of consultation is appropriate.

The methods of consultation for this set of accounts is described at the beginning of each stakeholder section.

Producers

Small farmers, craftspeople and their marketing organisations in the "third world" 106 producers in 26 countries.

Customers

All who buy Traidcraft's products for their own use or for resale. Customers include, mail order, Traidcraft's voluntary representatives, fair trade shops, general retailers and wholesalers and campaigning organisations whose mail order business is handled by Traidcraft:

- 40,500 mail order customers
- 1971 voluntary reps
- 570 retailers
- four contract clients – Greenpeace (UK), Amnesty International (UK), New Internationalist and Water Aid.

Employees

The 131 staff of Traidcraft Plc.

Shareholders

The 1,789,128 "B" shares are non-voting shares, except that "B" shareholders have the right to elect one director of the Board of the Company. The 55,165

"A" shares, which carry normal voting rights are held by the Trustees of the Traidcraft Foundation. Because of their responsibilities to the company's other stakeholders, set out in the Deed of Mutual Covenant and the Foundation Principles, neither the Trustees nor the Directors of the company contribute as stakeholders to the annual social accounts. 3,706 "B" shareholders

Wider public

Traidcraft's aims include raising public awareness about justice issues in trade with the "third world". It is also committed by its Foundation Principles to be a good citizen in the local community, a witness in the business community and an active partner with other organisations sharing a vision for a fairer world.

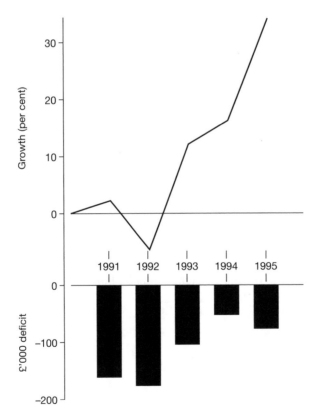

Figure A.1 Traidcraft plc's self-description

Trading background – 1994/95

The following directors' report on the company's financial performance in 1994/95 has not been audited as part of the social accounts.

The last year proved to be more difficult for trading than the board had expected. After two years of satisfactory sales growth, especially in our wholesale trade to other retailers, we placed orders with our overseas suppliers to match a higher planned level of sales for 1994/95.

The outcome fell well short of our targets. Sales grew by only 4% compared with an average of more than 9% pa over the two previous years. Sales demand was depressed in two key sales channels, which together account for two thirds of Traidcraft sales – mail order, which includes our contract mail order fulfilment services, and retail (where the plight of small high street retailers has been well publicised in the media). Only in the early part of the pre-Christmas season did we see significant growth on the previous year's sales volume.

The shortfall in planned sales has had short-term and long-term effects on Traidcraft as a business. The short-term effects have been:

- a trading loss of £33,000 for the year as promotional spending was not rewarded with sales.
- a large increase in stocks of goods yet to be sold which have to be funded by bank borrowing.

The long-term impact is a recognition that our central "Traidcraft 2000" aim – to double the volume of fair trade purchases from "third world" suppliers by the end of the decade – cannot be achieved without change within the company to match a changing external market environment. Traidcraft is now engaged in a Business Process Re-engineering review to identify what changes it can and should make to reposition itself for profitable growth in a more competitive marketplace.

There were high points as well as disappointments in the trading year. The customer response to the new Cafédirect freeze-dried instant coffee exceeded our expectations. Traidcraft sold 70,000 jars in barely 8 months, and nationwide more than 100 million cups of Cafédirect coffee have now been served since the brand was launched in 1991. Our voluntary reps increased their sales by 9% to a new record of £2.5 million.

Notes

1   The Foundation Principles state the aim of Traidcraft and the ethical principles for the achievement of that aim. It forms part of a Mutual Deed of Covenant between Traidcraft plc, Traidcraft Exchange Ltd and the Traidcraft Foundation. Copies of the Foundation Principles may be obtained from Traidcraft.

2   "Auditing the Market – a practical approach to social auditing" by Simon
     Zadek and Richard Evans (A5 60pp) was published in 1993 by
     Traidcraft Exchange and the New Economic Foundation to describe
     the initial development of their social accounting methodology and to
     stimulate debate. Copies can be obtained by sending £3.50 (includes
     postage) to Traidcraft Exchange, Kingsway, Gateshead, Tyne and Wear
     NE11 0NE, UK.

Financial Indicators

The value to producers of purchases from the third world (including those
attributable to our investment in Cafédirect) grew by over 30% in real terms
between 1990 and 1995, against a business target of 25%.

The loss in the year means that we have failed to clear the accumulated
deficit on our profit and loss account and are still unable to offer shareholders
a dividend.

Appendix 2. Traidcraft plc's Experience with
One of Its Stakeholder Groups

The early stages of Traidcraft plc's experience led us to believe that each of
the identified relationships needed to be described in some way which would
reflect the understanding of the parties to that relationship – noting that the
way in which they are accounted for will involve financial, quantitative and
descriptive elements. It is likely also that the way in which the *descriptors* of
the relationships are derived will be, in part, pragmatic – based on what *can*
be described and what data *can* be collated.

For illustration, we run through the a priori analysis of what (we believe)
is the most important of the Traidcraft relationships – the relationship
between Traidcraft and its developing country producers.

The producers (Third-World suppliers)

This is the dominant social relationship of Traidcraft plc. It is Traidcraft's
raison d'être without which Traidcraft, as it is currently conceived, would not
exist. This must, therefore, be one of the dominant areas of the social
account. The major elements of the relationship are derived from Traidcraft's
purchasing policy and are appropriately listed in the 1993 social accounts. In
addition, any account of its relationship with the producers needs to

●   be set in a context (of the range of suppliers, the products and the
     existing living/working conditions pre- and post-Traidcraft); and

- to explore the implied terms of the relationship – in particular the need to be in harmony with the local culture and to develop a closeness of relationship.

For each characteristic, the trick is to try to capture its essence and then to allow the producers themselves to speak about the characteristics of the relationship. The second part of this was done through direct (face-to-face) consultation with a selection of the producers and backed up by a distance questionnaire.[56] The results of this are recorded in the Traidcraft plc social accounting statements. The first of the two elements above – capturing the principle descriptors of the relationships – formed the basis of the social bookkeeping system (see Dey *et al.*, 1995). Our first attempt to articulate these descriptors – along with sources of information for the social account (that is, the means of social bookkeeping) – are shown in Table A1.

Table A1 Traidcraft's producers: performance indicators

Element of policy	Indicator(s) measure(s) related to purchasing policy	Source of data
Fair price and local value added	(TC price/local price) %	Accounting information system questionnaire
	Analysis of cost value added per product	Accounting information system
	(TC price/UK price) × (country average income/UK average income) %	Accounting information system *The Economist* × *The Economist*
Advances	(£Total advances/£Third World purchases) %	Accounting information system
Speed of payment	(Days from receipt invoice to payment from UK to producers)	Accounting information system
	ditto UK suppliers Ditto, but from receipt to producer receiving the money	Accounting information system questionnaire or Bank statements?
Continuity of orders	Net change % in sourcing from that country	Accounting information system
	(Average years of relationship/ average UK relationship) by country	Accounting information system
Product development and business management	What are the objectives here?	?
Environmental impact	Producer environmental audits undertaken	?
	Issues/objectives from reviews	?

Table A1 *continued*

Element of policy	Indicator(s) measure(s) related to purchasing policy	Source of data
Lobbying	Actions taken on specific issues	?
	Results claimed	?
Informing customers and reps about products	% of all TC products with producer information included	Marketing department?
	Number of enquiries for further information	Marketing department?
Producer objective 1: fair wage	By producer: (average wage average country wage) %	Questionnaire + visits + occasional audit
	By producer: (average wage country poverty level) %	Questionnaire + visits + occasional audit
Producer objective 2: working conditions	(Average working hours country average) %	Questionnaire + visits + occasional audit
Producer objective 3: participation	Statement of detail from producer	Questionnaire + visits + occasional audit
	Any evidence offered by producer	Questionnaire + visits + occasional audit
Closeness and harmony with local culture	Visit reports as now + table of visits made/not made	Cycle of visits + audits

HOW TO DO IT

Simon Zadek, Peter Pruzan and Richard Evans

There is a growing body of experiences in corporate SEAAR, particularly across Europe and North America.[1] Associated with this development has been the emergence of varied terminology and differing approaches. There are ethical accounts, social audits, ethical audits, social performance reports, and social reviews, just to name a few. In some cases these methodologies appear very similar. The ethical audit advocated by the European Institute for Business Ethics and the Nijenrode Business School,[2] for example, is similar in many respects to the social accounts method developed, adopted, and applied by Traidcraft plc and the New Economics Foundation.[3] The Body Shop International's ethical audit is, on the other hand, quite different since it represents a combination of social, environmental and animal testing audits.[4] This in turn is only comparable in parts to the 'ethical accounting' developed at the Copenhagen Business School and adopted by Sbn Bank and other companies and public sector organizations across Scandinavia.[5]

Much of the diversity in practice can be attributed to at least four significant differences in:

- interests on the part of those initiating the process;
- types of organisations;
- contexts; and
- theoretical and philosophical roots.

Many of these differences are entirely acceptable in that they reflect varied needs for which different methods are required. For example, organizations such as Sbn Bank in Denmark and Wøyen Mølle in Norway start with an emphasis on the evolution of shared values through ethical accounting. Not surprisingly, they focus on dialogue with key stakeholders rather than third-party verification. On the other hand, a company concerned with meeting the challenge of public accountability may well place far greater emphasis on securing adequate comparison with other companies or accepted social norms and benchmarks. For example, the move by companies in the textile, sportswear and toy sectors to adopt and comply with labour codes of conduct in their production in, and purchases from, the South, will focus on external verification precisely because the pressure comes from public consumer campaigns.[6] Similarly, a company principally concerned with public accountability may focus exclusively on the production of a report for external publication, whereas a company with an interest in SEAAR as a tool to facilitate internal change may have little or no interest in the published document, but may instead focus on the process of accounting, and the reports generated for internal use.

Identifying the right approach to SEAAR is therefore intimately related to *why* the particular organization engages in the exercise. This implies that there is no single approach that is correct for all situations: there is strength in diversity for diverse needs.

At the same time, there are variations between methods and practices that are not justified by any objective difference in circumstance and need. These are variations that may be rooted in two possible reasons for poor practices:

- an underspecification of the accounting, auditing and reporting process because of insufficient knowledge, skills, experience and/or resources applied in the process; and/or
- a deliberate attempt to underspecify the accounts and/or the verification process in order to report in a less than accurate, incomplete or unintelligible, manner.

For example, a company may undertake an externally verified exploration of the social impact of one area of its operations knowing full well that there is a critical problem associated with an area of work that they have chosen to omit from the assessment. An SEAAR exercise undertaken by a bank that did not deal with the nature of its investment portfolio, or an exercise by an advertising company that did not consider with care the nature of the images they were promoting and their effect, could not really be seen as being of adequate quality. Similarly, a company may forgo a dialogue with staff to determine key issues of concern because of inadequate resources, and as a result develop a survey that omits a range of critical issues that would profile the company in a negative light, or that are important for the staff and therefore for their prosperity to be responsible, committed and creative employees. It would not be appropriate, for example, for a fair trade organization (eg one seeking to offer a better deal to community suppliers in the South by offering such added benefits as a better price) to carry out an SEAAR exercise without adequate consultation with Southern suppliers.[7]

The challenge is to be able to distinguish between acceptable and unacceptable reasons for methodological (and terminological) differences. The failure to meet this challenge effectively will allow the 'bad to chase out the good', as companies and consultants alike find good reason to cut corners to save costs and to omit difficult areas from accounting, auditing and reporting. The ability to distinguish good from bad practice therefore provides a foundation on which standards can be set, a subject to which we return in Chapter 4.

A Brief History of 'How'

An extensive array of methods has been offered up over the years for assessing and reporting on corporate social and ethical performance. This is not the place to attempt a scholarly exposition of this history, which has been achieved more effectively elsewhere.[8] Of interest here is not so much the history of how social and ethical accounting and auditing have been talked about and practiced for their own sake. Rather, the intention is to show how today's emerging practice is informed by both the theoretical literature and earlier practical experience.

One of earliest proposed approaches to social auditing was that of the *cost* or *outlay audit*.[9] The basic idea, as the name suggests, was to specify the financial costs associated with social activities, and to set these out as an account of the social contribution made by the organization. The major disadvantage of this approach is that financial costs give little idea of the outcome's value. As one assessment of this method concluded: 'since the cost approach makes no effort to measure benefits to the corporation and others associated with the expenditures, it provides little evaluative information to the public.'[10]

Despite this very real limitation, the ready availability of financial data from conventional financial accounts and management systems has made this approach a durable one over the years. Many companies, for example, report on the amount of money that they donate to charitable causes, often expressed both as an absolute amount and as a percentage of pretax profits or gross earnings.[11] The cost or outlay approach has been formalized into a method also known as the *social balance*, effectively a record of financial costs based on a reanalysis of the audited financial accounts associated with actions that can be attributed to the company's social rather than its financial mission. This approach, for example, is currently being used by the Italian retail co-operative movement as the core of its *social balance* accounting, as in the case of Coop Italia.

A second methodological strand that has found its way into modern usage is *constituency accounting*, named by Grey in 1973.[12] Grey argued that traditional financial accounting could simply not accommodate the needs of SEAAR. Instead, an entirely new calculus was required. What he proposed was that companies should examine and report against the demands of key constituencies, whether inside or outside of the company concerned.[13]

There is little evidence of this 'constituency-based' approach having been taken up at the time that it was established at a theoretical level. As the US Department of Commerce commented at the time:

> While this approach attempts to assess benefits as well as costs, some critics believe that it does not state benefits in terms that are meaningful to constituencies outside the corporation. It has not been widely used in corporate social reporting.[14]

The concern raised about the accuracy and usefulness of benefits defined by constituents is one that warrants careful examination. However, such concerns have not prevented this form of consultation becoming a core part of many of the contemporary approaches to SEAAR in the guise of 'stakeholder consultation and dialogue'. As one senior corporate executive remarked at the time: 'All . . . [corporations] . . . must . . . be visibly attentive to public interest – to the public interest as the *public* views it.'[15] Consultation has not only become a vital means by which the views of key stakeholders can be elicited, it has also become a way of legitimising a company's social and ethical accounting process. Very recently, for example, the financial services company Allied Dunbar produced a publicly available report covering some of its philanthropic activities. Rather than report the financial costs of its contribution following the *outlay approach* described above, Allied Dunbar chose to follow more closely the *constituency* or *stakeholder approach*. In its summary of its *Stakeholder Accountability Report* for 1996, the company declares:

> 1996 marks the twenty-first anniversary of the Staff Charity Fund [SCF]. What better time to study the views of those with most interest in its work. The future will hold new challenges and the way the SCF develops the relationship it enjoys with its stakeholders lies at the heart of what happens next.[16]

Stakeholders' views have been increasingly seen as a critical part of any thorough accounting, auditing and reporting process. However, it has also been clear from an early stage that even the most accurate reporting of these perceptions may not be adequate. For example, in one social accounting and auditing exercise with a British company, staff repeatedly highlighted the view that they were being paid too little. In considering the wage data, it became clear to the auditors that they were in fact being paid just as much as people working for other companies that required broadly the same 'job of work' in the same region of the country. Eventually, the external auditor understood that since the company declared itself to have unusually high moral and ethical codes and values, staff expected to be paid what they saw as a *decent* rather than a *comparable* wage. What needed to be highlighted in this case was the tension revealed by examining the relationship between normal comparative financial indicators and staff perceptions. To omit either would have been to miss the point (or at least *this* point).

The limitations of using financial data are not therefore seen as a reason for rejecting all manner of quantification. Similarly, the limitations in working with people's subjective views are not a reason to ignore or marginalize them.'

Financial data, furthermore, has only been one element of the quantified information about social and ethical performance that has been publicly available. What has emerged from the early 1970s has been the practice of *corporate rating* against key social and ethical performance criteria. While many different approaches to this have been adopted, the essence of the practice has been to rate companies in one or both of two possible ways: against predetermined 'binary' criteria that seek the answer to the question: 'Is this company doing this?'; and against scaled criteria that seek to answer the question: 'How is the company doing in this area?'

One of the earliest documented users of this approach was the Interfaith Centre on Corporate Responsibility (ICCR), which took a particular interest, for example, in the practices of companies doing business in South Africa. Probably the most well-known contemporary practitioner in this area is the Council on Economic Priorities (CEP), a public-interest organization based in New York. CEP has been producing corporate ratings against social and environmental criteria for over 25 years, with a particular focus on retail companies and the education of consumers in their purchasing decisions through its annually produced *Shopping for a Better World*.[17] Corporate rating has developed rapidly since the mid 1980s, with a host of public interest NGOs entering the field with their own rating systems aimed at feeding the consumer public, and/or the growing number of ethical investment funds, with information.[18] Most recently, a group of these organizations from North America and Europe have come together in an effort to share information and to move towards some level of convergence in the manner in which screening is being undertaken.

A related development emerged in the 1970s on the back of the so-called *social indicators* movement.[19] Whereas *corporate rating* was an exclusively external activity undertaken by public interest, non-profit organizations and researchers, companies became more involved in the development and application of social performance indicators. The drive towards defining social indicators was closely intertwined with the growing interest in what we would now call stakeholder dialogue. For example, the US Department of Commerce saw some form of community consultation process as initiating the development or selection of relevant social indicators.

> For example, in establishing annual objectives for a corporate community affairs program, a firm would first attempt to develop a quality of life profile for the community, using social indicators regarding unemployment, environmental quality, education, health, and so on. Thereafter a firm could establish performance indicators for some or all of its own activities in relation to these indicators, establish priorities in relation to each other and then measure performance in relation to objectives and their assigned importance.[20]

Community-based approaches to selecting indicators of social and environmental development have emerged as a major theme of community development in the 1990s, particularly following the historic signing of the so-called Local Agenda 21 at the Earth Summit in Rio in 1992.[21] While certainly intended as an empowering process, these approaches can equally suffer from identifying what is important and how best to measure it. As Kim Davenport comments:

> [An] objection is that the catalogue of social indicators is not truly comprehensive, but simply reflects the concerns of the most active or organized constituencies. Also, establishing a fixed catalogue of social indicators might give corporations permission to ignore those issues outside of the catalogue. Moreover, the fixed catalogue could also prove a hindrance to the development and adoption of new, more effective, indicators.[22]

These perceived shortfalls of the pure constituency-based approach to selecting social indicators have opened the door to a complementary approach to the selection process: through identifying best practice or conventionally used indicators and benchmarks. For example, any report on the issue of gender within an organization would today be quickly ridiculed and dismissed if it omitted to report the number of men and women in different positions within the organization, or failed to provide data regarding wages and salaries to allow the proposition 'equal pay for equal work' to be tested. Similarly, any corporate environmental report found to have omitted information on the company's failure to comply with statutory regulations of self-imposed standards would be challenged in today's environmental-compliance sensitized world. At any time there are key issues for which there exist performance indicators that are widely acknowledged as an appropriate and essential part of any performance assessment and disclosure process.

Contemporary forms of SEAAR have drawn inspiration from many earlier approaches and initiatives, such as those highlighted in this section. For example, the Ethical Accounting Statement approach that emerged in Denmark in the late 1980s, through the work of Peter Pruzan and Ole Thyssen at the Copenhagen Business School, has focused exclusively on what might in earlier times have been called constituency accounting, rather than stakeholder dialogue.[23] Similarly, the approach developed by Traidcraft and the New Economics Foundation has drawn on the inspiration and calculus of the social indicators movement, as well as the lessons gained through the development of environmental auditing in the 1980s.[24] More generally, the cases described in this book, and the analytic framework offered in the following paragraphs, certainly arise from the rich and complex history of SEAAR.[25]

Understanding Quality

This historical thumbnail sketch of how SEAAR has evolved highlights some of the key methodological strands, and their possible relationships with differing reasons for the implementation of specific practices. However, despite the need for continued sensitivity towards the needs of diversity, there are also good reasons for establishing methods to compare different approaches.

In short, we need to find ways to be able to tell if a specific exercise in social and ethical accounting, auditing and reporting is worth the candle?

We have developed for this purpose an analytic framework for exploring the quality of a particular experience or initiative in SEAAR. In doing so, we have been painfully aware of the sheer scale of experimentation in this area, and of its increasing quality across many different contexts. In this light, we offer the tool not as a finished product, but as a first stab at what needs to be continued over the coming period. The framework is a means of categorizing experiences or initiatives through:

- *principles* of 'good practice' in SEAAR,
- the *elements* into which the principles can be subdivided to enable more detailed analysis, and
- the *level and quality* of reporting.

Each of these elements of the framework are discussed below. The aim here has not been to judge the relative quality of the cases. At any rate each has been chosen for inclusion on the basis of representing good practice. Rather, the aim has been to use the case studies to demonstrate how the tool can be employed in assessing the relative merits of different approaches.

Table 1 *Typology*

Type	Name	Cases	Description
A	Corporate-Led Reporting	Glaxo Holdings plc	Statutory disclosure plus additional internally generated, non-verified discretionary disclosure
B	Ethical accounting	Aarhus Municipality Sbn Bank Wøyen Mølle	Non-statutory disclosure of unverified stakeholder perceptions based on stakeholder-selected issues and questions
C	Social evaluation	Ben & Jerry's Homemade, Inc.	Non-statutory disclosure of stakeholder views and social indicators based on exploration and views of external assessor
D	Social accounting & auditing	The Body Shop International plc Traidcraft plc	Statutory and non-statutory disclosure of stakeholder views, indicators and benchmarks with external verification of process
E	Outlay audit (social balance)	Co-op Italia	Non-statutory disclosure of reanalysis of audited financial data to reveal social costs
F	Disclosure ranking	VanCity Savings and Credit Union	Non-statutory disclosure by external body of extent of public disclosure

---

BOX 1 The eight principles of quality

- Inclusivity
- Comparability
- Completeness
- Evolution
- Management Policies and Systems
- Disclosure
- Externally Verified
- Continuous Improvement

An initial typology of cases

We begin by offering a simple typology for the nine cases. The six different types (A to F) set out in Table 1 are not intended to be exhaustive, but rather to illustrate some of the key dimensions of the cases in their respective clusters.

The 'quality' principles

By voicing the history of different approaches to SEAAR, we are provided with a ready list of hints as to what are some of the key dimensions against which quality needs to be assessed. These have been formalised into eight key principles of quality.

Inclusivity

The principle of *inclusivity* means that the social and ethical accounting and auditing must reflect the views and accounts of all principal stakeholders, not only the particular stakeholders who have historically had the most influence over the evolution of the organization's formal mission statement. What this means, furthermore, is that the assessment cannot be based on a single set of values or a single set of objectives. While over time the various stakeholder groups *may* come to agree on many things, the assessment process cannot assume this to be the case and must therefore accommodate such diversity.[26] It is important to distinguish between consultation in the form of one-way surveying – ie essentially market research – and dialogue, which can be understood as a two-way process that brings the views and interests of all parties to the table.[27]

Comparability

The principle of *comparability* is quite simply that SEAAR enables the performance of the organization to be compared as a basis of assessment. Comparison may be based on the organization's performance in different periods, or on external benchmarks drawn from the experience of other organizations, statutory regulations or non-statutory norms. It is important that external benchmarks are selected for their relevance and legitimacy, not only for their accuracy. For example, comparisons of wage rates with outside organizations need to select the appropriate types of organizations, and also need to draw the comparative data from sources that would be considered legitimate (such as government statistics, or labour-research bodies).[28]

Completeness

The principle of *completeness* means that no area of the company's activities can be deliberately and systematically excluded from the assessment. This principle is important to ensure that the company does not 'cherry-pick' the areas of its activities which will show – on inspection – the most positive social and ethical performance.

Comprehensiveness in combination with the principle of inclusivity raises major practical problems, given the potential magnitude of the assessment process. A major manufacturing company may have thousands of products produced and marketed in a large number of contexts and cultures.

What this means in practice is that not everything can be covered at once, or more specifically during any one cycle. The essence of this principle is therefore that no area of the organization's activities are necessarily excluded from any particular cycle because of any unwillingness on the part of the organization – ie no 'malicious exclusion'. Over several cycles, furthermore, all of the principal stakeholder groups would be covered through an exploration of all the effects of all the organization's activities.[29]

Evolution

It is not possible, as we have here noted, to cover an entire company's 'social footprint' at one time; furthermore, it is likely that this footprint will vary over time. Furthermore, the impact and meaning given to its footprint will also vary, as the composition and expectations of key stakeholder groups change over time. The implication of this is that one-off accounting exercises are not sufficient for the needs of management – in seeking to understand what is happening – or in terms of the company's accountability to the wider public. A key principle against which the practice of SEAAR needs to be judged is therefore whether the exercise is repeated in a manner that demonstrates learning and continual challenge. That is, the process must follow an *evolutionary* path over time.

Management policies and systems

As with both financial and environmental auditing, it is not enough for an organization to get a snapshot of its performance in order to secure its learning processes. It is essential for any systematic process that the organization develops clear policies covering each accounting area, and systems and procedures that allow the accounting process itself to be controlled and evaluated and the organization's awareness and operation of policies and commitments to be assessed through an audit process.

Disclosure

The question of whether the social and ethical accounting and auditing processes are intended primarily for an internal audience, ie as a management tool, or whether they are a means of contributing to organizational learning or to strengthening public accountability, is a conflict that has figured in both the reasons *why* companies engage in the process and the *means by which* the accounting is undertaken. Clearly the focus on an internal audience obviates any need to disclose the results to the public, or even perhaps within the organization beyond the management and board. At the same time, an interest in establishing and maintaining organizational learning and a dialogue culture as well as in strengthening the company's legitimacy in the public domain would require some sort of disclosure. Where a disclosure route is chosen, the matter of quality concerns the extent to which disclosure is a formality or an active means of communication with key stakeholders and the wider public. Merely publishing a document – however comprehensive – does not constitute good practice if the document is difficult to obtain, costly, misleading, or unintelligible to key stakeholders.

Externally verified

The need for external verification concerns, again, the relative emphasis between SEAAR as a management tool and as a means of organizational learning; or as a means of strengthening accountability and legitimacy. Clearly, an emphasis towards the latter implies the need for external verification of some kind. The challenge is, of course, what kind of external verification process will be of a sufficiently high professional quality and independence for it to validate the published material.

Continuous improvement

The aim of any SEAAR system must be to assess progress rather than merely retrospective performance. That is, any relevant system must be able to identify whether the organization's performance has improved over time in relation to the values, missions and objectives set by the organization and its stakeholders, as well as by those established through broader social norms. Moreover, beyond the measurement of progress is the need for a method that actively encourages 'raising the floor' of social and ethical performance.

These eight principles seem to represent the most basic dimensions of quality against which any social and ethical accounting, auditing and reporting process can and should be judged. That does not mean to say that a case where several principles are not being adhered to is necessarily 'poor' in quality. For example, the Scandinavian applications of Ethical Accounting do not include external verification (principle seven), yet this may well be because it is not required given the societal context or the particular applications. So the principles cannot, in isolation, be a basis for intercase judgement, although they *can* provide a checklist of things to look for in any assessment or selection process.

Scoring Quality

The eight principles are relevant in offering an initial basis for assessing the quality of any exercise in SEAAR. They are, however, too general to be of use in anything but the most basic assessment process. For example, how can one distinguish between stakeholder consultation (essentially limited and one way) and an approach to stakeholder dialogue that is intended to be more deeply participative? Similarly, there are clearly many different ways in which external verification, comprehensiveness, and disclosure can be interpreted in practice.

The approach taken here has been to consider in more depth the possible elements that define the quality of each principle set out above. Specifically, the principles have been broken down into 45 elements against which any particular social and ethical accounting and auditing process can be judged. These elements have been derived from the experience of the case studies, the broader experience of the editors and an analysis of the literature.[30]

The cases in the next section have been 'approximately rated' by these elements. The rating is approximate in that there has been no attempt to construct a numerical scoring system. To do so would imply, amongst other things, that there was some *a priori* basis on which these principles and elements can be seen to be more or less important. For example, it would be problematic to add up the smiling or gloomy faces in the table to determine which organization or method had proved more successful. This stage would require comparisons between organizations with similar aims and comparable contexts.

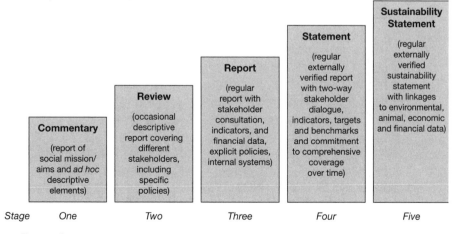

Figure 1 Social and ethical disclosure: assessing progress

Table 2 Quality rating against basic principles and elements

Case	Inclusivity	Comparability	Completeness	Evolution	Policies/Systems	External Verification	Disclosure	Continuous Improvement
Aarhus	●	○	●	●	●	□	●	●
Ben & Jerry's Homemade, Inc.	●	○	●	●	□	●	●	○
The Body Shop International	●	○	●	●	●	●	●	●
Coop Italia	□	●	□	□	□	□	●	□
Glaxo Holdings plc	□	○	□	□	○	□	○	○
Sbn Bank	●	○	●	●	●	□	●	●
Traidcraft plc	●	●	●	●	●	●	●	●
VanCity	○	●	○	○	○	○	●	○
Wøyen Mølle	●	○	●	●	●	□	●	●

● = method seeks to address principle

○ = method partially seeks to address principle

□ = method does not adequately seek to address principle

Assessing the Quality of Disclosure

The problems of *ranking* through such scoring and weighting have already been highlighted and concern, in particular, the need to recognize legitimate differences in SEAAR processes. At the same time, there is a demand by all stakeholders to be able to assess the quality of any *disclosure* of social performance, and therefore by implication of the accounting and auditing underlying the 'discovery process'. Drawing inspiration and method from work undertaken by the United Nations Environment Programme (UNEP) and the environmental consultancy SustainAbility Ltd, we have constructed a five-stage developmental model for social and ethical reporting.

The basis of scoring an organization against the five developmental stages of social and ethical reporting is, in the main, drawn from the principles set out above and the elements in the annex to this chapter. An analysis of Glaxo's experience, for example, would place it in stage one, although the availability of some financial data would give it elements of stage three characteristics. Similarly, a major difference between Sbn Bank and Traidcraft's experience, that of external verification, would separate them into stages three and four respectively.

This five-stage model clearly does take the step of defining, to a large degree, what principles and elements are more important than others. While this is a step cautioned against by the editors themselves in earlier sections, the model does illustrate where the whole assessment of the quality of SEAAR should go in the future. Specifically, *if* there is a need to be able to judge accounting, auditing and reporting against each other, some form of developmental model will almost inevitably be used, whether formally or implicitly.

Of course, the 'inevitability' of the need for some developmental model depends, in large part, whether or not some form of certification of quality is necessary, either now or in the future.

Notes

1   Published information on corporate social and ethical accounting and auditing almost exclusively covers Western Europe and the US. Research has revealed, however, that other experiences exist. One of the most important of these is probably the groundbreaking work of the Indian industrial conglomerate Tata Industries, which is covered in Institute of Social and Ethical Accountability (1997) *Sixth Environment Foundation Windsor Castle Roundtable on Social and Ethical Accounting* Auditing and Reporting Accountability Works 1, Institute of Social and Ethical Accountability, London.

2   Nijenrode University, The Netherlands Business School/European Institute for Business Ethics (1995) *The Technology of Ethical Auditing: An Outline* Nijenrode University, Breukelen.

3   S. Zadek and R. Evans (1993) *Auditing the Market: the Practice of Social Auditing* Traidcraft/New Economics Foundation, Gateshead.

4   *The Body Shop Approach to Ethical Auditing* The Body Shop International, Littlehampton, 1996. See also the entire *Values Report* (1996) which contains all three audits.

5   P. Pruzan (1995) 'The Ethical Accounting Statement', *World Business Academy Perspectives* Vol. 9, No. 2, 1995: pp. 35–46.

6   See, for example, the paper prepared on this subject by a group of Northern non-governmental organizations, Corporate Monitoring Working Group (1996) *Monitoring Codes of Conduct*, prepared by the New Economics Foundation and the Catholic Institute for International Relations, London.

7   See, for some discussion of this, S. Zadek and P. Tiffen (1996), 'Fair Trade: Business or Campaign' *Development* Autumn 1996: 3: pp. 48–53.

8   For those interested in some of the historical background that is at best only alluded to in this section, we would suggest R. Estes (1992) 'Social Accounting Past and Future: Should the Profession Lead, Follow – or Just Get Out of the Way?' *Advances in Management Accounting*, 1: pp. 97–108; R. Estes (1995) *Tyranny of the Bottom Line: Why Corporations Make Good People Do Bad Things* Berrett-Koehler, San Francisco; R. Gray, D. Owen & K. Maunders (1996) *Accounting and Accountability: Social and Environmental Accounting in a Changing World* Prentice Hall International, Hemel Hempstead; C. Medawar (1976) 'The Social Audit: A Political View', *Accounting, Organizations, and Society*, 1(4) pp. 389–394; and S. Zadek and P. Raynard (1995) 'Accounting Works: A Comparative Review of Contemporary Approaches to Social and Ethical Accounting', *Accounting Forum* 19 (2/3) Sept/Dec.

9   D. Blake, W. Frederick and M. Myers (1976) *Social Auditing: Evaluating the Impact of Corporate Programs* Praeger, New York.

10   US Department of Commerce (1979) *Corporate Social Reporting in the United States and Western Europe: Report of the Task Force on Corporate Social Performance* US Department of Commerce, Washington, DC: p. 6.

11   See, for example, D. Logan (1993) *Transnational Giving: An Introduction to the Corporate Citizenship Activity of International Companies Operating in Europe* The Directory of Social Change, London.

12   Discussed in M. Dierkes and R. Bauer (eds) (1973) *Corporate Social Accounting* Praeger, New York.

13   A related method, known as *human asset evaluation*, sought to measure the value of productive capability of the firm's human organisation, and simultaneously the loyalty of the firm's employees and other constituencies affected by the organisation. There is a very interesting development in this approach being trialed by the Swedish insurance company, Skandia, under the title intellectual capital valuation. See Skandia (1994) *Visualising Intellectual Capital in Skandia: Supplement to Skandia's 1994 Annual Report* Skandia, Sweden.

14   US Department of Commerce (1979), op cit: p. 6.

15   John Filer, CEO of Aetna Life and Casualty, quoted in US Department of Commerce (1979), *op cit*: p. vi.

16   Allied Dunbar (1996) *The Big Picture: A Summary of the Allied Dunbar Staff Charity Fund Stakeholder Accountability Report for 1996* Allied Dunbar, Swindon: p. 2. Based on the full report, *Staff Charity Fund Review & Stakeholder Accountability Report* Allied Dunbar, Swindon.

17   See also the British equivalent of this, A. Adams, J. Carruthers, and S. Hamil (1991) *Changing Corporate Culture: a Guide to Social and Environmental Policy and Practice in Britain's Top Companies* Kogan Page, London.

18   For example, Ethibel in Belgium, and EthicScan in Canada.

19   For a brief description of this movement and related references, see A. MacGillivray and S. Zadek (1995) *Accounting for Change: Indicators for Sustainable Development* New Economics Foundation, London.

20   US Department of Commerce (1979) *op cit*: p. 8.

21   See, for example, P. Walker (1995) 'Turning Dreams into Concrete Reality', *New Economics* Winter 1995: pp. 5–9; and J. Morris (1995) 'Indicators of Local Sustainability' *Town and Country Planning*, April 1995, Vol. 64 No. 4: pp. 113–119. For a review of some of the historical and contemporary strands of work in this area,

see A. MacGillivray and S. Zadek (1995) 'Accounting for Change: Indicators for Sustainable Development' WEF, London.

22   K. Davenport (1996) *Corporate Social Auditing* draft of unpublished thesis, Chapter two, p. 26.

23   P. Pruzan and O. Thyssen (1990), 'Conflict and Consensus: Ethics as a Shared Value Horizon for Strategic Planning', *Human Systems Development* 9 1990: pp. 134–152.

24   S. Zadek and P. Raynard (1995), 'Accounting Works: A Comparative Review of Contemporary Approaches to Social and Ethical Accounting', *Accounting Forum*, 19 (2/3) Sept/Dec.

25   For a more extensive description of some of the historical patterns that have been briefly alluded to in this section, see, for example, R. Gray, D. Owen, & K. Maunders (1996) *Accounting and Accountability: Social and Environmental Accounting in a Changing World* Prentice Hall International, Hemel Hempstead.

26   The principle of inclusivity can also be understood as the equivalent of the standard accounting principle of *materiality*. That is, the rights of stakeholders to choose performance indicators associated with their interests – in conjunction with the right of the organization to measure its performance against its own mission statement – is part of what secures information that is not only accurate but relevant or material.

     There is an interesting connection with Fourth Generation Evaluation here, which suffers from the methodological defect of requiring balanced power conditions from the outset of the evaluation process. See S. Zadek (1995) *Beyond Fourth Generation Evaluation* unpublished paper, New Economics Foundation, London.

27   There have been enormous strides forward in the last decade in developing more participative approaches to dialogue between institutions and their stakeholders. Some of the most interesting work has been in the development field, where participative learning methods have been developed to cope with gross imbalances of power between the dialoguing partners, for example, those that exist between development agencies and village communities in the South. See, for example, J. Pretty, I. Guijt, J. Thompson and I. Scoones (1995) *Participatory Learning and Action: A Trainer's Guide* International Institute for Environment and Development, London.

28   There has been intense activity in the area of social indicator development over the last decade, particularly since the Rio Summit under *Local Agenda 21*. A good review of some of this material is provided by A. MacGillivray and S. Zadek (1995) *Accounting for Change: Indicators for Sustainable Development* New Economics Foundation, London.

29   Note, too, that this may mean it is more realistic and relevant for a large, diversified company to develop different social and ethical accounts for different subunits instead of trying to develop one single accounting, auditing and reporting system for the whole organization.

30   A considerable debt is due to John Elkington and Andrea Spencer-Cooke for their work in benchmarking environmental reports. See in particular United Nations Environmental Programme (1994) *Company Environmental Reporting: A Measure of the Progress of Business & Industry Towards Sustainable Development* Technical Report 24, UNEP, Paris, and UNEP/SustainAbility (1996) *The Benchmark Survey: The Second International Progress Report on Company Environmental Reporting* UNEP, Paris.

Chapter 10

CSR strategy and implementation

I N THIS CHAPTER WE WILL:

- Discuss the key elements of managing CSR.
- Assess the specific challenge of integrating stakeholders into CSR implementation.
- Understand the nature and success factors of a CSR strategy.
- Explore the nature, use and limitations of codes of conduct as a CSR tool.
- Understand the potential and limits of CSR tools in the context of a broader CSR strategy.

Introduction

Given the breadth of the academic literature on CSR, it is somewhat surprising that there is very little to find on the actual management, implementation and operational side of CSR. Upon a closer look, and reflecting on what we have discussed so far in this book, in particular in Section B, this relative dearth of work on 'how to do CSR' is perhaps actually not so surprising. If we think of a company such as McDonald's when it develops a CSR strategy, this could feasibly entail virtually the whole company: from procurement, to production, R&D, marketing, human resource management, even finance – managers throughout the firm may have to be involved in developing responsible practices that impact positively on its various stakeholders. CSR, then, is more a new imperative, a new set of goals which need to be implemented across the board in all areas of the company, rather than in a special CSR department, similar to a marketing or finance department.

As CSR is a broad, and in many instances relatively new activity for many companies, it is no surprise that CSR implementation is mostly talked about in terms of a project management structure (Castka, Balzarova, Bamber and Sharp, 2004; Industry Canada, 2005; Sachs, Maurer, Rühli and Hoffmann, 2006). Typical steps would be a planning phase, an implementation phase and an evaluation phase, with the final phase potentially initiating a feedback loop to build on successes and learn from mistakes. In the following, we will have a look at each phase and the specific elements of CSR in an overview.

- *Setting goals for CSR.* The first step in implementing CSR is to identify the key areas where the company wants to achieve progress. Furthermore, the company needs to set specific targets of what to achieve in these areas and how progress towards these targets is going to be measured. In most large companies, these areas and targets would, first of all, be defined very broadly in terms of values or mission statements. Often, these mission statements are rather vague and the challenge is to break them down into concrete objectives. An example of such a mission statement was discussed in Case Study 2 with the ABN AMRO Bank's sustainability definition.

- *Designing CSR strategies.* Knowing what you want to achieve is one thing, but knowing *how* to achieve it is another. Designing CSR strategies is a matter of working out how the firm can get from its current position to a desired future state. While many strategies may be more emergent than planned, firms implementing CSR need to consider how to set the direction of the firm to achieve their CSR goals. The first reading in this chapter provides some clear insight into this area of CSR implementation.

- *Implementing CSR tools.* CSR management sometimes involves doing the same things as usual but with CSR added on – for instance, adding social criteria to supplier evaluation tools – and sometimes it involves doing things completely differently from the start – for example, building strategic management on the principles of stakeholder management. There are various CSR tools and techniques that can aid in these management processes, some of which are specific to a particular CSR area (e.g. audits in the workplace or cause-related marketing in the marketplace) while some cut across areas, such as stakeholder management tools, codes of conduct and risk management tools. We will discuss one of these tools, namely codes of conduct, in more detail in the second reading of this chapter.

- *Assessing the outcomes of CSR.* Finally, the results of CSR implementation need to be assessed, and much of what we discussed in Chapter 9 constitutes the core elements of this stage. CSR auditing and reporting are the key tools that help companies to assess their social performance and communicate it to audiences inside and outside the company.

Managing Stakeholder Relations

Throughout the process of planning, implementation and assessment a unique challenge for CSR lies in the management of the relations with different stakeholders. Managing responsibly is as much about the balancing of competing preferences, demands or claims of specific stakeholders as it is about anything else. Consequently, the management of stakeholder relations is a specific area of CSR management that managers need to handle quite carefully.

To begin with, there is often some ambiguity over who the relevant stakeholders are for a corporation in a given situation. If we think of Vodafone in Case Study 1 we find that the constituency of stakeholders in different parts of the world can vary quite significantly for a company, even on a single issue. Mitchell and co-authors (1997) therefore identify three criteria that may help us to identify 'who really matters' in terms of relevant stakeholders. This is determined by assessing 'stakeholder salience', consisting of three components:

1   *Power*. The perceived ability of a stakeholder to influence organizational action.
2   *Legitimacy*. Whether the organization perceives the stakeholders' actions as desirable, proper or appropriate.
3   *Urgency*. The degree to which stakeholder claims are perceived to call for immediate attention.

From a strategic perspective, a company should look in particular to engage with those stakeholders who are powerful, whose issues are considered legitimate and/or whose claims ask for the most immediate response. Apart from the decision about which group deserves most immediate attention, there is also a plethora of different ways in which a company may engage with stakeholders (Crane and Matten, 2007: 187–190). While in some cases it might be best to keep a distance from a certain stakeholder and to accept them just as a critical voice and benchmark for the company's CSR, other situations might call for more engagement through intensive dialogue or even through partnership and cooperation in certain projects.

Introducing the Readings

Both readings in this chapter focus on a specific element of the management of CSR – CSR strategy and CSR codes of conduct – in order to examine some of the key debates in this emerging area of the literature.

What makes a good CSR strategy?

The paper by Lee Burke and Jeanne Logsdon looks at the process of setting up a CSR strategy. The paper is based on an attitude to CSR which Garriga and Melé (chapter 3) would describe as 'instrumental': why should a company that is interested in long-term value creation engage in CSR? And what are the criteria of a successful CSR strategy? In doing so, the paper adopts an approach that would appeal to many business leaders because it mainly presents CSR as conducive to long-term profitability. The paper develops five criteria or 'dimensions' that a good CSR strategy could embrace. What makes the paper particularly valuable is that the authors also use a variety of CSR activities and ways of understanding strategy to illustrate their claims.

Codes of conduct as a CSR tool

Krista Bondy, Dirk Matten and Jeremy Moon provide an overview of the burgeoning theory and practice of codes of conduct. Codes are by now a common instrument of CSR management, especially in large corporations, and may be used to implement CSR commitments and communicate them internally and externally. The paper categorizes the field and develops a typology of the various codes that are currently used. Bondy *et al.* also contribute to our broader understanding of the recent surge in CSR as they embed the rise of this tool in wider societal and political changes in many industrialized countries over the past couple of years. Crucially, they venture a rather critical perspective on the effectiveness of codes to advance CSR-related goals. They conclude: 'Clearly, [codes of conduct] will only function if the broader culture of the organization is oriented towards sustainability and a code thus is just one supporting tool to foster this goal' (pp. 428–51).

This conclusion may in fact be generalized to most CSR efforts of companies. Similar to Burke and Logsdon's paper, the gist of Bondy *et al.*'s analysis is that more socially responsible behaviour of the company is critically dependent on a long-term, strategic commitment of the entire organization rather than as a result of implementing 'quick fixes' of CSR tools.

Study Questions

1   Discuss the specific challenges of managing CSR. Is CSR any different from other management areas such as finance, marketing or accounting?

2   What are the key elements of a successful CSR strategy?

3   Select a multinational corporation with which you are familiar and research its CSR activities on the web. Which of the five types of CSR behaviour in Burke and Logsdon's Figure 2 does the firm appear to engage in? To what extent would you say that it has adopted a strategic approach to these practices?

4   What are the specific advantages and drawbacks of codes of conduct? Answer the question by putting yourself in the shoes of both top management and lower-level employees. Are there specific CSR issues, challenges or situations where codes of conduct are likely to be more or less useful tools for managing responsibly?

5   Imagine a large multinational corporation with subsidiaries in all five continents trying to implement a code of conduct. What key problems will the company

encounter if implementing a globally homogeneous code? What solutions to these problems would you suggest?

References

Castka, P., Balzarova, M., Bamber, C., and Sharp, J.(2004) 'How Can SMEs Effectively Implement the CSR Agenda? A UK Case Study Perspective', *Corporate Social Responsibility and Environmental Management* 11: 140–149.

Crane, A. and Matten, D. (2007) *Business Ethics: Managing Corporate Citizenship and Sustainability in the Age of Globalization* (2nd edn), Oxford: Oxford University Press.

Industry Canada (2005) *Corporate Social Responsibility: An Implementation Guide for Canadian Business*, Ottawa: Industry Canada (http://strategis.ic.gc.ca).

Mitchell, R., Agle, B. and Wood, D. (1997) 'Toward a Theory of Stakeholder Identification and Salience: Defining the Principle of Who and What Really Counts', *Academy of Management Review* 22(4): 853–886.

Sachs, S., Maurer, M., Rühli, E. and Hoffmann, R. (2006) 'Corporate Social Responsibility from a "Stakeholder View" Perspective: CSR Implementation by a Swiss Mobile Telecommunication Provider', *Corporate Governance* 6(4): 506–515.

HOW CORPORATE SOCIAL RESPONSIBILITY PAYS OFF

Lee Burke and Jeanne M. Logsdon

Tougher competitive conditions in recent years have put pressure on firms to examine their philanthropy and other social responsibility activities. Cutbacks have occurred in many organizations because the rationales for continuing or upgrading these programmes have not been clearly articulated. However, a fundamental belief among its business supporters and business-and-society scholars is that corporate social responsibility "pays off" for the firm as well as for the firm's stakeholders and society in general. But the failure to find strong empirical support for the relationship between socially responsible behaviour and financial performance[1,2] has been troubling. Rightly or wrongly, this lack of a clearcut empirical relationship between social responsibility and the bottom line is perceived by some executives and students as evidence that it is irrelevant for successful corporate performance, perhaps even antithetical to it.

This article approaches the issue of linking corporate social responsibility (CSR) to the economic interests of the firm from a different perspective. Rather than focusing only on direct correlations between CSR programmes and short-term profits, the thrust of our approach is to examine the ways in which CSR programmes can create strategic benefits for the organization even when they are not readily measurable as separable contributions to the bottom line. The question that is addressed here is: *under what conditions does a firm jointly serve its own strategic business interests and the societal interests of its stakeholders?*

This is an important question for managers and for stakeholders because without a clearcut understanding of strategic benefits that may accrue to the organization, it is more likely that top management will not invest in CSR practices which contribute to the long-term success of the firm. While a few organizations with good reputations for CSR have encountered financial difficulties, we believe that the explanation for this decline lies not in their CSR activities but rather in their competitive environments and business decisions. A strategic reorientation of the firm's CSR philosophy can support its financial interests as well as other stakeholders' interests in the firm. How to reorient CSR toward a more strategic perspective is the key to inspiring more CSR activities, thus serving stakeholder and societal interests more fully.

A Tradeoff Between CSR and Profit? Historical Perspectives

The perception that CSR entails a zero-sum tradeoff with corporate economic interests is strongly identified with neo-classical economics. Even many defenders of CSR accept the zero-sum formulation, while at the same time embracing the social obligations of business. The classic literature in business and society asserted that while CSR might entail short-term costs, it paid off for the firm in the long run.[3,4] These scholars argued that firms would benefit from greater social legitimacy with less government regulation, and that a better society was simply good for long-term profitability. A complementary, though slightly different view held that CSR was appropriate for underwriting public goods which no single firm had a market incentive to provide.[5]

The next stage in the academic debate over social responsibility focused on clarifying and quantifying the benefits from CSR. Empirical analyses of the relationship between CSR and profitability began to appear in the mid-1970s, but did not result in consensus.[1,2] These studies have generally used a single measure of social performance (such as an external reputational index, content analysis of corporate annual reports or peer ratings) which was correlated with various measures of company economic performance. Researchers have usually acknowledged the weaknesses of these single CSR measures, but point out the extraordinary difficulty of gathering data about the wide range of CSR behaviours for a sufficient number of firms to perform statistical analyses. More recently, some have argued that fundamental definitional problems with the CSR construct itself, in addition to measurement problems, make the efforts to find statistical associations between CSR and profits highly problematic.[6]

While CSR researchers struggled with these issues, the field of strategic management was grappling with its own definitional problems. Just what exactly was business strategy? Some theorists defined strategy as the goals, mission, and objectives of the firm.[7,8] Others focused on strategy as plan,[9] pattern,[10,11] process[12] and positioning for competitive advantage.[13,14] Within the classic strategy literature, discussions of the firm's external environment expanded beyond the traditional economic or market context. Strategy theorists such as Andrews[10] identified the relationship between corporate strategy and "the economic and *noneconomic* contribution [the firm] intends to make to its shareholders, employees, customers, and communities" (p. 13, emphasis added). Ansoff[15] articulated the need for firms to develop societal strategies. As a result, environmental scanning and monitoring systems gained importance as elements of an effective information gathering system for strategy formulation.[16,17] Attempts to integrate the concepts of CSR and corporate strategy have included the stakeholder model of strategic management and the inclusion of social demands as strategic issues.[18,19] The integration of corporate social policy within the traditional strategy model was also furthered by the recognition that social response policies should be "strategically related to the economic interests of the firm" (Carroll and Hoy, p. 55).[20] The concept of strategic CSR builds on these efforts by demonstrating several fundamental ways in which CSR activities can be tightly linked to the strategy of the firm.

Strategic Corporate Social Responsibility

Corporate social responsibility (policy, programme or process) is *strategic* when it yields substantial business-related benefits to the firm, in particular by supporting core business activities and thus contributing to the firm's effectiveness in accomplishing its mission. While empirical studies to date have focused primarily on the link between CSR and financial performance (especially, short-term profits), we propose a more comprehensive basis for identifying the relationships between CSR and the firm's strategic interests. This broader set of criteria or dimensions attempts to capture the full range of strategic behaviour and opportunities for business to benefit from CSR. These dimensions are not intended to encompass all CSR activity. Much observed CSR behaviour remains nonstrategic, however valuable it is for stakeholders and society. Our attempt here is to develop better measures for assessing *when* and *in what ways* CSR activities jointly serve economic and societal interests.

We have identified five dimensions of corporate strategy which are both critical to the success of the firm and useful in relating CSR policies, programmes and processes to value creation by the firm. Value creation is commonly viewed as the most critical objective for the firm and its strategic decision-making process. In assessing the probable contributions of CSR activities to value creation, the five dimensions of strategic CSR are: centrality, specificity, proactivity, voluntarism and visibility. Figure 1 shows the development of these dimensions of value creation and their linkages to definitions of strategy found in the academic literature.

Centrality

Centrality is a measure of the closeness of fit between a CSR policy or programme and the firm's mission and objectives.[21] Centrality is a critical issue in most definitions of strategy as goals or objectives. It provides direction and feedback for the organization by revealing whether given actions or decisions are consistent with the mission, goals and objectives of the firm. Actions or programmes having high centrality are expected to receive priority within the organization and to yield future benefits, ultimately translated into profits for the organization. For example, in the product

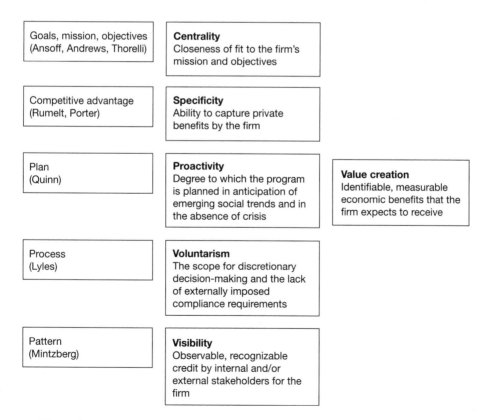

Figure 1

development area, funds spent by a pharmaceutical firm on new drug research and testing have very high centrality. By contrast, the internal auditing function, while important for the ultimate health and security of firms, generally has low centrality.

With respect to strategic CSR, programmes or policies which are related closely to the organization's mission or tightly linked to its accomplishment have much higher centrality than traditional broad-based corporate philanthropy programmes. For example, the design, testing and manufacture of air bags for automobiles – a socially responsible product – was highly central to TRW, as was the correction of safety problems with this product. Similarly, political activities in support of mandatory automobile safety equipment have high centrality for a manufacture of such equipment. But even philanthropy decisions can have a high degree of centrality. Merck's investment in developing and distributing the river blindness drug, Mectizan, is widely regarded as strategically astute as well as humanitarian. The 18 million Third World victims of this disease have clearly benefited from Merck's contribution, and Merck itself benefits because of its enhanced reputation in the industrialized world, including increased reputational leverage with medical professionals and government regulators. The company also benefits in terms of employee morale, productivity and retention by supporting the ethical motivations of the research staff.

Specificity

Specificity refers to the firm's ability to capture or internalize the benefits of a CSR programme, rather than simply creating collective goods which can be shared by others in the industry, community or society at large.[13,14] Externalities (whether positive or negative) and public goods are by definition non-specific. By contrast, investments in research and development leading to patentable products are highly specific.

Many CSR behaviours, including many philanthropic contributions, create non-specific public goods that are broadly available to a local or national community. For example, corporate donations to the San Francisco Symphony benefit Bay Area symphony-goers and others in the community who feel pride in or value the excellence of the local classical music scene. Neither of these benefits is specific to the donating firm since there is no exclusive enjoyment granted to the firm (although some of the firm's employees may hold symphony tickets). Similarly, smokestack scrubbers or waste water treatment facilities create public benefits (or avoid the creation of negative pollution externalities) which are available to the entire community. The firm discharging "clean" smoke or "pure" water benefits only to the extent that it shares in the enjoyment of a healthier environment and avoids censure or fines associated with failure to meet federal pollution enforcement standards. For a firm that *exceeds* existing standards for waste treatment, the benefit stream produced by pollution reductions beyond minimal compliance levels is public, i.e. nonspecific to the firm. One might argue that the firm may be motivated by the desire to save on future compliance costs. If so, the CSR behaviour may be strategic in terms of proactivity, another of the dimensions of strategic CSR.

Contrast this with the case of a firm investing in cogeneration technology which recaptures heat discharged through smokestacks and converts it to energy which substitutes electrical power purchased from the local utility. In this case, the benefits of cogeneration are highly specific to the firm in the form of energy costs saved. The benefit spillover to the public is the firm's contribution to aggregate energy conservation. Cause-related marketing programmes offer similar specific benefits to the sponsoring firm as well as to recipient nonprofit organizations.

Proactivity

Proactivity reflects the degree to which behaviour is planned in anticipation of emerging economic, technological, social or political trends and in the absence of crisis conditions. Proactivity has long been identified by business strategists as an important characteristic of planning and scanning systems.[9,10,22] In turbulent environments firms must constantly scan their environments to anticipate changes likely to affect the firm. Such changes can range from new market opportunities to emerging social issues or threats.

The firm that recognizes critical changes early will be better positioned to take advantage of opportunities or to counter threats. For example, a firm which introduces an employee education and retraining programme in advance of coming technological changes requiring more skilled or differently skilled labour will be better prepared to shift to new technologies and will encounter less resistance in doing so. Motorola has excelled in providing remedial education and specialized training for employees so that Total Quality Management and other improvement programmes could be implemented more effectively by a more qualified workforce.

An example of proactivity in the CSR context is a manufacturer monitoring emerging social trends and regulatory initiatives regarding pollution control. A company whose active investigation identifies new smokestack technologies to meet forthcoming or prospective regulations at a low cost would clearly gain a long-term competitive advantage over its competitors. But even more proactive is the firm which fosters pollution reduction throughout the organization because it has anticipated that pollution-related costs will increase over the long term. For example, 3M Company developed the Pollution Prevention Pays (3P) programme in 1975 and had reduced pollutants by over 575,000 tons by the early 1990s. The 3P Plus programme was recently introduced to provide an even more holistic approach to pollution prevention.[23] Similarly, a consumer products firm pursuing an environmental marketing strategy would be better positioned to roll out environmentally friendly packaging in a timely fashion for the "green" decade of the 1990s, as Procter & Gamble has done. By contrast, cutting back on R & D aimed at finding substitutes for CFCs in the early 1980s may have hurt DuPont's dominance of that market niche more than the cutbacks helped the immediate bottom line.

Voluntarism

Voluntarism indicates the scope of discretionary decision-making by the firm and the absence of externally imposed compliance requirements. Voluntarism is closely linked to proactivity, especially to the extent that it presumes the absence of regulatory or other mandates. In general, philanthropic contributions are assumed to be voluntary – although executives are often subject to social networks pressure to contribute to favourite charities.[24]

Firms regularly engage in voluntary behaviours in their core business functions, e.g. in decisions regarding product line and new product introductions. In general, normal business activities are considered voluntary in the sense that firms maintain high levels of control and discretion over day-to-day operations. In the CSR domain, the firm which exceeds minimum standards for quality or safety, such as an airline which exceeds FAA inspection and maintenance requirements, exhibits voluntarism. These activities offer both strategic and social responsibility payoffs. In many cases additional mandates come into play only when such voluntary behaviour ceases, often in the face of short-run financial pressures. For example, the perceived decline in US airline performance in the late 1980s with respect to on-time arrivals and baggage handling led to new requirements for airlines to publicly report performance in these areas.

Visibility

Visibility denotes both the observability of a business activity and the firm's ability to gain recognition from internal and external stakeholders. Visibility can have both positive and negative consequences for firms. Positive forms of visibility involving normal business activities include favourable media mentions, strong earnings announcements, stock price run-ups (not associated with impending hostile takeovers) and successful new product launches. Instances of negative visibility include government investigations of contract fraud, the indictment or sentencing of company officials, the discovery of dangerous side effects from otherwise beneficent drugs, cases of poisoning and other forms of commercial terrorism, or the disclosure of toxic contamination in waste disposal sites.

Visibility for CSR activities is less likely to be negative, although the CSR behaviour and resulting publicity may arise from initially negative events. For example, the discovery of toxic shock syndrome and its link to tampon use were certainly negative events. But Procter & Gamble's response, in the form of its recall of Rely tampons, generated significant positive visibility for the company and, by extension, enhanced the perceived reliability of its many other products.[25] Similarly, Johnson & Johnson's rapid and complete response to the Tylenol poisonings underscored the firm's concern for its customers and brought high visibility to its long-standing corporate code of conduct. An unanticipated consequence of the Tylenol episode is that Johnson & Johnson's code is now the most widely known corporate code among business students, often used in business-and-society courses as a model for all firms.

Clearly these two well-known cases illustrate voluntary CSR responses which resulted in positive visibility in the wake of negative initial events. This contrasts with Exxon's experience with the Valdez oil spill. In that case, negative visibility resulting from the initial event increased when the expected response capability failed to materialize. Exxon's treatment of, and information releases about, the extent and nature of the oil spill further reinforced the already negative publicity surrounding the initial event.

Visibility, unlike most of the other dimensions, may be particularly relevant with respect to the firm's internal constituency – its employees. For example, creative and extensive employee benefit programmes, such as comprehensive health care, on-site day care and continuing educational benefits, are likely to be highly visible within the firm, even if not to the outside world. They may also produce economic benefits for the firm by improving productivity, morale or loyalty, thus making it easier for the firm to attract and retain the best employees.

Value creation as strategic outcome

The ultimate measure of strategic benefits from CSR activities is the value they create for the firm. Value creation refers to the readily measurable stream of economic benefits that the firm expects to receive. This dimension also most closely approximates the attempts by earlier researchers to find relationships between social responsibility and economic performance. Firms create or attempt to create value in their ongoing business activities through investments in new technology, new products, brand awareness, production facilities, training and customer service. To the extent that some of these also constitute or are integrated with CSR objectives or goals, these CSR programmes are among the most likely to create demonstrable economic benefits to the firm. Figure 2 provides a number of examples of potentially strategic CSR activities and the benefits which they offer to firms.

	Centrality	Specificity	Proactivity	Voluntarism	Visibility	Value created
Philanthropic contributions ($, product, time)	Computer donations to schools by computer mfrs. Engineering research fellowships	Accustom new users to firm's products vs competitors'		Community support		Customer loyalty Future purchasers
Employee benefits (direct or indirect)		Health/wellness Day care Flex-time	New or uncommon benefits Higher employee loyalty	Employee loyalty and morale	Internal: employee loyalty and morale	Productivity gains
Environment management (health, safety, pollution)	New products e.g. 'green' Process innovation esp. re pollution	Patent or innovation edge in product or process development	Learning curve advantages	Positive relations with regulators	Public relations and/or marketing advantage	New products or markets
Political activity (PAC, lobby or information, independent or industry)	Favourable change in economic or social regulations	New business opportunities if pre-positioned to take advantage of new rules	Pre-positioning for changes in regulations			New product or geographic market opportunities
Product or service related characteristics, innovations or processes	Product reformulations e.g. 'green'; improved design, e.g. fuel efficiency; new products, e.g. airbags	Patent or innovation edge first-to-market brand loyalty	Environmental scanning to create edge in design or product ideas		First-to-market or leadership benefits	New product on new markets Edge in meeting emergency needs

Figure 2

Once the concept of strategic CSR is accepted by executives as feasible, the next step is to develop methods of analysis and guidelines to capitalize on these opportunities.

Implications for Management Practice and Research

Increasing competitive pressures have caused executives to examine the nature and extent of their firms' CSR activities. At the same time, governmental capabilities for solving social problems have been called into question, and in many cases society is looking to the business sector for assistance in identifying and implementing remedies. Meanwhile, many of these social problems are becoming more acute. It is critical for executives to consider the consequences of these trends. They do not bode well for communities or for firms.

One answer is strategic corporate social responsibility. By becoming more aware of the benefits to both the firm and its stakeholders, managers can make better decisions about CSR activities. For example, in a community suffering from a high drop-out rate in secondary schools, managers can design and implement many effective programmes for keeping at-risk teenagers in school. Many of these programmes are not very costly to firms, particularly when they encourage employees to volunteer. In addition, there are often payoffs to firms which employ and sell products or services within these communities.

If we recognize the long-term investment characteristics of CSR (as opposed to thinking of CSR merely as current period expenditures), then normal business decision rules would select CSR activities which *1*. yield the highest total payoffs in terms of collective benefits to the firm and its stakeholders and *2*. fall within the range indicated for *strategic* CSR. To identify such projects, the firm should incorporate CSR planning and investment within its corporate planning function. Specifically, the firm should carry out the following analysis:

- Identify the stakeholders which are critically important for achieving the firm's mission, goals or strategic objectives.
- Determine the socially valuable CSR policies, programmes and projects which address the needs and interests of these stakeholders.
- Assess the opportunities offered by these CSR projects to enhance the firm's attainment of strategic objectives or to solve significant problems and threats facing the firm. (Centrality.)
- Assess the degree to which these CSR projects offer benefits which can be captured and/or internalized by the firm as opposed to all firms in the industry or society at large. (Specificity.)
- Anticipate future changes in the firm's environment and changes in the needs of its key stakeholders which could be addressed through proactive CSR policies and activities. (Proactivity.)

- Determine the baseline of mandated requirements in order to identify the opportunities for voluntary activities. (Voluntarism.)
- Identify opportunities to create positive visibility with key internal or external stakeholders from CSR activities. (Visibility.)
- Measure and compare the value or potential value expected from various CSR projects. (Value creation.)

To the academic community, the concept of strategic CSR provides an opportunity to measure the benefits of CSR in a broader context than simple correlations between philanthropic contributions and profits. Recent literature in the business-and-society field implicitly or explicitly takes a more strategic orientation to various components of CSR.[26,27] Greater precision in specifying the attributes of strategic CSR will help future researchers to identify the broad range of business activities which represent CSR behaviour. In this vein, work needs to be done on *1.* creating sound measures of strategic CSR for empirical research; *2.* exploring the linkage between CSR and the alliance behaviours of firms; *3.* examining the role of industry leaders in establishing norms for CSR and in innovating strategic CSR. A comprehensive framework should help managers to identify opportunities for and justify greater attention to CSR behaviour which can be linked to the strategic interests of the firm.

Notes

1   A. Ullmann, Data in search of a theory: a critical examination of the relationships among social performance, social disclosure, and economic performance of US firms, *Academy of Management Review* 10(3), 540–557 (1985).

2   D. Wood and R. Jones, Research in corporate social performance: what have we learned? Paper presented at the Conference on Corporate Philanthropy, Case Western Reserve University, April (1994).

3   K. Davis, The case for and against business assumption of social responsibilities. In A. Carroll (ed.), *Managing Corporate Social Responsibility*, Little, Brown & Co. Boston, MA (1977).

4   G. Steiner, An overview of the changing business environment and its impact on business. In L. Preston (ed.), *Business Environment / Public Policy: 1979 Conference Papers*, pp. 3–18, AACSB, St Louis, MO (1980).

5   W. Baumol, Enlightened self-interest and corporate philanthropy. In *A New Rationale for Corporate Social Policy*. Committee for Economic Development, New York (1970).

6   M. Starik and A. Carroll, In search of beneficence: reflections on the connections between firm social and financial performance. *Proceedings,*

Several of these ideas appeared in a paper with Martha Reiner which was presented at the International Association for Business and Society 2nd annual conference in Sundance, UT.

International Association for Business and Society 1990 Annual Meeting, pp. 1–15 (1990).

7   H. Ansoff, *Corporate Strategy: an Analytic Approach to Business Policy for Growth and Expansion*, McGraw-Hill, New York (1965).

8   H. Thorelli (ed.), *Strategy Plus Structure Equals Performance*, Indiana University Press, Bloomington, IN (1977).

9   J. Quinn, *Strategies for Change: Logical Incrementalism*, Richard D. Irwin, Homewood, IL (1980).

10   K. Andrews, *The Concept of Corporate Strategy*, Richard D. Irwin, Homewood, IL (1980).

11   H. Mintzberg, Opening up the definition of strategy. In J. Quinn, H. Mintzberg and R. James, *The Strategy Process*, Prentice Hall, Englewood Cliffs, NJ (1988).

12   M. Lyles, Strategic problems: how to identify them. In L. Fahey (ed.), *The Strategic Planning Management Reader*, Prentice Hall, Englewood Cliffs, NJ (1985).

13   M. Porter, *Competitive Advantage*, Free Press, New York (1985).

14   R. Rumelt, The evaluation of business strategy. In W. F. Glueck, *Business Policy and Strategic Management*, 3rd edn, McGraw-Hill, New York (1980).

15   H. Ansoff, Societal strategy for the business firm. In *Advances in Strategic Management*, Vol. 1, pp. 3–29, JAI Press, Greenwich, CT (1983).

16   J. Camillus and D. Datta, Managing strategic issues in a turbulent environment, *Long Range Planning* 24(2), 67–74 (1991).

17   R. Lenz and J. Engledow, Environmental analysis: the applicability of current theory, *Strategic Management Journal* 7(4), 329–346 (1986).

18   A. Carroll, F. Hoy and J. Hall, The integration of corporate social policy into strategic management. In S. Sethi and C. Falbe (eds), *Business and Society: Dimensions of Conflict and Cooperation*, pp. 449–470, Lexington Books, Lexington, MA (1987).

19   R. Freeman, *Strategic Management: a Stakeholder Approach*, Pitman, Boston, MA (1984).

20   A. Carroll and F. Hoy, Integrating corporate social policy into strategic management, *Journal of Business Strategy* 4(3), 48–57 (1984).

21   H. Ansoff, Managing surprise and discontinuity: strategic response to weak signals. In H. Thorelli (ed.), *Strategy Plus Structure Equals Performance*, pp. 53–82, Indiana University Press, Bloomington, IN (1977).

22   A. Cooper and D. Schendel, Strategic responses to technological threats, *Business Horizons* 19(1), 61–69 (1976).

23   R. Bringer and D. Benforado, Pollution prevention and total quality environmental management. In R. Kolluru (ed.), *Environmental Strategies Handbook*, pp. 165–197, McGraw-Hill, New York (1994).

24   L. Burke, J. Logsdon, W. Mitchell, M. Reiner and D. Vogel, Corporate community involvement in the San Francisco Bay Area, *California Management Review* 28(3), 122–141 (1986).

25   E. Gatewood and A. Carroll, The anatomy of corporate social response: the Rely, Firestone 500, and Pinto cases, *Business Horizons* 24(5), 9–16 (1981).

26   J. Logsdon, M. Reiner and L. Burke, Corporate philanthropy: strategic

responses to the firm's stakeholders, *Nonprofit and Voluntary Sector Quarterly* 19 (2), 93–190 (1990).

27   J. Mahon, Corporate political strategy, *Business in the Contemporary World* 2(1), 50–62 (1989).

CODES OF CONDUCT AS A TOOL FOR SUSTAINABLE GOVERNANCE IN MNCs

Krista Bondy, Dirk Matten and Jeremy Moon

Introduction

This chapter discusses and analyses an increasingly popular tool that companies use to meet the goal of corporate sustainability. Codes of conduct (CoC), codes of ethics and codes of practice, have become extremely popular over recent years and have been widely adopted across industries, countries and sectors (Leipziger 2003; Sethi 2003; Wood *et al.* 2004). While initially codes have tended to focus on corporate governance issues (Aguilera and Cuervo-Cazurra 2004), this has increasingly shifted towards broader societal issues. In particular multinational corporations (MNCs) have adopted CoCs in the context of growing public concern about working conditions in their overseas operations and the responsible use of their economic power more generally (e.g. Emmelhainz and Adams 1999; Gordon and Miyake 2001; Kolk 2005; Kolk and van Tulder 2004; Kolk *et al.* 1999; Pearson and Seyfang 2001).

Elsewhere in this volume the concept of sustainability has been discussed at length and we follow a similar path in this chapter by understanding sustainability as the simultaneous effort of balancing economic, social and environmental goals for a corporation, often epitomized in the popular concept of the 'triple bottom line'. As such, sustainability is another metaphor for describing corporate social responsibility, corporate citizenship or ethical business conduct and for the purpose of this chapter we will use sustainability as a synonym for these concepts.

The chapter begins by describing the context in which codes exist and the importance of self-regulation (codes more specifically) in governing corporate attitudes and behaviours, particularly when operating in a trans-boundary environment. Codes are then defined, described and characterized to ensure a thorough understanding of what codes are and how they can be used by organizations. Lastly, the chapter discusses the issue of codes, sustainability and governance, and where and how codes can be used most effectively to further societal objectives.

Codes of Conduct as Reflexive Regulation

CoCs are an approach of voluntary corporate self-regulation. As such they represent a clear contrast to governmental, mandatory regulation. To better understand the function, role and constraints of CoCs for sustainable corporate governance, it is helpful to discuss the antecedents and characteristics of the social, political and economic factors that have encouraged this trend towards more self-regulation of industry. We would like to highlight three crucial developments.

First, the *institutional failure* of governmental institutions in most developed economies to maintain a consistently high level of regulation in the last quarter century or so. Some have argued there is a more fundamental failure of modern democracy in regulating societies towards sustainability (e.g. Beck 1994, 1996, 1997a; Giddens 1990). They suggest that while a highly regulated welfare state was a key element of the 'modernization' process of western society over the last two centuries, we have entered a phase where governments are increasingly faced with the – mostly unintended – 'consequences of modernity' (Giddens 1990). While these governmental institutions have been able to implement the logic of wealth distribution, they are intrinsically unable to serve as institutions which 'manage' the side effects of industrial modernity. As Beck argues, societies as a result are governed by a form of 'organized irresponsibility' which leaves in particular the ecological, economic and social risks of modern societies unaddressed. Consequently, at the heart of the new epoch of 'reflexive modernity' we witness the emergence of a political arena below the institutions of traditional political actors. In this sphere of 'subpolitics' (Beck 1997b) these 'consequences of modernity' are tackled by a plethora of actors, including civil society groups and – most notably – corporations which, due to resource and power differentials in relation to other civil society actors, take a dominant role in this process – a role which in many cases replaces or at least eclipses those of governments (Moon 2002). CoCs play a crucial element in this process, and as we will discuss later in this chapter, this often results from collaboration between multi stakeholders from civil society.

A second reason for governmental retreat from direct regulation is of a more *political* and *ideological nature* (White 2003: 8–15). Partly informed by institutional failure of the classic welfare state but also as a phenomenon in its own right, there has been a significant shift in political thinking and practice since the 1980s in most liberal democracies. The more extreme view, on the right of the political spectrum, is highly suspicious of the idea of a government responsible for so many aspects of its citizens' life. At the core of this libertarian model is the key importance of private property, a free market economy and a limited state. Consequently, beginning with the Reagan and Thatcher governments, we witnessed a reduction of state involvement which leaves significant areas of former governmental functions delegated to private actors or simply abandoned.

The new centre-left governments in Europe in the late 1990s, most notably in the UK, have followed a similar approach. In principle, the state is still responsible for guaranteeing basic citizenship rights but in practice it ensures access to the goods and services for its citizens by enabling their provision by private actors. The 'enabling state' (Deakin and Walsh 1996; Gilbert and Gilbert 1989) involves corporations increasingly delivering goods and services which in the initial liberal model were clearly a responsibility of governments. However the more corporations deliver telecommunications, public transport or health services, the higher are the public demands that the companies involved adhere to certain standards and be accountable to the public about the quality and price of their services. CoCs are a tool enabling corporations to address these issues.

The third contributing factor to this shift in regulatory approaches is the increased internationalization of economic, social and political processes, often referred to as '*globalization*' (Turner 2000). The central characteristic of globalization is the progressive *deterritorialization* of social, political, and economic interaction (Scholte 2000), whereby a growing number of social activities are now taking place beyond the power and influence of the nation state. This development is closely linked to the rise of new libertarian political thinking which in particular encouraged liberalization of world trade, reduction of regulation for foreign direct investment and increased economic freedom for corporate actors. Theoretically the governments of nation states still have full sovereignty in their own territories. However crucial changes effected by globalization place limitations on the exercise of that sovereignty because: (a) nation states are exposed to economic, social, and political action beyond their own control; and (b) actors within their own territories encounter less constraints on relocating activities into territories beyond the control of their original government. While the first aspects put governments under pressure to provide more freedom to economic actors in order to secure employment and attract investment, the latter exposes government to the constant threat by corporations to exit if the government imposes unacceptable levels of regulation, taxation and control, sometimes referred to as the 'race to the bottom'. Thus globalization provides an incentive to governments to refrain from the often costly and controversial regulation of sustainability related issues, such as environmental issues or protection of workers' rights. At the same time, corporations are increasingly exposed to public scrutiny of and outrage at many of their (perceived) shortfalls in achieving sustainability. As a consequence, in the absence of governmental regulation some corporations increasingly resort to self-regulation.

Governments also encourage corporate self-regulation as a way to meet societal objectives with alternatives (primarily CoCs) that sidestep the limitations associated with more traditional forms of legislation and regulation discussed above (e.g. International Council on Human Rights Policy 2002; Lenox and Nash 2003; Ruhnka and Boerstler 1998). These self-regulatory strategies involve participation from non-legal bodies in the development, monitoring and enforcement of desired social objectives (Wotruba 1997; Carroll and McGregor-Lowndes 2001; Martin 2003; Ruhnka and Boerstler 1998). Self-regulatory initiatives offer a means to control corporate behaviour across borders as they are not tied to any particular political system or territory, and therefore can be applied in a variety of locations within corporations, industries or sectors, depending on the scope of the initiative and the will of the corporation in implementation.

In the context of decreased governmental influence on regulatory processes CoCs are part of a wider trend in regulation which has been discussed under the label of 'reflexive regulation'. Reflexive regulation can be defined as 'a legal theory and a practical approach to regulation that seeks to encourage self-reflective and self-critical processes within social institutions concerning the effects they have on the natural environment' (Orts 1995b: 780; see also Orts 1995a). Reflexive regulation contrasts to the conventional models in sustainability related regulation. Reflexive models of environmental politics are to be found in many forms and appearances (Gibson 1999; Ten Brink 2002). Common to all is the fact that the corporations are no longer only the object of environmental regulation, but are also becoming active participants in the regulatory process also referred to as 'responsive' or 'enforced' self-regulation (Ayres and Braithwaite 1992). On the transnational level, voluntary codes of conduct adopted by MNCs have become the most common form of reflexive regulation of the last decades (Kaptein 2004).

Basic Types of Codes of Conduct

There is no standard definition of CoCs. Virtually every piece of literature on codes has its own definition, although the definitions are largely similar. Whether written by the corporation, or by a multistakeholder alliance for a wide range of corporations, CoCs can be defined as a voluntary set of commitments that either influence corporate attitudes and behaviours or are undertaken by the corporation to define their intentions and/or actions with regard to ethical and other issues, or towards a range of stakeholders from a market-based perspective (Kolk *et al.* 1999; Kaptein and Wempe 2002; United States Council for International Business 2000; ILO n.d.a; ILO n.d.b; Forcese 1997; Alexander 1997; Dickerson and Hagan 1998; OECD 2001; Diller 1999).

As with definitions, there are a variety of ways to understand the types of codes. Some are typified by the organization that created the code, some by the kind of content found in the codes, some by the intended function of the code and some by the progression of codes over time. Table 1 summarizes different ways in which codes have been categorized.

The literature on code types suggests two main debates: First, should codes be written by corporations, or should they be written by external

Table 1 Summary of code types

Code types	Example of criteria used	Real world example of codes
Author Organization (e.g. Jenkins, 2002; World Resources Institute 2003; Wotruba 1997)	● Company ● Industry association ● Model (acts as an example – created by variety or organizations) ● Inter-governmental ● Multistakeholder (negotiated between numerous stakeholders)	● Nike Code of Conduct ● Responsible Care (chemical industry) ● International Code of Ethics for Canadian Business ● OECD Guidelines for Multinational Enterprises ● CERES Principles
Content (e.g. Langlois and Schlegelmilch 1990; ILO n.d.a; Rezaee et al. 2001)	● Regulatory ● Philosophical ● Social responsibilities ● Management philosophy ● High road (aspirational)/ Low road (rules of behaviour)	● Vodafone Code of Ethics ● Global Compact (quasi-code) ● Social Venture Network Standards of Corporate Responsibility ● Nike Code of Conduct ● Global Sullivan Principles/Glaxosmithkline Code of Conduct
Code Function (e.g. Kolk et al. 1999; ILO n.d.c; Diller 1999)	● Guide or restrict corporate behaviour ● Influence other actors/ carry out self-regulation ● Operational or subscription ● Model (acts as an example)	● Virtually all codes ● Ethical Trade Initiative Base Code ● Social Venture Network Standards of Corporate Responsibility ● International Code of Ethics for Canadian Business
Progress Over Time/ Historical Progression (e.g. Mendes and Clark 1996)	● First generation ● Second generation ● Third generation ● Fourth generation ● Fifth generation	● Bell Canada Enterprises ● WPP Code of Business Conduct ● Royal Bank of Canada Code of Conduct ● Responsible Care ● CAUX Round Table Principles for Business

bodies, and, second, should code content be written as principles or rules as both have different implications for understanding and implementing the code from various stakeholder perspectives? The next section discusses the debate within the literature on these questions.

Corporate vs. multistakeholder codes

Company codes provide limited information on CSR and the kinds of initiatives expected of corporations operating in a global market due largely to the structure of the code document and the fact that guidance or clarification on code commitments are usually found within a separate document (Bondy 2003). They are typically written by a representative of the company or industry, with little or no input from outside groups and are often a vision of where the managing group or board of directors would like the company to be in the future. Therefore they do not reflect the way in which the corporation currently operates, nor do they typically meet the needs of other stakeholders affected by the corporation. Furthermore, company codes are also subject to the whims of senior management (Sodeman 1995).

The Clean Clothes Campaign (1998) lists four major drawbacks of company codes:

1   Vaguely defined – corporate codes do not specify precisely the limits of their responsibility;
2   Incomplete – many company codes exclude the right to organize, refer only to child labour or in other ways are not complete;
3   Not implemented – an important flaw in company codes of conduct is the lack of information on how these codes are being implemented or monitored;
4   Not independently monitored – controlled or internal monitoring assumes a willingness to take the company at its word only.

The two major benefits associated with company codes are the assumption that by virtue of creating the code, the corporation recognizes the importance of mitigating CSR issues at least superficially and that the code and resulting changes are driven from within and thus likely to be more successful where there is an intention to implement (WBCSD 2000).

Multistakeholder codes on the other hand are generally not aspirational, but determine the bare minimum of acceptable commitments to a wide variety of interested stakeholders. This results from a process of bargaining, negotiating and compromise between diverse groups coming from government, business coalitions, NGOs, and academia for example, where the aim is to meet as many of the needs as possible through generating consensus. According to Dickerson and Hagen (1998), these codes are actually superior as they produce a minimum normative consensus that can be applied universally. Both Dickerson and Hagen (1998) and Kolk van Tulder and Welters (1999) would agree that multistakeholder codes are better at articulating, guiding and assessing corporations on the business–society interface than are individually created or company codes. Resulting from the consensus process, Jeffcott and Yanz (2000) suggest that multistakeholder codes are seen to be more effective in dealing with issues related to the developing world and to supply chain management.

The resulting multistakeholder code can provide consistency and standardization of wider stakeholder expectations for companies participating in the codes and the stakeholders affected by the corporations. Also, it is argued that multistakeholder codes provide SMEs with an opportunity to participate in the use of codes without having to undertake development costs, particularly those associated with stakeholder engagement (Blowfield 2000).

Multistakeholder codes also require more transparency and accountability from member corporations, as audit reports from company codes are usually provided only to management (Blowfield 2000) where assessments on implementation of multistakeholder codes are generally required by the organization who created the code and are therefore available publicly. Also, when corporations commit to these externally created codes, they create a more visible accountability relationship with key internal and external stakeholders.

What makes this argument so interesting is that although the literature suggests corporations should be using multistakeholder codes, the vast majority used by corporations are those created internally (OECD 1999; Bondy *et al*. 2004). This issue will be discussed in more detail below.

Principles- vs. rules-based codes

Principles-based codes are typically a short list of statements that can cover a wider variety of issues because the commitments are not targeted at specific behaviours or actions and are meant to guide behaviour in a variety of contexts. Thus, they are more flexible and relevant over longer periods of time. By nature of their structure, they require individuals to think before acting to ensure their behaviour is in line with the code. However, this flexible structure invites a variety of possible interpretations for each statement, and makes them notoriously difficult to measure and thus report.

Rules-based codes can be a large list of more specific behavioural commitments, although this is not always the case. The rules tell individuals what they can and cannot do based on commitments made in the code. This provides a clear indication of expected behaviour surrounding particular issues, and provides external parties with a clear indication of the commitments and actions to be taken by the organization. Rules-based codes can also be much easier to measure. The major problem with rules-based codes is that they cannot cover every situation that arises and thus will not be an effective guide in areas not covered by the code, and must be constantly updated to address omissions and the changing situations faced by corporations.

The most effective CSR code of conduct is one that combines both principles and rules. The code would include an introductory section describing the author's perspective on CSR, codes of conduct, the appropriate role for corporations in society, and instructions on how to use the code. The introduction would indicate priorities and anticipated timelines for implementation of different phases (if a company code) etc., confirm that the code is not intended to act as a list of do's and don'ts, but that it provides specific commitments to attitudes and behaviour which may be more or less appropriate depending on the specific organizational context. The remaining text of the code would comprise each individual principle, with definitions of key terms (particularly those with vague or multiple meanings), how the term has been operationalized for action (or the rules for implementation), and the indicators to measure and report on progress.

The different types of codes and classification systems found in the literature help to highlight four important elements in understanding codes of conduct. The four elements: code author, content, function within the corporation and 'genre', indicate the importance of these code characteristics in the literature and thus in analysing and understanding codes. In other words, by using these characteristics to classify the types of codes available, the authors have emphasized the overall importance of the four elements in understanding codes. These typologies provide a somewhat specific understanding of some of the important characteristics of codes.

Code Characteristics

After having identified the nature and key types of codes we will now discuss in more detail the various characteristics of CoCs. Wotruba (1997) provides a succinct summary of the literature on the major dimensions upon which codes can be characterized. He lists five separate continuums under which all codes can be characterized to varying degrees.

1   *Specific vs. General* – This dimension describes to what degree the commitments found in codes are focused on specific behaviours or general statements. Operational codes fall on the specific side as they indicate expectations for specific kinds of behaviour. By contrast, model codes are on the general side as they typically suggest more sweeping comments on preferred philosophies and appropriate corporate intentions towards particular issues or groups.

2   *Comprehensive vs. Selective* – This dimension focuses on the breadth of topics covered by the code. Individual corporate codes are usually more selective as they include only issues appropriate to the unique operating conditions of the corporation. Multistakeholder codes usually attempt to be more comprehensive and cover a wider range of issues to be applicable to more organizations or industries.

3   *Positive vs. Negative* – This dimension describes the tone of the code. Some codes are written as aspirational statements about intentions for

behaviour in the future and therefore are more positive in nature (such as many internally written codes and/or principles-based codes) (Aaronson and Reeves 2002; Lad 1991). Other codes are written as a set of rules that indicate unacceptable behaviours (rules-based codes), indicating what members 'shall not do' and thus are negative in nature.

4   *Voluntary vs. Mandatory* — This dimension indicates the degree to which corporations undertake codes voluntarily. Although defined as a voluntary tool based on market issues, some codes are effectively mandatory for certain corporations in particular contexts. For instance, in the UK corporations must comply with the Combined Code if they want to be listed on the London Stock Exchange. Chemical industry associations require their members to comply with Responsible Care as part of their membership with the association, ensuring social and environmental impacts of the industry are prevented or mitigated. In these contexts, corporations are essentially forced to comply with the codes, making them mandatory.

5   *Equilegal vs. Supralegal* — This dimension describes the degree to which commitments listed in the codes are mere reflections of already existing legislation and standards (equilegal) or have moved beyond the minimum requirements of the legal environment (supralegal).

Each of the four code typologies differentiate between codes on content and structure, although in some cases this is done implicitly such as with the author typology. Therefore, these typologies would appear differently on Wotruba's (1997) five continuums of code characteristics. For instance, the code type 'model' from within the author typology would tend towards the general, selective and positive sides of the first three continuums. By definition, these codes would certainly be voluntary (fourth continuum) and might fit anywhere on the fifth continuum depending on the focus of the individual code. A regulatory code from the content typology however is likely to be on the specific, selective, negative ends of the first three spectrums, varied where it sits on the fourth continuum and likely to be on the equi-legal side of the fifth continuum. Thus, code type indicates a likelihood towards the appearance of certain content and structure.

The location of the respective codes on these five continuums can also indicate the likelihood of code effectiveness if implemented efficiently, and the credibility of the code according to external parties. As credibility depends on effective monitoring, enforcement and transparency (ILO n.d.a.) codes written in such a way as to lend simplicity to these processes will be viewed as more effective. They will therefore generate more credibility for the corporation and its CSR initiatives and create a stronger accountability relationship with key stakeholders.

Evaluating Codes of Conduct as a Tool for Sustainable Corporate Governance

There is ongoing debate about whether codes of conduct are effective corporate governance tools which move organizations towards increased sustainability and conformity to societal expectations. Discussions of code effectiveness inevitably evaluate their structural and functional benefits and limitations particularly to determine if codes are in fact capable of helping facilitate changes in the impacts of corporations on society. A variety of perspectives influence this debate.

Industries, businesses, NGOs and governments each have their own reasons for supporting or being concerned with codes, and may push for changes to make codes more effective for their own needs. The following discussion is summarized in Table 2 below and a more complete list of benefits and limitations can be found in Appendix A.

Benefits of codes

Primarily, codes are flexible documents that can be tailored to individual corporations, industries, countries, international contexts, issues or groups (Aaronson and Reeves 2002). Therefore, corporations can identify those

Table 2 Summary of code benefits and limitations

Benefits	Limitations
• Flexible, can be uniquely tailored	• Lack accountability mechanisms (monitoring, sanctions)
• Relatively inexpensive	
• Provide space for innovation and creative problem solving of targeted issues	• Cannot enforce proper implementation
	• Often written as broad philosophical statements therefore hard to measure
• Create potential for competitive advantage	• Adopters already leaders in industry and with CSR issues
• Mitigate need for governmental regulation or intervention	• Over-represented in industries with high visibility, customer products, focus on brand image or reputation and large environmental or social impacts, and under-represented in industries with low visibility, primarily business to business sales or where production costs are a large part of final sale price
• Level playing field of competitors within same industry	
• Create order and structure in transboundary environment	
• Enhance trust, customer loyalty and reputation	
• Allow stakeholder influence in governance decisions	• Lack expectations for suppliers
	• Unknown to majority of employees
• Create pressure to follow through on commitments through formalization and publication of commitments	• Do not include complaints process or whistleblower protection
• Create benchmark for measurement and identification of progress	

commitments applicable to their operational considerations, stakeholder base and governmental requirements (as is the case in the US) (Ruhnka and Boerstler 1998). This flexibility allows for creative and innovative solutions to complex social and environmental problems, and also allows for rapid changes to commitments required to keep pace with the changing needs of the marketplace, corporation and/or stakeholders (Australian Government 1997; WBCSD 2000).

Codes are less costly to create, implement, administer, monitor and enforce than legislation or legal regulation. The reduced costs of regulation achieved through codes are in essence transferred from governments to corporations, as all costs of internal codes are borne by the corporation. The same is true of corporations that implement multistakeholder codes. However, as the corporation only commits to activities applicable to its operations, the costs are less for them in the long-term as they only deal with appropriate issues and not those mandated for all corporations by legislation. Not only do codes reduce the cost of regulation with regards to development and implementation, they also reduce costs to the legal system as stakeholders use avenues other than the courts to seek remedies from the corporation. Code disputes must be addressed through non-legal or market routes such as trade associations or consumer groups (Gibson 2000; Wotruba 1997; Carroll and McGregor-Lowndes 2001) as they are not enforceable in law except as part of a contract.

If codes based on certain issues are used by a large enough percentage of corporations, the codes can mitigate the need for additional government legislation. This is particularly true when the codes proactively cover issues of potential concern to stakeholders, which in turn can help corporations avoid external pressure such as negative media attention and consumer boycotts that in some cases can be the impetus for government legislation (Gibson 2000; Wotruba 1997).

Industry or multistakeholder codes can ensure a level playing field where all corporations within a set of criteria undertake the same costs of implementation and administration of the code, therefore, maintaining fair competition between the corporations. These external codes can also create a transparent benchmark from which to build trust with stakeholders and create confidence in the industry (Martin 2003; Gibson 2000).

Codes are also very important in regulating corporations across borders. Governments and corporations recognize the importance of codes in being able to create some consistency in cross-border operations and transactions resulting from the lack of effective international institutions in creating structure in the international context (Martin 2003; Carroll and McGregor-Lowndes 2001).

Codes can actually provide economic benefits to corporations through increased customer loyalty and reputation, and can enhance trust in corporations that make steps to effectively implement the code (Sethi 2002; Wotruba 1997). Creating and effectively implementing a code can create a competitive advantage for the corporation and/or help to create a niche market with stakeholders who judge corporations by not only what they produce but also how they produce it. The competitive advantage created by codes can also restrict new entrants to the market because of the costs associated with competing on CSR issues as well as product and price issues (Gibson 2000; Wotruba 1997).

Development and implementation of effective and credible codes requires the creation of partnerships with other organizations, or disclosure to other organizations not solely focused on profit motives. Thus, codes allow other organizations to influence the philosophies or decisions corporations make regarding their social and environmental impacts and/or leverage their behaviour (Jenkins 2002; Sethi 2002; World Resources Institute 2003; Martin 2003).

By virtue of making public commitments to social and environmental issues, corporations make themselves more visible and vulnerable to external pressure and negative attention should they fail to achieve their social and environmental objectives (Gibson 2000; Jenkins 2002). This visibility that results from code adoption also helps create an accountability relationship with key stakeholders because it identifies responsibilities and commitments and suggests intended actions. This in turn gives stakeholders some power to ask questions surrounding implementation and performance, and to demand rectification of identified problems. In essence, committing to a code provides a subtle power shift away from corporations to interested stakeholders by allowing them a voice and the opportunity to directly affect corporate decision-making.

Codes can also create a benchmark from which corporations can be measured, audited and held publicly accountable and can encourage corporations to place the same expectations on their suppliers, thereby inducing more corporations to be socially and environmentally responsible (World Resources Institute 2003; Jenkins 2002). Thus codes, whether multistakeholder or company code, can act as a set of criteria in enabling the measurement of corporations and other organizations in relation to their non-economic issues and commitments.

Limitations of codes

The two most common critiques of codes are the lack of accountability mechanisms such as monitoring provisions and sanctions, and the inability or unwillingness of corporations to effectively implement code commitments. Many areas for concern with codes deal with the way in which they are written. Many codes are written as vague and/or broad philosophical concepts with little to no information on specific actions to be taken or plans for implementation, and the meaning of commitments can vary depending on the perspective and intent of the reader. The impact of codes with more general commitments are difficult to measure and it can therefore be hard to determine if the corporation is in fact living up to them. Often codes deal with specific issues that result from negative media attention, such as Nike and child labour, or are specific to a certain group of issues such as labour or the environment, without the inclusion of other pertinent issues from different areas. For instance, many organizations such as the ILO, Ethical Trading Initiative etc. have developed codes dealing only or primarily with labour issues. These codes lack the same attention to other issues such as human rights, environment, community issues etc. and thus only deal with one area of corporate impact.

Codes with vague or broad commitments also create problems because they are open to a wide variety of interpretations which in turn create unforeseen expectations from stakeholders who understand the commitment differently from the corporation. This problem is enhanced because corporations have limited resources and must choose appropriate initiatives which are within their means to implement. This means that not all issues mentioned by stakeholders can be dealt with by corporations regardless of their sincerity to act.

Since codes are intended to fill regulatory voids, the concern over implementation and enforcement is a serious one. If corporations effectively implement codes and work on continual improvement of their social and environmental objectives, codes become increasingly difficult to implement. The easiest and most obvious areas for improvement are usually the first to be accomplished. Although these early successes help to encourage buy-in from corporations and their employees, once the easiest tasks are completed, it becomes increasingly difficult to continue the same level of progress in achieving new social and environmental objectives. This is the problem of 'low-hanging fruit' – once it is gone, the amount of resources required to continue 'picking fruit' may outweigh the benefits to the corporation and its stakeholders.

Another critique is that individual corporations who adopt codes are usually already leaders in the industry or innovative with regards to CSR issues and it is usually the same corporations who are members of multiple voluntary initiatives. Multistakeholder codes suffer from low membership and are typically used as model codes, not adopted as written.

Codes are also found to be over-represented in industries with highly visible consumer products, brands or corporate images (such as apparel or other consumer goods industries) or large environmental or social impacts (such as extractive or pharmaceutical industries) and under-represented in industries with low consumer visibility, business-to-business sales or where the cost of production is high in proportion to the price of the product. In practice, codes are often found to have few provisions requiring social and environmental responsibility of suppliers, and focus primarily on issues that are either of large importance in the media, or have the ability to heavily impact the corporation in some way.

There is also a concern that corporations do not make their employees or other stakeholders aware of codes they have committed to, nor are they translated into languages that employees in other countries can understand. In other cases, the codes are critiqued for not having complaints procedures or secure channels for employees to indicate non-compliance within the corporation without fear of retaliation (Sethi 2002; World Resources Institute 2003; Martin 2003; Jenkins 2002; Carroll and McGregor-Lowndes 2001; Wotruba 1997; Diller 1999; Gibson 2000).

Often, this debate includes the use of different code types to illustrate benefits and limitations identified by the author. For instance, business coalitions tend to favour model or corporate codes because of the flexibility (structural) and transboundary (functional) nature of these code types. Many NGOs on the other hand favour intergovernmental or operational codes as they often prescribe right and wrong action (functional) and create minimum thresholds based on stakeholder consensus (structural).

In essence, the literature suggests that codes have the potential to be a powerful tool for self-regulation of corporations but only where the intent to implement co-exists with adoption. Codes can fill a global regulatory and governance gap that can be unique to specific corporate contexts or stakeholder viewpoints, where corporate intentions are formalized, creating greater transparency and accountability with respect to its business–society interface. However, the code must be developed with at least minimal consideration of affected stakeholders, methods for measuring corporate performance with it, and how it will be implemented for it to be an effective and credible tool amongst stakeholders.

Encouraging Sustainability by CoCs?

Clearly, the literature indicates that codes are quite varied in type, content, structure and use. But how does this translate into MNC practices? This final section will discuss motivations for corporations using codes, the relationship between codes and broader sustainability goals and finally look at whether codes are an effective tool for encouraging sustainability within corporations.

It turns out that MNCs, regardless of their home culture, may in fact articulate a small set of similar motivations for code adoption. Although the motivations articulated are generally in keeping with the four main groups assumed in the literature (stakeholder regulation, stakeholder communication, competitive advantage and mitigation of risks and/or threats), these motivations appear to be similar in different cultures. Figure 1 is based on our study of the top 50 MNCs in Canada, the UK and Germany and illustrates the most common motivations presented by corporations across these cultures (Bondy *et al.* 2004).

Based on this research, when MNCs provide a motivation for adopting a code that is not mandatory,[i] they list guides for behaviour, protection

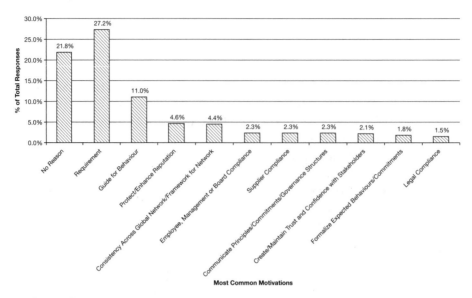

Figure 1 Most common motivations articulated for adopting codes

and/or enhancement of corporate reputation, consistency across a global framework, compliance of key stakeholders, communication of commitments, creating and/or maintaining trust, formalization of commitments and legal compliance most commonly. Thus, motivations for MNCs using codes to engage in CSR seem to be converging on a global scale around areas related to strategic business interests, communication and compliance.

Interestingly, there does not appear to be a relationship between the type of code used by the corporation and their reason for adopting it. In some cases there was a synergy between the type of code and the motivation (such as an industry code and adopting it to gain membership with the industry and to protect its reputation), while in other cases the type of code and the motivation for adopting it were disconnected (such as a company code and adopting it to create or maintain trust of key stakeholders). The code type, and the benefits and limitations associated with these did not appear to have any kind of systematic impact on the motivations presented for adopting codes, regardless of the type adopted.

Evidence from this study suggests that in fact codes are not primarily a tool of sustainability-related goals. To foster those, companies tend to resort more to other tools such as reports, policies, dedicated websites etc. Going back to the definition of sustainability provided at the start, this study suggests that codes on aggregate, do not in fact significantly further social and environmental imperatives for business success nor do they deal in any meaningful way with the social and environmental externalities of business activities. However, some of the codes in our sample are excellent examples of both furthering sustainability imperatives and including some externalities of business functions, but this is not true in the aggregate. Thus, codes are more often tools for governing organizational imperatives rather than governing the corporation towards increased sustainability.

Conclusion: Can Codes Encourage Corporations to Act Sustainably?

Arguably, codes are not a panacea for solving problems in the business–society interface and corporations, governments and the public need to better understand the nature, potential, restrictions and appropriate contexts of codes. They are certainly not, and cannot be, a catch-all solution to regulating corporations and the business–society interface. Codes provide one way of helping corporations understand the complexities of sustainability, and act as a guide for awareness and implementation of these issues. Inside a corporation, codes need to be a part of a much larger system of cultural commitments, values, accountability, actions and continual improvement etc. They need to be embedded within the corporation's attitudes and actions, while enhancing its strategic direction.

Codes though may have a particular potential in the areas of risk identification and management. Codes written by external parties can help the corporation to identify additional areas of potential risk on non-economic issues. They may help to identify potential threats to brand image or reputation, physical environmental liabilities, or processes, facilities, products or services with potential for environmental and social liabilities. Due to the flexibility of codes, as new risks are identified based on changes within the global market place, they can easily be modified and enhanced to respond with commitments to reducing negative and enhancing positive impacts, thus becoming part of a risk management strategy. In this way, codes can also be a powerful tool for risk management and an impetus for corporate scanning of potential future issues.

Codes themselves cannot change a corporation's behaviour. The success or failure of a code is dependent on the corporation's desire, ability and available resources to implement code commitments. Therefore, a good code, with clear language, strong commitments and a base philosophy similar to the one of the adopting corporation is much more likely to produce effective initiatives, but cannot determine how successfully a corporation will engage in CSR. In the literature on CoCs, there are few unequivocal recommendations with regard to implementation. Exceptions include Newton (1992), who stressed the importance of maximising the *participation* of organization members in the development stage in order to encourage commitment and 'buy-in' to the principles and rules of the code. Webley (2001) further contends that in order for codes to have credibility, companies must be willing to *discipline* employees found in breach of them. Similarly, Treviño *et al.*'s (1999) survey revealed that *follow-through* (such as detection of violations, follow-up on notification of violations, and consistency between the policy and action) tended to be much more influential on employee behaviour than the mere presence of a code, regardless of how familiar employees might be with it. These are sensible suggestions and findings. However, clear research findings relating to the effect of codes and their implementation on employee decision-making and behaviour are still relatively limited (Cassell *et al.* 1997).

These considerations about the key role of code implementation are linked to a more fundamental debate about the relation between bureaucratic control – of which CoCs are an important mechanism – and the ethical behaviour of individuals (Crane and Matten 2004: 132–137). This issue is critical in determining the potential of CoCs to foster sustainable corporate behaviour. Bureaucracy has been argued to have a number of effects on ethical decision-making (Weber 1947; Jackall 1988; Bauman 1989, 1993; ten Bos 1997; Kornberger *et al.* 2004). In particular, sceptics argue that individual morality tends to be subjugated to the functionally-specific rules and roles of the bureaucratic organization. Thus, effective bureaucracy essentially 'frees' the individual from moral reflection and decision-making since s/he needs only to follow the prescribed rules and procedures laid down to achieve organizational goals. This can cause employees to act as 'moral robots', simply following the rules rather than thinking about why they are there, or questioning their purpose. This particular criticism has been reiterated in some recent studies on CoCs (Kornberger *et al.* 2004; Schwartz 2000). Clearly, CoCs will only function if the broader culture of the organization is oriented towards sustainability and a code thus is just one supporting tool to foster this goal (Sims and Brinkmann 2003).

Most importantly, codes, if developed appropriately, can provide a set of criteria for use by corporations and their auditors to measure performance on social, environmental and economic related initiatives and actions. Codes can thus become a powerful tool useful to all key stakeholders in strengthening the business–society relationship and rebalancing power between groups within society. This process will take time, as corporations and key stakeholders determine what the critical terminology means and how codes are to be operationalized, implemented, administered and measured.

Note

i   Mandatory codes refer to those codes corporations must comply with to become members of certain bodies or groups. For instance, to be listed on the London Stock Exchange, companies are expected to comply with the Combined Code which deals specifically with corporate governance issues. Other examples of codes deemed mandatory in this study include the German Code of Corporate Governance and Responsible Care.

References

Aaronson, S. and Reeves, J. (2002) *The European Response to Public Demands for Global Corporate Responsibility*, National Policy Association. Available HTTP: <http://www.bitc.org.uk/docs/NPA_Global_CSR_survey.pdf> (accessed 3 November 2003).

Aguilera, R. and Cuervo-Cazurra, A. (2004) 'Codes of Good Governance Worldwide: What Is the Trigger?', *Organization Studies* 25(3): 415–443.

Alexander, J. (1997) 'On the Right Side', *World Business* 3(1) Jan/Feb: 38–41.

Australian Government (1997) 'Grey-Letter Law: Report of the Commonwealth Interdepartmental Committee on Quasi-regulation', Commonwealth Interdepartmental Committee on Quasi-regulation. Available HTTP: <http://www.pc.gov.au/orr/greyletterlaw/chapter3.pdf> (accessed 23 April 2002).

Ayres, I. and Braithwaite, J. (1992) *Responsive Regulation: Transcending the Deregulation Debate*, New York: Oxford University Press.

Bauman, Z. (1989) *Modernity and the Holocaust*, Cambridge: Polity Press.

Bauman, Z. (1993) *Postmodern Ethics*, London: Blackwell.

Beck, U. (1994) 'The Reinvention of Politics: Towards a Theory of Reflexive Modernization', in U. Beck, A. Giddens and S. Lash (eds) *Reflexive Modernization*, Stanford: Stanford University Press: 1–55.

Beck, U. (1996) 'Risk Society and the Provident State', in S. Lash, B. Szerszynski and B. Wynne (eds) *Risk, Environment and Modernity*, London: Sage: 27–43.

Beck, U. (1997a) *The Reinvention of Politics*, Cambridge: Polity Press.

Beck, U. (1997b) 'Subpolitics, Ecology and the Disintegration of Institutional Power', *Organization and Environment* 10(1): 52–65.

Blowfield, M. (2000) 'Ethical Sourcing: A Contribution to Sustainability or a Diversion?', Natural Resources Institute. Available HTTP: <http://www.eti.org.uk/pub/resources/othpub/pdfs/nret-susdev.pdf> (accessed 2 June 2002).

Bondy, K. (2003) *A New Method for Evaluating the Quality of Corporate Social Responsibility Codes of Conduct*, MEDes Degree, University of Calgary: Calgary.

Bondy, K., Matten, D. and Moon, J. (2004) 'The Adoption of Voluntary Codes of Conduct in MNCs: A Three-Country Comparative Study', *Business and Society Review* 109(4): 449–477.

Carroll, P. and McGregor-Lowndes, M. (2001) 'A Standard for Regulatory Compliance? Industry Self-regulation, the Courts and AS3806–1998', *Australian Journal of Public Administration* 60(4): 80–91.

Cassell, C., Johnson, P. and Smith, K. (1997) 'Opening the Black Box: Corporate Codes of Ethics in Their Organizational Context', *Journal of Business Ethics* 16: 1077–1093.

Clean Clothes Campaign (1998) 'Codes of Conduct for Transnational Corporations: An Overview', Clean Clothes Campaign. Available HTTP: <http://www.cleanclothes.org/codes/overview.htm> (accessed 12 August 2002).

Crane, A. and Matten, D. (2004) *Business Ethics – A European Perspective. Managing Corporate Citizenship and Sustainability in the Age of Globalization*, Oxford: Oxford University Press.

Deakin, N. and Walsh, K. (1996) 'The Enabling State: The Role of Markets and Contracts', *Public Administration* 74 (Spring): 33–48.

Dickerson, C. and Hagen, K. (1998) *Corporate Codes of Conduct*, American Society of International Law, Proceedings of the Annual Meeting, Washington: 265–277.

Diller, J. (1999) 'A Social Conscience in the Global Marketplace? Labour Dimensions of Codes of Conduct, Social Labelling and Investor Initiatives', *International Labour Review* 138(2): 99–129.

Emmelhainz, M. and Adams, R. (1999) 'The Apparel Industry Response to "Sweatshop" Concerns: A Review and Analysis of Codes of Conduct', *The Journal of Supply Chain Management* Summer: 51–57.

Forcese, C. (1997) *Commerce with Conscience: Human Rights and Corporate Codes of Conduct*, Canada: International Centre for Human Rights and Democratic Development.

Frankel, M. (1989) 'Professional Codes: Why, How and with What Impact?', *Journal of Business Ethics* 8: 109–115.

Gibson, R. (ed.) (1999) *Voluntary Initiatives and the New Politics of Corporate Greening*, Peterborough, Ontario: Broadview Press.

Gibson, R. (2000) *Encouraging Voluntary Initiatives for Corporate Greening: Some Considerations for More Systematic Design of Supporting Frameworks at the National and Global Levels*, Voluntary Initiatives Workshop United Nations Environment Programme. Available HTTP: <http://www.uneptie.org/outreach/vi/reports/encouraging_voluntary_initiatives.pdf> (accessed 7 November 2003).

Giddens, A. (1990) *The Consequences of Modernity*, Stanford: Stanford University Press.

Gilbert, N. and Gilbert, B. (1989) *The Enabling State: Modern Welfare Capitalism in America*, Oxford: Oxford University Press.

Gordon, K. and Miyake, M. (2001) 'Business Approaches to Combating Bribery: A Study of Codes of Conduct', *Journal of Business Ethics* 34: 161–173.

International Council on Human Rights Policy (2002) *Beyond Voluntarism: Human Rights and the Developing International Legal Obligations of Companies*, International Council on Human Rights. Online. Available HTTP: <http://www.cleanclothes/ftp/beyond_voluntarism.pdf> (accessed 17 November 2003).

International Labour Organization (n.d.a) *Corporate Codes of Conduct*, ILO Bureau for Workers' Activities. Available HTTP: <http://www.itcilo.it/english/actrav/telearn/global/ilo/code/main.htm> (accessed 17 March 2004).

International Labour Organization (ILO) (n.d.b) *Codes of Conduct for Multinationals*, ILO Bureau for Workers' Activities. Available HTTP: <http://www.itcilo.it/english/actrav/telearn/global/ilo/code/main.htm> (accessed 17 March 2004).

International Labour Organization (ILO) (n.d.c) *Private Initiatives and Labour Standards: A Global Look*, ILO Online. Available HTTP: <http://www.unglobalcompact.org/un/gc/unweb.nsf/content/ilostudy.html> (accessed 18 October 2001), no longer available.

Jackall, R. (1988) *Moral Mazes*, Oxford: Oxford University Press.

Jeffcott, B. and Yanz, L. (2000) *Codes of Conduct, Government Regulation and Worker Organizing*, Maquila Solidarity Network. Available HTTP: <http://www.maquilasolidarity.org/resources/codes/bluebooklet.htm> (accessed 20 February 2002).

Jenkins, R. (2002) 'Corporate Codes of Conduct: Self-Regulation in a Global Economy', in *Voluntary Approaches to Corporate Responsibility: Readings and a Resources Guide*, United Nations Non-Governmental Liaison Service. Available HTTP: <http://www.unsystem.org/ngls/documents/publications.en/development.dossier> (accessed 6 November 2003).

Kaptein, M. (2004) 'Business Codes of Multinational Firms: What Do They Say?', *Journal of Business Ethics* 50: 13–31.

Kaptein, M. and Wempe, J. (2002) *The Balanced Company: A Theory of Corporate Integrity*, Oxford: Oxford University Press.

Kolk, A. (2005) 'Corporate Social Responsibility in the Coffee Sector: The Dynamics of MNC Responses and Code Development', *European Management Journal* 23(2): 228–236.

Kolk, A. and van Tulder, R. (2004) 'Ethics in International Business: Multinational Approaches to Child Labor', *Journal of World Business* 39: 49–60.

Kolk, A., van Tulder, R. and Welters, C. (1999) 'International Codes of Conduct and Corporate Social Responsibility: Can Transnational Corporations Regulate Themselves?', *Transnational Corporations* 8(1): 143–180.

Kornberger, M., Clegg, S. and Rhodes, C. (2004) 'Everyday I write the book' – On the relationship between ethics, practice and rules in organizations', *University of Technology Sydney Working Paper*.

Lad, L. (1991) 'Industry Self-regulation as Interfirm and Multisector Collaboration: The Case of the Direct Selling Industry', *Research in Corporate Social Performance and Policy* 12: 155–178.

Langlois, C. and Schlegelmilch, B. (1990) 'Do Corporate Codes of Ethics Reflect National Character? Evidence from Europe and the United States', *Journal of International Business Studies* 21(4): 519–539.

Leipziger, D. (2003) *The Corporate Social Responsibility Code Book*, Sheffield: Greenleaf Publishing.

Lenox, M. and Nash, J. (2003) 'Industry Self-regulation and Adverse Selection: A Comparison Across Four Trade Association Programs', *Business Strategy and the Environment* 12: 343–356.

Martin, J. (2003) *Industry Self-regulation and Small Business: Voluntary Codes – Industry Self-regulation vs. Co-regulation vs. Government Regulation*, Australian Competition and Consumer Commission, Speech presented to National Alternative Dispute Resolution Advisory Council, 4 September. Available HTTP: <http://www.accc.gov.au/speeches/2003/Martin_Voluntary_4903.pdf> (accessed 7 November 2003).

Mendes, E. and Clark, J. (1996) 'The Five Generations of Corporate Codes of Conduct and Their Impact on Corporate Social Responsibility', Human Rights Research and Education Centre, University of Ottawa. Available HTTP: <http://www.cdp-hrc.uottawa.ca/publicat/five.html> (accessed 17 March 2004).

Moon, J. (2002) 'The Social Responsibility of Business and New Governance', *Government and Opposition* 37(3): 385–408.

Newton, L. (1995) 'The Many Faces of the Corporate Code', reprinted in W. Michael Hoffman and Robert E. Frederick (eds) *Business Ethics: Readings and Cases in Corporate Morality* (3rd edn), McGraw-Hill.

Organization for Economic Cooperation and Development (OECD) (1999)

Corporate Codes of Conduct: An Inventory, OECD. Available HTTP: <http://wwwl.oecd.org/ech/docs/codes.htm> (accessed 12 February 2002).

Organization for Economic Cooperation and Development (OECD) (2001) *Private Initiatives for Corporate Responsibility: An Analysis*, OECD Directorate for Financial, Fiscal and Enterprise Affairs. Available HTTP: <http://www.oecd.org/pdf/M000013000/M00013735.pdf> (accessed 22 January 2002).

Orts, E.W. (1995a) 'Reflexive Environmental Law', *Northwestern University Law Review* 89(4): 1227–1340.

Orts, E.W. (1995b) 'A Reflexive Model of Environmental Regulation', *Business Ethics Quarterly* 5(4): 779–794.

Pearson, R. and Seyfang, G. (2001) 'New Hope or False Dawn? Voluntary Codes of Conduct, Labour Regulation and Social Policy in a Globalizing World', *Global Social Policy* l(1): 49–78.

Rezaee, Z., Elmore, R. and Szendi, J. (2001) 'Ethical Behaviour in Higher Education Institutions: The Role of the Code of Conduct', *Journal of Business Ethics* 30(2): 171–183.

Ruhnka, J. and Boerstler, H. (1998) 'Governmental Incentives for Corporate Self-regulation', *Journal of Business Ethics* 17(3): 309–326.

Scholte, J. (2003) *Globalization: A Critical Introduction* (2nd edn), Basingstoke: Palgrave.

Schwartz, M. (2000) 'Why Ethical Codes Constitute an Unconscionable Regression', *Journal of Business Ethics* 23: 173–184.

Sethi, P. (2000) 'Gaps in Research in the Formulation, Implementation and Effectiveness Measurement of International Codes of Conduct', in O. Williams (ed.) *Global Codes of Conduct: An Idea Whose Time Has Come*, Indiana: University of Notre Dame Press, pp. 117–128.

Sethi, P. (2002) 'Standards for Corporate Conduct in the International Arena: Challenges and Opportunities for Multinational Corporations', *Business and Society Review* 107(1): 20–40.

Sethi, S. (2003) *Setting Global Standards: Guidelines for Creating Codes of Conduct in Multinational Corporations*, Hoboken, NJ: J. Wiley.

Sims, R. and Brinkmann, J. (2003) 'Enron Ethics (Or: Culture Matters More Than Codes)', *Journal of Business Ethics* 45: 243–256.

Snyder, F. (1999) 'Governing Economic Globalisation: Global Legal Pluralism and European Law', *European Law Journal* 5(4): 334–374.

Sodeman, W. (1995) 'Advantages and Disadvantages of Using the Brown and Perry Database', *Business and Society* 43(2): 216.

ten Bos, R. (1997) 'Business Ethics and Bauman Ethics', *Organization Studies* 18(6): 997–1014.

ten Brink, P. (ed.) (2002) *Voluntary Environmental Agreements*, Sheffield: Greenleaf Publishing.

Thompson, Dixon (ed.) (2002) *Tools for Environmental Management*, British Columbia, Canada: New Society Publishers.

Treviño, L., Weaver, G., Gibson, D. and Toffler, B.(1999) 'Managing Ethics and Legal Compliance: What Works and What Hurts', *California Management Review* 41(2): 131–151.

Turner, B. (2000) 'Review Essay: Citizenship and Political Globalization', *Citizenship Studies* 4(1): 81–86.

United States Council for International Business (2000) *Corporate Codes of Conduct: Overview and Summary of Initiatives*, United States Council for International Business. Available HTTP: <http://www.uscib.org/index.asp?document ID=1434> (accessed 17 March 2004).

Weber, M. (1947) *The Theory of Social and Economic Organization*, trans. A. Henderson and T. Parsons, Oxford: Oxford University Press.

Webley, S. (2001) 'Values-based Codes', in C. Moon and C. Bonny (eds) *Business Ethics: Facing up to the Issues*, London: The Economist Books, pp. 159–160.

White, A. (1999) 'Sustainability and the Accountable Corporation: Society's Rising Expectations of Business', *Environment* 41(8): 30–43.

White, S. (2003) *The Civic Minimum*, Oxford: Oxford University Press.

Wood, G., Svensson, G., Singh, J., Carasco, E. and Callaghan, M. (2004) 'Implementing the Ethos of Corporate Codes of Ethics: Australia, Canada, and Sweden', *Business Ethics: A European Review* 13(4): 389–403.

World Business Council for Sustainable Development (WBCSD) (2000) *Corporate Social Responsibility: Making Good Business Sense*, World Business Council for Sustainable Development. Available HTTP: <http://www.wbcsd.ch/printpdf/CSR2000-Making%20Good%20Business%20Sense.pdf> (accessed 18 February 2001).

World Resources Institute (2003) *World Resources 2002–2004: Decisions for the Earth: Balance, Voice, and Power*, United Nations Development Programme, World Bank, World Resources Institute. Available HTTP: <http://pubs.wri.org/pubs_content_print.cfm?ContentID=1835>(accessed 14 October 2003).

Wotruba, T. (1997) 'Industry Self-regulation: A Review and Extension to a Global Setting', *Journal of Public Policy and Marketing* 16(1): 38–54.

Appendix A

Advantages and limitations of voluntary initiatives and codes of conduct

Structural

Advantages

- Code is applicable across boundaries and government jurisdictions
- Better-suited to rapidly changing or complex contexts than regulations
- Allow for flexibility and creativity in designing solutions, helps to create best practice
- Emphasis on prevention

Limitations

- Limited implementation or process information
- Limited scope of content
- Content not appropriate in certain industries or contexts

- Lack of monitoring, auditing or verification commitments
- Lack of information disclosure, reporting or feedback mechanisms
- Vague, ill-defined responsibilities towards suppliers, business partners, contractors and subcontractors
- Content focused on issues highly damaging to reputation
- Drafted with little or no help from variety of stakeholders
- Commitments weak or vague
- Cannot set or enforce limits specific to individual facilities
- Cannot deal with negligent or poor performers (free-riders)

Individual Corporations

Advantages

- Influence corporate behaviour
- Acceptance by firms of responsibility for activities
- Acceptance by firms of responsibility for supplier/ business partner, contractor and subcontractor activities
- Protect or enhance reputation
- Not required to sign other agreements
- Establishes management commitment
- Competitive advantage/race to the top
- Long-term cultural changes in business management
- Implemented wisely, can achieve change without forcing early retirement of capital stock and resultant loss in economy and jobs
- Encourage awareness of new or more efficient technologies

Limitations

- May have negative, unintended effects
- Costs of development, implementation, auditing and/or certification
- Cannot be applied where no business self-interest
- Finite resources

Societal

Advantages

- Corporations accountable externally for code provisions
- Emphasizes business not separate from remainder of society
- Creates stakeholder confidence in corporation
- Improved dialogue and trust between industry and other two sectors
- Promotes partnerships and shared ownership
- Can provide useful product information to consumers, reducing information asymmetries
- Helps reduce compliance and enforcement costs

Limitations

- Limited adoption to date
- Adopted only by industry leaders
- Adopted due to external pressures, not for ethical or business reasons
- Concentrated in consumer goods sector
- Concentrated in firms that export or have overseas operations
- Codes seen as panacea
- Too many codes in existence
- Confusion over which codes are credible
- Suppliers faced with variety of different codes from different corporations
- Codes may undermine the position of trade unions
- Fear codes may replace regulations and government control over corporations
- Risk of creating trade barriers

Chapter 11

Globalization and CSR

I N THIS CHAPTER WE WILL:

- Understand the phenomenon of globalization in a CSR context.
- Discuss the key implications of globalization for corporations.
- Analyse the potential of corporations to address poverty and development in the global South.
- Understand the specific role multinational companies can assume with regard to global social and environmental standards.
- Reflect on the potential and limits of CSR in a global context.

Introduction

We are coming to the last chapter of the book, and you will have noticed that many examples, issues and challenges that we have discussed so far have dealt with global contexts – whether they are multinational companies, markets or supply chains in the developing world, global warming, or the global spread of HIV/AIDS. In short, as the subtitle of this book suggests, most of the CSR issues discussed so far have some sort of global dimension to them. This is by no means a coincidence. Arguably, one of the reasons why CSR has gained so much interest in the first place lies in the phenomenon of globalization.

Globalization is a result of some severe changes in the global economy over the past two decades. The most important ones are (Scherer and Palazzo, 2008):

- *Political factors.* Especially since the fall of the communist bloc in 1989, the exchange of people, goods and services across borders has become considerably easier. Furthermore, since then most countries in the world have put substantial effort into lowering trade barriers and making it easier for companies to invest in foreign countries. Parallel to that we have witnessed a number of efforts in creating international trade agreements which make it easier to exchange goods and services across borders.

- *Technological factors*. Owing to technological advancement in transportation and communication technologies, the costs of sea and air transport and tele-communications have been lowered dramatically over the past years. This has led to an unprecedented increase in the exchanges of goods, services and people across the globe. A particular development is the internet, which enables people from all over the world to communicate and interact for social, economic or political reasons.
- *Social and cultural factors*. Across the globe, people increasingly consume the same global brands, listen to the same music and watch the same movies. Simultaneously, with the spread of English as a new global 'lingua franca', communication barriers have decreased considerably. Similarly, we also witness a convergence of educational models across the globe, in particular in professions relevant for corporations, such as business, economics and engineering.

As a result of these factors we see an unprecedented growth in economic and social relations across borders and a sharp growth in the interdependence of social and political actors all over the world. This new world order of economics and politics is the main constituent feature of globalization – though many people also use the term in a much looser way.

Globalization and Changes in Political Governance

In the context of CSR, one of the key implications of globalization is its effect on nation-state governments and their capacity to govern, i.e. regulate and control economic activities. This applies, first of all, to those global business activities that are beyond the control of the nation state, such as global financial markets or the internet: globalization creates new economic spaces which are no longer linked to any territories that the nation state can control. These spaces are frequently governed, if at all, by business actors – and it is at this stage that corporations have to find solutions to govern these spaces responsibly.

Second, the decline in nation-state governance also applies to activities within the borders of a country: when it is easy for a company to relocate its manufacturing to another country or to sell its goods and services internationally, this brings companies into a relatively more powerful position with the country's government. It is frequently suggested that many governments these days, in the industrialized let alone in the developing world, are very reluctant to issue or properly enforce legislation which is unfavourable to (large) corporations out of fear that companies might relocate elsewhere, thereby leading to job losses, reduced tax incomes and so on. This opens up the space for some discretion for companies to decide whether or how to meet the expectations of stakeholders rather than being subject to high levels of regulation.

Finally, globalization creates a new political sphere where governments are only one player among many in governing global society: the tackling of global warming, the global response to terrorism, or battling against global diseases such as 'bird flu' or HIV/AIDS, just to name a few issues, cannot be tackled by governments alone, since they can only really exert authority over a relatively small territory. Governing issues of *transnational* concern therefore also involves other global actors, most notably multinational corporations and NGOs (Ruggie, 2004). Many even argue that corporations, in this new sphere of global governance, are in some respects the most powerful actors: some are economically more powerful than nation states; some command a global network of subsidiaries through which they significantly impact on other countries; some have financial and technical resources far in excess of other actors for use in tackling such issues.

CSR in a Global Context

As we have seen so far, the crucial point about CSR in a global context is that many stakeholder expectations are no longer expressed and enforced on the corporation by the legal framework issued by (national) government. However, even if, for instance, the government of El Salvador does not prevent a French clothing manufacturer from employing 12-year-old children in its El Salvadoran factories, this does not mean that the company's own stakeholders (e.g. customers, local communities, or retailers) will accept this as a legitimate practice and idly stand by. On the other hand, 'global CSR' in many ways may be seen as an attempt to replace absent or failing governmental action, even if it is simply because these stakeholders pressure the company into acting 'responsibly' (Matten and Crane, 2005). As a consequence, according to Ruggie (2004), we can identify three particular challenges for CSR in this new arena of global governance:

- *Building new social capacities.* When operating in countries with poor or corrupt governance, corporations are expected to take responsibility for working conditions, basic education or healthcare, respect for human rights and many other issues. This confronts companies not only with a new role but also with some completely new areas beyond their traditional expertise. The same applies to corporate involvement in global issues, such as the fight against HIV/AIDS or the protection of endangered species. The development of partnerships with NGOs and governments – often a popular way to address these issues – is a relatively novel area for CSR.
- *Involvement in rule-making.* Given the nature of global governance, nearly all larger trade agreements, standardization efforts and economic agreements involve corporations at some stage in setting the rules of engagement for business. In addition, as we have seen in Chapter 10, corporations are involved in rule-making by way of joining and/or adopting a plethora of codes of conduct. These developments thrust corporations into the role of rule-makers as well as rule-takers. The underlying rationale for creating such 'private regulation' is

manifold: while many may seek to create a level playing field for all players in one industry or market, others help to standardize what could be considered 'best practice' in CSR.

● *Broader accountability.* In Chapter 9 we discussed the role of accountability in CSR. At the global level, this call for accountability becomes even more pronounced and delicate: as we have seen, CSR at the global level often involves corporations in issues that traditionally nation states were held accountable for: the enforcement of human rights, basic healthcare or education, or tackling global poverty are just some examples. What we increasingly observe is that the more corporations attempt to live up to these expectations through CSR, the higher the level and quality of accountability that stakeholders expect from the company.

Introducing the Readings

Both of the readings pick up a specific CSR issue and develop a comprehensive rationale for understanding the wider implications for corporations in a global context.

The 'bottom of the pyramid' concept (BOP)

In 2006, on the first anniversary of the G8 Summit in Gleneagles and the global series of Live-8 concerts, the director of the Shell Foundation, Kurt Hoffman, was invited to assess the outcomes of the summit and of the broader 'Make Poverty History' campaign:

> [T]he difficulty is that these campaigners and the G8 leaders have a common problem: all the aid and debt relief in the world won't drag Africa out of poverty. The only proven route to this goal is delivering sustainable economic growth. And that means the private sector – behaving responsibly and soundly regulated – has to play a lead role: from multinationals to Africa's millions of budding potential entrepreneurs. . . . The good news is that the past year has seen a growing acknowledgement among the aid community that the private sector is a huge part of the solution. . . . The challenge for it now is to fully grasp the implications of this ideological nettle and place the private sector at the very heart of the war on poverty.[1]

This quote reflects a fairly broad shift in how CSR is being considered in developing countries. After more than fifty years of spending millions of development aid with relatively little impact on changing living conditions, there is increasingly a debate on how private companies can do a better job in these countries. The paper by C. Prahalad and Allen Hammond is one in a series of publications by Prahalad and various co-authors in setting out what is becoming known in CSR as the 'BOP concept'. The core idea is quite simple, and the many examples in the paper suggest rather convincingly that (Western multinational) corporations can achieve two things at the same time: (1) raising standards of living in formerly poverty-stricken parts of the world by enabling billions of potential consumers in the global South to participate more fully in consumption and production; (2) while at the same time enabling corporations to reap the 'fortune' that serving these markets can unleash. Again, despite the clear political message here, this is a classic instrumental case for CSR that offers win–win solutions for poor communities and powerful companies.

Raising global standards through CSR

The article by Andreas Georg Scherer and Marc Smid provides a comprehensive overview of some of the key issues and debates that multinational corporations face in the context of CSR: the power of large multinationals, key international rule-making systems, the relevance of NGOs, the 'race to the bottom', the role of human rights for global CSR, and the necessity for corporations to assume responsibility.

As one solution to the problems, the paper introduces the 'US Model Business Principles'. This serves well as an illustration of the potential and limits of even the most powerful nation state in governing the overseas activities of its multinational corporations. It may be worth mentioning that the paper was written at a time when one of the more recent and widespread global principles for responsible business, the UN Global Compact, was implemented. In many ways the Global Compact attempts to address many of the issues Scherer and Smid raise in this far-sighted piece – how can corporations raise global standards through their voluntary CSR efforts in the absence of effective regulation?

Study Questions

1   What are the key drivers of globalization? What role do corporations have in propelling this process?
2   What are the specific challenges that globalization poses for CSR?
3   Critically reflect on the BOP concept. What are the specific strengths of this approach? Do you see any limits?
4   What do we understand by the 'race to the bottom'? Do you see any opportunities for an individual corporation to escape this rationale?
5   What potential do you see for corporations to address global environmental, social and economic problems? Critically discuss the potential of CSR in this context.

Note

1   *Observer*, Poverty Supplement, 2 July 2006, p. 1.

References

Matten, D. and Crane, A. (2005) 'Corporate Citizenship – Toward an Extended Theoretical Conceptualisation', *Academy of Management Review* 30(1): 166–179.

Ruggie, J. (2004) 'Reconstituting the Public Domain – Issues, Actors, and Practices', *European Journal of International Relations* 10(4): 499–531.

Scherer, A. and Palazzo, G. (2008) 'Globalization and CSR', in A. Crane, A. McWilliams, D. Matten, J. Moon and D. Siegel (eds) *The Oxford Handbook of CSR*, forthcoming, Oxford: Oxford University Press.

SERVING THE WORLD'S POOR, *PROFITABLY*

C. Prahalad and Allen Hammond

Consider this bleak vision of the world 15 years from now: The global economy recovers from its current stagnation but growth remains anemic. Deflation continues to threaten, the gap between rich and poor keeps widening, and incidents of economic chaos, governmental collapse, and civil war plague developing regions. Terrorism remains a constant threat, diverting significant public and private resources to security concerns. Opposition to the global market system intensifies. Multinational companies find it difficult to expand, and many become risk averse, slowing investment and pulling back from emerging markets.

Now consider this much brighter scenario: Driven by private investment and widespread entrepreneurial activity, the economies of developing regions grow vigorously, creating jobs and wealth and bringing hundreds of millions of new consumers into the global marketplace every year. China, India, Brazil, and, gradually, South Africa become new engines of global economic growth, promoting prosperity around the world. The resulting decrease in poverty produces a range of social benefits, helping to stabilize many developing regions and reduce civil and cross-border conflicts. The threat of terrorism and war recedes. Multinational companies expand rapidly in an era of intense innovation and competition.

Both of these scenarios are possible. Which one comes to pass will be determined primarily by one factor: the willingness of big, multinational companies to enter and invest in the world's poorest markets. By stimulating commerce and development at the bottom of the economic pyramid, MNCs could radically improve the lives of billions of people and help bring into being a more stable, less dangerous world. Achieving this goal does not require multinationals to spearhead global social development initiatives for charitable purposes. They need only act in their own self-interest, for there are enormous business benefits to be gained by entering developing markets. In fact, many innovative companies – entrepreneurial outfits and large, established enterprises alike – are already serving the world's poor in ways that generate strong revenues, lead to greater operating efficiencies, and uncover new sources of innovation. For these companies – and those that follow their lead – building businesses aimed at the bottom of the pyramid promises to provide important competitive advantages as the twenty-first century unfolds.

Big companies are not going to solve the economic ills of developing countries by themselves, of course. It will also take targeted financial aid from the developed world and improvements in the governance of the developing nations themselves. But it's clear to us that prosperity can come to the poorest regions only through the direct and sustained involvement of multinational companies. And it's equally clear that the multinationals can enhance their own prosperity in the process.

Untapped Potential

Everyone knows that the world's poor are distressingly plentiful. Fully 65% of the world's population earns less than $2,000 each per year – that's 4 billion people. But despite the vastness of this market, it remains largely untapped by multinational companies. The reluctance to invest is easy to understand. Companies assume that people with such low incomes have little to spend on goods and services and that what they do spend goes to basic needs like food and shelter. They also assume that various barriers to commerce – corruption, illiteracy, inadequate infrastructure, currency fluctuations, bureaucratic red tape – make it impossible to do business profitably in these regions.

But such assumptions reflect a narrow and largely outdated view of the developing world. The fact is, many multinationals already successfully do business in developing countries (although most currently focus on selling to the small upper-middle-class segments of these markets), and their experience shows that the barriers to commerce – although real – are much lower than is typically thought. Moreover, several positive trends in developing countries – from political reform, to a growing openness to investment, to the development of low-cost wireless communication networks – are reducing the barriers further while also providing businesses with greater access to even the poorest city slums and rural areas. Indeed, once the misperceptions are wiped away, the enormous economic potential that lies at the bottom of the pyramid becomes clear.

Take the assumption that the poor have no money. It sounds obvious on the surface, but it's wrong. While individual incomes may be low, the aggregate buying power of poor communities is actually quite large. The average per capita income of villagers in rural Bangladesh, for instance, is less than $200 per year, but as a group they are avid consumers of tele-communications services. Grameen Telecom's village phones, which are owned by a single entrepreneur but used by the entire community, generate an average revenue of roughly $90 a month – and as much as $1,000 a month in some large villages. Customers of these villages phones, who pay cash for each use, spend an average of 7 percent of their income on phone services – a far higher percentage than consumers in traditional markets do.

It's also incorrect to assume that the poor are too concerned with fulfilling their basic needs to "waste" money on nonessential goods. In fact, the poor often do buy "luxury" items. In the Mumbai shantytown of Dharavi, for example, 85 percent of households own a television set, 75 percent own a pressure cooker and a mixer, 56 percent own a gas stove, and 21 percent have telephones. That's because buying a house in Mumbai, for most people at the bottom of the pyramid, is not a realistic option. Neither is getting access to running water. They accept that reality, and rather than saving for a rainy day, they spend their income on things they can get now that improve the quality of their lives.

Another big misperception about developing markets is that the goods sold there are incredibly cheap and, hence, there's no room for a new com-petitor to come in and turn a profit. In reality, consumers at the bottom of the pyramid pay much higher prices for most things than middle-class consumers do, which means that there's a real opportunity for companies, particularly big corporations with economies of scale and efficient supply chains, to capture market share by offering higher quality goods at lower prices while maintaining attractive margins. In fact, throughout the devel-oping world, urban slum dwellers pay, for instance, between four and 100 times as much for drinking water as middle- and upper-class families. Food also costs 20 percent to 30 percent more in the poorest communities since there is no access to bulk discount stores. On the service side of the economy, local moneylenders charge interest of 10 percent to 15 percent *per day*, with annual rates running as high as 2,000 percent. Even the lucky small-scale entrepreneurs who get loans from nonprofit microfinance institutions pay between 40 percent and 70 percent interest per year – rates that are illegal in most developed countries. (For a closer look at how the prices of goods compare in rich and poor areas, see Figure 2, "The High-Cost Economy of the Poor.")

It can also be surprisingly cheap to market and deliver products and services to the world's poor. That's because many of them live in cities that are densely populated today and will be even more so in the years to come. Figures from the UN and the World Resources Institute indicate that by 2015, in Africa, 225 cities will each have populations of more than 1 million; in Latin America, another 225; and in Asia, 903. The population of at least 27 cities will reach or exceed 8 million. Collectively, the 1,300 largest cities will account for some 1.5 billion to 2 billion people, roughly half of whom will be bottom-of-the-pyramid (BOP) consumers now served primarily by informal economies. Companies that operate in these areas will have access to millions of potential new customers, who together have billions of dollars to spend. The poor in Rio de Janeiro, for instance, have a total purchasing power of $1.2 billion ($600 per person). Shantytowns in Johannesburg or Mumbai are no different.

The slums of these cities already have distinct ecosystems, with retail shops, small businesses, schools, clinics, and moneylenders. Although there are few reliable estimates of the value of commercial transactions in slums, business activity appears to be thriving. Dharavi – covering an area of just 435 acres – boasts scores of businesses ranging from leather, textiles, plastic recycling, and surgical sutures to gold jewelry, illicit liquor, detergents, and groceries. The scale of the businesses varies from one-person operations to bigger, well-recognized producers of brand-name products. Dharavi generates an estimated $450 million in manufacturing revenues, or about $1 million per acre of land. Established shantytowns in São Paulo, Rio, and Mexico City are equally productive. The seeds of a vibrant commercial sector have been sown.

While the rural poor are naturally harder to reach than the urban poor, they also represent a large untapped opportunity for companies. Indeed, 60 percent of India's GDP is generated in rural areas. The critical barrier to doing business in rural regions is distribution access, not a lack of buying power. But new information technology and communications infrastructures – especially wireless – promise to become an inexpensive way to establish marketing and distribution channels in these communities.

Conventional wisdom says that people in BOP markets cannot use such advanced technologies, but that's just another misconception. Poor rural women in Bangladesh have had no difficulty using GSM cell phones, despite never before using phones of any type. In Kenya, teenagers from slums are being successfully trained as Web page designers. Poor farmers in El Salvador use telecenters to negotiate the sale of their crops over the Internet. And women in Indian coastal villages have in less than a week learned to use PCs to interpret real-time satellite images showing concentrations of schools of fish in the Arabian Sea so they can direct their husbands to the best fishing areas. Clearly, poor communities are ready to adopt new technologies that improve their economic opportunities or their quality of life. The lesson for multinationals: Don't hesitate to deploy advanced technologies at the bottom of the pyramid while, or even before, deploying them in advanced countries.

A final misperception concerns the highly charged issue of exploitation of the poor by MNCs. The informal economies that now serve poor communities are full of inefficiencies and exploitive intermediaries. So if a microfinance institution charges 50 percent annual interest when the alternative is either 1,000 percent interest or no loan at all, is that exploiting or helping the poor? If a large financial company such as Citigroup were to use its scale to offer microloans at 20 percent, is that exploiting or helping the poor? The issue is not just cost but also quality – quality in the range and fairness of financial services, quality of food, quality of water. We argue that when MNCs provide basic goods and services that reduce costs to the poor and help improve their standard of living – while generating an acceptable return on investment – the results benefit everyone.

The Business Case

The business opportunities at the bottom of the pyramid have not gone unnoticed. Over the last five years, we have seen nongovernmental organizations (NGOs), entrepreneurial start-ups, and a handful of forward-thinking multinationals conduct vigorous commercial experiments in poor communities. Their experience is a proof of concept: Businesses can gain three important advantages by serving the poor – a new source of revenue growth, greater efficiency, and access to innovation. Let's look at examples of each.

Top-line growth. Growth is an important challenge for every company, but today it is especially critical for very large companies, many of which appear to have nearly saturated their existing markets. That's why BOP markets represent such an opportunity for MNCs: They are fundamentally new sources of growth. And because these markets are in the earliest stages of economic development, growth can be extremely rapid.

Latent demand for low-priced, high-quality goods is enormous. Consider the reaction when Hindustan Lever, the Indian subsidiary of Unilever, recently introduced what was for it a new product category – candy – aimed at the bottom of the pyramid. A high-quality confection made with real sugar and fruit, the candy sells for only about a penny a serving. At such a price, it may seem like a marginal business opportunity, but in just six months it became the fastest-growing category in the company's portfolio. Not only is it profitable, but the company estimates it has the potential to generate revenues of $200 million per year in India and comparable markets in five years. Hindustan Lever has had similar successes in India with low-priced detergent and iodized salt. Beyond generating new sales, the company is establishing its business and its brand in a vast new market.

There is equally strong demand for affordable services. TARAhaat, a start-up focused on rural India, has introduced a range of computer-enabled education services ranging from basic IT training to English proficiency to vocational skills. The products are expected to be the largest single revenue generator for the company and its franchisees over the next several years.[1] Credit and financial services are also in high demand among the poor. Citibank's ATM-based banking experiment in India, called Suvidha, for instance, which requires a minimum deposit of just $25, enlisted 150,000 customers in one year in the city of Bangalore alone.

Small-business services are also popular in BOP markets. Centers run in Uganda by the Women's Information Resource Electronic Service

Most companies target consumers at the upper tiers of the economic pyramid, completely over-looking the business potential at its base. But though they may each be earning the equivalent of less than $2,000 a year, the people at the bottom of the pyramid make up a colossal market – 4 billion strong – the vast majority of the world's population.

Purchasing power parity
(in U.S. dollars)

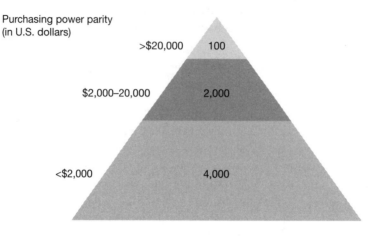

>$20,000   100

$2,000–20,000   2,000

<$2,000   4,000

Population (in millions)

Figure 1 The world pyramid

(WIRES) provide female entrepreneurs with information on markets and prices, as well as credit and trade support services, packaged in simple, ready-to-use formats in local languages. The centers are planning to offer other small-business services such as printing, faxing, and copying, along with access to accounting, spreadsheet, and other software. In Bolivia, a start-up has partnered with the Bolivian Association of Ecological Producers Organizations to offer business information and communications services to more than 25,000 small producers of ecoagricultural products.

It's true that some services simply cannot be offered at a low-enough cost to be profitable, at least not with traditional technologies or business models. Most mobile telecommunications providers, for example, cannot yet profitably operate their networks at affordable prices in the develop-ing world. One answer is to find alternative technology. A microfinance organization in Bolivia named PRODEM, for example, uses multilingual smart-card ATMs to substantially reduce its marginal cost per customer. Smart cards store a customer's personal details, account numbers, trans-action records, and a fingerprint, allowing cash dispensers to operate without permanent network connections – which is key in remote areas. What's more, the machines offer voice commands in Spanish and several local dialects and are equipped with touch screens so that PRODEM's customer base can be extended to illiterate and semiliterate people.

Another answer is to aggregate demand, making the community – not the individual – the network customer. Gyandoot, a start-up in the Dhar district of central India, where 60 percent of the population falls below the poverty level, illustrates the benefits of a shared access model. The company has a network of 39 Internet-enabled kiosks that provide local entrepreneurs with Internet and telecommunications access, as well as with governmental, educational, and other services. Each kiosk serves 25 to 30 surrounding villages; the entire network reaches more than 600 villages and over half a million people.

Networks like these can be useful channels for marketing and distributing many kinds of low-cost products and services. Aptech's Computer Education division, for example, has built its own network of 1,000 learning centers in India to market and distribute Vidya, a computer-training course specially designed for BOP consumers and available in seven Indian languages. Pioneer Hi-Bred, a DuPont company, uses Internet kiosks in Latin America to deliver agricultural information and to interact with customers. Farmers can report different crop diseases or weather conditions, receive advice over the wire, and order seeds, fertilizers, and pesticides. This network strategy increases both sales and customer loyalty.

Reduced costs. No less important than top-line growth are cost-saving opportunities. Outsourcing operations to low-cost labor markets has, of course, long been a popular way to contain costs, and it has led to the increasing prominence of China in manufacturing and India in software. Now, thanks to the rapid expansion of high-speed digital networks, companies are realizing even greater savings by locating such labor-intensive service functions as call centers, marketing services, and back-office transaction processing in developing areas. For example, the nearly 20 companies that use OrphanIT.com's affiliate-marketing services, provided via its tele-centers in India and the Philippines, pay one-tenth the going rate for similar services in the United States or Australia. Venture capitalist Vinod Khosla describes the remote-services opportunity this way: "I suspect that by 2010, we will be talking about [remote services] as the fastest-growing part of the world economy, with many trillions of dollars of new markets created." Besides keeping costs down, outsourcing jobs to BOP markets can enhance growth, since job creation ultimately increases local consumers' purchasing power.

But tapping into cheap labor pools is not the only way MNCs can enhance their efficiency by operating in developing regions. The competitive necessity of maintaining a low cost structure in these areas can push companies to discover creative ways to configure their products, finances, and supply chains to enhance productivity. And these discoveries can often be incorporated back into their existing operations in developed markets.

For instance, companies targeting the BOP market are finding that the shared access model, which disaggregates access from ownership, not only widens their customer base but increases asset productivity as well. Poor people, rather than buying their own computers, Internet connections, cell phones, refrigerators, and even cars, can use such equipment on a pay-per-use basis. Typically, the providers of such services get considerably more revenue per dollar of investment in the underlying assets. One shared

When we compare the costs of essentials in Dharavi, a shantytown of more than 1 million people in the heart of Mumbai, India, with those of Warden Road, an upper-class community in a nice Mumbai suburb, a disturbing picture emerges. Clearly, costs could be dramatically reduced if the poor could benefit from the scope, scale, and supply-chain efficiencies of large enterprises, as their middle-class counterparts do. This pattern is common around the world, even in developed countries. For instance, a similar, if less exaggerated, disparity exists between the inner-city poor and the suburban rich in the United States.

Cost	Dharavi	Warden Road	Poverty premium
credit (annual interest)	600%-1,000%	12%-18%	53X
municipal-grade water (per cubic meter)	$1.12	$0.03	37X
phone call (per minute)	$0.04-$0.05	$0.025	1.8X
diarrhea medication	$20	$2	10X
rice (per kilogram)	$0.28	$0.24	1.2X

Figure 2 The high-cost economy of the poor

Internet line, for example, can serve as many as 50 people, generating more revenue per day than if it were dedicated to a single customer at a flat fee. Shared access creates the opportunity to gain far greater returns from all sorts of infrastructure investments.

In terms of finances, to operate successfully in BOP markets, managers must also rethink their business metrics – specifically, the traditional focus on high gross margins. In developing markets, the profit margin on individual units will always be low. What really counts is capital efficiency – getting the highest possible returns on capital employed (ROCE). Hindustan Lever, for instance, operates a $2.6 billion business portfolio with zero working capital. The key is constant efforts to reduce capital investments by extensively outsourcing manufacturing, streamlining supply chains, actively managing receivables, and paying close attention to distributors' performance. Very low capital needs, focused distribution and technology investments, and very large volumes at low margins lead to very high ROCE businesses, creating great economic value for shareholders. It's a model that can be equally attractive in developed and developing markets.

Streamlining supply chains often involves replacing assets with information. Consider, for example, the experience of ITC, one of India's largest companies. Its agribusiness division has deployed a total of 970 kiosks serving 600,000 farmers who supply it with soy, coffee, shrimp, and wheat from 5,000 villages spread across India. This kiosk program, called e-Choupal, helps increase the farmers' productivity by disseminating the latest information on weather and best practices in farming, and by supporting other services like soil and water testing, thus facilitating the supply of quality inputs to both the farmers and ITC. The kiosks also serve as an e-procurement system, helping farmers earn higher prices by minimizing transaction costs involved in marketing farm produce. The head of ITC's agribusiness reports that the company's procurement costs have fallen since e-Choupal was implemented. And that's despite paying higher prices to its farmers: The program has enabled the company to eliminate multiple transportation, bagging, and handling steps – from farm to local market, from market to broker, from broker to processor – that did not add value in the chain.

Innovation. BOP markets are hotbeds of commercial and technological experimentation. The Swedish wireless company Ericsson, for instance, has developed a small cellular telephone system, called a MiniGSM, that local operators in BOP markets can use to offer cell phone service to a small area at a radically lower cost than conventional equipment entails. Packaged for easy shipment and deployment, it provides stand-alone or networked voice and data communications for up to 5,000 users within a 35-kilometer radius. Capital costs to the operator can be as low as $4 per user, assuming a shared-use model with individual phones operated by local entrepreneurs. The MIT Media Lab, in collaboration with the Indian government, is developing low-cost devices that allow people to use voice commands to communicate – without keyboards – with various Internet sites in multiple languages. These new access devices promise to be far less complex than traditional computers but would perform many of the same basic functions.[2]

As we have seen, connectivity is a big issue for BOP consumers. Companies that can find ways to dramatically lower connection costs, therefore, will have a very strong market position. And that is exactly what the Indian company n-Logue is trying to do. It connects hundreds of franchised village kiosks containing both a computer and a phone with centralized nodes that are, in turn, connected to the national phone network and the Internet. Each node, also a franchise, can serve between 30,000 and 50,000 customers, providing phone, e-mail, Internet services, and relevant local information at affordable prices to villagers in rural India. Capital costs for the n-Logue system are now about $400 per wireless "line" and are projected to decline to $100 – at least ten times lower than conventional telecom costs. On a per-customer basis, the cost may amount to as little as $1.[3] This appears to be a powerful model for ending rural isolation and linking untapped rural markets to the global economy.

New wireless technologies are likely to spur further business model innovations and lower costs even more. Ultrawideband, for example, is currently licensed in the United States only for limited, very low-power applications, in part because it spreads a signal across already-crowded portions of the broadcast spectrum. In many developing countries, however, the spectrum is less congested. In fact, the U.S.-based Dandin Group is already building an ultrawideband communications system for the Kingdom of Tonga, whose population of about 100,000 is spread over dozens of islands, making it a test bed for a next-generation technology that could transform the economics of Internet access.

E-commerce systems that run over the phone or the Internet are enormously important in BOP markets because they eliminate the need for layers of intermediaries. Consider how the U.S. start-up Voxiva has changed the way information is shared and business is transacted in Peru. The company partners with Telefónica, the dominant local carrier, to offer automated business applications over the phone. The inexpensive services include voice mail, data entry, and order placement; customers can check account balances, monitor delivery status, and access prerecorded information directories. According to the Boston Consulting Group, the Peruvian Ministry of Health uses Voxiva to disseminate information, take pharmaceutical orders, and link health care workers spread across 6,000 offices and clinics. Microfinance institutions use Voxiva to process loan applications and communicate with borrowers. Voxiva offers Web-based services, too, but far more of its potential customers in Latin America have access to a phone.

E-commerce companies are not the only ones turning the limitations of BOP markets to strategic advantage. A lack of dependable electric power stimulated the UK-based start-up Free-play Group to introduce hand-cranked radios in South Africa that subsequently became popular with hikers in the United States. Similar breakthroughs are being pioneered in the use of solar-powered devices such as battery chargers and water pumps. In China, where pesticide costs have often limited the use of modern agricultural techniques, there are now 13,000 small farmers – more than in the rest of the world combined – growing cotton that has been genetically engineered to be pest resistant.

Strategies for Serving BOP Markets

Certainly, succeeding in BOP markets requires multinationals to think creatively. The biggest change, though, has to come in the attitudes and practices of executives. Unless CEOs and other business leaders confront their own preconceptions, companies are unlikely to master the challenges of BOP markets. The traditional workforce is so rigidly conditioned to operate in higher-margin markets that, without formal training, it is unlikely to see the vast potential of the BOP market. The most pressing need, then, is education. Perhaps MNCs should create the equivalent of the Peace Corps: Having young managers spend a couple of formative years in BOP markets would open their eyes to the promise and the realities of doing business there.

To date, few multinationals have developed a cadre of people who are comfortable with these markets. Hindustan Lever is one of the exceptions. The company expects executive recruits to spend at least eight weeks in the villages of India to get a gut-level experience of Indian BOP markets. The new executives must become involved in some community project – building a road, cleaning up a water catchment area, teaching in a school, improving a health clinic. The goal is to engage with the local population. To buttress this effort, Hindustan Lever is initiating a massive program for managers at all levels – from the CEO down – to reconnect with their poorest customers. They'll talk with the poor in both rural and urban areas, visit the shops these customers frequent, and ask them about their experience with the company's products and those of its competitors.

In addition to expanding managers' understanding of BOP markets, companies will need to make structural changes. To capitalize on the innovation potential of these markets, for example, they might set up R&D units in developing countries that are specifically focused on local opportunities. When Hewlett-Packard launched its e-Inclusion division, which concentrates on rural markets, it established a branch of its famed HP Labs in India charged with developing products and services explicitly for this market. Hindustan Lever maintains a significant R&D effort in India, as well.

Companies might also create venture groups and internal investment funds aimed at seeding entrepreneurial efforts in BOP markets. Such investments reap direct benefits in terms of business experience and market development. They can also play an indirect but vital role in growing the overall BOP market in sectors that will ultimately benefit the multinational. At least one major U.S. corporation is planning to launch such a fund, and the G8's Digital Opportunity Task Force is proposing a similar one focused on digital ventures.

MNCs should also consider creating a business development task force aimed at these markets. Assembling a diverse group of people from across the corporation and empowering it to function as a skunk works team that ignores conventional dogma will likely lead to greater innovation. Companies that have tried this approach have been surprised by the amount of interest such a task force generates. Many employees want to work on projects that have the potential to make a real difference in improving the lives of the poor. When Hewlett-Packard announced its e-Inclusion division, for example, it was overwhelmed by far more volunteers than it could accommodate.

Making internal changes is important, but so is reaching out to external partners. Joining with businesses that are already established in these markets can be an effective entry strategy, since these companies will naturally understand the market dynamics better. In addition to limiting the risks for each player, partnerships also maximize the existing infrastructure – both physical and social. MNCs seeking partners should look beyond businesses to NGOs and community groups. They are key sources of knowledge about customers' behavior, and they often experiment the most with new services and new delivery models. In fact, of the social enterprises experimenting with creative uses of digital technology that the Digital Dividend Project Clearinghouse tracked, nearly 80 percent are NGOs. In Namibia, for instance, an organization called SchoolNet is providing low-cost, alternative technology solutions – such as solar power and wireless approaches – to schools and community-based groups throughout the country. SchoolNet is currently linking as many as 35 new schools every month.

Entrepreneurs also will be critical partners. According to an analysis by McKinsey & Company, the rapid growth of cable TV in India – there are 50 million connections a decade after introduction – is largely due to small entrepreneurs. These individuals have been building the last mile of the network, typically by putting a satellite dish on their own houses and laying cable to connect their neighbors. A note of caution, however. Entrepreneurs in BOP markets lack access to the advice, technical help, seed funding, and business support services available in the industrial world. So MNCs may need to take on mentoring roles or partner with local business development organizations that can help entrepreneurs create investment and partnering opportunities.

It's worth noting that, contrary to popular opinion, women play a significant role in the economic development of these regions. MNCs, therefore, should pay particular attention to women entrepreneurs. Women are also likely to play the most critical role in product acceptance not only because of their childcare and household management activities but also because of the social capital that they have built up in their communities. Listening to and educating such customers is essential for success.

Regardless of the opportunities, many companies will consider the bottom of the pyramid to be too risky. We've shown how partnerships can

---

Sharing Intelligence

What creative new approaches to serving the bottom-of-the-pyramid markets have digital technologies made possible? Which sectors or countries show the most economic activity or the fastest growth? What new business models show promise? What kinds of partnerships – for funding, distribution, public relations – have been most successful?

The Digital Dividend Project Clearinghouse (digitaldividend.org) helps answer those types of questions. The Web site tracks the activities of organizations that use digital tools to provide connectivity and deliver services to underserved populations in developing countries. Currently, it contains information on 700 active projects around the world. Maintained under the auspices of the nonprofit World Resources Institute, the site lets participants in different projects share experiences and swap knowledge with one another. Moreover, the site provides data for trend analyses and other specialized studies that facilitate market analyses, local partnerships, and rapid, low-cost learning.

limit risk; another option is to enter into consortia. Imagine sharing the costs of building a rural network with the communications company that would operate it, a consumer goods company seeking channels to expand its sales, and a bank that is financing the construction and wants to make loans to and collect deposits from rural customers.

Investing where powerful synergies exist will also mitigate risk. The Global Digital Opportunity Initiative, a partnership of the Markle Foundation and the UN Development Programme, will help a small number of countries implement a strategy to harness the power of information and communications technologies to increase development. The countries will be chosen in part based on their interest and their willingness to make supportive regulatory and market reforms. To concentrate resources and create reinforcing effects, the initiative will encourage international aid agencies and global companies to assist with implementation.

All of the strategies we've outlined here will be of little use, however, unless the external barriers we've touched on – poor infrastructure, inadequate connectivity, corrupt intermediaries, and the like – are removed. Here's where technology holds the most promise. Information and communications technologies can grant access to otherwise isolated communities, provide marketing and distribution channels, bypass intermediaries, drive down transaction costs, and help aggregate demand and buying power. Smart cards and other emerging technologies are inexpensive ways to give poor customers a secure identity, a transaction or credit history, and even a virtual address – prerequisites for interacting with the formal economy. That's why high-tech companies aren't the only ones that should be interested in closing the global digital divide; encouraging the spread of low-cost digital networks at the bottom of the pyramid is a priority for virtually all companies that want to enter and engage with these markets. Improved connectivity is an important catalyst for more effective markets, which are critical to boosting income levels and accelerating economic growth.

Moreover, global companies stand to gain from the effects of network expansion in these markets. According to Metcalfe's Law, the usefulness of a network equals the square of the number of users. By the same logic, the value and vigor of the economic activity that will be generated when hundreds of thousands of previously isolated rural communities can buy and sell from one another and from urban markets will increase dramatically – to the benefit of all participants.

Since BOP markets require significant rethinking of managerial practices, it is legitimate for managers to ask: Is it worth the effort?

We think the answer is yes. For one thing, big corporations should solve big problems – and what is a more pressing concern than alleviating the poverty that 4 billion people are currently mired in? It is hard to argue that the wealth of technology and talent within leading multinationals is better allocated to producing incremental variations of existing products than to addressing the real needs – and real opportunities – at the bottom of the pyramid. Moreover, through competition, multinationals are likely to bring to BOP markets a level of accountability for performance and resources that neither international development agencies nor national governments have demonstrated during the last 50 years. Participation by MNCs could set a new standard, as well as a new market-driven paradigm, for addressing poverty.

But, ethical concerns aside, we've shown that the potential for expanding the bottom of the market is just too great to ignore. Big companies need to focus on big market opportunities if they want to generate real growth. It is simply good business strategy to be involved in large, untapped markets that offer new customers, cost-saving opportunities, and access to radical innovation. The business opportunities at the bottom of the pyramid are real, and they are open to any MNC willing to engage and learn.

Notes

1   Andrew Lawlor, Caitlin Peterson, and Vivek Sandell, "Catalyzing Rural Development: TARA-haat.com" (World Resources Institute, July 2001).
2   Michael Best and Colin M. Maclay, "Community Internet Access in Rural Areas: Solving the Economic Sustainability Puzzle," *The Global Information Technology Report 2001–2002: Readiness for the Networked World*, ed. Geoffrey Kirkman (Oxford University Press, 2002), available on-line at http://www.cid.harvard.edu/cr/gitrr_030202.html.
3   Joy Howard, Erik Simanis, and Charis Simms, "Sustainable Deployment for Rural Connectivity: The n-Logue Model" (World Resources Institute, July 2001).

THE DOWNWARD SPIRAL AND THE US MODEL BUSINESS PRINCIPLES: WHY MNEs SHOULD TAKE RESPONSIBILITY FOR THE IMPROVEMENT OF WORLD-WIDE SOCIAL AND ENVIRONMENTAL CONDITIONS[1]

Andreas Georg Scherer and Marc Smid

Introduction

In the course of globalization, different locations compete for investments and jobs. The reduction of trade and capital transfer barriers, the new possibilities offered by information technologies, the reduction of transport costs, as well as the improved infrastructure and educational standards in many countries of the world enable a high mobility of capital and investments. These conditions permit multinational enterprises (MNEs) to create supply chains on a world-wide basis or reallocate resources within a short period of time. It is a consequence of the market economy that capital seeks out the cheapest offers of factors of production. In the wake of this development, the business activities of MNEs are gradually distancing themselves from the regulatory limits of individual nation states, without a sufficient legal system being established at a transnational level (Ohmae 1995, Orts 1995, Reich 1991, Thurow 1996).

Many regions in the industrialized countries have experienced factory closings in entire branches of their industries. Many businesses have either moved abroad or have declined. This can partly be explained by the lower production costs in non-industrialized countries. The textile and sports utility industries, the steel industry, ship-building, and the computer and semi-conductor industries are but a few of the examples which can be mentioned here (Greider 1997, Longworth 1998). However, it is not only the lower labor costs that attract capital into other countries. Many emergent and developing countries have conditions where regulations on safety and health at work, trade union activities, co-determination, and environmental protection are unknown, where wages are below the subsistence level, and where child labor and discrimination against women and ethnic minorities are the rule. These conditions are an additional attraction for investment, because they reduce costs in those industries where largely semi-skilled workers are used (Greider 1997, Martin/Schumann 1996).

The power of individual nation states to define the rules of the economic system and to influence the policy of MNEs is fading (Vernon 1998). At the same time, the efforts of intergovernmental organizations such as the United Nations, the International Labor Organization, or the World Trade Organization have not yielded much progress in enforcing social and environmental standards for business world-wide. Though paperwork has been done for decades, these organizations are still unable to enforce and control business conduct effectively because they depend on the executing bodies of individual nation states. In many cases, nation states have no interest in monitoring the behavior of multinational firms, because they want to hold or lure foreign investments. Because of these difficulties, the US government proposed the so-called Model Business Principles in the summer of 1995. These principles state that MNEs should use their economic power and political influence to create humane working conditions world-wide. The idea of these principles is that the multinational firm should behave as a moral actor, as long as there is no political world order available that defines and enforces social and environmental standards.

In this paper we will consider the process of globalization and the role that MNEs are playing in this process. We will emphasize the new power of the multinational firm first. Then we will describe the difficulties that individual nation states have in defining the rules of the economic system during the process of globalization. Next we will focus on the efforts of intergovernmental organizations to create a new economic world order. Finally, we will describe the US Model Business Principles and provide a philosophical and economical justification for these principles. We are aware that we cannot develop definite answers to the emerging problems we deal with. This paper has to be seen as a first step toward a normative theory of the multinational enterprise in a globalized economy, a theory that transcends the mainstream economic theory of the firm (Scherer/Löhr 1999, Scherer 2000).

The Power of the Multinational Enterprise

We see *globalization* as a process of movement toward the creation of a global economy, which enables entrepreneurs to raise money anywhere in the world, to use technology, supplies, labor, and management from different locations, and to produce and sell products or to create services anyplace. Today, the network structures of MNEs permit an operational flexibility that makes the realization of arbitrage advantages possible. These advantages are created by the exploitation of differences in the law and cost structures in different countries (Kogut 1985). Multinationals move from country to country in order to compete more successfully on labor and other costs. In some cases, they search for those national legislations which have the laxest labor standards (Boje 1998, Boyer/Drache 1996, Greider 1997, Mokhiber/ Weissman 1999). By transferring activities to countries with less restrictive labor legislation corporations buffer themselves from the restraint of individual nation states and act in a permissive legal environment. These practices may lead to a world-wide lowering of wages and working conditions.

However, the power of MNEs means more than these evasive actions. Their economic superiority can also put direct political pressure on smaller nations. "Because corporations are seen as powerful and influential actors . . . they often acquire the capacity to control the host country's economy and even [its] . . . future" (Petrella 1996, p. 64). Some MNEs have a turnover which is higher than the gross national product of many nation states. During the era of modernization business acquired more and more power to tighten or even cut the material lifelines of individual nations and societies. Because of the fact that the MNEs provide jobs, taxes, and investments, they are able to put pressure on many national economies and to get involved in politics. But this has happened without a democratic legitimization by the population (Beck 1997, Orts 1995), which makes the exercise of power questionable. Such an authoritarian exercise of power by MNEs undermines democratic principles, because it answers political questions only through economic criteria (Scherer/Löhr 1999, Scherer 2000).

Nation States Under Pressure: The Downward Spiral

Many developing and newly industrialized countries do not mind this influence. They want to use their comparative cost advantage to attract MNEs by maintaining low standards (see e.g. Greider 1997). They impede the passing of general social and environmental standards for international business in the multinational negotiations of GATT, WTO, UNCTAD, and ILO (see e.g. ILO 1993, UNCTAD 1994, WTO 1996). The corresponding initiatives of the western industrialized countries are criticized in particular by representatives of emergent and developing countries (and in part also by the industrialized nations, see below) as protectionist measures that are to prevent the critics from using their cost advantages and gaining an entry to world markets (The Economist 1996, Krauss 1997). Also, the suggestions of the industrialized countries are discredited as introducing a new phase of imperialism, where western values dominate over others, especially Asian cultural values (Lal 1998, Lee 1994, Mahatir 1995, Sanger 1994). In many developing and emergent countries, the validity of human rights is not automatically recognised (Marglin 1990).

Even in those areas where multinational committees have already reached agreement on social and environmental standards, the implementation of those standards is at risk, as many states try to attract foreign capital and to get multinational enterprises to make direct investments by watering down the standards (Deetz 1995, Thurow 1996). The authorities in these countries "frequently have erratic or poor human rights records. Simultaneously, they promote ambitious economic development plans that invite foreign investment and they court corporations by offering conditions that will be attractive to them. Governments in China, Indonesia, and Mexico, for example, are all too willing to ignore irresponsible corporate practices" concludes the human rights activist group Human Rights Watch (1997). Regarding environmental standards, the practices of many emergent and developing countries parallel their policies on labor and social standards. The low standards in many countries are marketed as competitive advantages, and supported indirectly by foreign investment. It is to be feared, therefore, that a larger and larger part of the world's economic production will be generated under worsening labor and environmental conditions, so that a downward spiral will be put into motion (Deetz 1995, Greider 1997, Longworth 1998, Martin/Schumann 1996).

In the process of globalization, both nation states and MNEs feel subject to increasing world-wide competition. It seems irrelevant how competitive advantages are realized, whether "by the mobilization of the resources of an authoritarian achievement-oriented society, by low wages, by technological superiority, by making use of stable industrial relations or by a hybrid mixture of these factors" (Altvater/Mahnkopf 1996, p. 54, translation by the authors). When a MNE starts negotiating for the transfer of its production into low wage areas, a political bargaining process begins, in which governments compete for the new factories. This includes political favors like tax exemptions, state suppression of workers, or the assignment of export privileges (Greider 1997). The consequence is a ruinous competition, a "race to the bottom," that hurts those countries that pursue reasonable development the most. But countries that tried to compete with relatively low standards in the past did not turn out to be "capital magnets" (Großmann/Koopmann 1994). This strategy apparently does not pay either in a mid-term or a long-term perspective.

The increasing world-wide mobility of capital and production factors tends to make national regulations more and more a "merchandise" in the global market (Strange 1996). Low social standards are seen and marketed as competitive advantages in many developing countries, because nations with high working standards are disadvantaged in wage costs. In the past, governments of industrialized countries have tried to control MNEs with traditional trade restrictions and monetary regulations. But today, when trade liberalization and deregulation are on the top of the political agenda world-wide, these means seem obsolete. As a result, multinationals have often "enjoyed the economic nirvana of a regulative vacuum" (Kolde 1982, p. 295).

Defining the Rules of the Game: The Insufficient Attempts of Intergovernmental Organizations to Establish World-wide Standards

Until recently, the nation state system was successful in providing the conditions necessary for peaceful coexistence within national territories. But in the context of globalization, the nation state is less and less in a position to create these conditions and to maintain growth, stability, and a minimum standard of living. Multilateral agreements and intergovernmental organizations are seen as possible cooperative solutions for the problems that arise in a competitive global market. The strategy of coordinating separate national economic policies originated in the Versailles Treaty in 1919. The member states obligated themselves to secure and maintain fair and humane working conditions at home and in every country they kept economic relations with (Peace Treaty of Versailles, part 1, article 23a). We now examine the following organizations more closely, assessing their potential to establish world-wide standards for all nation states and for multinational corporations: International Labor Organization (ILO), United Nations (UN), General Agreement on Tariffs and Trade (GATT), World Trade Organization (WTO), Organization for Economic Cooperation and Development (OECD), and International Non-Governmental Organizations (NGO).

International Labor Organization (ILO)

Based on the Versailles Treaty, the *International Labor Organization* (ILO) grew out of Article 19. The preamble of the constitution of the ILO reads: "the failure of any nation to adopt humane conditions of labour is an obstacle in the way of other nations which desire to improve the conditions in their own countries" (quoted in Sengenberger/Wilkinson 1995, p. 115). The ILO became one of the first international economic institutions, and the very first international social institution. The organization's main activity is drawing up conventions that demand minimum binding standards from the countries that ratify them. From the beginning, it was understood that the conventions have to take into account the particular needs of developing countries. The conventions for the abolishment of prison labor, for the freedom of coalition, for the right for collective negotiations, for the equal payment of men and women, and for the elimination of discrimination were ratified by more than 100 states each. In order to ensure enforcement of the ILO conventions, the possibility of economic and legal sanctions was originally considered, but those means were never brought into action. Instead, the ILO tries to ameliorate working standards by convincing governments that following their conventions is for their own benefit, because the legitimacy advantages are higher than the costs (cf. Charnovitz 1995, p. 173). However, Preston and Windsor (1997, p. 199) point out that "the ultimate success of an international agreement appears to require a judicious combination of sticks and carrots, rigorous enforcement by local and national authorities on the one hand and economic inducements on the other hand." But today the obligations agreed upon in the ILO conventions are only binding for the national states. No direct pressure can be put by the ILO on regional governments, single industries, or multinational enterprises.

United Nations (UN)

In 1945 the *United Nations* (UN) was born with the aim of ensuring lasting peace in the world. The organization follows several principles, which are: protecting world peace and international security, the development of friendly relations between states, cooperation in the solution of international economic, social, cultural, and humanitarian problems, and the establishment of human rights. Furthermore, balancing the interests of the Northern and the Southern hemispheres has become a major part of the UN's activities. For this reason, the United Nations Conference on Trade and Development (UNCTAD) was founded in 1964 as a recurrent meeting in which the developing countries were more heavily represented than was the case with the GATT (see below). In 1976 negotiations started concerning a UN "Code of Conduct on Transnational Corporations," but they were never concluded. Nevertheless, the draft of this UN code can be seen as the best of several international codes, guidelines, and declarations that guide business behavior in the world markets (cf. Windsor 1994, p. 165).

The UN principle of national sovereignty constitutes the main problem for asserting an effective transnational code that could deal with some of the problems brought about by globalization. The principle makes a consensus necessary, with an international consensus being a gradual and lengthy process. Therefore, it is unlikely that the draft of the UN code will become a comprehensive framework for conduct in international business in the near future (cf. Windsor 1994, pp. 171–173). Besides, the attitude of the UN towards multinational corporations has changed fundamentally. While it has always been critical of their activities, the UN nowadays spends a large part of its time advising countries on how to attract multinationals (cf. The Economist 1993, p. 5). In addition, the UN now asks MNEs for their support to maintain humane working conditions world wide (Annan 1999).

General Agreement on Tariffs and Trade (GATT)

The *General Agreement on Tariffs and Trade* (GATT) is part of the Bretton Woods Agreement between Great Britain and the USA, which aimed at reviving the world economy after World War II. The Bretton Woods Agreement laid the foundations for a cooperative international economic structure by creating three institutions. First, the International Monetary Fund (IMF) was established to secure exchange rate stability and give support to countries that have financial problems. The International Bank for Reconstruction and Development (IBRD) had the mandate to provide capital for the reconstruction of the destroyed economies in Europe. Today this institution is known as the World Bank, and focuses upon support of the developing countries. The third institution created was the International Trade Organization (ITO), which was to begin negotiations toward a new multilateral, liberal world trade regime (cf. Trebilcock/Howse 1996, p. 20). But because of the resistance of the US Congress, which feared that the organization would limit US national sovereignty too much, the ITO was never started. Instead, the originally provisional GATT, negotiated in 1947 between 23 important trading countries, became the basis for the current international trade regime. The GATT has achieved considerable reductions in trade restrictions in the last few decades (Hoeckman/Kostecki 1995, Trebilcock/Howse 1996). In contrast to the ITO, the GATT contains no statement concerning labor standards, except article XX (e), which prohibits the trade of goods manufactured with prison labor. The GATT is primarily seen as a trade agreement and, therefore, the prevailing belief is that social standards should be taken care of in the ILO, the institution designated for this (cf. Charnovitz 1995, p. 171).

World Trade Organization (WTO)

The *World Trade Organization* (WTO) was established on January 1, 1995, as a result of the 1994 Uruguay round of the GATT and replaces this organization. The WTO pursues stable world trade within a system based on rules. The member countries consider trade liberalization to be an essential condition for economic stability, growth and development. The WTO sees itself as an organization based on consensus, but the WTO treaty also contains the authority to impose trade sanctions on countries that do not follow the conventions. During the first ministerial conference of the WTO in Singapore in 1996, it was agreed that member countries should abide by the most important internationally acknowledged labor standards, that the ILO was the institution in charge of labor standards, and that these standards are supported by growth due to trade liberalization (WTO 1996). However, under no circumstances should labor standards be used for protectionism or to interfere with the comparative advantages of countries (Ruggiero 1998). The efforts of the USA and France to include social clauses in the WTO treaty failed because of the resistance of the European Union countries, mainly Great Britain and Germany, and the developing countries (cf. Cassen 1996, p. 18). At the 2000 ministerial conference in Seattle the WTO member states could not even agree upon a common declaration. So far, the WTO, which pursues the promotion of international trade within a rule system, has succeeded only in deregulating world trade. Besides the vague agreement about labor standards, no progress has been made regarding workplace regulations. The relationships with developing countries and policies on investment, competition, and labor standards will remain some of the main challenges. "The WTO will face a rather daunting agenda in the decades to come" (Hoekman/Kostecki 1997, p. 265).

Organization for Economic Cooperation and Development (OECD)

The *Organization for Economic Cooperation and Development* (OECD) was created by the industrialized countries in 1961. It pursues a policy of enabling the member states to obtain optimal economic development and employment, and a rising standard of living, while maintaining financial stability (OECD 1997, p. 2). The "OECD Guidelines for Multinational Enterprises," written in 1976, were an effort to translate these goals into a policy for regulating the activities of multinational corporations. The code was written by the industrialized nations and shows the strong common convictions of the contributing governments. It does not differ much from corporations' usual practices. Therefore, this code was the most prominent one for a long time (cf. Mahari 1985, pp. 702–705). But the code places few obligations on multinational corporations, even if it is strongly propagated by the member governments. Furthermore, it is questionable whether the world economy will comply with a code which was determined only by industrialized nation states. The OECD's current activities are much friendlier towards the multinational corporations than their guidelines written in the seventies. Since 1995 the "Multilateral Agreement on Investment" (MAI) proposal, which aims to remove protectionist obstacles to direct investment, has been discussed within the OECD. The proposal has been heavily criticized because of the asymmetry of rights and duties in favor of multinational corporations. For example, the proposal suggests that a company can directly sue a country in international court for compensation payments if the enterprise faces higher costs due to environmental regulations. Opponents speak of a contract of dominance of the corporation and the decline of democracy (Brunner 1998). Because of these concerns the MAI negotiations were postponed.

Non-Governmental Organizations (NGOs)

International *Non-Governmental Organizations* (NGOs) are non-official international organizations which keep contact with the Economic and Social Council of the United Nations. The most important functions of NGOs are observation of nation states, multinational enterprises, and other global actors, and the publication of information about misconduct. Well-known NGOs of this type are Amnesty, Greenpeace, Human Rights Watch, Corporate Watch, and Sweatshop Watch. The organizations' international network structures are similar to those of the multinational corporations, and therefore permit them to follow corporate activities in other countries and to make undesirable practices public, e.g. by using the Internet. The mobilization of the public is the strongest means of intervention for the NGOs. Prominent examples include the boycott campaign initiated by Greenpeace, which forced Royal Dutch/Shell to change its usual practice of disposing of old oil rigs (see Osterloh/Tiemann 1995), and the various initiatives of Corporate Watch, Sweatshop Watch, and other NGOs against the sports utilities manufacturer Nike. The latter actions were in response to sweat shop conditions in Nike's subcontractors' production plants in South East Asia (see e.g. Boje 1998, Mokhiber/Weissman 1999, Scherer 2000). But even though the NGOs have a strong influence on public opinion, their power to bring about legal, binding regulations depends on the cooperation of official international organizations or powerful nation states that have the necessary sovereignty. Thus, the problems of the NGOs reflect those of other international organizations.

Summarizing the difficulties encountered by the international organizations reviewed above, a major problem is the nature of consensus-based decision-making, which is considered to be essential for long-lasting agreements, but is too lengthy for fast solutions. The international organizations are still very much dependent on the nation states, who are reluctant to transfer their sovereignty to supernational institutions. Furthermore, it is unclear how individual groups and ethnic categories can be adequately represented in global institutions. This is particularly true when certain nation states claim that the humane standards advanced by the industrialized nations are based on Western values that have no basis in other cultures.

It remains to be seen whether after a longer period of time a "cosmopolitan order" (Held 1997) can be established, in which democratic law-making and administrative bodies work on a global basis to define the rules for the economic and political system (see Albrow 1997, Beck 1998a, 1998b, Chwaszcza/Kersting 1998, Habermas 1998). In political science there is currently a debate about whether developments will finally lead to a "clash of civilizations" (Huntingdon 1996) or to a convergence of economic and political institutions (Fukuyama 1992). However, in this intermediate period, when on the one hand "the end of the nation state" (Ohmae 1995) has almost come, and on the other hand a democratic world order has not emerged, one has to act to prevent the drastic conflict scenarios some students of political science describe (e.g., Huntingdon 1996). We therefore suggest an analysis of how the economic power and political influence of MNEs can be used to make a step forward toward humane working and living conditions world-wide, and thus to contribute to the promotion of a global democracy.

How to Use the Power of the MNE to Promote Human Rights: The Case for the Model Business Principles

The US Model Business Principles

Since the efforts at an international political level have not really achieved much to date, the US government has made an effort to use the power of the global enterprise to create world-wide validity for common social and environmental standards that are oriented to human rights. In the summer of 1995, the US government issued the so-called *Model Business Principles*, by which American enterprises were to be called upon voluntarily to keep to a number of principles (see Figure 1). The principles are primarily concerned with creating workplaces that are non-detrimental to health, abstaining from discrimination, child and forced labor, and recognising the right to form trade unions. Corporations are further urged to obey existing laws, to stop corruption and bribery, and to compete fairly. The Model Business Principles advise companies to write formal principles of ethical behavior and to communicate them to all members of their organization. US Secretary of State Madeleine K. Albright (1998) has strongly encouraged multinational corporations to develop and observe the Principles, in order to build a world where "global norms of worker rights and environmental protection rise, so that profits increasingly result from inspiration and perspiration, not exploitation." The US Department of Commerce (1998) has introduced an Information Clearinghouse, through which interested companies can be informed about the practical experiences of other companies with these principles.[2] In order to promote the success of these measures, a Best Global Business Award is presented each year to a company that has involved itself in an exemplary fashion with the Model Business Principles, and has therefore promoted human rights. In June of 1997, the Californian consulting company Asia Pacific Resources, Inc. (APR) was presented with the award for standing up for human rights in China: "President Clinton has made clear that the US business community can play a positive and important role in promoting human rights, protecting the environment and creating more open societies . . . APR's activities embody the essence of the Model Business Principles and serve as an example for setting high standards for business practices," emphasized Under Secretary of State Stuart Eizenstat at the award ceremony (US Department of Commerce 1997).[3] In addition, the Model Business Principles were coordinated with the programmes of other US government departments and organizations, and were integrated into a policy to support world-wide standards of business activity (US Department of State 1997, Albright 1999a, Koh 1999). The US government believes that other industrialized countries should also be encouraged to support this policy, because "the United States has a vital strategic interest in strengthening the international system by bringing nations together around the principles of democracy, open markets, and the rule of law" (Shattuck 1998).

However, the attempt to use the power of MNEs to promote social and environmental standards poses many problems (see also Steinmann/Scherer 1998). Because of the high degree of connectivity in their supplier networks and the economic importance that many MNEs have in their host countries, it is indisputable that MNEs can exert great pressure on the politics and the culture of those countries (Boddewyn 1995, The Economist 1996, Orentlicher/Gelatt 1993, Orts 1995). What guarantees are there, however, that this influence will be executed in a responsible manner? What incentives are there for the enterprise to avoid undercutting social and environmental standards, and to reject the tax gifts of the host countries? Are these not exactly the special economic advantages of multinational enterprises that they can flexibly react to the cost differences of various locations (Kogut 1985, Rosenzweig 1998)? Furthermore – and this is a very difficult question – is the initiative of the US Government totally legitimate? Should the moral claim that is formulated by the Model Business Principles be understood as representing values whose legitimacy can be taken for granted so that the implementation of these principles is only a socio-technical task? Or is the achievement of legitimacy itself linked to the implementation of values, so that the moral charge to the MNEs must be seen as a demand to get involved in a process of justification with the particular cultures in question?

Recognizing the positive role of U.S. business in upholding and promoting adherence to universal standards of human rights, the Administration encourages all businesses to adopt and implement voluntary codes of conduct for doing business around the world that cover at least the following areas:

1   Provision of a safe and healthy workplace;
2   Fair employment practices, including avoidance of child and forced labor and avoidance of discrimination based on race, gender, national origin, or religious beliefs; and respect for the right of association and the right to organize and bargain collectively;
3   Responsible environmental protection and environmental practices;
4   Compliance with U.S. and local laws promoting good business practices, including laws prohibiting illicit payments and ensuring fair competition;
5   Maintenance, through leadership of all levels, of a corporate culture that respects free expression consistent with legitimate business concerns, and does not condone political coercion in the workplace; that encourages good corporate citizenship and makes a positive contribution to the communities in which the company operates; and where ethical conduct is recognized, valued, and exemplified by all employees.

In adopting voluntary codes of conduct that reflect these principles, U.S. companies should serve as models and encourage similar behavior by their partners, suppliers, and subcontractors.

Adoption of codes of conduct reflecting these principles is voluntary. Companies are encouraged to develop their own codes of conduct appropriate to their particular circumstances. Many companies already apply statements or codes that incorporate these principles. Companies should find appropriate means to inform their shareholders and the public of actions undertaken in connection with these principles. Nothing in the principles is intended to require a company to act in violation of host country or U.S. law. This statement of principles is not intended for legislation.

Source: U.S. Department of Commerce 1995

Figure 1 Model business principles

In the following section we will discuss some of these questions. Rather than giving definite answers, we want to sketch the philosophical difficulties that are yet to be resolved in order to legitimately use the influence of MNEs to establish humane working conditions world-wide. In our opinion, the US initiative implicitly assumes that there are universally valid standards whose realization can rightly be demanded of all cultures. The initiative could then be seen as an "emancipatory anticipation" in the sense of the philosopher Karl-Otto Apel (1980) – as an attempt with strategic means to help the Western idea of a good and just life succeed. Seen in this way, however, the basic ideas expressed in the Model Business Principles are subject to debate, not only in discussions of world politics but also in philosophical reflection on basic principles (for an overview see Steinmann/ Scherer 1997, 1998).

The Philosophical Agenda: How to Justify Human Rights

The *fundamental philosophical* question that is relevant here is the possibility of justifying universalistic positions in principle (Steinmann/Scherer 1997, 1998). Only when such a justification is possible the US initiative can be considered as legitimated. Otherwise, this initiative would be an expression of the use of power. It would be an expression of a distribution of power in whose service the MNEs would be placed.

The philosophical dispute between "universalists" and "relativists" (or "postmodernists") involves the question of whether and how a unified concept of reason can be found, in view of the variety of cultures, norms, and values in existence (Habermas 1994, Rorty 1985). This question is particularly relevant where cultures with different interpretive schemes and norms come in contact (Gergen 1995). Within cultures individuals have always possessed common sources of meaning and values that have been constituted via common actions, and that helps ensure coordination of social actions in everyday life, in the family, in politics, and in the business sphere (Giddens 1984). In view of globalization the problem is that cultures with incommensurable values are now meeting each other. Therefore, cross-cultural coordination may lead to misunderstandings and conflicts of values. This is likely to happen because norms that would enable reasonable decisions and actions are not automatically available as the actors cannot refer to an existing practice of interaction that has already proved successful (Wohlrapp 1998).

Human rights are often seen as enjoying a basic consensus when dealing with intercultural contacts. However, the idea of human rights emerged during the European Enlightenment, and therefore, they are to be seen as (legal) products of Western civilization (Galtung 1994, Kühnhardt 1991). According to the Western formulation, human rights are universal, because they claim to represent all human beings, who are all equal. Their universal character suggests that they are to be respected by all humans. But there are two critical points that arise (cf. Welsch 1995, pp. 739–747). First, the opponents of human rights point out that these norms are characterized by Eurocentrism, and therefore cannot be considered universal (Banuri 1990, Lal 1998, Marglin 1990). Second, the idea of human rights itself requires the recognition of differing opinions, which even includes tolerance of disapproving attitudes toward human rights. Both points undermine the universal validity of human rights.

The philosopher Wolfgang Welsch (1995) has responded to these critiques. He emphasizes that human rights must not be understood in fixed terms, but as a historical achievement (see also Senghaas 1998). Human rights cannot be deduced from first principles, that are once and for all legitimate, but are to be recognized as the expression of "good experiences" and are embedded in social practices rather than in ahistorical principles. They are the expression of a stage of cultural evolution, and are open for further developments as new (good) experiences unfold. Therefore, material human rights are always to be measured and verified against this idea of human rights as cultural achievements, and, if necessary, to be changed. Due to this self-critical structure of the human rights concept, one-sidedness can be corrected, and this defuses the critique of Eurocentrism. In addition, Welsch (1995) offers a response to the justification problem that defends the idea of human rights by "negative reasoning." Negative reasoning means the identification of the evidently false, of what is to be avoided in all cases. In the case of human rights, this leads to the realization that only the recognition of these rights can guarantee that different cultures will not be threatened by violence, destruction, and extermination. Considering today's world situation, Welsch (1995) develops a defense of the *pragmatic universality* of human rights: the European model is the only known model that actually raises the question of how different cultures can peacefully live together, and develops possible solutions for this problem. "This pragmatic distinction justifies the right to put this concept – because there is no better one – at the basis of the coexistence of the different cultures and even to demand and impose it on other cultures. In this sense – and only in this sense – the pragmatic universalization of the 'European' human rights conception is justified" (Welsch 1995, p. 746, translation by the authors).

In the context of globalization, human rights are reflected primarily in efforts to establish social and environmental standards. These standards are based on the idea of fundamental human rights, but widen the focus from the moral to the economic and socio-political dimensions. The establishment of world-wide workplace standards as part of a global economic order is of great importance, because an increase in human rights violations is likely in the 21st century. The population explosion, the extensive migrations of people, technological and scientific progress, and the possibility of controlling intelligence offer the potential for new human rights violations. However, neither human rights nor social or environmental standards should be understood as strict measures which could be literally applied under all conditions. Rather, the idea of human rights should be understood as a means to initiate a learning process which is directed towards the improvement of social and environmental conditions step by step. It is also our suggestion to understand the Model Business Principles as an invitation for MNEs to engage in such a learning process.

The Economic Agenda: Why Is It Reasonable to Promote Social and Environmental Standards?

Apart from these philosophical considerations, there are also *economic reasons* for multinational companies to observe social and environmental standards (Wieland 1999). For example, there are NGOs and critical publics that have followed the activities of MNEs in developing countries, and have sanctioned unethical behavior in various ways. One has only to consider the Nigeria Affair of the Royal Dutch/Shell oil company, or the criticism that Nike, an American sportswear company, had to endure because a large proportion of its products was made in developing countries under sweatshop conditions (Gibbs 1996, Mokhiber/Weissman 1999). These problems have caused many enterprises in the clothing and sports wear businesses to establish guidelines for ethical behavior in international business. The jeans manufacturer Levi Strauss & Co. and the sports wear manufacturers Nike and Reebok now claim to lead the way in protecting human rights (Paine 1996, Rosenzweig 1995). However, many enterprises seem still to shun having their activities monitored by a neutral party. For example, Nike and Reebok are measured by their own claims, and are regularly criticized (for the case of Nike see Boje 1998 and Mokhiber/Weissman 1999). The human rights organization Human Rights Watch (1997) complained that many enterprises are very open to discussing human rights questions, but not so open to disclosure of their activities.

Human Rights Watch (1997) has observed that companies in the textile and sports wear industries are more likely to support initiatives on human rights and the establishment of social standards than are MNEs of the heavy industries or oil and mining companies. This is because the success of consumer goods is very closely linked to the reputation of its brand name. The oil company Royal Dutch/Shell, however, learned through the events surrounding the planned sinking of the Brent Spar oil platform, and also through the Nigeria Affair, that an observant public can swiftly react with boycotts. Managers of the capital goods and basic industries may therefore want to put more emphasis on human rights and social and environmental standards when making decisions in the future (The Economist 1996).

Companies are becoming increasingly aware that they can only survive in a healthy environment, and, therefore are motivated to take responsibility for their social and natural environment. This is also the case for MNEs, who in the end have to inhabit specific locations. If economic actors expected that their particular business partners were exploiting existing contracts opportunistically whenever possible, with no consequences or costs, business would not take place at all (cf. Wieland 1993, p. 26). A voluntary self-commitment to ethical norms is therefore in the own interests of MNEs, because an increase of conflicts is related to a decrease in productivity and profits. In the long run, an increase of conflicts may even lead to a strengthening of international institutions, and therefore to increased restriction of business activities (cf. Kumar/Sjurts 1991, pp. 181–182). Furthermore, business ethics are a potential success factor in international competition, because they are on the one hand the basis for the justification of sacrifices regarding cost-cutting (Kothen/McKinley/Scherer 1999) and on the other hand a useful device for the promotion of innovation (Steinmann/Scherer 2000).

In the meantime, many initiatives have been started to label ethically sound products. In Germany, for instance, a label was introduced by carpet importers to show that the products were manufactured without child labor. In the US, Congressman George Miller suggested that US firms should introduce a label that showed that products were manufactured under humane working conditions. This suggestion has been adopted by the US Department of Labor, and has been publicised as the so-called "No-sweat initiative" (Human Rights Watch 1997, US Department of Labor 1997). Another opportunity for companies to demonstrate their commitment to best practice in the ethical manufacture and supply of the goods they sell is the *Social Accountability 8000* initiative, a global standard for ethical sourcing and a certification procedure launched by the Council on Economic Priorities on October 15, 1997.[4] Companies like Toys R Us, Avon, and Otto Versand (a German mail order firm) already have made commitments to adopt the standard, which is based on conventions of the ILO and other international human rights organizations (EBEN 1998).

Conclusion

It is clear that a world-wide improvement of social and environmental conditions will be costly. Consumers and enterprises should participate jointly in this effort: the consumers by sanctioning or rewarding the behavior of the enterprises, and the enterprises by adopting acceptable standards not only for economic reasons, but to make peace more stable. The confidence of people in the justice and fairness of competition is a precondition for global stability and the prosperity of the world economy. Governments, corporate actors, intergovernmental organizations, and NGOs are called upon to contribute to the maintenance of this confidence, as US president Bill Clinton (1998) recently pointed out at the 1998 WTO ministerial meeting in Geneva:

"We must do more to make sure that this new economy lifts living standards around the world, and that spirited economic competition among nations never becomes a race to the bottom in environmental protections, consumer protections and labour standards. We should level up, not level down. Without such a strategy, we cannot build the necessary support for the global economy. Working people will only assume the risks of a free international market if they have the confidence that this system will work for them."

The Model Business Principles are an important measure to contribute to such a policy. Let us convince MNEs to take part in this endeavor.

Notes

1   Parts of this paper were presented at the Critical Management Workshop at the Academy of Management (AoM) Annual Meeting in San Diego, Aug. 1998, and at the AoM meeting in Toronto, Aug. 2000. We would like to thank several institutions

and individuals for their kind help. This paper has greatly benefited from discussions with Jean Boddewyn (CUNY), Thomas Olbrich (Erlangen-Nuremberg), Eric Orts (Wharton), Stephen Payne (Georgia College), Karl Albrecht Schachtschneider (Erlangen-Nuremberg), and Horst Steinmann (Erlangen-Nuremberg). William McKinley (Southern Illinois Univ.) gave very helpful comments on earlier drafts of this paper. The Dr. Alfred Vinzl-foundation (Erlangen) provided financial support for our attendance at the 1998 and 2000 AoM conferences.

2   The Information Clearinghouse can be found on the internet at http://www.ita.gov/bgp/clearing.html.

3   More recently, two further companies were awarded. The sugar company F. C. Schaffer & Associates was honored for its activities in Ethiopia, and Xerox Corp. was awarded for its community involvement program in Brazil (Albright 1999b).

4   The SA 8000 initiative can be found on the internet at: http://www.cepaa.org.

References

Albright, M. (1998) *Secretary of State Albright Speaks Out Against Child Labor*. Commencement Address at the University of Maryland on May 22, 1998, http://www.usis.usemb.se/regional/nea/sasia/topics/sec5.htm, 09/24/1998.

Albright, M. (1999a) *Secretary of State Madelaine K. Albright, Remarks at Conference on the Domestic Impacts of Foreign Policy*, Wesleyan University, Middletown, Connecticut, February 6, 1999, http://secretary.state.gov/www/statements/1999/990206.html, 02/06/1999.

Albright, M. (1999b) *Secretary of State Madelaine K. Albright, Remarks at Presenting Inaugural Corporate Excellence Awards to Francis Schaffer, President, F. C. Schaffer & Associates, and to Richard Thoman, Chief Executive Officer, Xerox Corp.*, Washington, D.C., December 21, 1999, http://secretary.state.gov/www/statements/1999/991221a.html, 06/28/00.

Albrow, M. (1997) *The Global Age: State and Society Beyond Modernity*, Stanford: Stanford University Press.

Altvater, E. and Mahnkopf, B. (1996) *Grenzen der Globalisierung: Ökonomie, Ökologie und Politik in der Weltgeschichte*, Münster: Westfälisches Dampfboot.

Annan, K. (1999) *A Compact for the New Century*. Speech before the World Economic Forum, Davos, January 31, http://www.un.org/partners/business/davos.htm, July 9, 1999.

Apel, K.-O. (1980) *Towards a Transformation of Philosophy*, trans. G. Adey and D. Frisby, London: Routledge & Kegan Paul.

Banuri, T. (1990) 'Development and the Politics of Knowledge: A Critical Interpretation of the Social Role of Modernization Theories in the Development of the Third World', in F. A. Marglin and S. A. Marglin (eds.), *Dominating Knowledge: Development, Culture, and Resistance*, Oxford: Clarendon Press, pp. 29–72.

Beck, U. (1997) *Was ist Globalisierung?*, Frankfurt a.M.: Suhrkamp.

Beck, U. (ed.) (1998a) *Politik der Globalisierung*, Frankfurt a.M.: Suhrkamp.

Beck, U. (ed.) (1998b) *Perspektiven der Weltgesellschaft*, Frankfurt a.M.: Suhrkamp.

Boddewyn, J. (1995) 'The Legitimacy of International-Business Political Behavior', *The International Trade Journal* IX(1): 143–161.

Boje, D. M. (1998) *While Coyote meets Roadrunner: Nike's Postmodern Encounters with*

Entrepreneurial Activists http://cbae.nmsu.edu/mgt/handout/boje/coyote/index.html.

Boyer, R. and Drache, D. (eds) (1996) *States Against Markets: The Limits of Globalization*, London: Routledge.

Brunner, M. (1998) 'Ein multilaterales Investitionsabkommen soll der Weltwirtschaft noch weitgehendere Freiheiten bringen: Chance oder Gefahr?', *Wirtschaftkurier* 40 (3): 1.

Cassen, B. (1996) 'Modestes propositions pour sortir de la crise . . . La "clause sociale", un moyen de mondialiser la justice', *Le Monde Diplomatique* 503, 43, 02: 18–19.

Charnovitz, S. (1995) 'Promoting Higher Labor Standards', *The Washington Quarterly* 3, pp. 167–190.

Chwaszcza, C. and Kersting, W. (eds) (1998) *Politische Philosophie der internationalen Beziehungen*, Frankfurt a.M.: Suhrkamp.

Clinton, B. (1998) *Statement by H. E. Mr. William J. Clinton, President, Speech Before the WTO Ministry Conference*, http://www.wto.org/wto/anniv/clinton.htm, 09/23/1998.

Deetz, S. (1995) 'Transforming Communication, Transforming Business: Stimulating Value Negotiation for More Responsive and Responsible Workplaces', *International Journal of Value-Based Management* 8: 255–278.

EBEN – European Business Ethics Network, A Global Ethical Sourcing Standard (1998) *The European Business Ethics Newsletter* no. 1, March.

Economist (1993) *A Survey of Multinationals: Everyone's Favorite Monster*, 03/27/1993.

Economist (1996) *Companies and Their Conscience*, 07/20/1996.

Fukuyama, F. (1992) *The End of History and the Last Man*, New York: Free Press.

Galtung, J. (1994) *Menschenrechte – anders gesehen*, Frankfurt a.M.: Suhrkamp.

Gergen, K. (1995) 'Global Organization. From Imperialism to Ethical Vision', *Organization* 2: 519–532.

Gibbs, N. (1996) 'Cause Celeb', *Time* 147 (25), 06/17/1996.

Giddens, A. (1984) *The Constitution of Society: Outline of the Theory of Structuration*, Cambridge: Polity Press.

Grieder, W. (1997) *One World, Ready or Not: The Manic Logic of Global Capitalism*, New York: Simon & Schuster.

Großmann, H. and Koopmann, G. (1994) 'Sozialstandards für den internationalen Handel?', *Wirtschaftsdienst* XI: 585–591.

Habermas, J. (1994) 'The Unity of Reason in the Diversity of Its Voices', in J. Habermas, *Postmetaphysical Thinking: Philosophical Essays*, trans. W. Hohengarten, Cambridge: MIT Press, pp. 115–148.

Habermas, J. (1998) 'Die postnationale Konstellation und die Zukunft der Demokratie', in J. Habermas, *Die postnationale Konstellation*, Frankfurt a.M.: Suhrkamp, pp. 91–169.

Held, D. (1997) 'Democracy: From City-states to a Cosmopolitan Order?', in R. E. Goodin and Ph. Pettit (eds) *Contemporary Political Philosophy*, Oxford: Blackwell, pp. 78–101.

Hoekman, B. and Kostecki, M. (1997) *The Political Economy of the World Trading System – From GATT to WTO*, Oxford: Oxford University Press.

Human Rights Watch (1997) *Corporations and Human Rights*, http://www.hrw.org/about/initiatives/corp.html, 09/09/1997.

Huntingdon, S. (1996) *The Clash of Civilization*, New York: Schuster & Schuster.

International Labour Conference (1994) *Resolution calling upon the ILO to resist the introduction of the social clause in international trade and to review ILO standards*, submitted by the Government delegation of Indonesia, Malaysia, Philippines, Singapore and Thailand, 1993, in International Labour Conference Provisional Record, 1, Eighty-first Session, Geneva, pp. 1/4–1/5.

Kogut, B. (1985) 'Designing Global Strategies: Profiting from Operational Flexibility', *Sloan Management Review* 27: 27–38.

Koh, H. (1999) *Promoting Human Rights in the Pursuit of Peace: Assessing 20 Years of US Human Rights Policy*, address by H. H. Koh, Assistant Secretary for Democracy, Human Rights, and Labor, to the US Institute of Peace Symposium, Washington, DC, March 17, 1999, http://www.state.gov/www/policy-Remarks/1999/990317_koh_usips.html, 06/02/1999.

Kolde, E.-J. (1982) *Environment of International Business*, Belmont: Kent.

Kothen, C., McKinley, W. and Scherer, A. (1999) 'Alternatives to Organizational Downsizing: A German Case Study', *Management* 2 (3).

Krauss, M. (1997) *How Nations Grow Rich: The Case for Free Trade*, New York: Oxford University Press.

Kühnhardt, L. (1991) *Die Universalität der Menschenrechte*, Bonn: Bundeszentrale für Politische Bildung.

Kumar, B. and Sjurts, I. (1991) 'Multinationale Unternehmen und Ethik', in M. Dierkes and K. Zimmermann (eds) *Ethik und Geschäft – Dimensionen und Grenzen unternehmerischer Verantwortung*, Frankfurt a.M.: FAZ-Verlag, pp. 159–186.

Lal, D. (1998) 'Social Standards and Social Dumping', in H. Giersch (ed.) *Merits and Limits of Markets*, Heidelberg: Springer, pp. 255–274.

Lee Kuan Yew (1994) 'Ich sage, wir hängen sie auf, Lee Kuan Yew interviewed by M. Naß', *Die Zeit* 49 (49), 12/02/1994.

Longworth, R. (1998) *Global Squeeze: The Coming Crisis of First World Nations*, Chicago: NTC Contemporary Publishing.

Mahari, J. (1985) *Codes of Conduct für Multinationale Unternehmen*, Wilmington: Morgan Internat. Institution.

Mahatir, M. (1995) 'Sie zelebrieren das Chaos, Malaysia's Premier Mohamad Mahatir interviewed by E. Follath and B. Schwarz', *Der Spiegel* 34: 136–139.

Marglin, S. (1990) 'Towards the Decolonization of the Mind', in F. A. Marglin and S. Marglin (eds) *Dominating Knowledge: Development, Culture, and Resistance*, Oxford: Clarendon Press, pp. 1–28.

Martin, H.-P. and Schumann, H. (1996) *Die Globalisierungsfalle: Der Angriff auf Demokratie und Wohlstand*, Reinbek bei Hamburg: Rowohlt.

Mokhiber, R. and Weissman, R. (1999) *Corporate Predators: The Hunt for Mega-Profits and the Attack on Democracy*, Monroe, ME: Common Courage Press.

OECD (1997) *Aufbruch in ein neues globales Zeitalter*, Paris.

Ohmae, K. (1995) *The End of the Nation State: The Rise of Regional Economics*, New York: Free Press.

Orentlicher, D. and Gelatt, T. (1993) 'Public Law, Private Actors: The Impact of Human Rights on Business Investors in China', *Northwestern Journal of International Law and Business* 14: 66–129.

Orts, E. (1995) 'The Legitimacy of Multinational Corporations', in L. Mitchell (ed.) *Progressive Corporate Law*, Boulder, CO: Westview Press, pp. 247–279.

Osterloh, M. and Tiemann, R. (1995) 'Konzepte der Wirtschafts- und Unternehmensethik', *Die Unternehmung* 5: 321–338.

Paine, L. (1996) 'Levi Strauss & Co.: Global Sourcing (A)', in L. Paine *Cases in Leadership, Ethics, and Organizational Integrity*, Chicago: Irwin, pp. 346–376.

Peace Treaty of Versailles (1998) http://www.lib.byu.edu/~rdh/wwi/versa/versa1.html, 09/30/1998.

Petrella, R. 'Globalization and Internationalization: The Dynamics of the Emerging World Order', in R. Boyer and D. Drache (eds) *States Against Markets: The Limits of Globalization*, London: Routledge, pp. 62–83.

Preston, L. and Windsor, D. (1997) *The Rules of the Game in the Global Economy: Policy Regimes for International Business*, Norwell: Kluwer.

Reich, R. (1991) *The Work of Nations*, New York: Alfred A. Knopf.

Rorty, R. (1985) 'Solidarity or Objectivity', in J. Rajchman and C. West (eds) *Post-Analytic Philosophy*, New York: Columbia Press, pp. 3–19.

Rosenzweig, P. (1995) 'International Sourcing in Athletic Footwear: Nike and Reebok', in C. A. Bartlett and S. Ghoshal (eds) *Transnational Management* (2nd edn), Chicago: Irwin, pp. 170–182.

Rosenzweig, P. (1998) *Winning the Global Game: A Strategy for Linking People and Profits*, New York: Free Press.

Ruggiero, R. (1998) *The general director of the WTO, the WTO and the 'wired' global economy*, http://www.itu.int/newsroom/press/WTPF98/WTOandGlobal economy.html, 03/19/1998.

Sanger, D. (1994) 'Trade Agreement Ends Long Debate, But Not Conflicts', *New York Times*, December 4.

Scherer, A. (2000) *Die Rolle der Multinationalen Unternehmung im Prozeß der Globalisierung: Vorüberlegungen zu einer Neuorientierung der Theorie der Multinationalen Unternehmung*, Habilitationsschrift, Univ. Erlangen-Nürnberg, Nürnberg.

Scherer, A. and Löhr, A. (1999) Verantwortungsvolle Unternehmensführung im Zeitalter der Globalisierung – Einige kritische Bemerkungen zu den Perspektiven einer liberalen Weltwirtschaft, in B. Kumar, M. Osterloh and G. Schreyögg (eds) *Unternehmensethik und Transformation des Wettbewerbs: Festschrift für Horst Steinmann*, Stuttgart: Schaeffer-Poeschel, S. 261–290.

Sengenberger, W. and Wilkinson, F. (1995) 'Globalization and Labour Standards', in J. Michie and J. G. Smith (eds) *Managing the Global Economy*, New York: Oxford University Press, pp. 111–134.

Senghaas, D. (1998) *Zivilisierung wider Willen*, Frankfurt a.M.: Suhrkamp.

Shattuck, J. (1998) *Assistant Secretary of State for Democracy, Human Rights and Labor, Human Rights and Democracy, Statement before the House Committee on Appropriations, Subcommittee on Foreign Operations*, Washington D.C., 04/01/1998, http://www.state.gov/www/policy_remarks/ 1998/980401_shattuck_hr_dem.html.

Steinmann, H. and Scherer, A. (1997) 'Intercultural Management Between Universalism and Relativism: Fundamental Problems in International Business Ethics and the Contribution of Recent German Philosophical Approaches', in S. Urban (ed.) *Europe in the Global Competition: Problems–Markets–Strategies*, Wiesbaden (Germany): Gabler, pp. 77–143.

Steinmann, H. and Scherer, A. (1998) 'Corporate Ethics and Global Business: Philosophical Considerations on Intercultural Management', in B. N. Kumar and H. Steinmann (eds) *Ethics in International Management*, Berlin: de Gruyter, pp. 14–46.

Steinmann, H. and Scherer, A. (2000) 'Corporate Ethics and Management Theory', in P. Koslowski (ed.) *Historism as a Challenge to Economic Ethics and Philosophy*, Berlin/Heidelberg/New York: Springer.

Strange, S. (1996) *The Retreat of the State: The Diffusion of Power in the World Economy*, Cambridge: Cambridge University Press.

Thurow, L. (1996) *The Future of Capitalism: How Today's Economic Forces Shape Tomorrow's World*, New York: William Morrow & Co.

Trebilcock, M. and Howse, R. (1995) *The Regulation of International Trade*, London: Routledge.

U.S. Department of Commerce (1995) *Model Business Principles*, New York Times, May 27; see also: http://www.depaul.edu/ethics/principles.html.

U.S. Department of Commerce (1997) *Asia Pacific Resources Honored as Recipient of Best Global Practices Award*, U.S. Department of Commerce News, 06/06/1997, http://www.ita.doc.gov/media/bestp.htm.

U.S. Department of Commerce (1998) *Best Global Practices – Information Clearinghouse*, http://www.ita.doc.gov/bgp/clearing.html, 09/30/1998.

U.S. Department of Labor (1997) *Secretary of Labor Unveils New No-Sweat Garment Initiative for Teens*, U.S. Department of Labor – Office of Public Affairs, 10/16/1997, http://www2.dol.gov/dol/opa/public/media/press/opa/opa97370.htm.

U.S. Department of State Publication 10486, Released June 1997, Bureau of Democracy, Human Rights and Labor: *Promoting the Model Business Principles*, http://www.state.gov/www/global/human_rights/business_principles.html.

United Nations Conference on Trade and Development (UNCTAD) (1994) Relationship Between the Trading System and Internationally Recognized Labour Standards, in United Nations *Conference on Trade and Development, the Outcome of the Uruguay Round: An Initial Assessment*, Supporting Papers to the Trade and Development Report, Annex 4, pp. 245–247.

Vernon, R. (1998) *In the Hurricane's Eye: The Troubled Prospects of Multinational Enterprises*, Cambridge, Mass.: Harvard University Press.

Welsch, W. (1995) *Vernunft*, Frankfurt a. M.: Suhrkamp.

Wieland, J. (1993) *Formen der Institutionalisierung von Moral in amerikanischen Unternehmen – Die amerikanische Business-Ethics-Bewegung: Why and How They Do It*, Bern: Haupt.

Wieland, J. (1999) *Die Ethik der Governance*, Marburg: Metropolis.

Windsor, D. (1994) 'Toward a Transnational Code of Business Conduct', in W. Hoffman, J. Kamm, R. Frederick and E. Petry, Jr. (eds) *Emerging Global Business Ethics*, Westport: Quorum, pp. 165–176.

Wohlrapp, H. (1998) 'Constructivist Anthropology and Cultural Pluralism: Methodological Reflections on Cultural Integration', in B. Kumar and H. Steinmann (eds) *Ethics in International Management*, Berlin: de Gruyter, pp. 46–63.

World Trade Organization (WTO) (1996) Singapore Ministerial Declaration, Ministerial Conference, Singapore, 9–13 Dec. 1996, http://www.wto.org/ wto/archives/wtodec.htm, 11/19/1998.

Nike's global supply chains: stepping up to the mark?

Introduction

In this case study, written by Simon Zadek, Chief Executive Officer of AccountAbility, a discussion and analysis is presented of the CSR process which the US sports apparel manufacturer Nike has gone through since the 1990s. Although it is not the only company to come under public and NGO fire for its highly cost-efficient but ethically questionable labour standards in its global supply chains, Nike has become the major example of a corporation struggling to deal with its public image and supply chain practices in such a way as to show that it takes CSR *really* seriously.

Zadek provides considerable insight into how CSR has been managed at Nike, describing the implementation of the company's global code of conduct and associated auditing and reporting practices. These he considers in the context of a broader transition towards greater transparency and accountability in the firm's global operations. He also offers a helpful typology of the stages of organizational learning that firms such as Nike go through when developing strategies of social responsibility. Finally, Zadek considers the inherently global aspects of Nike's path to CSR, and provides a fascinating glimpse into how large organizations might take their responsibilities sufficiently seriously to seek engagement with suppliers and other stakeholders to take an active leadership role in developing global standards for business conduct. As Zadek puts it, Nike came to view CSR 'as integral to the realities of globalization – and a major source of learning, relevant to its core business strategy and practices'.

Study Questions

1   Who is Nike accountable to, and to what extent has the company satisfied the requirements for accountability as set out by the two readings in Chapter 9?

2   Has the CSR strategy developed by Nike paid off in terms of creating value for the company? Discuss in terms of Burke and Logsdon's model of CSR strategy in Chapter 10.

3   To what extent can Nike's code of conduct act as a tool of 'sustainable governance' (Bondy *et al.*, Chapter 10). What else has or should Nike do to achieve improved governance of labour conditions in developing countries?

4   Is it reasonable to expect a large company in one part of the world to be responsible for the activities of suppliers in another? What are the arguments for and against such an 'extended responsibility' for the improvement of worldwide social and environmental conditions?

THE PATH TO CORPORATE RESPONSIBILITY

Simon Zadek

Nike's tagline, "JUST DO IT," is an inspirational call to action for the millions who wear the company's athletic gear. But in terms of corporate responsibility, the company hasn't always followed its own advice. In the 1990s, protestors railed against sweatshop conditions at its overseas suppliers and made Nike the global poster child for corporate ethical fecklessness. Nike's every move was scrutinized, and every problem discovered was touted as proof of the organization's irresponsibility and greed. The real story, of course, is not so simple.

Nike's business model – to market high-end consumer products manufactured in cost-efficient supply chains – is no different from that of thousands of other companies. But the intense pressure that activists exerted on the athletic giant forced it to take a long, hard look at corporate responsibility faster than it might have otherwise. Since the 1990s, Nike has traveled a bumpy road on this front, but it has ended up in a much better place for its troubles. And the lessons it has learned will help other companies traverse this same ground.

Over the past decade, I have worked with many global organizations, including Nike, as they grappled with the complex challenges of responsible business practices. This experience has shown me that while every organization learns in unique ways, most pass through five discernible stages in how they handle corporate responsibility. Moreover, just as organizations' views of an issue grow and mature, so does society's. Beyond getting their own houses in order, companies need to stay abreast of the public's evolving ideas about corporate roles and responsibilities. A company's journey through these two dimensions of learning – organizational and societal – invariably leads it to engage in what I call "civil learning." (To map this process for your organization, see Figure 3, "The Civil-Learning Tool.")

Organizational Learning

Organizations' learning pathways are complex and iterative. Companies can make great strides in one area only to take a few steps backward when a new demand is made of them. Nevertheless, as they move along the learning curve, companies almost invariably go through the following five stages (see Figure 1).

"It's not our job to fix that." In the *defensive* stage, the company is faced with often unexpected criticism, usually from civil activists and the media but sometimes from direct stakeholders such as customers, employees, and investors. The company's responses are designed and implemented by legal and communications teams and tend to involve either outright rejections of allegations ("It didn't happen") or denials of the links between the company's practices and the alleged negative outcomes ("It wasn't our fault"). Think of Royal Dutch/Shell's handling of the controversy around carbon emissions. For years, the company – along with the rest of the energy sector – denied its responsibility for emissions created by the production and distribution of its energy products. Today, Royal Dutch/Shell acknowledges some accountability. But unlike some of its competitors, the company continues to resist environmentalists' demands that it accept responsibility for emissions from its products after they have been sold.

"We'll do just as much as we have to." At the *compliance* stage, it's clear that a corporate policy must be established and observed, usually in ways that can be made visible to critics ("We ensure that we don't do what we agreed not to do"). Compliance is understood as a cost of doing business; it creates value by protecting the company's reputation and reducing the risk of litigation. Until recently, for example, much of the food industry has understood "health" as the avoidance of legally unacceptable "non-health." When Nestlé came under fire for the health dangers of its infant formula – activists claimed that mothers in developing countries would end up mixing the power with contaminated water, thereby compromising their children's health – its response for many years was to shift its marketing policies to make this hazard clear to new mothers rather than, for example, trying to educate them generally about ways to ensure their babies' overall nutrition. The current public debate on obesity highlights the same dynamics – food companies' instinct is to simply aim for compliance, while the public clearly wants a far greater commitment from them.

"It's the business, stupid." At the *managerial* stage, the company realizes that it's facing a long-term problem that cannot be swatted away with attempts at compliance or a public relations strategy. The company will have

to give managers of the core business responsibility for the problem and its solution. Nike and other leading companies in the apparel and footwear industries increasingly understand that compliance with agreed-upon labor standards in their global supply chains is difficult if not impossible without changes to how they set procurement incentives, forecast sales, and manage inventory.

"It gives us a competitive edge." A company at the *strategic* stage learns how realigning its strategy to address responsible business practice can give it a leg up on the competition and contribute to the organization's long-term success. Automobile companies know that their future depends on their ability to develop environmentally safer forms of mobility. Food companies are struggling to develop a different consciousness about how their products affect their customers' health. And pharmaceutical companies are exploring how to integrate health maintenance into their business models alongside their traditional focus on treating illnesses.

"We need to make sure everybody does it." In the final *civil* stage, companies promote collective action to address society's concerns. Sometimes this is linked directly to strategy. For instance, Diageo and other top alcohol companies know that as sure as night follows day, restrictive legislation will come unless they can drive the whole sector toward responsible practices that extend well beyond fair marketing. Among other activities, these companies have been involved in educational initiatives that promote responsible drinking. Likewise, energy companies understand that their industry has to grapple with the sometimes unethical ways in which governments use the windfall royalties they earn from oil and gas extraction. So they are supporting the UK's Extractive Industries Transparency Initiative, which urges governments to report the aggregate revenues they derive from resource extraction. Some organizations look even further ahead and think about metastrategy: the future role of business in society and the stability and openness of global society itself.

Societal Learning

A generation ago, most people didn't think tobacco was a dangerous health threat. Just a few years ago, obesity was seen as a combination of genetics and unhealthy lifestyle choices – certainly not the responsibility of food companies. Today, ageism is rarely seen as a corporate responsibility issue beyond compliance with the law – but in an era of dramatic demographic shifts, it soon will be.

The trick, then, is for companies to be able to predict and credibly respond to society's changing awareness of particular issues. The task is daunting, given the complexity of the issues as well as stakeholders' volatile and sometimes underinformed expectations about business' capacities and responsibilities to address societal problems. Many civil advocates, for instance, believe pharmaceutical companies should sell life-saving drugs to the poor at reduced prices; after all, the drug companies can afford it more than the patients can. The pharmaceutical industry has claimed over the years that such price limits would choke off its research and development efforts. But today, drug companies are exploring how to sustain R&D while pursuing price reductions in developing countries and how to integrate the prevention of illness into their business models.

Danish pharmaceutical company Novo Nordisk has created a practical tool to track societal learning on some of its core business issues – animal testing, genetically modified organisms, and access to drugs. The drugmaker's approach can be adapted and used by any company facing any number of issues. (See Figure 2, "The Four Stages of Issue Maturity.") In the early stages, issues tend to be vague and their potential significance well below conventional thresholds used by the financial community to determine materiality. These issues are often first identified through a company's interactions with non-traditional sources of knowledge, such as social activists. As one senior business manager explains, when he deals with nongovernmental organizations, "I see the future of our markets, our products, and this business."

As issues mature, they become absorbed into mainstream professional debate and eventually into practice. Once leading companies adopt unconventional commitments and practices around certain societal issues, laggards must either follow suit or risk the consequences. In 1991, when Levi Strauss publicly launched its "terms of engagement" – which defined the labor standards for Levi's business partners and was one of the world's first corporate-conduct policies – every other company in its industry looked the other way, arguing that labor standards in other people's factories weren't their responsibility. When the Body Shop adopted human rights policies in the mid-1990s, most mainstream companies deemed its practices unfeasible. And when BP CEO Sir John Browne acknowledged in his infamous Stanford Business School speech that BP had a co-responsibility to address the challenges associated with global warming, he was taking a leadership role and betting that others would have to follow – as indeed they did. Each of these actions played a big part in dragging the rest of the players in the industry toward common approaches to responsible business practices.

How Nike Just Did It

Nike's story illuminates better than most the tensions inherent in managing corporate performance and societal expectations. In the 1990s, the company was blindsided when activists launched an all-out campaign against it because of worker conditions in its supply chain. There's no doubt that Nike managed to make some extraordinary errors. But it also learned some important

When it comes to developing a sense of corporate responsibility, organizations typically go through five stages as they move along the learning curve.

STAGE	WHAT ORGANIZATIONS DO	WHY THEY DO IT
DEFENSIVE	Deny practices, outcomes, or responsibilities	To defend against attacks to their reputation that in the short term could affect sales, recruitment, productivity, and the brand
COMPLIANCE	Adopt a policy-based compliance approach as a cost of doing business	To mitigate the erosion of economic value in the medium term because of ongoing reputation and litigation risks
MANAGERIAL	Embed the societal issue in their core management processes	To mitigate the erosion of economic value in the medium term and to achieve longer-term gains by integrating responsible business practices into their daily operations
STRATEGIC	Integrate the societal issue into their core business strategies	To enhance economic value in the long term and to gain first-mover advantage by aligning strategy and process innovations with the societal issue
CIVIL	Promote broad industry participation in corporate responsibility	To enhance long-term economic value by overcoming any first-mover disadvantages and to realize gains through collective action

Figure 1 The five stages of organizational learning

lessons. Today, the company is participating in, facilitating, convening, and financing initiatives to improve worker conditions in global supply chains and promote corporate responsibility more generally.

From denial to compliance. Nike's business model is based exclusively on global outsourcing. Simply put, the company has rarely produced a shoe or a T-shirt outside of its design studio. By the time the company was singled out in a 1992 *Harper's Magazine* article for the appalling working conditions in some of its suppliers' factories, almost all of its competitors were using a similar sourcing model. Labor activists in the early 1990s were exerting enormous pressure on premium-brand companies to adopt codes of conduct in their global supply chains. These groups targeted Nike because of its high-profile brand, not because its business practices were any worse than its competitors'.

Pharmaceutical company Novo Nordisk created a scale to measure the maturity of societal issues and the public's expectations around the issues. An adaptation of the scale appears below and can be used by any company facing any number of societal issues.

STAGE	CHARACTERISTICS
LATENT	• Activist communities and NGOs are aware of the societal issue. • There is weak scientific or other hard evidence. • The issue is largely ignored or dismissed by the business community.
EMERGING	• There is political and media awareness of the societal issue. • There is an emerging body of research, but data are still weak. • Leading businesses experiment with approaches to dealing with the issue.
CONSOLIDATING	• There is an emerging body of business practices around the societal issue. • Sectorwide and issue-based voluntary initiatives are established. • There is litigation and an increasing view of the need for legislation. • Voluntary standards are developed and collective action occurs.
INSTITUTIONALIZED	• Legislation or business norms are established. • The embedded practices become a normal part of a business-excellence model.

Figure 2 The four stages of issue maturity

The company's first reaction was defensive. "We said, 'Wait a minute; we've got the best corporate values in the world, so why aren't you yelling at the other folks?'" one of Nike's senior managers recalls. "That was a stupid thing to do. It didn't get us anywhere. If anything, it raised the volume higher." The company realized it couldn't just shut out the noise. It eventually responded to activists' demands for labor codes and after further pressure, agreed to external audits to verify whether these codes were being enforced.

Nike hired high-profile firms or individuals to conduct the audits, which were initially one-off events. But these companies and individuals had little actual auditing experience or credibility in labor circles, and the approach backfired. Statements such as former UN Ambassador Andrew Young's casual conclusions that all was well in Nike's supply chains were publicly challenged and subsequently proved to be flawed or overly simplistic. Consequently, many labor activists believed Nike's early, failed attempts at building credibility were proof of insincerity.

Companies frequently resist accepting new responsibilities because they see how risk-taking organizations are criticized for their efforts to do just that. But the pressure on Nike was so intense that it couldn't afford to wait until the whole sector advanced. Labor activists' demands for action were cascading into Nike's core and highly profitable youth markets in North America and Europe. So in 1996, Nike "went professional" in creating its first department specifically responsible for managing its supply chain partners' compliance with labor standards. And in 1998, Nike established a Corporate Responsibility department, acknowledging that acting responsibly was far more than just reaching compliance; it was an aspect of the business that had to be managed like any other.

Managing responsibility. By the turn of the millennium, Nike's labor-compliance team was more than 80 strong. The company had also hired costly external professionals to audit its roughly 900 suppliers. Even so, new revelations about Nike's failure to adhere to its own labor codes constantly came to light. Many outsiders took this as proof that the company still lacked any real commitment to address labor standards. Those inside Nike's walls were incredibly frustrated by their failure to move past this ongoing crisis. After a particularly painful documentary on Nike aired in the United Kingdom, the CEO assembled a team of senior managers and outsiders led by Nike's vice-president for corporate responsibility, Maria Eitel. The team was instructed to leave no stone unturned in figuring out how to get beyond the company's continued failure to effectively comply with its own labor codes.

The team's review didn't focus on the behaviors of factory managers and workers, as many previous studies did; the group considered issues at the factory level to be symptoms of a larger systemic problem. Instead of looking down the supply chain, the team studied the upstream drivers. After six months, it concluded that the root of the problem was not so much the quality of the company's programs to improve worker conditions as Nike's (and the industry's) approach to doing business.

Like its competitors, Nike offered performance incentives to its procurement teams based on price, quality, and delivery times. This standard industry practice undermined Nike's many positive efforts to comply with its own codes of conduct; it had the unintended effect of actively encouraging its buyers to circumvent code compliance to hit targets and secure bonuses. And there were other tensions between Nike's short-term financial goals and its longer-term strategic need to protect the brand. For instance, the company's tight inventory management often led to shortages when forecasting errors were made. That created urgent short-term needs for more goods to satisfy market demand, which drove procurement teams to take what they could get. Often, this would force suppliers to cut corners to push the envelope on delivery times, which would drive up overtime in the factories – exactly what Nike's labor code was trying to prevent. To cap it all, when something went wrong and Nike's reputation took a hit, the

The civil-learning tool is intended to help companies see where they and their competitors fall on a particular societal issue. It can help organizations figure out how to develop and position their future business strategies in ways that society will embrace.

The tool factors in the two different types of learning, organizational and societal. When an issue is just starting to evolve, companies can get away with defensive actions and deflections of responsibility. But the more mature an issue becomes, the further up the learning curve an organization must be to avoid risk and to take advantage of opportunities.

As the tool makes clear, there is a point where the risky red zone turns into the higher-opportunity green zone. The question for most companies is, "Where is that line for my organization?" The answer depends on a host of factors, and a company's actions can actually shift the line in its favor. A company might step way out in front of an immature issue while most of its rivals are still in defensive mode. Cases in point: BP's aggressive stance on publishing the amount of royalties it pays to host governments; Rio Tinto's adoption of a human rights policy when most companies would not go near the idea; and Levi Strauss's groundbreaking "terms of engagement," which set out the company's responsibilities to workers in its global supply chains.

Additionally, events in one industry can affect companies in a different industry or organizations in the same industry that are facing different issues. For example, the heated public debate about the pricing of drugs in poorer communities has created a broader debate about the fundamentals of intellectual property rights and the merits of a preventive approach to health at a time when the pharmaceutical industry makes its money from treating illnesses. Similarly, the emergence of obesity as an issue for the food industry has been accelerated by both rising health care costs and the devastating impact of litigation on the tobacco industry.

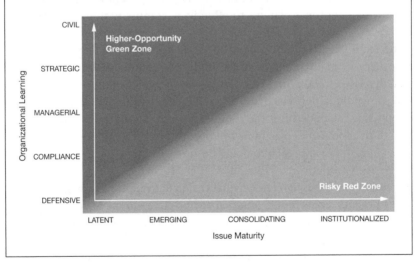

Figure 3 The civil-learning tool

procurement, marketing, and inventory management teams weren't the ones that suffered financially. The brand shouldered the burden, and the legal and other costs were charged to the corporate center, not to those whose behavior had caused the problem in the first place.

Nike realized that it had to manage corporate responsibility as a core part of the business. Technically, it was relatively easy to reengineer procurement incentives. The review team proposed that Nike grade all factories according to their labor conditions and then tax or reward procurement teams based on the grade of the supplier they used. But commercially and culturally, it wasn't so simple. Nike's entrepreneurial culture extended from brand management to procurement. Any challenge to that spirit was considered by many as an affront to a business model that had delivered almost continual financial success for three decades.

Nike's resistance to shifting its procurement methods cannot be dismissed as some irrational distaste for change. It knew that constraining its procurement teams would involve real costs and commercial risks. And the hard reality was that Nike's efforts to secure adequate worker conditions delivered little to the financial bottom line in the short term – which was the sole focus for the bulk of the company's mainstream investors. (For more on the business implications of doing good, see the box "Being Good Doesn't Always Pay.") Nike's challenge was to adjust its business model to embrace responsible practices – effectively building tomorrow's business success without compromising today's bottom line. And to do this, it had to offset any first-mover disadvantage by getting both its competitors and suppliers involved.

It has turned out to be a long and rocky path for Nike and other companies working to get the labor piece right. Several multistakeholder initiatives were launched that focused on the development of credible and technically robust approaches to compliance. Most well-known in the United States are the Fair Labor Association (FLA), which was initially established with support from the Clinton administration as the Apparel Industry Partnership, and the SA8000 standard, which evolved with help from parties outside the United States. The multistakeholder Ethical Trading Initiative (ETI) emerged from the United Kingdom. Each initiative has distinct characteristics, involves diverse companies, and associates with different NGOs, labor organizations, and public bodies. But all have broadly responded to the same need to develop, monitor, and comply with now commonly accepted labor standards underpinned by UN conventions.

Responsible business strategies

Nike's underlying business strategy wasn't static as it moved up the corporate responsibility learning curve. The prevailing trade agreement in the apparel industry, the Multifiber Arrangement (MFA), was nearing its end. The MFA had established country-based garment import quotas to the all-important U.S. market. The growth of Nike's apparel supply chains during the 1990s was partly driven by cost grazing – the ongoing search for lower prices. But the MFA had reinforced that need to graze because companies had to search the world for spare quota. The MFA also inhibited businesses like Nike from making longer-term procurement commitments to their

Being Good Doesn't Always Pay

There is no universal business case for being good, despite what we might wish. Civil regulation, attacks by NGOs to damage corporate reputations, and the like rarely cause measurable, long-term damage to a fundamentally strong business. In the short term, which is what most investors focus on, variations in financial performance are usually attributable to business fundamentals such as design, cost of sales, and market forecasting.

Nike has been highly profitable the past three decades – a period in which it was also subjected to continuous and vociferous opposition to its business practices. Consider the global media coverage of the company's alleged malpractices and the widespread anti-Nike protests at North American universities (a core market segment for Nike). Yet institutional investors have shown a startling disinterest in Nike's handling of its labor standards.

The high-profile, two-year case of activist Marc Kasky versus Nike brought the company before the California and federal supreme courts for allegedly misrepresenting the state of labor standards in its supplier factories. Even now, after an out-of-court settlement, the case raises the spectre of further legal action against Nike and others based on similar claims of commercial misstatements. Yet the case has barely raised an eyebrow from the mainstream investment community. Coping with such challenges, it seems, is simply an acceptable overhead cost of doing business.

That's not to say, however, that responsible business practices cannot pay. As with any business opportunity, the chances to make money by being good must be created, not found. Reinventing one's business isn't easy. And doing so in socially responsible ways involves a major shift in managerial mind-set – from a risk-based, reputational view of corporate responsibility to one focused on product and process innovations that will help to realign the business and the market according to shifting societal concerns.

suppliers and thwarted the stable conditions needed to advance opportunities for brands to invest in technological and managerial progress.

The MFA's expiration on January 1, 2005, will accelerate the consolidation of supply chains. With disperse supplier relationships and no quotas to destabilize, experts argue, the scene is set for changes in the apparel industry that will be as significant as the advent of globalized supply chains themselves, which was a major factor in Nike's original success.

It's not just that there will be fewer and larger suppliers. Intensified competition is pushing apparel makers to shorten the time between design and market even as they continue to cut costs. The industry will probably move to some form of lean manufacturing – shifting away from traditional top-down managerial styles toward greater worker self-management that delivers more flexibility and productivity. Some estimates suggest possible manufacturer cost savings of up to 25 percent.

In terms of worker conditions, the move toward lean manufacturing could reduce the total number of people employed, especially if fewer, more stable supply chains lead to advanced production technologies. But the shift could also improve conditions for the remaining workers over time. Because lean manufacturing requires employees to learn new skills, it would put upward pressure on wages and improve management's behavior toward workers. Clearly, Nike and its competitors will soon have new opportunities to create value and new ways to align those opportunities with responsible business practices. The challenge is to manage the transition to a post-MFA world in a responsible fashion.

Nike's 2004 acquisition of the athletic apparel and footwear brand Starter also affects Nike's strategy in terms of corporate responsibility. Starter is sold at large retailers such as Wal-Mart, Kmart, and Target, and the acquisition is a key element of Nike's growth strategy as the company reaches the limits of organic growth in some of its core markets. Now that it has entered the world of value-channel economics, Nike must concern itself with high product volumes and low margins while also maintaining its commitment to its labor codes.

Although it is a king-size operator in the market for premium goods, Nike has far less leverage in the market for value items, in which it must deal with retailers like notorious cost-squeezer Wal-Mart. Furthermore, value customers focus on price and are generally less responsive to ethical propositions – particularly those involving faraway problems like worker conditions in Asia or Latin America. Nike's public position on these issues is clear: It is committed to maintaining its labor compliance standards in all product lines and in all supply chains. But the business model underlying value-channel economics requires that Nike find new ways to keep its social commitments. Part of Nike's response to this challenge has been to argue for regulated international labor standards, which would offset any possible competitive disadvantage that Nike would incur if it had to go it alone.

Collective responsibility simply makes sense. After the acquisition of Starter, Nike sent out letters to stakeholders explaining its approach: "Whatever the channel where Nike products are sold, we have a growing conviction that it is essential to work with others to move toward the adoption of a common approach to labor compliance codes, monitoring, and reporting to help ensure broader accountability across the whole industry. This will take time, but through these efforts and with the active participation of all the major players, we believe we can further contribute

to the evolution of supply chain practices, including in the value channel."
Nike recognized that its long-term success required it to expand its focus
from its own practices to those of the entire sector.

Toward civil action

Nike has been involved in various initiatives designed to bridge corporate
responsibility and public policy, starting with the FLA in 1998. In July
2000, CEO Phil Knight attended the launch of the Global Compact, UN
Secretary-General Kofi Annan's multistakeholder initiative designed to
encourage responsible business practices. Knight was one of the 50 or so
chief executives of companies, NGOs, and labor organizations from around
the world who were at the event. He was the only CEO of a U.S. company
in attendance; since then, many more U.S. organizations have associated
themselves with the initiative. At the launch, Knight announced Nike's
"support of mandatory global standards for social auditing," asserting that
"every company should have to report on their performance" against these
standards. His proposal meant that Nike's suppliers and competitors would
have to share the financial burden of securing a regulated level of worker
conditions in global supply chains. When the social performance records
of all the companies were made public, Knight believed, Nike would be
revealed as a leader, which would help protect the brand.

In early 2004, Nike convened high-profile players from the international
labor, development, human rights, and environmental movements at its
Beaverton, Oregon, headquarters. Their willingness to attend was itself
a testament to how far Nike had progressed – from a target of attack to a
convenor of erstwhile critics. Even more notable was the fact that the topics
discussed weren't specific to Nike's operations. The conversations focused
on the potential negative fallout from the MFA's demise.

The end of the agreement raises the challenge of how to assist countries
with garment industries that may be suddenly rendered far less competitive
in international markets. For example, a significant portion of the export-
oriented garment industry in Bangladesh is at risk. Today, that sector employs
upward of two million people and accounts for 75 percent of the country's
foreign-exchange earnings. Similar data for countries in Latin America,
Africa, and Asia highlight the potentially disastrous social and economic
fallout if the transition to a post-MFA world is botched.

The MFA is ending partly because of the lobbying by NGOs and
governments of key exporting countries; they argued that the agreement
was a barrier to trade for developing countries. Even though companies
will be downsizing, relocating, and consolidating in response to the MFA's
demise, the business community was not a significant player in this trade
change and, in fairness, cannot be held responsible. However, the public
is already focusing on which companies are laying off workers and with

what effects. Nike is one of a few companies that believe, regardless of how this situation arose, they must be part of the solution if they don't want to be seen as part of the problem.

So Nike has joined a group of organizations – including companies such as U.S. retailer the Gap and UK retailer Asda; NGOs such as Oxfam International and AccountAbility; labor organizations such as the International Textile, Garment, and Leather Workers Federation; and multistakeholder initiatives such as the ETI, the FLA, and the Global Compact – to explore how such an alliance could help to address the challenges of a post-MFA world. This alliance might be well placed to advise governments and agencies like the World Bank on ways to develop public programs to assist workers in the transition; establish a framework to guide companies in their realignment of their supply chains; or lobby for changes to trade policies that would confer benefits to factories and countries that took labor issues into greater account.

Nike is, of course, a business, and as such is accountable to its share-holders. But the company has taken significant steps in evolving a strategy and practice that shifts it from being an object of civil activism to a key participant in civil society initiatives and processes.

In dealing with the challenges of corporate responsibility, Nike has come to view the issue as integral to the realities of globalization – and a major source of learning, relevant to its core business strategy and practices. That learning prompted the company to adopt codes of labor conduct, forge alliances with labor and civil society organizations, develop nonfinancial metrics for compliance that are linked to the company's management and its broader governance, and engage in the international debate about the role of business in society and in public policy.

As Nike's experience shows, the often talked-up business benefits of corporate responsibility are, at best, hard-won and frequently, in the short term, ephemeral or nonexistent. When accusations arise, it's easy for companies to focus on the low-hanging fruit – employee morale, for instance, or the immediate need to defend the brand. But making business logic out of a deeper sense of corporate responsibility requires courageous leadership – in particular, civil leadership – insightful learning, and a grounded process for organizational innovation.

Subject index

Authors index

Company index